Baedeker
Greece

Baedeker

Greece

200 colour photographs (credits at end of book)
25 situation plans, 25 general maps, 21 ground plans, 15 drawings, 16 town plans, 1 large map of Greece

Text: Monika A. Baumgarten, Vera Beck, Dr Otto Gärtner, Prof. Wolfgang Hassenpflug, Prof. Ernst Homann-Wedeking, Peter M. Nahm

Consultant: Axel Kramer

Editorial work: Baedeker-Redaktion

Design and layout: Baedeker-Redaktion

General direction: Dr Peter Baumgarten, Baedeker Stuttgart

Cartography: Gert Oberländer, Munich; Mairs Geographischer Verlag, Ostfildern-Kemnat (large map of Greece)

English language edition: Alec Court

English translation: James Hogarth
Updating: Margaret Court, Crispin Warren

4th English edition

Published in the United States by:
Macmillan Travel
A Simon & Schuster Macmillan Company
15 Columbus Circle
New York, NY 10023

Macmillan is a registered trademark of Macmillan, Inc.

Distributed in the United Kingdom by the Publishing Division of The Automobile Association, Fanum House, Basingstoke, Hampshire, RG21 2EA.

A CIP catalogue record for this book is available from the British Library.

Licensed user:
Mairs Geographischer Verlag GmbH & Co., Ostfildern-Kemnat bei Stuttgart

Printed in Italy by G. Canale & C. S.p.A. – Borgaro T.se – Turin

ISBN 0–02–860119–X US and Canada
0 7495 0403 X UK

Contents

The Principal Sights at a Glance

The places listed above are merely a selection of the principal sights – places of interest in themselves or for attractions in the surrounding area. There are of course innumerable other sights throughout Greece, to which attention is drawn by one or more stars.

Preface

This guide to Greece is one of the new generation of Baedeker guides.

These guides, illustrated throughout in colour, are designed to meet the needs of the modern traveller. They are quick and easy to consult, with the principal places of interest described in alphabetical order, and the information is presented in a format that is both attractive and easy to follow.

The present guide covers the whole of Greece, including both the mainland and the islands. The guide is in three parts. The first part gives a general account of the country, its geology, climate, flora and fauna, population, government and society, economy and transport, history, art and culture. A number of suggested routes for visitors provide a lead-in to the second part, in which places and features of tourist interest – cities and towns, the different regions and islands – are described. The third part contains a variety of practical information. Both the sights and the practical information are listed in alphabetical order.

The new Baedeker guides are noted for their concentration on essentials and their convenience of use. They contain numerous specially drawn plans and colour illustrations; and at the end of the book is a large map making it easy to locate the various places described in the "A to Z" section of the guide with the help of the co-ordinates given at the head of each entry.

How to use this book

Following the tradition established by Karl Baedeker in 1844, sights of particular interest are distinguished by either one ★ or two ★★.

To make it easier to locate the various sights listed in the "A to Z" section of the Guide, their co-ordinates on the large map of Greece are shown in red at the head of each entry.

Only a selection of hotels can be given: no reflection is implied, therefore, on establishments not included.

The symbol ⓘ on a town plan indicates the local tourist office from which further information can be obtained. The post-horn symbol indicates a post office.

In a time of rapid change it is difficult to ensure that all the information given is entirely accurate and up to date, and the possibility of error can never be completely eliminated. Although the publishers can accept no responsibility for inaccuracies and omissions, they are always grateful for corrections and suggestions for improvement.

Facts and Figures

Greece, the cradle of western culture, has long attracted scholars and travellers interested in its classical past; but in recent years it has also been discovered by a wider public who have come to appreciate its many other attractions. The visitors who are now drawn to Greece in such large numbers do not go only to see its ancient sites and recall the contribution it has made to European cultural and intellectual life, but to enjoy the extraordinary beauty of its scenery, the Mediterranean charm of its islands, the ready hospitality of its people and its beautiful beaches – all combining to form a marvellously seductive holiday land.

General

Situation

Greece, a southern outpost of the Balkans lying at the south-eastern extremity of Europe, consists of the Greek mainland territory (including the Peloponnese), a number of large islands and countless smaller ones, between latitude 36° and 41° north and longitude 20° and 26° east. It is bounded on the north by Albania, Yugoslavia, Bulgaria and Turkey and surrounded by the sea on the west, south and east.

Territory

Greece is a relatively small country, with a land mass of only 131,944 sq.km/50,944 sq. miles, but the area of sea which it occupies is something like 400,000 sq.km/154,500 sq. miles. About a fifth of its land area – 25,166 sq.km/9717 sq. miles – is accounted for by islands. The sea cuts deeply into the land from the west in the Gulf of Corinth and carves the eastern and southern coasts into a complex pattern of promontories and inlets, peninsulas and bays, linking them up with the scatter of islands to the south and east. Of the country's total coastline of 15,021km/9334 miles some 11,000km/6835 miles are contributed by the islands, over 2000 in number. Greece's land frontiers amount to only 1170km/727 miles – 247km/153 miles with Albania, 246km/153 miles with Yugoslavia, 475km/295 miles with Bulgaria and 203km/126 miles with Turkey.

Topography

No other country is so characteristic of the Mediterranean world as Greece. Slender and intricately articulated, surrounded by a multitude of islands of all shapes and sizes, it pulls away from the more solid structure of south-eastern Europe, reaching far out into the sea to Europe's most southerly outpost, the long island of Crete. It is a land of mountains, deeply penetrated by the ubiquitous sea and wrapped in the mantle of a climate which is everywhere the same. Greek land and the Greek seas – the Ionian Sea in the west, the Aegean in the east – are parts of an indivisible whole, one of which cannot be conceived without the other. No part of the Peloponnese or central Greece is much

◀ *View of the plain of Sparta from the ruined town of Mistra* more than 50km/30 miles from the sea, and even in northern Greece the maximum distance from the sea is not much more than 100km/60 miles.

Mainland Greece

Characteristics

Mainland Greece, bounded by mountainous territory on the west, has an open seaboard on the east, with coastal plains and natural harbours. The mountains rise for the most part above 1000m/3300ft, frequently exceeding 2000m/6600ft, and reaching their highest point in Mount Olympus (2917m/9571ft). They appear even higher than they are, rising directly out of the sea and in many rugged coastal areas rearing up in sheer cliffs to the summits. They are very different from the Alps, however, since they have been shaped not by glaciers but by weathering and water erosion. There are no jagged peaks or arêtes; the hills are predominantly of gentle rounded form, characterised more by horizontal than by vertical lines. There are few areas of lower hills, and the mountains are always visible in the background; low-lying land is the exception. There are, it is true, many areas of plain; but they are small, frequently at a high altitude and always framed by hills. Many of them are connected with basins which frequently have no drainage to the exterior and are occupied by lakes and bogs. Others lie on the coast or are washed by the sea, which penetrates far inland in deeply indented gulfs and inlets. Everywhere there are sudden alternations within a small area between high land and low land.

It is these plain areas that provide the people of Greece with their main living space. They are usually cut off from one another by inhospitable mountain barriers and linked only by roads running over passes; often it is easier to get from one to another by sea. The size of these plain areas increases from south to north; the only plains of any considerable extent are in the north (Thessaly, Macedonia) and in Laconia. In ancient times this fragmentation of Greek territory led to the formation of many small independent states, consisting of the *polis* (city) and the immediately surrounding area.

Rivers of any considerable size are found only in the north, in Thessaly, Macedonia and Thrace – the Pinios, the Axios, the Strymon, the Nestos and the Evros. They give Greece a series of fertile alluvial plains in which agriculture has made substantial progress in recent years. In the rest of the country the rivers mostly dry up in summer but during the rainy season swell into raging torrents.

Natural regions

The division of Greece into natural regions is determined mainly by the Dinaric–Hellenic system of folded mountains which extends from north to south, continuing down the Peloponnese and then circling in a wide arc by way of Crete and Rhodes into Asia Minor (Turkey).

Northern Greece

The backbone of northern and central Greece is the Pindos mountain range, rising to a height of 2637m/8652ft in Mt Smolikas. West of Pindos are the barren but attractive uplands of Epirus, while to the north-east are the Macedonian hills, surrounding the fertile coastal region round Salonica. South-east of Salonica the peninsula of Chalcidice, famed for its beautiful bathing beaches, extends its three "fingers" (Kassandra, Sithonia and Athos) into the northern Aegean.
In the extreme north-east Greece takes in part of the region of Thrace, patterned by the foothills of the Rhodope range and the river basins of the Nestos and the Evros (Maritsa).
South-west of Salonica is the crystalline massif of Mount Olympus (2917m/9571ft), Greece's highest mountain. The Thessalian basin, on

The Taygetos range, dominating the southern Peloponnese

the boundary between northern and central Greece, is enclosed on the north by Mount Olympus, on the east by the Thessalian coastal hills and on the west by the Pindos range.

Central Greece

Central Greece, bounded on the south by the long arm of the sea consisting of the Gulf of Patras and the Gulf of Corinth, takes in the Aetolian/Acarnanian coastal region, the mountain barrier formed by Mts Giona, Parnassus and Parnis, the Boeotian basin and the peninsula of Attica, with the national capital, Athens, the country's largest port, Piraeus, and the Attic coastal plain, together with the island of Euboea to the north-east.

Southern Greece

The heartland of the Peloponnese, a peninsula extending to the south of the Gulf of Corinth in the shape of a hand, is the upland region of Arcadia, from which ranges of hills reach south and south-east like fingers, enclosing a series of coastal plains.

The Greek Islands

The intricate coastal topography of mainland Greece has its counterpart in the multitude of islands scattered in the Aegean to the east and the Ionian Sea to the west, which in ancient times developed the seafaring skills of the Greeks and made them at an early stage the economic and cultural mediators between the three continents of the ancient world.

Aegean islands

The most densely clustered of the Greek islands are those in the Aegean, between the Greek mainland and the Turkish coast. Euboea (Evvia), the largest of the islands in central Greece, is, like the Northern

Mountains, Rivers and Lakes of Greece

Sporades to the north-east, a continuation of the Othrys range on the mainland, and was considered in ancient times as a detached part of Boeotia. The Cyclades, lying around the island of Delos in the southern Aegean, are the farthest south-easterly extension of Euboea and Attica. Kythira, south-east of the Peloponnese, is a stepping-stone on the way to Crete, the largest of the Greek islands (if the independent island of Cyprus, at present divided, is excluded), which closes off the Aegean on the south; straggling from east to west, it is a continuation of the mountain ranges of Anatolia.

Crete

Off the south-west coast of Asia Minor, between Rhodes and Samos, extends a string of islands, the Southern Sporades, most of them belonging to the Dodecanese. Widely dispersed in the north-eastern Aegean are the large islands of Chios, Lesbos, Lemnos, Samothrace and Thasos.

Ionian Islands

Off the west coast of Greece lie the Ionian Islands (Corfu, Lefkas, Ithaca, Kefallonia, Zakynthos, etc.), the central group of which is - ethnologically and historically associated with the nearby mainland of central Greece.

The Greek islands – a sailing paradise

Geology

Folded mountains

The mountain ranges and massifs of Greece form a pattern of great complexity and variety. In the west they are comprehended under the term Hellenides (Dinarides), which in the Greek peninsula run from north-west to south-east and extend in a wide arc by way of Crete and Rhodes to Asia Minor. They are folded mountains of Alpine structure, formed fairly late in geological time and consisting mainly of Mesozoic and Tertiary rocks, in particular limestones, sandstones, marls and conglomerates. Apart from this folding the territory of Greece has been subjected to violent upthrusting and downfaulting at various periods in the earth's history, continuing into quite recent times. In the Peloponnese late Tertiary deposits laid down by the sea are found at an altitude of 1800m/5900ft.

Ancient mountains

Quite different formations occur in the eastern part of the peninsula and in the Aegean.

In early geological times the Aegean basin was occupied by a folded range of ancient mountains, mostly of crystalline and metamorphic rocks, whose eroded remains survive in Thrace and Macedonia (the Rhodope massif), the Cyclades and the southern Peloponnese (the Pelagonian massif) and whose peaks emerge from the sea in the form of islands.

In the Mesozoic era these ancient hills were covered by the Tethys Sea, which left massive deposits of slates, sandstones and limestones. During the Pleistocene, after the withdrawal of the sea, they formed a land bridge between Greece and Asia Minor.

Marine depressions

In the Quaternary era this land link was broken up by three large marine depressions – the northern Aegean basin (up to 1950m/6400ft deep), to the north of an imaginary line from the Magnesian peninsula by way of Lemnos to the Gallipoli peninsula (the Dardanelles being a drowned river valley); the central Aegean basin (up to 4850m/15,900ft deep) between Euboea, the Cyclades, Samos and Chios; and the southern Aegean basin (up to 4453m/14,610ft deep), north of a line from Kythira by way of Santorin (Thera) to Rhodes. These depressions are separated from one another by ridges at a depth of around 500m/1640ft, and are marked off from the south-eastern Mediterranean by a shelf at a depth of some 800m/2625ft.

Faults and fractures

It is a reflection of this highly unstable structure that the territory of Greece, even more markedly than the rest of the Mediterranean, is fragmented by countless faults and fractures, to an extent found hardly anywhere else on earth. The faults have affected both the folded rocks and the ancient basement, producing a mosaic of hills of varying height and countless little basins and plain areas, forming deep bays, long promontories and peninsulas, a scatter of islands, rugged cliffs and a fantastically patterned coastline.

Vulcanism

In the fault zones there was violent volcanic activity, decreasing in more recent times, with its accompaniment of earth tremors and thermal springs.

Karstic formations

The folding and faulting of limestones has produced the karstic formations to be found all over Greece and on the islands.

Climate

Greece reaches out from the Balkan land mass far into the eastern Mediterranean, with numerous peninsulas and islands; and its climate depends, therefore, on a corresponding variety of influences.

In general Greece has a typical Mediterranean climate, with hot, dry summers and wet, cool winters. In comparison with the holiday areas of the western Mediterranean, Greece is much more exposed to continental influences. As a result, with comparable average temperatures, the daily and annual temperature ranges are markedly greater in Greece. In the climatic diagrams this is measured by the breadth of the temperature bands.

Climatic Diagrams

Temperatures and rainfall

The climatic diagrams on page 15 show temperatures and rainfall over the year as recorded at selected weather stations. The blue columns show average monthly precipitation (rainfall) in millimetres. Temperatures (in degrees Celsius) are represented as an orange band, the upper edge of the band showing average maximum day temperatures and the lower edge average minimum night temperatures.

Weather Stations (see map on page 15)

The variety of climate within Greece is illustrated by the data for four weather stations – Kerkyra (Corfu), Kavala, Athens and Iraklion (Crete) – each representative of a larger region. There are of course transitions between the different areas.

Kerkyra

Kerkyra is representative of the relatively wet and mild climate of western Greece, including the Ionian Islands.

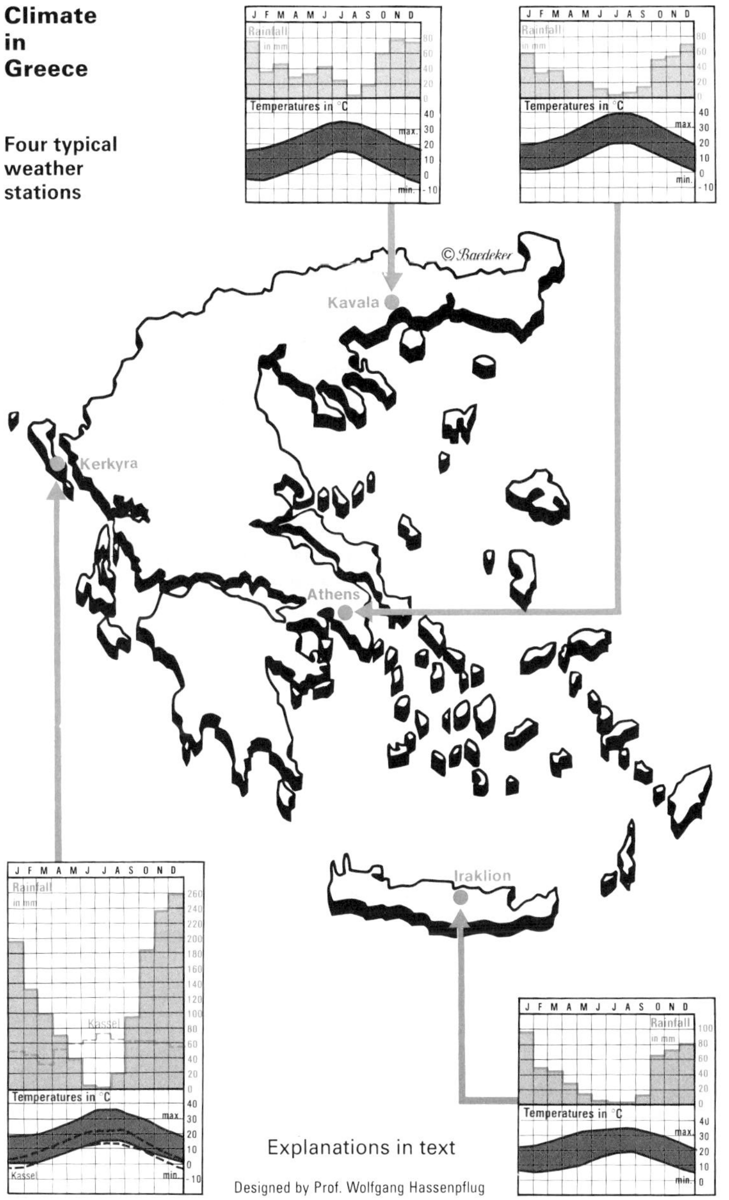
Climate in Greece
Four typical weather stations
J F M A M J J A S O N D
Rainfall in mm
Temperatures in °C
max.
min.
Kavala
Kerkyra
Athens
Iraklion
Kassel
© Baedeker
Explanations in text
Designed by Prof. Wolfgang Hassenpflug

Climate

Region	Temperatures in °C (°F)							Average annual rainfall in mm (inches)
	Air					Sea		
	Annual average	Jan.	July/Aug.	Minimum for yr	Maximum for yr	Jan.	July/Aug.	
Athens	**17.8 (64.0)**	**9.3 (48.7)**	**27.5/27.5 (81.5/81.5)**	**−5.5 (22.1)**	**43.0 (109.4)**	**14.8 (58.6)**	**24.9/25.6 (76.8/78.1)**	**401 (16)**
Salonica	**16.4 (61.5)**	**5.0 (41.0)**	**26.6/26.3 (79.9/79.3)**	**−9.5 (14.9)**	**41.6 (106.9)**	**11.5 (52.7)**	**24.5/24.8 (76.1/76.6)**	**477 (19)**
Corfu	**17.4 (63.3)**	**10.0 (50.0)**	**26.7/26.6 (80.1/79.9)**	**−2.8 (27.0)**	**41.0 (105.8)**	**15.5 (59.9)**	**25.7/26.8 (78.3/80.2)**	**1137 (45)**
Crete	**19.0 (66.2)**	**12.3 (54.1)**	**25.9/25.6 (78.6/78.1)**	**+0.1 (32.2)**	**45.7 (114.3)**	**15.2 (59.4)**	**25.9/25.6 (78.6/78.1)**	**539 (21)**

Average duration of Sunshine: 2500–3000 hours in year

Kavala

Kavala is representative of northern and eastern Greece, where continental influences are stronger.

Athens

Athens is representative of central Greece, to the east of the mountainous mainland regions and on the western fringes of the Aegean islands.

Iraklion

Iraklion is representative of the southern Greek islands.

Climatic Characteristics

The climate of any particular place can be estimated with the help of the diagrams, making allowance for local factors like the pattern of relief and taking account of the following general rules.

Continental influences are strongest in the north and in the interior of the country, which have the largest temperature variations between day and night and between summer and winter. Towards the south, particularly on the islands, the variations are smaller.

Dry months

Temperatures and aridity in summer increase from north to south. In northern Greece there are three to four arid months (i.e. months in which evaporation is greater than rainfall), in central Greece four to five, in southern Greece and the Aegean five to six, on Santorin seven. In southern Greece three to four months are practically rainless. Thanks to the dryness of the air and the high rate of evaporation, however, the heat of summer is relatively tolerable.

The west side of Greece is distinctly wetter than the east side, since the rain-bringing winds of the winter months come from the west and have discharged their rain by the time they reach the east of the country, in the lee of the mountains (compare the climatic diagrams for Kerkyra and Kavala). The climate of western Greece is also considerably milder (average January temperature in Kerkyra 10°C/50°F, in Salonica 5.5°C/42°F).

Winds

Climate is also influenced by the local winds. The etesians (the ancient Greek term) or *meltemia* (in modern Greek) are dry winds which blow in summer from the north across the Aegean, rising to considerable violence in the early afternoon and dying down towards the evening. They may create difficulties for shipping, but on land they serve a useful purpose in driving the numerous windmills used for grinding grain or raising water for irrigation. They are associated with areas of low pressure over western and southern Asia.

Prickly pears on the Gulf of Corinth

Sirocco

In the southern islands (the Cyclades, Crete) the sirocco, a south wind, blows in winter and spring, bringing with it mild, wet weather and a sultry air which can be oppressive. It originates on the fronts of depressions moving eastward over the Mediterranean area.

Upland regions

Mountainous and hilly regions, which make up the greater part of Greece, have a climate of their own, very different from that of the lower-lying basins and coastal areas. With increasing height the climate becomes cooler and wetter, with average temperatures falling by around 0.5° to 0.8°C (0.9° to 1.4°F) for every 100m/330ft of height. Average annual rainfall at a height of 800m/2625ft can be twice as high as at sea level, as it is, for example, on the north side of Crete. Snow is rare on low-lying ground, but may lie for a considerable time at altitudes above 1000m/3300ft. In the mountains in summer thunder showers are by no means rare.
In general the climate in the mountains of Greece is similar to that of Central Europe.

Greek seasons

Greece has only three seasons – the period when nature comes to life and vegetation grows and ripens (March to June), the dry season (June or July to October) and the rainy season (October to March or April).

Flora and Fauna

Flora

Trees and shrubs

The flora of Greece is of typically Mediterranean character, with leathery-leaved evergreens and succulents; the trees never exceed a very moderate height. In the fertile depressions and coastal regions, up to a height of around 800m/2625ft, mixed forests of oaks, planes, Aleppo pines, carob-trees, etc., alternate with a macchia (Greek *longos*) of holm oaks, kermes oaks, arbutus, mastic bushes, laurel, broom, oleander and wild olives. In the wetter regions of western Greece the macchia is found higher up (800–2000m/2625–6560ft), in the drier south-east at lesser heights, becoming increasingly sparse and merging into the type of dry macchia known as *frygana,* with semi-shrublike plants, junipers, heaths and spurges, providing meagre grazing for sheep and goats. Mixed deciduous forests of beech, chestnut, plane, maple and elm are found up to heights of over 1500m/4900ft, particularly in the mountains of northern and central Greece, coniferous forests to heights of over 1700m/5600ft. Above these heights, up to 2000m/6560ft, only the Apollo fir is found. Above the tree line are scanty Alpine meadows – in so far as the karstic formations of the limestone hills permit the growth of any vegetation at all.

Cultivation and wasteland

The natural landscape of Greece is characterised not by the luxuriance of the south but by tracts of bare and barren countryside. Since ancient times the natural cover of forest and macchia has been largely destroyed by the extension of arable land and animal grazing. At best it has given place to olive-groves, fig plantations and vineyards; at worst it has reverted to wasteland. In recent years, however, efforts have been made to halt this latter trend by reafforestation.

Imported species

Additions to the native flora of Greece have been the agave and prickly pear from Central America and the date palm from Africa, originally introduced as an ornamental tree but now also found growing wild.

The donkey – still a valued and uncomplaining beast of burden

Fauna

Game

The extensive devastation of the flora has considerably reduced the habitats, and consequently the variety of species, of the fauna of Greece. Some deer and wild pigs are still to be found in the mountains, and in the northern mountain regions bears are now more frequently encountered.

Mountain goats

The wild bezoar goat (*Capra aegagrus*), the ancestral form of the domestic goat, is still found on Crete.

Reptiles

Greece has a variety of reptiles (lizards, snakes, tortoises and turtles), the Greek tortoise being particularly common. The breeding sites (e.g. on Zakynthos) of the loggerhead turtle, an endangered species, are now statutorily protected.

Birds

Countless species of birds pass through Greece on their southward migration. The shooting of birds (particularly quails) and also of rabbits is a popular Greek sport.

Marine fauna

Apart from the various species of fish to be found all over the Mediterranean, octopuses, shellfish, lobsters and spiny lobsters are caught round the coasts.
The monk seal, another endangered species, still survives in sea-caves.
Sponges are found all over the Aegean.

Population

Numbers and density

The Greek population of something over 10 million is confined to a relatively small area of cultivable land, at the high density of 220 to the sq.km (570 to the sq. mile), compared with the overall density of 78 to the sq.km (202 to the sq. mile).

Structure

The Greek people are of mixed origin, with Slav, Albanian and other European elements, but their consciousness of national identity, based on a common language and a common religion, has down the centuries shown an astonishing persistence and an astonishing power of assimilation. They withstood almost 400 years of Turkish rule, with the drain of so many of their boys into the Turkish service, without yielding and without giving up hope. When the new kingdom of Greece was established in 1830 it was necessary to set up two lawcourts in Athens, one for Greeks and the other for Albanians, since the population of Attica was then predominantly Albanian; but this has long ceased to be a problem, and the Albanians, particularly on the islands of Hydra and Spetsai, were among the most ardent and energetic of Greek patriots during the struggle for liberation from the Turks.
A distinctive imprint was left on the Dodecanese by the long period of Turkish and later Italian rule, and on the Ionian Islands by the British protectorate in the 19th century, which gave these islands an enduring link with western European culture.

The unity of the population was increased by the events following the First World War, when around 1.5 million Greek refugees came to Greece from Asia Minor and 518,000 Turks and 92,000 Bulgarians left Greece.

The population of Greece is now 98.5% Greek. There are now only small minorities of Turks (0.8%; in Thrace and on Rhodes and Kos),

Bulgarians (0.3%; in Macedonia), Armenians (0.2%) and Koutzovlachs (Arromans) in Thessaly, together with some nomadic gipsy tribes.

In spite of all modern developments the family and the habit of living harmoniously together in a strict hierarchy of age remain determining factors in Greek life. Men still retain their predominance, and the move towards equal rights for women is still only in its early stages.

The great majority of the population are basically country people, and even in large towns many districts preserve the atmosphere of country life. It remains true, nevertheless, that in recent years the large towns have grown with alarming rapidity at the expense of the country areas, creating both social problems and problems of infrastructure. Of the working population of some 4 million 40% work in the tertiary sector (administration, services, commerce, transport, tourism), 30% in productive industry and 27% in agriculture, forestry and fishing.

Distribution

Something like a third of the population live in the country, mostly in villages of closely packed houses. The determining factor in the siting of a village is the availability of drinking water, and the village well or fountain is usually the hub of village life. Isolated farms and hamlets are rare.

Towns feature less prominently in the total picture, though they are now rapidly increasing in number and size; they are to be found mainly in the eastern half of mainland Greece, and are mostly of small or medium size, showing the same closely huddled pattern as the villages.

There are only a few cities of any size. Athens and the adjoining port town of Piraeus, with their suburbs, form a conurbation of some 3.5 million inhabitants. The north of the country is dominated by Salonica, with a population of some 750,000 including suburbs. The largest town in the Peloponnese is Patras, with 155,000 inhabitants. Then follow Iraklion (110,000) on Crete and, in central Greece, Volos (107,000) and Larisa (102,000).

Flight from the land; emigration

In contrast to the towns on the mainland, most of the islands show a steady decline in population, and some, like Kastellorizo (far to the south-east, off the Turkish coast), are faced with total depopulation. The poor quality of the soil and the fragmentation of holdings by inheritance have so reduced the standard of living that many young people prefer to seek a better livelihood on the mainland, in the industrialised countries of western Europe or overseas (particularly in the United States). In quite recent years, however, many young Greeks, disillusioned with town life, are returning to the land, and a modest degree of "industrialisation" of agriculture is developing in the main farming regions.

Some 3 million Greeks live outside Greece. Many of them help to support members of their family who have remained at home, and they frequently return home when they retire from active life; this is true particularly of Greeks from the islands.

Language

The national language of Greece is modern Greek. Although the modern language is directly descended from ancient Greek and uses the same alphabet, it has undergone considerable changes in grammar, syntax, vocabulary and above all in pronunciation. There is also

the peculiarity that the language exists on two levels, demotic and *katharevousa.* Demotic (*dimotikí*) is the ordinary colloquial language which has developed naturally down the centuries. When the new Greek state was established in 1829–30, however, some Greek scholars sought to create an artificial idiom closer to ancient Greek, and this form, known as *katharevousa* ("purified"), was adopted as the official language of Greece. It remained the language of administration, the law, scholarship and largely of the press until 1975, when the Greek Parliament adopted the demotic form of Greek as the national language of Greece.
See also Literature, page 93.

Religion

In spite of the regional differences that have developed in the course of history and the sharp geographical fragmentation of their country the Greeks have preserved a profound consciousness of their national identity. A unifying factor, particularly in hard times, has been the Greek Orthodox church, whose influence in both private and public life has remained strong. Since 1833 the church of Greece has been autonomous, and in 1850 it was recognised by the Oecumenical Patriarchate in Constantinople (Istanbul) as an autocephalous church (i.e. with its own synod and the power to appoint its own bishops). It has been the state church of Greece since 1864. Its head is the Archbishop of Athens.

The islands of the Dodecanese, reunited with Greece only in 1912–13, and the monastic republic of Athos remain subject to the jurisdiction of the Patriarchate of Constantinople.
Crete occupies a special position as a semi-autonomous province of the church.

Some 98% of the population profess the Greek Orthodox faith. There are also small numbers of Muslims (1.3%), Protestants, Catholics (a legacy of Venetian rule in the Cyclades) and Jews.

Government and Society

A Democratic State

Since the fall of the military dictatorship in 1974 and the national referendum, which showed a large majority in favour of the abolition of the monarchy, Greece, under the 1975 constitution (with additions and amendments in 1985 and 1986), has been a democratic parliamentary republic.

National flag

The Greek flag, flown for the first time in March 1822, has a Greek cross in the top left-hand corner and nine alternating blue and white horizontal stripes, representing the nine syllables of the Greek battle-cry during the war of liberation from Turkish rule, *"E/lef/the/rí/a i thá/na/tos"* ("Freedom or death").

National emblem

Since the abolition of the monarchy in 1975 the Greek national emblem or coat of arms has been a silver Greek cross on a blue shield encircled by a green laurel wreath.

National anthem

The text of the Greek national anthem, adopted in 1865, was taken from the "Hymn to Freedom" by Dionysios Solomos (1798–1857), the first considerable Greek lyric poet of modern times; the tune, composed in 1828, is by Nikolaos Mantzaros (1795–1872). The first line is

Greece
(Hellenic Republic)

Regions

- A Thrace
- B Macedonia
- C Epirus
- D Thessaly
- E Central Greece
- F Peloponnese
- G Ionian Islands
- H Crete
- I Aegean Islands

Nomoi (chief towns in parentheses)

1 Evros (Alexandroúpolis)
2 Rodopi (Komotini)
3 Xanthi
4 Kavala
5 Drama
6 Serrai
7 Kilkis
8 Salonica
9 Lésbos (Mytilíni)
10 Chalcidice (Poliyiros)
11 Pieria (Katerini)
12 Imathia (Veria)
13 Pella (Edessa)
14 Florina
15 Kastoria
16 Kozani
17 Grevena
18 Ioannina
19 Thesprotia (Igoumenitsa)
20 Preveza
21 Arta
22 Trikala
23 Karditsa
24 Larissa
25 Magnesia (Volos)
26 Evritania (Karpenision)
27 Aetolia/Acarnania (Agrinion)
28 Phthiotis (Lamia)
29 Phocis (Amfissa)
30 Euboea (Khalkis)
31 Boeotia (Levadia)
32 Attica (Athens)
33 Corinth
34 Achaea (Pátras)
35 Elis (Pýrgos)
36 Arcadia (Tripolis)
37 Argolid (Nauplia)
38 Messenia (Kalamata)
39 Laconia (Sparta)
40 Corfu
41 Lefkás
42 Kefallinía (Argostóli)
43 Zakynthos
44 Chaniá
45 Réthymnon
46 Iráklion
47 Lasíthi (Ayios Nikólaos))
48 Dodecanese (Rhodes)
49 Cyclades (Ermoúpolis)
50 Sámos (Vathý)
51 Chíos

"Se gnorízo apó tin kópsi tou spathioú" ("I know you by the cut of your sword").

Universal suffrage

All Greek men and women over the age of 18 have the vote.

Parliament

The Greek Parliament has 300 members, elected by a free and secret vote for a four-year term. Parliament in turn elects the President of Greece by a two-thirds majority for a five-year term of office.

Parties

The following parties are represented in the Greek Parliament: the conservative New Democracy (ND), the Pan-Hellenic Socialist Movement (PASOK) and the communist Alliance of the United Left (KKE).

Military service

Military service is compulsory for all Greek males.

International bodies

Greece is a member of the United Nations and most of its subsidiary organisations, the European Union, the Council of Europe, NATO, OECD and a number of other international bodies.

Administrative Divisions (see map on page 22)

Hellenic Republic

The territory of the Hellenic Republic (*Ellinikí Dimokratía*, "Hellenic Democracy") is divided into ten geographical regions, which in turn are divided into 51 districts (*nomí*, singular *nomós)*.
The districts are made up of 147 provinces (*eparkhíes*, singular *eparkhía)*, with 264 urban communes or municipalities (*dími*, singular *dímos)*, 5672 rural communes (*kinótites*, singular *kinótis*) and 11,691 "settlements" (*ikismí*, singular *ikismós)*.

Athos

The monastic republic on Mount Athos (Ayion Oros, the Holy Mountain) enjoys complete domestic self-government. See A to Z, Athos.

Education

Under a new law passed in 1976 school attendance is compulsory for a total of nine years, six in the primary school (*dimotikó skholeío*) and three in the secondary school (*gymnásio)*.

Kindergartens, the number of which is increasing, take children from the age of 3½. Attendance is not compulsory.

After secondary school young people can spend a further three years in a general, technical or vocational college in order to gain a university entrance qualification.

Higher education

Greece has six universities, at Athens, Salonica, Patras, Ioannina, in Thrace (Xanti and Komotini) and on Crete (Iraklion and Rethymnon), and six other higher educational establishments – colleges of political science, economics and commerce, agriculture and art in Athens and colleges of industrial research and planning in Salonica and Piraeus.

Adult education

The government has been concerned to supplement the well established traditional educational system by developing adult education. In general, however, these efforts have been successful only in relation to people under 40; less has been achieved with the older age groups, partly as a result of the still relatively high illiteracy rate in Greece.

Fishing boats, Lefkas

Cultural Life

See page 92

Economy

In consequence of its unfavourable geographical and geological structure Greece has long been one of the economically backward countries in Europe. In antiquity this was one of the reasons for the foundation of colonies, and it still leads many Greeks, particularly in the younger age groups, to emigrate to the New World or to seek employment as "guest workers" in the industrialised countries of Western Europe.
Hitherto agriculture, in spite of its relatively low economic yield, has been the dominant element in the Greek economy. Industry is now developing rapidly, and the services sector – the most important branch of the economy in terms of numbers employed and value of output – is destined to increase still further in importance through the development of commerce and transport and the still growing tourist trade.

Agriculture

The broad base of the Greek economy is still agriculture, although the proportion it contributes to the national income is now declining. Its main products, sometimes grown on laboriously built up terraced fields, are grain (wheat, barley, maize, rice), wine (as well as table grapes, raisins, currants and sultanas), tobacco, cotton, sugar-cane, melons, fruit (including southern fruits), figs, nuts (almonds, pistachios, groundnuts) and early vegetables (tomatoes, aubergines, gherkins). The olive-tree makes a major contribution (olive oil, olives).

Stock farming is mainly concerned with sheep (about 8 million), goats (about 4.5 million) and smaller animals.
Beekeeping provides honey and wax.
A quarter of the population is engaged in agriculture (compared with the European Community average of 7.6%), although it contributes only 15% of the gross domestic product. Poor soil, local shortages of water, relatively low pay, lack of skilled workers and structural problems – almost three-quarters of all agricultural holdings are under 5 hectares/12½ acres – all hinder the development of agriculture. In spite of this, however, Greek agriculture still largely meets the needs for home consumption and in addition produces substantial quantities of produce for export.

Fishing

The Greek fisheries are unproductive as a result of inadequate regeneration of the food supply and continued over-fishing, and it is necessary to import fish to supply domestic needs.
Sponge-fishing: see below, Economy of the Greek Islands

Mining

Greece is well supplied with minerals – bauxite, pyrites, magnesite, iron, chromium, zinc, lead and other ores – but capital is lacking to import the coal necessary for smelting, and although there are some deposits of lignite this is an inadequate substitute.
Marble, much used in building, is quarried in many places.

Power supplies

The development of new sources of power is a matter of great urgency. Fully 90% of the country's electricity is supplied by thermal power stations using native lignite and imported coal and oil. The rest comes from hydroelectric power stations (e.g. on the river Akheloos in central Greece), but although the capacity of these stations has been increased they contribute a steadily declining proportion of national requirements. Plans to build nuclear power stations (e.g. at Lavrion, south-east of Athens) have been deferred because of seismic activity in the region.
At the beginning of 1974 considerable reserves of oil and natural gas were found by underwater drilling off the island of Thasos in the northern Aegean; but these reserves are also claimed by Turkey, and their discovery has added a further strain to the relations between the two countries. It is estimated that oil from this Prinos field will in future supply 13% of Greece's requirements of power.
Considerable reserves of natural gas were also found in the western Peloponnese in 1981.

Productive industry

Industry and craft production provide employment for around a third of the working population and contribute a similar proportion of the gross domestic product. In addition to the traditional forms of industry – foodstuffs (canned produce, fruit juices, wine, spirits) and tobacco goods, textiles (carpets, clothing), leather goods, furs (Kastoria) – there are also shipbuilding, chemicals and metal-processing, with industrialisation proceeding at a rapid pace. A bauxite plant on the Gulf of Corinth (near Delphi), to which there have been objections on ecological grounds, supplies aluminium to the Soviet Union and Bulgaria.

Industrial centres

A third of the population of Greece live in the Athens conurbation (including Piraeus and the bay of Eleusis), which produces almost two-thirds of the country's total industrial output. This extreme concentration of industry, due to be still further increased, gives rise to grave environmental problems, long evident in the blanket of smog which frequently covers the area. Other industrial centres are Salonica in northern Greece and Patras in the Peloponnese.

Economy

Tertiary sector

Some 40% of the working population are now employed in the various service industries – the civil service, commerce, banking, transport, hotels and restaurants. The tertiary sector is thus the most important part of the Greek economy.

Foreign trade

Greece became an associate member of the European Economic Community in 1962 and a full member of the European Community in 1981. The resultant reduction in customs and commercial barriers brought a radical change in the economic situation. Between 1970 and 1980 industrial production and exports multiplied eleven-fold. Whereas in 1960 more than 90% of all exports consisted of agricultural produce, by 1984 the proportion had fallen to 22% and industrial products made up almost half the total volume of exports.

Greece's most important trading partners are the members of the European Union, particularly Germany, Italy and France, followed by the United States and up until 1990 the Soviet Union.

In spite of the increase in exports Greece has been unable to reduce the deficit on its balance of trade, the increased revenue from exports being more than swallowed up by increased population and higher domestic consumption.

Income

The average income of employed persons in Greece is at 6800 dollars (1991) still considerably below the level of other European Union countries.

Inflation, unemployment

Inflation (14–20% between 1989 and 1991) and unemployment (approaching 8%) are both high.

Tourism

An element of major importance in the economy of Greece is tourism, which in 1988 brought some 8 million foreign visitors into the country – roughly four-fifths of its normal population. The needs of these visitors have been catered for by the provision of additional hotels and other accommodation and the construction of new roads; but the government is also very conscious of the possible drawbacks which this constantly increasing influx of tourists may bring with it. Nevertheless it must be expected that with its unique remains of one of the world's great civilisations, its beautiful climate and its magnificent scenery Greece will continue in the coming years to attract increasing numbers of visitors.

Economy of the Greek Islands

The islands are among the least developed parts of Greece. There is practically no industry, and commerce and craft production depend on agriculture, which is the islands' principal source of income. (With 546,200 hectares/1,350,000 acres of cultivable land, the islands account for 13.4% of the national total.) While the smaller islands can do little more than supply their own needs, the larger ones export agricultural produce to the mainland and to other countries.

Agricultural produce

The main products of the islands since ancient times have been olives (both for oil and for eating), wine, honey or wax, and in more recent times also melons and early vegetables, tomatoes (Cyclades) for the making of tomato purée, sultanas, almonds and groundnuts (Crete), table grapes and currants (Ionian Islands), cotton, tobacco, mastic (Chios), and peaches, apricots, apples and pears (canning factory on Crete). Sheep and goats are still, as in the past, the main suppliers of milk and meat. The poor road system on many of the smaller islands means that donkeys and mules are still indispensable as draught animals and beasts of burden.

Fishing, sponge-fishing

The island fisheries are no more productive than in the rest of Greece. Sponge-diving, once a major source of income in the eastern Aegean, is declining as a result of competition from synthetic sponges, and is now concentrated in the waters off the North African coast. The Greek sponge-fishing fleet is traditionally based in the Dodecanese, where there are small boatyards which build and repair the local caiques.

Mining

The working of minerals in the islands (by small and medium-sized undertakings with no more than 400 workers) is confined to small deposits of iron, manganese, nickel, zinc, lead and molybdenum (Euboea, Melos). World-famous marble has been worked since ancient times on Tinos, Chios, Naxos and Paros. Pozzolana, a volcanic earth found on Santorin and Melos, was already valued in ancient times as a mortar used in the construction of harbour installations.

Craft production

Craft production is based on local supplies of clay (pottery, ceramics) and on the rearing of sheep and goats (woollen carpets, textiles, leather-working).

Transport

Roads

Given the topography of the country, Greece has an excellent road system, with some 40,000km/25,000 miles of roads, around four-fifths of which are in satisfactory condition or are being rapidly improved. Increased attention is now being given to the construction of expressways, sections of which are of motorway standard or are being brought up to that standard, and bypasses for through traffic round towns. It is now possible to drive all over Greece, including the Peloponnese and the larger islands, without difficulty, even in the mountainous areas.

The backbone of the road system of mainland Greece is the expressway (partly of motorway standard, with dual carriageways) which runs from the Yugoslav frontier by way of Salonica, Larisa and Lamia to Athens, continuing along the south side of the Gulf of Corinth to Patras and on to Olympia. Other major roads which present no difficulties for the driver and are constantly being improved are the east–west links in northern and central Greece (crossing numerous passes), the road which runs south-east from the ferry port of Igoumenitsa on the Ionian Sea by way of Arta, Nafpaktos, Delphi and Livadia to Athens (with multi-lane carriageways approaching Athens), and various roads running diagonally across the Peloponnese.

Signposting

In general Greek roads are excellently signposted, with names of places in both Greek and Latin script. There are also helpful signs indicating place of tourist interest (archaeological sites, museums, churches, natural beauties, etc.).

Railways

The Greek railway network, run by the state-owned Organismós Siderodrómon Elládos (OSE), is relatively small (2500km/1550 miles). Much of the system, which is predominantly of the standard European gauge, is single-track, and no progress has been made with the electrification of the system. There is one trunk line providing a connection with Central Europe, from Athens via Salonica and Belgrade.

Narrow-gauge lines

The Peloponnese line, which runs south from Athens and Piraeus through the Peloponnese, and the east–west line from Volos to Kalambaka in central Greece, are both narrow-gauge.

Athens suburban line

The Athens conurbation is served by a Metro, running underground in the city centre, the Ilektrikós – the only one of its kind in Greece.

Buses

The rather inadequate Greek rail system is supplemented by a dense network of bus services, some of them run by the State Railways but most of them by private companies. There are regular long-distance services (mostly with air-conditioned buses) between the larger towns and adequate regional and local services, making it possible to reach even the remotest places in the country.

Tourist buses

In addition, particularly in Athens, there are numerous excursions designed for visitors, usually in modern luxury coaches.

Air Services

There has been a considerable development of air services in Greece in recent years, and the country is now linked with the international air network both by the national airline, Olympic Airways (established by Aristoteles Onassis in 1957, state-owned since 1975), and by numerous foreign airlines and charter companies. In addition Olympic Airways fly a dense network of domestic services, particularly in the Aegean islands.

Airport

The most important Greek international airport by far is Athens/Ellinikó (south-east of the city), which in addition to its busy tourist and business traffic to Greece provides a link between south-eastern Europe and the Middle East. Other major airports are Salonica and Iraklion (Crete).

Shipping Services

Given the interpenetration of land and sea in the geography of Greece, it is not surprising that shipping plays an important part in the country's economy. After suffering heavy losses in two world wars the Greek merchant fleet occupies fourth place in the world ranking list, with 2700 vessels over 300 tons and a total capacity of 49 million tons (including 20 million tons of tanker capacity).
In addition there are a number of vessels belonging to Greek shipowners which sail under flags of convenience (Liberia, Panama).

Coastal shipping and ferries

The Greek merchant fleet not only plays an important part in international shipping but also serves the considerable coastal traffic and the busy and well organised network of ferry services between mainland Greece and numerous islands in the Aegean and the Ionian Sea.

Ports

The largest and most important Greek port is Piraeus, which has been since ancient times the gateway to the metropolis, Athens. In Piraeus and the neighbouring bay of Eleusis there are large shipyards.
Other large ports are Patras, Salonica, Volos and Iraklion (Crete). In addition there are countless smaller commercial and ferry ports and boating harbours all over the Greek coasts and on the islands.

Tourism

See page 26

History

Myths

Polytheism

As a result of the mingling of the beliefs of the pre-Greek population with those of the Greek incomers, the earlier worship of natural forces developed in Greece before the beginning of historical times into a polytheistic system of religious beliefs centred on a pantheon of supernatural beings, comprising numerous major and minor divinities conceived as distinctive personalities together with countless local divinities and spirits of nature.

Anthropomorphism

In the works of Homer the Greek myths – that is, the legends of the world of the gods – are developed on an epic scale, and in the process the gods are largely humanised. They are represented like human beings, but immortal and all-powerful, and the world of the gods on Olympus is conceived as resembling in social structure the world of humans. The early writers, Homer and Hesiod, established a kind of genealogy of the gods.

The Greek Pantheon

In this account the Greek names of the gods and goddesses are accompanied by their Roman equivalents.

Origins

It was believed that out of the primal Chaos (etymologically a "yawning" void or abyss) there emerged the first divine couple, Ouranos (the sky) and Gaia (the earth), from whom the divine race of Titans – four brothers and four sisters, associated in pairs (Okeanos and Thetys, Hyperion and Theia, Kronos and Rheia, Koios and Phoibe) – were descended. There was a great war (Titanomachy) between the Titans and the gods of Olympus in which the Olympians were victorious.

Principal gods and goddesses

The principal gods of Olympus were the sky god and ruler of the world Zeus (Jupiter), his consort Hera (Juno; goddess of marriage and birth), Pallas Athene (Minerva; goddess of wisdom), Apollo (God of light and of prophecy), Artemis (Diana; goddess of hunting), Ares (Mars; god of war), Aphrodite (Venus; goddess of beauty), Hermes (Mercury; messenger of the gods and god of trade), Hephaistos (Vulcan; god of fire and of metalworking) and Hestia (Vesta; goddess of the domestic hearth).

Subsidiary gods and goddesses

Subsidiary divinities were the love god Eros (Amor), the nine Muses – Klio (history), Melpomene (tragedy), Terpsichore (dance and choral lyric poetry), Thalia (comedy), Euterpe (music and lyric poetry), Erato (love poetry and dancing), Urania (astronomy), Polyhymnia (serious poetry, dance and mime) and Calliope (epic and elegiac poetry) – Themis and the Horai (Eunomeia, Dike and Eirene), Nike (Victoria; goddess of victory), Iris (messenger of the gods), Hebe (Juventus; goddess of youth), and Ganymede, cupbearer of the gods; Helios (Sol; the sun), Selene (Luna; the moon) and Eos (Aurora; the dawn); the stars and the winds; Nemesis (goddess of punishment), Tyche (Fortuna; good fortune) and the Moirai (Parcae) or Fates, Klotho, Lachesis and Atropos.

Divinities of the sea and the waters

The principal divinities of the sea were Poseidon (Neptune) with his trident, his wife Amphitrite and his son Triton. Other water gods and goddesses were Nereus and the Nereids, Proteus, Glaukos, Ino and

Melikertes, the Sirens and the Oceanids, descendants of the Titan Okeanos.

Divinities of the earth and the underworld

These included Gaia (Tellus), the primal earth mother, and her daughter Rheia (Cybele); Dionysus (Bacchus), god of wine; the nymphs (naiads, oreads, dryads), the satyrs (fauns) and Silene; the shepherd god Pan with his flute and Priapos (god of fields and gardens); Demeter (Ceres), goddess of fertility and the earth's bounty, and Persephone (Proserpina), goddess of the underworld; Hades (Pluto), ruler of the underworld (the kingdom of the dead beyond the river Acheron) and his servants the Erinyes (Furies); Hekate, goddess of night terrors; and the brothers Hypnos (Sleep) and Thanatos (Death).

Heroes

Heroes, in the myths of the ancient Greeks, were god-like beings, usually the offspring of a god or goddess and a mortal (demigods). They were not essentially different in nature from ordinary men: like men, they were mortal, but they possessed superhuman powers. The best known of the heroes was Herakles (Hercules); others were Theseus, Perseus, Sisyphos and Bellerophon.

Oracles

In early times oracles played an important role and enjoyed great respect and confidence. The major oracles had shrines at which those who came to seek the oracle's advice had the god's pronouncements conveyed to them by a seer (Greek *mantis*) or priest. Much attention was also paid to such auguries as the observation of the flight of birds and the interpretation of the entrails of sacrificial animals or unusual natural phenomena (springs being particularly important in this respect).

The best known oracular shrines in ancient Greece were Dodona in Epirus, Delphi (where the oracle was pronounced by the Pythia) and, in Asia Minor, Klaros (near Kolophon) and Didyma. Although the importance of the oracles declined from the 4th century B.C. onwards as a result of the rationalist teachings of the sophists they took on a fresh lease of life under the Romans and survived into the 4th century A.D.

Chronology

Neither in ancient times nor in later centuries is it possible to think in terms of a general history of Greece: the history of the country is to be seen rather as a series of individual histories of particular cities or regions.
The efforts to achieve a unified Greek policy which are associated with the name of Perikles were of a purely ephemeral nature; and the amphictyonies (associations of neighbouring states with a common shrine, like Delphi or Delos) were of much greater religious than political importance.
The attempts of the Macedonian dynasty to win the leadership of Greece had only a superficial appearance of success within Greece itself, and led in the end to the intervention of Rome and the end of the league of Greek states.
It was only in the 19th century that the Greeks were able to recover their independence and establish a unified state.

From the Earliest Times to the Persian Wars

(3rd millennium to about 500 B.C.)

During the 3rd millennium B.C. the Sesklo culture and later the Dimini culture flourish in mainland Greece, while on the Aegean islands the Cycladic culture emerges, and on Crete the Minoan culture, which reaches its peak about 2000 B.C. and is economically and culturally dominant until its sudden collapse in the 15th century B.C.	3rd millennium B.C.
Early Minoan: Pre-Palatial periods I, II and III.	2600–2000
Beginning of the Indo-European migration from the Balkans into Greece. These early Greeks (Achaeans) develop around 1580 the Mycenaean government and economic system, whose trading activities extend as far as Sicily in one direction and the eastern Mediterranean countries in the other. On the Acropolis in Athens, in the Argolid (Mycenae, Tiryns) and in other parts of Greece (Thebes, Pylos) local ruling princes build citadels, usually surrounded by cyclopean walls, which show the influence of Minoan civilisation.	about 2000
Middle Minoan, also with three periods: MM I (about 1900): the first palaces at Knossos and Phaistos on Crete MM II (about 1800): the heyday of Minoan culture (Kamares ware) MM III (about 1700): rebuilding, after earlier destruction, of the (second) palaces of Knossos (the "Labyrinth") and Phaistos; building of the palace of Ayia Triada.	2000–1600
Late Minoan: collapse of the Minoan empire (about 1400), perhaps as a result of an earthquake on Thera (Santorin); further rebuilding of the (third) palace of Knossos by Mycenean Greeks.	1600-1400
Sub-Minoan period: Dorian migration into Greece; the Cyclades and Euboea remain Ionian.	1400–1000
Further incursion by northern tribes (the Sea Peoples). The Achaean Greeks (Aeolians and Ionians) withdraw eastward and around 1000 B.C. found colonies on the west coast of Asia Minor and the islands of the eastern Aegean.	about 1200
In subsequent centuries there develop the little states, each confined to its own small territory, which make up the map of Greece until the Macedonian period.	after 1200
Trojan War, brought about by Paris's abduction of Helen. The Greeks, under Agamemnon's leadership, conquer Troy with the help of the wooden horse, a stratagem devised by Odysseus. Homer's "Iliad" tells the story of the war; his "Odyssey" tells of Odysseus's return home to Ithaca.	1194–1184 (?)
The Dorians, led by the Heraclids, occupy the Peloponnese.	1104
Geometric style in pottery.	1000–700
Foundation of Sparta.	about 950
Legislation of Lycurgus (Lykourgos) in Athens.	about 820
Homer and the Homerids.	about 800
Traditional date of foundation of the Olympic Games; starting-point of Greek reckoning of dates by olympiads (periods of four years).	776

8th century	In the course of the 8th century the Greek states, frequently directed by the oracle at Delphi, found colonies all over the Mediterranean.
740–720	Sparta's attempt to conquer Messenia leads to the First Messenian War; the Achaeans are driven out of Achaea and settle in the Ionian islands.
734	Foundation of Syracuse (Sicily) by the Corinthians.
707	Foundation of Taras (Tarentum) by the Spartans.
about 700	End of the Dorian migration. Aeolians now begin to settle in the eastern Aegean (Lesbos) and on Cyprus, Ionians in the northern Sporades, Euboea, the Cyclades (round a central cult site on Delos), Chios, Samos and Ikaria, and Dorians on Crete, Melos, Thera (Santorin), Anaphe (Anafi), the Dodecanese and the Ionian islands.
650–630	Second Messenian War; period of the Spartan poet Tyrtaios (war songs).
632	Rising in Athens, led by Kylon. Murder of Kylon; banishment of the Alcmaeonids.
621	Legislation of Draco in Athens.
about 600	The poetess Sappho and the poet Alcaeus (Alkaios) on Lesbos. Flowering of sculpture and architecture on Naxos, Delos and Samos. Invention of hollow casting of bronze.
600–590	The Sacred War: Athens and Sikyon make war on, and destroy, Krisa and Kyrrha.
594	Solon gives Athens a constitution.
about 570	The philosopher Pythagoras born on Samos (d. about 500–480 at Metapontion in southern Italy).
560–510	Athens ruled by Peisistratos and his sons Hippias and Hipparchos. The Greek colonies in Asia Minor fall under the control of Persia.
after 550	Naxos flourishes under the tyrant Lygdamis, Samos under Polykrates.
532	Introduction of the cult of Dionysos in Athens. The first tragedy is performed.
528	Death of Peisistratos.
514	Hipparchos is murdered by Harmodios and Aristogeiton.
after 512	Northern coast of the Aegean occupied by the Persians.
510	Hippias driven out of Athens (d. 490). Reform of the Solonic constitution by the Alcmaeonid Kleisthenes.

From the Persian Wars to Alexander the Great
(*c.* 500 to 338 B.C.)

500–494	Rising of the Ionian Greeks, led by Histiaios of Miletus and Aristagoras, against the Persians.

First Persian campaign against Greece. Aegina submits to Mardonios and is then laid waste by Sparta and Athens under Miltiades. Persian fleet wrecked on Athos. 492

Second Persian campaign: Persian army led by Datis and Artaphernes defeated by the Athenians under Miltiades. 490

Unsuccessful expedition led by Miltiades against Paros; his death. 489

Third Persian campaign, led by Xerxes. Battle of Thermopylai (Leonidas), followed by naval battle of Artemision and Greek victory, under the leadership of Eurybiades of Sparta and Themistokles of Athens, over the Persian fleet at Salamis. 480

This great victory arouses the Greeks' consciousness of their common identity as an ethnic and cultural community, in spite of their political fragmentation into small city states (*poleis*, singular *polis*).

Hymns of Pindar; tragedies of Aeschylus.

Fighting continues against the Persians who are still in Greece, led by Mardonios. Battle of Plataiai (Pausanias of Sparta, Aristeides of Athens). Naval battle at Mykale (Leotychides of Sparta, Xanthippos of Athens). 479

Athens takes over the leadership of the Greek cities. 478/477
Formation of a maritime league of Greek states, the Confederacy of Delos.

The Athenian general Kimon defeats the Persians on land and sea in the battle of the river Eurymedon. Conquest of the Chersonese. 465

A devastating earthquake in the Peloponnese destroys the city of Sparta and kills several thousand people. 464

Themistokles is exiled from Athens. about 462

Hippokrates, the great Greek physician, is born on Kos (d. *c.* 370 in Larisa). about 460

Third Messenian War. Athenian auxiliaries sent back by the Spartans; Athenian alliance with the Argives (457). 459–450

Unsuccessful Athenian expedition to Egypt. 456–450

The Athenians defeated in the Argolid but victorious at sea over the allied fleet of Corinth, Epidauros and Aegina. 456

Kimon exiled from Athens. 455

Athens at war with the Spartans and Boeotians. The Athenians are defeated by the Spartans at Tanagra (455), but defeat the Boeotians at Oinophyta (455). 455–451
Conquest of Aegina.
Kimon recalled to Athens (452).
Armistice between Athens and Sparta (449).

Laws of Gortyn (Crete). after 450

Chronology

449	Naval victory over the Persians. Kimon dies during the siege of Kition (Cyprus), but his fleet defeats the Persians at Salamis (Cyprus). End of the Persian wars.
442–429	The golden age of Athens under Perikles; work on the Acropolis by Pheidias, Iktinos and Mnesikles. Polygnotos (painter); "Histories" of Herodotus; tragedies of Sophocles.
433	The victory of Korkyra (Corfu), with Athenian help, over Corinth in the Sybota islands leads to the Peloponnesian War.
431–404	The Peloponnesian War (interrupted by the Peace of Nikias in 421) ends in the defeat of Athens. The Spartans appoint the Thirty Tyrants to rule Athens. History of the war by Thucydides; tragedies of Euripides; comedies of Aristophanes; Polykleitos (sculptor); Hippokrates of Kos (physician); Socrates and the sophists.
431	Attack on Plataiai by the Thebans. The Spartans invade Attica.
430	Plague in Athens.
429	Death of Perikles.
428	The island of Lesbos defects from the Athenian cause.
427	The philosopher Plato born in Athens (d. there in 347). Fall of Plataiai. Successful expedition into Acarnania led by Demosthenes. The Athenians reconquer Lesbos.
425	Demosthenes lands in Messenia and fortifies Pylos. The Spartan general Brasidas occupies Sphakteria, which falls to the Athenians, led by Kleon. The island of Kythera is occupied by the Athenians. Raid into Boeotia; Athenians defeated at Delion.
422	Battle of Amphipolis: Brasidas is victorious, but dies from his wounds; Kleon killed while fleeing.
421	Peace of Nikias.
418	Battle of Mantineia: Athenians and Argives defeated by the Spartans.
416	The island of Melos is captured by the Athenians.
415–413	Athenian expedition to Sicily, led by Alkibiades, Nikias and Lamachos. Alkibiades is accused of sacrilege and flees to Sparta. Annihilation of the Athenian army and fleet at Syracuse (413).
413	On Alkibiades' advice the Spartans occupy Dekeleia and make an alliance with the Persians against Athens. Athens is abandoned by its allies.
412	Victory of the Athenian fleet at Miletus.
411	Overthrow of the Athenian constitution; Alkibiades recalled. Athenian naval victories at Abydos.
410	Alkibiades defeats the Spartan fleet at Kyzikus; Athens regains control of the sea.

The Spartan Lysander defeats the Athenian fleet at Notion. Alkibiades 407
dismissed (d. 404).

Victory of the Athenian fleet at Arginousai. 406

Lysander destroys Athenian naval power in the battle of 405
Aigospotamoi.

Athens surrenders to Lysander: the Thirty Tyrants. 404

Thrasyboulos restores democracy. 403

Campaign of Cyrus the Younger against his brother Artaxerxes Mne- 401
mon. Battle of Kunaxa. Retreat of the Ten Thousand, led by Xenophon.

Flowering of painting (Zeuxis, Parrhasios). 400

The philosopher Sokrates (b. 470) condemned to death for corrupting 399
youth; dies by drinking hemlock.

Sparta at war with Persia; Agesilaos victorious in Asia (396). 396–394

Corinthian War: Argos, Athens, Corinth and Thebes against Sparta. 395–387

Battle of Haliartos; the Spartan leader Lysander is killed. 395

Battle of Knidos: the Spartan fleet is defeated by the Athenian general 394
Konon and the Persian Pharnabazos.
Battle of Koroneia: Agesilaos defeats the allies.

The Spartan leader Antalkidas makes peace with the Persians. 387

War between Sparta and Thebes; Pelopidas frees Thebes. 379–362

Establishment of the second Athenian maritime league by the Athe- 377
nian generals Chabrias, Iphikrates and Timotheos.

Severe earthquake in central Greece; destruction at Delphi and 373
elsewhere.

The Theban leader Epameinondas defeats Sparta at Leuktra and 371
establishes the dominance of Thebes.

The Thebans in the Peloponnese. Messenia independent; Megalo- 370
polis capital of Arcadia.

Battle of Kynoskephalai: Pelopidas victorious, but is killed in the 364
battle.

Battle of Mantineia: Epameinondas victorious, but killed in the battle. 362

Philip II becomes king of Macedon. 359
Agesilaos in Egypt to support rebels, but dies on the voyage home
(358).
Praxiteles (sculptor).

Allies at war with Athens. 357–355
Battle of Amphipolis: Athens against Philip II.

Sacred War against Phocis. 355–346

352	Philip II victorious in Thessaly, but halted by the Athenians at Thermopylai.
348	Olynthos destroyed by Philip II.
346	Peace between Philip II and Athens. Aischines (orator).
343	Philip II summons the philosopher Aristotle (b. 384 at Stageira in Macedonia, d. 322 at Chalkis on Euboea) to be tutor to his son Alexander (b. 356).
340	Philip II conquers Thrace and besieges Byzantium. Athens declares war on him and compels him to raise the siege.
339–338	Sacred War against Amphissa.
338	The Macedonians defeat the Athenians and the Thebans in the battle of Chaironeia. Philip II becomes commander in chief of the Hellenes for the war with Persia.

From Alexander the Great to the Destruction of Corinth
(336–146 B.C.)

336	Alexander the Great succeeds his murdered father, destroys Thebes (335) and thereafter establishes the Macedonian world empire. Diogenes (philosopher); Lysippos (sculptor); Apelles and Protogenes (painters).
335	Alexander destroys Thebes.
334	Alexander in Asia; battle of the Granikos. Chios and Lesbos temporarily in Persian hands.
333	Battle of Issos: Alexander defeats the Great King, Darius III, near what is now the Turkish port of Iskenderun.
332	Siege of Tyre; foundation of Alexandria.
331	Battle of Arbela.
330	Darius III murdered.
327	Spartan rising: King Agis II killed at Megalopolis.
323	After Alexander's death, struggles between his successors (the Diadochoi).
323–322	Lamian War.
321	Murder of Perdikkas.
319	Death of Antipatros.
306	Antigonos and Demetrios Poliorketes assume the title of king.
301	Battle of Ipsos; Antigonos killed. Aetolian League.
300	Epicurus (Epikouros) and Zeno (philosophers); comedies of Menander.

Death of Kassandros.	296
King Pyrrhos of Epirus in Italy. The Gauls invade Macedonia and Greece.	287–275
Achaean League.	280
Antigonos Gonatas king of Macedon.	278
Aratos, general of the Achaean League, frees Sikyon.	251
King Agis IV of Sparta seeks to reform the state.	241
King Kleomenes III of Sparta overthrows the ephors.	225
Battle of Sellasia: Achaeans and Macedonians defeat Kleomenes (d. 219).	221
Rome steadily increasing in strength.	from 220
War between the Aetolian and Achaean Leagues.	220–217
Philip V of Macedon allied with Hannibal; the Aetolian League with Rome. First Macedonian War.	215
Philopoimen, general of the Achaean League (the "last of the Greeks"), defeats the Spartans at Mantineia.	207
Peace between Philip V and the Aetolian League.	206
Philip V at war with Rome: Second Macedonian War.	200
The Roman consul Flaminius defeats the Macedonians at Kynoske-phalai; Greece remains independent.	197
Battle of Magnesia: Roman victory over Antiochos of Syria. End of the Aetolian League.	190
Perseus of Macedon at war with Rome: Third Macedonian War.	171–168
Aemilius Paulus defeats Perseus at Pydna.	168
War between the Achaean League and Rome; Roman victory at Skarphaea.	148
The Romans destroy Corinth. End of the Achaean League. Greece and Macedon become the Roman province of Macedonia.	146

Greece under Roman and Byzantine Rule
(2nd/1st century B.C. to A.D. 1453)

Slave revolts in Attica.	about 133 B.C.
The Greeks take part in the Mithridatic War.	88–87 B.C.
Battle of Orchomenos: Sulla victorious.	85 B.C.
Julius Caesar defeats Pompey at Pharsalos.	48 B.C.

Chronology

42 B.C.	Antony and Octavian defeat Caesar's murderers, Brutus and Cassius, at Philippi.
31 B.C.	Octavian (Augustus) defeats Antony at Actium (Aktion) in Epirus.
31 B.C. to A.D. 14	Augustus sole ruler of Rome. Greece a Roman province under the name of Achaea. Revival of local confederacies of Greek cities.
A.D. 49–54	The Apostle Paul preaches Christianity in Salonica (Thessalonica), Athens and Corinth.
A.D. 117–138	Much building in Greece in the reign of the Emperor Hadrian. The sophist Herodes Atticus in Athens.
about 170	Pausanias writes his famous "Description of Greece".
249–251	Emperor Decius. First appearance of the Goths on the frontiers of Greece.
253–260	Emperor Valerian. Walls built round Athens.
260–268	Gothic incursions into Greece; Athens defended by Dexippos.
323–337	Emperor Constantine the Great. Byzantium (Constantinople) becomes capital of the Roman Empire. Triumph of Christianity.
361–363	The Emperor Julian (the Apostate) favours the Greeks. Unsuccessful attempt to restore paganism.
379–395	Emperor Theodosius I.
393	Last Olympic Games of antiquity.
395	Division of the Roman Empire. The Goths, led by Alaric, destroy Eleusis, storm Athens and devastate the Peloponnese.
467–477	Incursions of the Vandals into Greece.
527–565	Emperor Justinian I.
529	The school of philosophy in Athens is closed.
540	Slav invasion of Greece.
6th century	Severe earthquake in the Peloponnese: Olympia destroyed.
end of 6th century	Avars and Slavs advance through Greece and into the Peloponnese.
717–741	Emperor Leo III.
727	Greek rising; unsuccessful naval expedition to Constantinople.
746–747	Plague in Greece. The Slavs spread over the Peloponnese.
about 805	Defeat of the Slavs at Patras.

Emperor Basil I. The Slavs in the Peloponnese are converted to Christianity. Photius patriarch of the Greek church: beginning of the schism between the Greek and Latin churches (formally declared in 1054).	867–886
The Emperor Basil II defeats the Bulgars at Thermopylai and Athens. First appearance of Albanians in Greece.	1019
Norwegians ("Varangians"), led by Harold Hardrada, in Athens.	1040
The Normans in Thessaly. Successful defence of Larisa.	1084/1085
An Italian noble, Orsini, seizes the islands of Kefallonia, Ithaca and Zakynthos.	1194
The Venetians gain control of Crete, Kythira and the southern tip of the Peloponnese.	beginning of 13th century
The Crusaders take Constantinople and set up the Latin Empire. Boniface de Montserrat, king of Salonica, conquers Boeotia and Attica (d. 1207). Othon de la Roche is granted the fiefs of Athens and Boeotia, and in 1205 becomes "Megaskyr" (Grand Duke) of Athens. Geoffroy de Villehardouin conquers the west coast of the Peloponnese with the help of Guillaume de Champlitte, who in 1205 becomes first Prince of the Morea (the Peloponnese).	1204
Marco Sanudo, a Venetian, conquers Naxos and founds the duchy of Naxos or the Twelve Islands (Archipelagos).	1207
Demetrius king of Salonica.	1207–1222
Geoffroy de Villehardouin second Prince of the Morea. Conquest of Corinth.	1210
Conquest of Nafplion and Argos.	1211–1212
After the death of Geoffroy de Villehardouin his son Geoffroy II (d. 1245) becomes third Prince of the Morea and is recognised by the Latin Emperor Pierre de Courtenay as Duke of Achaea.	1218
Theodoros Angelos Komnenos conquers Salonica and is crowned Emperor.	1222
Guillaume II de Villehardouin follows his brother Geoffroy as Prince of the Morea (d. 1278).	1245
Emperor Vatatzes of Nicaea reunites Salonica with Constantinople.	1246
Monemvasia conquered by Guillaume II.	1248
Guy I becomes Duke of Athens.	1258
Emperor Michael VII Palaeologus.	1259–1282
Michael VIII conquers Constantinople. End of the Latin Empire.	1261
Guillaume II de Villehardouin is compelled to cede to Constantinople the castles of Mistra, Monemvasia and Maina in the Peloponnese.	1262

	Beginning of the Byzantine reconquest of the peninsula, followed by an intellectual and artistic flowering in Mistra.
1267	Baldwin II, the last Latin Emperor, cedes to Charles of Anjou his feudal superiority over the principality of Achaea.
1308	Gautier de Brienne becomes Duke of Athens.
1311	Defeat of an army of French knights by Catalan mercenaries; Gautier de Brienne is killed.
1312	Roger Deslaur becomes Duke of Athens.
1364	Death of Robert of Taranto, last Prince of Achaea.
1380	Robert's nephew Jacques des Baux conquers the Morea, but dies in 1383.
1389	The Venetians occupy Nafplion and extend their rule over the whole of Greece and the islands.
1394	Rainerio Acciaiuoli, ruler of Corinth, becomes Duke of Athens. Argos occupied by the Venetians.
1395	Theodore I Palaeologus (1383–1407) recovers Corinth.
1396	Pierre Bordeaux de Saint-Supéran is recognised by King Ladislas of Naples as Prince of the Morea (d. 1432).
1404	Centurione Zaccaria, a Genoese, becomes Prince of the Morea (d. 1432).
1430	The Morea is recovered by the Palaeologi.
1435	Thebes occupied by the Turks.
May 29th 1453	Mehmet II conquers Constantinople. End of the Byzantine (Eastern Roman) Empire.

Greece under Turkish Rule

(*c.* 1450 to 1828)

1456	The Turks occupy Athens. Beginning of almost 400 years of Turkish rule in Greece.
1460	The Turks conquer the Peloponnese, with the exception of the Venetian possessions.
1463	Argos is conquered by the Turks but recovered by the Venetians.
1464	The Venetian admiral Vettore Cappello conquers the island of Euboea.
1470	Euboea retaken by the Turks.
1499–1501	Sultan Bayezit II captures the ports of Lepanto, Modone, Korone and Navarino from the Venetians, but fails to take Nafplion and Monemvasia.
1503	Peace between Turkey and Venice.

Nafplion and Monemvasia taken by the Turks.	1540
As a Turkish province the Dodecanese is granted extensive autonomy in domestic affairs.	16th century
Naval battle of Lepanto (October 6th): the young Don John of Austria, with a fleet of Venetian and Spanish galleys, inflicts an annihilating defeat on the Turks in the Ekhinades islands, off the mouth of the river Akheloos. Lepanto (Nafpaktos) was a Turkish naval base.	1571
Peace treaty between Venice and the Ottoman Empire: the Turks are left in possession of the whole of Greece.	1573
The Venetian duchy of Naxos falls to the Turks.	1579
Unsuccessful war by Venice against the Turks.	1645–1669
Conquest of the Peloponnese (Morea) by the Venetians, led by Francesco Morosini.	1685–99
Morea lost to the Turks.	1715
Peace of Passarowitz, confirming the Turks in possession of the Morea.	1718
Unsuccessful Greek rising, supported by Russian forces under Orlov. Many Albanians flee to the islands.	1770
Ali Pasha, an Albanian (born c. 1744) becomes Vizier of Ioannina. He establishes a quasi-sovereign state in Albania and northern Greece which lasts for more than 30 years. The principal European states, including Britain and France, maintain consulates in Ioannina, which plays the part of a capital.	1778
Hassan Pasha defeats an Albanian rising at Tripoli.	1779
The Hetairia Philikon ("Friendly Society"), a secret society for the purpose of preparing and organising the Greek fight for liberation, is established in the Russian Black Sea port of Odessa.	1814
British protectorate over the Ionian Islands.	1815
War of Greek Liberation.	1821–28
Alexander Ypsilanti, leading the forces of the Hetairia, crosses the river Prut and calls on the Greeks to fight for their freedom (March 7th), but suffers an annihilating defeat at the Romanian town of Drăgăşani (June 19th) and is forced to flee to Austria. On March 25th (now the Greek National Day), in the Ayia Lavra monastery in the Peloponnese, Germanos, metropolitan of Patras, calls on the Greeks to rise against the Turks. The Ottoman government holds the Oecumenical Patriarch, Gregorios V, responsible for this, and he is hanged at the entrance to the Patriarchate in Istanbul.	1821
A National Congress in Epidavros proclaims the independence of Greece and promulgates a national constitution (January 13th). A Turkish force of 50,000 men is sent against Ali Pasha, who had rebelled against Sultan Mahmud II, and after a 15-month siege of his citadel he is captured and executed.	1822

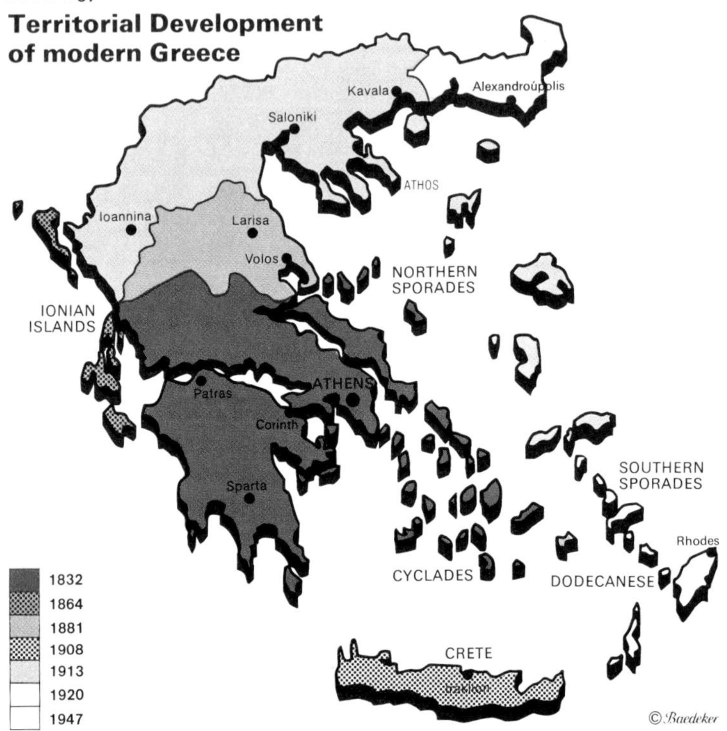

Dramalis is defeated by Kolokotronis and Nikitas.
Kurshid Pasha defeats a Greek force at Peta.
Athens is occupied by the Greeks.

1823 Omer Vriones is defeated by the Greeks at Karpenisi.

1824 Ibrahim Pasha recovers the Peloponnese.

1826 Fall of Mesolongi.
The Turks recapture Athens.

1827 John Kapodistrias is elected head of the Greek free state.
Naval battle of Navarino (October 20th): a combined British, French and Russian fleet destroys most of the Turkish fleet in the bay of Pylos (Navarino).

1828 Kapodistrias takes office as head of the Greek government (January 7th).
Ibrahim Pasha leaves the Peloponnese.
A French expeditionary force lands in Greece.

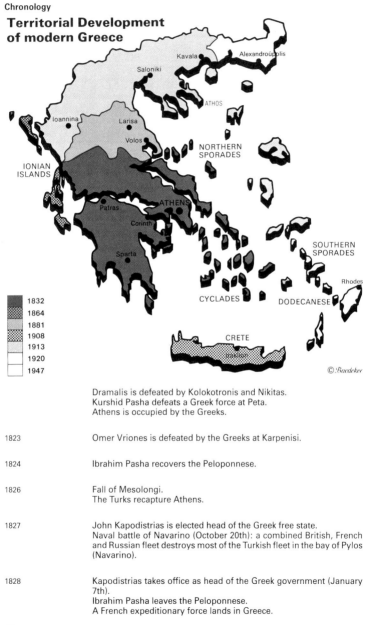

The Kingdom of Greece
(1830–1973)

Under the Peace of Adrianople (Edirne) Turkey is compelled to recognise the independence of Greece – which, however, is still required to pay tribute to Turkey. 1829

London Protocol (February 3rd): the protecting powers (Britain, France and Russia) guarantee the independence of Greece, now recognised as a sovereign kingdom. 1830

John Kapodistrias is murdered (September 27th); his brother Augustine becomes President (resigns in 1832). 1831

Prince Otto von Wittelsbach, son of King Ludwig I of Bavaria, is installed by the great powers as King of the Hellenes (Otto I), and is confirmed by the Greek National Congress. As he is not yet of age Greece is governed by a Bavarian regency council. 1832

Otto comes to Greece and at first resides in Nafplion. 1833
Kapodistrias makes the national Greek church independent of the Patriarchate in Constantinople.

The king transfers his residence to Athens, which thereafter acquires many buildings in neo-classical style, mostly designed by German architects. 1834

Otto I comes of age. 1835

Rising in Athens. 1843
First Greek constitution of modern times.

Piraeus blockaded by the British navy. 1850
The Patriarch of Constantinople confirms the autocephaly (independence) of the national Greek Orthodox church.

French forces seize Piraeus and the Greek fleet (which they hold until 1857) in view of Greek support for Russia in the Crimean War. 1854

Catastrophic earthquake on Crete. 1856

After a number of risings King Otto I leaves the country and returns to Bavaria. 1862

A Danish prince, William of Sonderburg-Glücksburg, becomes king as George I. 1863

Britain returns the Ionian Islands to Greece. 1864
New Greek constitution.

Greece acquires Thessaly and part of Epirus. 1881

Piraeus is blockaded by the European powers. 1886
A severe earthquake devastates towns and villages in Messenia.

The Greek government declares the country bankrupt. 1893

After a rising on Crete against Turkish occupation Greece fights an unsuccessful war against Turkey. 1897
Treaty of Constantinople: Greece is required to pay a large sum by way of reparations and to cede to Turkey important strategic points on

	the borders of Thessaly and Macedonia. An international commission is established to control Greek finances.
1898	Crete is granted self-government under Turkish suzerainty.
1909	Military coup d'état at Goudi, near Athens.
1910	Eleftherios Venizelos, a Cretan, becomes prime minister.
1912	Italy occupies most of the Dodecanese.
1912–13	As a result of the Balkan Wars Greece makes territorial gains. Under the treaty of London (May 30th 1913) it acquires Epirus and the islands of Crete, Samos, Lesbos, Tenedos, Imbros and Thasos; but Italy holds on to the Dodecanese. Under the treaty of Bucharest (August 10th 1913) Greece acquires part of Macedonia, including Salonica and Kavala.
1913	After the murder of King George I his son becomes king as Constantine I. Crete is united with Greece.
1914–18	During the First World War part of Greece is occupied by Allied troops.
1915	The king dismisses Prime Minister Venizelos, who supports the Allies.
1917	Constantine abdicates in favour of his second son Alexander as regent. Greece breaks with the Central Powers.
1919–20	Under the treaties of Paris and Sèvres Greece receives southern Albania, western Thrace from Bulgaria and eastern Thrace and a mandate over Smyrna (from Turkey).
1920	After the death of Prince Alexander and Venizelos's defeat in an election King Constantine is recalled to Greece.
1920–22	The Greco-Turkish War ends in the defeat of Greece. Constantine abdicates in 1922 in favour of his son George II.
1923	The treaty of Lausanne provides for an extensive exchange of populations. Greece loses the territories in Asia Minor which had been occupied by Greeks since ancient times, together with the islands of Imbros and Tenedos. Over 1.4 million refugees flee to Greece. Turkey cedes the Dodecanese to Italy.
1924	Proclamation of a Republic (March 25th), confirmed by a plebiscite (April 14th). This is followed by much unrest and frequent changes of government.
1926	A severe earthquake devastates the east coast of Rhodes.
1928	Corinth is largely destroyed by an earthquake.
1928–32	Eleftherios Venizelos returns to power.
1930	Treaty of Ankara, settling differences with Turkey.
1935	After a national referendum the monarchy is restored. King George II returns to Greece.

Coup d'état by General Metaxas; establishment of dictatorship. 1936

After occupying Albania the Italians march into Greece, but are driven 1940
back and lose part of Albania to Greece.

Death of Metaxas (January 29th). 1941
German forces cross the Yugoslav and Bulgarian frontiers into Greece (April 6th), occupy Salonica (April 9th), enter Athens (April 17th) and force Greece to surrender (April 20th–21st).
On the island of Crete, to which the Greek king and government had withdrawn (later moving to Egypt), a German airborne landing meets fierce resistance from Cretans and from British forces. The German advance, however, compels British forces to withdraw both from Crete and from mainland Greece.

A variety of resistance groups are formed in Greece. Ruthless reprisals 1942
by the German occupying forces: atrocities of all kinds, shooting of hostages, mass executions of men, women and children and the destruction of whole villages, particularly in southern Greece.

The Bulgarians, who had moved into northern Greece in the wake of 1943
the German forces, seek to establish their authority in this area.

A severe earthquake devastates the west coast of the Mani peninsula 1944
in the Peloponnese.
After the withdrawal of German forces from Athens (October 14th) British troops enter the town (October 16th) and at first tolerate a "government of national unity" led by Yeoryios Papandreou, but after conflicts between different Greek factions are compelled to intervene militarily (the "battle of Athens"). Papandreou resigns, and the king appoints Archbishop Damaskinos of Athens as Regent (December 31st).

A bloody and damaging civil war between the government and left- 1945–49
wing groups hinders all efforts at reconstruction after the ravages of war; Greece remains in a chaotic state.

After a national referendum George II returns to Athens, but dies in the 1946
following year.

Italy is compelled to return the Dodecanese to Greece. 1947
George II is succeeded by his brother, Paul I.

Government forces win a decisive victory over the Communists. 1949
The last British troops leave Greece.

A referendum on Cyprus produces a 78% majority in favour of union 1950
with Greece (Enosis).

New Greek constitution. 1952
Greece joins NATO.

Greece, Yugoslavia and Turkey sign a treaty of friendship, the Balkan 1953
Pact.
Agreement between Greece and the United States on the use of air and naval bases by US forces.
Devastating earthquake in the Ionian Islands.

Tug-of-war between Greece, Britain and Turkey over the political 1954–60
future of Cyprus. In 1960 it becomes independent, with Archbishop Makarios as President.

1961–62 Greece becomes an associate member of the European Economic Community.

1964 Death of King Paul I; he is succeeded by his son Constantine II.

1967 Coup d'état by Colonel Papadopoulos, followed by the establishment of a military dictatorship. After an unsuccessful attempt at a counter-coup the king flees to Rome (and later to London). General Zoitakis becomes Regent.

1968 New Greek constitution (the "constitution of November 15th").

1969 Greece leaves the Council of Europe and withdraws from the International Convention on Human Rights.

1971 Greece re-establishes diplomatic relations with Albania.

1972 Zoitakis is relieved of his office as Regent; Papadopoulos becomes head of state.

1973 A government-managed national referendum decides on the abolition of the monarchy in favour of a Republic (a parliamentary presidential democracy). Papadopoulos becomes President; Markezinis heads a civilian government.
Greece establishes diplomatic relations with the German Democratic Republic.
The bloody repression of a student rebellion in Athens by armoured units of the army (November 17th) leads to a military revolt led by General Ioannidis. Papadopoulos is overthrown and General Gizikis becomes President.

Hellenic Republic
(from 1974)

1974 After a coup d'état by the Greek-officered Cypriot National Guard Turkish armed forces land on Cyprus and occupy the north of the island.
President Gizikis recalls Konstantinos Karamanlis, a former prime minister, from his exile in Paris. He forms a democratic civilian government. Greece withdraws from NATO.
Greece applies to rejoin the Council of Europe.
In the first free election (November 17th) after seven years of military dictatorship Karamanlis's party, New Democracy (ND), gains an absolute majority in Parliament.

1975 A new constitution comes into force (June 11th).
Konstantinos Tsatsos is elected President (June 19th).
Earthquake in central Greece.
Trial of the leaders of the 1967 military coup. Colonels Papadopoulos, Pattakos and Makarezos are condemned to death, a sentence commuted by the government to life imprisonment.

1976 Greece aims at increased economic cooperation with both capitalist and socialist states.
When a Turkish research vessel begins sounding operations in the Aegean, in an area of the continental shelf claimed by Greece, the Greek government puts its forces in a state of alert and appeals to the UN Security Council and the International Court in the Hague against the Turkish action.

Greece concludes a four-year defence agreement with the United States. 1977
In a parliamentary election on November 20th New Democracy, the government party, suffers losses; the strongest opposition party is PASOK, the Pan-Hellenic Socialist Movement.

A severe earthquake in northern Greece causes much destruction, particularly in Salonica. 1978
The foreign minister. Yeoryios Rallis, visits the Soviet Union (the first Greek government representative to do so since the Second World War).

A treaty on Greece's entry into the European Community is signed in Athens on May 28th and ratified by the Greek Parliament on June 28th. 1979

Greece opposes the extension of Turkish air control over the Aegean (February). 1980
Konstantinos Karamanlis is elected President (May 5th) after the premature resignation of President Tsatsos. Yeoryios Rallis becomes prime minister.
Greece rejoins NATO (October).

Greece becomes the tenth member of the European Community (EC; in Greek EOK) on January 1st. 1981
Queen Frederica, widow of Paul I, dies in exile in Madrid (February 6th). Ex-King Constantine II returns briefly to Greece (for the first time since the 1967 coup) for her funeral on the royal family's private estate at Tatoi (north of Athens).
A series of severe earthquakes cause heavy damage in central and southern Greece, particularly in the Corinth area (February–March).
Negotiations on the renewal of the agreement with the United States on military bases in Greece.
In a parliamentary election on October 18th PASOK wins an absolute majority; Andreas Papandreou becomes prime minister.
Government plans for the "socialisation" of important branches of the economy.

Papandreou's social policy is aimed at adjusting pay in line with rising inflation, with particular regard for the lower income groups. 1982

Further negotiations with the United States on military bases in Greece (July). 1983
The drachma exchange rates ceases to be linked to the US dollar.
At a conference of European Community foreign ministers in Athens Greece blocks a proposal to condemn the Soviet Union for the shooting down of a South Korean airliner (September).
The Greek Parliament ratifies an agreement on the stationing of American forces in Greece until 1988 (November).

Conference in Athens on making the Balkans a nuclear-weapons-free zone, in which Greece, Yugoslavia, Bulgaria and Romania take part, with Turkey as an observer (January). 1984
The Greek government terminates a 38-year-old civil aviation agreement with the United States (beginning of February).
A further conference in Athens on the establishment of a nuclear-weapons-free zone in the Balkans ends without result (February).
Following a controversy with Turkey over the military status of the island of Lemnos Greece refuses to take part in NATO's autumn manoeuvres.

1985 In a controversial election Khristos Sartzetakis becomes President (February).
In an election following an early dissolution of Parliament PASOK again wins; Andreas Papandreou remains prime minister.
Greece ends the state of war with Albania which has existed since 1940.
Delegates from NATO, the Warsaw Pact and non-aligned countries meet in Piraeus for discussions on peace.
The socialist government introduces a two-year wage-freeze.

1986 A constitutional reform restricts the powers of the President in favour of the prime minister and Parliament (March 7th).
In local government elections (October 12th/19th) the government party suffers considerable losses, particularly in the towns.
Large-scale demonstrations and a wave of strikes against the government's economy measures (December).

1987 The introduction of a value-added tax (January 1st) sparks off three 24-hour general strikes (January–February).
In the dispute over the use of the Aegean Turkey abandons for the time being its prospecting for oil in international waters on the continental shelf claimed by Greece.
The Greek Parliament passes a very controversial law on the expropriation of land owned by the Greek Orthodox church (April 6th), but the government, bowing to the influence of the church, withdraws it (August 18th).
Heat wave in Greece, with temperatures of up to 46°C/115° F and very high air humidity (end July).

1988 In the course of an international economic forum at Davos in Switzerland (end January) the Greek prime minister, Andreas Papandreou, and the Turkish head of government, Turgut Özal, declare that Greece and Turkey desire in future to seek lasting friendly relations between the two countries.
Turgut Özal visits Athens for political discussions (June 13th–15th).
A terrorist attack on the "City of Poros", an excursion ship returning from Hydra to Athens, causes eleven deaths (July 11th).
Greece terminates the 1983 agreement with the United States on military bases.
Some 8 million foreign tourists come to Greece in 1988.

1989 In a parliamentary election on June 18th PASOK, the government party, loses its predominance, partly at least as a result of the Koskotas scandal. Yeoryios Koskotas, Director of the Bank of Crete, who is charged with corruption, declares that the prime minister and his government had also received bribes from him. None of the other parties can achieve the necessary majority for forming a government; and in order to resolve this stalemate the New Democracy party and the Communist alliance of the "United Left" agree, surprisingly, on the formation of a transitional government headed by the conservative politician Tsannis Tsannetakis. The Tsannetakis government calls a new election and determines, in a programme of "purification" (katharsis), to clear up the financial and economic scandals of Papandreou's PASOK government.
The fresh election on November 5th produces no decisive result.

1990 In a further election (April 8th) the New Democracy party (ND) falls short of an absolute majority by a single vote; but it achieves this

majority (151 out of 300 members) when the representative of the Democratic Renewal party (DEANA) joins ND and enables it to form a government under Konstantinos Mitsotakis.
By means of a package of drastic fiscal measures the new government sets out to tackle the country's appalling economic problems – high inflation, public debts amounting to the equivalent of a year's gross national product, tax evasion estimated at a level of 50% of the GNP, unprofitability of state-owned enterprises (approx. 80% of Greek business firms are state-controlled), as well as financial privileges granted to government officials. With its narrow majority it is not possible, however, for the government to pursue its policy of national rehabilitation effectively and it meets with opposition from trade unions, socialists and communists, who counter with general strikes. A terrorist organisation, "the 17th November", justifies its bomb attack on an industrialist by its declared struggle against privatisation and foreign (in particular German) investment ("dehellenisation").

The neighbouring former Yugoslavian republic of Macedonia, having 1992
gained the status of sovereign state, wishes to call itself the "Republic of Macedonia", a move fiercely resisted by Greece, which fears claims against its territorial sovereignty.

In March a motion of no confidence lodged by the socialist opposition 1993
against Mitsotakis fails.
In parliamentary elections on October 12th the Panhellenic Socialist Movement gains an absolute majority (46.9%). The PASOK leader Papandreou is entrusted with the task of forming an administration.

Art and Culture

Ancient Greek Art

Prehistory

Neolithic

No other prehistoric discoveries have aroused so much excitement as the royal graves of Mycenae and the palaces of Crete. Much more modest, but much older, are the finds of Neolithic material in Thessaly and Boeotia, on Samos and Crete and in Chalcidice and the Peloponnese. In contrast to the rather meagre Palaeolithic material so far discovered, these point to the existence of substantial settlements with a considerable level of cultural achievement. It is not yet possible, however, to say much about the people who occupied Greece in the centuries after 3500 B.C. The layouts of their houses show a predominance of straight lines, with an attempt, usually successful, to achieve rectangular structures.

Sesklo culture

On the basis of the finds of pottery it is possible to distinguish two geographical areas – one in the south-east, taking in Crete, the Cyclades and Samos (museums of Iraklion, Rhodes and Pythagorion), and the other in central and northern Greece, the area of the Sesklo culture, which is named after the type site in Thessaly (Volos and Chaironeia museums). The pots are elegantly shaped, at first burnished red and black ware, occasionally with incised designs, later with painted decoration. A variety of decorative techniques are used – red designs on a light ground or white designs on a dark ground. Pottery or, more rarely, stone idols with strongly emphasised female sexual characteristics were found in settlement levels but not in burials.

Dimini culture

In the Dimini culture of Thessaly, which begins after 2900 B.C. and has close relationships with the Danube area, spiral motifs appear in the pottery decoration and curved lines occasionally occur in the plans of buildings. The lines of the pots are less finely articulated than in the Sesklo culture. The vessels become rounder and fuller in other parts of Greece as well during the 3rd millennium B.C. (Archaeological Museum, Salonica). More organic forms find their best expression in zoomorphic (animal-shaped) vases, with rather abstract variants in the so-called "sauce-boats", duck-shaped vessels and beaked jugs (Nafplion and Tegea museums). The source of these types is to be found in north-western Anatolia. The islands lying off the coasts of Asia Minor were so closely bound up with the eastern cultural sphere during this period that they have quite appropriately been called Western Anatolia.

A distinctive local style was developed in the Cyclades, where vessels and utensils were made from the local marble as well as from clay. The marble idols of the Cyclades (National Archaeological Museum and Goulandris Museum of Cycladic Art, Athens) were exported to other parts of Greece.

Cycladic idol

The finest flowering of prehistoric culture, however, was achieved on Crete.

Snake goddess from Knossos

Harvesters Vase from Ayia Triada

Crete

Early Minoan

In the Early Minoan period (before about 2000 B.C.) there were numerous small flourishing settlements in the Gortys plain, on the Gulf of Mirabello and on the little islands of Mokhlos and Psyra. Grave goods, sometimes of great richness, were buried with the dead.

The large palaces of Knossos and Phaistos were built in a later period and enlarged between 1900 and 1800 B.C.; they contain numerous rooms of different shapes and sizes laid out round interior courtyards, with a complex system of staircases and light shafts and with unusually shaped columns tapering towards the base. Here and at Malia open-air theatres were used for ceremonies and acrobatic performances. Large rooms alternate with smaller ones, and there are a variety of cult rooms, bathrooms (sometimes with a terracotta bath), lavatories, store-rooms and cellars.
Similar, though on a smaller scale, is the palace at Ayia Triada, the last to be built; but here are to be seen the oldest fresco paintings, and it was only at Ayia Triada that new buildings of any size were erected after the destruction of the Cretan palaces around 1400 B.C. The inhabitants of Knossos and Phaistos were content with makeshift accommodation rigged up in the ruins of the old palaces. Apart from the palaces the remains of other houses have been preserved.

At Gournia in eastern Crete the layout of a whole town has been recovered, with the foundations of houses and the street pattern so clearly visible that it takes only a little imagination to visualise the life of this little Minoan town of the 2nd millennium B.C.

The development of Minoan culture can be charted with the help of dated Egyptian imports, and a relative chronology can be established on the basis of the rich finds of pottery (Iraklion Museum).

The Kamares style, named after a cave on the slopes of Mt Ida, was dominant in the first quarter of the 2nd millennium B.C. The contours of the vases are compact and clear, and they are decorated with brightly coloured and freely drawn patterns of spirals, stylised flowers, stars, etc.

Late Minoan

In the Late Minoan "Palace style" the forms become slenderer and more elegant, with flowing lines and types of handle which at times take on a Baroque exuberance, and the vases are strikingly decorated with floral patterns and double-axe motifs. The finest artistic achievements of Late Minoan Crete are the wall paintings, sometimes preserved only in fragments (Iraklion Museum).
Natural though this painting appears, it cannot be described as naturalistic. It reproduces sensuous movement in forms and colours; it is based on the observation of nature, but conveys that observation in the form of impressions, without seeking to impose any preconceived structure on the material.

Melos

Paintings of this kind have also been found in the Minoan settlement at Fylakopi on the island of Melos. This island had long been of importance as the source of the obsidian used in making knives and arrowheads; for although the men of the 3rd millennium had copper they knew nothing of bronze. It was not until the beginning of the 2nd millennium that the technique of adding tin to copper to produce bronze came into use throughout the eastern Mediterranean.

Mycenae

Peloponnese

While the Cretan empire was at the peak of its power the Peloponnese, and in particular the Argolid, was pursuing its own course of de-

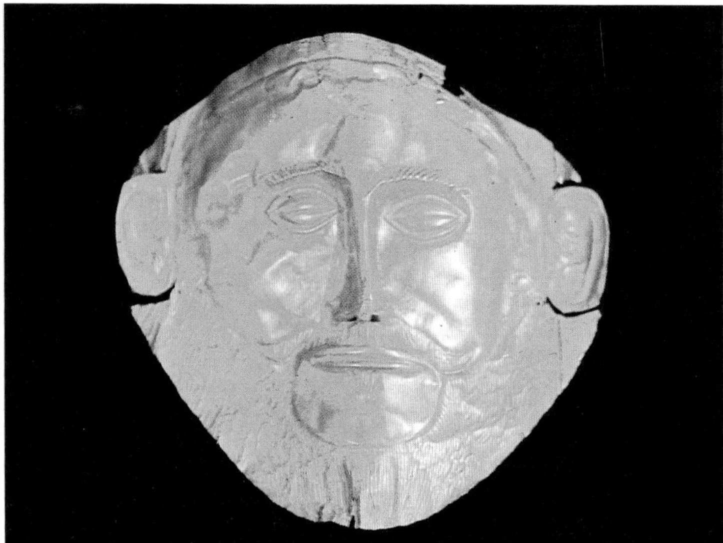

Gold mask from Mycenae

velopment. The Mycenaean culture certainly developed out of a close contact with Crete, but the Argolid was never a Cretan cultural province in the same way as Melos and Thera.

Defensive structures

From about 1600 B.C. Mycenae was the dominant power in the Peloponnese; but here, as at Tiryns, a short distance away to the south-east, the buildings are not palaces but strongholds designed with an eye to defence. Mycenae occupies a commanding situation surrounded by massive walls within which the buildings are closely fitted together. In contrast to the irregular layout of the Cretan palaces, there seems at Mycenae to be an attempt to achieve some degree of symmetry.

Frescoes

Here too, in the later phases, large wall paintings are found. The artists may well have been Cretans, but they had to adapt themselves to the requirements of their patrons, both in the themes (including battle and hunting scenes which are not found on Crete) and in the composition, which shows a stronger tectonic sense and sometimes a certain rigidity.

Grave goods

The valuable grave goods found in the shaft graves (14th c. B.C.) bear witness to the power of the ruling family; they included almost 14kg/31lb of gold in the form of ornaments and utensils. A characteristic feature is the presence of large numbers of weapons; for this was a very different world from the peaceful Cretan empire, which no doubt relied on a powerful fleet for protection but needed no other defences.

Monumental architecture

The most striking examples of the monumental architecture of the later Mycenean period are the Lion Gate and the beehive-shaped tomb (*tholos*) known as the "Treasury of Atreus", both still in situ. Tombs of this type are found at many other places in the Peloponnese (e.g. at Vaphio, famous for the two gold cups discovered there and for the earliest use of iron) and in mainland Greece.

Inscriptions

Important light has been thrown on the history of the second half of the 2nd millennium by material discovered at the settlement of Ano Englianos (Messenia), which has been thought to be the Homeric Pylos, home of Nestor. This evidence takes the form of inscribed clay tablets, excellently preserved by being baked in the fire which destroyed the building in which they were found. The script, known as Linea B, was deciphered after the last war by the English architect Michael Ventris, who showed the language to be Greek, although written in a script which was certainly not devised for Greek. The 600 tablets found here, still under study in the National Archaeological Museum in Athens, were merely administrative records, but nevertheless can be made to yield valuable information about the political and social structure of the period and, even more significantly, about its religious conceptions: there are references in the texts to Dionysos and Paian (Apollo).

Population

This material, and the prospect of finding and interpreting similar texts at Mycenae and on Crete, raise the problem of the original population of Greece on to a new plane. The script and language of the tablets have made it possible to confirm earlier hypotheses. The literary tradition of the settlement of the Greek islands by Carians can be related in time to the 3rd millennium and the introduction of Anatolian pottery types. From about 2000 B.C. the Carians were caught between two other population groups. On the one hand there were Cretans, like the Carians a non-Greek people, whose Minoan culture cannot have originated in Greece or any of the neighbouring countries. Comparisons have been made with the early Indus culture (Mohenjo Daro, in present-day Pakistan); although the similarities are unlikely to reflect any actual movement of peoples, but may perhaps be the result of influences from the village cultures of the Taurys and Iran, moving both east and west. The other peoples from the mainland of Greece and the Peloponnese who pushed back the Carians in the Bronze Age, however, were Greek. The dead who were buried in the shaft graves of Mycenae were still honoured as heroes in the period of the tholos tombs; there had, therefore, been no change of dynasty. These kings of the Argolid must have been heroes of the kind celebrated in the "Iliad". The inscribed tablets now tell us that not only was Greek spoken throughout the Peloponnese but that it was used in those parts of Crete in which the palaces were destroyed about 1400 B.C.

Pottery

The pottery, with its astonishing abundance and wide distribution, provides evidence of the development and expansion of Mycenaean culture. The pottery is often decorated with patterns of Cretan origin but, unlike the vessels of precious metal, is locally made, and does not match the quality of the best Cretan products. Like the wall paintings of the Argolid, it shows a stronger tectonic structure and uses only a selection from the range of Cretan motifs. The vessel forms include both imitations of Cretan vessels and specifically indigenous types. This ware was exported to Asia Minor (Troy), Cyprus, Syria, Palestine, Egypt, Sicily and probably also Spain. From about 1300 B.C. signs of decadence begin to appear in the vase decoration; the style becomes steadily more schematic, and finally degenerates completely. Although in the final stages new subjects begin to appear (human figures, horses, domestic animals) the artists have no longer the skill to give them convincing expression.

Geometric Style

Although after the collapse of the Minoan and Mycenean civilisations some historical memories and religious conceptions were handed on, together with certain technical skills, Greek art – the development of which was indirectly affected by the Dorian migration (*c.* 1200 B.C.) – made a fresh start. The achievements of the civilisations of previous centuries were abandoned, and ritual and political forms, customs and practices underwent radical change. A new conception of the world was given expression in the simplest form. The buildings now erected were small, and at first of perishable materials; the vessels and utensils used were modest, through produced with great care; the pottery ash urns and grave goods had only the most limited decoration. This new decorative style, with its lines and circles, is known as the Geometric style. The characteristic motif is the meander, though this does not appear in the first ("Proto-Geometric") phase. In later stages we find more valuable bronze articles (votive offerings), small sculpture in clay, ivory and metal, and jewellery. The Geometric period extended over some four centuries. The oldest temple of which remains survive on Samos is dated to around 800 B.C.

Pottery

Geographical differences can be recognised in the development of the Geometric style. The best pottery was produced in Athens, and only in the final phases was Attic ware surpassed in quality by Corinthian. The vessel forms are precise, clearly articulated and of simple lines; so too are the figures of humans and animals which begin to appear in the

decoration about 900 B.C. The themes, sometimes involving numerous figures, include mourning for the dead, biers and funeral processions, battles on land and sea, gymnastic and musical performances, dances, birds and other animals. The development of the style can be observed in the serried ranks of vases in the Kerameikos Museum in Athens, recovered from the cemetery outside the Dipylon, the double gate in the old town walls. Some of the amphoras used as funerary monuments were over 1.5m/5ft high (National Archaeological Museum, Athens).
The artists who painted the vases were less concerned with the purely optical impression than with the idea they wanted to convey – for example in a human figure the head and the lower part of the body may be shown in profile and the torso frontally – and individual characteristics are of less importance than what is felt to be typical. The main principles of composition are symmetry and arrangement in regular rows; and when both these principles are combined they produce a dense centralised composition.

Small sculpture

Although the Near Eastern countries had shown the way, and Syria in particular had produced some notable small sculpture, all this work was surpassed by the Greek achievement, introducing a whole new repertoire of forms. Even in small statuettes the limbs are clearly detached from one another, though the figures are not properly balanced: except where they formed part of a larger whole, whether as a member of a group or as an element in some implement or utensil, they must either have been leaned against something or merely laid down. While the figures in vase paintings remain within the upper and lower margins of a frieze or are strictly confined within a rectangular frame, the small sculpture makes a freer use of space: the outlines of the figures are not of the same geometric precision, the impetuous vigour of their bearing and their glance is not always subject to the same discipline of form (helmeted man with legs apart: National Archaeological Museum, Athens). This freer treatment is most notable in representations of the human figure. Such items as the hundreds of little bronze horses in the museum at Olympia are less different from their counterparts on vases than are the bronzes and terracottas of human figures from the warriors and mourning women depicted on vases.
The leading bronze foundries were evidently in the Peloponnese and in Athens.

Archaic Period

(*c.* 670–490 B.C.)

Large sculpture

Considerable as were the originality and the artistic achievement of the Geometric period, the period immediately following was no less remarkable. Its most important contribution to Greek art – and to Western culture as a whole – was a new conception of the life-size statue.
Large sculpture had long been produced in the East, particularly in Egypt; and the Greeks had now reached a stage in their own development, a moment of maturity, when they were ready to follow these earlier examples. But here again they remained largely independent. In comparison with Egyptian work the earliest Greek statues may at first sight appear somewhat primitive. They are not direct copies – certainly not copies of the cult images in their temples, which were frequently no more than large statuettes, though sometimes reaching a height of 2m/6½ft. These divine images were either not shaped by human hand at all or only very crudely hewn into the likeness of

Archaic horseman (c. *560* B.C.)

Peplos Kore (c. *530* B.C.)

human form – sacred objects which were supposed to have fallen from heaven or to have been found in marvellous circumstances in some wild part of the country. The men of the Geometric period had conceived their divinities in the form of such images, which later Greek writers referred to as "unhewn blocks of wood". The images were clad in cloth garments and on the occasion of ritual festivals were bathed and anointed. They were thus treated as having a real existence, as being natural beings.

Oldest known draped figure

In contrast to these images, the oldest large marble figure that has come down to us (*c.* 600 B.C.; National Archaeological Museum) is a deliberately created artistic form. An inscription on this draped figure of the goddess Artemis, Apollo's sister, records that it was dedicated by a woman named Nikandre of Naxos. It was found in the temple of Artemis on the island of Delos, and is identified as the goddess herself by the holes bored in her hand, presumably for her bronze bow and arrows. This earliest example of Greek monumental sculpture shows not only great sureness of touch in the individual forms – still visible in spite of the weathering of the surface and the loss of the original colours – but also an exact proportion between the parts and the whole. The structure of this whole is admittedly conceived only from the front, and the figure is flatter than the Geometric bronzes and terracottas; but it shows the unified composition and the single dominant rhythm which had previously been found only in vase paintings and not in small sculpture. One consequence, however, was the loss of the earlier dynamic expressiveness, the free extension of the body in space; for the monumentality of large statuary could at first be achieved only by using the simplest forms. The oldest marble statues show less of the overflowing creative power found in the earlier statuettes; and the sculpture of the 7th century has none of the luxuriance of Oriental imagery found in the vase paintings of the same period. Nevertheless the fact that in the very beginnings of large sculpture those types were created which influenced the whole development of ancient sculpture, and indeed have continued to influence sculptors down to our own day, demonstrates the intensity of final effect produced by this deliberate limitation.

Early figures of *kouroi*

Alongside the draped figures of women there now appears the type of the *kouros,* an unclothed figure of a youth. The earliest examples of the type are fragments found at the same site and made of the same material as the statue dedicated by Nikandre (Delos Museum). They can be reconstructed on the basis of a well preserved bronze statuette of a youth with a tiered hair-style and a wide belt in the Delphi Museum. The fact that these figures wear a belt on their otherwise naked body indicates that their nakedness did not represent the way they went about in everyday life but was a stylistic form deliberately selected on ethical and artistic grounds. Slightly later are the *kouroi* found on the island of Santorin (Thera), which have a more elaborate hair-style but no belt. These figures, unfortunately in a poor state of preservation, are the earliest examples of over-lifesize figures in Greek sculpture.

Euthykartides

Even allowing for the chances of preservation, the figures found in the Cyclades mark these islands out as one of the centres of Greek sculpture in the earliest period. The flowering of sculpture in the Cyclades was undoubtedly promoted by the excellent stone available there: the marble quarries of Naxos are inexhaustible, and the marble of Paros was famed as the finest material for the sculptor. It is perhaps no accident, therefore, that the earliest sculptor whose name is recorded, Euthykartides, describes himself as a Naxian (Delos Museum: triangular base with inscription, ram and Gorgons' heads, *c.* 620 B.C.; only feet of statue preserved). The name suggests a man of noble family; the inscription refers to him as both the donor and the sculptor of the statue.

Unknown master

The forms created in the Cyclades, however, became the model for the whole of Greece only through the work of the great creative artists of Athens. The name of the leading master of his day, a contemporary of Euthykartides, is not known to us. His principal work was a statue 2.5m/8ft high which stood on a tomb outside the Dipylon in Athens. The head (National Archaeological Museum, Athens), hands, shoulder and knee (Agora Museum) have been preserved. There is another statue by the same sculptor – smaller, but still more than life-size – in the Metropolitan Museum of Art, New York. In the vigour of their lines, the clear structure of the planes on all four sides and the rendering of detail, the perfection of which is almost reminiscent of mineralogical forms, these figures are quite without peer.

Later *kouroi*

Later stages in the development of the kouros type are represented by the colossal figure from Cape Sounion (*c.* 600 B.C.: National Archaeological Museum, Athens), the figures of Kleobis and Biton (*c.* 590 B.C.: Delphi Museum), the torso from Megara (*c.* 570–560 B.C.: National Archaeological Museum), the kouros from Tenea (*c.* 560 B.C.: Glyptothek, Munich) and the funerary statues of Kroisos (*c.* 530 B.C.) and Aristodikos (*c.* 510 B.C.: both National Archaeological Museum).

Draped female figures

From about 640 B.C. the draped figures of women gain greater plastic fullness and spatial quality without losing their tectonic structure and precision (half life-size statue from Auxerre, now in the Louvre, Paris). In the headless statue of Hera from Samos (Louvre) the flat planes and four-square structure of the earlier examples are merged into a more unified, almost columnar, composition. The delicate modelling of the surface (almost entirely covered with an intricate pattern of pleats) betrays the hand of a master – whose name is unknown, for the inscription mentions only the donor, Cheramyes (who appears on at least two other votive inscriptions). Roughly contemporary with this statue (*c.* 560 B.C.) is a group of four (originally six) figures on a large base, with an inscription naming the persons represented and also the sculptor, Geneleos (Vathy Museum).

Korai

Among later figures of this type (*korai,* maidens; singular *kore*) one (in the Acropolis Museum) returns to the simpler angular forms of the 7th century but shows a feeling of individuality in the taut features and tense glance, while others enrich the tradition by still more elegantly draped robes and the dreamy beauty of the lowered eyelids (Acropolis Museum). The 5th century kore dedicated by Euthydikos (also in the Acropolis Museum) has, unlike her predecessors, a serious and indeed melancholy expression.

Temples

The Greek temple achieved monumentality not in the 7th century like the sculpture but some 70 years later, in the early 6th century.

Corfu

On the island of Corfu, within the Corinthian sphere of influence, there was built about 590 B.C. a temple of Artemis which already shows the canonical forms of Doric architecture (see pages 90–91). Particularly notable is the well preserved sculpture from the west pediment (Corfu Museum), which has figures of Medusa and her sons Chrysaor and Pegasos, flanked by wild beasts, in the centre, a scene from the destruction of Troy to the left and Zeus fighting giants to the right.

Athens and Samos

Some twenty years later, almost contemporary with one another, were the Doric temple built to house the old image of Athena on the Acropolis in Athens and the huge temple of Hera on Samos, with no fewer than 134 columns, built by Rhoikos and Theodoros. In spite of the difference between their absolute dimensions (the one 44m/144ft long, the other 105m/345ft) the proportion of breadth to length is about the same (1:2) in both temples. Earlier temples had been much longer in proportion to their breadth (1:4 or 1:5).

While the temple of Athena has in all essentials the proportions of the canonical temple *in antis* surrounded by columns, the temple of Hera is typical of the colossal temples of the Ionic order in its size, its magnificence and the multiple ranks of columns enclosing the naos. From this temple there is a direct line leading to Hadrian's completion, in the Corinthian order, of the temple of Zeus in Athens.

The plan of Rhoikos's temple on Samos is known to us, but only from the trenches dug by stone-robbers. The only column still standing belongs to a more recent temple completed centuries later. This later structure, however, gives a striking impression of the size of the early temple, for its dimensions and proportions, as seen from the well preserved foundations, correspond exactly to those of Rhoikos's temple, although the later temple was moved some 40m/130ft west.

The foundations of the old temple of Athena on the Acropolis are still easily distinguishable, and there are many fragments of the superstructure in the Acropolis Museum, including some of the sculpture from the pediments. The temple was pulled down when the Erechtheion was built as a replacement a little to the north.

Corinth

A good impression of the Doric order of the mid 6th century B.C. can be gained from the remains of the temple of Apollo in Corinth. The columns, firmly based on the three-stepped crepidoma, rear massively up, the very incarnation in stone of static forces, topped by

Temple of Apollo, Corinth

capitals which seem flattened by the weight of the roof structure, now represented only by a few blocks of the architrave.

Greek Temples (see plans on page 60)

The temple ranks with the theatre (see page 74) as one of the supreme achievements of ancient Greek architecture. It was not designed as a meeting-place of the faithful, but as the home of the cult image, and thus of divinity itself. The earliest temples were built in the 9th century B.C., but since they were built of timber and clay no remains survive. The first temples in stone – usually marble – date only from the second half of the 7th century.

Development

The form of the Greek temple is derived from the rectangular main room (megaron) of a Greek house, preceded by an antechamber, such as can be seen in the throne-rooms of Mycenaean palaces. The windowless main chamber of the temple is known in Greek as the *naos,* in Latin as the *cella.* The entrance to the temple was normally at the east end, with the divine image facing it against the west wall of the naos, which was divided up by one or two rows of columns. The roof was low-pitched, with triangular pediments containing sculpture at each end.

Temple *in antis*

Different types of temple developed from the earliest times. The simplest form is the temple *in antis,* in which the naos is preceded by an antechamber (the pronaos) flanked by *antae* (forward projections of the side walls of the naos). Between the antae are two columns supporting the pediment (Treasury of the Athenians, Delphi). A temple with a second antechamber (the *opisthodomos*) at the far end is known as a double anta temple (temple of Aphaia, Aegina).

Types of Greek Temple

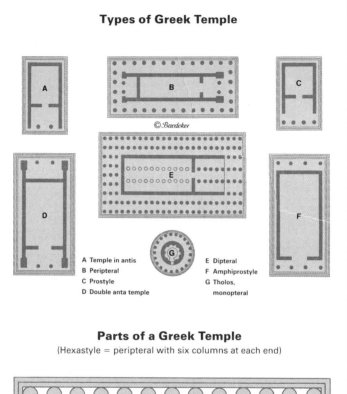

A

B

C

© Baedeker

D

E

F

G

A Temple in antis
B Peripteral
C Prostyle
D Double anta temple

E Dipteral
F Amphiprostyle
G Tholos, monopteral

Parts of a Greek Temple

(Hexastyle = peripteral with six columns at each end)

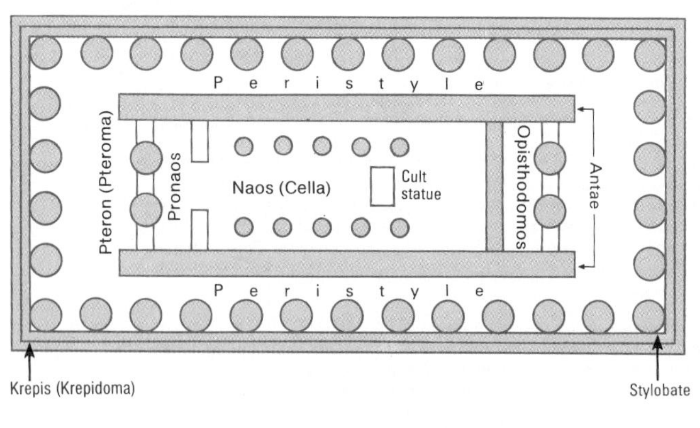

Prostyle

Where there is another row of columns in front of the antae, supporting the projecting pediment (one column in front of each of the antae, with two or four between), the temple is known as prostyle (eastern temple in the Erechtheion, Athens).

Amphiprostyle

If there is a similar row of columns on the rear end of the temple it is known as amphiprostyle (Temple of Nike, Acropolis, Athens).

Peripteral

From the second half of the 7th century the classical form was the peripteral temple, in which the naos was surrounded on all four sides by a colonnade (*peristasis).* At one end was the entrance, with the pronaos; at the other end was a rear chamber, the opisthodomos. In the 6th century an elongated ground-plan was favoured, with six columns at the ends and 16 along the sides (temple of Hera, Olympia; temple of Apollo, Delphi, with 6 + 15 columns). In the 5th century the classical proportions of the temple were developed, with *x* columns at the ends and 2*x*+1 along the sides (Temple of Zeus, Olympia, 6 + 13 columns; Parthenon, Athens, 8 + 17).

Dipteral
Pseudo-dipteral

If the temple has a double row of columns on all four sides it is known as dipteral (Olympieion, Athens). If the inner row of columns is omitted to leave room for a wider naos, the temple is known as pseudo-dipteral.

Tholos

A less common type of temple is the *tholos,* on a circular ground-plan, with a ring of columns round the naos. Examples of this type can be seen at Delphi (Marmaria) and Epidauros.

Temples differ not only in ground-plan but also in the form and proportions of the columns and roof structure. See the description of the classical orders on pages 90–91.

Pottery of the Archaic period

In the painted pottery of the early Archaic period four very different local types can be distinguished.

Corinth

The leading place in number of potters' workshops and quality of work was taken by Corinth. The material used was the local clay, yellowish-white to light green in colour. Most of the vessels are small, designed to contain oil for cosmetic purposes. They are frequently decorated with tiny friezes of animals, and sometimes also with mythological scenes, mainly found on larger vessels (examples in Corinth and Aegina museums; outstanding pieces are a jug formerly in the Chigi collection and now in Rome, and a mixing jar depicting Eurytios's banquet, now in the Louvre). The Corinthian potters devised the technique of black-figure decoration, the figures standing out in black on a clay-coloured ground and the details being incised with a hard point.

Black-figure ware

Rhodes

The second group of workshops was in the eastern Aegean islands; the largest quantity of material has been found on Rhodes. Animal friezes predominate in the decoration, and the general effect is more Oriental, more "carpet-like" than in the rest of Greece (examples in Rhodes Museum; outstanding piece a jug formerly in the Lévy collection and now in the Louvre).

Cyclades

The third group was in the Cyclades (Naxos, Paros, Melos). Here individual human figures and animals (lions, horses) are drawn with evident care. Pairs of figures and individual heads are found which in their flatness, their contours and their proportions are strikingly reminiscent of the earliest examples of large sculpture. Examples can be seen in the Mykonos and Naxos museums and in the National Archaeological Museum in Athens.

Mixing jar (krater)

Votive jug

Athens

Finally there was Athens, which evolved a distinctive form of dramatic narrative decoration, used on vases which were sometimes of very considerable size. Even the animal friezes and the individual figures seem to be there for their contribution to the subject-matter rather than on artistic or formal grounds, and this gives expression to the idea behind the decoration more strongly than in the work of the other groups.

This expressive tendency can be seen as looking forward to the later achievements of Attic painting. In the 6th century this style dominated the field: the only new development was the Spartan school of vase painting, which was mainly confined to drinking cups. By the end of the 6th century all the other workshops had been driven out of business by competition from the Attic potters.

Exekias

Rather earlier, between 550 and 525 B.C., an Attic potter and painter, still practising the black-figure technique, had reached one of the summits of Greek painting. This was Exekias, nine signed examples of whose work have been preserved (e.g. Herakles and Geryon, in the Louvre; Leda and her sons, in the Vatican Museums, Rome).

Red-figure ware

But even while Exekias was painting his last works a new technique of red-figure decoration was developing. This method, specifically Attic, uses the same kind of colour contrasts as in the mature black-figure style, but in reverse. The ground is now painted black, and it is the figures that retain the reddish colouring of the clay. The details are no longer incised, but are painted in brilliant black or in thub matt lines. The figures now gain in plastic quality as compared with the silhouette figures of the black-figure technique.

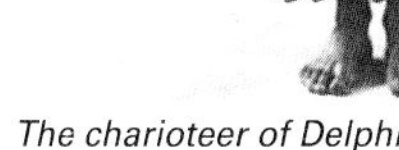

The charioteer of Delphi

Spartan warrior (Leonidas)

Severe Style

(*c.* 490–450 B.C.)

The "Severe" style is the very apt name given to a distinct and characteristic phase of Greek art. The term, applied in the first place to sculpture, is not to be understood as marking a contrast to the preceding Archaic period but as the first phase in the development of mature classical art. The later phases of classical art are sometimes, less aptly, described as the "rich", the "beautiful" or the "free" style; in contrast to these the Severe style reflects an awareness of the serious, and indeed the tragic, quality of human existence.

Sculpture

There is an anticipation of this in the melancholy expression of Euthydikos's kore, although her posture is still typical of the korai of the Archaic period. Figures of men and youths evidently broke free at an earlier stage than the korai from the old axial and symmetrical canons of composition. A group by Antenor glorifying the liberation of Athens from tyranny (510 B.C.) may already have shown the freer and livelier forms of the Severe style; but we know it only from copies of a version dating from 476 B.C. A chronological reference point is given by the Persian capture of the Acropolis of Athens in 480 B.C., when many votive offerings were damaged, including a statue of a youth of the highest quality, of which at least two fragments have been preserved (Acropolis Museum, Athens; lower part of body).

We know the names of some of the leading sculptors of this period – Kritios, Nesiotes, Kalamis, Dionysios, Onatas, Pythagoras, Myron. A group of Athena and Marsyas and a statue of a discus-thrower can be confidently ascribed to Myron.

"Critian Boy"

The "Critian Boy" in the Acropolis Museum (illustration, page 70) shows clearly the change in posture which now came into vogue. The weight of the body is no longer borne equally on both legs: a clear distinction is made between the leg which supports the body and the one that remains free, and this difference is reflected in the whole muscular structure of the figure right up to the shoulders. The most notable feature is that the front of the torso and the face are no longer in the same plane, the head being turned to the right.

Representation of men and gods

The discovery of man as an individual, and the realisation of his own personal responsibility within the bonds of religion and the community, now found expression in art, and the thousand-year-old representational conventions which remained predominant in Egypt and the ancient East were now cast aside by the contemporaries of Herakleitos. This new conception of man's dignity as man and this new severity of artistic expression were displayed in the votive gift of a four-horse chariot presented to the sanctuary of Apollo at Delphi by the ruler of Syracuse, of which the charioteer has survived (Delphi Museum: also a good example of the technical skills of the period, with inset eyes and eyelashes).

But this period also saw the beginnings of a consistent practice of differentiating between the representations of gods and of men. The marble torso of a Spartan warrior (Sparta Museum) may be a representation of Leonidas, the hero of Thermopylai; but the bronze statue of an unclothed bearded man in the National Archaeological Museum, Athens, which shows a similar liveliness of representation, depicts a figure from an altogether different sphere. The effortless power of the arm, drawn back to hurl a weapon (no doubt Poseidon's trident), and the tranquil majesty of the features can belong only to a god.

Roman copies

Hardly a single example of this later sculpture has survived, and none of the most famous works of the period. The precious metals and the bronze were subsequently melted down, the marble broken up and used in building or burned to produce limestone. But the originals survived at any rate into the Roman period, when numerous reproductions of them were made, and many of these works, therefore, are known to us in copies, and sometimes in numerous copies. Examples of such copies of works in the Severe style are a marble statue of Apollo found in the Theatre of Dionysos in Athens (National Archaeological Museum) and five clothed statues in bronze from Herculaneum, reduced to six-sevenths the size of the originals (National Museum, Naples).

Small sculpture

There are, however, very numerous original pieces of small sculpture – thousands of bronze statuettes, various articles incorporating figural decoration, including in particular stands for circular metal mirrors, and terracottas. The high quality and craftsmanship of these small items reflects the increased national confidence which followed the defeat of the Persians, high artistic dedication and an intimate fusion of art and technical skill; and their survival is at least some compensation for the loss of the larger works. The figure supporting a hemispherical bronze bowl (National Archaeological Museum, Athens) can stand beside the finest works on a similar theme; the figure, a consummate example of the mature Severe style, is not only perfectly conceived to serve its function as a support but can stand on its own as an independent work of art.

Painting

The painting of this period was of equally notable artistic quality.

Polygnotos

The greatest master of the period was Polygnotos of Thasos, whose best known works were in Athens (of which he was made an honorary citizen) and in an assembly hall at Delphi. He used the technique of

fresco, painting his works on prepared wall surfaces or wooden panels. Although we have detailed descriptions of his paintings, particularly those at Delphi, the most vivid impression of his composition and draughtsmanship is to be had from a number of vase paintings which are evidently based on monumental paintings (Louvre, Paris).
The scale and the focal point of all such paintings, even those with seventy or more figures, was determined by the individual human figure. Some degree of perspective effect was contrived for the purpose of representing movement by foreshortening of the limbs and emphasis on weapons and accoutrements like shields. There was, however, no sense of perspective in the composition as a whole: the individual figures were not seen from a common viewpoint but were depicted in a single plane surface.

Vase painters

Those vase painters who were not directly basing their work on mural or panel paintings perfected their art within the framework of the genre. The remark already made about the small sculpture of the period is equally true of the vase painting: at no other time in the history of Greek art was such perfection of individual forms combined with such harmony between form and function. An incomparable example of this relationship between the vase and the vase painting is provided by a drinking bowl bearing the signature of Brygos (Martin von Wagner Museum, Würzburg). It is significant that consummate effects of this kind were achieved even with the simplest subjects, indicating that the artists were catering for a large clientele of education and taste.

Relief sculpture

The Greek art of relief sculpture – including the fully rounded figures in temple pediments – is a genre closer to painting than to free-standing sculpture. Reliefs and paintings, however different in other respects,

Herakles with apples of Hesperides

Olympian Zeus (reconstruction)

have a common feature in the background which links together the separate elements in the scene depicted on it or in front of it. Already in the Archaic period a narrow slab of stone with a representation in low relief or painting within incised lines sometimes took the place of a free-standing statue on a tomb, and the tradition of the funerary relief was continued in the Severe style (Palazzo dei Conservatori, Rome; National Archaeological Museum, Athens; Archaeological Museum, Salonica). When two figures were represented they were now not always merely set behind one another, facing in the same direction, but were related to each other (Louvre, Paris). This opened up new compositional possibilities and challenges. The same characteristics are found in votive reliefs, such as the figure of a boy (formerly with a gilded bronze garland) found at Sounion (National Archaeological Museum, Athens) or a relief showing Athena in front of an inscribed stone (Acropolis Museum, Athens).

The finest examples of relief carving in the Severe style, however, are to be found in architectural sculpture – the sculpture in full relief on the pediments of temples.

Temple of Aphaia, Aegina

The temple of Aphaia near the east coast of Aegina was built about 500 B.C., but some of the figures in the battle scene on the east pediment were damaged and renewed, probably before 480 B.C.; and the transition from the Archaic to the Severe style took place between the carving of the original sculpture on both pediments and the renewal of the east pediment (Glyptothek, Munich). The earlier work forces the figures into a schematic composition of parallel lines, while the later work from the east pediment shows a unified and organic composition with a feeling of movement.

Temple of Zeus, Olympia

The temple of Zeus at Olympia (completed in 456 B.C.) still resembles the temple of Aphaia in detailed architectural form; for although it was not so squat as earlier reconstructions suggested it must undoubtedly have had a certain heaviness of effect. The column drums of muschelkalk limestone still litter much of the site of this temple, the largest in the Peloponnese. The roof and the sculptural decoration were of Parian marble (Museum, Olympia).

In addition to the pediment sculpture there were twelve metopes with relief decoration (fragments in the Louvre, Paris) on the front and the rear end of the naos, depicting the twelve labours of Herakles. Athena frequently appears in these scenes as the hero's divine patroness and helper. In addition to "action" scenes (e.g. the cleansing of the Augean stables) in a diagonal compositional pattern there are quieter and more static scenes (e.g. Atlas with the apples of the Hesperides) of a type particularly characteristic of the Severe style.

The east pediment represents a legend featuring Zeus as a judge, Oinomaos (a mythical king of Elis) and Pelops (a hero particularly revered at Olympia) and recalling the establishment of the Olympic chariot races.

The west pediment depicts the fight between Greek heroes and centaurs at a wedding feast, with Apollo standing majestically between the contestants – the counterpart to the figure of Zeus on the east pediment. The imposing figures of the gods have the same visionary character as the statue of Poseidon already referred to.

Pheidias's famous statue of Zeus, one of the seven wonders of the world, was probably set up in the naos some 25 years after the completion of the temple.

Pheidias and Polykleitos

These two names mark the high point of Greek art. Both were sculptors, although Pheidias also painted in his earlier days. They differed, however, in the subjects they chose: Pheidias owed his fame to his statues of gods, while Polykleitos devoted himself mainly to human figures.

This difference was merely the external reflection of their personal and profoundly different conceptions of the function of art; but seen from our later point in time and against the whole background of the development of art they move closer together, with their diverse aspects complementing one another to form a single culminating point in the history of the art of antiquity.

Pheidias

Pheidias was born in Athens, probably at the beginning of the 5th century B.C. He inscribed his name and that of his father on the base of what was probably his last work, the statue of Zeus at Olympia. This statue was completed about 430 B.C., and Pheidias is believed to have died soon afterwards, perhaps in 428. There are divergent traditions about the teacher from whom Pheidias learned his craft. At a later stage in his career he worked in collaboration with the painter Parrhasios, and it has been suggested that Pheidias may have been a pupil of Euenor of Ephesus, Parrhasios's father. This theory is based on the possibility that a column bearing Euenor's signature which was set up on the Acropolis of Athens about 475 B.C. bore a small statue of Athena by the youthful Pheidias. The statue has been preserved and is now in the Acropolis Museum; and in fact it has the appearance of an early forerunner of the statues of Athena carved by the mature Pheidias. It is a work of notable quality, and in various details (the left hand resting on the hip) anticipates the full classical style. The figure as a whole, of course, still bears the mark of the Severe style; but Pheidias must have been at work during that period, even though his principal works belong to a later period.

Principal works

The two large votive offerings which the Athenians commissioned from Pheidias after their victory at Marathon in 490 B.C. – a bronze group at Delphi and a bronze figure of Athena Promachos, 16.5m/54ft high, on the Acropolis – were probably produced between 460 and 450; and thereafter a whole series of works, known to us only from copies and descriptions, followed in quick succession. On the Acropolis there were a bronze figure of Apollo (statue in Kassel, head in National Archaeological Museum, Athens) and a bronze figure of Athena Lemnia (probably 448–447 B.C.; statue in Dresden, head in Bologna), in Ephesus a bronze Amazon (Vatican Museums, Rome).

In 447 B.C. work began on the building of the Parthenon, one of Perikles's great enterprises, and, as Plutarch tells us, the general oversight of the project was entrusted to Pheidias. Two architects were responsible for the building of the temple, and numerous sculptors worked on the relief decoration on the metopes (before 442–441 B.C.), the best preserved of which are the fights with centaurs (British Museum, London), and on the frieze (Acropolis Museum and British Museum) and pediments (438–432 B.C.; British Museum). The chryselephantine cult image (438 B.C.) was the work of Pheidias himself.

When Pheidias later created the chryselephantine statue of Zeus at Olympia he was clearly following up the experience he had gained in setting up the image of Athena Parthenos in Athens.

Although Pheidias maintained, and indeed enhanced, the visionary aspect of the divine images in the Severe style, he departed from the earlier pattern of representation. It has been well observed of the statue of Apollo in Kassel that scant attention is paid to the proper distribution of weight, since although the supporting leg shows an outward curve the free leg is not correspondingly concave (Khr. Karousos). As a result the side with the supporting leg conveys an impression of movement, while the other side is vertical, as if rooted

to the ground; and the almost mincing posture suggests a certain instability. The unity of the figure does not reside in its physical structure: the god is superior to the laws of gravity, and both the body and the face show that this is a divine and transcendent being.
This is also the case with the Dresden figure of Athena, who is depicted presenting weapons to a warlike group of settlers setting out for Lemnos. The face of the Bologna head shows that the figure forms part of something very different from the ordinary genre scene.
The statues in the Parthenon and the temples at Olympia not only reached out beyond all accustomed degrees of grandeur and splendour but were seeking to achieve entirely new effects. An important factor in this respect is the space which these statues occupied within the temple, taking up its full height and breadth, almost bursting out of its confines. And the wealth of attributes and the detail of the carving are beyond all numbering here.

Parthenon frieze

This transcendental, superhuman vitality of the gods is no less evident in the Parthenon pediments (east pediment, birth of Athena; west pediment, contest between Athena and Poseidon for possession of Attica); but the frieze takes us into a different world. It represents the procession during the Panathenaic festival which took Athena's new robe to the Acropolis, where the assembled divinities of Olympus awaited it. Here the sculptors give expression to all the beauty of the human body and all the grace of youth. We are at once reminded of the finest of the funerary reliefs of Attica, the sculptors of which no doubt also worked on the Parthenon – of the magnificent figure of a youth in the act of releasing a bird from a cage, as the soul is released from the body (National Archaeological Museum, Athens), or the intimately associated figures of two women on the grave stele of Hegeso (also in the National Archaeological Museum), in an almost circular composition of consummate harmony.

The influence of such works by Pheidias as the relief of a horseman in the Villa Albani, Rome, is still seen in the stele of Dexileos (394 B.C.; Kerameikos Museum, Athens).
In this context, too, we must consider the lekythoi (oil-flasks), with scenes painted or drawn in colour on a white ground, which were used only as grave goods to accompany the dead (National Archaeological Museum and Kerameikos Museum, Athens). On these we see representations of the monument over the tomb, the dead persons, their relations and friends, the life of this world and the next, often indiscriminately mingled.

Reliefs and painting

The designs for the carving on the shield of Athena Promachos were drawn by Parrhasios, but of this work nothing has survived, even in the form of copies. We have in fact none of the work of Parrhasios or of any of the other famous Greek painters; but we have such excellent descriptions of his style and draughtsmanship that it has been possible to show that some of the vases with decoration on a white ground were influenced by him, including some original works.
The Acropolis Museum contains a work by Alkamenes, a sculptor of rather conservative bent, depicting a woman with a small boy snuggling against her; and we also have a fragment and parts of the base of a statue of the goddess Nemesis (Retribution) carved by the more impulsive Agorakritos for the town of Rhamnous in Attica (British Museum, London; National Archaeological Museum, Athens).

The total work of art

In addition to altering the strict rules of construction in sculpture Pheidias also presided over a mingling and modification of the canonical orders of architecture. The shaping of the interior of the Parthenon

was determined by the form and intended effect of the cult statue: the temple was, as it were, made to measure for the statue. The number and proportion of the columns were unusual, and the frieze was an element from the Ionic order which did not properly belong to the Doric order. The continuation of the interior row of columns round the back of the cult image must be seen as reflecting the special status of the image: the effect aimed at is that of a total work of art.
A similar tendency is seen in the later work on the Parthenon by Iktinos and in the temple of Apollo at Bassai, in which Corinthian capitals were used for the first time. The Propylaia of the Acropolis, built by Mnesikles in the time of Pheidias, have both Doric and Ionic columns. But during the period of building activity which began with the Parthenon even purely Ionic forms were modified in a specifically Attic way (temple of Nike, Erechtheion), while Doric buildings like the splendidly preserved temple of Hephaistos (wrongly called the Theseion) in Athens and the temple of Poseidon on Cape Sounion are barely conceivable without the model provided by the Parthenon.

Polykleitos

Polykleitos of Argos was some 15 years younger than Pheidias. We have only copies of his statues, but some of the original bases and inscriptions have been preserved (Kyniskos, Pythokles, Xenokles; Museum, Olympia). His earliest work was the Diskobolos (Discus-Thrower; Vatican Museums, Rome), the style of which is better preserved in a winged head in the Pergamon Museum (Berlin) than in complete statues. An Amazon now in Rome (Capitoline Museum) and the "Westmacott Athlete" (British Museum), probably belonging to the Kyniskos base, both date from the middle of the 5th century. A much more famous work was the Doryphoros (Spear-Bearer), of which over 40 copies are known (4th c. relief, with addition of horse; National Archaeological Museum, Athens). A Herakles now in Rome (Museo Baracco) and a youth tying a ribbon round his head (National Archaeological Museum, Athens) are probably late works. The originals of all these statues were in bronze.
Polykleitos also worked in the chryselephantine technique. His last work, a statue of Hera for the temple at Argos, which was burned down in 423 B.C. and had to be rebuilt, was in the same technique as Pheidias's temple statues and according to Strabo was in no way inferior to them in magnificence and grandeur.

Polykleitos's statues were governed by strict rules, both in respect of the form of the body and the facial features. The marks of the feet in surviving statue bases, and the copies of the statues themselves, show that, even more markedly than in the "Critian Boy", one leg bore most of the weight. To an even greater extent than in the Critian Boy, too, the whole body was governed by a system of correspondences: to the free leg corresponded the arm which was in active movement, to the supporting leg the arm which hung quietly by the figure's side. This resulted in a completely balanced and harmonious composition. This harmony extends to every detail of Polykleitos's figures, including the faces, which have none of the spiritualisation of Pheidias's gods. Polykleitos's statues achieve their artistic unity by a precise observance of the laws of structure and mathematical proportion. At the same time the creative process depended in the last analysis on an element of the irrational, as Polykleitos himself emphasised in a theoretical treatise.
It is not surprising, however, that he was criticised for the uniformity of his figures, which were in fact merely variations on the same general scheme. That is true enough, but the criticism is misconceived; for it is precisely this that makes Polykleitos a supreme representative of Greek art, which from its very beginnings showed both the will and the

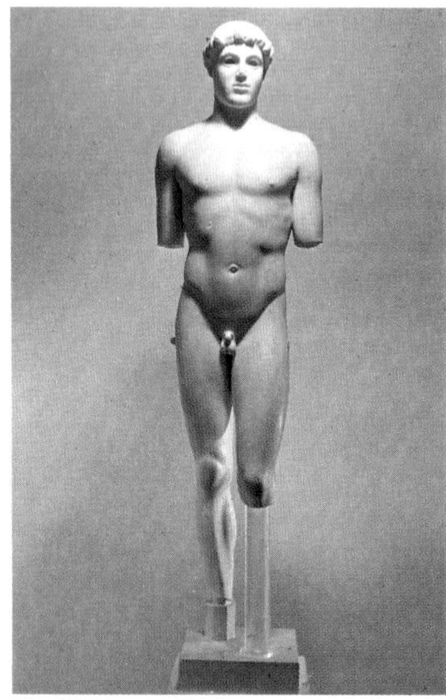

The "Critian Boy"

Hermes, by Praxiteles

ability to create types. In this respect the artist of the high classical period proves himself the heir to the art of the Archaic period. In his statues of youths Polykleitos gives expression to the same ideas, though at a higher stage of development, as another sculptor from Argos had expressed a century and a half earlier in his statues of Kleobis and Biton.

Late Classical Art

(*c.* 390–330 B.C.)

Painting

While in the Severe style even the paintings of Polygnotos and the work of the vase painters had sought to achieve a plastic effect, the development of the classical school after Pheidias and Polykleitos shows a painterly trend.

During the last decades of the 5th century B.C. large-scale painting was already seeking to contrive new effects by the use of light and shade on garments and male bodies. The painters were now not merely producing frescoes and panel paintings but also decorating rooms in private houses and painting architectural scenes as stage settings.

Once again we see a reflection of this in vase painting, which achieves more colourful effects by the use of a white ground colour, gilding and even relief moulding of certain parts. The themes become lighter, gentle, sentimental.

Funerary reliefs

In the earlier reliefs the figures had been related to one another either by the action or by the mood of the scene. In the numerous Attic funerary reliefs of the 4th century B.C. (National Archaeological Museum, Athens) – which were forbidden by sumptuary legislation about 310 B.C. – the mere existence of the figures is sufficient. To an increasing extent they become isolated from one another, standing out like individual statues against the background of the relief. This does not mean, however, that the figures themselves are given greater plasticity: instead, the architectural framework of the scene gains in importance, so that the figures are set within a niche. The artistic theme of these reliefs thus became the relationship between the figures and the frame within which they were enclosed. The figures, moulded in the round though they were, could now be seen from only one viewpoint – that of the spectator face to face with the relief background.

Praxiteles

This is true also of the statues of the most celebrated creator of divine images after Pheidias, Praxiteles. They too are designed to be seen from only one viewpoint, and they too are spatial compositions which, like the reliefs, seek to achieve a picture-like effect by the use of highlights, deep shadows and transitional nuances. At the same time there was a more vivid use of colour than had previously been usual. It is significant that Praxiteles believed his finest statues to be those which had been painted by the contemporary painter Nikias. We can get some idea of the nature of the colouring from those of the little terracotta figures from Tanagra which have preserved their surface coating of clay and their painting (National Archaeological Museum, Athens, and Thebes Museum).

Statues of gods

In the interpretation of his themes Praxiteles showed a very individual approach. He represented Apollo as a youthful figure barely beyond adolescence and still with the interests of a boy – leaning against a tree in a relaxed posture and reaching out with his right hand to catch a lizard which is climbing up the trunk (marble copy of a bronze original; Vatican Museums, Rome).

In his Aphrodite of Knidos (50 copies in many museums) Praxiteles ventured for the first time in Greece to depict a goddess completely naked.

A similar conception of the weightless being of the gods is expressed in a late work, not quite finished, representing Hermes with the infant Dionysos, the original of which was found at Olympia (Museum, Olympia).

Three original reliefs by Praxiteles from the bases of statues by him at Mantineaia (National Archaeological Museum, Athens) depict clothed figures – Apollo with six Muses, Marsyas challenging Apollo to a musical contest, and the flaying of the defeated Marsyas.

Mausoleum

Other examples of the painterly treatment of relief are the friezes on the gigantic funerary monument (the Mausoleum) of King Mausolos of Caria (d. 353 B.C.), the best preserved fragments of which, depicting a fight with Amazons, are in the British Museum. Attempts have been made to distinguish four different groups within the considerable amount of material that survives, corresponding to the four famous contemporaries of Praxiteles – Timotheos, Skopas, Leochares and Bryaxis – who were traditionally believed to have carved the sculptured decoration on each of the sides of the monument, which was almost square in plan.

Timotheos

Timotheos also worked on the pediments of the temple of Asklepios at Epidauros (*c.* 375 B.C.: National Archaeological Museum, Athens). A statue of Leda by him is preserved in a poor copy (Capitoline Museum, Rome), and an Artemis by him is represented, together with a figure of Apollo in a long robe playing the lyre, on a statue base found in Italy (Sorrento Museum). Both statues were set up in the temple of Apollo on the Palatine in the time of Augustus; they probably stood originally in a temple at Rhamnous.

Tholos, Delphi

Monument of Lysikrates, Athens

Skopas

Skopas, an architect as well as a sculptor, was responsible for the rebuilding, probably around 340 B.C., of the temple of Athena Alea at Tegea, which had been destroyed by fire in 395 B.C. The sculpture on the pediments of the temple (National Archaeological Museum, Athens) was probably also by Skopas, or at least produced in his workshop and under his direction. In concentrated power of movement, the passionate facial expressions and the high quality of the carving this surpasses even the best parts of the Mausoleum frieze. The vast pediment depicted the hunting of the Calydonian boar by Meleager, the west pediment probably a warlike encounter between Herakles and Achilles.

Leochares and Bryaxis

Leochares and Bryaxis were also noted for their figures of gods. The bronze original of the Apollo Belvedere (Vatican Museums, Rome) was probably by Leochares.
Bryaxis – who, to judge from his name, was probably of Carian origin – was in his younger days, when he worked on the Mausoleum, pioneer of a modern style with a diagonal compositional axis; towards the end of his life, which extended into the 3rd century, he might rather stand as a representative of the final phase of the late classical style.

Painterly trend

In spite of their diversity of individual temperament, origin and technique, however, all these artists are at one as representatives of a particular stage in the development of art in which painterly tendencies constantly recur. In sculpture external forms are depicted by the effects of light and shade in the treatment of the surfaces and by the disposition of the composition within a flat area of space.

Grave relief from Ilissos

The clearest example of the dissonant elements in the late classical style, which are combined to form a work of art only through the achievement of a painterly or picturesque effect, both in spatial and in atmospheric terms, is the grave relief from the Ilissos (National Archaeological Museum), which shows affinities with the style of Skopas. The figure of the dead youth is typical of one composed in a flat area of space. He stands in a relaxed pose, leaning back and looking at the spectator with an almost indifferent glance, while his aged father, sharply drawn in profile, stands leaning on his staff, with his left hand raised to his chin, and gazes at his son, deep in thought, but receives no answering glance. The diagonally composed steps and the pillar on which the young man has laid his cloak represent the tomb. Associated with him, both formally and personally, are the small servant who squats sleeping on the steps and the dog sniffing about on the ground: they are both now lost and abandoned. To questions about the meaning of death or of life there is no answer but the beauty created by art.

Rotundas
Delphi
Epidauros

A characteristic feature of the architecture of the late classical period is the rotunda. The earliest example of the type was the round temple in the precinct of Athena Pronaia at Delphi (Marmaria), followed by the Thymele at Epidauros. In both of these buildings, as in the earlier temple of Apollo at Bassai and the later temple of Athena Alea at Tegea, the Doric order was used on the exterior and the Corinthian order in the interior. A magnificent Corinthian capital found at Epidauros probably served as the model for all the others on that site. The Philippeion (second half of 4th c. B.C.) at Olympia has Ionic columns on the exterior and Corinthian half-columns in the interior. A small rotunda in Athens, the choregic monument of Lysikrates (333 B.C.), has only Corinthian half-columns, now used on the exterior; on this monument, too, relief decoration reappears in the form of a Dionysiac frieze. The occasion for the erection of the monument (the victory of a choir financed by Lysikrates in a dramatic competition) and the decorative themes (Dionysos and satyrs, the transformation of Tyrrhenian pirates into dolphins) bring us back to the theatre.

Olympia

Athens

Theatres

This period saw the first monumental theatres – the theatre at Epidauros, finely designed as a total work of art, and the rebuilding of the theatre at Athens (completed 330 B.C.). Both of these are masterly achievements in terms of both architecture and acoustics.

The Greek Theatre (see plan, page 74)

The origins of the European theatre lie in ancient Greece. The first dramatic performances were associated with the cult of Dionysos, in which a choir performed round dances, accompanied by singing, in honour of Dionysos, god of fertility and of wine. About 535 B.C. the semi-legendary Thespis of Athens introduced the figure of a narrator or speaker as counterpart to the choir in the performance of a tragedy and thus took the first step towards a dramatic presentation in the theatre. Aeschylus introduced a second actor and Sophocles a third.

Performances were given in the open air on the *orkhestra,* a circular dancing floor on which there was probably also the altar of Dionysos (*thymele*).
Originally the spectators probably stood round the dancing floor; later they sat on simple timber stands; and finally these gave place to the characteristic semicircular *theatron* (originally meaning "audience"), with tiers of benches rising up the slope of a hill in the auditorium (Greek *koilon,* Latin cavea).

Opposite the auditorium, on the far side of the *orkhestra,* was the stage building (*skene*), several storeys high. This was originally a timber structure, which in the post-classical period was elaborated into a palatial edifice in stone.
The *skene* was then supplemented by the *proskenion* (proscenium), an additional stage raised above the *orkhestra.*
Between the stage and the auditorium, which extended slightly beyond a semicircle, were the *parodoi,* the entrances for the chorus.

The classical form of Greek theatre developed in Athens and spread from there throughout the whole Greek world. Most of the ancient Greek theatres, the largest of which could accommodate many thousand spectators (Theatre of Dionysos, Athens, 17,000; Epidauros 14,000), have now been either completely or partly excavated; some are excellently preserved, and some have been restored. Some of them are now again in use for the performance of plays, both ancient and modern, and musical works, such as the theatres of Epidauros, Philippi, Thasos and Dodona and the Odeion of Herodes Atticus in Athens.

The Romans at first used simple wooden structures, with or without a cavea, for their theatrical performances, but later followed the Greek example and built large stone structures. These were no longer built into a hillside like the Greek theatres but were free-standing masonry

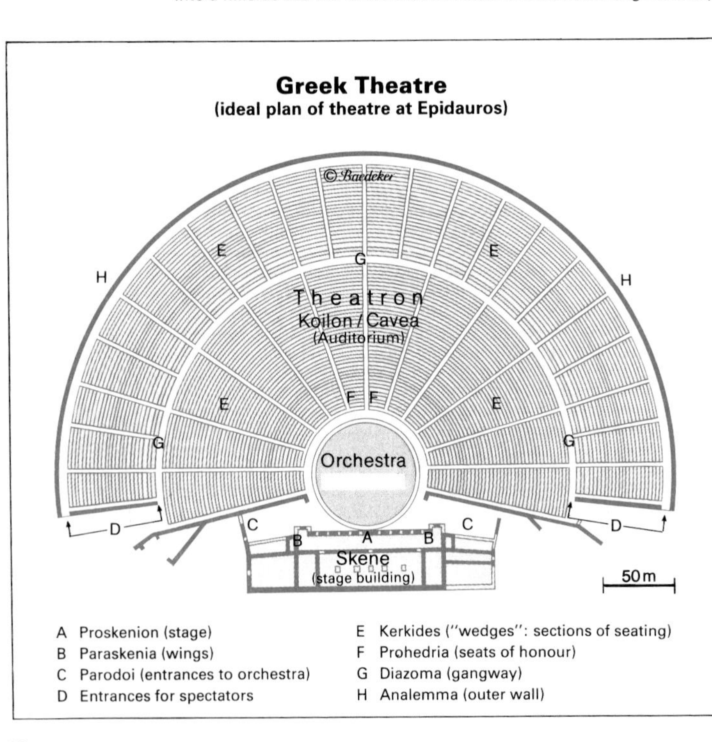

buildings, with access to the auditorium by doorways and staircases in the outer walls.
A distinctive Roman development was the amphitheatre, a large arena without a stage, surrounded by tiers of seating for the spectators, which was used for large-scale performances of various kinds (mock battles, wild beasts, gladiatorial contests, etc.). The best known example is the Colosseum in Rome.

The basic idea of the Greco-Roman theatre was taken up and developed at the Renaissance; but theatres were now always roofed and the auditorium constantly elaborated in form. The type of auditorium with boxes came into vogue in the Baroque period.

Odeion

The *odeion* was a small roofed theatre mainly used for musical performances (e.g. the Odeion of Perikles in Athens, near the Theatre of Dionysos). Numbers of these ancient concert and lecture halls were built in the Hellenistic and Roman periods (Latin *odeum*).
The modern Odeion in Athens is the Conservatoire (College of Music).

Apelles and Lysippos

Apelles

It is difficult to assess the quality and the influence of works of art which have not survived even in copies and have not even left any mark on other artistic genres. While we can see some reflection of the wall paintings of Polygnotos or Parrhasios in contemporary vase painting, and have excellent ancient copies of paintings by contemporaries of Apelles ("Perseus and Andromeda" by Nikias, "Alexander's Battle" by Philoxenos: National Museum, Naples), we have no evidence of this kind about the work of Apelles himself. The remains of his work, indeed, are in inverse proportion to his fame. But the subjects of his paintings, his virtuoso-like mastery of his craft, his position as a contemporary of the great events of Alexander's reign and his friendship with Alexander himself all make it necessary to mention his name here.

Apelles (*c.* 370–310 B.C.) was born in the Ionian city of Kolophon in Asia Minor, learned his craft in the painting school at Sikyon in the Peloponnese, later lived on the island of Kos and perhaps died there. He was one of a group of three artists who had a kind of monopoly in the portrayal of Alexander the Great. There are references in classical literature to at least eighteen portraits by him, including five portraits of Alexander, two of which were taken to Rome and set up by Augustus in his Forum. We know the measurements of these pictures (2.65m/9ft by 2.35m/8ft), since the positions they occupied are still visible. The quality of these portraits must have lain both in the fidelity of the likeness and in their magnificent expression of the "imperial idea" which led Augustus to display them in the most prominent position in Imperial Rome. In each of these portraits Alexander was shown with the attributes and insignia of his power – on horseback, with a thunderbolt, with the Dioskouroi, in a chariot – in the role known to the Romans as Triumphator.

Portraits of Alexander

Self-portrait

But Apelles was also the first artist who is known to have painted a self-portrait, no doubt showing the same truth to life and the same spiritual interpretation of the physical features as his other portraits. This was the first self-portrait only in the sense that the artist now became the subject of the picture without any attempt at disguise; for earlier artists had no doubt created a projection of their own ego in the legendary figures they portrayed.

Mythological themes

A notable feature of Apelles' other paintings was that he rarely depicted actions or events: scenes from the old myths and legends are absent from his work. Gods and heroes were depicted either as individual figures or surrounded by other mythological personages. His most famous picture was one of Aphrodite rising from the sea which later found its way to Rome. Like all of his work, so far as we know, it was a panel picture, not a wall painting, and used only the colours black, white, yellow and red. Although we have insufficient information about the style and composition of his pictures to be able to assert that he marked the culmination of the picturesque tendencies of the late classical period and in his use of spatial and aerial perspective prepared the way for Hellenistic art, it is clear at any rate from the literary evidence that his importance at a turning-point in the history of art was at least as great as that of Lysippos.

Lysippos

Lysippos (*c.* 395–300 B.C.), a native of Sikyon, worked even more exclusively than Polykleitos in bronze; but he was not confined to the Peloponnesian tradition of the great masters of Argos. Although he spoke of Polykleitos's Doryphoros as his model, he is also said to have declared that he was no man's pupil: artists must follow nature, not their predecessors. He was credited with producing some 1500 statues, and he was Alexander the Great's favourite sculptor, as Apelles was his favourite painter.

His work is poorly represented, however, among the surviving copies: his sculpture was not "classical" enough and therefore was not popular during the great age of copying. Among the many sculptured representations of Alexander which are preserved in copies or in variants the official portraits by Lysippos (Louvre, Paris; Archaeological Museum, Istanbul) do not take a high place. Of the four statues of Zeus by Lysippos which are referred to in the literary sources we can form no conception, while his other portrayals of gods and heroes may be represented by a number of statues of Herakles, including the late work, best known in a copy (National Archaeological Museum, Athens) in the Farnese collection, which in another copy (Palazzo Pitti, Florence) has an inscription ascribing it to Lysippos. As with Polykleitos, we also have some of the original bases for statues by Lysippos, including one (Poulydamas: Museum, Olympia) which preserves some remains of relief carving.

Apoxyomenos

We do not know, however, whether Lysippos's most famous statue, the Apoxyomenos (an athlete scraping himself with a strigil), preserved in a single copy in the Vatican Museums, Rome, may have come from one of these bases. This work is very characteristic of Lysippos's style. Departing from the canon of rather thickset figures, it shows slender proportions: the head is smaller in relation to the rest of the figure, and the supporting and the free leg are more sharply distinguished than in Polykleitos's work. This difference between the two legs, however, no longer determines the structure of the figure. The stance is now almost labile: it appears as if the weight might be transferred at any moment to the free leg. The object is to achieve a posture which has been aptly called the "pendulum position". The transitory effect is produced not only by this latent possibility of a change of position but also by the smoothly flowing contours and above all by the slight turn of the body on its axis – as if inviting the spectator to walk round the statue without taking his eyes off it. The figure is designed to be seen not merely from a single viewpoint but from all round, and thus achieves a new kind of spatial effect. But the matter goes farther than this: an element of space is caught up into the statue itself. The wide stance and the reaching-out movement of the arms involve the immediately surrounding space so intimately with the figure that the plastic surfaces no longer mark the boundaries of the artistic composition. The statue now stands within an area of space which in a sense is shaped and influenced by its form.

These innovations seem to have brought Lysippos to the very frontiers of his art, and to mark the end of an epoch. In the words of J. G. Droysen, "the name of Alexander marks the end of an era in world history and the beginning of a new one"; and this is true also of art. Lysippos marked not only the culmination of one phase in Greek art but the first intimation of a new and final phase, the Hellenistic period.

Hellenistic Period

(323–27 B.C.)

The Hellenistic period in art lasted from the death of Alexander (323 B.C.) to the establishment of the Roman province of Achaea (27 B.C.), which marked the end of Greece as an independent political and cultural organism. During these three centuries there came into being – alongside the old artistic centres in the Peloponnese, Athens and its dependent territories, and the old established Greek colonies on the coast of Asia Minor – the new capitals of the independent kingdoms which had been carved out of Alexander's empire, chief among them Alexandria and Pergamon.

Sculpture

In sculpture it might appear that in the early years of the period the achievements of Lysippos were not followed up. Numerous works of art of the late 4th century – still continue late classical traditions.

Ariadne

One masterpiece of this period survives only in a fragment – a female head found on the southern slopes of the Acropolis of Athens and now in the National Archaeological Museum. The passionate mouth and the fiercely yearning glance have led to its identification as Ariadne. What makes this head particularly notable is not only the rarity of surviving examples of original free-standing sculpture of the highest quality, but also the opportunity it gives us of comparing the fire and delicacy of the original with the sentimental trivialisation of a copy which also survives (Pergamon Museum, Berlin). It is clear, therefore, that the Ariadne was a celebrated work of sculpture, an *opus nobile.*

Niobe

The creator of the Ariadne figure had close affinities with the sculptor who produced the large group of Niobe and her children (copies in the Uffizi, Florence), probably originally set up in the open air, which connoisseurs of the Imperial period ascribed to either Praxiteles or Skopas. The figures of Ariadne and the Niobids do indeed show a development of the style of these two great sculptors; but they were created at a time when Praxiteles and Skopas were both dead.

Chairestratos

Polyeuktos

It would be natural to suppose that the introduction of new impulses by Lysippos would lead to the dying out of the older tradition; but it is remarkable that in fact post-Lysippan sculpture in purely Hellenistic style appears resistant to his conception of the statue and his use of space. Numbers of works produced in the first half of the 3rd century are clearly not designed to be seen from a variety of standpoints: cf., for example, a figure of a divinity like the statue of Themis by Chairestratos (original; National Archaeological Museum, Athens), which stood in a temple at Rhamnous, or a portrait statue such as the figure of Demosthenes by Polyeuktos (Vatican Museums, Rome). The classical appearance of these works, however, is deceptive: the sculptured surfaces are instinct with the mobility of the Lysippan manner, apparently only just under control, and the figure of Demosthenes expresses a spiritual tension richer in contrast and in complexity than is found in any portrait of the classical period.

It is not surprising, therefore, that towards the end of the century the Hellenistic feeling for space, which is present in these works, as it were, in repressed form, achieves full and powerful expression. This trend can be detected in the "Barberini Faun" (Glyptothek, Munich), depicted asleep but on the point of awakening. It is seen in fully developed form in two other over-lifesize compositions. The first of these is the great monument erected by Attalos I of Pergamon to commemorate a victory over the Galatians in 230 B.C., of which there survive the inscribed base and copies of the principal figures ("Dying Gaul", Capitoline Museum, Rome).

Monument of Attalos

Victory of Samothrace

The new trend is also seen in the famous Victory of Samothrace (original; Louvre, Paris). The Victory (Nike), dated to the beginning of the 2nd century B.C., probably commemorates a Rhodian victory over Antiochos III of Syria in 190 B.C. When compared with the vigour and panache of this work even the liveliest figures of the classical period appear subdued. And yet the vehement movement which carries the winged goddess on to meet the wind does not seem overdone, and the passionate intensity with which every fold in her robe and every feather in her wings is delineated appears, both in total effect and in detail, entirely unforced and free of empty rhetoric.

Pergamon

This cannot perhaps be said of every detail of the carving on the monumental Altar of Zeus from Pergamon (Pergamon Museum, Berlin); but certainly in terms of richness of composition and power of execution the frieze depicting a fight between gods and giants, which dates from the reign of Eumenes II (197–159 B.C.), need fear no comparisons. The smaller frieze depicting the mythological genealogy of the ruling family of Pergamon, executed during the reign of Attalos II (159–138 B.C.), shows a quieter, almost idyllic trend. It is notable that the first deliberate copies of earlier work were made at Pergamon. The city apparently had cultural links with Athens, and reproductions of Attic figures of divinities were set up in its temples. They are distinguished from later copies by the enthusiasm of their assimilation, which militated against the fidelity of the reproduction.

Venus de Milo

This trend, however, reflected a gradual decline in creative force. After such works as the world-famed Aphrodite of Melos (Venus de Milo; Louvre, Paris) and the Poseidon also found on Melos (National Archaeological Museum, Athens), both of which are dated to around the middle of the 2nd century B.C., all art forms become forced, imitative, academic – characteristics quite alien to the natural and unconstrained quality of Greek art.

Laokoon group

But that even in these circumstances great artists could still produce notable work is demonstrated by fragments of the group of gods by Damophon of Messene (after 150 B.C.; National Archaeological Museum, Athens, and Lykosoura Museum) and the famous Laokoon group by Hegesandros, Polydoros and Athanadoros (Vatican Museums, Rome), a work of the late Hellenistic period shortly before its end.

Architecture

In architecture the Ionic order was predominant during the Hellenistic period. In addition to temples – and the great temples of eastern Greece were all rebuilt or renovated in late classical and Hellenistic times – changed political and social conditions called for a variety of other buildings, including council chambers, stoas, and imposing and luxurious residences.

Hellenistic mosaic, Pella

The stoa

The stoa, a long hall with one or more rows of columns along its open side, was a feature particularly characteristic of Hellenistic architecture, found in sacred precincts and in the market-places which were the main centres of public life. Notable examples can be seen in the cities of Asia Minor and, since the excavations of the last few decades, in the Agora of Athens. The stoa built in the Athenian Agora by Attalos II of Pergamon was rebuilt by the American excavators and now houses a museum of material found in the Agora.

Painting

Painting still clung to the traditions of the preceding period; but the use of perspective was developed, and the figures had the proportions established by Lysippos. Among notable surviving examples of the work of this period are numerous painted grave stelae from Pagasai (Volos Museum) and the monumental dome frescoes of Kazanlăk (Bulgaria).
The art of vase painting had completely disappeared.

Mosaics

The art of the mosaic developed and advanced in the Hellenistic period. The earliest mosaics (5th and early 4th c.; Athens, Olynthos) were pebble mosaics, which had a great flowering at Pella in the time of Alexander the Great. From the 3rd century onwards coloured tesserae were used (e.g. in houses on Delos).

Roman Period

(2nd/1st c. B.C.–4th c. A.D.)

When the Roman general Aemilius Paullus defeated King Perseus of Macedon in 168 B.C. he set up a monument celebrating his victory in the sanctuary at Delphi, with a frieze depicting the decisive battle of Pydna which is purely Hellenistic in style.

Tower of the Winds, Roman Agora, Athens

Portrait statues

By about 100 B.C., however, a distinctive style had been evolved on Delos for the portrait statues commissioned by Italian patrons (National Archaeological Museum, Athens). The bodies were based on earlier models (statues of gods or heroes), almost unchanged; but while in Greek sculpture, even in portrait statues, the figure was conceived and depicted as a whole, in Roman work the head took on a special importance of its own. Actual likenesses of individuals now became possible for the first time, whether in the form of statues, busts or herm portraits. Whereas in Greek representations of human beings the general always predominated over the individual, the Romans sought to depict the distinctive characteristics of the sitter. The individual personality was now mirrored with uncompromising fidelity in Roman portraits. This basic difference from the Greek portrait was maintained even in the neo-classical work of the Augustan period, when the aim, particularly in portraits of members of the Imperial house (Pythagorion Museum, Samos), was to achieve a kind of tranquil simplicity in detail as well as in general effect. And although all the portraits produced in Greece during the Roman period still show a last dying touch of Hellenistic grace this does not obscure the fact that they are quite different from earlier Greek work.

Architecture

Athens

The architecture of the Roman provinces, making much use of the arch and the vault, surpassed Hellenistic architecture in scale and boldness of construction. In Athens, however, the buildings erected at the beginning of the Roman period were still relatively modest, like the Tower of the Winds, which was equipped with a water-clock and a sundial by a certain Andronikos. The neo-classical style of the early Empire is represented by the remains of the circular temple of Rome and Augustus to the east of the Parthenon, some of the ornament of which was painstakingly copied from the Erechtheion. The reliefs on the stage building of the Theatre of Dionysos reproduce classical types of divine figures. The Monument of Philopappos (grandson of the last ruler of Commagene), on the hill south-west of the Acropolis (*c.* A.D. 115), is also in neo-classical style. A new Roman market had been built near the old Agora about A.D. 5, and in the reign of Hadrian a whole new district was built. The Arch of Hadrian has an inscription referring to the older city to the west as the city of Theseus and the new area to the east, which included the temple of Zeus, as the city of Hadrian. The Odeion of Herodes Atticus, named after the wealthy private citizen who built it, also dates from the time of Hadrian.

Historical reliefs

In spite of its splendour this architecture of the late period has a rather contrived and stereotyped air. Greece was now a mere Roman province, and as such was exposed to Rome's glorification of its own history. The historical relief, familiar on the triumphal arches of Italy and on the columns of Trajan and Marcus Aurelius, now came to Macedonia, and the Arch of Galerius in Salonica (*c.* A.D. 300) depicts victorious Roman armies, battle and marching scenes, the Roman general among his legionaries, and the goddess Fortuna, ruler of the world: a greater contrast to the frieze in Delphi depicting the battle of Pydna can hardly be imagined. The composition is no longer related to the human figure with its established proportions, and the crowded scenes lack any sense of plastic form. The details of costume and weapons, standards, exotic animals and a variety of accessories are meticulously depicted; but exact delineation of the scene and the action, of the various arms and the various ranks, is lost in the overcrowded and formless profusion of the whole. Within this whole the proliferation of circumstantial detail becomes a stylistic element of subordinate importance, and the total effect is almost of an abstract pattern in a single plane.

Byzantine Period

(4th–15th c. A.D.)

Christian art

In Byzantine art, particularly in mosaics and paintings, the individual figure again comes into its own, but this time in the new setting of Christianity. The Byzantine monuments (mainly churches and monasteries) in which Athens and the rest of Greece are so rich owe nothing to ancient Greek art: they belong to a new phase in history and in art which must be seen in the wider framework involving not only Constantinople (Istanbul) itself but taking account of Ravenna and influences from the eastern Mediterranean world, and indeed of the whole of Roman/Christian art.

Bas-reliefs
Icon-painting
Mosaics

In the 4th century A.D. a strictly frontal pose came into favour in relief sculpture (reliefs on the base of the obelisk in the Hippodrome, Constantinople), and this also became predominant in many aspects of Byzantine art, particularly in icons. This new Christian art preferred relief carving to sculpture in the round for the transcendental representation of sacred figures and found expression particularly in painting, including mosaics.

Byzantine art was above all a religious art, which sought to create buildings in the image of the divine cosmos. Of central importance in this respect is the cruciform ground-plan of the domed Byzantine churches which in the Middle Byzantine period (Macedonian dynasty, 867–1056; Comnenian dynasty, 1081–1185) replaced the older basilican form; and equally significant is the decoration of the churches with figures of Christ Pantokrator (Ruler of All), the Mother of God, saints and church festivals, to be seen notably in the mosaics of a number of 11th century monastic churches (e.g. Osios Loukas and

Vividly coloured icons in the Byzantine Museum, Athens

Dafni on the mainland and the Nea Moni on the island of Chios) and in the frescoes in the churches of Mistra, near Sparta (Peloponnese), which date from the Late Byzantine period (Palaeologue dynasty, 1259/61–1453). Salonica has preserved a few mosaics and paintings of the Early Byzantine period (e.g. 7th–9th century work in the church of Ayios Dimitrios).

After 1453

With the conquest of Constantinople by the Turks in 1453 the Byzantine Empire came to an end and the fate of Byzantine culture was sealed, though Russia later claimed its inheritance. The so-called post-Byzantine art of the Balkans fell far below the standard of earlier centuries. Nevertheless the traditions of Byzantine art were carried on during the period of Ottoman rule, for example in Meteora's "monasteries in the air" (Thessaly; 14th–16th c.), on Mount Athos, the Holy Mountain, and in the numerous churches of Kastoria in northern Greece.

Byzantine Museum, Athens

In addition to the old churches and monasteries themselves and the numerous smaller collections to be found all over Greece and on the islands, the richly stocked Byzantine Museum in Athens offers a comprehensive view of Byzantine art and its successive phases throughout the Greek world, including Asia Minor (church architecture, icons, reliefs, liturgical utensils, etc.).

The Greek Church

(see plans, page 83).

When Christian worship was officially permitted in the 4th century the first churches began to be built.

Greek Churches

Early Christian basilica

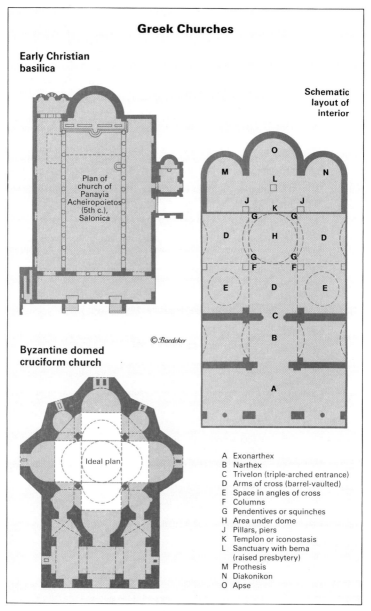

Plan of church of Panayia Acheiropoietos (5th c.), Salonica

Schematic layout of interior

Byzantine domed cruciform church

A Exonarthex
B Narthex
C Trivelon (triple-arched entrance)
D Arms of cross (barrel-vaulted)
E Space in angles of cross
F Columns
G Pendentives or squinches
H Area under dome
J Pillars, piers
K Templon or iconostasis
L Sanctuary with bema (raised presbytery)
M Prothesis
N Diakonikon
O Apse

The basilica	The predominant form was the basilica, with a nave flanked by one or two lower lateral aisles and the altar in an apse at the east end. The entrance was at the west end, with a narthex (porch) preceding the nave, and frequently with an atrium outside the entrance. This type was found throughout the Roman world, from Rome to Jerusalem.
The domed cruciform church	In the 9th century a new type of church developed in Greece, based on a centralised rather than a longitudinal plan. This was the domed cruciform church, which thereafter became predominant. The central dome is supported either on sections of wall or on columns, occasionally on two sections of wall and two columns. It may span either the nave alone or (with eight supports) the nave and aisles. The chancel, with the altar, was originally separated from the body of the church by a low stone screen, which later developed into the iconostasis. It is flanked by two small rooms, the prothesis and diakonikon, which serve liturgical purposes; and, matching this tripartite structure, the church usually has three apses. At the west end of the church there is often an exonarthex (outer narthex) preceding the narthex. The wall and dome paintings in the interior of the church reflect the heavenly hierarchy, with Christ at the highest point of the dome and the Mother of God (the Virgin), patriarchs, prophets and saints at lower levels. The exterior walls are in stone and brick, often elaborately patterned. In post-Byzantine times there was sometimes a reversion to the old basilican type of church, usually small, with one to three aisles.

Glossary of Technical Terms (Art, History, Mythology)

Abacus — The upper part of the capital of a Doric column, a square slab above the echinus. See diagram, page 90.

Abaton, Adyton — The innermost sanctuary of a temple, to which only priests were admitted.

Acanthus — A spiny-leaved plant used in the decoration of Corinthian and Byzantine (Justinianic) capitals.

Acropolis — The highest part of a Greek city; the citadel.

Acroterion — A figure or ornament on a roof ridge or the top of a pediment. See diagram, page 90.

Adyton — See Abaton.

Agora — The market-place of a Greek city, the main centre of public life.

Alabastron — An oil-flask without base or handles.

Amazonomachia — A fight between Greeks and Amazons.

Amphiprostyle — (Temple) with columned portico at both ends. See diagram, page 60.

Amphora — A two-handled jar of bulbous form.

Annulus — A ring round the shaft of a Doric column below the echinus.

Anta — A pillar-like projection at the end of the side wall of a temple.

A horizontal stone lintel resting on the columns of a temple. See diagram, page 90.	**Architrave**
The highest official of a Greek city.	**Archon**
A spherical oil-flask.	**Aryballos**
Sanctuary of Asklepios.	**Asklepieion**
The beaded moulding of the Ionic order.	**Astragal**
King.	**Basileus**
1. Originally a royal hall, usually divided into aisles, used for commercial or judicial purposes. 2. The standard form of Christian church developed in the 4th century, with three or five aisles. See plan, page 83.	**Basilica**
1. A platform used by orators. 2. The sanctuary of a Christian church.	**Bema**
A square altar.	**Bomos**
A pit for offerings.	**Bothros**
Council chamber; the meeting-place of the council (*boule*) of a Greek city.	**Bouleuterion**
The moulded or carved top of a column or pillar, supporting the entablature. See diagram, page 90.	**Capital**
A female figure supporting an entablature.	**Caryatid**
The auditorium (seating) of a theatre.	**Cavea**
The enclosed chamber of a temple: the Latin equivalent of Greek *naos.* See diagram, page 60.	**Cella**
A fight between Lapiths and Centaurs.	**Centauromachia**
A pleated linen garment worn with a belt, mostly in Ionia.	**Chiton**
A short cloak.	**Chlamys**
"Choir-leader": a person who financed the choir performing in a tragedy.	**Choregos**
(Sculpture) of gold and ivory on a wooden core.	**Chryselephantine**
(Divinities) of the earth.	**Chthonian**
The three-stepped platform of a temple. See diagram, page 90.	**Crepidoma**
(Walls) of large irregular blocks, ascribed in antiquity to the Cyclopes.	**Cyclopean**
A wave moulding with double curvature.	**Cyma**
A room in the right-hand lateral apse of a Byzantine church. See diagram, page 83.	**Diakonikon**
The gangway between tiers of seating in a theatre.	**Diazoma**

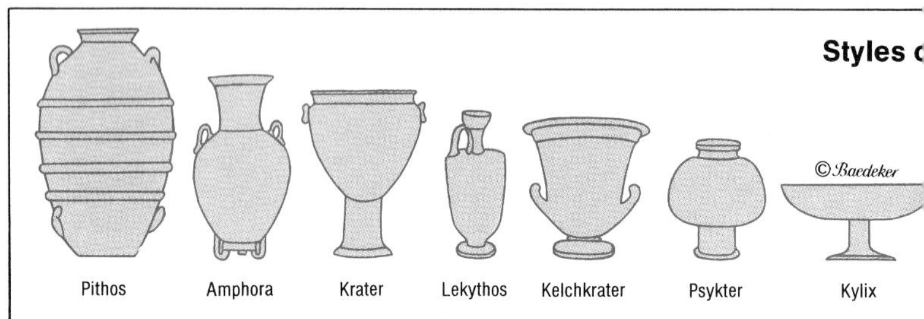

Dipteral	(Temple) surrounded by a double row of columns. See diagram, page 60.
Dipylon	A double gateway.
Double anta temple	A temple with antae at both ends.
Dromos	A passage; specifically, the passage leading into a tomb.
Echinus	A convex moulding under the abacus of a Doric capital. See diagram, page 90.
Entablature	The superstructure carried by columns.
Entasis	A swelling in the lower part of a column. See diagram, page 90.
Ephebe	A youth who was not yet a full citizen.
Epigonoi	Descendants of the Seven against Thebes.
Esonarthex	The inner narthex of a church.
Exedra	A recess, usually semicircular, containing benches.
Exonarthex	The outer narthex of a church.
Frieze	A decorative band above the architrave of a temple; in the Doric order made up of metopes and triglyphs, in the Ionic order plain or with continuous carved decoration. See diagram, page 90.
Geison	The cornice of a temple. See diagram, page 90.
Gigantomachia	A fight between gods and giants.
Gymnasion	A school for physical training and general education, consisting of a square or rectangular courtyard surrounded by colonnades and rooms of varying size and function.
Heraion	A temple or sanctuary of Hera.
Herm	A square pillar with a head of Hermes or some other god; later with a portrait head.
Heroon	The shrine of a hero.
Hieron	A sanctuary.

Greek Vases

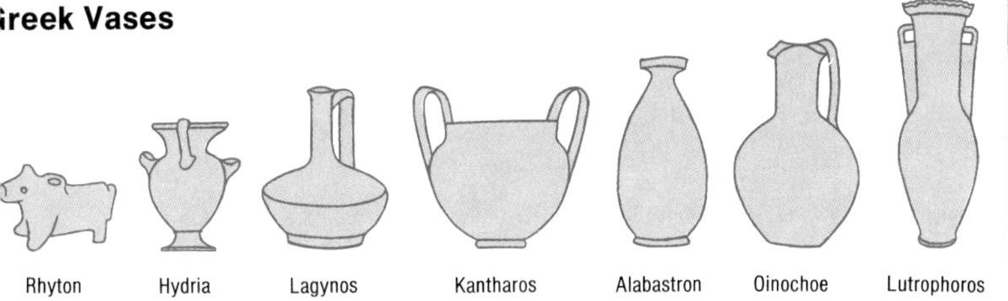

The priest of a mystery cult.	**Hierophant**
A cloak worn over the chiton.	**Himation**
An elliptical course for chariot races.	**Hippodrome**
A heavily armed foot soldier.	**Hoplite**
A water jar.	**Hydria**
An under-floor heating system for baths, etc.	**Hypocaust**
An underground vault, especially one used for burials.	**Hypogeum**
(Hall, etc.) having a roof supported by columns.	**Hypostyle**
A screen in a Byzantine church between the sanctuary and the main part of the church, bearing tiers of icons.	**Iconostasis**
Horizontally coursed (masonry).	**Isodomic**
A drinking cup with two handles and a high foot.	**Kantharos**
Castle, usually Byzantine or Venetian.	**Kastro**
A bishop's throne.	**Kathedra**
The principal church of a monastery.	**Katholikon**
A stringed instrument; Apollo's lyre.	**Kithara**
Well-house, cistern; water-clock.	**Klepsydra**
Maiden, girl; statue of a girl.	**Kore** (plural korai)
Youth; statue of a naked youth.	**Kouros** (plural kouroi)
A two-handled jar for mixing water and wine.	**Krater**
A shallow drinking-cup with horizontal handles.	**Kylix**
A legendary people in Thessaly.	**Lapiths**
A narrow-necked oil-flask.	**Lekythos**
Assembly room, club-house.	**Lesche**

Glossary of Technical Terms (Art, History, Mythology)

Maeander	A continuous fret or key pattern
Megaron	The principal room in a Mycenaean palace.
Metope	A rectangular panel between the triglyphs in the frieze of a Doric temple, either plain or with relief decoration.
Metroon	Sanctuary of the Great Mother.
Monopteral	(Temple) without a naos, usually circular. See diagram, page 60.
Naiskos	A small temple.
Naos	The enclosed chamber of a temple: the Greek equivalent of the Latin *cella.* See diagram, page 60.
Narthex	A rectangular entrance hall preceding the nave of a church. Sometimes there may be both an outer and an inner narthex (exonarthex and esonarthex). See diagram, page 83.
Necropolis	Cemetery ("city of the dead").
Nekromanteion	Oracle of the dead.
Nomos	Administrative district, province.
Nymphaeum	Fountain-house.
Odeion	A hall (usually roofed) for musical performances, etc.
Oinochoe	A wine-jug.
Olympieion	Sanctuary of Olympian Zeus.
Opisthodomos	A chamber at the rear end of a temple. See diagram, page 60.
Orchestra	A circular or semicircular area between the stage and the auditorium of a theatre in which the chorus danced. See diagram, page 74.
Orthostat	A large block of stone, set vertically, in the lower part of a temple wall.
Ostracism	A system of voting on potsherds (*ostraka*) for the banishment of a citizen.
Palaistra	A training school for physical exercises (wrestling, etc.).
Panayía	"All-Holy"; the Mother of God, the Virgin.
Pantokrator	"Ruler of All"; Christ.
Parekklesion	A subsidiary church or chapel.
Parodos	Side entrance to the orchestra of a theatre.
Pediment	The triangular termination or gable of a pitched roof.
Pendentive	A triangular section of vaulting forming the transition from a square base to a circular dome.
Peplos	A woollen cloak worn by women.

The enclosure wall of a sacred precinct.	**Peribolos**
(Temple) surrounded by a peristyle. See diagram, page 60.	**Peripteral**
A colonnade surrounding a building. See diagram, page 60.	**Peristyle**
A large storage jar.	**Pithos**
(Masonry) of irregularly shaped stones.	**Polygonal**
A kind of limestone.	**Poros**
A seat of honour in a theatre or stadion. See diagram, page 74.	**Prohedria**
A vestibule at the entrance to a temple. See diagram, page 60.	**Pronaos**
A monumental form of propylon.	**Propylaia** (plural)
Gateway.	**Propylon**
Fore-stage. See diagram, page 000.	**Proskenion**
(Temple) with columned portico in front. See diagram, page 60.	**Prostyle**
A room in the left-hand lateral apse of a Byzantine church. See diagram, page 83.	**Prothesis**
Office of the *prytanes* (city councillors).	**Prytaneion**
Tower, bastion.	**Pyrgos**
A cylindrical vase.	**Pyxis**
A drinking vessel, often in the form of an animal's head.	**Rhyton**
The gutter of a building, with lion's-head water-spouts. See diagram, page 90.	**Sima**
The stage building of a theatre. See diagram, page 74.	**Skene**
A drinking-cup with two horizontal handles.	**Skyphos**
The rounded end of a stadion.	**Sphendone**
A small arch built obliquely across the angles of a square tower in order to support a circular dome.	**Squinch**
1. A measure of length, 600 feet; a stade. 2. A running track 600ft long. 3. A stadium, with a running track and embankments or benches for spectators.	**Stadion**
An upright stone slab (often a tombstone), usually with an inscription and frequently with relief carving.	**Stele**
A portico; a hall with columns along the front.	**Stoa**
A curved blade used to scrape dust and oil off the body after physical exercise.	**Strigil**
The uppermost step of a temple platform. See diagram, page 90.	**Stylobate**

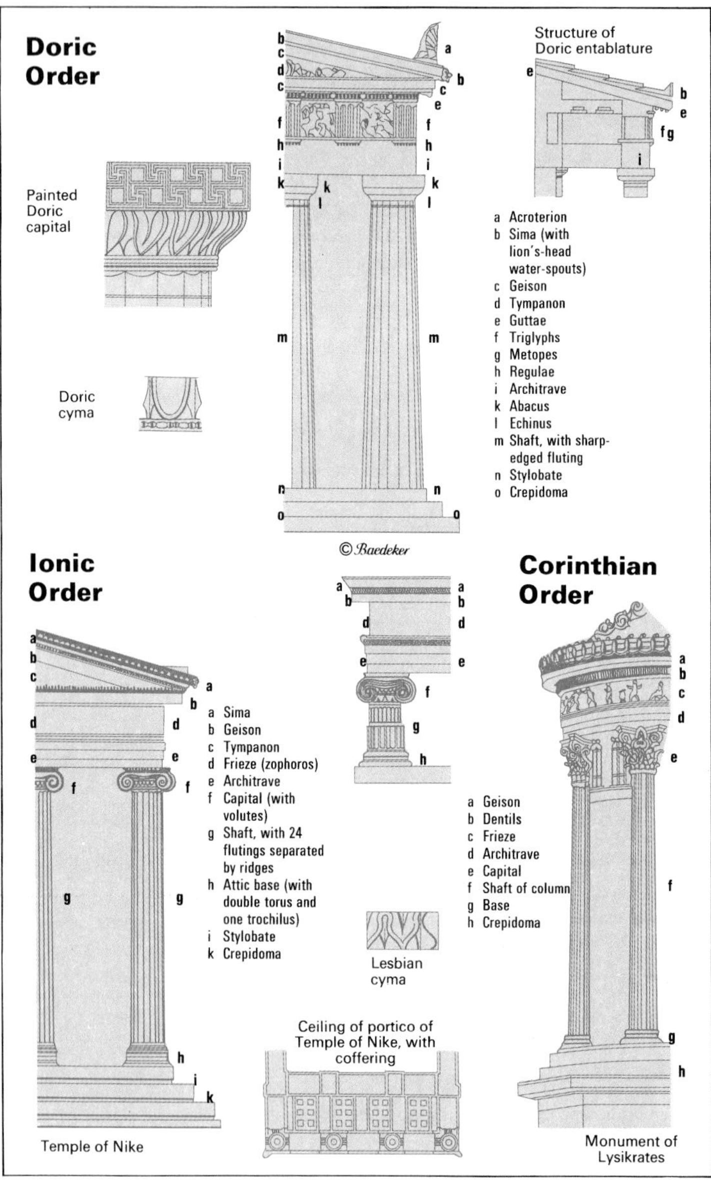
Doric Order
Painted Doric capital
Doric cyma
Structure of Doric entablature
a Acroterion
b Sima (with lion's-head water-spouts)
c Geison
d Tympanon
e Guttae
f Triglyphs
g Metopes
h Regulae
i Architrave
k Abacus
l Echinus
m Shaft, with sharp-edged fluting
n Stylobate
o Crepidoma
© Baedeker
Ionic Order
a Sima
b Geison
c Tympanon
d Frieze (zophoros)
e Architrave
f Capital (with volutes)
g Shaft, with 24 flutings separated by ridges
h Attic base (with double torus and one trochilus)
i Stylobate
k Crepidoma
Lesbian cyma
Temple of Nike
Ceiling of portico of Temple of Nike, with coffering
Corinthian Order
a Geison
b Dentils
c Frieze
d Architrave
e Capital
f Shaft of column
g Base
h Crepidoma
Monument of Lysikrates

Stone benches for the clergy in the apse of a Byzantine church.	**Synthronon**
A sacred precinct.	**Temenos**
A low stone screen in an Early Christian or Byzantine church separating the sanctuary from the rest of the church.	**Templon**
(Temple) with four columns on the façade.	**Tetrastyle**
Treasury.	**Thesauros**
A circular building, rotunda; a domed Mycenaean tomb.	**Tholos**
An altar in the orchestra of a theatre.	**Thymele**
A convex moulding of semicircular profile. See diagram, page 90.	**Torus**
A projecting member, with two vertical channels, between the metopes of the Doric order. See diagram, page 90.	**Triglyph**
A convex moulding. See diagram, page 90.	**Trochilus**
The rear wall of a temple pediment. See diagram, page 90.	**Tympanon**
The spiral scroll of an Ionic capital. See diagram, page 90.	**Volute**
An archaic wooden cult image.	**Xoanon**

The Classical Orders

Doric Order

In the Doric order the shaft of the column, which tapers towards the top and has between 16 and 20 flutings, stands directly, without a base, on the stylobate above the three-stepped crepidoma or platform. A characteristic feature is the entasis (swelling) of the columns, which together with the frequently applied curvature of the crepidoma relieves the austerity of the structure.
The capital consists of the echinus, curving up from the shaft, and the square abacus. It carries the architrave with its frieze of triglyphs and metopes, which may be either plain or with relief ornament. Between and below the triglyphs are the drop-like guttae. The tympanon is enclosed by the horizontal cornice (geison) and the oblique mouldings which form an angle with it, and usually contains the pediment figures. The sculptured decoration normally consists of the carving on the metopes and the pediment figures, but may extend also to the front of the pronaos.

Where limestone rather than marble was used it was faced with a coat of stucco. The surface was not left in its natural colour but was painted, the dominant colours being blue, red and white.

Ionic Order

The Ionic order has slenderer and gentler forms than the Doric, the "male" order. The flutings of the columns are separated by narrow ridges. The column stands on a base, which may be either of the Anatolian type (with several concave mouldings) or the Attic type (with an alternation between the convex torus and the concave trochilus). The characteristic feature of the capital is the spiral volute (scroll) on either side. The architrave is not straight, but made up of three sections, each projecting over the one below. The frieze is continuous, without triglyphs to divide it up.

The Ionic type of temple, which originated in the territories occupied by the Ionian Greeks, was well adapted to the development of large structures, such as the gigantic temples on Samos and at Ephesus, Sardis and Didyma in Asia Minor.

Corinthian Order

The Corinthian order is similar to the Ionic except in the form of the capital.
The characteristic feature of the Corinthian capital is the acanthus foliage which encloses the circular body of the capital, with tendrils reaching up to the concave architrave (the "master capital" in Epidauros Museum; Olympieion, Athens).

Composite capital

The Corinthian capital was particularly popular in the Imperial period, which also evolved the "composite" capital, a marriage of the Ionic and Corinthian forms, and developed ever more elaborate decorative schemes.

Modern Greek Culture

Art and Architecture

19th century

After Greece's liberation from Turkish rule in the first third of the 19th century there was a return, in part at least, to Byzantine models (Ophthalmic Clinic and New Mitropolis church, Athens).
In art the influence of the Munich school, which came to Greece in the train of the country's first king, a Bavarian prince, was at first predominant. Architects and town planners such as the Danish brothers Christian and Theophil Hansen, the Germans Friedrich von Gärtner and Eduard Schaubert, and Stamatios Kleanthes, however, looked for their inspiration to antiquity. Examples of this trend are a series of neo-classical buildings in Athens, including the University, the Academy, the National Library and the Royal Palace, as well as the marble Stadion, rebuilt in its original form between 1896 and 1906.
For the artists of the late 19th century the standards were set by Paris.

20th century

Twentieth century Greek art has been marked by increasing contact with the influential international centres in Europe and North America. All the main trends in modern art have reached Greece, though usually with a certain time-lag. Greek artists lean on the one hand towards the maintenance of old-established traditions, but at the same time are very ready to entertain new trends from abroad, sometimes evolving unusual fusions of styles.
It is notable that many Greek artists work both in Greece and abroad, and that not a few have left the country for good – no doubt influenced by the precarious economic situation in what is a relatively poor country. In spite of this the number of artists working in Greece is comparatively high. It is not possible, however, to identify any characteristically Greek artistic movement which has had influence beyond the bounds of Greece.

The work of contemporary Greek architects and town planners is in sharp contrast to the creations of antiquity. There is much building activity at many places in mainland Greece and the islands; but with a few laudable exceptions the results show a lack of any dominant idea. It is not only in the larger cities and towns that the development of industry and new housing is getting out of hand: even smaller towns are reaching out beyond their original bounds to accommodate the inflow of population from declining rural areas.

In the towns and villages of mainland Greece visitors are likely to be struck by the large numbers of unfinished houses and makeshift temporary buildings (e.g. car repair workshops) and by the uniformity of building style which produces a kind of facelessness – though the farther away from large towns a place is, the more individuality it is likely to have.

On the Greek islands, where industrialisation has made little headway, there is much less modern development of this kind. In the islands it is mainly the tourist trade, with its rash of hotel building, that has destroyed the charm of so many once idyllic areas.

Literature

Origins

The beginnings of modern Greek literature can be traced back to Byzantine times, in the form of the ballads celebrating the exploits of the freedom-loving popular hero Digenis Akritas, who was also the subject of an epic poem written in the 11th/12th century.

Turkish period

The Turkish conquest of Constantinople and much of Greece brought a deep and lasting break in Greek cultural and literary development. Only in folk poetry was the tradition carried on, with the lyrical ballads about the klephts, the "freedom fighters" of Greece and Albania. The flight of many Greek scholars to Italy led to the intellectual impoverishment of Greece, and the only focal point of Greek culture was the Greek enclave in the Phanar district of Istanbul.

From the end of the 15th century, however, there was a lively development of literary activity in Crete, which was not yet under Turkish rule but was under Venetian influence, culminating in the 17th century in the plays of G. Khortatsis and the poems of V. Kornaros.

18th century

New impulses came to Greece in the second half of the 18th century from the Danube principalities, which were relatively independent of Turkish control. Greek politicians and scholars living in these territories wrote essays and learned works in *dimotikí* (Demotic), the colloquial language of Greece.

Linguistic dualism

This was an important step forward in solving the problem of Greece's linguistic dualism, the existence of two different levels of the Greek language. This dualism had begun in the time of Alexander the Great, when the *koine* ("common" language), a colloquial form of Greek, developed out of classical Greek and became an international lingua franca (the language in which the New Testament was originally written), while scholars continued to take classical Attic Greek as their model.
In Byzantime times Greek authors still wrote in Atticising Greek, while the colloquial language, continuing to develop on its own, was excluded from serious literature. It was not until the "literary revolution" of 1888 that Demotic was recognised as a literary language.

Meanwhile, following the foundation of the new Greek state in 1829–30, the academic Establishment had created a "purified" form of Greek related to the classical language, *katharévousa,* which remained the official language of Greece until 1975.

Towards Political Freedom

Adamantios Korais (1748–1833), who lived for many years in France, played a major part in the development of a "committed" modern Greek literature, which reached eloquent expression in the poems of Dionysios Solomos (1798–1857), author of the Greek national anthem. Under Solomos's influence writers in the Ionian Islands also wrote in Demotic.

During the fifty years after the liberation of Greece many literary works were written in the artificial Katharevousa but achieved no popular success.

The appearance in 1888 of a book by Yannis Psykharis (1857–1929), "To Taxídi mou" ("My Journey"), written in Demotic, sparked off an enthusiasm for the colloquial language among Greek writers and marked the final breakthrough to a recognised modern Greek literary language.

Thereafter Greek writers took an increasing interest in the folk traditions and way of life of the people of Greece and in human conflicts. An outstanding representative of the modern Greek *roman de mœurs* was Alexandros Papadiamantis (1851–1911), with his descriptions of life on his native island of Skiathos.

Turn of the century

Around the turn of the 19th century a new generation of writers came to the fore, much influenced by the lyric poetry of Dionysios Solomos; its most prominent representative was Kostis Palamas (1859–1943), a writer of great expressive power. Other young Greek writers followed contemporary literary trends in western Europe, particularly the French Symbolists, but also looked to Scandinavia and Russia.

The modern school

The forerunner of the undramatic modern school of writers was an expatriate Greek, Konstantinos Kavafis (1863–1933), born in Alexandria. Its real beginning was marked by the appearance in 1931 of a volume of poems, "Strofí" ("Turning-Point"), by Yeoryios Seferis (1900–71), who together with other lyric poets – among them the Surrealist "poet of the Aegean" Odysseas Elytis (Odysseas Alepoudelis, b. 1911 in Iraklion, Crete) – edited a literary journal, "Néa Grámmata" ("New Writing") from 1935 to 1939.

Second World War and Civil War

The events of the Second World War and the civil war that followed it were reflected in numerous literary works – novels, short stories and poems. The literature of the Resistance began immediately after the Italian attack in 1940 and the German occupation of Greece in 1941. The poems of Angelos Sikelianos (1884–1951) and other writers dedicated to the idea of freedom circulated clandestinely in occupied Greece. In his "Heroic and Mournful Song on the Lieutenant Killed in Albania" (1945) Odysseas Elytis celebrated the Greek struggle for freedom.

Post-war period

The Greek writers who had initiated the new literary era in the thirties were able to get their work published again after the war. Most of the works of Nikos Kazantzakis (1883–1957), including his famous novel "Zorba the Greek", were not published until after 1945.

Dictatorship

With the seizure of power by the military junta in 1971 Greek literary life suffered a severe setback, as a result of censorship, the deportation of some writers and other restrictions. This led to the development of a new literature of resistance, some of it written in exile.

The contemporary literary scene is characterised on the one hand by the large number of "committed" writers and the correspondingly large number of works published, and on the other by an extraordinary variety of styles and themes. Every conceivable trend has its representatives, but a distinct movement can be observed towards works of social criticism.

Contemporary writers

The only Greek writers who have so far won the Nobel Prize for literature are Yeoryios Seferis (1963) and Odysseas Elytis (1979).

Nobel Prizes

Drama

In contrast to ancient Greece, the birthplace of western drama, the modern Greek theatre has produced little of significant importance to the development of drama.

The modern Greek theatre had a first flowering in the 15th–17th centuries on Crete, brought to an end by Turkish occupation. The works produced during this period mostly showed strong Italian influence.

Italian influence

After the foundation of the new Greek state in 1829–30 the Greeks tried to develop a theatre of their own, but until about 1870 this did not develop beyond the amateur level. One difficulty was the problem of language (the Katharevousa/Demotic controversy). Towards the end of the 19th century the influence of the naturalism then predominant in the European theatre began to be felt in Greece.

Amateur theatre

Regular theatrical activity became possible with the establishment of the Basilikón Théatron (Theatre Royal) and the Néa Skiní (New Theatre) in Athens in 1901. The New Theatre was dedicated to Naturalism, while the Theatre Royal went in for Expressionism.
In 1932 a third large theatre, the Ethnikón Théatron (National Theatre), was opened. Here D. Rontiris, who had worked with Max Reinhardt in Berlin, put on very successful productions of ancient Greek dramas.

New theatres

Mention should also be made of the Greek liking for light entertainment in the form of farces, cabaret shows, etc.

Farces, etc.

The German occupation during the Second World War brought Greek theatrical life to an almost complete standstill, although a few travelling amateur companies played to audiences of resistance fighters and partisans.

Wartime close-down

A new trend in dramatic subject-matter and technique was introduced in the mid fifties by Iakovos Kambanellis (b. 1919), a master of contemporary dramatic language who seeks his themes in the world of the under-privileged and oppressed.
The great majority of present-day theatres, however, offer lighter dramatic fare (farces, musicals, cabaret).

Kambanellis

Some 70% of present-day productions are works by Greek dramatists; the rest are translations and adaptations from other languages and cultures.

Special types of theatre are puppet theatres, "box" theatres, the shadow theatres inherited from the 19th century, student theatres and children's theatres.

Special types of theatre

The most important large theatres in Greece are the National Theatre in Athens; the National Theatre of Northern Greece (founded 1961) in

Principal theatres

Salonica, with its subsidiaries the Thracian and Pontic Theatres; the travelling "Waggon of Thespis" company (founded 1976); and the Arts Theatre.

Private theatres

In addition there are a number of semi-national and private theatres, including the Amphi-Theatre and several district theatres in Athens, the Piraeus Theatre, the Thessalian Theatre in Larisa, the Theatre of Epirus, the Peloponnesian Theatre, the Cretan Theatre, the Theatre of the Cyclades, the Volos Theatre Club, the Bourini Theatre in Mytilini (Lesbos) and the Desmí ("Bonds") travelling company.

Drama festivals

Every year in summer there are dramatic festivals in Athens and Epidauros, which have been sponsored since 1955 by the National Tourist Organisation of Greece.

Athens

The Athens International Festival is held in the restored Odeion of Herodes Atticus and the modern open-air theatre on Lykabettos.

Epidauros

The Epidauros Festival is held in the ancient theatre, which is famed for its magnificent acoustics.

Philippi, Thasos

A Festival of Ancient Drama has been promoted since 1964 by the National Theatre of Northern Greece in the ancient theatres in Philippi and on the island of Thasos.

Dodona

The Athens National Theatre company performs from time to time in the theatre at Dodona, famed in antiquity for its oracle.

Music

For many years after Greece achieved independence in 1829–30 Greek music (apart from folk music: see below) was under the influence of contemporary Italian music. Greek musical life was almost exclusively dominated by Italian opera companies, and the Ionian school of music was a direct scion of Italian opera.

On Corfu (Kerkyra) Nikolaos Mantzaros (1795–1872), the first considerable modern Greek composer, made great efforts to promote musical education and a specifically Greek identity. He was also the composer of the Greek national anthem.

Spyridon Xyndas (1812–96) wrote the first purely Greek opera, "O Ypopsérios Voulevtís" ("The Parliamentary Candidate", 1867), with a Greek libretto, and the productive operatic composer Dionysios Lavrangas (1860?–1941) broke away from Italian models. Manolis Kalomiris (1883–1962), regarded by Greek musicians as the father of Greek music, pursued an entirely independent course.

Marios Varvoglis (1885–1967) and Emilios Riadis (1886–1935) were influenced by French Impressionism in music (Debussy, Ravel).

Around the turn of the 19th century German and other western European influences made themselves felt in Greek music.

Subsequently Greek composers were torn between a tendency to follow trends in other countries and a concern with native Greek traditions. Another feature of Greek musical life in this period was the fact that some Greek composers studied and worked outside Greece.

Modern composers

Notable among the numerous contemporary Greek composers have been Dimitris Mitropoulos (1896–1960), who had a great influence on Greek musical life as director of the Athens Symphony Orchestra from 1927 to 1939; Antiokhos Evangelatos (b. 1903) and Iannis Konstantinidis (b. 1903), who used motifs from Greek folk music; and Nikos Skalkottas (1904–49), a pupil of Schönberg, who also enjoyed an international reputation.

Representatives of post-war Greek music include Dimitris Dragatakis (b. 1904), Anestis Logothetis (b. 1921), Iannis Xenakis (b. 1922), Iani Khristou (born in Egypt; 1926–70) and the very productive Theodoros Antoniou (b. 1935).

Hadjidakis and Theodorakis

Two composers, both born in 1925, enjoy great popularity both in Greece and abroad: Manos Khatzidakis (Hadjidakis) and Mikis Theodorakis, who with their rehabilitation of the *rembétiko* songs (see below) have created a serious and distinctively Greek alternative to western light music.

Musical institutions

The chief centres of musical activity in Greece are Athens and the northern Greek city of Salonica, which have the country's most important musical institutions.
The Greek academies of music are the Odeion in Athens (founded 1871), the Piraeus Conservatoire (1904), the State Conservatoire in Salonica (1915) and the Hellenic Conservatoire (1919) and National Conservatoire in Athens (1926).
The Greek National Opera, founded in 1939, was the only opera house in Greece until the establishment in 1978 of the Salonica Opera, a branch of the State Theatre of Northern Greece.
The internationally known Athens State Orchestra (reconstituted in 1942 as the KOA) was originally the orchestra (established 1912) of the Odeion. From 1927 to 1939 it was directed by the composer and conductor Dimitris Mitropoulos; its present director is Manos Khatzidakis (Hadjidakis). The Salonica State Orchestra (KOTh) was founded in 1959.
The Athens Festival, held annually in summer, includes concerts and recitals of music as well as drama.

Customs and Traditions

Folk events

Greece's richly developed folk culture, still firmly anchored in tradition, finds expression on the occasion of the numerous church festivals (particularly the Easter celebrations and patronal festivals) and on family occasions in country areas.

Costumes

Although in recent years Greek traditional costumes have become rarer, they are still an established feature of popular life in some parts of the country.

Fustanella

In northern Greece men wear the fustanella, a white knee-length skirt decorated with bells and coins and usually accompanied by a white shirt and an embroidered jacket.

Vraka

On Crete men can sometimes be seen wearing the traditional vraka (baggy black breeches) and black head-scarf.
Old costumes can also be seen on the island of Karpathos, in the southern part of Rhodes, on Corfu (Kerkyra) and in the Pindos range in central Greece.

Evzones

The colourful uniform of the Evzones ("finely belted"), the former royal bodyguard, is derived from a traditional Albanian costume. It is still worn by soldiers mounting guard at the National Monument in front of the Parliament Building in Athens.

Folk dances

Dancing and music have been associated in Greek tradition since time immemorial. Ancient vases depict dancers performing round dances, and according to Greek legend Rheia, mother of Zeus, herself taught her priests the original dances.
Two different types of dance can be distinguished, the measured tread of the *syrtos* dances and the impetuous movements of the *pidik*

A Greek folk dancing group

dances – though every island and every part of mainland Greece has developed its own style and its own variations.
The best known Greek folk dance is undoubtedly the *syrtáki,* a round dance led by a principal dancer. The better the leader is, the more improvisations he devises before handing on to the next dancer.
The ring dances, in which the dancers hold each other's hands or hold on to handkerchiefs, are now danced by men and women together, though originally they were danced by the sexes separately.

Mime

Popular events during the Carnival are mime dances in which the dancers imitate particular social classes or occupational groups and dances by men in women's dress recalling the deeds of the klephts (guerrilla fighters) of the Greek struggle for liberation in the 18th and 19th centuries.

Folk music
Folk songs
Klepht songs

The past lives on, too, in Greek folk songs. Particularly popular are the melancholy klepht songs ("robbers' songs", "thieves' songs"), which date from the period of Turkish rule. Their themes are heroic deeds and hardships in the mountains, separation from loved ones, the longing for freedom, the blue sea and the wildness of nature. The songs are accompanied by the shepherd's pipe and the lyre, a predecessor of the violin.

With the continuing development of the country and the growing appeal of the towns urban influences have increasingly crept into folk music and led to a combination of folk songs, Byzantine and Turkish music, the Italian-influenced *kantades* of the Ionian Islands and imports from the countries of the West (particularly the tango).

Bouzoúki

Within recent years Greek folk music, which with its characteristic rhythms and unusual intervals has had a major influence on contemporary Greek light music, has become better known in the rest of Europe. The singing is accompanied by the popular bouzoúki, a mandoline-like stringed instrument, the santoúri, a kind of dulcimer, and various woodwind instruments.

Rembétiko

The *rembétiko* is a type of song, now widely popular, which originated in the 1920s in the slums and tavernas of Piraeus among the *rembetes,* the outcasts of society, unemployed or doing hard and heavy work in the docks, who had developed a life-style of their own, involving drugs but also leaving a place for music. They wrote sharply satirical songs, not uncommonly composed in prison, which were accompanied on a home-made bouzoúki, the *baglama,* formed from a hollowed-out pumpkin, a piece of wood and a few wire strings. The rembétiko sang in highly colloquial language of the deeds of "cabbage-pickers" (pickpockets), of "eating wood" (getting a beating), of faithless street-girls. When General Metaxas banned the use of drugs many of the musicians retired to Salonica, out of the way of the authorities in Athens. Finally the recording industry took up the rembétiko and made it socially acceptable.

"Greek music"

"Greek music" tends nowadays to mean songs like those written by Manos Khatzidakis (Hadjidakis) and Mikis Theodorakis, whose tunes hark back to the turn of the 19th century. Theodorakis, a very popular singer, ranks in other countries as a kind of cultural ambassador of Greece. He became internationally known through his music for the famous film "Zorba the Greek", which is set on the island of Crete.

Mass Media

Press

The eventful history of the modern Greek state has repeatedly involved the press – the oldest of the mass media – in the hurlyburly of social and political conflicts and changes.

The first Greek newspapers appeared during the period of Turkish rule – not in Greece but in Vienna (1784), Paris and London. After the beginning of the war of liberation, in 1821, the first newspaper printed on Greek soil, the "Sálpinx Elliniki" ("Greek Trumpet"), the organ of the then revolutionary government, was founded.
With the establishment of the new Greek state in 1829–30 the freedom of the press was severely restricted, and it was not restored until 1864. The first daily newspaper, the "Efimeris", began to appear in 1873, to be followed by a number of other papers, some of which still survive. The Greek press was subjected to strict controls and censorship during the German occupation of 1941–44 and again under the military dictatorship of 1967–74. The position of the press is now safeguarded by the 1975 constitution (Article 14), which establishes press freedom and prohibits censorship.

Newspapers

Athens is the newspaper capital of Greece as well as its political capital. The overwhelming majority of Greece's newspapers and periodicals are published in Athens, with Salonica as a poor second. There are also numerous smaller regional and local papers.
A Greek peculiarity is the relatively large number of regional papers, through which people in provincial towns and country areas can keep in touch with relatives and friends who have moved to the big towns.

The following are the largest and most important of the Greek newspapers (more than three-quarters of which appear in the afternoon or evening):

Athens

"Ethnos" ("Nation"; circulation over 200,000)
"Ta Nea" ("News"; over 150,000)
"Apogevmatini" ("Afternoon Journal"; *c.* 130,000)
"Eleftheriotypia" ("Free Press"; *c.* 100,000)
"I Vradyni" ("Evening Journal", founded 1922; over 70,000)
"Avriani" ("Morning Journal"; over 70,000)
"Akropolis" (founded 1883; over 50,000)
"I Katherimini" ("Daily", founded 1919; *c.* 50,000)
"Rizospastis" ("Radical"; the Moscow party line; just under 50,000)
"Express" (an economic journal; *c.* 35,000)
"Athlitiko Ikho" ("Sports Echo", daily; *c.* 25,000)
"I Avyi" ("Dawn"; Euro-Communist; just under 10,000)
"Athens News" (English-language daily; *c.* 10,000)
"To Vima" ("The Tribune"), formerly a daily, now appears only once a week (35,000)

Salonica

"Makedonia" (*c.* 50,000)
"Thessaloniki" (*c.* 35,000)

News Agency

The Greek News Agency is based in Athens and signs its reports ANA (Athenagence).

Radio

The history of radio in Greece goes back to the year 1923, when a naval station sent a message by radio for the first time. The first official radio transmission went on the air on the Greek National Day (March 25th) in 1938 (although a private radio station in Salonica had previously been responsible for the first broadcast in the Balkans in 1936).

Now Greek Radio and Television (ERT: see below) broadcasts on medium and short waves and VHF. There are short news and weather bulletins in English in the morning, afternoon and evening.

The possible establishment of private radio stations is under discussion.

Television

The Greek National Radio Corporation, Ethnikón Idryma Radiofonías (EIR) broadcast its first television programme on February 23rd 1966, and, after a change of name to Ethnikón Idryma Radiofonías Tileoráseos (EIRT) in 1970 and to Ellinikí Radiofonía Tileórasis (ERT: Greek Radio and Television) in 1975, began transmitting in colour (on the French SECAM system) in 1978; there are now two channels.

Suggested Routes

The following routes are intended merely as suggestions to guide visitors in planning their trip to Greece, leaving them free to select and vary the routes in accordance with their particular interests and preferences.
The suggested routes take in all the main tourist sights in Greece; but not all the places of interest described in this guide lie directly on the routes, and to see them it will be necessary to make detours from the main routes. The descriptions in the A to Z section of the guide, therefore, contain numerous suggestions and recommendations for detours, excursions and round trips to see these other sights. This applies particularly to the Greek islands.
The suggested routes can be followed on the map enclosed with this guide, which will help with detailed planning.

Travelling to and from Greece

The journey from Britain to Greece by road is a long one, since it involves travelling from the Channel port across Europe and then down through Italy. From here take one of the car ferries from Italian ports (Ancona, Bari, Brindisi) to the Greek ports of Igoumenitsa, Patras or Piraeus (Athens). This does, however, call for exact timing, since places on the ferries must be booked well in advance.

Travellers should seek advice before choosing a route through former Yugoslavia.

General notes

In these routes the names of places which are the subject of a separate entry in the A to Z section of the guide are given in **bold** type.

All the places mentioned – towns, villages, regions, islands, rivers and isolated features of interest – are included in the Index at the end of the guide, making it easy to find the description of any sight.

The distances given in brackets at the head of each route are rounded figures for the main route. The additional distances involved in the various detours and excursions are indicated in each case.

Northern and Central Greece

1: Salonica to Athens (520km/325 miles)

Main route

This route between Greece's two largest cities, the main axis of the Greek road network, is part on the transcontinental highway E 75. It is an expressway (toll payable) for its whole length, with some sections of motorway standard.

The route runs along the Gulf of Salonica, the northwestern tip of the Aegean, into which flow the large rivers Gallikos, Axios (Vardar), Loudias and Aliakmon, and then through Greek **Macedonia**, over the featureless plain of Kampania. It then skirts the eastern foothills of the

Pieria range and after passing the little town of Katerini runs close to the Thermaic Gulf, on a magnificent stretch of road at the foot of **Mount Olympus**, home of the gods and Greece's highest mountain (2917m/9571ft). After passing the Crusader castle of Platamón the road passes through the beautiful Vale of **Tempe**, between Olympus and Mount Ossa, into the fertile plains of **Thessaly**, which has been the granary of Greece since ancient times. Here, on the river Pinios, is **Lárisa**, chief town of Thessaly.
The road continues south-west, passing the port of **Vólos** (off the road to the left), describes a wide arc to the east and south of the Óthrys range and comes to **Lamía**, chief town of the nomos of Phthiotis. From there it continues past **Thermopylai** – no longer the narrow pass it was in ancient times – and the seaside resort of **Kaména Voúrla** and along the south coast of the Gulf of Euboea.
Soon afterwards the road turns inland and enters **Boeotia**, passing the massive Mycenaean stronghold of **Gla** (to left) and the ancient city of **Thebes**, to the south. It then comes into the peninsula of **Attica**, runs round the east side of Mount **Parnis** (Oros Párnitha) to enter **Athens**.

Detours and variants

The little hill town of **Litókhoron**, at the foot of Mount **Olympus**, is the starting-point for the ascent of the mountain.
A few kilometres north of Litókhoron are the interesting excavations of the Macedonian town of **Dion**.
From **Lárisa** there is a good road running west (85km/53 miles) to **Tríkala** and the extraordinary "monasteries in the air" of **Metéora**.
From **Vólos** an excursion can be made eastward to Mount **Pelion**, with its remote and picturesquely situated mountain villages.

From **Lamía** a winding road runs west through the southern **Pindos** to **Agrínion** (see Route 2), chief town of the nomos of Aetolia. The road follows the valley of the Sperkhiós, passes the mountain village of Karpenísi, at the foot of Mt Tymfristós (2315m/7596ft; winter sports), crosses an offshoot of the long artificial lake on the river Akheloos (Lake Kremastá) and continues to Agrínion (just under 200km/125 miles).

From **Lamía** or **Thermopylai** a short excursion can be made westward to the village of Gorgopótamos, where during the Second World War British soldiers and Greek Resistance fighters blew up the railway viaduct over the river Gorgopótamos and thus interrupted the main supply line for the German forces.
From Lamía there is also a charming mountain road leading south into Phocis, passing through Vrálos and continuing by way of **Amfissa** to **Delphi**, shrine of the famous oracle, situated at the foot of Mount **Parnassus** (95km/59 miles).

Those who cannot face the prospect, after a long day's drive, of the chaotic Athens traffic should turn off the expressway at Ritsona (75km/47 miles before Athens) and take the road which runs north-east to Khalkis (Khalkída) on the island of **Euboea** (Évvia), here separated from the mainland by a narrow channel (interesting old traversing bridge; new bridge under construction nearby).

For the journey from Khalkis to Athens it is worth taking a rather longer way round via the ancient oracular shrine, the **Amphiareion** (near the coastal town of Skála Oropoú on the Gulf of Euboea) and the battlefield of **Marathón**. From there a beautiful hill road crosses the **Pentelikon** range (marble quarries) to Diónysos, a favourite Athenian weekend resort.

2: Igoumenítsa via Delphi to Athens (530km/330 miles)

Main route

This route is designed for visitors arriving in Greece by way of Italy and the car ferry to Igoumenítsa.
From **Igoumenítsa**, which has ferry connections with the Italian and Yugoslav Adriatic ports and with the island of **Corfu** (Kérkyra), the road runs south-east, at some distance from the coast of the Ionian Sea, through the hilly region of **Epirus**, passes the little town of Mesopótamos, with the **Nekromanteion Ephyras** (the oracle of the dead), and then continues close to the sea to the port of **Préveza**, at the narrow mouth of the Ambracian Gulf, a large and almost totally land-locked bay, which is crossed on a car ferry to Aktion. The road then turns east, passes through **Vónitsa** and comes to Amfilokhía, an attractive little holiday resort at the head of an inlet at the south-eastern tip of the Ambracian Gulf.
Soon afterwards the road crosses the north end of Lake Amvrakía on a causeway and continues down the east side of the lake, through an intensively farmed agricultural area, into the wide valley of the river Akhelóos (which is dammed farther north to supply electric power) and reaches the village of Strátos, on the site of the ancient city of that name, once chief town of Acarnania (circuit of walls, with towers and gates; temple of Zeus). Crossing the stony bed of the Akhelóos, here divided into several arms (hydroelectric station), the road continues through a barren upland region to **Agrinion**, chief town of the nomos of Aetolia, from which an interesting mountain road runs north-east through the **Pindos** range to **Lamía** (see Route 1).
The route continues south from Agrínion, between Lake Lysimákhia (to the west) and the larger Lake Trikhonída (to the east: not visible), and then crosses a pass between the sheer rock walls of the Klisoúra gorge and descends, passing extensive salt-pans and the little town of Aitolikó, on a lagoon, to **Mesolóngi**, famed for its part in the Greek war of liberation. The main road bypasses the town, still partly surrounded by its old walls, and runs east to Antirrion (Andírrio), with the old fortress of Roumeli, on the Strait of **Ríon** (the Little Dardanelles: car ferry to the Peloponnesian side), at the narrow west end of the Gulf of Corinth.
From here the route follows the north side of the Gulf of **Náfpaktos** (in Venetian times known as Lepanto), on a beautiful stretch of road which keeps close to the shore for most of the way, with magnificent views of the hills of the Peloponnese to the south. At Erátini there is a first glimpse of Mount **Parnassus**.
Shortly before the little port town of Itéa the road passes the unsightly Parnassus aluminium workings. From Itéa it continues north over a plain covered with large olive plantations and then climbs, with many bends but fine views, to **Delphi**, passing through the modern tourist town with its hotels, restaurants and shops and then coming to the excavated site (or rather sites) of the ancient oracular shrine, in a magnificent mountain setting.
From Delphi the road runs east by way of the picturesquely situated tourist centre (and winter sports resort) of Arákhova, the Boeotian capital of **Levadia** (Livadiá), the important ancient city of **Thebes** (Thíva) and **Eleusis**, shrine of the Eleusinian mysteries, now surrounded by the industrial town of Elefsína, to **Athens**.

Variants

For a less direct but very attractive alternative route from Igoumenítsa to Athens, take the road which leads inland and in 100km/60 miles, on a good road through beautiful mountain country, reaches **Ioánnina**, chief town of **Epirus**, beautifully situated on its lake. From here the road turns south and descends the beautiful valley of the river Loúros (trout) to **Arta** with its interesting Byzantine churches. This was ancient Ambrakia, which gave its name to the Ambracian Gulf to the south of the town.

Those who prefer to avoid the ferry crossing from Préveza to Aktion should take a road (No. 21) which goes off on the left 17km/10½ miles before Préveza and runs north-east to join the variant route from Ioánnina to Arta.

From Vónitsa there is an alternative route leading south by way of Astakós to Aitolikó and then joining the main route from Amfilókhia via Agrínion to Mesolóngi.

From Antírrion, on the Strait of Ríon, an alternative to the route via Delphi is to take the car ferry across the strait to **Ríon**, in the **Peloponnese**, follow the expressway (toll) along the south side of the Gulf of Corinth to **Corinth**, cross the Corinth Canal and continue via Mégara and **Eleusis** to **Athens** (see Route 7, in the reverse direction).

Detours

From the road going south-east from Igoumenítsa to Préveza a short detour can be made to the seaside resort of **Párga**, in a pretty little bay. Near Préveza are the extensive excavations of the city of **Nikopolis**, founded by Octavian.

After crossing the Préveza–Aktion ferry it is possible to visit the Ionian island of **Lefkás**, which is separated from the mainland only by a narrow channel and can be reached by way of a causeway and a bascule bridge.

From the road running inland from Igoumenítsa by way of **Ioánnina** there are a number of possible excursions: to the Pérama stalactitic cave, a little to the north of the Lake of Ioánnina; north-west on the road to the Albanian frontier (see Route 3, in the reverse direction) to the interesting mountain village in the Zagória range and the deeply slashed Víkos gorge; south-west to **Dodona**, famed in antiquity for its oracle, with an ancient theatre in which performances are still given. From Ioánnina a beautiful road runs east via **Métsovo**, over the Katára pass (new section of road, with tunnel, under construction) and through the imposing mountain world of the **Pindos** range to the extraordinary monasteries of **Metéora** (125km/78 miles).

Visitors who have insufficient time to see the many sights in the **Peloponnese** (see Routes 7 and 8A–D) should at least make a short excursion to see **Olympia**. This can be done by crossing from Antírrion to **Ríon** and continuing from there via **Patras** and **Pýrgos**. Except within the built-up area of Patras the road is an expressway for almost the whole distance (120km/75 miles).

Between Delphi and Athens there are numerous places of interest to be seen just off the main road, which it might perhaps be better to visit by following Route 6 or by making detours from a base in the Athens area. One sight of great interest that can best be taken in on the present route, however, is the monastery of **Ósios Loukás** with its magnificent 11th century mosaics, which is reached on a side road from Arákhova.

Just off this road lies the village of Dístomo, where in 1944 the German occupying forces massacred more than 200 Greeks.

3: Salonica via Kastoriá to Ioánnina (450km/280 miles)

Main route

This route through the far north of Greece runs through a beautiful region away from the main roads frequented by tourists but with much of interest to offer. The first part of the route follows the line of the old Roman road, the Via Egnatia, which ran from Dyrrhachium (the

Italian Durazzo, now Durrës in Albania) to Constantinople. At first the route traverses mainly flat or gently rolling country, then comes into a hilly region.
From **Salonica** the road turns west over the wide Macedonian coastal plain (Kampania), crosses the expressway from the Yugoslav frontier (Skopje–Salonica–Athens: see Route 1) and the broad river Axios (Vardar), passes the remains of **Pella**, once capital of the kingdom of Macedon, and the little country town of Yiannitsá, near which was the large Lake of Yiannitsá, now drained, and comes to **Édessa**, on a plateau in the foothills of Mt Vermion.
Beyond Édessa the road runs round the north end of Lake Vegorítida, passes through the villages of Kélla and Vévi and comes to **Flórina**, chief town of a nomos. From here a trunk road goes north to the Yugoslav frontier, continuing via Bitola to Lake Prespa and Lake Ohrid.
From Flórina the route leads west and then south, following a winding course through hilly country near the meeting-place of Greece, Yugoslavia and Albania, to **Kastoriá**, a picturesque old town with numerous Byzantine churches situated on a peninsula in Lake Kastoriá.
South of Kastoriá we join the main road from **Kozáni** (see Route 5), which leads west, at first through beautiful upland country and then through magnificent mountain scenery, into **Epirus**. At this point the road, following for much of the way rivers with an abundant flow of water, keeps close to the Albanian frontier. At Kónitsa (above the road on the left) it descends into an extensive and well cultivated plain, and after a further winding stretch through hills runs down, with the Zagória range to the left, into the broad basin containing Lake **Ioánnina**.

Detours

From Ioánnina it is 100km/60 miles west to the port of **Igoumenítsa** (see Route 2, first variant).
For possible excursions to the Ioánnina area and the Metéora monasteries, see Route 2.

4: Salonica via Kavála to Istanbul (650km/400 miles)

Main route

This route, which is relatively fast because of its long straight stretches, is the only land link between Greece and Turkey, and for part of the way follows the old Via Egnatia (see Route 3). From the Gulf of **Salonica** it runs at first through the southern part of Greek **Macedonia**, passing close to Lakes Korónia and Vólvi. To the south is the "three-fingered" peninsula of **Chalcidice**.
Beyond Rendína the road reaches the coast of the Strymonic Gulf (Kólpos Orfánou) and continues through the seaside resorts of Asprovälta and Kerdýlia to the mouth of the river Strymon (Bulgarian Struma). Just before the bridge is a stone lion from nearby **Amphipolis**. The road then continues along the coast, passes through the seaside resort of Loutrá Eleftheró, crosses the marshy plain of **Philippi** and comes to the Gulf of Kavála, with the charmingly situated port of **Kavála**.
Soon after Kavála the road crosses the river Nestos (Bulgarian Mesta), which has formed a large and fertile coastal plain to the south-east of the road. Here the road crosses from Macedonia into **Thrace**. As a result of its long period under Ottoman rule western Thrace, which has belonged to Greece since the end of the First World War and before that was briefly held by Bulgaria, has more of an Oriental character than any other part of Greece, and in spite of the population exchange between Greece and Turkey in 1923 still has a substantial Muslim minority.

Beyond **Xánthi** the road traverses a narrow strip of land between Lake Vistonis and a bay on the Aegean to Porto Lago, and then continues to **Komotiní**, below the Rhodope range (most of which is in Bulgaria). It then crosses the western Thracian plain and through rocky upland country to the port of **Alexandroupolis**, the last place of any size before the Turkish frontier. From there the direct road to Istanbul crosses the river Évros (Turkish Meriç Nehri), which marks the frontier, and continues through Turkish Thrace, for the most part a steppe-like region traversed by numerous small rivers, and then along the steadily narrowing Thracian Peninsula between the Black Sea and the Sea of Marmara. At Tekirdağ it reaches the Sea of Marmara and continues, on or near the coast, to Istanbul (see the AA/Baedeker guide "Istanbul"). From Istanbul it is possible to return to Greece or to an Adriatic port by ferry.

Detours and variants

If time permits it is worth while making an excursion from Salonica into the peninsula of **Chalcidice**, with numerous attractive holiday resorts on the two western "fingers" of the peninsula, Kassándra and Sithonía. On the third finger is the monastic republic of **Athos**, which can be visited only by adult males and only with special permission. A few kilometres north of Néa Kerdýlia are the remains of ancient **Amphipolis**.

From Kavála and Keramotí there are ferries to the island of **Thásos**, and from Alexandroúpolis a ferry to **Samothrace**.

South of Xánthi are the remains of the ancient port of Abdera, excavated in the 1950s.

Between Alexandroúpolis and Istanbul it is worth while taking the longer way round (about 80km/50 miles more) via the Turkish town of Edirne (Adrianople) to see the Mosque of Selim, one of the most magnificent in the whole of Turkey.

An alternative to the direct road between Salonica and Kavála is the inland route via **Dráma** and **Serrai** (Sérres; about 40km/25 miles longer). Although the road itself is less attractive, this route runs through typical Thracian lowland country (tobacco-growing) and passes the site of ancient **Philippi**.

5: Salonica via Kozáni to the Monasteries of Metéora (270km/170 miles)

Main route

From **Salonica** this route begins by following Route 1, but just before crossing the Aliakmon bears off on the right and follows the broad river westward to the pleasant town of **Véria**, situated on a terrace in the foothills of Mt Vérmion.

From there the route continues south-west and crosses the Khantova pass, between Mt Vérmion to the west and the Piéria range to the east. It then runs down into the extensive Kozáni basin, passes a large lignite-fired power station and comes to **Kozáni**, chief town of a nomos.

The route then follows an expressway (No. 5), running west from Kozáni, and in 30km/19 miles turns left into a road (No. 15) which runs south-west, crossing the upper Aliakmon, to Grevená, continues through the Khásia range to enter **Thessaly** and comes to **Kalambáka**, from which the famous "monasteries in the air" of **Metéora** can be visited.

Detours and variants

From Véria a short detour can be made to **Vergína**, where the tomb of Philip II of Macedon was discovered.

From Kozáni a road (No. 3) runs south-east to **Lárisa** (145km/90 miles: see Route 1), crossing the large artificial Lake Aliakmon on a bridge

more than 2km/1¼ miles long and passing through **Sérvia**, Elassóna and Tírnavos.
From Kalambáka through the **Pindos** range to **Ioánnina**: see Route 2, detours.
Kalambáka via **Lamía** to **Athens**: see Route 6 (in the opposite direction).

6: Athens via Lamía to the Monasteries of Metéora (360km/225 miles)

Main route

This route runs north-west from **Athens** on the expressway to Corinth, passing the monastery of **Dafní** and the industrial installations which disfigure the Bay of Eleusis and at **Eleusis** (Elefsína) itself turning right into a road (No. 3) which leads north and follows a winding route through the Attic uplands. Beyond Erythrai (Erythrés) the road passes the battlefield of **Plataiai** (on left), where the Greeks defeated the Persians in 479 B.C., and soon afterwards reaches the famous ancient city of **Thebes** (Thíva), 6km/4 miles north of which is the Athens–Lamía–Lárisa–Salonica expressway.
Beyond Thebes the road (still No. 3) continues through the Boeotian capital **Livadiá** and **Chaironeia**, where Philip II of Macedon defeated a Greek army led by Demosthenes, an Athenian, in 338 B.C. (monumental lion marking the grave of the Thebans who fell in the battle). From here the road ascends the valley of the Kifisós, passing Amfíklia, with the rock walls of Mount **Parnassus** to the south, and Brálos, to the Pournaraki pass, on the watershed between the river systems of the Kifisós and the Sperkhios and on the boundary between the nomoi of Phocis and Phthiotis. The road then runs down into the broad and fertile valley of the Sperkhios, crosses the river and enters **Lamía** (see Route 1), chief town of the nomos of Phthiotis.
North of Lamía is the Óthrys range, through which the road follows a winding course to the Foúrka Pass (Stená Foúrkas), which until 1881 lay on the frontier between Greece and Turkey.
Some 55km/34 miles beyond Lamía, at Néo Monastíri, the road forks. The road to the right (No. 3) goes north-east to **Fársala** and **Lárisa** (60km/37 miles: see Route 1). The road to the left (No. 30), which is followed by the present route, leads north-west over the western Thessalian plain to **Karditsa**, **Tríkala** and **Kalambáka**, near which are the famous monasteries of **Metéora**.

Variants

Between Lamía and Athens there are several possible alternative routes:
The expressway (see Route 1, in the reverse direction) is faster than the route just recommended but from the sightseeing point of view the least interesting of the possible routes.
From Livadiá there is an attractive route running west below the south side of Mount **Parnassus** and through the picturesque little hill town of Arákhova to **Delphi** (see Route 2, in the opposite direction; possible detour via Dístomo to the monastery of **Ósios Loukás**), and from there via **Ámfissa** to rejoin the main route at Brálos (*c.* 50km/30 miles extra).
From Brálos there is an alternative route to Lamía on a road going north-east into the marshy plain around the mouth of the Sperkhios; then, after a short detour to **Thermopylai** (see Route 1), it is not far north-west to **Lamía**.
Kalambáka via **Kozáni** to **Salonica**: see Route 5 (in opposite direction).
Kalambáka through the **Pindos** to **Ioánnina**: see Route 2, detours.

Detours

At Panakton, an old frontier stronghold in the Attic uplands, a road goes off on the left to the seaside resort of **Pórto Yermenó**, in a bay at the east end of the Gulf of Corinth, on the site of ancient Aigosthena.

From Erythrai it is a short distance to the excavations of ancient **Plataiai**.
Just beyond Livadiá a short detour can be made to **Orkhomenós**, with the remains of ancient Orchomenos, a city with its origins in mythic times.
Lamía to the historic railway viaduct of Gorgopótamos: see Route 1, detours and variants.

Southern Greece (Peloponnese)

7: Athens via Corinth to Patras (220km/135 miles)

Main route

This route follows the important east–west connection (toll expressway, with some sections of motorway standard) between Athens and the largest city in the Peloponnese. It is of particular importance to visitors travelling by car and using the ferry service to or from Patras.
From Athens the road runs north-west on the line of the old Sacred Way, through the Aigaleos hills and past the monastery of **Dafní** to the Bay of **Eleusis**, now disfigured by intensive industrial development. Offshore is the island of **Salamis**. Beyond Mégara the road skirts the Saronic Gulf at the foot of the Yeránia range of hills, crosses the Corinth Canal (Dioriga Korinthou), passing **Isthmia**, and comes to **Corinth**.
The expressway now follows the north of the Peloponnese for the whole length of the Gulf of Corinth, bypassing such coastal towns and villages as Kiáton, **Xylókastro**, Trápeza, Diakoftó and **Aíyion**. Beyond the Strait of **Ríon** (the Little Dardanelles), in the Bay of Patras, is the large port of **Patras** (Pátra).

Variants

Those who are not pressed for time may prefer the old coast road, which keeps close to the shores of the gulf for most of the way. Although there may be traffic hold-ups in the towns and villages, this road offers more varied scenery than the expressway. Extensive coastal plains with olive-trees, cypresses and other southern species and currant-drying fields alternate with narrow strips of coast hemmed in by high hills and traversed by many mountain streams which are usually dry but after heavy rain may flood the road.

Detours

Immediately before the bridge over the Corinth Canal a minor road branches off on the right to the seaside resort of **Loutráki**, in a bay at the east end of the Gulf of Corinth, and beyond this is **Perakhóra**, with an ancient temple of Hera.
From the not particularly interesting modern town of Corinth it is a short distance to the important remains of ancient **Corinth**. It is well worth while also to drive up to the top of the castle-crowned hill of Acrocorinth, from which there is a celebrated view.
From the little town of Kiáton, on the coast road, it is 40km/25 miles south-west to the Stymphalian Lake, scene of one of the labours of Herakles.
Another attractive possibility is a trip from Trápeza (30km/19 miles) or by rack railway from Diakoftó (23km/14 miles), through lonely hills, to the monastery of Megaspílaion, the largest in Greece, and the tourist centre of **Kalávryta**, where in December 1943 the German occupying forces massacred more than 1400 people and burned the town down. A short distance away is the Ayía Lávra, the monastery in which the Greek war of liberation from the Turks was proclaimed in 1821.
Patras to **Olympia**: see Route 2, detours.

8: Circuits of the Peloponnese

The large peninsula in southern Greece known as the **Peloponnese** (the "Island of Pelops"; in the Middle Ages called the Morea, the "mulberry orchard"), which has some of the most important ancient sites in Greece, ranking with Athens and Delphi, consists predominantly of mountain country, much of it forest-covered. It is now well served by roads, including a new trunk road (not yet completed) running diagonally across the peninsula from Corinth via Trípoli to the south.
It should be borne in mind, however, that many of the ancient sites and beauty spots in the Peloponnese are quite remote and that any thorough sightseeing programme will involve much travelling on winding mountain roads. It is advisable, therefore, to avoid trying to pack too much into one day, and the routes suggested in this section are therefore relatively short.
Those who are pressed for time may be able to combine two or more routes, or selected sections of them.

Starting point

At first sight the obvious base from which to explore the Peloponnese is **Trípoli**, situated in the centre of the peninsula at the junction of several roads. This town, however, has little to offer apart from its situation. A more suitable place – in spite of its peripheral situation on the east side of the Peloponnese – would be the port of **Náfplion**, in a picturesque setting at the north end of the Argolic Gulf. With its rich historical past – from 1828 to 1834 it was capital of the new kingdom of Greece – its scenic attractions (two imposing fortresses above the town and a small island stronghold in the bay), its excellent communications both by land and by sea, its numerous hotels and restaurants, its shops, its churches and museums, the many ancient sites in the surrounding area and the beautiful beaches round the town, Náfplion is an excellent base from which to explore the Peloponnese, a good place to return to after a day's sightseeing.

All over the Peloponnese visitors will see roadside monuments commemorating the many people who lost their lives during the German occupation in 1941–44.

8A: The Argolid and the Corinth Area

Since there are so may interesting ancient sites to be seen, particularly in the **Argolid**, these suggested routes exclude the sites of **Tiryns**, **Argos** and **Mycenae**, which are within easy reach of Náfplion.

Main route

From **Náfplion** the route runs east by way of Ligoúrio to **Epidauros** (Palaiá Epídavros), with the remains of the sanctuary of the healing god Asklepios and the completely preserved ancient theatre, famed for its excellent acoustics, scene of a cultural festival during the summer months.
From Epidauros a road to the north above the much indented coast of the Saronic Gulf passes the little port of Palaiá Epídavros, the village of Néa Epídavros and the monastery of Agnounda; then, beyond Almyri, it descends to the shores of the Saronic Gulf at the spa of Loutró Elénis. After passing the site of the ancient Corinthian port of Kenchreai (some remains visible under water), it comes to **Isthmia**, on the south side of the Isthmus of Corinth.
From here the route runs a few kilometres west on the Athens Patras expressway, and just before **Corinth** takes a road on the left which runs south into the Peloponnese. After passing through Fikhtio and

Argos this road skirts the hill crowned by the ancient stronghold of **Tiryns** (Tíryntha) and returns to the starting-point of the route at **Náfplion**.

Detours

From Epidauros there are a number of side roads running south-east to various seaside resorts in bays on the Argolic peninsula: e.g. to **Pórto Khéli** (60km/37 miles; boats to the nearby island of **Spetsai**), Ermióni (boats to the island of **Hydra**) and Petrothalassa, and via ancient **Troizen** to the health resort of Méthana (65km/40 miles).
From the junction with the Athens–Patras expressway a short detour can be made to the bridge over the Corinth Canal (Dioriga Korinthou).
The access road to the interesting excavations of ancient **Corinth** (Palaiá Kórinthos; with possible drive up Acrocorinth) is clearly signposted on the Corinth–Argos road.
Also well signposted are the roads to **Nemea** (west from railway station) and, from Fikhtio, to **Mycenae** (Mykínes).
11 km/7 miles north-east of Argos, at the village of Khónikas, is the Argive Heraion.

8B: Via Trípoli to Olympia and Back (450km/280 miles)

Main route

The route leads north-west from **Náfplion** and round the shores of the Argolic Gulf to Myli. From there a road (No. 7) runs west into the northern part of the Mt **Parnon** range, with ever finer rearward views of the gulf, and comes to **Trípoli**, chief town of Arcadia and an important road junction.
From Trípoli the route turns north, traverses the Maínalon range of hills, with constantly changing scenery, passes through Levídi, Vlakhérna, Vytína, Karkaloú and Langádia, goes over several low passes, enters the wide valley of the Ládon and crosses the river Erymanthos to enter the district of Elis. After passing through an area of forest it comes to the famous ancient site of **Olympia**, place of origin of the Olympic Games. On the far side of the river Kladeos is the tourist centre of Olympia, on the northern edge of the plain of the river Alpheios (Alfiós).

Variants

For the return to Náfplion there are two alternative routes: either the road (an expressway for almost its whole length) via **Pýrgos** and **Patras** to **Corinth** and then via Argos (a detour of 50km/31 miles) or the road which runs south-east from Pýrgos along the coast of the Ionian Sea (the Cyparissian Gulf) to **Kaiáfas** and Kaló Neró. From there a road leads inland, through mountainous country for part of the way, to **Megalopolis**, from there to **Trípoli** and then back to **Náfplion**.

Detours

At Mýli (ruins of a medieval castle on Mt Pontinos) is the abundant spring of Amymone, at which Herakles killed the Lernaean hydra with the help of the burning brands provided by Iolaos. To the south-east are the excavations of the prehistoric settlement of Lerna.
Just north of Trípoli a side road on the right leads to the remains of ancient **Mantineia** (Mandínia), the scene of an indecisive battle between Thebes and Sparta in 362 B.C. in which the Theban leader Epameinondas was killed.

The return journey can be by way of the expressway from Patras. From Olympia the route runs north via Pýrgos, cutting across the **Kyllíni** peninsula. From Gastoúni it is a short distance to the seaside resort of Loutrá Kyllínis (good sandy beach), at the western tip of the Peloponnese, off which is the Ionian island of **Zákynthos**. A short distance away is the village of Kástro, with the mighty medieval Frankish stronghold of Khlemoutsí.

8C: To Laconia and Back (480km/300 miles)

Main route

From **Náfplion** the route follows Route 8B as far as **Trípoli**. It then continues south through a fertile valley basin, passing (on right) the Taka marsh, a lake which is now almost completely silted up, and then, after a hilly stretch (with views of the **Taýgetos** range to the right), descends into the intensively cultivated Sparta basin, crosses the river Evrótas and comes to the ancient and famous city of **Sparta** (Spárti), which preserves little trace of its former glory.
From Sparta the route continues south, at first over a plain planted with olive-trees and then through an upland region between the Evrótas on the left and the majestic Taýgetos range on the right. After passing through Khánia it reaches the little town of **Gýthion** on the Laconian Gulf, once the naval harbour of Sparta and now a port shipping the produce of Laconia.
The road then runs down the **Máni** peninsula to Areópoli, and from there turns north-west along the shores of the Messenian Gulf, passing through Áyios Nikólaos and the picturesque village of Kardamýli, to the Messenian port of **Kalamáta**, which has been repeatedly shaken by severe earthquakes.
From Kalamáta the route turns inland, goes over a ridge in the **Taýgetos** range on a beautiful road with a succession of sharp bends and then leads down through the impressive Langáda gorge to **Sparta**. The return to Náfplion via Trípoli is on the same road as on the outward journey.

Detours

A few kilometres south of Trípoli a side road branches off to the site of ancient **Tegea**, of which little is left but the remains of a marble temple of Athena Alea.
Shortly before Sparta a road runs south-east through the **Parnon** range to **Geráki** (40km/25 miles), with a Frankish Crusader castle.
A few kilometres west of Sparta (signposted) are the ruins of the Byzantine town of **Mistra**, straggling up the slopes of a hill crowned by a castle.
From Khánia a road runs 70km/43 miles south-east to **Monemvasía**, a little medieval walled town at the foot of a mighty crag projecting into the sea near the south-eastern tip of the Peloponnese.
Another fascinating trip (from Gýthion by way of Areópoli) is into the **Máni** peninsula, with the characteristic defensive towers erected by the leading families of the area. A circuit of the peninsula from Areópoli is about 60km/37 miles. An additional attraction is provided by the stalactitic caves of Dýros.

8D: To Messenia and Back (450km/280 miles)

Main route

From **Náfplion** the route follows Routes 8B and 8C to **Trípoli**. From there it runs south-west, along the edge of the Arcadian plain, then on a hilly stretch of road to **Megalopolis**, past large mining installations with a coal-fired power station, over the Xerillas, a source stream of the Alpheios (Alfiós), and finally over a range of hills into the intensively cultivated Messenian plain, watered by the river Pamisos.
Beyond the **Kalamáta** airfield, at Asprókhoma, a road goes off on the right, crosses the river Pamisos, passes the little town of Messíni and follows the Messenian Gulf at some distance from the coast. It then cuts across the south-western tip of the Peloponnese to **Pylos**, in the beautiful Bay of Pylos, which is sheltered from the Ionian Sea by the island of **Sfaktiría**. The bay is better known as Navarino Bay, the scene of a naval defeat inflicted on the Turkish fleet in 1827.
From Pylos the route turns north, at first keeping close to the coast, with a fine view of Navarino Bay, and then bearing inland to the well

kept excavations of the Mycenaean "Palace of Nestor". There is a museum in the nearby village of Khóra.

Thereafter the route broadly follows the coast, and then pursues a winding course, out of sight of the sea, through a hilly region with olive-groves, vineyards and arable fields (early vegetables grown under cover). At Gargaliáni there is a beautiful view of the coastal lowlands. The road then continues through garden-like country by way of Filiatrá to the Triphylian town of **Kyparissía**.

Soon afterwards, at Kaló Neró, the route leaves the coast and turns inland, accompanied by the railway (Peloponnesian Railway). A pleasant mountain road runs via Dório to join the road from Kalamáta. The return to Náfplion is on the same route as on the outward journey, passing through Megalopolis and Trípoli.

Detours

From Megalopolis there is a rewarding trip by way of **Karítaina** and Andrítsaina to the well preserved temple of Apollo Epikourios at **Bassai** (Vassés; 60km/37 miles), in a lonely and beautiful mountain setting.

From Tsoukalaíika, on the road (No. 7) crossing the Messenian plain to Kalamáta, a secondary road (signposted to Ithomi) runs south-west via Lámbaina to Mavrommáti (20km/12½ miles), a village below the south side of triple-peaked Mt Ithomi, on the site of ancient **Messene**. An attractive road follows the west coast of the Messenian Gulf to the little port of **Koróni** (30km/19 miles from the turn-off on the Kalamáta–Pylos road), below a mighty medieval stronghold.

From Pylos a visit should be paid to the port of **Methóni** (12km/7½ miles south), with the massive ruins of the largest Venetian castle in Greece. Offshore is the island of Sapientza.

The Acropolis of Athens ▶

Ancient harbour

Below the temple to the south was the ancient commercial harbour (now silted up); when the sea is calm the old quays can be seen under the water. The modern harbour, on the site of the ancient naval harbour, is still protected by the ancient breakwaters. On the long northern breakwater is the early 19th century chapel of Áyios Nikólaos.

Tomb of Phokos

1.5km/1 mile north of the town is an artificial mound (6th c. B.C.) similar to the one at Marathon (see entry), traditionally believed to be the tomb of Phokos, half-brother of Pelesus and Telamon, who killed him.

From here the road to the temple of Aphaia (13km/8 miles east of Aíyina) runs through hilly country, partly wooded and partly under cultivation, passing the church of the Áyii Theodóri (frescoes), built in 1289 with stone from ancient temples.

Palaiokhóra

In 8km/5 miles the road comes to Palaiokhóra, chief town of the island until its abandonment around 1800, with the monastery of Áyios Nektários, named after Archbishop Nektarios (d. 1920, canonised 1961), whose tomb attracts many pilgrims. Above the monastery are the ruins of a medieval castle. In the ruins of Palaiokhóra, scattered about on a hill, are more than twenty whitewashed churches of the 13th and 14th centuries, some of them with frescoes.

Mesagró

Farther on are the scattered houses of Mesagró. Soon after this a steep path leads up to the temple.

★★Temple of Aphaia

The Temple of Aphaia (5th c. B.C.), dedicated to a daughter of Zeus, a divinity associated with Artemis who was revered as a protectress of women (dedicatory inscription; terracottas), is built on the foundations of an earlier 6th century temple, on the site of a pre-Greek shrine. It is a peripteral temple of 6×12 columns, with a pronaos and opisthodomos in antis. The roof of the naos was supported on two rows of columns. In the opisthodomos is a stone altar-table. There survive 23 columns of yellowish limestone, mainly at the east end and the adjoining sides, still preserving remains of the original stucco facing; most of the columns are monolithic. The roof and sculptural decoration were in Pentelic marble. Unusual features are irregularities in the floor of the naos and the subdivision of the opisthodomos. In the floor can be seen holes left by the railing behind which votive offerings were kept.

The sculpture from the pediments is now in the Glyptothek in Munich, and there are some other remains of sculpture in the National Archaeological Museum, Athens, and the Aíyina Museum.

Outside the east end of the temple and connected with it by a ramp are the foundations of an altar, and to the south of this is the Propylon, with octagonal pilasters, by which the temple was approached. The temple stood on a terrace built up to a level surface and retained partly by the natural rock and partly by masonry walls. Systematic excavations in recent years have brought to light fragments of the earlier temple of around 580 B.C., enabling the façade to be partly reconstructed. This reconstruction, with other material from the site, is in the excavators' store (at present closed) to the west of the temple.

In the surrounding area are the remains of dwellings of the Neolithic period (4th–3rd millennium B.C.).

From the temple precinct there are magnificent views over the Saronic Gulf to the mainland, from Athens to Cape Soúnion.

Greece from A to Z

Greek names

There is no generally accepted system for the transliteration of modern Greek place-names and personal names into the Latin alphabet, and visitors to Greece will find much diversity and inconsistency of spelling, for example on signposts and in guidebooks and other literature in English. The situation is still further complicated by changes in pronunciation which have taken place since ancient times, so that many familiar old classical names look very different in modern Greek: thus the ancient Hymettus or Hymettos may appear as Imittós.

In this guide modern Greek place-names and personal names are transliterated in a form approximating to their pronunciation. Classical names are given in their "Greek" rather than their "Latin" forms (e.g. Polykleitos rather than Polyclitus), except where there is an accepted English form (Athens, Piraeus) or where the name is so familiar in its Latin form that it would be pedantic to insist on the Greek spelling (e.g. Thucydides rather than Thoukydides).

In the headings of entries in this section of the guide the place-names are given in the most readily understandable form. Below this are the name in its modern Greek form and a transcription in the Latin alphabet as an aid to pronunciation.

Alternative forms of place-names are given in the text where necessary.

Aegina H 6

Αίγινα
Aíyina

Nomos: Attica
Area of island: 83 sq.km/32 sq. miles
Altitude: 0–532m/0–1745ft
Population: 12,000
Chief town: Aíyina

Boat services

Boat and hydrofoil services several times daily between Athens (Piraeus) and the ports of Aíyina, Souvála and Ayía Marína, and between Méthana and Aíyina.
Local boat services to Ankístri.

Situation and characteristics

Aegina, lying in the Saronic Gulf some 19km/12 miles south-west of Piraeus, is a hilly but fertile island of marly limestones and schists, with a few rounded hills of volcanic origin. The coasts are mostly fringed by cliffs, with only a few sheltered coves. The inhabitants live by agriculture, producing and exporting excellent pistachio nuts. Other contributions are made to the island's economy by fishing, sponge-diving and the manufacture of pottery. The locally made *kannatia* (water-coolers) are wide-necked, two-handled jars of porous fabric which keep the water cool by evaporation.
With its mild climate and low rainfall, Aegina has long been a favourite summer resort for prosperous Athenians, and in recent years it has become increasingly popular with foreign holidaymakers.

Myth and history

According to the ancient legend the progenitor of the Aeginetans was Aiakos, son of Zeus and Aigina and father of Peleus and Telamon, a wise and just ruler who became one of the judges of the Underworld along with Minos and Rhadamanthys.
The oldest traces of Pelasgian settlement date back to the 3rd millennium B.C. In the 2nd millennium the island carried on a considerable trade in pottery and ointments, evidence of which has been found in the areas of Helladic, Cycladic and Minoan culture.
Aegina first appears in history as a colony of the Dorian city of Epidauros, ruled in the 7th century B.C. by Phaidon of Argos. After breaking away from Epidauros in the 6th century it enjoyed a period of considerable prosperity, which brought it into competition with Corinth. The Aeginetans had trading posts in Umbria, on the Black Sea and in Egypt, and their shipowners became the wealthiest in the Greek world. The coins of Aegina, bearing the island's emblem of a turtle, were the earliest in Europe, and were already circulating widely by 656 B.C.; and Aeginetan weights and measures were used throughout the Greek world until Roman times.
At the beginning of the Persian wars Aegina was at the peak of its power. After the battle of Salamis, to which the island sent thirty ships, an Aeginetan vessel was awarded the prize for the greatest display of valour. Against this was the fact that Aegina, with commercial interests in mind, offered earth and water to Darius's envoys in token of submission. As a result, after being called to account on a complaint by Sparta, it came into conflict with Athens, which saw the powerful island as an obstacle to the expansion of its naval power.
After two Athenian naval victories in quick succession, at Kekryphaleia (Ankístri) and off Aegina, the island city was forced, after a nine-month-long siege, to surrender, and in 456 B.C. it was compelled to pull down its walls, hand over its warships and pay tribute to Athens. Finally at the beginning of the Peloponnesian War, in 431, the Aeginetans were driven off their island and their land was distributed to Attic settlers. After the overthrow of Athens in 404 B.C. many of them were able to return, but the island's prosperity was gone for good. A series of military campaigns brought it again under the control of Athens, whose destinies it henceforth shared.
Aegina was the capital of Greece from January 12th to October 3rd 1828.

Aegina Town (Aíyina)

The island's capital, Aíyina (pop. 5000), lies on the gentle slopes above a wide bay at the north end of the west coast, roughly on the site of the larger ancient city. From the harbour, protected by a breakwater, there are fine views of the little islands of Metópi and Ankístri to the south-west and Moní to the south and of the hills round Epidauros. The Archaeological Museum contains material recovered from the temples of Aphaia and Aphrodite and much else besides, ranging in date from the 3rd millennium B.C. to Roman times.

Kolóna

On the hill of Kolóna, to the north of the town, is an 8m/26ft high Doric column, all that is left of a temple by the harbour (460 B.C.), according to Pausanias a temple of Aphrodite but now known to have been dedicated to Apollo. Under the temple were found remains of Mycenaean and pre-Mycenaean settlement (3rd millennium B.C.); to the west were two smaller temples, probably dedicated to Artemis and Dionysos. The "Aeginetan sphinx" (*c.* 480 B.C.) discovered here in 1904 is now in the Archaeological Museum.

Ancient harbour

Below the temple to the south was the ancient commercial harbour (now silted up); when the sea is calm the old quays can be seen under the water. The modern harbour, on the site of the ancient naval harbour, is still protected by the ancient breakwaters. On the long northern breakwater is the early 19th century chapel of Áyios Nikólaos.

Tomb of Phokos

1.5km/1 mile north of the town is an artificial mound (6th c. B.C.) similar to the one at Marathon (see entry), traditionally believed to be the tomb of Phokos, half-brother of Pelesus and Telamon, who killed him.

From here the road to the temple of Aphaia (13km/8 miles east of Aíyina) runs through hilly country, partly wooded and partly under cultivation, passing the church of the Áyii Theodóri (frescoes), built in 1289 with stone from ancient temples.

Palaiokhóra

In 8km/5 miles the road comes to Palaiokhóra, chief town of the island until its abandonment around 1800, with the monastery of Áyios Nektários, named after Archbishop Nektarios (d. 1920, canonised 1961), whose tomb attracts many pilgrims. Above the monastery are the ruins of a medieval castle. In the ruins of Palaiokhóra, scattered about on a hill, are more than twenty whitewashed churches of the 13th and 14th centuries, some of them with frescoes.

Mesagró

Farther on are the scattered houses of Mesagró. Soon after this a steep path leads up to the temple.

★★Temple of Aphaia

The Temple of Aphaia (5th c. B.C.), dedicated to a daughter of Zeus, a divinity associated with Artemis who was revered as a protectress of women (dedicatory inscription; terracottas), is built on the foundations of an earlier 6th century temple, on the site of a pre-Greek shrine. It is a peripteral temple of 6×12 columns, with a pronaos and opisthodomos in antis. The roof of the naos was supported on two rows of columns. In the opisthodomos is a stone altar-table. There survive 23 columns of yellowish limestone, mainly at the east end and the adjoining sides, still preserving remains of the original stucco facing; most of the columns are monolithic. The roof and sculptural decoration were in Pentelic marble. Unusual features are irregularities in the floor of the naos and the subdivision of the opisthodomos. In the floor can be seen holes left by the railing behind which votive offerings were kept.

The sculpture from the pediments is now in the Glyptothek in Munich, and there are some other remains of sculpture in the National Archaeological Museum, Athens, and the Aíyina Museum.

Outside the east end of the temple and connected with it by a ramp are the foundations of an altar, and to the south of this is the Propylon, with octagonal pilasters, by which the temple was approached. The temple stood on a terrace built up to a level surface and retained partly by the natural rock and partly by masonry walls. Systematic excavations in recent years have brought to light fragments of the earlier temple of around 580 B.C., enabling the façade to be partly reconstructed. This reconstruction, with other material from the site, is in the excavators' store (at present closed) to the west of the temple.

In the surrounding area are the remains of dwellings of the Neolithic period (4th–3rd millennium B.C.).

From the temple precinct there are magnificent views over the Saronic Gulf to the mainland, from Athens to Cape Soúnion.

1 Outer terrace
2 Stoa
3 Priests' lodgings (5th c.)
4 Propylon (5th c.)
5 Priests' lodgings (7th c.)
6 Altar (5th c.)
7 Altar (6th c.)
8 Altar (7th c.)
9 Propylon (6th c.)
10 Peribolos (7th c.)

Temple of Aphaia on the island of

Aegina

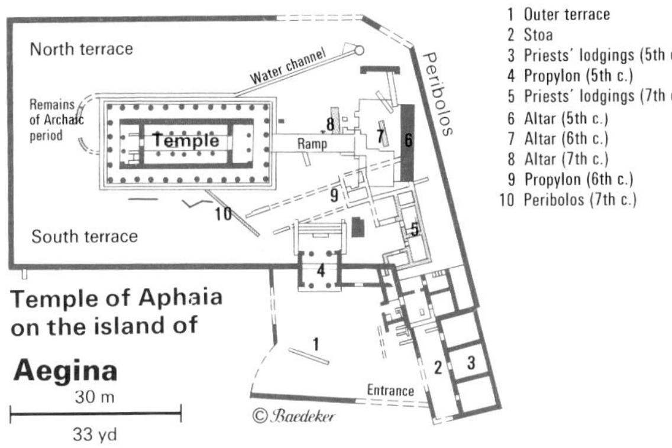

Ayía Marína

Below the temple of Aphaia (3km/2 miles south), in a wide bay on the east coast of Aegina, is the busy modern seaside resort of Ayía Marína.

★Oros

Oros (532m/1745ft), the "Mountain", also known as Profítis Ilías after a chapel on top of the hill, is the most prominent landmark in the Saronic Gulf. It can be climbed on a steep and difficult path from the village of Marathón (6km/4 miles south of Aíyina). ★ View

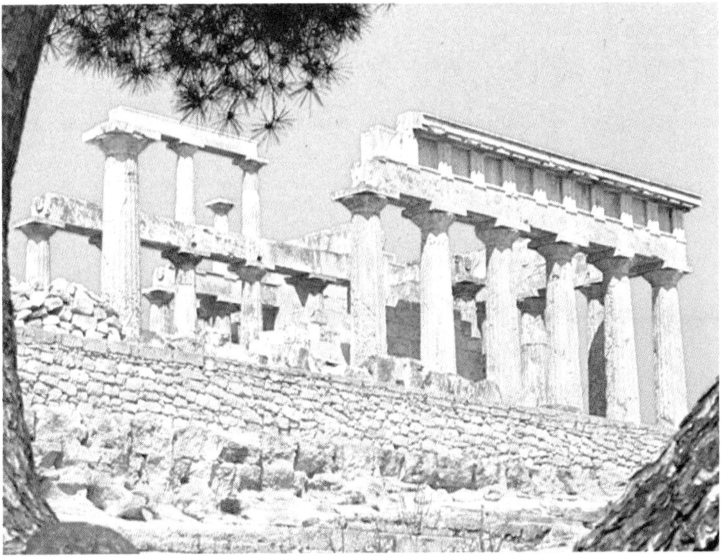

Temple of Aphaia

In Mycenaean times (13th c. B.C.) there was an extensive settlement, surrounded by cyclopean walls, on the terraces round the summit. From here there are tremendous views extending over almost the whole island and over the Saronic Gulf to Salamis, the Methourides (Troupika and Revitousa), the Diaporia, Ankístri, the Méthana peninsula and the islands of Poros and Hydra.

Below the north side of the summit, near the chapel of the Taxiarkhes, was the 5th century temple of Zeus Panhellenios.

Ankístri

Some 5km/3 miles south-west of Aegina lies the wooded island of Ankístri (area 12 sq.km/4½ sq. miles; alt. 0–216m/0–709ft), whose 700 inhabitants are the descendants of Albanians who settled on the island in the 16th century.

Agathonísi L/M 6

Αγαθονήσι
Agathonísi

Nomos: Dodecanese
Area of island: 13 sq.km/5 sq. miles
Altitude: 0–212m/0–696ft
Population: 180
Chief place: Megálo Khorió

Boat services

Local connections with Sámos, Pátmos, Lipsí and Arkí.

Situation and characteristics

Agathonísi (formerly called Gaidouronísi), the most northerly island in the Dodecanese, lies off the coast of Asia Minor, half way between Sámos and Léros. It was ancient Tragia, where in 76 B.C. the young Julius Caesar was captured by pirates. The whole coastline of this karstic island, 7km/4½ miles long by up to 3km/2 miles across, is ringed by sheer cliffs, with little in the way of sheltered anchorages. Off the north, east and south sides of the island are seven uninhabited islets, some land on which is farmed from Agathonísi. The inhabitants live modestly by farming and fishing. With no sandy beaches and no ancient monuments, Agathonísi has remained completely untouched by tourism – an example, now difficult to find, of a totally unspoiled Aegean island.

Agrínion F 5

Αγρίνιον
Agrínion

Nomos: Aetolia
Altitude: 90m/295ft
Population: 34,300

Transport

Bus connections with Athens.

Situation and characteristics

Agrínion, situated just north-west of Lake Trikhonis, is chief town of the nomos of Aetolia and centre of the local tobacco trade.

Thérmos

★ Temple of Apollo

27km/17 miles east of Agrínion, on the northern shore of Lake Trikhonis, is the temple of Apollo at Thérmos. Here, near an earlier Helladic megaron, a first temple of Apollo was built in the 10th–9th century B.C. Its successor, of which some remains survive, was built about 625 B.C.

Aíyion G 5

Αίγιον
Aíyion

Nomos: Achaea
Altitude: 15m/50ft
Population: 21,000

Transport

Railway station on the Corinth–Patras line.
Bus connections with Corinth and Patras.

The town of Aíyion lies on the south side of the Gulf of Corinth, 35km/22 miles east of Patras (see entry). It is situated on a rocky plateau above the beach, at the foot of which are springs which were already known in ancient times.

Ancient Aigion was a member of the Achaean League. In the Middle Ages, under the name of Vostitsa, it was for a time the seat of a Crusader baron.

Archaeological Museum

An archaeological museum was opened in Aíyion in August 1994. It has exhibits documenting human settlement on the Peloponnese from the Stone Age to the Roman era.

Diakoftó

Diakoftó, 15km/9 miles east of Aíyion, is a railway station on the Patras–Corinth line, from which a rack railway goes up to Kalávryta (see entry). From the upper station at Megaspilaion it is a 45 minutes' walk to the cave monastery of Megaspilaion, founded in the 5th century.

Alexandroúpolis K 3

Αλεξανδρούπολι
Alexandroúpoli

Nomos: Evros
Altitude: 10m/35ft
Population: 34,500

Transport

Air connection with Athens.
Railway station on Salonica–Istanbul railway line.
Boat connection with Samothrace.

Situation and characteristics

Alexandroúpolis (Alexandrople) is the most easterly town on the coast of Thrace, near the frontier with Turkey on the river Evros. It was founded by the Turks under the name of Dedeağaç ("grandfather's tree"), and became Greek in 1912. Now a centre of the local tobacco trade, the town has no features of particular interest.

Surroundings of Alexandroúpolis

Alexandroúpolis is a good base from which to visit the island of Samothrace (see entry). The ferry takes between 5 and 7 hours.

It is also a convenient centre from which to explore Thrace (see entry), which has a Turkish and Muslim minority. Two towns of particular interest are Komotiní and Xánthi (see entries).

Alónnisos H 4

Αλόννησος
Alónnisos

Nomos: Magnesia
Area of island: 72 sq.km/28 sq. miles
Altitude: 0–476m/0–1562ft
Population: 1550
Chief place: Patitíri

Boat services

Regular services (boats and hydrofoils) several times weekly from Vólos, Áyios Konstantínos and Kými (Euboea) via Skíathos and Skópelos.

Situation and characteristics

The long rocky island of Alónnisos (formerly Khiliondrómia; in antiquity Ikos), one of the more secluded places in Greece, lies in the middle of the chain of the Northern Sporades, which runs west from Skíathos. Along the whole length of the island extends a ridge of hills which reaches its highest point in Mt Kouvoúli (476m/1562ft). The north-west coast is fringed by cliffs; on the gentler south-east coast there are a number of sheltered bays. Here there are traces of settlement going back to Neolithic times.

Sights

Patitíri
Alónnisos (Khorió)

The population, mainly farmers and fishermen, almost all live in the fertile southern part of the island. In this area are the port, Patitíri, and, 1km/¾ mile north-west of this, commandingly situated above the sea, the island's old capital Alónnisos (Khorió), which was largely abandoned after an earthquake in 1965 but is now being developed as a tourist centre (magnificent views).

Vótsi

1km/¾ mile east of Patitíri is the modest fishing village of Vótsi, with houses for holiday visitors.

Ikos

The ancient settlement of Ikos is believed to have been at Kokkinókastro on the south-east coast, where remains of a town wall and tombs have been brought to light.

Peristéra

Off the south-east coast of Alónnisos, separated from it by a sheltered sound, lies the barren island of Peristéra (area 14 sq.km/5½ sq. miles; alt. 0–250m/0–820ft), also known as Xeró.

Skántzoura

This island (area 7 sq.km/2¾ sq. miles; alt. 0–107m/0–351ft), which belongs to the monastic republic of Athos (see entry) and is used for

View from Khorió

the grazing of goats, lies some 20km/12½ miles south-east of Alónnisos. It is occasionally visited for the sake of its sea-caves and its underwater fishing.

Pélagos

Some 13km/8 miles north-east of the northern tip of Alónnisos is the wooded island of Pélagos (area 25 sq.km/9½ sq. miles; alt. 0–302m/0–991ft), known in antiquity as Euthyra. It is also called Kyrá Panayía after the monastery of that name on its east coast. The monastery, which is under the jurisdiction of Athos, has an 11th century church with old icons.

Ghioúra

The next island to the north-east in the chain of the Northern Sporades is Ghioúra (area 9 sq.km/3½ sq. miles; alt. 0–570m/0–1870ft), with a ruined monastery; it is now a reserve for wild goats (bezoar goats). On the south coast are the Caves of Cyclops, which according to legend were the home of Polyphemos.

Piperi

Farther east is the little island of Pipéri (area 7 sq.km/2¾ sq. miles; alt. 0–354m/0–1161ft), a seal reserve.

Psathoúra

The volcanic island of Psathoúra (area 6 sq.km/2¼ sq. miles; alt. 0–20m/0–65ft) lies at the north-eastern tip of the chain of the Northern

Sporades. There are remains of buildings belonging to an ancient city under the sea just off the coast of the island.

Amfissa G 5

Άμφισσα
Ámfissa

Nomos: Phocis
Altitude: 180m/590ft
Population: 7000

Situation and characteristics

Ámfissa (Amphissa), now a country town in Phocis, 14km/8½ miles north-west of Itéa on the road from Itéa to Lamía, lies on a hill surrounded by olive-groves. In antiquity it was the chief town of the Locrians.

The medieval castle, dating from the time when the town was held by Frankish knights and was known as Salona, is built on the polygonal walls of the ancient acropolis.

Amorgós K/L 7

Αμοργός
Amorgós

Nomos: Cyclades
Area of island: 130 sq.km/50 sq. miles
Altitude: 0–826m/0–2710ft
Population: 1650
Chief place: Amorgós (Khóra)

Boat services

Weekly connections with Piraeus, several times weekly with Náxos, Íos and Santorin.

Situation and characteristics

Amorgós is a bare, rocky, mountainous island 33km/22 miles long by 2–6.5km/1¼–4 miles across. The south-east coast mostly falls steeply down to the sea; the north-west coast is gentler, with two deep bays, the sheltered Katápola Bay to the south-west, with the island's principal harbour, and Aiyiáli Bay to the north-west. The islanders – declining in numbers as a result of emigration – live by farming and fishing.

History

The remains of several ancient towns, extensive cemeteries, finds of coins and rock inscriptions show that in Minoan and Hellenistic times Amorgós was an important port of call on the sea route between Melos and the south-eastern Aegean. In Roman times a place of exile and in later centuries much harried by pirates, the island has never been a place of any economic or political importance, and as a result has remained largely unspoiled. In recent years, however, this very beautiful island has increasingly suffered from the visitations of large numbers of backpackers.

Sights

Amorgós

The chief place on the island, Amorgós (Khóra), lies on a hill, its typical white Cycladic houses, its many barrel-vaulted family churches and windmills huddling round a ruined 13th century Venetian castle on the hilltop. A number of ancient reliefs can be seen built into house walls.

★ Monastery of Panayía Khozoviótissa

From the town it is a 30 minutes' walk (or donkey ride) to the little Byzantine monastery of Panayía Khozoviótissa (founded 1088), built into a recess in a sheer rock face 367m/1204ft above sea level. From the lower terrace there are fine views of the sea.

Katápola
Minoa

4km/2½ miles west of the Khóra is the port of Katápola. At the south end of the bay, on the hill of Mountiliá, are the remains of the ancient town of Minoa, believed to have been founded by Cretans in the 2nd millennium B.C.

Kastrí

On the southern tip of the island, at Kastrí, near the pretty village of Arkesíni, are the remains of a town which was inhabited from Mycenaean to Roman times.

Kríkelos

Near the north end of the island, in Aiyiáli Bay, are remains of a settlement founded by Milesians. From here Mt Kríkelo (826m/2710ft), the island's highest peak, can be climbed.

Levíta group

The Levíta group, north-east of Amorgós, consists of two main islands, Levíta (area 5 sq.km/2 sq. miles; alt. 0–167m/0–548ft) and Kínaros (area 9 sq.km/3½ sq. miles; alt. 0–329m/0–1050ft), and a number of small islets, mostly uninhabited. Here it is still possible to find beautiful lonely beaches, since none of these islands has any regular boat services or accommodation for visitors.

Panayía Khozoviótissa monastery

Amphiareion

H 5

Αμφιαρείο
Amfiarío

Nomos: Attica

Situation

The Amphiareion is an ancient sanctuary, the shrine of an oracle, beautifully situated in a quiet wooded valley in northern Attica, south-east of Oropós.The site is reached from Athens by taking the express-way, leaving it at the Kapandríti exit (30km/19 miles) and continuing via Kapandríti and Kálamos in the direction of Oropós. The entrance to the site is on the right after a right-hand bend, 4km/2½ miles beyond Kálamos and 49km/30 miles from Athens.

Myth and history

Amphiaraos was a mythical king of Argos who had the gift of clairvoyance. On his way to Boeotia during the expedition of the Seven against Thebes he was victorious in a contest at Nemea (see entry) during the funeral ceremony of the young prince Opheltes. During the battle for Thebes he was snatched away by Zeus and disappeared into a cleft in the earth, but later re-emerged on the borders of Attica and Boeotia and was revered in a sanctuary at a sacred spring as a seer and a hero who brought salvation and healing. The cult and the sanctuary have much in common with the Asklepieion at Epidauros (see entry). The site was excavated by Leonardos and Petrakos.

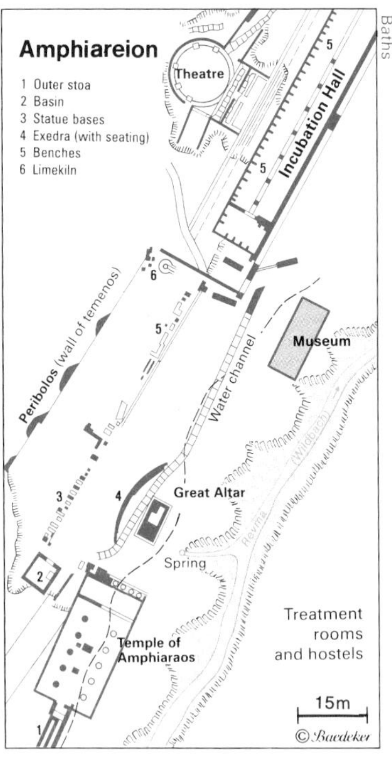

The ★Site

Temple

A path runs downhill from the entrance. Immediately on the right is the temple of Amphiaraos (4th or 3rd c. B.C.). The front of the temple has six Doric columns between antae, which were in the form of half-columns. The interior is divided into three aisles by two rows of five columns. A porch built on to the rear of the temple had a second door leading to the priests' lodgings. Against the rear wall of the naos can be seen the base for the cult image; in the centre is an offerings table.
In front of the temple, beside the sacred spring, is the

Great Altar, which according to Pausanias was dedicated to Amphiaraos and numerous other divinities. Below the altar is a well, in which large numbers of coins – votive offerings from people who had been cured – were found.

Incubation hall

Beyond this, on the left, are statue bases of the Roman period. Farther along is the 110m/360ft long incubation hall (4th c. A.D.), in which worshippers seeking a cure slept, wrapped in the skin of a ram which they had sacrificed at the altar. The hall is divided into two aisles by a row of 17 Ionic columns and has 41 Doric columns along the exterior. Against the rear wall are stone benches. The two corner rooms were probably meant for women.

Theatre

Beyond the incubation hall is the theatre, with five marble seats of honour round the orchestra (dancing floor) and a well preserved stage building. The auditorium now has pines growing in it. In this theatre musical contests were held every five years from 332 B.C. onwards.

Farther down the stream are the remains of Roman baths. On the far side of the stream are a clepsydra (water-clock) and remains of houses and other installations.
There is a small museum displaying interesting local finds.

Surroundings of the Amphiareion

Oropós

On the coast 6km/4 miles north-west lies the pretty little fishing port of Oropós or Skála Oropoú, with some attractive tavernas on the seafront.

Amphipolis H 3

Αμφίπολη
Amfípoli

Region: Macedonia
Nomos: Serrai

Situation

This ancient Macedonian city, 60km/37 miles west of Kavála (see entry) near the mouth of the river Strymon, was a major Greek stronghold and in Roman times an important staging-point on the Via Egnatia, the great highway running from the Adriatic to Constantinople.

The Site

★ Lion Statue

The site extends out into the sea. Greek excavations have revealed sections of the town walls, and in 1972 brought to light a building which has been identified as a gymnasium. The most striking monument is a majestic stone lion of the Hellenistic period which stands outside the ancient city, immediately west of the bridge over the Strymon.

Anafi K 7

Ανάφη
Anáfi

Nomos: Cyclades
Area of island: 36 sq.km/14 sq. miles
Altitude: 0–584m/0–1916ft
Population: 300
Chief place: Anáfi (Khóra)

Boat services

Regular services several times weekly from Athens (Piraeus). Passengers are landed in small boats.

Situation

This hilly island in the Cyclades lies 22km/14 miles east of Santorin.

According to the ancient legend Apollo caused the island to emerge from the sea to provide a place of refuge for the Argonauts returning from Colchis.
The islanders draw a very modest livelihood from agriculture and a little fishing.

Sights

Anáfi (Khóra)

The chief place, Anáfi (Khóra), lies in the south of the island; it is gradually losing its population. Above the village, on a spur of rock, can be seen the ruined walls of a 14th century Venetian castle.

North-east of the Khóra, on a rocky hill, is the site of ancient Anaphe, littered with the remains of walls and fragments of sculpture.

Zoodókhos Piyí

In the east of the island is the monastery of the Zoodókhos Piyí (Lifegiving Spring) or Káto Kalamiótissa, built on the site of a temple of Apollo and incorporating fragments of ancient masonry. Farther north are the ruins of another Venetian castle.

Bell-cote, Anáfi

Panayía Kalamiótissa

At the eastern tip of the island, prominently situated on Mt Kálamos (396m/1299ft), a limestone crag falling steeply down to the sea, is the little church of the Panayía Kalamiótissa (1715). From the top of the hill there are extensive views, extending in clear weather as far as Crete.

Lying south-east of Anáfi are the three rocky islets of Ftená, Pakhiá and Makrá.

Ándros I/K 5/6

Άνδρος
Ándros

Nomos: Cyclades
Area of island: 374 sq.km/144 sq. miles
Altitude: 0–994m/0–3261ft
Population: 10,500
Chief town: Ándros (Khóra)

Boat services

Daily connection with Rafína (Attica).

Situation and characteristics

The wooded island of Ándros, the most northerly and, after Náxos, the largest of the Cyclades, is separated from Euboea (see entry) – its south-easterly continuation – by the Pórthmos Kafiréfs (Italian Canale d'Oro), a busy but stormy strait 12km/7½ miles wide. To the south-east it is separated from the neighbouring island of Tínos by a channel 1200m/1300yds wide. In the island's four ranges of hills, the highest of which, Mt Pétalon, reaches 994m/3261ft, are marble quarries which were already being worked in ancient times. Thanks to its abundance of water Ándros has a flourishing agriculture. Several important Greek shipowners have homes on the island.

Myth and history

In antiquity Ándros was dedicated to Dionysos, and its celebrations of his cult were widely famed.
Originally colonised by Ionians, the island soon came under the control of Eretria. In the 7th century B.C. Ándros itself sent settlers to Chalcidice in Thrace. After the battle of Salamis Themistokles made war on Ándros, which had supported the Persians, but it did not become a dependency of Athens until some time later. In 338 B.C. it fell into the hands of Macedon and after the defeat of Macedon passed into Roman control.
From A.D. 1207 Ándros was ruled by Venetian dynasts, and the island has many watch-towers dating from the period of Venetian rule. In the early 15th century many Albanians settled in the north of the islands, and their descendants preserved their own language until the 20th century. Ándros was occupied by the Turks in 1566, and remained under Turkish rule until its incorporation in the new kingdom of Greece in the 19th century.

Sights

Ándros (Khóra)

The island's chief town, Ándros or Khóra (pop. 2000), lies in the poorly sheltered central bay on the east coast. From the harbour a picturesque flight of steps leads up to the old town, situated on a rocky promontory with a ruined medieval castle. The newer part of the town, with its market square and its busy wide main street, extends farther inland.

★ Zoodókhos Piyí

The principal features of interest in Ándros are the Orthodox church of the Zoodókhos Piyí (Lifegiving Spring), with an iconostasis of 1717, the Roman Catholic church of St Andrew (15th c., rebuilt in 18th c.), the little museum of seafaring and the Museum of Modern Art, opened in the early 1980s. This museum is the only one of its kind in Greece and has an international reputation. (Open: Wed.–Mon. 10am–2pm, 6–9pm.)

★★ Museum of Modern Art

Some 5km/3 miles north-west of the Khóra is the spring of Apíkia, which produces the well known Sáriza mineral water.

Mesariá

5km/3 miles west of the Khóra, in the fertile Mesariá valley with its characteristic dovecots, lies the pretty village of Mesariá, with a church dating from 1158.

Kórthion

10km/6 miles south of the Khóra is Kórthion, with a Venetian castle.

Ancient capital

The island's ancient capital, which flourished into Byzantine times, lay 16km/10 miles west of the present town in a wide bay on the west coast, near the tiny village of Palaiópolis. There are remains of the acropolis, the harbour, etc.

Gávrion

The bay of Gávrion on the west coast, with the fishing village of that name, the island's port, formed a sheltered harbour in late antiquity. Part of the medieval harbour can be seen at the Ayía Moní (monastery).
2km/1¼ miles north-west, higher up, at the village of Áyios Pétros, stands a Hellenistic watch-tower (magnificent views).

Batsí

8km/5 miles south-east of Gávrion is the seaside resort of Batsí, starting-point of the ascent of Mt Kouvára (975m/3199ft; 4–5 hrs).

Arcadia F/G 6

Αρκαδία
Arkadía

The upland region of Arcadia, in the centre of the Peloponnese, reaches its highest points in the north: Erymanthos (2224m/7297ft), Khelmós (2355m/7727ft) and Kyllíni (2376m/7796ft). The few areas of plain are concentrated round Trípoli and Megalópolis. The most important river is the Alfiós (Alpheios), with its tributaries: other parts of the region have no drainage to the sea, leading to the formation of bogs.

History

In the 2nd millennium B.C. this inaccessible region was occupied by the Arcadians, and their possession of the territory was not contested by the Dorians when they moved into the Peloponnese. Their ancestral shrine, dedicated to Zeus, was on Mt Lykaion. For long the people of Arcadia maintained their simple peasant way of life, and the earliest city states, such as Tegea and Mantineia (see entries) grew up on the fringes of the region. In the 5th century B.C., and again in 250 B.C. the Arcadians formed themselves into a league. According to Strabo the region was derelict and almost depopulated in the early Imperial period – by which time it had already become the setting for pastoral poetry.
During the Crusading period (13th c.) many Frankish barons built their castles on the hills of Arcadia, for example at Níkli (near Tegéa), Veligósti (Megalópolis), Karítaina (above the river Alfiós) and Ákova (on the river Ládon). During the Turkish period Tripolitsa (Trípoli: see entry) was founded as the seat of the Pasha of the Morea.

Only within recent years has Arcadia become less isolated as a result of an extensive programme of road-building, but away from the main roads it has preserved much of its original sequestered character. Although this seclusion may appeal to the tourist, however, it has led many of the younger generation of Arcadians to drift away from the land into the towns.

Argolic Islands H 6

Αργολικές Νησιά
Argolikés Nisiá

The name of Argolic Islands covers all the islands off the coasts of the Argolid and in the Argolic Gulf. They include Hydra (see entry), Dokós, Spétsai (see entry), the smaller islands of Tríkeri, Spetsopoúla, Psilí and Platía, and numerous isolated rocks. They form the most southerly and westerly group of the Saronic Islands (see entry).

Argolid G/H 6

Αργολίδα
Argolída

The Argolid, Homer's "horse-rearing Argolis", in the north-eastern Peloponnese, played a central part in the history of Greece. Already settled in Neolithic times, it was occupied by the Achaeans around 2000–1900 B.C., and in the Mycenaean period (1580–1100 B.C.) was the most densely populated part of Greece. Mycenae, Tiryns and Argos (see entries), as well as such lesser cities as Mideia and Prosymna, were centres of power, of economic activity and of a rich culture. The excavations of Heinrich Schliemann from 1874 onwards led to the rediscovery of this forgotten world.

Myth and history

Many of the Greek myths were associated with this region. Akrisios, king of Árgos in succession to Danaos and Lynkeus, drove out his twin brother Proitos, who fled to nearby Tiryns and had it fortified by Cyclopes from Asia Minor, and was succeeded by his son Megapenthes. Akrisios had a daughter called Danaë, who was visited by Zeus in the form of a shower of gold. Their son Perseus killed the Gorgon, freed Andromeda, accidentally killed his father while throwing the discus, handed over Árgos to his cousin Megapenthes in exchange for Tiryns, surrounded Mycenae and Mideia with walls and incorporated them in his dominions. Sthenelos, son of Perseus and Andromeda, married Nikippe, daughter of Pelops, and their son Eurystheus was the last of the Perseids. It was in his service that Herakles performed his famous labours.
Eyrystheus later drove out the sons of Herakles, whose descendants in the fourth generation returned in the time of Oxylos.
The intervening period was filled by the descendants of Pelops, the Pelopids or Atreids, among whom, at the time of the Trojan War, were Agamemnon, his wife Klytaimnestra and their children Orestes, Iphigeneia and Elektra. Orestes' son Tisamenos was the last Mycenaean king of Sparta, and his death was followed by the "return of the Heraclids" – i.e. the migration of the Dorians into the Peloponnese, the claim to descent from Herakles giving the newcomers an honourable ancestry.

If the mythic tradition is considered with the archaeological evidence and the historical course of events, the Perseid dynasty can be dated to about 1600 B.C. (shaft graves, Mycenae), the Pelopid dynasty to about 1400 B.C. (tholos tombs, Mycenae) and the Heraclids to the time of the Dorian migration (12th c. B.C.).
In the Dorian period Argos became the most powerful city in the region, and the Heraion of Argos gained increasing importance as its central shrine. There was also an important shrine dedicated to Zeus at Nemea in the north-western Argolid.
Under Venetian rule Náfplion (see entry), then called Napoli di Levante ("Naples of the East"), became a powerful stronghold, taking in the hills of Akronáfplia and Palamídi.

Sights

Nowadays the coastal resorts of Náfplion and Tolón (see entry), together with resorts farther east such as Ermióni and Pórto Khéli (see entry) and the offshore islands of Spétsai and Hýdra (see entries), are major centres of the tourist trade. The ancient sites still exert their fascination, however, on visitors interested in the past of this beautiful part of Greece.

Argos G 6

Άργος
Árgos

Nomos: Argolid
Altitude: 15m/50ft. Population: 20,700

Transport

Station on Corinth–Trípoli railway line; bus connections with Náfplion and Palaiá Epídavros.

Situation

Árgos, in the Argolid (see entry), is a country town situated in a fertile plain near the Gulf of Náfplion, at the foot of two hills – Lárisa (289m/948ft), crowned by a castle, and the low dome of Aspís (80m/260ft).

History

The site of Árgos was occupied in pre-Greek times, and during the Mycenaean period it became the seat of the Danaid dynasty. After the coming of the Dorians, in the 1st millennium B.C., it grew into a place of considerable importance, although during the 7th and 6th centuries it exhausted itself in strife with Sparta. In the 5th century the Árgos school of sculptors produced the great Polykleitos, who perfected the canon (the ideal human figure) of Doric sculpture. In 146 B.C. the city became Roman. In A.D. 267 and 305 it was plundered by the Goths. During the Middle Ages and the early modern period it was held at different times by the Venetians (1388–1463, 1686–1715) and the Turks (1463–1686, 1715–1826). National assemblies were held in the ancient theatre in 1821 and 1829.

Sights

St Peter's church
★ Archaeological Museum

In the town's central square, the Platía, are St Peter's church and the Archaeological Museum, the most notable exhibits in which, in addition to the pottery and mosaics, are the finds from Lerna.
On the road to Trípoli are the excavated remains of the Agora, and opposite, on the lower slopes of Lárisa, the theatre and remains of

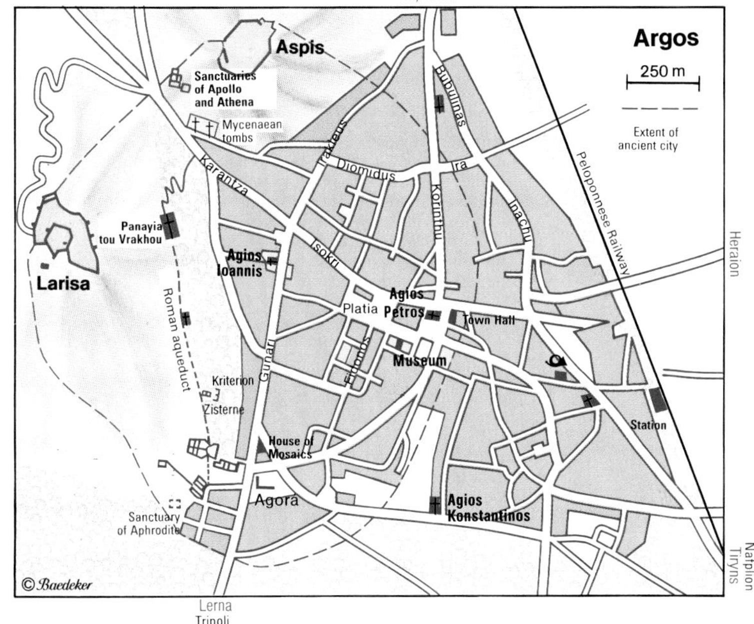

Roman baths. The ancient town walls took in both Aspís and Lárisa. The latter hill can be climbed in 45 minutes; half way up is the Panayía monastery, and on the summit is a medieval castle (views). In the lower ground between the two hills temples dedicated to Apollo and Athena and Mycenaean graves were found.

★Heraion

Location
11km/7 miles
NE of Árgos

The Argive Heraion is reached by way of the village of Khónika. From Mycenaean times onwards this was the principal Argive sanctuary. In its present form, laid out on terraces on the slopes of a hill (600m/1970ft), it dates from the 8th–5th centuries B.C. On the south side a broad flight of steps leads up to a stoa and the foundations of the 5th century temple of Hera, which contained a chryselephantine statue of the goddess by Polykleitos. On the next terrace was the older (7th c.) temple which was destroyed by fire in 425 B.C. Beside this temple were other stoas. The impressiveness of this site is due not so much to the meagre remains as to its grandiose and solitary situation.

Mérbaka

Location 8km/5 miles
east of Árgos

The road from Khónika to Náfplion runs past the village of Mérbaka, named after a 13th century Roman Catholic bishop of Corinth, William of Moerbeke. In the churchyard is one of the most beautiful churches in the region.

Kefalári

Location
5km/3 miles
south of Árgos

5km/3 miles from Árgos on the road to Trípoli a minor road (signposted) branches off to the village of Kefalári, famed for its large plane-tree. A spring which emerges from the rock here was believed by Strabo to be the outflow of the Stymphalian Lake (see Xylókastro, Surroundings). Here, where once Pan and the nymphs were worshipped, there now stands a chapel dedicated to the Mother of God as the Zoodókhos Piyí ("Lifegiving Spring"). Nearby is the "Pyramid" of Kefalári, which is frequently interpreted as a mausoleum but in fact was certainly part of a military control system of the 4th century B.C.

Kókla

Near Kefalári is the little village of Kókla, where a Mycenaean tholos (domed) tomb was discovered in 1981.
1km/¾ mile from Kefalári on the Árgos road a side road goes off on the left and in 2km/1¼ miles comes to Kókla. The tomb, which dates from around 1400 B.C., is notable for its magnificent situation, its size and the fact that it had not been robbed. In recesses in the entrance passage (dromos) were found two skeletons. The tomb itself was hewn from the rock to a depth of 7.5m/25ft and then completely faced with dressed stone. It contained rich grave goods, including gold and silver bowls. Other graves of the 16th–13th centuries B.C. were found in the surrounding area.

★Lerna

Location
12km/7½ miles
south of Árgos

Just beyond the village of Mýli on the Trípoli road can be seen (on the left, close to the sea) the roofed-over American excavations of Lerna, a site occupied from Neolithic times onwards. Here a double line of defensive walls of the Early Helladic period was found built over a Neolithic dwelling of the 4th millennium B.C. In the centre of the site is an Early Helladic palace, known as the "House of the Tiles", which was built about 2200 B.C. and burned down about 200 years later. Measuring 24m/79ft by 11m/36ft, it is the largest building of the pre-Greek period in Greece. After its destruction it was buried under a mound of earth enclosed by a large circle of stones. Two Mycenaean shaft graves provide evidence of Mycenaean occupation of the site about 1600 B.C.
Immediately north of the site is the Spring of the Hydra, which is associated with one of the labours of Herakles.

Arki L 6

Αρκοί
Arkí

Nomos: Dodecanese
Area of island: 7 sq.km/2¾ sq. miles
Altitude: 0–115m/0–375ft
Population: 50
Chief place: Arkí (Khóra)

Boat services

Occasional connections with Pátmos and Lipsí.

The barren and forlorn island of Arkí, known in antiquity as Akrite, lies 12km/7½ miles north-east of Pátmos in the Southern Sporades. The island's few inhabitants live very modestly, with no modern infrastructure. They earn their livelihood mainly from fishing, with some stock-farming.

Situation

Arkí is surrounded by numbers of smaller islets and isolated rocks, some of which provide grazing for goats.

Árta E 4

Άρτα
Árta

Nomos: Árta
Altitude: 0–30m/0–100ft
Population: 18,300

Transport

Bus connections with Athens and towns in Epirus.

Situation

Árta, chief town of a nomos in Epirus, lies on the left bank of the river Árakhthos, on the site of ancient Ambrakia, which gave its name to the almost completely land-locked Ambracian Gulf on the Ionian Sea.

History

Founded in the 7th century B.C. by settlers from Corinth, Ambrakia became in 297 B.C. the capital of the Molossian king Pyrrhos of Epirus. In 31 B.C. the population of the town was transferred to the newly founded city of Nikopolis.

In the 13th century A.D. the town, now known as Árta, became capital of the Despotate of Epirus, the rulers of which were related to the Imperial house of the Angeloi and for a time, during the Frankish occupation of Constantinople, themselves bore the title of emperor. This period left its mark on Árta in the form of the castle built on the site of the ancient acropolis (now occupied by the Xenia Hotel) and a number of churches in the town and monasteries in the surrounding area.

In 1318 Árta fell into the hands of the Norman lordship of Kefalloniá; in 1340 it returned briefly to Byzantine control; in 1348 it became part of the Serbian principality of Ioánnina; in 1449 it was occupied by the Turks; and in 1881 it was united with Greece.

Sights

★ Panayía Parigorítissa

On a hill on the north side of the town, near Platía Skoufas, stands the church of the Panayía Parigorítissa (Mother of God the Swiftly Consoling), built about 1290 by Despot Nikifóros, a massive and imposing cube-shaped structure, with three superimposed tiers of columns supporting the 24m/79ft high dome. The church was partly built with material from the ruins of the Roman city of Nikopolis (see entry). The dome has mosaics of Christ Pantokrator and prophets. On the iconostasis is an icon of the church's patroness, the Mother of God the Swiftly Consoling.

Ayía Theodóra

The church of Ayía Theodóra also dates from the 13th century. It was enlarged by the mother of Despot Nikifóros, Theodóra (later recognised as a saint), after the murder of her husband, Michael II (1271). In the narthex is her sarcophagus, the front of which has a fine relief carving of Theodóra and her small son. Her dual role as ruler and as saint is expressed by her dress, with a nun's veil over her royal robes,

Panayía Parigorítissa

and her attitude, with her right hand holding a sceptre and her left raised in the gesture of blessing.

Áyios Vasílios

★ Turkish bridge

Other features of interest are the 14th century church of Áyios Vasílios, with brick and tile decoration on the exterior, and a gracefully arched Turkish bridge over the Árakhthos (on the right of the road to Ioánnina).

Around the town are numerous churches and monasteries, notably the church of Káto Panayía to the north and the Vlakhernai monastery to the north-east (both 13th c.). On the road to Nikópolis is the castle of Rógi (see Nikópolis, Surroundings).

Astypalaia L 7

Αστυπάλαια
Astipálaia

Nomos: Dodecanese
Area of island: 99 sq.km/38 sq. miles
Altitude: 0–482m/0–1581ft
Population: 1100
Chief place: Astypálaia (Khóra)

Boat services

Twice weekly from Athens (Piraeus); local services (Kos–Kálymnos–Astypálaia), weekly.

Khora, Astypalaia

Situation and characteristics

The arid karstic island of Astypálaia, the most westerly of the Dodecanese, lying between Kos (40km/25 miles away), Amorgós (35km/22 miles) and Anáfi (40km/25 miles), has close affinities in topography and culture with the Cyclades. Two wide bays on the north-west and south-east sides of the island divide it into a higher western half (482m/1581ft) and a lower eastern half (366m/1201ft), linked by the isthmus of Áyios Andréas, which is only 110m/120yds wide. Stock-farming (cheese), the growing of fruit and vegetables and fishing bring the inhabitants a modest degree of wellbeing.

Sights

Astypálaia (Khóra)

The island's picturesque chief town, Astypálaia (Khóra), is finely situated on a bare rocky hill above the harbour (Skála), dominated by a Venetian castle (13th–16th c.).

Livádia valley

Below the Khóra, to the west, is the fertile Livádia valley, the main area of agricultural land on the island.

Scattered all over the island are some 200 churches and chapels, mostly founded by local families and now frequently in a ruinous state.

There are numerous small islets and isolated rocks, some of which provide grazing for goats. 35–45km/22–28 miles south-east are the lonely little islands of Seírina and Tría Nisía.

Athens H 5/6

Αθήνα
Athína

Nomos: Attica
Altitude: 0–150m/0–490ft
Population: 930,000 (conurbation, including Piraeus, 3.5 million)

The description of Athens in this guide is abridged, since there is a detailed account of the city in the AA/Baedeker guide "Athens".

Transport

With an international and domestic airport, bus services radiating to all parts of Greece, rail services and a network of shipping services from Piraeus (see entry), Athens is an ideal starting-point for journeys to any part of Greece.

Air services

The airport for both international and domestic flights is at Ellinikó, to the south of the city, with an East Terminal for international airlines and a West or National Terminal for international and domestic services by Olympic Airways.
There are domestic services from Athens to Aktion, Alexandroúpolis, Chios, Corfu (Kérkyra), Ioánnina, Iráklion (Crete), Kalamáta, Kastoriá, Kavála, Kefalloniá, Khaniá (Crete), Kýthira, Kos, Kozáni, Lárisa, Léros, Lemnos, Lésbos, Melos, Mýkonos, Páros, Rhodes, Salonica, Sámos, Santorin (Thera), Skiáthos, Skýros and Zákynthos.

Rail services

Trains to Salonica and Alexandroúpolis leave from the Central Station (Stathmós Larísis), trains to Corinth and the Peloponnese (Kalamáta) from the nearby Peloponnese Station.

Bus services

Within Athens and its suburbs there are yellow trolleybuses and green buses. There are also many country bus services to towns all over Greece. Many services leave from Sýntagma Square, Akadimías Street and Káningos Square (near Omónia Square). There are also bus services run by the State Railways.

Metro (Ilektrikós)

The Metro (Ilektrikós) runs (partly underground) from Piraeus through the city centre to Kifissiá in the north. Important stations in the central area are Thísion (north-west of the Agora), Monastiráki, Omónia, Viktória (west of the Pedion Areos) and Attikís (north-east of the Central Station).

Traffic in central Athens tends to be chaotic, and makes a major contribution to the dangerously heavy air pollution.

Useful Addresses

Department of Antiquities and Restoration: Aristídou 14, tel. 3 24 30 56.
Greek Automobile and Touring Club (ELPA): Mesoyion 2, tel. 7 79 16 15 (information on road conditions).
First aid: dial 166.
KAT (Accident and Orthopaedic Hospital): Kifissiá Street, tel. 8 01 44 41.

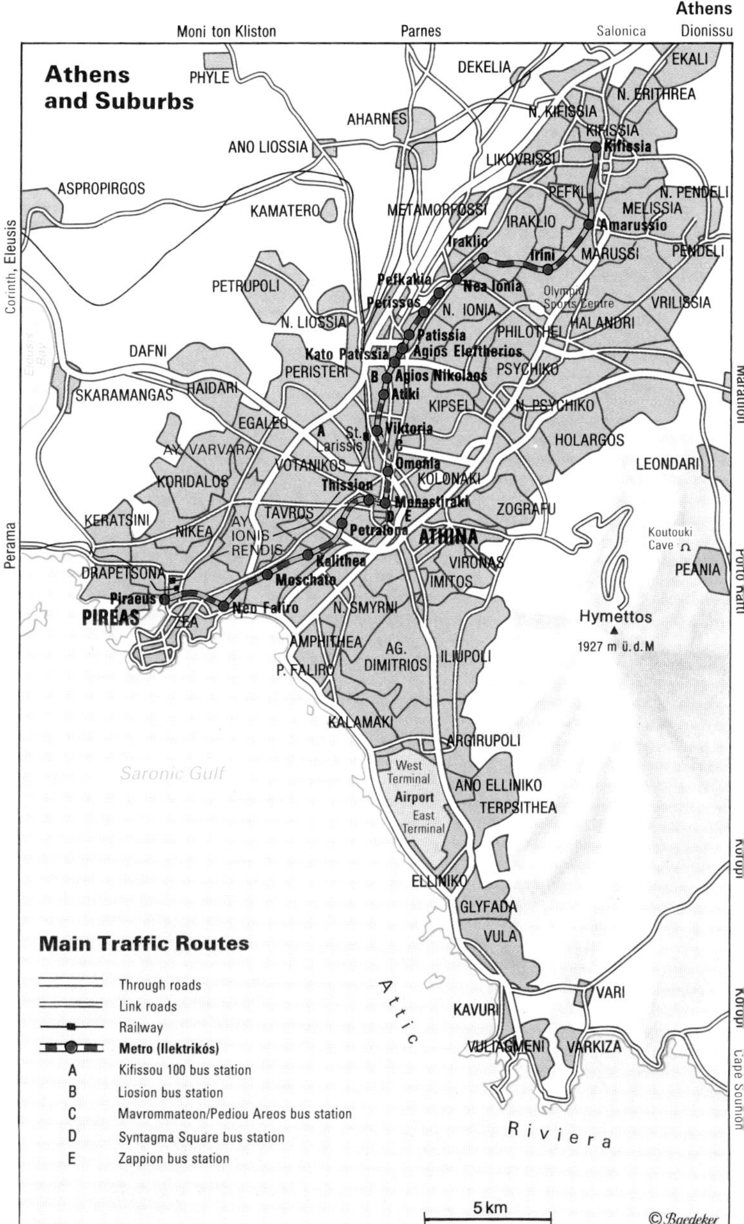
Moni ton Kliston
Parnes
Salonica
Dionissu
Athens and Suburbs
Main Traffic Routes
Through roads
Link roads
Railway
Metro (Ilektrikós)
A Kifissou 100 bus station
B Liosion bus station
C Mavrommateon/Pediou Areos bus station
D Syntagma Square bus station
E Zappion bus station
Corinth, Eleusis
Perama
Saronic Gulf
Attic
Riviera
Hymettos
1927 m ü.d.M
Koutouki Cave
5 km
© Baedeker

Embassies

See Practical Information, Embassies and Consulates.

Events

Athens Festival, in Odeion of Herodes Atticus, July–September (drama, opera, music, ballet); folk dancing in Philopappos Theatre, May–September; *son et lumière* shows on Pnyx, April–October.

Entertainment

Most places of entertainment are in the picturesque old Plaka district, a favourite haunt of tourists, well provided with restaurants, cafés and tavernas with bouzouki music.
Eight theatres offer a wide choice of entertainment to visitors who have some knowledge of modern Greek.
Many of the cinemas are open-air establishments.

Beaches

On the Attic Riviera (the Coast of Apollo): see Attica.

Shopping

Most of the shops selling folk art are situated around Monastiráki Square, where there is also a flea market on Sundays.
Good-quality gold and silver jewellery can be seen in jewellers' shops, most of which are north of Sýntagma Square.
Reproductions of ancient jewellery and ornaments in gold and silver can be bought in the National Archaeological Museum, which also sells reproductions of other museum exhibits.
Visitors should think twice before purchasing any antiques, since the export of works of art of this kind is prohibited.

Modern Athens

Other worthwhile buys are precious stones, leather goods, furs and records, discs or cassettes (particularly folk music and contemporary light music).
The most fashionable shopping district is between Sýntagma and Kolonáki Squares, to the south of Lykabettós.

The City

Athens (in modern Greek Athína), a city which has grown enormously in size over the last 150 years (from a population of only 6000 in 1834), lies just to the north of the Gulf of Aegina (Saronic Gulf) and now extends over the whole of the main Attic plain, which is watered by the Kifissos and Ilissos and bounded on the north and west by the Párnis and Aigaleos ranges of hills, on the north-east by Mt Pentelikon, famed for its Pentelic marble, and on the east and south-east by Mt Hymettos (Imittós).
Now as in antiquity Athens is the intellectual and artistic centre of Greece, and also, with the port of Piraeus (see entry), the country's economic centre. Its predominant position within Greece is illustrated by the fact that almost a quarter of the country's population live in and around the capital.

The political centre of Attica since the "synoecism" (unification) attributed to Theseus and capital of Greece since 1834, Athens has long been the largest and most important city in Greece. It has a University and a College of Technology; it is the seat of the Archbishop of Athens and of Greece; and it is the country's economic, commercial and

banking centre. Its historic buildings and its museums hold incalculable treasures. Its importance as a tourist centre is matched by the steadily increasing hotel resources within the city and its suburbs and along the coast of Attica towards Soúnion, the improvement of the road system and the development of the coastal strip along the bay of Fáliron into an attractively laid-out and excellently equipped holiday area.

Athens lies in the wide coastal plain on a site which provided its early inhabitants with a sufficiency of agricultural land, an easily defensible hill and good harbours within easy reach, but yet was far enough away from the sea to give security against surprise attack. The plain is surrounded by hills which form natural frontiers marking off Attica from the rest of Greece. To the west are Korydallos (468m/1536ft) and Aigaleos (453m/1486ft); to the north Parnis (1413m/4636ft) and Pentelikon (Pentéli; 1109m/3639ft); and to the east the broad ridge of Hymettos (Imittós; 1027m/3370ft). Between the various ranges of hills gaps and passes facilitate communications with the rest of Greece.

A number of lower hills rise out of the plain of Attica, among them Lykabettos (Lykavittós; 277m/909ft), now crowned by a chapel dedicated to St George, and Tourkovoúnia (the "Turkish Hills", known in antiquity as Anchesmos; 338m/1109ft), both of which lay outside the ancient city and have only been brought within the built-up area in recent times. The hill of most importance in the history of Athens, however, was the Acropolis (156m/512ft), which was built on as early as Mycenaean times and was ideally suited to be the site of a fortress, with its moderate height, sufficient area and access only on the west side. To the south of the Acropolis, a short distance away, are the Hill of the Nymphs (105m/345ft), with the Observatory, the Pnyx (110m/361ft), meeting-place of the Assembly in ancient Athens, and the Hill of the Muses (147m/482ft), crowned by the monument commemorating Philopappos, prince of Commagene.

The area of Athens is ill provided with natural watercourses, and since they are now largely built over they play little part in the pattern of the city. The ancient city was traversed by the Eridanos, which rises on Lykabettós, leaves the city precincts near the Sacred Gate in the Kerameikos, where it can still be seen, and flows west to join the Ilissos. The Ilissos itself rises on the south-western slopes of Hymettós and flows westward between the Olympieion and the Stadion to join the city's principal river, the Kifissos, which, rising at Kifissiá on the slopes of Pentelikon, flows south, to the west of the ancient city, to reach the sea in the bay of Fáliron.

Art and culture

With its University, College of Technology, Academy of Sciences, College of Commerce and Academy of Art, Athens is the cultural centre of Greece. It has several libraries and eight theatres which offer a varied repertoire. During the annual Athens Festival (July–September) there are dramatic and operatic productions, concerts and recitals of the highest quality. A great range of museums devoted to ancient and Byzantine culture, art galleries and natural history collections provide interest and fascination throughout the year.

Commerce and industry

The Athens conurbation is the heartland of Greek commerce and industry. All the Greek banks and most of the country's large businesses and shipping lines have their headquarters in Athens. Of particular importance are the industrial installations on the bay of Eleusis (see entry) and the numerous insurance corporations.
Tourism also plays a major role in the economy of Athens. In addition to the ancient sites in and around the city it offers the attractions of the seaside resorts on the Saronic Gulf.

Myth and History

Mythic origins

The early days of Athens were associated with the names of a series of mythical kings. According to traditions recorded by Apollodoros and others the first king of Athens was Kekrops, part man and part serpent, who was credited with the first numbering of the people, the first laws and the introduction of monogamy and the alphabet. His reign saw the conflict between Poseidon and Athena for the land of Attica, from which Athena emerged victorious. The tomb of Kekrops was incorporated in the Erechtheion, the shrine of a later king, Erechtheus, and now lies under the Caryatid porch. Close by is an olive-tree, marking the spot where Athena was said to have planted the first olive-tree in Attica.

Kekrops was succeeded by Kranaos, who ruled at the time of the Great Flood of Greek mythology and was deposed by Amphiktyon. After ruling for twelve years Amphiktyon was in turn displaced by Erichthonios, son of Hephaistos and Athena or the Earth Mother, who, like Kekrops, had the form of a serpent. Erichthonios set up a wooden cult image of the goddess and initiated the Panathenaic festival. He was succeeded by his son Pandion, and Pandion by his son Erechtheus, whose "well-founded citadel" is referred to by Homer ("Iliad", 2, 547). His twin brother Boutes was a priest of Athena and Poseidon, whose cult was later celebrated in the Erechtheion. Erechtheus was succeeded by his descendants Kekrops II and Panadion II, the latter of whom was deposed and fled to Megara. His son Aigeus returned to Athens, and it is from him that the Aegean takes its name. Legend had it that he flung himself into the sea when he saw ships with black sails returning from Crete and believed that his son Theseus had failed in his mission.

This Theseus, who was believed to have united all the inhabitants of Attica under the leadership of Athens (the "synoecism"), was the tenth of the mythical kings and the great hero of Athens. He destroyed Prokroustes (Procrustes) and other robbers who infested the road between Troizen, where he had been brought up, and Athens; he killed the Minotaur and ended the tribute paid by Athens to King Minos of Crete; with his friend Peirithoos he fought the Centaurs, and with Herakles the Amazons; and he abducted the youthful Helen from Sparta to Aphidna in Attica. He was killed on the island of Skyros by his host, King Lykomedes; and many centuries later, about 475 B.C., his remains were brought back to Athens by Kimon and the Theseion erected in his honour.

The last king of Theseus's line was Thymoites, who, in gratitude for military assistance, assigned the crown to Melanthos, driven out of Pylos by the invading Dorians. From Melanthos the throne passed to his son Kodros, who sacrificed his life in 1068 B.C. to save Athens from the Dorians. According to some traditions Kodros was the last of the kings; according to others he was succeeded by his son Medon, while other sons began the settlement of the west coast of Asia Minor. Thus Neleus was credited with the foundation of Miletus, Androklos with that of Ephesus.

Early history

These mythic traditions reflect the history of Athens from early Mycenaean times to the turn of the 2nd–1st millennium. In fact, however, the history of the city goes much further back. Finds on the southern slope of the Acropolis and in the Agora show that the site of Athens was already occupied in the Neolithic period, around 3000 B.C. After the arrival of the early Greek peoples Athens participated in the development of the Mycenaean world. About 1400 B.C. the Acropolis became the site of a royal stronghold (Kekrops) and was surrounded by a cyclopean wall, the whole course of which has been established;

part of this wall, the Pelargikon, is still preserved near the temple of Nike. The palace was on the north side of the Acropolis, where, near the old temple of Athena, the stone bases of two timber columns can be seen, protected by gratings.

The Acropolis, which then covered an area of 35,000 sq.m/42,000 sq.yds (Mycenae 30,000 sq.m/36,000 sq.yds, Tiryns 20,000 sq.m/24,000 sq.yds), no doubt served as a place of refuge for the inhabitants of the settlements round the Agora, at the Dipylon and on the Hill of the Muses and the Areopagos. The Dorian migration of the 12th century passed Attica by (cf. the myth of Kodros), and accordingly the Athenians regarded themselves in historical times as the indigenous inhabitants. The city did, however, give asylum to refugees from the Peloponnese, and the resultant population pressure led to the colonisation of western Asia Minor and its offshore islands. Thucydides saw the activities of Theseus as historical facts, and regarded the synoecism by which he established the unity of Attica as the foundation of Athens's later greatness. Nevertheless the history of the period of kingly rule is wholly obscure: all that is known is that after the end of the monarchy the functions of the kings passed to the archons, who changed every year. Thereafter there came into being, probably in the 8th century B.C., an aristocratic state the great families of which supplied the nine annually appointed members of the government – the *archon,* who gave his name to the year (*archon eponymos*); the *basileus,* who performed the cult functions of the earlier kings; the *polemarchos* or military commander; and six *thesmothetai* (lawgivers). The Areopagos (lawcourt), which met on the Hill of Ares (Areios pagos), was made up of former archons. The popular Assembly met in the Agora.

From Solon to Perikles

In the 7th century B.C. there were severe social tensions in Athens, since the nobility possessed almost all the land, while the mass of the population, their tenants, fell into debt and sank to the condition of serfs. This situation was remedied by the first Attic legislators, Drakon (*c.* 624 B.C.) and Solon, scion of the old royal family of the Medontids, who was elected archon and arbiter, with full powers, in 594/593 B.C. Solon's reforms wiped out all public and private debts and abolished the practice, previously common, of selling debtors into slavery. He also limited individual holdings of property and reformed the system of weights and measures and the coinage. The population was divided into four classes according to their taxable income. The highest class consisted of the archons; the second and third (knights and yeomen) occupied the other government posts and were responsible for defence; while the fourth, the *thetes,* were members of the popular Assembly (Ekklesia) and Court (Heliaia). Alongside the Areopagos was established the Council of 400. In the words of H. Bengtson: "With Solon's creation the history of the conception of a state in Europe begins".

After the time of Solon further tensions arose between the inhabitants of the different parts of Attica – in the Kephisos valley, in the coastal areas and among the peasant farmers of the interior. This last group, the poorest, found a leader in Peisistratos, a noble from Brauron, who occupied the Acropolis with his bodyguard in 561/560 and made himself sole ruler (*tyrannos,* "tyrant") of Athens. He was compelled to flee from the city more than once, but from 546 until his death in 528/527 he ruled with absolute power. His reign was one of the most brilliant periods in the history of Athens. Democratic rather than tyrannical, in the judgment of Aristotle, he erected fine new buildings in Athens and Eleusis, including the temple of Athena Polias, built on the site of the old royal palace on the Acropolis. He also reinstituted the Panathenaic festival, introduced the cult of Dionysos and with it the performance of tragedy, and caused the Homeric poems to be collected.

After the death of Peisistratos his sons Hippias and Hipparchos took over the government. In 514 B.C. Hipparchos was murdered in an act of private revenge, and although Harmodios and Aristogeiton were later honoured as the tyrant-killers who had cast off the yoke of tyranny Hippias in fact continued to rule as a particularly ruthless tyrant until 510, when he was overthrown and expelled from Athens by the Alcmaeonids.The leading representative of the Alcmaeonids was Kleisthenes, who reformed the constitution of Athens in 508/507 B.C. and introduced democracy. The basis of the system was the organisation of the population into *phylai* (tribes). Attica was divided into three parts – the city, the coast and the interior – and each of these parts into ten *trittyes.* The ten tribes were then formed by taking one *trittys* from each of the three regions. Each tribe sent 50 representatives to the Council of 500, which met in the Bouleuterion in the Agora. As a further precaution against excessive political ambition and influence Kleisthenes introduced the system of "ostracism", an effective weapon in the hands of the Assembly which brought down many prominent politicians.

The following decades were dominated by the struggle with Persia. On the advice of Hippias, who had fled to Persia, Persian forces landed in the bay of Marathon in 490 B.C. but were defeated by the Athenians with the assistance of Plataiai; the Spartans arrived too late.

The following years were used by Themistokles to build up a strong fleet. When the Persians returned in 480 the Athenians were compelled to abandon Attica and evacuate the population, but the Athenian fleet was victorious in a naval battle at Salamis, which, with the battles of Plataiai and Mykale (479 B.C.), put an end to the danger from Persia. As a protection against further attacks Athens was surrounded by the "Themistoclean walls", still to be seen (as strengthened by Konon in the 4th century) in the Kerameikos area.

The Persian wars had so enhanced the position of Athens within the Greek world that it became leader of the Confederacy of Delos, the first Attic maritime league, which was established in 478 B.C. In 454 the league's treasury was transferred from the island of Delos to Athens, where it was used by Perikles to finance the construction of the Parthenon and other buildings on the Acropolis – the most splendid achievement of Athens in its great age, the 5th century.

Perikles, who succeeded Kimon as the dominant figure in Athens in 461 B.C., maintained his position, in spite of much opposition, until his death in 429. Seeing Sparta and Persia as the main enemies, he strengthened the naval alliance, which the island of Aegina and other city states were forced to join. The buildings on the Acropolis, which was no longer a stronghold of the city's rulers but a citadel of the gods, still bear witness to the spiritual and artistic power of the age of Perikles.

Later antiquity

This great flowering of art, to which artists from all over Greece contributed, was ended by the Peloponnesian War (431–404), a conflict between Athens and Sparta which fatally weakened all the participants. The Athenian empire was destroyed, and Athens itself fell under the reign of terror of the Thirty Tyrants. In 403, however, democracy was restored. The conflict with Sparta revived in the 4th century, and in 377 Athens established the second Attic maritime league, seeking to maintain its position by changes in its alliances. But now a new power was rising in the north, the Macedon of Philip II, which

began by capturing Attic possessions in the north, including Amphipolis (357), and in the battle of Chaironeia (338) established its dominance over the whole of Greece. The age of the democratic city state, the *polis,* was at an end.
The reign of Philip's son Alexander marked the beginning of an age of peace and prosperity for Athens, interrupted by periods of occupation. Alexander respected Athens for its intellectual achievement; and this fame sustained the city during the subsequent period, when it was a place of no political importance and declined into a small country town. Later it was embellished by Hellenistic rulers with imposing buildings like the Stoa of Attalos and the Stoa of Eumenes. Its nadir came in 86 B.C., when it was sacked by Roman troops under Sulla. Under the Empire it enjoyed a further period of prosperity. The Roman Agora dates from the time of Augustus, but a major contribution to the development of Athens was made by Hadrian, who built the "city of Hadrian" round the Olympeion, which he completed, with a gateway between his city and the "city of Theseus". In this period too Herodes Atticus, a native of Marathon, erected other fine buildings (the Odeion, the Stadion). The city's schools of rhetoric now became famous.
In A.D. 267 Athens was captured and plundered by the Herulians, an East Germanic people. Thereafter it was surrounded by defensive walls enclosing a much smaller area. The walls ran north from the Propylaia to the Stoa of Attalos, then east across Hadrian's Market and finally south to the east side of the Acropolis. Much stone from buildings in the Agora was used in the construction of the walls.
The schools of Athens maintained their importance in subsequent periods, and about 400 a large new Gymnasion was built in the Agora – the home of the University of Athens.

Medieval and modern times

Athens now gradually declined into a provincial town in the Byzantine Empire. Christianity had long been established in the city, and in 426 the great pagan temples were closed. In 529 the University and the Platonic Academy were also closed down. The first Christian church in Athens was built in Hadrian's Market (the "Library of Hadrian") in the 5th century, and in the 5th or 6th century the Parthenon, the Erechtheion and the temple of Hephaistos were also given over to Christian worship. The town was now remote from the centre of events and was visited only once by an Emperor – Basil II in 1085, a few years after the foundation of the monastic church of Dafni by an imperial official (*c.* 1080).
After the 4th Crusade (1203–04) Athens became the seat of a Frankish duke, who built his palace in the Propylaia on the Acropolis, now once again a fortress. In 1457, three years after the fall of Constantinople, the town was taken by Mehmet II, and it remained in Turkish hands until the liberation of Greece in the 19th century. The Parthenon, long a Christian church and since 1204 a Roman Catholic cathedral, now became a mosque. The Turkish commandant resided in the Propylaia, and his harem was accommodated in the Erechtheion. In 1775 the population of Athens consisted of some 3000 Turks in the fortress, 5000 Greeks in the area north of the Late Roman walls (the "Valerian walls") and some 1000 Albanians of the Christian faith in the Plaka, under the north side of the Acropolis. (This compares with Attica's estimated population, in the time of Perikles, of 170,000 citizens, 30,000 *metoikoi* or foreign settlers and 115,000 slaves.) Only two of the mosques of the Turkish period have been preserved, without their minarets – Syntrivani in Monastiráki Square and Fethiye Camii near the Tower of the Winds. During the 17th century a number of Europeans visited Athens, and to their accounts we owe our knowledge of the condition of the Parthenon before its destruction by a Venetian grenade in 1687.

During the 19th century war of liberation Athens was the object of bitter fighting. In 1821–22 it was taken by the Greeks, but in 1826 the town and in 1827 the fortress were recaptured by the Turks, who were not finally expelled until April 12th 1833.
A new period of development began when King Otto I made Athens capital of the new kingdom of Greece on January 1st 1834. After independence the population of Athens increased by leaps and bounds, from 8000 in 1823 to 42,000 in 1860, 105,000 in 1889 and 600,000 in 1928. Extensive new districts were developed when, after the catastrophe in Asia Minor in 1923, 300,000 refugees flooded into Athens and Piraeus, creating a problem which it took decades to resolve. Athens and Piraeus have long formed a single urban area in which modern buildings are totally dominant. Greater Athens, with nine city wards and 38 associated communes extending in a vast sea of houses over the plain of Attica between the sea and Pentelikon, now has a population of some 3.5 million and is the undisputed economic as well as political capital of Greece.

Pausanias, the "Baedeker of Antiquity"

An invaluable guide to the topography of ancient Athens, supplementing the evidence provided by the surviving remains, is the first book of the "Description of Greece" written by Pausanias in the 2nd century A.D. This work, justly famed as the "Baedeker of Antiquity", has proved of great value in guiding excavation and interpreting its results.
Pausanias, coming from Sounion, arrived in Piraeus and entered Athens, after passing the tombs outside the walls, by the Dipylon (Double Gate) in the Kerameikos area. From there he went along the Panathenaic processional way to the Agora, of which he gives a detailed though not complete account, also covering the hill to the west with the temple of Hephaistos. His next section is devoted to the area around the Olympieion and the Ilissos, where he mentions numerous temples and the Gymnasion of Kynosarges, home of the Cynic philosophical school founded by Antisthenes, the approximate situation of which on the left bank of the Ilissos has now been established.
Pausanias also refers to another philosophical school, the Lykeion (Lyceum) in which Aristotle once taught, situated in the area of what is now Sýntagma Square. Then, after the Stadion, he turns his attention to the Acropolis. Going along the Street of the Tripods (in which he fails to mention the Monument of Lysikrates, still visible today), he comes to the Theatre of Dionysos and then finds his way up the southern slope of the hill, passing the sanctuary of Asklepios, to the Acropolis. From the Propylaia he makes for the sanctuary of Artemis Brauronia and then for the altar of Zeus Polieus, on the highest point of the hill, the Parthenon and the Erechtheion. Then follows a description of the courts of Athens, the Areopagos and the Heliaia (which has been identified at the south-west corner of the Agora). Finally Pausanias describes numerous tombs on the road to the oldest philosophical school in Athens, Plato's Academy, the Academy itself, the Kolonos Hippios where Oedipus died and the Sacred Way to Eleusis.

A translation of Pausanias's guide by Peter Levi has been published by Penguin Books. This edition, with helpful footnotes, will be found invaluable by anyone who wants to get the feel of ancient Athens (or of other ancient sites in Greece).

Athens

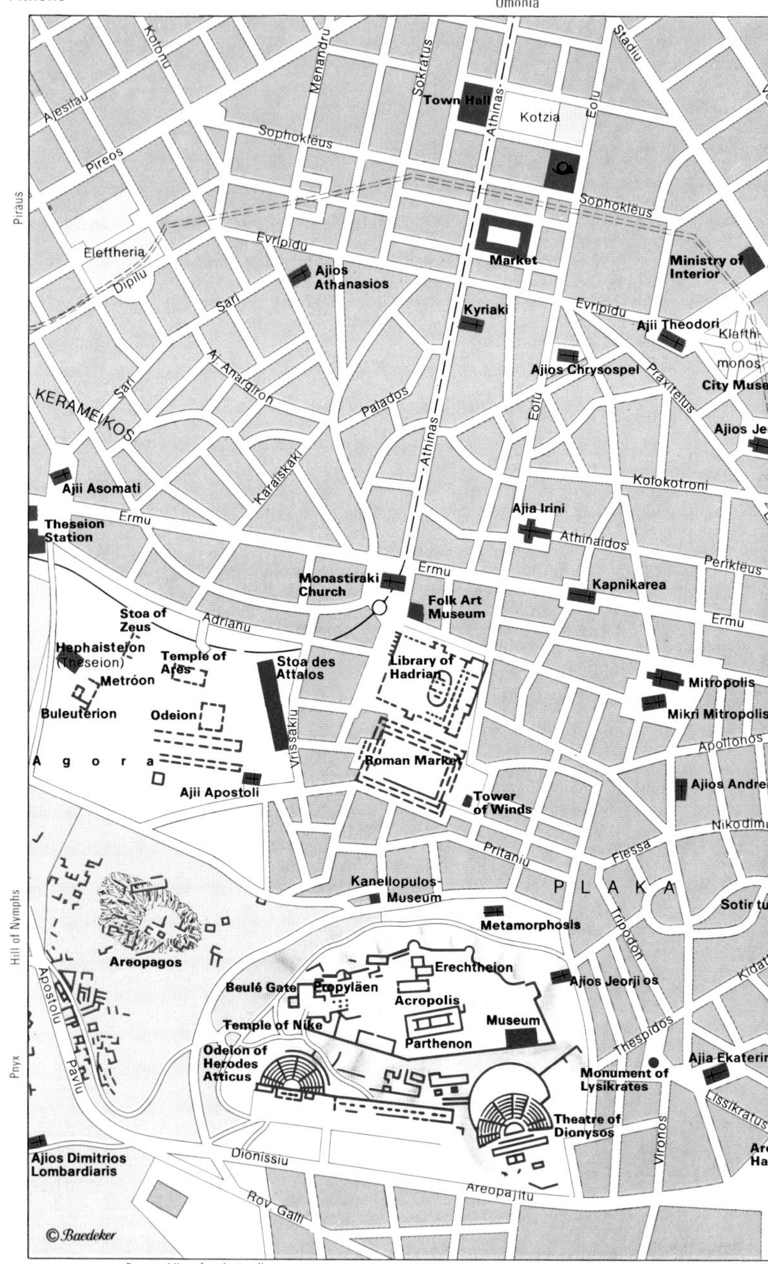
National Archaeological Museum
Omonia
Kotonu
Menandru
Sokratus
Stadiu
Ajesilau
Town Hall
Kotzia
Athinas
Eolu
Sophokleus
Pireos
Piraus
Eleftheria
Dipilu
Evripidu
Ajios Athanasios
Market
Ministry of Interior
Sari
Kyriaki
Evripidu
Ajii Theodori
Klafthmonos
Aj. Anargiron
Ajios Chrysospel
Praxitelus
City Muse
KERAMEIKOS
Palados
Athinas
Eolu
Ajios Je
Karaiskaki
Ajii Asomati
Kolokotroni
Ajia Irini
Theseion Station
Ermu
Athinaidos
Perikleus
Monastiraki Church
Ermu
Kapnikarea
Folk Art Museum
Stoa of Zeus
Adrianu
Ermu
Hephaisteion (Theseion)
Temple of Ares
Stoa des Attalos
Library of Hadrian
Metroon
Mitropolis
Mikri Mitropolis
Buleuterion
Odeion
Vrissakiu
Apollonos
A g o r a
Roman Market
Ajii Apostoli
Tower of Winds
Ajios Andre
Nikodim
Pritaniu
Flessa
Kanellopulos-Museum
P L A K A
Sotir
Hill of Nymphs
Metamorphosis
Areopagos
Erechtheion
Apostolu
Beulé Gate
Propyläen
Ajios Jeorjios
Tripodon
Acropolis
Kidat
Temple of Nike
Museum
Thespidos
Parthenon
Odeion of Herodes Atticus
Monument of Lysikrates
Ajia Ekaterir
Pnyx
Pavlu
Lissikratus
Theatre of Dionysos
Vironos
Ajios Dimitrios Lombardiaris
Dionissiu
Areopajitu
Rov. Galli
© Baedeker
Presumed line of ancient walls
Airport

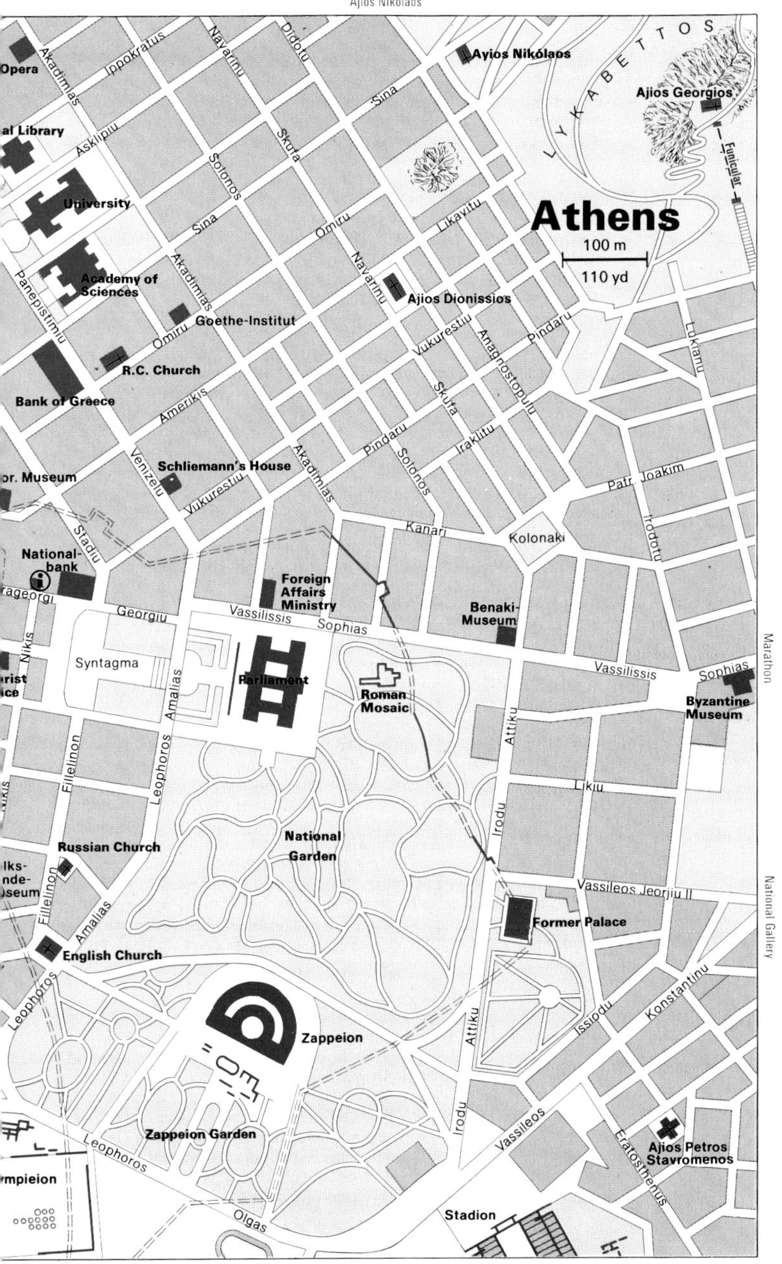
Ajios Nikolaos
Athens
100 m
110 yd
LYKABETTOS
Ajios Georgios
Funicular
Ayios Nikólaos
Opera
al Library
University
Academy of Sciences
Goethe-Institut
R.C. Church
Bank of Greece
Ajios Dionissios
Schliemann's House
or. Museum
National-bank
Foreign Affairs Ministry
Benaki-Museum
Kolonaki
Syntagma
Parliament
Roman Mosaic
Byzantine Museum
National Garden
Russian Church
English Church
Former Palace
Zappeion
Zappeion Garden
Ajios Petros Stavromenos
Stadion
mpieion
Akadimias
Ippokratus
Navarinu
Didotu
Sina
Skufa
Solonos
Asklipiu
Omiru
Likavitu
Panepistimiu
Vukurestiu
Anagnostopulu
Pindaru
Lukianu
Amerikis
Iraklitu
Venizelu
Stadiu
Patr. Joakim
Irodotu
Kanari
Vassilissis Sophias
Georgiu
Amalias
Leophoros
Filellinon
Nikis
Attiku
Irodu
Likiu
Vassileos Jeorjiu II
Konstantinu
Issiodu
Vassileos
Eratosthenus
Olgas
Marathon
National Gallery
Metro

Ancient Athens

The limestone plateau of the Acropolis, situated in the middle of the plain of Attica, was a site well suited for the fortified "upper town", originally a royal fortress and a precinct enclosing the most sacred shrines of Athens, later the exclusive stronghold of the gods. This religious centre of ancient Athens, given its classical form in the age of Perikles, thus became a monument to the Greek sense of human values, reflecting standards which have remained valid down to our own day. In spite of the destruction they have suffered down the centuries – not least the devastating explosion in 1687, when a Venetian grenade blew up the Turkish powder magazine in the Parthenon and brought it down in ruin – these buildings still convey something of the splendour of the age of Perikles, when Athens stood at the centre of the Greek world in intellectual and artistic as well as in political terms.

The 19th and early 20th centuries did a great deal, by the removal of later buildings and the restoration of the ancient ones, to restore the structures on the Acropolis to their original 5th century state. The work began in 1836, immediately after the liberation of Greece from the Turks, with the re-erection (by Ludwig Ross, a member of King Otto's staff) of the temple of Athena Nike, which had been incorporated in a Turkish bastion, and culminated in the re-erection of the columns along the north side of the Parthenon in the twenties of the present century.

But our own century has also done more damage to the Acropolis within a few decades than the previous two and a half millennia. As a result of the waste gases and exhaust fumes produced by a huge modern city, the taking off and landing of thousands of aircraft (which are now prohibited from overflying the Acropolis) and the tramping of the three million visitors who climb up to the Acropolis every year, the rock surface and the marble facing are being worn away, the Pentelic marble is breaking down into gypsum, the surviving pieces of classical sculpture (e.g. on the west frieze of the Parthenon) are flaking off, and altogether destruction is proceeding at an alarming rate and on an alarming scale. Accordingly a 15 million dollar programme for saving the Parthenon was launched by UNESCO. The first measures taken were the laying of a wooden floor over the central passage of the Propylaia, the provision of a protective roof over the Caryatid porch of the Erechtheion and the exclusion of visitors from the interior of the Parthenon. Further measures are under way for the protection of the Bouleuterion. Visitors and tour operators could also help if they could agree that not every casual day tripper need actually set foot on the Acropolis. It remains to be seen, however, how far the various measures taken or planned will succeed in preserving this incomparable monument of antiquity from the devastating effects of modern technological civilisation.

Pnyx

Excellent views of the Acropolis – offering a valuable preliminary to a visit or an informative general impression for visitors with little time at their disposal – are to be enjoyed from various points in the city. The north side can be seen from the Agora, the south-east side from the Olympieion, the west side (in particular the monumental Propylaia) from the Pnyx.

The Pnyx was the meeting-place of the popular Assembly after Kleisthenes' reform of 507 B.C., the place where statesmen such as Themistokles and Perikles appeared before the people of Athens. Visitors can still see the rock-hewn tribune from which the orators spoke, the altar of Zeus (*c.* 400 B.C.) and the retaining wall of the auditorium, constructed of gigantic blocks of stone about 330 B.C. Here too can be seen some remains of the shorter circuit of town walls (the diateichisma) built in 337 B.C.

★ Hill of the Muses

The finest view of the Acropolis, however, is the view of its south side from the Hill of the Muses. From the car park we go east along the rocky ridge towards the conspicuous Monument of Philopappos, commemorating a prince of Commagene in south-eastern Anatolia who was exiled to Athens by the Roman authorities and died there in A.D. 116. In gratitude for his munificence the Athenians allowed his tomb to be erected on this exceptional site – an honour, it has been remarked, that in the great days of Athens was not granted even to such a man as Perikles. On the frieze round the base Philopappos is shown as a Roman consul driving in a chariot and accompanied by lictors. Above this are seated figures of the dead man and (on left) Antiochos IV (Philopappos's grandfather), last king of Commagene (until A.D. 72).

On the way to this monument to a personality cult under the Roman Empire we pass various cisterns and rock-cut chambers, one of them misnamed the Prison of Socrates. Along the way, too, there are attractive and constantly changing views of the Acropolis, with the various buildings clearly visible – on the Acropolis itself the Propylaia, the Erechtheion and the Parthenon, on its southern slopes the Odeion of Herodes Atticus, the Stoa of Eumenes, the Theatre of Dionysos and the columns of the Monument of Thrasyllos. In the background is the pointed summit of Lykabettós.
The hill is a popular resort in the warm afternoon light, but it is also well worth coming here in the very early morning.

★★Acropolis

The rocky crag of the Acropolis measures 320m/350yds from east to west and 156m/170yds from north to south, and is 156.2m/512ft high at its highest point. It drops precipitously on the north, east and south sides, so that access from the earliest times was always from the west.

History

In Mycenaean times the cyclopean walls of the fortress closely followed the lie of the land. On the north side were two small gates leading to the Klepsydra spring and the caves in the north face of the rock. On the site later occupied by the older temple of Athena stood the royal palace, and to the east of the Erechtheion were other dwellings. There are remains of at least ten buildings dating from the Archaic period (7th and 6th centuries) as well as the remains of two temples. One of these, the early 6th century temple of Athena, was built on the site of the Mycenaean megaron. The naos of this temple, which was not surrounded by columns, was 100 feet long by 50 feet across and was accordingly known as the Hekatompedon (the "hundred-footer"). The large pediment of poros limestone now in the Acropolis Museum (in the centre bulls attacked by lions, to the left Herakles and Triton, to the right a figure with three bodies, perhaps Nereus) probably belonged to this temple. About 520 B.C. Peisistratos built a temple with a colonnade of 6×12 columns – either a reconstruction of the Hekatompedon or a new building – in which marble was used for the first time in the figures on the pediment (Athena and a battle with giants). This "Old Temple" succeeded the Hekatompedon as the sanctuary of Athena Polias and housed the old wooden cult image. Its ground-plan can be identified immediately south of the Erechtheion.

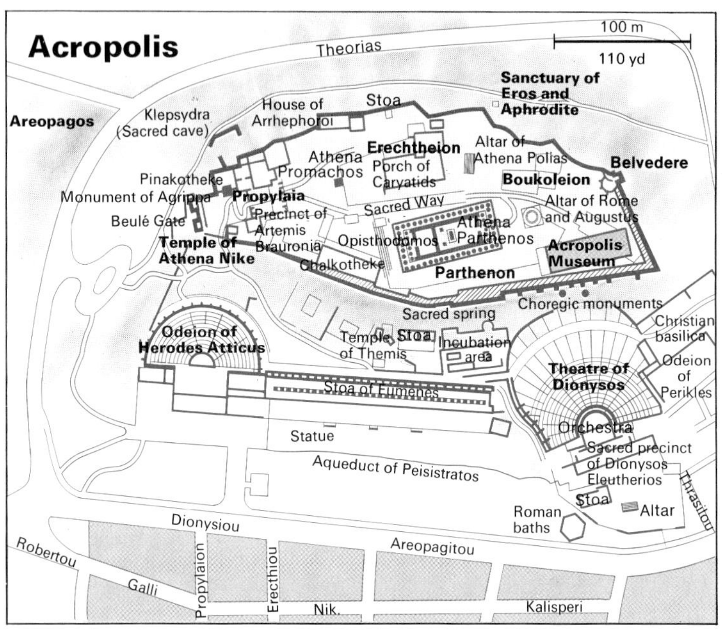

All the buildings of the Archaic period were destroyed by the Persians in 480 B.C. The remains of the Old Temple were razed to the ground in 406, after the removal of the cult image (*xoanon*) to the new temple of Athena in the eastern part of the Erechtheion. In the rebuilding by Themistokles immediately after the destruction column drums and fragments from the entablature were used, as can still be seen in the north wall. Some time later, after 467, the line of the defences on the south side of the Acropolis was altered by Kimon, who built the present straight wall. The ground level behind the walls built by Themistokles and Kimon was raised, using debris from the buildings and sculpture destroyed by the Persians; and excavations in this rubble carried out by Panayiotis Kavvadias in 1885–86 yielded numerous pieces of sculpture and architectural fragments, including the many figures of *korai* (maidens) which are now among the principal treasures of the Acropolis Museum.

Within the fortified area as extended by Kimon the great building and rebuilding programme of the classical period was carried out by Perikles. The Parthenon was built between 447 and 438, the Propylaia between 437 and 432, the temple of Athena Nike between 432 and 421, the Erechtheion between 421 and 406.

The only structure dating from a later period of which remains are still to be seen is a round temple of Rome and Augustus, dating from the early Empire, below the east end of the Parthenon.

Beulé Gate

The Acropolis is now entered by the Beulé Gate, built after the Herulian raid of A.D. 267, using stone from destroyed buildings, among them the Dorian monument of Nikias from the southern slope of the Acropolis. Tickets are sold here.

★ Propylaia

Immediately in front rear up the Propylaia, built by Mnesikles in 437–432 B.C. He had conceived a monumental and symmetrical structure consisting of three wings, but the daring original plan had to be modified to take account of the old temple of Athena Nike on the projecting spur of rock to the right (the "Pyrgos" or Tower of Nike). Traces of the earlier Propylon of the 6th century B.C. can still be seen. On top of the native rock is a flight of steps, the lowest step being of grey Eleusinian marble and the rest of Pentelic marble. The central structure of the Propylaia consists of a portal with five gateways which increase in height towards the centre. The architrave of the central gateway is enlarged by the addition of a metope – a device used here for the first time which later became common. In front of the portal is a deep vestibule, the central carriageway of which is flanked by three Ionic columns on each side; the front pediment is supported by six Doric columns. While this western portico makes an imposing entrance, the corresponding portico at the east end, also with Doric columns, is shorter and lower; seen from above it appears small and modest, subordinate to the more important cult buildings.

Monument of Agrippa

The west portico is flanked by side wings. To the left is the Pinakotheke, which housed a collection of pictures, and to the west of this is the high base of the Monument of Agrippa, (Augustus's son-in-law), erected in 27 B.C. It was originally planned to have a building similar to the Pinakotheke on the south side, but this was reduced to a narrow passage or vestibule giving access to the temple of Athena Nike.

★ Temple of Athena Nike

The temple of Athena Nike (Athena who brings Victory) was built between 432 and 421 B.C., with four Ionic columns at each end. This type of column was then already old-fashioned, leading Carpenter to suggest that in this temple, built after the time of Perikles, an older design by Kallikrates was used (see the account of the architectural history of the Parthenon, below). In front of the little temple the remains of an altar can be identified, and opposite this a fragment of the Mycenaean walls, the Pelargikon. Under the 5th century paving within the temple can be seen remains of earlier structures. The temple platform was originally surrounded by a parapet. Finds from the site are in the Acropolis Museum.

The present state of the Propylaia and the temple of Nike is the result of 19th and 20th century restoration, for both buildings had been damaged and disfigured from the 13th century onwards by their use as the residence of Frankish dukes and Turkish commandants and for the purposes of defence.

Beyond the Propylaia the bare rock of the Acropolis, worn smooth by the feet of countless visitors, rises in a gentle slope. Numerous cuttings in the rock mark the positions of the cult images and votive monuments which once stood here, many of them mentioned by Pausanias. Among them was a figure of Athena Hygieia (semicircular base for a bronze statue against the southernmost column of the east portico of the Propylaia, together with an altar, still visible). Exactly on the axis of the central roadway of the Propylaia stood a bronze statue of Athena Promachos, a celebrated work by Pheidias which was later carried off to Constantinople and was destroyed in 1203 during the Crusaders' siege of the city. The goddess, whose lance was visible far and wide, stood on a marble base, part of which, with an unusually large egg-and-dart moulding, has survived in situ.

Brauronion

Immediately to the right (south) of the Propylaia are the remains of the Brauronion, the cult precinct of Artemis of Brauron, who was brought

The Parthenon

Chalkotheke

to Athens by Peisistratos, and the Chalkotheke, in which works of art in bronze were kept. Beyond this a broad flight of steps hewn from the rock leads up to the higher level on which the Parthenon stands. The ancient processional way ran along the north side of the temple (opposite the seventh column of which is a rock-cut dedication to Ge, the Earth Mother) to the entrance at the east end.

★★ Parthenon

The Parthenon, the temple of the Maiden Athena (Athena Parthenos), built between 447 and 458 B.C. (pediment sculpture completed 432), was the master-work of the architect Iktinos and of Pheidias, to whom Perikles had entrusted the overall direction of the building work on the Acropolis. The architectural history of the Parthenon, which was based on an earlier building on the site, has been established, with a high degree of probability, by the work of Hill, Dinsmoor and Carpenter.

Architectural history

The foundations of the first Parthenon, consisting of 22 courses of masonry with a height of up to 10.75m/35ft, were built and the lower drums were laid in 490 B.C., or soon afterwards; but the building, designed to have 6×16 columns, was still unfinished at the time of the Persian invasion in 480, and the column drums were damaged by fire. In 468 Kimon continued the work, with Kallikrates as architect, but the building of this first Parthenon was halted on Kimon's death in 450.
In 447, under Perikles, the new master of Athens, the erection of the present Parthenon was begun. Kallikrates was replaced by Iktinos, who used the column drums and metopes already available in his altered plan. The foundations were adapted to accommodate the new and wider ground-plan; the older foundations, extending farther to the east, can be clearly distinguished on the south side.
Standing on a substructure (the crepidoma) with steps 52cm/20in high, the temple now had eight columns along the ends and seven-

teen along the sides (compared with the previous 6×16). The Doric columns stand 10.43m/34ft high, with a diameter at the base of 1.9m/6ft 3in and at the top of 1.48m/4ft 10 in. They have twenty flutings and show a distinct swelling in the middle (the feature known as entasis). Similarly the crepidoma shows a gentle curve, rising towards the middle (best seen on the uppermost step, the stylobate). These features (entasis and curvature), together with the slight inward inclination of the columns (the corner columns leaning diagonally inward), were deliberately contrived to avoid any impression of heaviness or rigidity and to create the effect of an organically developed structure.

The building was roofed with marble slabs. The lions' heads at the corners of the roof were not pierced to serve as water-spouts but were purely ornamental; the water simply ran off at the corners without any channel. On the architrave at the east end are dowel holes marking the place where shields captured by Alexander the Great at the battle of the Granikos in 334 B.C. were suspended.

The interior of the temple (now closed to visitors) is in two parts. At the west end is a square chamber, with remains of painting dating from the time when it was used as a Christian church, leading into the Parthenon proper, the roof of which was borne on four Ionic columns. At the east end the pronaos leads into the naos, in which stood the chryselephantine statue of Athena, known to us only from descriptions and later copies. The cavity for the base on which it stood can be seen in the floor of the naos. The statue, completed in 438 B.C., stood some 12m/39ft high; the face and hands were of ivory, the garments of gold (weighing, we are told, over a ton). The statue was later taken to Constantinople and was destroyed there. Marks in the floor show that a two-tier Doric colonnade ran along the sides and to the rear of the statue – an entirely new conception of the interior of a temple. It has been supposed that the broader ground-plan of the Parthenon, with eight instead of six columns along the ends, was necessary to accommodate this arrangement: the earliest example of a temple in which the overall plan was determined by the form of the interior.

No less celebrated than the statue of Athena was the sculpture on the exterior of the Parthenon – the east and west pediments, the Doric metopes and the Ionic frieze along the top of the naos wall. Some of the sculpture is in the Acropolis Museum and some in the Louvre, but most of it is in the British Museum (the "Elgin marbles", taken to London by Lord Elgin in 1801).

The pediments, completed in 432 B.C., depicted the birth of Athena from the head of Zeus (east pediment) and the contest between Athena and Poseidon for the possession of Attica (west pediment). In the east pediment are copies of the figure of Zeus and the heads of the Sun god's and Moon goddess's horses at each end, in the west pediment King Kekrops and one of his daughters (original). The 92 metopes depicted a gigantomachia (battle of giants: east end), a fight with Centaurs (south side: the best preserved), fighting with Persians (or Amazons: west end) and the Trojan War (north side).

The frieze along the outer wall of the naos is 1m/40in high and 160m/525ft long. It depicts not a mythical or historical theme but a great occasion in the life of Athens in the classical period, the Panathenaic procession which took place every four years, making its way from the Gymnasion through the Dipylon and over the Agora to the Acropolis. The procession begins at the south-west corner of the naos and runs along the west end, where the slabs are still in situ, and the north side to the east end, where it met the other half of the procession along the south side.

Temple of Rome and Augustus

Outside the east end of the Parthenon is the little temple of Rome and Augustus, dating from the early Imperial period, the decorative forms of which were modelled on the Erechtheion. To the north of the temple, on the highest point of the Acropolis, are cuttings in the rock which mark the position of the temple of Zeus Polieus. A short distance east is the Belvedere, from which there are extensive views of the city.

★★ Erechtheion

The Erechtheion (restoration work in progress), on the north side of the Acropolis, was built between 421 and 406 B.C. It has a complex ground-plan, since it had to be accommodated to a number of earlier shrines on the site. At the east end was the temple which housed the old wooden cult image of Athena Polias, patroness of Athens; at the west end were the tomb of Erechtheus, the tomb of Kekrops – below the Caryatid porch which projects on the east side, its entablature borne by six figures of maidens (copies: originals in Acropolis Museum) – and, in the floor of the north porch, the marks left by Poseidon's trident. On the naos wall, above a band of elegant palmette ornament, is a frieze of grey Eleusinian marble on which white marble figures were applied.
Immediately south of the Erechtheion can be seen the foundations of the Old Temple of Athena (6th c.), which was destroyed in 480, and two column bases, protected by gratings, from the megaron of the Mycenaean palace.

Pandroseion

To the west of the Erechtheion is an olive-tree, commemorating the first olive-tree planted by Athena. In this area was the Pandroseion, the temple of the dew goddess Pandrosos. To the north-west can be seen the remains of the House of the Arrhephoroi, in which during the four years between Panathenaic festivals four girls between the ages

The Erechtheion

of seven and eleven lived as temple servants and assistants to the priestess of Athena. It was one of their tasks to make the peplos (robe) in which the image of the goddess was arrayed for the festival. From the courtyard beside the House of the Arrhephoroi a staircase leads down through an opening in the Acropolis walls to a sanctuary of Eros and Aphrodite, from which the arrhephoroi brought up certain secret objects (hence their name: "bearers of that which must not be spoken of"). Farther west, built against the north wall of the Acropolis, are the remains of a building which is presumed to have been the dwelling of the priestess of Athena.

★★Acropolis Museum

The Acropolis Museum, built between 1949 and 1953 and inconspicuously sited low down at the south-east corner of the Acropolis, contains one of the world's finest collections of Greek sculpture.

The east end of the museum (to the left) contains material dating from the Archaic period (6th c.) recovered from the rubble left by the Persian destruction: pediments of temples and treasuries, votive statues and – extending into the west end – figures from the marble pediment of the Old Temple (Rooms I–IV). The other rooms to the west (VI–IX) are mainly devoted to sculpture of the classical period (5th c.). The vestibule is dominated by a large owl, the emblem of Athena (No. 1347; beginning of 5th c.), and also contains a marble statue of Athena from the Propylaia (No. 1336; end of 5th c.), a marble base with a relief of a dancing soldier (No. 1338; 4th c.) and a marble funerary lekythos (No. 6407; end of 4th c.). We now turn into Room I, which contains material of the early 6th century. To the left is a pediment of painted poros limestone (No. 1; *c.* 600 B.C.) depicting Herakles and the Hydra,

Forequarters of a horse (c. *485* B.C.)

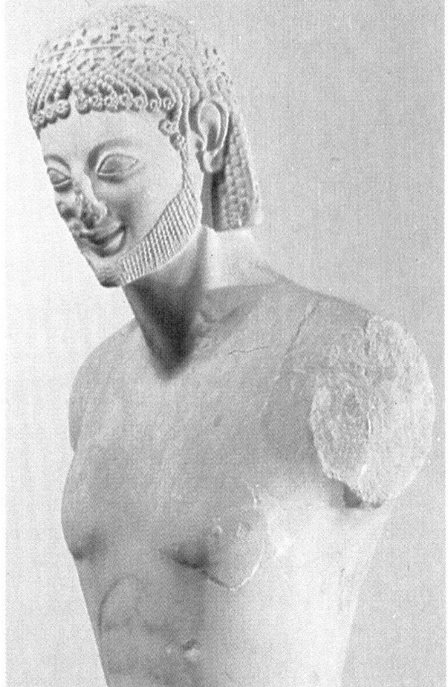

The Rampin Horseman (c. *550* B.C.)

the charioteer Iolaos and the crab which bit Herakles's foot. Opposite the entrance doorway is a lioness rending a young bull, from a large pediment of poros limestone (No. 4; *c.* 490). To the right is a Gorgon (No. 701; early 6th c.).

Room II contains the two halves of the "Red Pediment", the right-hand half with the introduction of Herakles into Olympus (No. 9+55; *c.* 580), the left-hand half with the fight between Herakles and Triton (No. 2; *c.* 560); the "Pediment of the Olive-Tree", probably depicting the story of Troilos; an interesting model of a temple, beside a figure of a female water-carrier (No. 52; *c.* 570); and two parts of a pediment of poros limestone, probably from the Hekatompedon, with Herakles and Triton to the left and a figure with three bodies, now thought to be Nereus, to the right (No. 35; 580–570). The central part of the pediment was probably the group in Room III depicting two lions rending a bull (No. 3). Also in Room II are the famous Moschophoros, the figure in Hymettian marble of a man carrying a calf, a votive offering by one Rhombos (N0. 624; *c.* 570), and the earliest of the *korai* (votive offerings to Athena which were set up in large numbers on the Acropolis). This Attic work shows the maiden holding a pomegranate in one hand and a garland in the other (No. 593; early 6th c.).

Room III, contains, in addition to the fragment of a pediment already mentioned, the torsos of two *korai,* probably from Naxos or Samos (Nos. 619 and 677; 580–550).

Room IV, a long hall, contains a whole series of master works. First there are four or five works ascribed to the same sculptor, Phaidimos. The earliest is the "Rampin Horseman" (the head is a cast: original in the Louvre), part of the oldest known equestrian group in Greece, the other horseman in the group being represented only by fragments. It has been supposed that the group depicted the sons of Peisistratos, Hippias and Hipparchos, or alternatively Castor and Pollux (No. 590; *c.* 550). The Peplos Kore, named after the Dorian peplos she wears, is a mature work by the same sculptor (No. 679; *c.* 530). A lion-head spout from the Old Temple of Athena (No. 61l; *c.* 525) and a hound from the Brauronion (No. 143; *c.* 520) are also attributed to Phaidimos. Another equestrian statue of a figure wearing Persian or Scythian dress probably represents Miltiades (No. 606; *c.* 520).

The central features of the rear part of Room IV are the *korai,* figures of girls wearing a peplos and in the later examples a more richly decorated chiton, over which they usually wear a cloak (himation). As a rule one hand gathers up the peplos, while the other holds an offering. The figures, usually larger than life-size, stood in the open air, and many of them show evidence of the crescent-shaped iron cover which was let into their head to protect them from bird droppings. They were originally painted, and some traces of colouring can still be seen, particularly on their garments.

We first note a kore with a serious expression, in Ionian costume (No. 673; 520–510), an elegant kore from Chios with a beautifully draped painted chiton (No. 675; *c.* 510) and a magnificent head of a kore (No. 643; *c.* 510). Then, in a large semicircle, come (from left to right) a large kore from Chios (No. 682; *c.* 520), a finely modelled kore, probably from the Peloponnese (No. 684; *c.* 490), the enigmatic "Kore with the Sphinx's Eyes" (No. 674; *c.* 500) and a kore clad only in a chiton (No. 670; *c.* 510). A large seated figure of Athena in the middle of the group, a work by Endoios, is followed by the clothed figure of a youth (No. 633; late 6th c.), the "Severe Kore", the only one not gathering up her garment (No. 685; *c.* 500), a kore from the Ionian Islands, preserved almost intact (No. 680; *c.* 520) and a large kore which has also survived almost undamaged (No. 671; *c.* 520).

In Room V are the 2m/6½ft high Kore of Antenor, with a base bearing the names of the donor, Nearchos, and the sculptor, Antenor (Nos. 681

and 681A; *c.* 525), and figures from the pediment of Peisistratos's Old Temple representing Athena in a battle with giants (No. 631; *c.* 525). In the alcove to the left is a collection of fine pottery ranging in date from the Geometric to the late Classical period.

Room VI brings us to the early 5th century B.C., with the beginnings of classical art, the earliest examples of which date from before the fateful year 480, the year of the Persian conquest. It includes also works in the Severe style. Of particular interest are the "Sulky Kore", dedicated by Euthydikos (Nos. 696 and 609; *c.* 490), the "Kore of the Propylaia", set up shortly before the Persian attack (No. 688; *c.* 480), a figure of Athena (No. 140; 480–470), the relief of a potter (No. 1332; *c.* 500), the head of a youth from the workshop of Pheidias (No. 699; 450–440) and the forequarters of a horse (No. 697; a noble work of 490–480). Celebrated works of the early classical period are the "Fair-Haired Youth", a figure of unusual melancholy beauty (No. 689; shortly before 480), a relief of "Mourning Athena" (No. 695; 460–450) and the oldest of the group, the "Critian Boy", ascribed to Kritios or his workshop (No. 698; 485). The torso and the head of this figure were found separately in 1865 and 1888. It is the earliest statue known to us in which the Archaic posture, with each leg bearing an equal weight, gives place to the classical pose with one leg bearing the weight and the other free. In this respect Kritios was a forerunner of the art of the classical period.

The following rooms are devoted to the buildings of the classical period on the Acropolis. Room VII contains plaster reproductions of the Parthenon pediments, a metope from the south side (Centaurs fighting a Lapith: No. 705), a torso of Poseidon from the west pediment (No. 885) and two horses' heads from Poseidon's team (Nos. 882 and 884), all from the Parthenon.

Room VIII contains large sections of the Parthenon frieze (1m/40in high, 160m/525ft long) depicting the Panathenaic procession and giving a vivid impression of life in Athens in the Periclean period. The north frieze shows horsemen, *epibatai* (who jump on and off moving chariots), marshals, musicians, youths carrying hydrias, and sacrificial animals; the last slab (No. 857) is undoubtedly the work of Pheidias himself. From the south frieze there are figures of horsemen; from the east frieze Poseidon, Apollo and Artemis, probably by Alkamenes, a pupil of Pheidias.

On the projecting wall which divides the room into two are parts of the Erechtheion frieze, carved some decades after the Parthenon frieze, between 409 and 405 B.C. The reconstruction shows the technique used, the figures in light-coloured Pentelic marble being attached to the background of darker Eleusinian marble with metal pegs. The significance of the figures is unclear.

Finally there are a series of slabs from the parapet round the temple of Nike, which are dated to around 410 B.C. They show Athena enthroned on a rock (No. 989) with a series of goddesses of victory, including the famous "Nike loosing her sandal" (No. 973).

Room IX contains a large mask of a deity (No. 6461), a bas-relief of an Attic trireme (No. 1339) and an idealised portrait of the young Alexander (No. 1331), probably carved by Leochares or Euphranor after Alexander's visit to Athens about 335 B.C.

The Areopagos and the Slopes of the Acropolis

Areopagos

The Acropolis rock was circled in ancient times by a footpath, known from inscriptions to have been called the Peripatos, which can still be followed for much of the way. If we turn right at the foot of the road

The Areopagos, the supreme court of ancient Athens

running down from the Acropolis we come, before reaching the path along the north side, to the Areopagos (Areios pagos, the Hill of Ares), with rock-cut steps leading to the top. This rocky hill, 115m/377ft high, was the seat of the supreme court of ancient Athens. Here in Mycenaean times, as Aeschylus relates in his "Eumenides", Orestes was called to account for the murder of his mother Klytaimnestra. The goddess Athena herself secured his acquittal, whereupon the Erinnyes or Furies who had been relentlessly pursuing him – and who had a cave sanctuary on the Areopagos – turned into the Eumenides or "Kindly Ones". The occasion was commemorated by an altar dedicated to Athena Areia by Orestes, to which Pausanias refers. Of this and other buildings on the site nothing now remains.

Chapter 17 of the Acts of the Apostles records the address which the Apostle Paul gave to the "men of Athens" on this ancient site on "Mars' Hill" in the year 60, referring to Christ as the "unknown god" to whom one of the many altars on the hill was dedicated. A modern bronze tablet (to the right of the steps up the hill) is inscribed with this text, and on the northern slopes of the Areopagos are the remains of a basilica dedicated to Dionysios, a member of the Areopagos, who was Paul's first convert in Athens.

Chamber tombs

The remains on the lower slopes of the Areopagos are more easily visible than those on the hill itself. On the north side are Mycenaean chamber tombs with an 11m/36ft long entrance passage (dromos), no doubt the graves of kings who resided on the Acropolis, and to the south-west, at the foot of the hill, a residential quarter (seen from Apóstolou Pávlou Street) has been excavated. At a street corner can be seen the trapezoid Amyneion, the shrine of an ancient local healing god, Amynos.

★ View of Agora

Although the smoothness of the rock does not make for easy walking, it is well worth while climbing the Areopagos for its magnificent view of the Propylaia and the excellent general view which it affords of the Agora. This view of the Agora can also be enjoyed from the modern path which runs east, roughly on the line of the ancient Peripatos. On the right of this path can be seen, on the northern slope of the Acropolis, the masonry of the Klepsydra, the spring which supplied the Acropolis with water from the most ancient times. Above it are two prominent caves, the Cave of Apollo Pythios (below the Pinakotheke) and to the left of this the Cave of Pan. The old shepherd god Pan was particularly honoured in Athens after the Persian wars, since the Athenian victory at Marathon in 490 B.C. was believed to be due to his help. Farther along, below the House of the Arrhephoroi, is the Cave of Aglauros.

The remains on the south side of the Acropolis are more abundant and more important, extending from prehistoric times to the 2nd century A.D., and indeed into the Christian period.

In the 6th century B.C. Peisistratos transferred the cult of Dionysos from Eleutherai in the Kithairon Hills (on the road to Thebes) to Athens, where accordingly the god was known as Dionysios Eleuthereus, and a temple was built to house the old cult image from Eleutherai.

★Theatre of Dionysos

In association with the cult of Dionysos – the god of drunkenness, of transformation, of ecstasy and the mask – the Theatre of Dionysos was built in a natural hollow on the slopes of the Acropolis. Nine building phases have been distinguished by Travlos, the first two dating from the 6th and 5th centuries B.C. The theatre and the temple precinct were separated about 420 B.C. when a stoa facing south was built, involving the transfer of the temple to another site. The breccia foundations of this later temple, for which Alkamenes made a chryselephantine cult image, can be seen to the south of the remains of the stoa. About 330 B.C. the theatre's present stone tiers of seating were built; they rise up to directly below the rock of the Acropolis, where there is a cave formerly dedicated to Dionysos and now occupied by the chapel of the Panayía Spiliótissa (Our Lady of the Cave). Above the entrance was a tripod, part of a choregic monument erected by one Thrasyllos in 320–319 B.C.; the two columns still visible are tripod bases of the Roman period. The 67 tiers of seating, which could accommodate some 17,000 spectators, are divided into three sections by transverse gangways, and the lowest section is divided vertically into thirteen wedges separated by staircases. In the front row are seats of honour inscribed with the names of the occupants, and in the centre is the seat reserved for the priest of Dionysos Eleuthereus, decorated with reliefs and with post-holes in the ground pointing to the existence of a canopy. Behind the priest's seat is a seat of honour for the Emperor Hadrian. The orchestra is paved with marble slabs and is surrounded by a marble barrier to provide protection from the wild beasts which took part in shows during the Roman period. The stage buildings, to the south, were several times rebuilt. Here there are striking reliefs of Dionysiac scenes, which according to a recent theory were re-used in an orator's tribune (*bema*) of the 5th century A.D.

The importance of the Theatre of Dionysos – of which there is a fine general view from the south wall of the Acropolis – is that it was built at a time when tragedy was being introduced, and indeed created, in Athens. The first drama was performed in 534 B.C., probably in the Agora, by Thespis, who travelled about Greece with his company in a wagon. This early form, in which a single actor performed with a chorus, was the beginning of a development which led in the 5th century – the period of pride and confidence after the Persian wars – to the brilliant flowering of Greek tragedy. The works of the three great Attic tragedians were first performed in the Theatre of Dionysos in celebration of the Dionysiac cult; and here Aeschylus – who had fought as a hoplite at Marathon and made a point of having this recorded on his tombstone – Sophocles and Euripides appeared in person. Thus the Theatre of Dionysos became the cradle of the European theatre.

East of the theatre stood the square Odeion, built at the expense of Perikles.

Stoa of Eumenes

Adjoining the Theatre of Dionysos on the west is the 163m/535ft long Stoa of Eumenes, built by King Eumenes II of Pergamon (197–159 B.C.), who not only erected magnificent buildings in his own city (Great Altar of Pergamon) but sought to do honour to Athens by the erection of this stoa. His example was followed by his brother and successor Attalos II (159–138 B.C.), who built the Stoa of Attalos in the Agora, probably employing the same architect as his brother.

The Stoa of Eumenes differed from the Stoa of Attalos in having no rooms behind the double-aisled colonnade. It was thus not designed for the purposes of business but was merely a spacious promenade for visitors to the temple and theatre of Dionysos. It was two-storeyed, with Doric columns on the exterior, Ionic columns on the ground floor of the interior and columns of Pergamene type on the upper floor. Since the stoa was built against the slope of the hill, it was protected by a retaining wall supported by pillars and round-headed arches; the arcades, originally faced with marble, can still be seen.

Monument of Nikias

In front of the east end of the Stoa of Eumenes are the foundations of a choregic monument erected by Nikias in 320 B.C. Stones from this monument were used in building the Beulé Gate after the Herulian raid in A.D. 267.

★Odeion of Herodes Atticus

Immediately west of the Stoa of Eumenes is the Odeion of Herodes Atticus, built by the great art patron of that name (A.D. 101–177), a native of Marathon, after the death of his wife Regilla in 161. Its proximity to the Theatre of Dionysos provides a convenient demonstration of the difference between the Greek and the Roman theatre. The Greek theatre fitted its auditorium into a natural hollow, and the rows of seating extended round rather more than a semicircle. The orchestra was originally exactly circular, with the low stage structure (*skene*) on one side. Between the auditorium and the stage were open passages (*parodoi*) for the entrance of the choir.

The principles of Roman theatre construction were quite different. The auditorium (*cavea*) was exactly semicircular, the side entrances were vaulted over and the stage, which in the later period was raised, was backed by an elaborate stage wall (*scenae frons*) of several tiers, lavishly decked with columns and statues, which rose to the same height as the top rows of seating or the enclosure wall of the auditorium. The auditorium and the stage thus formed an architectural unity, and the theatre became a totally enclosed space. The theatre was open to the sky, but an odeion (odeum), intended for musical performances, would be roofed. The 32 steeply raked rows of seating in the Odeion of Herodes Atticus could accommodate 5000 spectators, and were faced with marble (recently restored). The structure, which was incorporated in the defences of the medieval castle, is in such an excellent state of preservation that it is used during the Athens Festival every summer for dramatic performances and concerts by leading European artistes.

Asklepieion

Between the Odeion of Herodes Atticus and the Stoa of Eumenes is a path leading up to the terrace above the stoa, on which are the remains of the Asklepieion, the shrine of the healing god Asklepios. This was established here, beside a sacred spring, in 420 B.C., when the cult of Asklepios was brought to Athens from Epidauros. Within the rectangular precinct, just below the Acropolis rock, here hewn into a vertical face, is a stoa 50m/165ft long, originally two-storeyed, which was built in the 4th century B.C. to accommodate the sick who came here to seek cure. Associated with it is a cave containing the sacred spring. The spring is still credited with healing powers, and accordingly the cave is now used as a chapel.

Parallel to this stoa another similar building, of which some remains are still to be seen, was erected in Roman times along the south side of the sacred precinct. Both of these buildings faced inwards towards the centre of the precinct, in which stood the temple. This was oriented to the east and had four columns along the front (prostyle/tetrastyle). The foundations of the temple and the altar which stood in front of it can still be distinguished. In early Christian times a basilica was built over the remains of the temple and the altar, and some architectural fragments bearing Christian crosses can be seen lying about the site.

At the north-west corner of the sacred precinct is a *bothros,* a round pit for offerings, which was originally surrounded by columns bearing a canopy. To the west of this are the foundations of another stoa and a small temple lying at an angle to the other buildings – perhaps the first temple of Asklepios, dating from the late 5th century B.C.

Farther along the path, which leads to the entrance to the Acropolis, can be seen traces of the prehistoric settlement which lay on the southern slopes of the Acropolis.

The Agora

To the north of the Acropolis lay a number of large open squares: the Agora, the Roman Market and the Library of Hadrian.

A good general view of the Agora, the market square of ancient Athens, can be had from the north wall of the Acropolis, the Areopagos hill, the path which runs east from the Areopagos along the northern slopes of the Acropolis, or the path along the foot of the Acropolis. It is also a help towards understanding the site to study the layout plan displayed at the north entrance, reached by way of Hermes Street (Ermoú) or Hadrian Street (Adrianoú).

★ Agora

The Agora was excavated and studied by American archaeologists in 1931–41 and 1946–60 after the demolition of a whole district of the city which had grown up on the site, and the remains now lie within an attractive park. In recent years further excavations have been carried out north of the Piraeus railway line, which previously marked the boundary of the excavation site, and to the east of the Agora, where, under a modern road, excavation has revealed the ancient road linking the Agora with the Roman Market, together with the buildings flanking the road.

From the Mycenaean period until the end of the 7th century B.C. this was a cemetery area. It began to be used as an agora (market place) in

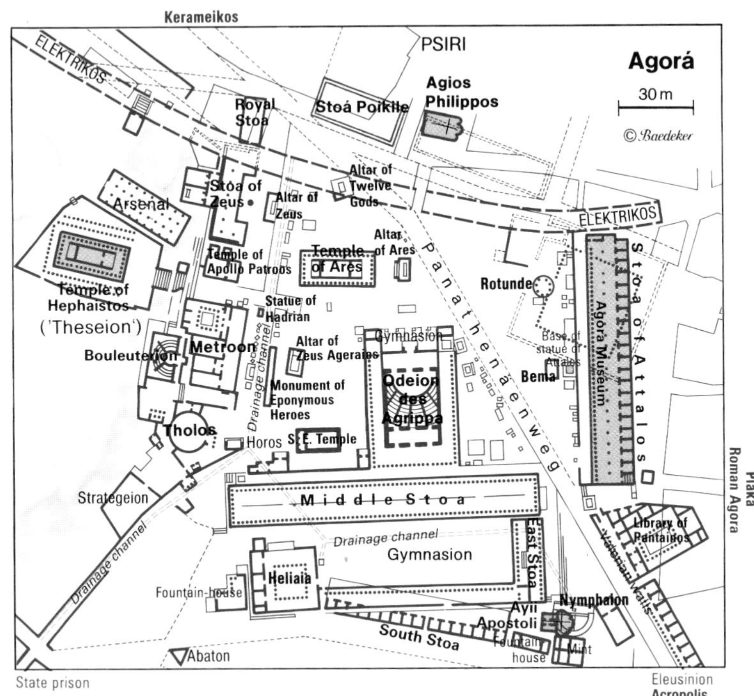

the early 6th century, in the time of Solon, and the first buildings were erected at the west end of the site, below the Agora hill. Thereafter it remained for many centuries the centre of the city's public life, each century erecting new buildings, frequently at the expense of earlier ones.

To the time of Peisistratos (*c.* 600–528) belong the Altar of the Twelve Gods, the Tyrant's House at the south-west corner and the Enneakrounos fountain at the south-east corner. After the reforms of Kleisthenes (508 B.C.) there was much new building – the courthouse of the Heliaia (on the site of an earlier Solonic building), the large drainage channel on the west side of the site, the old Bouleuterion for the Council of 400 and the Metroon, a small temple dedicated to the Mothers. After the destruction by the Persians (480–479 B.C.), the time of Kimon, the circular Tholos was built. Other buildings erected in the course of the 5th century included the Temple of Hephaistos, the Stoa of Zeus and the South Stoa. The temples of Apollo Patroos, Zeus Phratrios and Athena Phratria were built in the period after 350 B.C. The 2nd century B.C. contributed large stoas on the south side of the Agora, the Stoa of Attalos and a new Metroon. Sulla's campaign in 86 B.C. caused much destruction in the Agora. Later, around 20 B.C., the open area in the centre of the Agora was built up for the first time, with the erection of the Odeion of Agrippa and, near this, a new temple of Ares. The 2nd century A.D. saw the erection of the Library of Pantainos. In the following century, however, the Herulian invasion (267) brought a further catastrophe, and thereafter the Stoa of Attalos was incorporated in the Late Roman walls which enclosed the reduced area of the city. For more than a hundred years the Agora, lying outside the walls, lay empty and abandoned; then, about 400, there was a fresh burst of building activity. The Tholos was restored, a Gymnasion was built to house the University of Athens and the temple of Hephaistos became a Christian church. This was the last phase in the history of the Agora: by about 550 it was abandoned, and it was not reoccupied until the 11th century, when it began to develop into the populous quarter which was pulled down to allow the 20th century excavations to proceed.

Panathenaic Way

From the north entrance there is a general view of the spacious rectangular area of the Agora, bounded on the east (left) by the Stoa of Attalos and on the west by the Agora hill, with the well preserved temple of Hephaistos. The Panathenaic Way, still retaining some of its original paving, cuts diagonally across the area. This was the route followed by the Panathenaic procession on its way from Kerameikos to the Acropolis.

Stoa of Attalos

Turning left, we come to the Stoa of Attalos, in front of which are the remains of a small building and a circular fountain-house (at the north end) and of an orator's tribune (*bema*) and the base for a statue of Attalos (half way along). The stoa, 116m/381ft long, was built by King Attalos II of Pergamon (159–138 B.C.), brother and successor of Eumenes II, who built the Stoa of Eumenes on the south side of the Acropolis. It was (and is, since the faithful reconstruction of the Original building in 1953–56) two-storeyed, with Doric columns fronting the lower floor and Ionic columns on the upper floor. The stoa proper, which is backed by a series of rooms (originally 21) to the rear, is

Athens, from the Stoa of Attalos to Lykabettos

divided by Ionic columns into two aisles. The reconstruction has restored the impressive spatial effect of the long pillared hall.
The object of the rebuilding was to provide an appropriate home for the Agora Museum.

★ Agora Museum

The display of sculpture in the portico begins at the south end with a colossal statue of Apollo Patroos (S2154; 4th c. B.C.), which Pausanias ascribed to the sculptor Euphranor. Then follow two statues (opposite the 2nd column) representing the "Iliad" and the "Odyssey" (S2038 and 2039; early 2nd c. A.D.); a priestess (opposite the 4th column; S1016, 4th c. B.C.), flanked by two herms, the one on the right bearing a child (S33 and S198; Roman); a marble stele inscribed with a law against tyranny and a relief depicting Democracy crowning the people of Athens (at the 5th column; I6524, 336 B.C.); sculpture from the temple of Hephaistos (opposite the 11th column); and acroteria from the Stoa of Zeus (S312 and S373; *c.* 410 B.C.).
To the rear of the portico, at the south end, are four small rooms containing two Ionic columns from an unknown building of the 5th century B.C., a shop and a collection of wine amphoras.
The long main hall displays in chronological order a large collection of material, most of which is notable not so much for its artistic quality as for the evidence it gives of life in ancient Athens. The collection begins with the Neolithic period (3rd millennium B.C.). The Mycenaean period (1500–1100 B.C.) is represented by vases and grave goods, including two ivory caskets carved with griffins and nautiluses (Case 5, BI 511 and 513). From the early Iron Age (11th–8th c. B.C.) date 9th century tombs with their grave goods, and also Proto-Geometric and Geometric vases (Cases 11, 17 and 18). Then come vases in Orientalising style, a mould for casting a bronze statue dating from the Archaic period (6th c.) and a beautiful 6th century terracotta figure of a kneeling boy (P1231). There are numerous items illustrating the everyday life of the classical period (5th c.) – inscriptions, a machine for the selection of public officials by lot (I3967), sherds used in the process of ostracism (including one with the name of Themistokles: Case 38), a terracotta child's commode, domestic utensils, etc. On either side of the exit are Cases 61 (finds from a well, ranging in date from the 1st to the 10th century A.D. and 63 (material of the Byzantine and Turkish periods).

Library of Pantainos

Proceeding south-east from the Stoa of Attalos along the Panathenaic Way, we see on the left the Library of Pantainos (2nd c. A.D.). In front of it are remains of the Late Roman town walls (after A.D. 267), with many re-used fragments from earlier buildings. Outside the Agora enclosure, on the left of the ancient road, are remains of the sanctuary of the divinities of Eleusis.

Church of the Holy Apostles

Turning right at this point, we come to the church of the Holy Apostles, the only surviving church in this quarter. The church, built in the 11th century over a semicircular nymphaeum, was subsequently much altered by has now been restored to its original state. Dome borne on four columns; semicircular apse and transepts; good frescoes in the interior. In the narthex are wall paintings (*c.* 1700) from the nearby church of St Spyridon, demolished in 1939. Immediately south of the church there once stood the Athenian mint and the Enneakrounos fountain.

South Stoa II

To the west of the church are the remains of South Stoa II, the Middle Stoa, running parallel to it on the north, and the East Stoa, linking the two (all 2nd c. B.C.). Adjoining the west end of the South Stoa is the square building of the Heliaia (5th c. B.C.), on the north side of which was a water clock of about 350 B.C.

Odeion of Agrippa

A large and well preserved Corinthian capital marks the position of the Odeion of Agrippa, lying north of the Middle Stoa in the centre of the Agora. Built about 20 B.C. by the Roman general Agrippa, it was a square building with a stage and eighteen rows of seats which could accommodate an audience of 1000 (some remains preserved). In the 2nd century A.D. a new entrance was constructed on the north side, with three tritons and three giants supporting the roof of the portico; three of these figures are still erect. After the destruction of the original building by the Herulians in A.D. 267 the site was used about 400 for the erection of a Gymnasion to house the University of Athens, which was closed down by the Emperor Justinian in 529; the foundations of this building can still be seen.
Going west from here, we see on a lower level a boundary stone (*horos*) dating from about 500 B.C., and after crossing the large drainage canal come to the buildings on the west side of the site.

Metroon
Bouleuterion

The first of these is the circular Tholos (diameter 18.3m/60ft), which once housed the sacred hearth and was the meeting-place of the 50 *prytaneis*, the city councillors (*c.* 465 B.C.). To the north of this is the Metroon (temple of the Mothers), with the Bouleuterion (5th c. B.C.) to its rear. In the 2nd century B.C. a colonnade was built in front of the vestibule of the Bouleuterion and the Metroon in order to unify the side facing the Agora. The present floor surface of the Metroon belongs to a Christian church installed in the ancient building in the 5th century A.D.

Temple of Apollo Patroos
Stoa of Zeus

The next building – also surviving only in the form of foundations – is the temple of Apollo Patroos (4th c. B.C.), the cult image from which is now in the Stoa of Attalos. In an annexe to the temple the earliest register of the population of Athens was kept. Immediately beyond the temple, extending to the Piraeus railway line (the construction of which destroyed its north end), is the Stoa of Zeus Eleutherios (Bringer of Freedom). The stoa, originally 46.55m/153ft long, with projecting wings at each end, was built about 430 B.C., probably by Mnesikles, the architect of the Propylaia. In front of it, on a round base, stood a statue of Zeus Eleutherios. During the Roman period a square annexe was built on to the rear of the stoa, perhaps for the purposes of the Imperial cult. Pausanius tells us that the Stoa of Zeus contained pictures, including representations of the Twelve Gods, Theseus and the battle of Mantineia.
It used to be thought that the Stoa of Zeus was the same as the Royal Stoa (Stoa Basilike), but this has now been identified in the excavation area beyond the Piraeus railway line. There too were found the west end and part of the superstructure of the Stoa Poikile (Painted Stoa), built in the first half of the 5th century B.C., which was famed for its pictures by Polygnotos of Thasos, Mikon of Athens and other painters. The Royal Stoa, like the Stoa of Zeus, had projecting wings at the ends, but was considerably smaller (18m/59ft by 6.2m/20ft). This was the seat of the Archon Basileus, the official who took over the cultic functions of the kings. Among these functions was the trial of offenders accused of impiety (*asebeia*), and accordingly this stoa may have been the scene of Socrates' trial in 399 B.C., when he was condemned to death by drinking hemlock, after defending himself against charges of impiety and the corruption of youth in the "Apology" recorded by his pupil Plato.
Two other dialogues by Plato, the "Crito" and the "Phaedo", are set in the prison in which Socrates spent his last days in the company of his pupils. The Prison, which had traditionally but erroneously been located on the Hill of the Muses, has now been identified by an American archaeologist, E. Vanderpool, in a building 100m/110yds

south-west of the Tholos along the main drainage channel. The building, dated to the middle of the 5th century B.C., measured 37.5m/123ft by 16.5m/54ft and had an open passage down the middle, flanked by cells and a bath-house. The entrance was at the north end, and at the south end was a courtyard. The first two rooms on the right-hand side communicate with one another and thus match Plato's description. Among the finds were thirteen vessels only 4cm/1½ in high – just large enough to contain a fatal dose of hemlock – and a statuette of Socrates.

In front of the buildings along the west side of the Agora are numerous monuments – a long base which once supported statues of the eponymous heroes of the ten Athenian tribes (second half of 4th c. B.C.); the altar of Zeus Agoraios; farther north a statue of the Emperor Hadrian (2nd c. A.D.); the temple of Ares, a large rectangular structure originally built about 440 B.C. on another site and moved here in the Augustan period; and finally, close to the railway line, one corner of the altar of the Twelve Gods (6th c. B.C.).

From the Tholos an attractive path leads up the Agora hill (Kolonos Agoraios) to the Hephaisteion, the temple of Hephaistos. The erroneous name of Theseion still stubbornly persists (and is perpetuated by the name of the nearby station on the Piraeus line); but the actual situation of the real Theseion, in which the remains of the Attic hero Theseus were deposited after being brought back from the island of Skyros by Kimon in 475 B.C., remains unknown.

★★ Hephaisteion

The Hephaisteion, situated near the smiths' and craftsmen's quarter of Athens, was dedicated to the divinities of the smiths and of the arts, Hephaistos and Athena. It is one of the best preserved of surviving Greek temples, thanks to the conversion into a Christian church which saved it from destruction.

This Doric temple, with the classical ground-plan of 6×13 columns, was built about the same time as the Parthenon but is considerably smaller (columns 5.71m/18ft 9 in high, Parthenon 10.43m/34ft 3 in). In general it is more austere and conservative than the Parthenon, but has certain features (e.g. Ionic friezes instead of Doric triglyphs on the façades of the pronaos and opisthodomos) which appear to be modelled on the Parthenon. The explanation is that building began, probably under the direction of Kallikrates, before 449 B.C. but was suspended to allow concentration of effort on Perikles's great building programme on the Acropolis and resumed only during the Peace of Nikias (421–415 B.C.), after Perikles's death. This late date explains the more recent aspect of the east end, with the entrance to the temple. Here the portico, the coffered ceiling of which is completely preserved, is three bays deep (compared with one and a half at the west end) and is tied in to the axis of the third column; the pronaos frieze is carried across to the north and south peristyles; and the metopes have carved decoration, while elsewhere they are plain. All these are changes which give greater emphasis to the east end, departing from the earlier principle of a balance between the two ends.

The damaged pronaos frieze depicts battle scenes, the west frieze fighting between Lapiths and Centaurs (in the centre the invulnerable Lapith being driven into the ground by Centaurs). In spite of its small size the naos had columns on three sides framing the cult images of Hephaistos and Athena by Alkamenes which were set up in the temple about 420 B.C.: again an imitation of the Parthenon. The naos walls were roughened and covered with paintings.

When the temple was converted into a Christian church dedicated to St George in the 5th century it became necessary to construct a

The Temple of Hephaistos ("Theseion"), above the Agora

chancel at the east end in place of the previous entrance. A new entrance (still preserved) was therefore broken through the west wall of the naos and the old east entrance wall was removed, along with the two columns of the pronaos, and replaced by an apse. At the same time the timber roof structure normal in Greek temples was replaced by the barrel vaulting which still survives. When King Otto entered the new capital of Greece in 1834 a solemn service was held in St George's Church. Thereafter it became a museum, and continued in that function into the present century.

Roman Market and Hadrian's Library

Roman Market

Between the Stoa of Attalos and the Library of Pantainos is the beginning of an ancient road leading to the Roman Market. While the Greek Agora grew and developed over the centuries, this later market was laid out on a unified plan within a rectangular area measuring 112m/367ft by 96m/315ft. It has two gates: at the west end a Doric gateway built between 12 B.C. and A.D. 2, and at the east end an Ionic propylon probably dating from the reign of Hadrian (2nd c. A.D.). It was surrounded by colonnades, off which opened shops and offices, and on the south side was a fountain. During the Turkish period a mosque, the Fethiye Camii, was built on the north side of the market; it now serves as an archaeological store.

Tower of the Winds

The entrance to the Roman Market is at the east end, near the Tower of the Winds. This octagonal structure, 12m/39ft high, was built about 40 B.C. and housed a water clock. It owes its present name to the carved representations of the eight wind gods below the cornice. Under these figures are sundials.

Reliefs on the Tower of the Winds

To the south is a building with the remains of arches, the function of which is unknown (offices of the market police? Caesareum?). At the entrance to this excavation area is a marble latrine with almost 70 seats (1st c. A.D.).

Hadrian's Library

Parallel to the Roman Market, only 16m/52ft away, is another complex of similar character but different functions – Hadrian's Library, founded by the Emperor of that name in A.D. 132. This consisted of a colonnaded court measuring 122m/400ft by 82m/269ft, with exedrae (semicircular recesses) in the external walls. The original entrance was at the west end, part of which, with Corinthian columns, has been preserved. The present entrance, however, is at the east end, in Aeolus Street (Eólou). The central hall in the east range of buildings, much of which is still standing, was the actual library, with recesses for the book scrolls. The rest of the building probably served similar purposes. The courtyard was laid out as a garden, with a central pool.
The columns and other architectural elements now to be seen in the courtyard came from the 5th century church of the Megáli Panayía.

Kerameikos: the Cemetery on the Eridanos

Potters' quarter

Bordering the Agora on the north-west was the potters' quarter of ancient Athens, extending west to the Academy. Known as Kerameikos (after Keramos, patron of potters), this area where the Attic potters produced their magnificent work has, appropriately, given its name to the art and craft of ceramics. After 479 B.C., when Themistokles built walls round the city following the Persian invasion, part of the area lay within the walls and part outside them.
Only part of the old Kerameikos quarter has been excavated – the area lying in the angle between Hermes and Piraeus Streets (Ermoú and

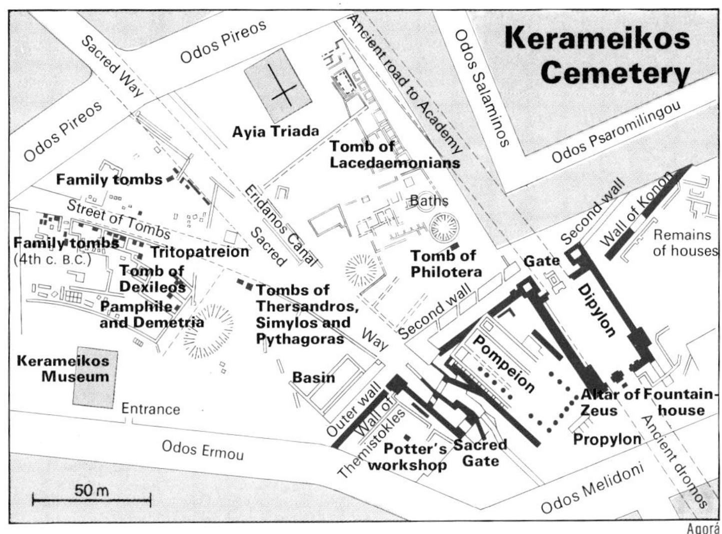

Pireos), beside the Ayía Triáda church. In this area there were two gates: the Sacred Gate by the Eridanos, through which the Sacred Way passed on its way to Eleusis, with a road to Piraeus branching off on the left within the excavated area, and the larger Dipylon (Double Gate), starting-point of the ancient road, 39m/128ft wide, which ran 1.5km/1 mile north-west to the Academy.
From the 11th century onwards this area, on both sides of the Eridanos, was used for burial, and a continuous sequence of tombs can be traced from the sub-Mycenaean period to late antiquity. The monumental funerary amphoras ("Dipylon vases") of the 8th century B.C., the starting-point from which we can follow the development of Attic art, are now in the National Archaeological Museum, and the remains now visible on the site are predominantly of the 5th and 4th centuries B.C.
Within the excavated area are many different types of tomb, either originals or reproductions – individual tombs, family burial plots or funerary precincts, terraces of tombs. This is the most thoroughly excavated of all Athenian cemeteries – by Greek archaeologists from 1863, by German archaeologists from 1907. Still little affected by mass tourism, it is quiet and full of atmosphere.

★ Kerameikos Museum

The entrance to the site is in Hermes Street (Ermoú), beside the Museum, which displays the more recent finds. Of particular interest is the large collection of pottery, which allows visitors to follow the history of the area and the development of Greek pottery. The first room contains sculpture from tombs. Immediately on the right is the stele of Ampharete, showing the dead woman with her infant grandchild (*c.* 410 B.C.), and opposite this is an equestrian relief of Dexileos, killed in a skirmish at Corinth in 394 B.C. Other items of interest are the Archaic stele of Eupheros (*c.* 500 B.C.), a sphinx as a tomb-guardian, an equestrian statue and statue bases with carved decoration (procession of horsemen, wild boar fighting a lion).

Street of Tombs

Going north from the museum on an ancient road, we pass on the left the tomb of two sisters, Demetria and Pamphile (*c.* 350 B.C.), and come to the Street of Tombs, on the road to Piraeus, flanked by tombs of the 5th and 4th (mainly 4th) centuries. Turning left (west) along this road, we pass the equestrian monument of Dexileos (original in museum), the tomb of Agathon and Sosikrates of Herakleia in Pontos (with three stelae), the tomb of Dionysios of Kollytos, topped by a fine figure of a bull, and the burial plot of Archon Lysimachides of Acharnai, built of polygonal blocks, guarded by a Molossian hound and decorated with reliefs (Charon, a funeral banquet). Behind this is a crudely constructed altar belonging to a cult precinct of Hekate.

Returning along the same road, we see on the left two interesting family burial plots – that of the family of Eubios (stele of Bion) and beyond this that of the family of Koroibos, with a funerary stele in the middle, a relief of Hegeso (*c.* 410 B.C.: cast) on the left and a *loutrophoros* (a large water jar for the bridal bath, set over the tomb of one who died unmarried) on the right. Then, in front of the small trapezoid sanctuary of the Tritopatreis (ancestor gods), with inscribed boundary stones at the north-east and south-east corners, is a large round tumulus of the mid 6th century B.C., constructed for one of the great families of that period, perhaps the family of Solon. Beyond this, on the right, are the simple tombs of ambassadors from Korkyra (*c.* 375 B.C.) and Pythagoras of Selymbria (*c.* 450 B.C.).

Sacred Way

Here the Street of Tombs meets the Sacred Way to Eleusis (see entry). Along this road to the left (away from the city) are the tombs of Antidosis and Aristomache, and beyond this the very beautiful loutrophoros of Olympichos. In the other direction, towards the city, the Sacred Way runs alongside the Eridanos to the Sacred Gate in the town walls, which were built by Themistokles in great haste in 479 B.C.,

Funerary monuments . . .

. . . in the Kerameikos quarter

using stone from numerous earlier tombs, and reinforced in the 4th century by the construction of an outer wall and a ditch. Turning left along the walls, we come to the Dipylon, which consists of two towers at the outer end, a rectangular court flanked by parallel walls and a double gateway at the inner (south-east) end. Immediately inside the gate are an altar dedicated to Zeus, Hermes and Akamas and a fountain-house.

On either side of the Dipylon, set against the town walls, are boundary stones (*horoi*) marking the width (39m/128ft) of the road to the Academy, which begins here. Along this road men who had fallen in war were buried in common graves, which were regarded with special honour. It was on one such occasion, at the beginning of the Peloponnesian War (431 B.C.), that Perikles pronounced the famous funeral oration recorded by Thucydides. One such tomb has been excavated – the state tomb of the Lacedaemonians (the Spartan officers who died in 403 B.C. fighting the Thirty Tyrants of Athens) on the south side of the road at the second boundary stone. Just at the edge of the excavated area are the remains of another tomb (anonymous). Pausanias refers to other tombs of special honour on the road to the Academy, including that of Harmodios and Aristogeiton, who killed the tyrant Hipparchos.

Pompeion

Between the walls, the Sacred Gate and the Dipylon is the Pompeion, named after the procession (*pompe*) to the Acropolis which formed up here during the Panathenaic festival. There are remains of two buildings, one overlying the other. The earlier one, dating from around 400 B.C., consisted of a court surrounded by 6×13 columns, identified as a Gymnasion. Objects used in the Panathenaic festival were found here. Wheel-ruts in the propylon show that the court was entered by wheeled vehicles. The rooms on the north side, which have preserved some remains of pebble mosaic paving, were probably the scene of the ceremonial banquet at the end of the Panathenaic festival; and it has been suggested by Hoepfner that the Panathenaic vases which were the prizes for victors in the contests may have been presented here.

This earlier building was destroyed by Sulla in 86 B.C., and much later, in the 2nd century A.D., was replaced by a three-aisled hall, which in turn was destroyed by the Herulians in 267. The plans of both buildings can be seen most clearly from outside the site in Melidoni Street (turn left along Ermoú when leaving the site and then immediately left again).

On the way out it is well worth looking at the collection of modest little funerary colonnettes (*kioniskoi*) which have been brought together in the pine-grove beside the museum. These simple monuments were erected after a sumptuary law of 317 B.C. banned the lavish tombs produced by the funerary art which had developed over the course of 400 years.

Academy

The broad road from the Dipylon led to the Academy, 1.5km/1 mile away, the meeting-place from 387 B.C. of Plato and his pupils, the first institution of its kind in the world. Excavations in Kimon Street, beyond the railway line, have yielded valuable results. Among the buildings found were a square hall (between Euclid and Tripoli Streets) and, immediately north of this, a small temple, possibly dedicated to the hero Akademos. There is also a large building laid out round an inner courtyard dating from the Imperial period. Of particular interest is a building measuring 8.5m/28ft by 4.5m/15ft (now covered by a protective roof) which dates from the early Bronze Age (2300–2100 B.C.) – the oldest building so far discovered in Athens.

Kolonos Hippios

From the site of the Academy Tripoli Street runs north-west to the Kolonos Hippios, the hill which gave its name to the deme of Kolonos, the home district of Sophocles (*c.* 496–406). This was the setting of "Oedipus on Colonos", written when Sophocles was 90. The hill now lies in a rather poor district of the city. On it are the tombs of two archaeologists, Carl Otfried Müller (1797–1840) and François Lenormant (1837–83).

The Olympieion and Surrounding Area

★ Olympieion

When Syngros Avenue (Leofóros Sýngrou), the road from Piraeus and Fáliron, was laid out in the 19th century it was aligned on two massive columns belonging to the Olympieion, which still dominates the area east of the Acropolis.

A temple to the supreme god of the Greek pantheon, who had previously been worshipped in the open air, was built on this site by Peisistratos at some time before 550 B.C. – a hundred years earlier than the temple of Zeus at Olympia. It measured 30m/100ft by 60m/200ft, rather less than the later Parthenon. Peisistratos's sons Hippias and Hipparchos resolved to replace it by a gigantic temple with a double colonnade (*dipteros*) measuring 41m/135ft by 107.75m/354ft, comparable with the temple built by Polykrates on the island of Samos (see entry). Work on this building, which was to have 8×21 columns, was suspended after the expulsion of Hippias in 510 B.C., and it lay unfinished for almost 350 years until about 175 B.C., when King Antiochos IV of Syria commissioned a Roman architect, Cossutius, to complete it. The new temple was designed to have a double colonnade of 8×20 Corinthian columns, 17m/56ft high, of Pentelic marble; but this temple too remained unfinished, and it was not completed for another 300

Temple of Olympian Zeus

years, until about A.D. 130, when Hadrian had it finished in accordance with Cossutius's plan. Its building had thus taken over 700 years.

Reflecting the tastes of the period of the tyrants, a Syrian king and a Roman emperor, this temple of Olympian Zeus was alien to the Greek sense of measure, and has always been overshadowed by the Parthenon, although its architectural qualities merit more attention than they have received. The cella, which contained a statue of Hadrian as well as the cult image of Zeus, has disappeared, as have most of the columns, to the making of which went no less than 15,500 tons of marble. The surviving remains, however – a group of thirteen columns, with part of the entablature, at the south-east corner, two isolated columns on the south side and another column which collapsed in 1852 – are still of imposing grandeur. It is not certain whether the thirteen columns on the south-east belong to the Hellenistic building and the three on the south side to the Roman one, or whether they are all of Roman date.
The entrance to the site is in Leofóros Ólgas. Near the entrance, in the old defensive ditch which surrounded Athens, are a number of column drums from the Peisistratid temple. Farther west are the remains of Roman baths and other buildings. Through the partly reconstructed propylon we enter the large rectangular precinct (*temenos*) in which the temple stands. From the south wall of the temenos we look down into an excavated area on a lower level in which, among other structures, the foundations of the temple of Apollo Delphinios and the large rectangle of the Panhellenion can be distinguished. They are among the many temples and shrines on the banks of the Ilissos, which flows through this area; others include the temple of Aphrodite in the gardens on the right bank of the stream, the Metroon and the shrine of Artemis Agrotera on the left bank. In Christian times a basilica was built here by the spring of Kallirhoe.

Arch of Hadrian

To the west of the Olympieion enclosure, beside the very busy Leofóros Amalías, stands the Arch of Hadrian (A.D. 131–132), which marked the boundary between the ancient city of Athens and the Roman extension of the city – between the "city of Theseus" and the "city of Hadrian", as an inscription on the arch records.

Monument of Lysikrates

Immediately opposite is Lysikrates Street, at the far end of which is the Monument of Lysikrates, a rotunda 6.5m/21ft high surrounded by Corinthian columns (illustration, page 72). The frieze round the top depicts scenes from the life of Dionysos (the transformation into dolphins of the pirates who captured Dionysos). The stone acanthus flower on the roof originally bore a bronze tripod and cauldron, the prize received by Lysikrates when the choir which he had financed as choregos was victorious in the tragedy competition in 334 B.C. Later incorporated in a Capuchin convent and used as a library – when it was known as the "Lantern of Diogenes" – this is the only surviving example of the numerous choregic monuments in the ancient Street of the Tripods. Other choregic monuments in Athens are the Monument of Nikias between the Theatre of Dionysos and the Stoa of Eumenes and the Monument of Thrasyllos above the Theatre of Dionysos.

★ Stadion

North-east of the Olympieion, between two low hills, is the Stadion. Although this large marble structure, with seating for 70,000 spectators, is modern, it has the same form and occupies the same site as its ancient predecessor, in which the Panathenaic games were held. It was provided with new marble seating in A.D. 140–144 by Herodes Atticus, whose tomb was on the hill to the north.

The Panathenaic Stadion, rebuilt on its original site

The Olympic Stadion

Herodes Atticus, who was born in Marathon in A.D. 101 and died there in 177, was one of the great art patrons of antiquity. He rose to high office under Hadrian and Antoninus Pius, becoming archon, chief priest, consul and tutor to future Emperors, though later he was charged with various offences in the Imperial court. He had a great reputation as a rhetor, but his writings did not outlive his own day. He was famous for his munificence, financing the Stadion and the Odeion which bears his name in Athens, the renovation of the Stadion at Delphi, the provision of a water supply and the building of a nymphaeum at Olympia and the renovation of the spring of Peirene at Corinth.

When the Stadion was rebuilt for the first Olympic Games of modern times in 1896 it was financed, as in the days of Herodes Atticus, by a wealthy private citizen, Yeoryios Averof, who thus – like other modern Greeks, particularly those who have made their money abroad – continued the ancient tradition of the *euergetes* ("benefactor").

Modern Athens

The modern city of Athens dates from the reign of King Otto I (1834–62), a scion of the Bavarian house of Wittelsbach. The plan for the conversion of a sleepy little provincial town into the new capital of Greece was the work of a number of Germans, two Danes, a Frenchman and a Greek. The general lines of the new town to be built north of the ancient city were laid down by a German, Eduard Schaubert, and his Greek friend Kleanthes in 1832–33, while the Greek government was still based in Náfplion.

Omonia Square

From Omonia Square (Platía Omonías, Square of Concord), originally conceived as the site of the royal palace, three streets fan out towards the south: Athena Street (Athínas), which runs due south to Monastiráki Square, with a vista of the Acropolis; Piraeus Street (Pireós), to the south-west; and Stadion Street (Stadíou) to the south-east, with Venizelos Street (Venizélou), also known as University Street (Panepistimíou), parallel to it.
Along the foot of the triangle formed by Athena and Stadion Streets runs Hermes Street (Ermoú), laid out by Leo von Klenze in 1834. During the construction of this street the Kapnikaréa church was preserved from demolition by the intervention of the king and his father, Ludwig I of Bavaria.

Sýntagma Square

At its east end, where it meets Stadion Street, Hermes Street meets another large square, known since the 1843 revolution as Sýntagma Square (Platía Syntágmatos, Constitution Square). On the higher side of the square, which is now surrounded by hotels, airline offices, etc., stands the former royal palace (by Friedrich von Gärtner, 1834–38), now the Parliament Building, with the Tomb of the Unknown Soldier, guarded by evzones, in front of it.

National Garden
Zappion Park

To the south and east of the Parliament Building extends the National Garden, originally the palace gardens laid out by Queen Amalia in what was then waste land. One of the city's relatively few open spaces, this is now a popular place of recreation and relaxation. Adjoining it on the south, in the direction of the Olympieion, is the Zappion Park, with the Zappion, an exhibition and congress hall designed by Ernst Ziller and built at the expense of the Zappas brothers.

Venizelos Street

A general impression of the modern city and of the efforts made in the reigns of Otto I and George I to dignify the new capital with imposing

Bird's eye view of Omonia Square

neo-classical architecture can be gained by walking along Venizelos Street (University Street) from Sýntagma Square. On the right, fronted by loggias, is the Ilíou Mélathron, built by Ernst Ziller as a residence for Heinrich Schliemann and his Greek wife Sophia. It is planned to establish a Schliemann Museum and a collection of coins in the house. Beyond this are the Byzantine-style Ophthalmic Clinic and Leo von Klenze's church of St Dionysius (Roman Catholic: King Otto did not adopt the Orthodox faith).

University

A dominant position, farther along the street, is occupied by the University (designed by the Danish architect Christian Hansen; begun 1837), flanked by two grandiose buildings by Hansen's younger brother Theophil, the Academy of Art (1859–85) on the right and the National Library (begun 1887) on the left. In front of the Academy – which after its recent restoration is a fine example of the vivid colouring of Athens's neo-classical architecture – are two columns bearing statues of Athena and Apollo, and flanking the steps leading up to the building are seated figures of Plato and Socrates. In front of the University are statues of Kapodistrias, who as Governor of Greece (1827–31) had proclaimed the establishment of the University, and the poet and scholar Adamantios Korais. King Otto, who initiated the building of the University, appears, surrounded by the Muses, in a painting above the entrance.
In the interior of the University building the staircase hall and Great Hall have preserved their original mural paintings.

The rest of Venizelos (University) Street is made up of modern shops and offices, with occasional remnants of the two-storey neo-classical buildings of the 19th century. It ends in the traffic roundabout of Omonia Square with its central pool and fountains.

The Academy

Klafthmon Square

Returning along Stadion Street, we come, half way along – just down from the University – to Klafthmon Square (Platía Kláfthmonos), at the west corner of which is the church of SS Theodore. Also in the square is the Museum of the City of Athens, the first section of which documents the reign of Otto I.

Farther along the street is the Old Parliament Building (by the French architect Boulanger, 1871), now occupied by the National Historical Museum. In front of it stands an equestrian statue of Theodóros Kolokotrónis, the great fighter for the freedom of Greece.

Lykabettos

For another walk starting from Sýntagma Square we go along Leofóros Vasílissis Sofías, to the left of the Parliament Building, and continue to the end of the National Garden. Here we can either turn right along Herodes Atticus Street (Iródou tou Attikoú), on the left of which is the former Crown Prince's Palace (by Ziller, 1890–98), later the residence of the king, or turn left to reach Kolonáki Square and from there climb Lykabettos (Lykavittós; 277m/909ft). On the top of the hill, which can also be reached by funicular from the end of Plutarch Street (Ploútarkhou) are a chapel dedicated to St George and a restaurant (views).

Monastiráki Square

Those who want to see something of the busy shops and markets of Athens should walk south from Omonia Square along Athena Street (Athínas), exploring its side streets, to Monastiráki Square, at the junction with Hermes Street (Ermoú). Here Hephaistos Street (Iféstou) goes off on the right and Pandrosos Street (Pandrósou) on the left, both lined with shops of every kind and bustling with activity. In Monastiráki Square is the Syntrivani Mosque, beyond which can be seen the pillared front of Hadrian's Library.

Pláka
(plan, p. 178)

This is the beginning of the Pláka, the old district of Athens lying between the north side of the Acropolis and Hermes Street and

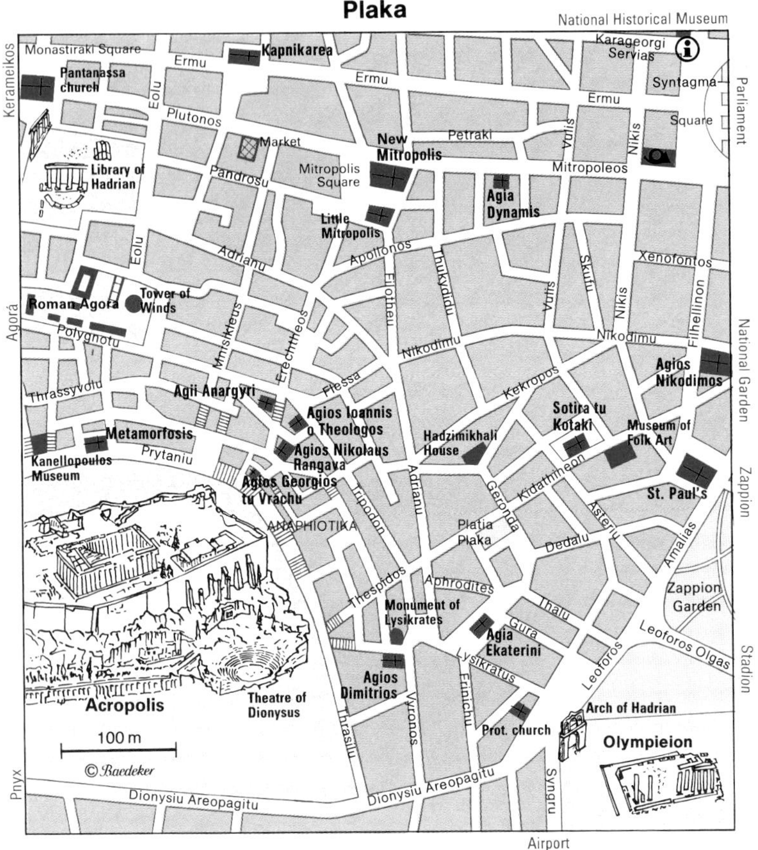

extending eastward almost to Leofóros Amalías. In its narrow streets and little squares are a number of small churches and modest houses of the neo-classical period. In Tholos Street (Tholou 5) is the house of Stamatios Kleanthes, who together with Eduard Schaubert drew up the plan for the new town of Athens. The house was occupied by Athens University before its move to the new building in University Street.

In recent years efforts have been made to stem the development of the Pláka into a noisy and garish tourist haunt, and it has begun to recover something of its old atmosphere.

The Churches of Athens

In the Christian period Athens was, politically and culturally, an unimportant provincial town within the Byzantine Empire. The buildings of this period, therefore, cannot compare with those to be seen in the capital, Constantinople, or the Empire's second largest city, Salonica. Nevertheless they are of considerable interest.

In the 5th–6th century the Parthenon was converted into the church of the Panayía Athiniótissa (remains of painting on outer wall of opisthodomos), the temple of Hephaistos became the church of St George and the church of the Megáli Panayía was built in Hadrian's Library. Finds from other buildings of this period are preserved in the Byzantine Museum. The surviving churches mostly date from the Middle Byzantine period (10th–12th c.) and are predominantly of the domed cruciform type. The ground-plan is in the form of a Greek cross, with four arms of equal length, and the church has a central dome (and sometimes smaller subsidiary domes over the arms of the cross).

St Nicodemus

Going south from Sýntagma Square along Leofóros Amalías, we see in the third street on the right the church of St Nicodemus, built in 1045, which has been a Russian Orthodox church since 1852, when the church (which had been damaged during the war of liberation) was purchased by the Tsar of Russia. The paintings in the interior, by Ludwig Thiersch, date from the subsequent restoration.
Farther along Leofóros Amalías is the neo-Gothic St Paul's Church (Anglican), designed by Kleanthes in the mid 19th century.

Sotíra Kottáki

A short distance south-west, in Kydathenaíon Street, is the 13th century church of Sotíra Kottáki, originally a domed cruciform church but later converted into a basilica. Turning left into Farmáki Street, we come to St Catherine's Church (Ayía Ekateríni), situated in a spacious palm-shaded courtyard behind the remains of a colonnade of the Roman Imperial period. Although later enlarged, the church preserves its 13th century dome and apses. Close by is the Monument of Lysikrates.

St Catherine's

Áyios Nikólaos Rangavá

Going north from here along Tripods Street (Tripódon) and then turning left into Epikhármou, we come to Áyios Nikólaos Rangavá, built in the 11th century within thc precincts of the palace of the important Rangavá family and later altered.

Áyios Ioánnis Theológos

Continuing along Tripods Street and then by way of Erotokritos Street (Erotokrítou) into Erechtheus Street (Erekhtheos), a stepped lane, we come the beautiful domed cruciform church of Áyios Ioánnis Theológos (13th c.), restored some years ago. At the top of the steps, on the right, is the entrance to a complex belonging to the monastery of the Holy Sepulchre in Jerusalem, in which is the church of the Anárgyiri, with a Baroque interior (17th c.).

Anárgyiri

St Simeon's

Higher up the hill is a settlement of immigrants from the island of Anáfi (Anafiotiká), with the little church of St Simeon (1847). To the west of this is the church of the Metamorphosis, a small domed cruciform church (14th c.), with an altar made out of an early Christian capital.

Metamorphosis

Going downhill from here past the Tower of the Winds to the east entrance of Hadrian's Library, we can see the remains of the 5th century Megáli Ekklisía (Great Church).

Megáli Ekklisía

Pantánassa

From here Pandrosos Street, to the left, leads to Monastiráki Square, in which, on a lower level, is the Pantánassa church, of basilican type. Going west from here along Hephaistos Street (Iféstou) and turning into the second little street on the left, we pass the church of St Philip and come to the entrance to the Agora, near which is the 11th century

The church of the Áyii Apostoli in the Agora

Holy Apostles
Áyii Asómati

church of the Holy Apostles. Returning to Hermes Street and going west, we come to the recently restored 11th century church of the Áyii Asómati (Incorporeal Spirits: i.e. angels).

Áyios Ioánnis Kolóna

From here Sarri Street runs north-east towards Euripides Street (Evripídou), in which is the tiny chapel of Áyios Ioánnis Kolóna, named after a Roman column which rears up above its roof; the assistance of John the Baptist is invoked here for the cure of ailments affecting the head.

Áyii Theódori

At the east end of Euripides Street is Klafthmon Square, in which stands the church of the Áyii Theódori (SS Theodore), a handsome 11th century church built of stone and brick, with a belfry.

Kapnikaréa

Going south from here by way of Márkou and Kalamióti Streets, we come back to Hermes Street, just at the Kapnikaréa church. This 11th century domed cruciform church, a very fine example of the type, was later enlarged by the addition of a porch and a chapel on the north side. The paintings cover the complete iconographic programme as developed in the Middle Byzantine period.

New Mitrópolis

Close by is Mitrópolis Square, in which are the old and the new Mitrópolis churches. The New Mitrópolis (1842–62) was designed by Schaubert, with the needs of the court and the capital in mind. In a shrine on the first pillar on the left are the remains of Patriarch Gregory V, who was hanged in Constantinople by the Turks (1821) and is honoured as a neomartyr.

★ Little Mitrópolis

The Little Mitrópolis, dedicated to the Panayía Gorgoepíkoos and Áyios Elefthérios, is a 12th century building of the greatest interest. Incorporated in the structure are a variety of ancient and medieval

Little Mitropolis

New Mitropolis

fragments of architectural ornament and sculpture, including two parts of an ancient calendar frieze (arranged in the wrong order) above the entrance, pilaster capitals, pediments from funerary aediculae, figural reliefs, etc. – all of the most charming effect.
From here we return to Sýntagma Square along Mitrópolis Street, passing on the right the tiny church of Ayía Dýnamis, carefully preserved under the corner of a large modern office block which has been built over it.

Modern cemetery

After visiting the ancient tombs of Athens some visitors may be interested in seeing a more recent cemetery, the principal cemetery of Athens. It is reached by going up Odos Anapáfseos (Street of Repose), which branches off Ardittos Street, a major traffic artery to the south of the Olympieion. Beside a chapel to the left of the entrance are the graves of archbishops of Athens, and beyond these the elaborate tomb of Yeoryios Averof, who financed the building of the Stadion. Higher up the slope is the temple-like mausoleum of Heinrich Schliemann (by Ziller), and near this the tomb of Kanaris. On the left of the main avenue which runs down to the second church is the tomb of Kolokotronis, hero of the struggle for liberation. Apart from such individual tombs this beautifully laid out cemetery is highly informative on Greek attitudes to death and burial in the 19th and early 20th centuries.

Kaisarianí Monastery

It is well worth taking a trip through the suburb of Kaisarianí to the monastery of Kaisarianí, situated in a valley on the reafforested slopes of Mt Hymettos.

The name comes from a spring close to a shrine of Aphrodite from which the Emperor Hadrian caused an aqueduct to be built to Athens (2nd c. A.D.): thereafter the spring was known as *kaisariane,* Imperial. It was (and is) credited with healing powers, particularly for women who desire to bear a child. The water of the spring still flows from an archaic ram's head in the forecourt of the monastery.

During the Turkish period the monastery was renowned for its library and for its learned abbots. Among the students of the seminary which flourished here for many years – one of the few in existence during that period – was the future Patriarch Gregory V, martyred in 1821. The last abbot died in 1855, and thereafter the monastery was abandoned and fell into decay. At last, in 1952, it was carefully restored at private expense. This restoration, combined with the reafforestation of the surrounding area, has made Kaisarianí one of the most attractive spots in the neighbourhood of Athens – an ancient monastery set amid trees, a spring of clear water and an antique column from a temple of Aphrodite set in a shady courtyard, all combining to make a haven of peace, a place for contemplation and repose.

The monastery church is of the domed cruciform type. It was erected around 1000 on the site of an earlier church, and is thus rather older than the buildings of this type in Athens itself. The dome is borne not on the walls but on four columns with Ionic capitals, giving the interior an air of lightness. A templon formed of marble screens separates the sanctuary (*bema*) from the rest of the church. The painting is much later than the church, having been done in the 16th century, during the Turkish period, probably by a monk from Athos. It is in strict accordance with the rules for the hierarchical disposition of the various themes – Christ Pantokrator in the dome, with the prophets below him and the four Evangelists in the pendentives; the Mother of God enthroned in the apse, with angels, the Communion of the Apostles and the Fathers of the Church below her; and on the barrel vaulting of the arms of the cross the various church festivals. In the porch is a fine representation of the Trinity. The porch, like the south chapel dedicated to St Antony, was added in the late 17th century, as was the bell-cote.

There are considerable remains of the conventual buildings. Entering by the main entrance, on the east, we see on the left a building which was originally a bath-house and later housed oil-presses. Beyond this, set back a little, are a two-storeyed range of cells and a tower house belonging to the Venizelos family of Athens, who were great benefactors of the monastery. In the right-hand corner are the kitchen and refectory, now housing a small museum.

On the hills outside the west gateway of the monastery (20 minutes' walk) are other remains of churches dating back to the 6th century, beside the old monks' cemetery. From here too there are wide views of Athens and the sea, with Kaisarianí lying below in its peace and seclusion.

The Museums of Athens

Acropolis Museum See page 155

Agora Museum See page 164

★Benáki Museum

The Benáki Museum, in Leofóros Vasílissis Sofías, grew out of the private collection assembled by Antonios Benakis. On its three floors it displays material illustrating the Greek struggle for independence, relics and mementoes of kings Otto I and George I, Byron and various heroes of the war of liberation, manuscripts, icons (including two attributed to El Greco), costumes from the different parts of Greece, ancient pottery and Islamic and East Asian material.

★Byzantine Museum

The Byzantine Museum, also in Leofóros Vasílissis Sofías, is housed in a palace built by Kleanthes in 1840 for the Duchesse de Plaisance, on a site which was then in open country. It contains a valuable collection of Byzantine art from Greece and Asia Minor.

In the courtyard are architectural fragments from Early Christian basilicas and Byzantine churches (5th–15th centuries) and a reproduction of a fountain depicted in a mosaic at Dafní.

The left-hand wing contains a large collection of icons, arranged partly in chronological order and partly according to iconographic types. There is a further display of icons in the right-hand wing.

The rooms on the ground floor of the main building illustrate the development of the church interior. Room 1 contains a scaled-down reproduction of an Early Christian basilica (5th–6th c.), showing the templon which separates the sanctuary (bema), with the altar and seating for priests (synthronon), from the rest of the church. The pulpit is copied from the one in Áyios Minás, Salonica. In Room 3 is a typical Middle Byzantine domed cruciform church (10th–11th c.), with a sculptured eagle on the floor, marking the omphalos (navel). Room 4 shows a post-Byzantine church with a carved and gilded iconostasis (17th–18th c.) and a bishop's throne from Asia Minor (18th c.). There are also some individual works of great interest, among them sculptured representations of the Good Shepherd (No. 92) in which the old type of the lamb-carrier, as seen in the Acropolis Museum, is applied to Christ, and Orpheus (No. 93), and also (in Room 2) some rare Byzantine reliefs.

On the upper floor large numbers of icons are displayed, including a fine 14th century mosaic icon of the Mother of God Episkepsis (No. 145), together with Gospel books, historical documents (e.g. a chrysobull of the Emperor Andronikos II dated 1301, in Room 1), gold jewellery from Lesbos (Room 2) and liturgical vestments and utensils, particularly notable among these being an epitaphios from Salonica (an embroidered cloth used in the representation of the Holy Sepulchre on Good Friday: 14th c.) in Room 4.

★Cycladic Museum

The Museum of Cycladic Art (Neofýtou Doúka 4, in the Kolonáki district) was opened in 1986. Its nucleus was the celebrated collection of Cycladic art assembled by the shipowner Nikolaos P. Goulandris. The principal treasures of the Museum, magnificently arranged and displayed, are the masterpieces of Cycladic art (3200–2000 B.C.). On the second floor is a fine and carefully selected collection of pottery, bronzes and glass ranging in date from the Geometric to the post-classical period.

Kanellópoulos Museum

The Kanellópoulos Collection was presented to the State by Pavlos and Alexandra Kanellopoulos in 1972 and opened as a museum in a neo-classical house on the upper edge of the Pláka (corner of Theorías and Pánou) in 1976. The exhibits (sculpture, pottery, icons) range in date from prehistoric times to the 19th century.

Kerameikos Museum

See page 169

Museum of Athens (King Otto Museum)

The King Otto Museum in Klafthmon Square, the first part of the Museum of Athens, was opened in 1980 in a modest house (1834) in which King Otto I and Queen Amalia lived from 1836 to 1842. On the ground floor is a model of Athens in 1842 (scale 1:1000), as well as the old kitchen. On the upper floor are the apartments occupied by the royal couple, furnished in Empire and Biedermeier style, with many mementoes.

Museum of Folk Art

The Museum of Folk Art, at Kydathinaíon 17, gives some impression of the richness, variety and distinctive characteristics of Greek folk art (embroidery, woodcarving, folk painting, etc.), the inheritor of Byzantine traditions.

★★National Archaeological Museum

The richly stocked National Archaeological Museum in Patission Street, built by Ludwig Lange in 1860 and considerably enlarged since then, is the finest collection of Greek art in the world. It would take repeated visits to get anything approaching a complete idea of its full range and richness: here we can do no more than refer to a selection of the outstanding exhibits.

Mycenaean Hall

The entrance lobby (sale of tickets, slides, books) leads straight into the Mycenaean Hall (Room 4), with material excavated by Heinrich Schliemann and others at Mycenae and other Mycenaean sites, illustrating the richness of a culture which combined the nobility and monumentality of Achaean Greek art with the refinement of Minoan Crete (1600–1150 B.C.).

The exhibits are not arranged chronologically but according to site or type. The front part of the hall is occupied by material from Mycenae itself, including the famous gold mask of a king from Shaft Grave V (253: *c.* 1580 B.C.), together with gold cups, vases, carved ivories, richly decorated daggers, boar's-tusk helmets, the "Warrior Vase" (1426: *c.* 1200 B.C.) and two half-columns from the entrance to the so-called "Treasury of Atreus".
Particularly notable items in the rear part of the room are the two famous gold cups (1758, 1759) from Vaphió, south of Sparta, which date from the 15th century B.C.

Neolithic Hall

To the left is the Neolithic Hall (Room 5), with material from the Greek mainland, including objects from Dímini (4th millennium B.C.), Sésklo (3rd millennium B.C.) and Orchomenos (3rd–2nd millennium B.C.).

Cycladic Hall

To the right is the Cycladic Hall (Room 6), with material of the 3rd and 2nd millennia B.C. Characteristic of the highly developed art of this insular culture are the Cycladic idols, the Cycladic "frying-pans", the

National Archaeological Museum

GROUND FLOOR

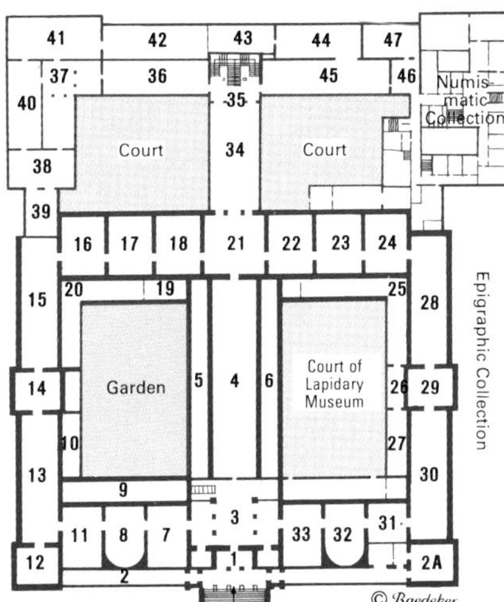

GROUND FLOOR
1 Entrance
2 North Hall
2A Display and sale of casts
3 Entrance Hall
4 Mycenaean art
5 Neolithic art
6 Cycladic art
7–12 Archaic art
13 Aristodikos Room
14, 15 First half of 5th c. B.C.
16–20 Classical period (5th c. B.C.)
21 Diadumenos and other statues
22 Sculpture from Epidavros
23, 24 Funerary stelae (4th c. B.C.)
25–27 Votive reliefs (4th c. B.C.)
28 Ephebe of Antikythira
29 Themis (3rd c. B.C.)
30 Hellenistic art
31 Temporary exhibition
32 Stathatos Collection
34 Votive reliefs
35 Stairs to upper floor
36 Karapanos Collection
37, 40 Bronzes
41–43 Greek sculpture of Hellenistic and Roman periods

Rooms not listed are not at present open to the public

UPPER FLOOR: Vase collection

Harp-Player (3908) and the flying-fish frescoes from Fylakopí on the island of Melos (5844: 16th c. B.C.).

Returning to the entrance lobby, we continue clockwise through the chronologically arranged collections, beginning with the Geometric period (9th–8th c. B.C.) and continuing through the Archaic (7th–6th c.) and Classical (5th–4th c.) to the Hellenistic (3rd–1st c.) and Roman periods.

In the centre of Room 7 is the Dipylon Vase from the Kerameikos cemetery, a monumental funerary vase in Geometric style with a representation of the lament for the dead, dating from the time of Homer (V804: *c.* 750 B.C.). On the right-hand wall is a flat relief from the island of Delos, dedicated by Nikandre (1: *c.* 650 B.C.). There are also metopes from the Archaic temple of Athena in Mycenae (2702, 2869, 2870, 4471: *c.* 620 B.C.).

Room 8 is dominated by two kouroi from Soúnion, some 3m/10ft high (2720, 3645: 626–600 B.C.). When Greek artists began to produce large sculpture around 600 B.C. they achieved monumental expression in over-lifesize figures of naked youths (*kouroi*). Characteristic of these figures are the rigidly frontal pose and the equal distribution of weight on both legs, with the left foot always in front of the right. Originally the hands were held close to the thighs, with clenched fists; later the arms hung free.
Also in this room are the head and hand of a kouros from Kerameikos (the "Dipylon Head", 3372: *c.* 600 B.C.).

Room 9 (to right) contains a winged Nike from Delos (21: *c.* 500 B.C.) and, to the right of this, a slim kouros from Melos (1558: *c.* 550 B.C.). Of particular interest is the excellently preserved kore holding a lotus

Pan and Aphrodite

Ephebe of Antikythira

flower in her left hand, with an inscription giving her name as Phrasikleia (4889). This figure was found by Mastrokostas in 1972 at Merénda, near Markópoulo (Attica), together with the kouros in Room 10, adjoining. Stylistic comparisons suggest that the figure of Phrasikleia was carved about 530 B.C. by Aristion, a sculptor from Paros working in Attica who was also responsible for the kouros from Anávyssos in Room 13 (see below). In Andrew Stewart's view the kore of Merénda and the Theseus and Antiope group from Erétria (Khalkís Museum) are also by Aristion or his school.
Also notable in Room 10 is the ephebe with a diskos from the Dipylon (*c.* 560 B.C.).

Returning to Room 8, we pass into Room 11, which contains the stele of Aristion, by Aristokles (29: *c.* 510 B.C.), and a kouros from the island of Kéa (3686: *c.* 530 B.C.). In Room 12, to the left, are a relief of a running hoplite from Athens (1959: *c.* 510 B.C.) and heads from the original east pediment of the temple of Aphaia on Aegina (*c.* 500 B.C.).

In Room 13, a long hall, are more kouroi, including a late Archaic figure with arms akimbo from the Ptoion (127: c. 510 B.C.) and the massive kouros of Anávyssos by Aristion of Paros (3851: 540–530 B.C.), with an inscription on the base: "Stop and weep at his grave for the dead Kroisos, destroyed by wrathful Ares while fighting among the warriors in the forefront of the battle."

In Room 14 we move from Archaic to classical art: relief of Aphrodite (?) from Melos (3990: 470–460 B.C.); relief of a youth with a garland (originally a metal attachment) from Soúnion (3344: *c.* 470 B.C.).

Room 15. – On the left an Eleusinian votive relief depicting Demeter giving the first ear of corn to the boy Triptolemos, with her daughter

Persephone or Kore (126: *c.* 440 B.C.). In the centre of the room is an over-lifesize bronze statue of a god found in the sea off Cape Artemision (northern Euboea). After much discussion of the god's identity (Zeus hurling a thunderbolt or Poseidon with his trident?) it is now generally agreed that he is Zeus. The figure, which is excellently preserved, lacking only the eyes and the thunderbolts, is dated to around 460 B.C. and was probably the work of Kalamis; but whoever the sculptor was it is one of the finest achievements of classical art.

Room 16 contains funerary monuments, including the large marble lekythos of Myrrhine (4485: *c.* 420 B.C.).
Room 17: a votive relief from Piraeus depicting Dionysos with actors (1500: *c.* 400 B.C.) and a head of Hera from the Argive Heraion (1571: *c.* 420 B.C.). To the right of this is the L-shaped Room 19–20, which contains a small Roman copy of Pheidias's Athena Parthenos, the Varvakion Statuette (129: 2nd–3rd c. A.D.). From here we can enter one of the Museum's four inner courtyards.
Returning to Room 17, we continue into Room 18, with the most celebrated monument from the Kerameikos cemetery, the relief of Hegeso and her maid (3624: *c.* 410 B.C.).
In Room 21 are the Diadumenos, a Roman marble copy of a lost bronze original by Polykleitos (1826: *c.* 440 B.C.), and the Hermes of Andros, a Roman copy of an original from the school of Praxiteles (218: 4th *c.* B.C.) – two works which exemplify the change from the vigorous but controlled representations of the 5th century to the spiritualised approach of the 4th. Also in this room is the lively figure of a boy rider, who has recently been mounted on a bronze horse (15177: 2nd *c.* B.C.).
Room 22: sculpture from Epidauros.
Rooms 23 and 24: funerary stelae of the 4th century B.C., including a stele from the Ilissos, perhaps by Skopas (578: *c.* 350 B.C.).
Room 25 (to right): statues and votive offerings dedicated to Amynos and Asklepios.
Room 28: the Ephebe of Antikythera, an original work in bronze (Br 13396: 340 B.C.); a figure of Hygieia, probably by Skopas (3602: *c.* 360 B.C.); a head of Asklepios from the island of Amorgós (4th c. B.C.).
Room 30: a figure of Poseidon from Melos (235: 2nd c. B.C.); bronze heads of a boxer from Olympia (Br 6439: *c.* 350 B.C.), a philosopher (Br 13400: 3rd c. B.C.) and a man from Delos (Br 14612: *c.* 100 B.C.).
Room 32 contains the Helene Stathatos collection.

From Room 21 we pass between two columns to enter the next section of the museum. Room 34 contains votive offerings to Pan and the nymphs. To the left, at the foot of the staircase leading to the upper floor, are Rooms 36 and 37, which contain the Karapanos Collection, with numerous small bronzes of the Archaic and classical periods, including a horseman from Dodona (16547: *c.* 550 B.C.), a goddess with a dove (Aphrodite or Dione) from the Pindos (460 B.C.), the well known statuette of Zeus hurling a thunderbolt from Dodona (16546: 450 B.C.), an Athena Promachos from the Acropolis (6446: *c.* 500 B.C.) and a head of Zeus from Olympia (6440: *c.* 500 B.C.). In the adjoining Room 41 are a number of large bronzes found by chance in Piraeus in 1959, including an Apollo (*c.* 510 B.C.) and an Artemis (4th c. B.C.), and the Ephebe of Marathon (*c.* 350 B.C.; probably school of Praxiteles), which was recovered from the sea in 1925.

On the upper floor are two collections which are very well worth seeing if time permits: the very comprehensive collection of vases (best seen with the aid of a guidebook by Varvara Philippaki which can be bought in the entrance lobby) and the sensational finds, including in particular wall paintings of about 1500 B.C., which have been made at Akrotíri on the island of Santorin since 1967 (and which it is planned to return to Santorin).

★National Gallery

The National Gallery, in Leofóros Vasiléos Konstantínou, contains a collection of Greek painting of the 19th and 20th centuries (Gisi, Volonkakis, Yakovidi, etc.).

National Historical Museum

The National Historical Museum, in the Old Parliament Building in Stadion Street (Stadíou), is devoted to the history of Greece in the 18th and 19th centuries. The main emphasis is on the period of the struggle for the liberation of Greece (1821). Among the relics of this period are Byron's helmet and sword.

Natural History Museum

The Natural History Museum, in the northern suburb of Kifissiá (Levidou 13), has large collections illustrating the biosphere of the Mediterranean region. Pride of place is taken by the skeleton of a dinosaur (Triceratops) almost 8m/26ft long. Also of great interest are the collections of butterflies and moths and of shells.

Theatre Museum

The Theatre Museum, housed in the basement of the Municipal Cultural Centre (Akadimías 50), near the University and the National Library, displays a variety of material of theatrical interest (costumes, directors' scripts, posters and mementoes of all kinds).

War Museum

The War Museum in Leofóros Vasilíssis Sofías, opened in 1975, displays material relating to wars of particular importance to Greece, like the Persian wars of the 5th century B.C. and the battle of Navarino in 1827.

Surroundings of Athens

Popular places of resort, particularly in summer, are two suburbs of Athens which lie higher up in the hills and accordingly have a very agreeable climate – Amaroússion (alt. 230m/755ft), which features in Henry Miller's "Colossus of Maroussi", and the even more attractive Kifissiá (alt. 267m/876ft; pop. 14,200). Other pleasant places to stay are in the hills of Mts Párnis and Pentélikon, north and north-east of the city (see entries).

Athos/Áyion Óros **I 3**

Άθως/Άγιον Όρος
Áthos/Áyion Óros

Region: Chalcidice
Political status: autonomous monastic republic
Area: 321 sq.km/124 sq. miles
Population: 1700

Transport

Boats from Trypití and Ouranópolis to Dafní.
Cruises along the south coast are run from Ammouliani and Ouranópolis; visits to monasteries are permitted only if the party consists solely of men.

★★ Situation

The Holy Mountain (Áyion Óros) of Athos, an autonomous region within Greece and for more than a thousand years a centre of Orthodox monasticism, is the most easterly of the three "fingers" of the Chalcidice peninsula. This "garden of the Mother of God", as it is known to the monks, is an area of great natural beauty, with its hilly landscape and great expanses of forest washed by the waters of the Aegean, and of extraordinary interest with its twenty great monasteries and its host of lesser houses and hermitages scattered about the peninsula – a corner of Byzantium that has survived into modern times.

History

The first settlers on this finger of land up to 5km/3 miles wide which reaches south-east for some 45km/28 miles and rises to a height of 2033m/6670ft in Mt Athos, were a few isolated hermits. Then in A.D. 963 Athanasios, a monk from Trebizond, established, with the support of the Emperor Nicephorus Phocas, the first monastery, the Meyísti Lávra, the Great Lavra, which is still the largest of the monasteries. This was followed by numerous other foundations, which followed a rule (typikon) laid down by the Emperor John Tzimisces (969–976). The pattern of monastic life was coenobitic (communal), with prayer in common, meals in common and an abbot elected for life to rule

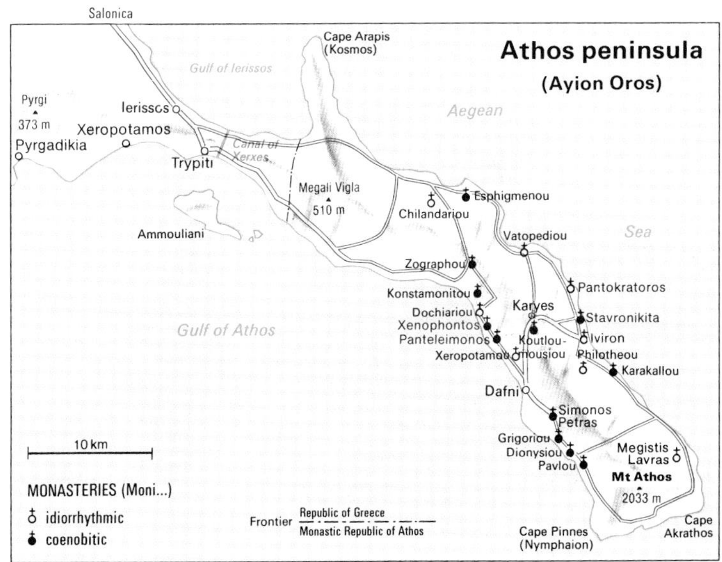

each monastery. With the mystical movement known as hesychasm (from *hesychos,* "tranquil, quiet") which developed in the 14th century a new form of monastic life known as idiorrhythmic emerged. Under this system, apart from prayers in common, each monk was left free to choose his own pattern ("rhythm") of life and to practise his own form of asceticism, each monastery being governed by three trustees with a restricted term of office. In time most of the monasteries adopted the idiorrhythmic pattern.

The ★★ monasteries

In recent years there has been a tendency to return to the stricter coenobitic system. At present sixteen of the twenty monasteries are coenobitic – Esphigménou, Stavronikíta, Philotheoú, Karakalloú and the Great Lavra on the north-east coast, Koutloumousíou in the centre of the peninsula and Zográphou, Konstamonítou, Dochiaríou, Xenophontos, Panteleímonos, Xeropotámou, Símonos Pétra, Grigoríou, Dionysíou and Pávlou on the south-west coast. The other four, all on the north-east coast, are idiorrhythmic – Chilandári, Vatopédi, Pantokrátoros and Ivíron. In addition to the twenty great monasteries there are several monastic villages, *kellía* occupied by "families" of three monks and, particularly on the steep south coast of the peninsula, small isolated hermitages. Most of the monks are Greek, but the other Orthodox nations are also represented – Russians in Panteleímonos, Bulgarians in Zográphou, Yugoslavs in Chilandári. Although political conditions have led to an ageing in the population of the Russian monastery, there has been an influx of young monks into some of the other houses in recent years. The affairs of the monastic republic as a whole are managed by the Sacred Council (Iera Epistasía) which meets in the village of Karyés; its members are appointed by the monasteries for a year at a time.

Dionysíou monastery

Visiting Athos

Athos is very different from a tourist area, and visitors must learn to fit in with the ways of this monastic republic. No women or "beardless boys" are admitted. Foreign visitors (who are limited to a daily quota) should obtain a letter of recommendation from their embassy, which must then be taken to the Ministry of Foreign Affairs in Athens or the Ministry of Northern Greece in Salonica, where they will obtain an authorisation for presentation to the authorities on Athos. From the landing-stage at Dafní they travel by bus to Karyés, where they must first register with the police and then go to the Epistasía, where they receive the *diamonitírion* which entitles them to receive hospitality (free of charge) in the monasteries. In each monastery there is a guest wing (*arkhondaríkion*), with a guest-master (*arkhondáris*) who is responsible for looking after visitors. The use of tape-recorders and ciné-cameras is prohibited, but cameras are permitted.

The monasteries are surrounded by massive walls, against which are built the monks' and guests' quarters and the tower housing the library. The principal church (Kathólikon) stands in the middle of the courtyard, usually with the fountain (*fyáli*) and refectory (*trápeza*) in close proximity. Most of the churches and refectories have fine wall paintings, and the libraries and treasuries contain many valuable books and precious objects.
In 1981 a fire devastated Koutloumousíou monastery, but the icons and manuscripts were saved.

From Karyés the various monasteries can be visited on foot, or it may be possible to hire a mule or, from Karyés to Ivíron, get a lift on a truck. Depending on weather conditions, and on the rather irregular boat services, many of the monasteries can be reached by sea. The mule-tracks and footpaths leading to the monasteries are of variable quality and frequently strenuous. In the area of the hermitages at the southern tip of the peninsula visitors should avoid disturbing the hermits.

Mount Athos

The ascent of Mount Athos (2033m/6670ft; 7 hrs from the Great Lavra), crowned by the chapel of the Transfiguration, to which there is an annual procession, is for good walkers only.

Attica H/I 5/6

Αττική
Attikí

Situation

Attica, the most easterly region of central Greece, is bounded on the south and east by the sea, on the north by Boeotia and on the west by the ancient territory of the Megarid. With an area of 3350 sq.km/1295 sq. miles, it is broken up by ranges of hills, between which are four plains: the one round the city of Athens, the Thriasian plain round Eleusis to the west, the Mesóyia ("Central Plain") between Hymettos and the west coast, and the plain of Marathón to the north-east.

History

Attica has been settled by man since the Neolithic period, and it has many fortified sites dating from pre-Greek and Mycenaean times. Tholos tombs have been found at Thorikós, Marathón and Menídi, pointing to the existence of separate principalities which lost their independence in Theseus's "synoecism" (see Athens, History). Although sanctuaries such as Eleusis with its mysteries and the temple of Poseidon on Cape Soúnion maintained their importance

throughout antiquity, Athens increasingly developed into the political, cultural and economic centre of Attica, helped by the proximity of the excellent natural harbour of Piraeus.
Since Greece achieved its independence and Athens became its capital in 1834 a huge modern metropolis has spread far out over the central plain, and the olive-groves which once lay between Athens and Piraeus have long since disappeared. The plain of Eleusis has been disfigured by industrial installations, but the Marathón and Mesóyia plains have largely preserved their agricultural character. The coastal strips have been developed, and a whole string of seaside resorts has grown up between Athens and Soúnion. The east coast, south of Marathón, is also a popular holiday area.

★Attic Riviera (Coast of Apollo)

The Attic Riviera is the stretch of coast between Athens and Cape Soúnion, also known as the Coast of Apollo. In antiquity there were a number of towns in this area, including the sites of Áyios Kósmas and Anaphlystos, near Anávyssos, which have yielded important finds, but in modern times the area was sparsely populated until the influx of refugees from Asia Minor after 1922 (the theme of Ilías Venésis's novel "Galini"). The south coast of Attica has been transformed by the development of mass tourism since the Second World War, and a whole series of popular resorts have sprung up (Palaion Faliron, Kalamaki, Glyfada, Kavouri, Vouliagmeni, Varkitsa, Lagonisi, Anávyssos, Legrena, etc.).

Áyios Efstratios I/K 4

Άγιος Ευστράτιος
Áyios Efstrátios

Nomos: Lésbos
Area of island: 43 sq.km/16½ sq. miles
Altitude: 0–303m/0–994ft
Population: 500
Chief place: Áyios Efstrátios

Boat services

Regular services several times weekly between Áyios Konstantínos or Kými (Euboea), Skópelos, Áyios Efstrátios and Lemnos; also local connections with Lemnos and Lésbos.

Situation

Áyios Efstrátios, known in antiquity as Halonesos and in the Middle Ages as Néon (Turkish Hagiostratı), is a rocky island of volcanic origin some 30km/20 miles south of Lemnos (see entry).
In ancient times the island protected the sea route between Athens and the islands of Lemnos and Imbros.

The little town and port of Áyios Efstrátios lies in the largest bay on the west coast of the island. Above the town are an old castle and windmills.

Áyios Yeoryios H 6

Άγιος Γεώργιος
Áyios Yeóryios

Nomos: Attica
Area of island: 9 sq.km/3½ sq. miles
Altitude: 0–329m/0–1079ft

Situation

The barren island of Áyios Yeóryios (lighthouse), some 20km/12½ miles south of Cape Soúnion, was used in antiquity as a penal colony and is now inaccessible.

Bassai F 6

Βασσές
Vassés

Region: Peloponnese
Nomos: Elis

Access

The best way to approach Bassai is from Trípoli by way of Megalópolis and Karítaina; an alternative route is from Pýrgos via Kréstena (south of the river Alfiós) to Andrítsaina and Bassai.

Situation and importance

The Temple of Apollo Epikouriios stands on a remote site (1130m/3708ft) on the slopes of Mt Lykaion, 14km/9 miles from the village of Andrítsaina, from which a road ascends to within a short distance of the site. Rediscovered in 1763, the temple has since then largely been re-erected. According to Pausanias, who regarded it as "second only to the temple at Tegéa for the beauty of its stone and its exact proportions", it was built by Iktinos, the architect of the Parthenon, as a thank-offering by the city of Phigaleia for being spared from the plague of 429 B.C. to which Perikles fell a victim in Athens.

★★Temple of Apollo

N.B.: The temple is at present under restoration and is covered by a temporary roof. Something of the structure can be seen, but parts are obscured by scaffolding.

The temple of Apollo at Bassai shows some unusual features. The column ratio (6 × 15) follows the Archaic pattern rather than the classical norm of 6 × 13, and the temple is oriented not to the east but to the north, though it has a doorway in the east wall of the naos. While the external columns are Doric the naos has two rows of Ionic columns – not free-standing but set close to the walls and engaged in projecting buttresses. A frieze (now in the British Museum) ran round the walls of the naos above the columns, a departure from the previously normal practice of having the frieze on the external walls. Iktinos thus showed himself, in Gruben's words, "a leader of the avant-garde in architecture", carrying a stage farther the trend towards increased emphasis on the interior of the temple which is already evident in the Parthenon.

At the far end of the naos, at the entrance to the adyton in which the cult image of the god was housed, there originally stood a column with a Corinthian capital – the earliest known use of this type. The capital was present when the temple was examined by Haller von

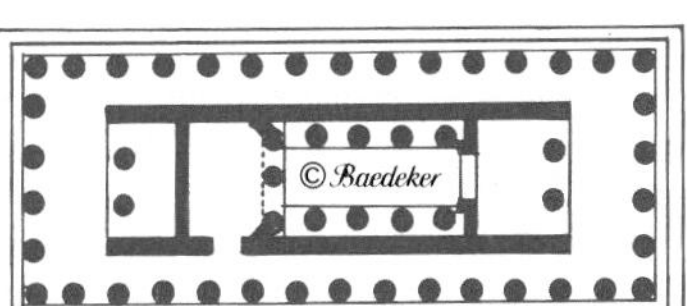

Bassai

Ground-plan of temple of Apollo Epikouris

N
10 m

The Temple of Apollo at Bassai in its lonely setting

Hallerstein in 1811 but subsequently disappeared and is known to us only from his drawing.

The adyton must have served some unknown cult purpose. With this separate holy of holies within the naos, with its elongated ground-plan and its 6 × 15 columns, this temple of Apollo is reminiscent of the temple in the central sanctuary of Apollo at Delphi (see entry), which Iktinos reproduced here, reducing it in size by exactly a third.

Phigaleia

It is a 2½ hours' walk from Bassai to Figalía, with the remains of ancient Phigaleia, continuing to the Néda gorge.

Boeotia G/H 5

Βοιωτία
Viotía

Boeotia occupies an area of 3000 sq.km/1160 sq. miles in central Greece, between the gulfs of Corinth and Euboea and between Phocis and Attica. The plain around its capital, Thebes, and in the Asopos valley – supplemented in modern times by the land won by the drainage of Lake Kopais – have made Boeotia an agricultural region since ancient times; and its inhabitants were traditionally regarded as rather uncouth rustics, in spite of the fact that Hesiod, Pindar and Plutarch all came from Boeotia. In the field of art it produced only the sculptor Kalamis, famed for his figures of horses.

History

In Mycenaean times Boeotia had important fortified towns such as Thebes, Orchomenos and Gla. In the historical period a league of cities was formed, of which Thebes became leader in the time of Epameinondas (371–361 B.C.). The city of Thebes was destroyed on several occasions, e.g. by Alexander the Great in 335 B.C. and by Catalan mercenaries in the 13th century, and did not recover its position until the 19th century. During the Turkish occupation the chief town of the region was Livadiá.

Sights

Although most visitors only pass through Boeotia on the way to somewhere else, it has a number of sites and monuments which are well worth seeing. The Mycenaean period is represented by Orchomenos and Gla (see entries), the 1st millennium B.C. by Chaironeia and the Kabirion of Thebes (see entries), and the Christian era by the churches of Skripoú, one of which can be seen when visiting Osios Loukás (see entry) or Orchomenos.

Brauron

I 6

Βραυρώνα
Vravróna

Region and nomos: Attica

★ Situation

At Brauron on the east coast of Attica, 8km/5 miles north-east of Markópoulo, Papadimitríou excavated between 1948 and 1963 a sanctuary of Artemis which has been excellently restored and is now a most impressive and interesting site.

History

The site was occupied from Neolithic times. Remains of Middle Helladic buildings (2000–1600 B.C.) were found on the acropolis hill, and there was evidence of dense occupation in the Late Helladic (Mycenaean) period (1600–1100 B.C.). After a period of abandonment the site was resettled in the 9th century B.C. Brauron's heyday was in the 5th and 4th centuries; but after 300 B.C. the land became waterlogged and the site was again abandoned. The cult of Artemis Brauronia was transferred from Braurion to the Acropolis of Athens in the 6th century by Peisistratos, himself a native of Brauron.

In Mycenaean times the goddess Artemis was known here as Artemis Iphigeneia; and according to Euripides Iphigeneia, daughter of king Agamemnon of Mycenae, was a priestess at Brauron after her return from the Tauric Chersonese until her death. In the classical period Athenian girls served in the sanctuary between the ages of five and ten. They were known as "little bears" (*arktoi*) from the saffron-coloured garments they wore, recalling a she-bear sacred to Artemis.

Sights

On the slopes of a hill, near a 12th century chapel of St George, is a small shrine, beyond which are the Cave of Iphigeneia (now roofless) and a "sacred house". To the north are the rock-cut footings of the temple of Artemis which replaced an earlier building in the first half of the 5th century B.C. Beyond this is a stoa built round three sides of a courtyard (430–420 B.C.), with the entrance on the west side, where there is an ancient bridge. The Doric columns of the stoa, which were of limestone, had marble capitals. Six rooms in the north wing and three in the west wing each contained eleven wooden beds for the "little bears".

Museum

The Museum contains finds from the site. Rooms 1–3 have material from the sanctuary of Artemis, Room 5 has pottery from the acropolis (Early to Late Helladic). Room 4 and the Atrium also display material from the Merénda necropolis (vases of the 9th–4th c. B.C., funerary stelae), Room 5 pottery from Anávyssos and the Peráti necropolis.

Surroundings of Brauron

500m/550yds inland can be seen the excavated remains of an Early Byzantine basilica and baptistery (6th c.).

Pórto Ráfti

See entry

Chaironeia G 5

Χαιρώνεια
Khairónia

Region and nomos: Boeotia

★ Lion of Chaironela

The monumental Lion of Chaironeia, 5.5m/18ft high, rears up against a backdrop of cypress trees by the roadside 14km/8½ miles north of Livadiá (see entry). It commemorates a battle in 338 B.C. in which the allied Greek city states were defeated by Philip II of Macedon and his 18-year-old son Alexander.
The battle marked the beginning of the Macedonian domination of Greece. The fallen Macedonians were buried in an earth mound on the battlefield (2km/1¼ miles east of the Lion), and Philip sent the ashes of the dead Athenians to Athens, while Thebes raised a tomb for its dead which was enclosed by a low wall and marked by the figure of the lion.

Old Town

Of the ancient city of Chaironeia (1.5km/1 mile west) there remains only a small theatre hewn from the rock on the slopes of the acropolis hill, now called Mt Petrakhos. This was the birthplace of the philosopher and biographer Plutarch, a priest of Apollo at Delphi (A.D. *c.* 45–*c.* 120), who returned to Chaironeia in his old age.

Chalcidice G–I 3/4

Χαλκιδική
Khalkidikí

Area: 3000 sq.km/1160 sq. miles

Transport

Chalcidice is traversed by two roads running from west to east, Salonica–Rendína–Kavála and Salonica–Polìyiros–Ierissós, from which side roads branch off and run south.
Bus connections with Salonica.
Boat service from Ouranópolis to Dafní on Athos.

Situation

The peninsula of Chalcidice, a hilly and well wooded region, lies south-east of Salonica, with three finger-like sub-peninsulas reaching out into the sea – to the west Kassándra, in the middle Sithónia (or Lóngos), to the east Athos (see entry). The name of the peninsula is a reminder that the Euboean city of Chalkis (see page 262) founded 32

Evening in Porto Karras, Chalcidice

cities here, including Olynthos (see entry). In recent years Chalcidice, with its magnificent long sandy beaches, has become a rapidly developing holiday region.

★ Beaches

Chios K/L 5

Χίος
Khíos

Nomos: Chios
Area of island: 842 sq.km/325 sq. miles
Altitude: 0–1267m/0–4157ft
Population: 49,800
Chief town: Chios

Transport

Air connections with Athens several times daily; also with Lésbos, Mýkonos and Sámos.
Regular boat services several times weekly from Athens (Piraeus); local connections with the neighbouring islands of Inoúsai and Psará. Ferry service to Çeşme (Turkey).

Situation and characteristics

The rugged island of Chios (known in Turkish as Sakıs Adası, "Mastic Island") lies in the eastern Aegean, just off the Çeşme peninsula on the south side of the Gulf of Smyrna, separated from the Turkish mainland only by the 8km/5 mile wide Strait of Chios. Most of the island is occupied by a range of craggy limestone hills traversing it from north to south, reaching its highest point in Mt Profítis Ilías, the ancient Pellinaion (1267m/4157ft), at the north end of the island. The hills fall steeply down to the sea, forming impressive cliffs, particularly on the east.

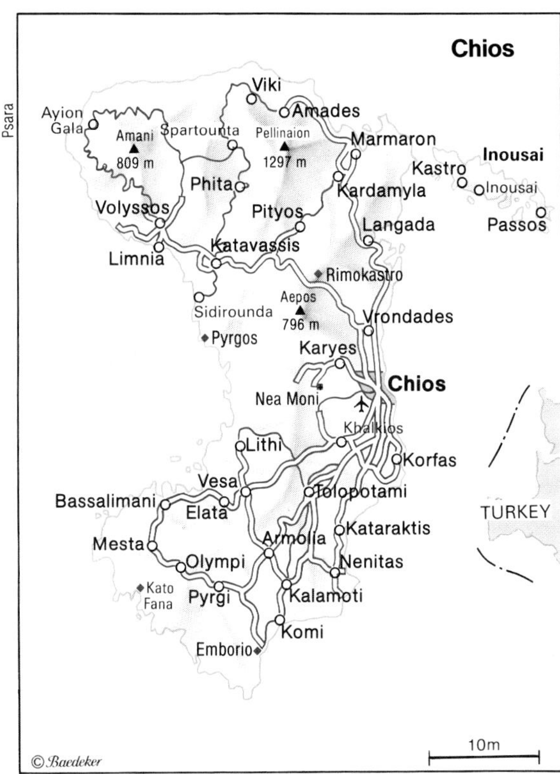

The population is concentrated mainly in the fertile southern part of the island, where olives, vines, figs and citrus fruits are grown. The island's major crop, however, is mastic, the aromatic resin of the mastic or lentisk tree (*Pistacia lentiscus* L.), which was already being exported in ancient times, making an important contribution to the island's prosperity. The mastic is also used to make *mastikha,* a bitter-sweet liqueur, and a rather sickly-sweet confection. Apart from agriculture the island's prosperity depends on commerce and shipping: something like a third of the Greek merchant fleet is based on Chios.

History

Excavation has yielded evidence of human settlement reaching back to the 4th millennium B.C. In the 8th century B.C. Ionian Greeks settled on Chios and made it one of the wealthiest and most important members of the Ionian League of cities which was established around 700 B.C. In the 6th century B.C. an important school of sculptors was active on the island.

From 512 to 479 Chios was under Persian rule, and thereafter became a member of the Attic maritime league, but was able to maintain its independence. In this period Chios is believed to have had a population of 30,000 free men and 100,000 slaves, and the islanders grew

wealthy from viniculture, commerce and industry (Chian beds). In 412 B.C. Chios broke away from Athens and in 392 from Sparta; then in 377 it became the first member of the second Attic maritime league, but soon left it. Under the Romans, with whom it sided in 190 B.C., it still maintained its independence.
Held from 1204 to 1304 by the Venetians and later by the Genoese, Chios became Turkish in 1566. The popularity, in the Sultan's harem, of the mastic which grew on the island and of the sweets made from it gave Chios a special status – although no Greeks were allowed to live within the Turkish citadel. In addition to its mastic Chios was famed for its silk-weaving, which also contributed to the island's prosperity.
Throughout their eventful history the Chians showed themselves to be skilled seamen and shrewd businessmen. They took an active part in the struggle for liberation from the Turks, and Chios was the scene in 1822 of the bloody massacres depicted in a famous painting by Delacroix. Severe devastation was caused by an earthquake in 1881.
In November 1912, during the Balkan War, a Greek squadron appeared off the island and captured it after a brief resistance by the Turks. After the First World War Chios lost its economic hinterland in Turkey and had to give asylum to many Greeks expelled from Asia Minor.

Sights

Chios Town

The island's chief town and principal port, Chios (pop. 24,000), lies half way down the east coast, roughly on the site of the ancient city. It extends in a semicircle round the harbour, dominated on the north by the dilapidated medieval Kastro (13th–16th c.; restoration planned). Little is left of the old part of the town, since the houses that survived the Turkish raid of 1822 were mostly destroyed in the 1881 earthquake. Features of interest in the town are the Archaeological Museum, with pottery from prehistoric times onward, coins and some sculpture; the Folk Museum; and the Korais Library, the third largest in Greece, with 140,000 volumes. The library is named after the Chios-born scholar Adamantios Korais (1748–1833), who later worked in Paris. In the same building is the Argentis family's large collection of paintings and folk art, presented to Chios by Filippos Argentis (bust in front of the building); the collection also includes a wealth of material on the history of Chios.

In the fertile Kampos to the south of the town is the mansion of the Argentis family, now open to the public. The house with its marble fountains and painted water-wheels, set in a large orange-grove, gives a picture of the way of life of the Genoese and native aristocracy.

★★ Néa Moní

From the town of Chios a road runs north-west by way of the colourful village of Karyés (5km/3 miles) and over a pass to the convent of Néa Moní, a straggling complex of buildings in a verdant setting now occupied only by a few nuns. The convent, founded by the Emperor Constantine IX Monomachos (1042–55), is notable for its magnificent mosaics on a gold ground, which rank with those at Dafní and Ósios Loukás (see entries) as the finest surviving examples of 11th century religious art.

Church

The dome of the church is borne, as at Dafní, on eight piers and spans the full width of the church, not merely the central aisle. The walls still have their original facing of red marble. Some of the mosaics were destroyed in the 1881 earthquake; in particular those on the dome, which collapsed, were lost. In subsequent restoration work the dome was rebuilt and the surviving mosaics made safe. Among the principal

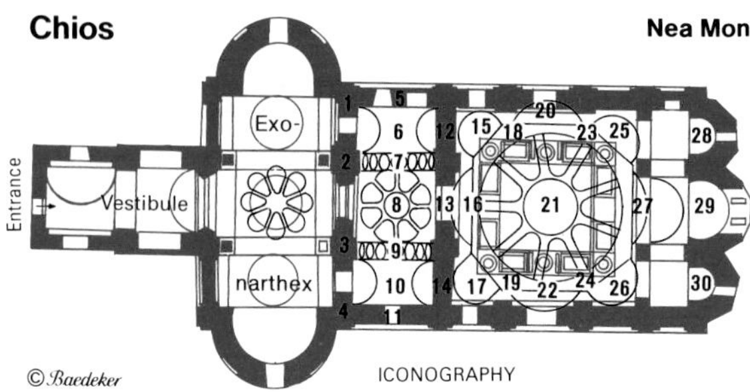

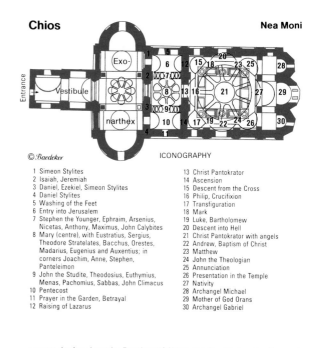

1 Simeon Stylites
2 Isaiah, Jeremiah
3 Daniel, Ezekiel, Simeon Stylites
4 Daniel Stylites
5 Washing of the Feet
6 Entry into Jerusalem
7 Stephen the Younger, Ephraim, Arsenius, Nicetas, Anthony, Maximus, John Calybites
8 Mary (centre), with Eustratius, Sergius, Theodore Stratelates, Bacchus, Orestes, Madarius, Eugenius and Auxentius; in corners Joachim, Anne, Stephen, Panteleimon
9 John the Studite, Theodosius, Euthymius, Menas, Pachomius, Sabbas, John Climacus
10 Pentecost
11 Prayer in the Garden, Betrayal
12 Raising of Lazarus
13 Christ Pantokrator
14 Ascension
15 Descent from the Cross
16 Philip, Crucifixion
17 Transfiguration
18 Mark
19 Luke, Bartholomew
20 Descent into Hell
21 Christ Pantokrator with angels
22 Andrew, Baptism of Christ
23 Matthew
24 John the Theologian
25 Annunciation
26 Presentation in the Temple
27 Nativity
28 Archangel Michael
29 Mother of God Orans
30 Archangel Gabriel

scenes depicted are the Baptism of Christ, the Crucifixion, the Descent from the Cross and the Descent into Limbo. In the main apse is the Mother of God, flanked by the Archangels Michael and Gabriel in the lateral apses.

There are also fine mosaics in the narthex – the Washing of the Feet, the Mother of God surrounded by local saints, the Betrayal. All these mosaics date from the time of the convent's foundation (*c.* 1050) and are thus rather later than those of Ósios Loukás and rather earlier than those at Dafní.

The frescoes in the exonarthex (among them a Last Judgment) date from the Late Byzantine period (14th c.).

The other conventual buildings were damaged during the Turkish punitive expedition of 1822, and many of them are now in a state of dilapidation, as are the hospices for pilgrims around the convent. By the gateway of the convent is a chapel commemorating those who were killed in 1822. Other notable features are the old refectory (*trápeza*) and a large cistern a few paces to the right of the main gateway. From the terrace of the new refectory (the one used by the nuns) there is a very beautiful view.

Tríon Patéron

A few kilometres above the convent on a narrow concrete road is the cave monastery of Tríon Patéron (the Three Fathers), which commemorates the three hermits who lived here and founded the Néa Moní.

Anávatos

A road continues north-west to the almost deserted village of Anávatos, impressively situated on the slopes of a hill. In the upper part of the village are two churches, at present under restoration.

North of the island

6km/4 miles north of Chios town is the villa suburb of Vrondádes (pop. 4700). At the north end of the town, near the sea, are the Pasha's Spring (Basávrysi) and a large block of dressed stone which was probably a shrine of Cybele. This is popularly known as the Daskalópetra (Teacher's Stone) or Skholí Omírou (School of Homer) – recalling the island's claim to be the birthplace of Homer.

Farther up the coast lies Langáda (15km/9 miles), near which there are the excavated remains of the Delphinion, a site fortified by the Athenians in 412 B.C. At Kardámyla (27km/17 miles; pop. 1300) a road goes off on the right to the little port of Mármaron (25km/15½ miles; pop. 2400), which has a sandy beach. Beyond Kardámyla the main road continues round the north of the island, passing through Víki and the picturesque village of Kéramos to reach Áyion Gála (50km/31 miles). Another road runs north-west from Chios town along the northern slopes of Mt Aepos to Vólyssos (40km/25 miles) and its harbour at Límnia. From Límnia there is a motorboat service to the island of Psará (see entry).

South of the island

Some 30km/19 miles south of Chios town, in the centre of the villages which produce mastic (*mastikhoría),* is Pyrgí, a picturesque little place dominated by a Genoese castle. The 12th century church of the Áyii Apóstoli (frescoes) follows the pattern of the Néa Moní, which also served as a model for other churches on the island. Many of the houses have attractive sgraffito decoration.

8km/5 miles south-west of Pyrgí is the archaeological site of Káto Fána, with remains of a temple of Apollo; 7km/4½ miles south-east is the site of Emborió. A road runs north-west from Pyrgí to the port of Ayía Anastasía or Basalimáni (43km/27 miles from Chios town), from

A sheltered harbour on Chios

which we can return to Chios by way of Eláta and the medieval village of Vésa.

Inoúsai Islands

North-east of Chios, at the north end of the Strait of Chios, are the Inoúsai Islands (formerly known as the Spalmatori), an archipelago extending north-west which consists of the main island, Inoúsai (school of navigation), the islets of Pásas, Gaváthion and Váton to the east, and numerous isolated rocks.

South-west of Chios, at the mouth of Elata Bay, are the little islands of Pelagonísos, Áyios Yeóryios and Áyios Stéfanos, with the remains of Hellenistic watch-towers.

Corfu/Kerkyra D/E 4

Κέρκυρα
Kérkyra

Nomos: Kérkyra
Area of island: 592 sq.km/229 sq. miles
Altitude: 0–906m/0–2973ft
Population: 100,000
Chief town: Kérkyra (Corfu Town)

Air services

Airport 5km/3 miles south of Corfu Town.
Scheduled flights from Athens several times daily (50 minutes). Direct flights from London and other UK airports.

Boat services

Ferry services Igoumenítsa–Corfu (10 daily); Patras–Corfu, weekly; also ferry connections with Italy (Brindisi, Bari, Ancona, Otranto) and Croatia (Dubrovnik).
Local services: Corfu–Paxí; Corfu–Erikoúsa–Mathráki–Othonian Islands; Corfu–Kefalloniá (Sámi)–Ithaca–Patras.

Situation

Corfu (Kérkyra), the most important and most northerly of the Ionian Islands, lies off the coasts of Albania and the Greek region of Epirus, at a distance ranging between 2.5 and 20km (1½ and 12½ miles). The beauty of its scenery, with gentle green hills in the south and rugged limestone hills in the north, rising to 906m/2973ft in the bare double peak of Mt Pantokrátor, its mild climate and its luxuriant southern flora make Corfu a very popular holiday area.
The island's main source of revenue, in addition to the increasing tourist trade, is agriculture.

Myth and history

Corfu (known to the ancient Greeks as Korkyra) is believed to be the Homeric island of Scheria, home of the Phaeacians and their king Alkinoos. The earliest traces of settlement point to the presence of farming peoples, perhaps incomers from Italy. Colonised by Corinth in 734 B.C., Korkyra developed into a considerable power which threatened Corinth itself. A Corinthian naval victory over Korkyra in 432 B.C. in the Sybota Islands (probably at the mouth, now silted up, of the river Kalamas) was a major factor in the outbreak of the Peloponnesian War. In 229 B.C. it was occupied by the Romans, who called it Corcyra. In the division of the Roman Empire in A.D. 395 Corfu fell to the Eastern (Byzantine) Empire.

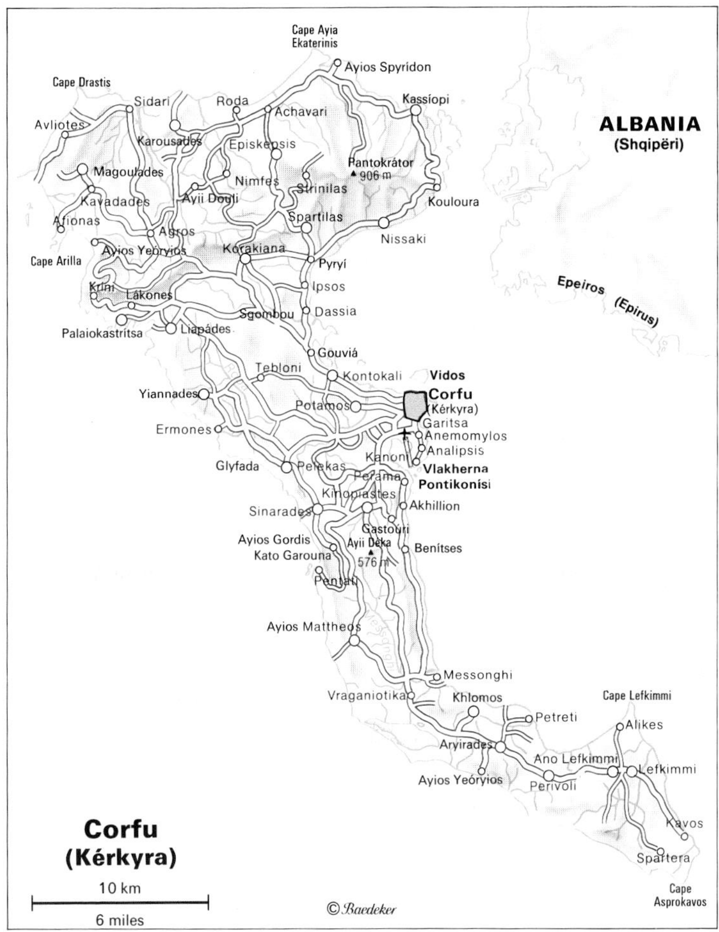

The medieval name of Corfu appears to be derived from the Greek name Koryphoi ("Peaks"). From 1386 to 1797 Corfu was held by the Venetians; then, after a brief period of French occupation, it passed to Britain in 1815 along with the rest of the Ionian Islands. It was returned to Greece in 1864.

In the course of its eventful history Corfu suffered frequent devastation, so that most of its ancient and medieval remains have been destroyed.

Corfu Town (Kérkyra)

The island's chief town is Kérkyra (pop. 30,000), beautifully situated on a promontory on the east coast and dominated by the New Fort. The ancient city lay farther south on the Kanóni peninsula. Kérkyra is now the seat of both a Greek Orthodox and a Roman Catholic archbishop.

New Fort

At the north end of the town is the harbour, with the massive New Fort (16th c.) rising above it on the south. Offshore to the north, 1km/¾ mile away, is the island of Vídos.

Spianada

From the harbour we can either go east along the high seafront road (views), passing the former royal palace, or south-east along Nikifóros Street, the town's busy main shopping street, to the Spianada (Esplanade), a large park-like area between the town and the Citadel.

Royal Palace
★ Museum of Asian Art

On the north side of the Spianada is the former Royal Palace, a neo-classical mansion built in 1816 for the British Lord High Commissioner which now houses the Museum of Byzantine and East Asian Art.

Citadel

From the east side of the Spianada, where there is a statue of Count Matthias Johann von der Schulenburg (1661–1747), who commanded the stubborn defence of the island against the Turks in 1716, a bridge leads over a ditch (the "contrafossa") to the Citadel, situated on a small island, with its dilapidated walls climbing up the slopes of a steep-sided double hill (70m/230ft; lighthouse). *Son et lumière* shows are given here in summer.

Old town

North-west of the Spianada stands the church of Áyios Spyrídon, with a silver sarcophagus containing the remains of the town's patron saint (processions on Palm Sunday, the Saturday before Easter, August 1st

Street scene in Corfu town

Beach, Glyfada

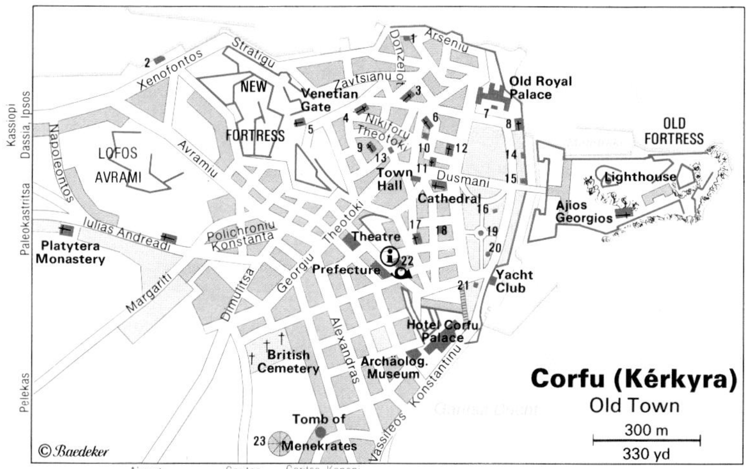

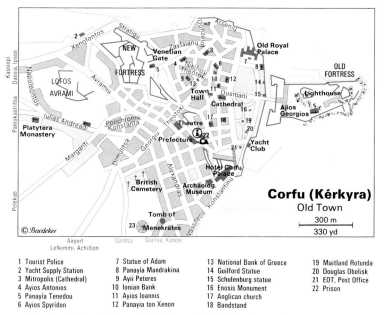

1 Tourist Police
2 Yacht Supply Station
3 Mitropolis (Cathedral)
4 Ayios Antonios
5 Panayia Tenedou
6 Ayios Spyrídon
7 Statue of Adam
8 Panayia Mandrakina
9 Ayii Peteres
10 Ionian Bank
11 Ayios Ioannis
12 Panayia ton Xenon
13 National Bank of Greece
14 Guilford Statue
15 Schulenburg statue
16 Enosis Monument
17 Anglican church
18 Bandstand
19 Maitland Rotunda
20 Douglas Obelisk
21 EOT, Post Office
22 Prison

and the first Sunday in November). To the north of the church extends the old town with its narrow lanes (many silversmiths' shops) and Italian- and Venetian-style houses.

To the west of the Spianada, in Theotoki Square, are the former Venetian Theatre (1663–93), which since 1902 has been the Town Hall, and the Roman Catholic Cathedral (16th c.), with a neo-classical façade. West of this is the former Archbishop's Palace (18th c.), now occupied by the National Bank of Greece.

Archaeological Museum
★ Gorgon Pediment

From the Spianada Leofóros Dimokratías runs south along the sea-front. 200m/220yds along this street, off on the right just beyond the Corfu Palace Hotel, is the Archaeological Museum; its most notable exhibit is the Gorgon Pediment (*c.* 585 B.C.) from the temple of Artemis (see below).

Tomb of Menekrates

500m/550yds beyond this, on the right in the garden of a police station, can be seen the Tomb of Menekrates (7th or 6th c. B.C.), a low circular structure resembling a fountain-house which was discovered in 1843 during the demolition of the old Salvator Bastion.
Leofóros Dimokratías ends at the bathing station of Mon Repos, at the south-eastern end of the suburban district of Garítsa.

Mon Repos
★ Park

500m/550yds south, set in a beautiful park, is the villa of Mon Repos, birthplace in 1921 of the Duke of Edinburgh. North of the park, near the ancient harbour of Anemomylos, now silted up, is the Byzantine church of SS Jason and Sosipater (11th–12th c.), partly built of stones from ancient buildings. Some 500m/550yds south-west is the ruined church of Áyia Kérkyra (originally 5th c.; frequently destroyed or damaged), formerly the basilica of Palaiopolis, built on the site of a late Hellenistic Agora (2nd–1st c. B.C.). Nearby are the remains of Roman baths.

Temple of Artemis

1km/¾ mile west, beyond the monastery of Áyios Theodóros, are the scanty remains of a temple of Artemis of the 6th century B.C.; its west pediment, known as the Gorgon Pediment, is now in the Archaeological Museum (see above).

★ Kanóni
★ Vlakhérna
★ Pontikonísi

From Garítsa a beautiful road runs 3km/2 miles south to the southern tip of a promontory between the sea and Lake Khalikiópoulos, with the tree-shaded terrace of Kanóni (views). In front are two small islets: on the nearer one, reached on a causeway, is the small monastery of Vlakhérna (17th c.), and beyond this is Pontikonísi ("Mouse Island"), with a Byzantine chapel. To the ancient Greeks Pontikonísi was the Phaeacian ship, turned to stone by Poseidon, which took Odysseus back to Ithaca ("Odyssey", 13, 163). On the west side of the Kanóni peninsula lies Lake Khalikiópoulos, now partly drained (airport) and partly marshland (wild ducks), which in ancient times was the island's principal harbour. The encounter between Odysseus and Nausikaa is said to have taken place on the south-west shore of the lake.

★ Achilleion

A favourite outing from Kérkyra is to the villa of Gastoúri (15km/9½ miles) and, 1km/¾ mile beyond this, the Achilleion (Akhíllion; alt. 145m/475ft), a villa in Italian Renaissance style built in 1890–91 for the Empress Elizabeth of Austria (d. 1898) and acquired by Kaiser Wilhelm II in 1907. State property since 1928, it is now a casino. It contains mementoes of the Empress and the Kaiser. It has a beautiful park with numerous statues and fine views.

Benítses

3km/2 miles south of the Achilleion is the charming fishing village of Benítses, with the remains of a Roman villa.

The islands of Vlakhérna and Pontikonísi, the "Mouse Island"

From here or from the Achilleion the return to Kérkyra is on the road along the east coast (17km/10½ miles or 20km/12½ miles).

Áyii Déka

13km/8 miles from Kérkyra on the road to Gastoúri a side road goes off on the right to the village of Áyii Déka (the "Ten Saints"; alt. 206m/676ft), from which it is an hour's climb (with guide; stout footwear required) to the summit of Mt Áyii Déka (576m/1890ft); magnificent views.

Kérkyra to Palaiokastrítsa

From Corfu Town the road runs north-west, close to the coast, passing the old fort of Abramo on a hill on the left. Farther on the island of Lazaretto can be seen in the sea to the right.
10km/6¼ miles: Gouviá, with a Venetian arsenal of 1716.

Mt Pantokrátor

Just beyond this a road branches off on the right and runs by way of Ípsos, Pyrgí and Spartílas (alt. 424m/1391ft) to Striníla s. From here it is an hour's climb (or a drive on a poor road) to a small rest-house, from which it takes 10 minutes to reach the summit of Mt Pantokrátor (906m/2973ft; views), the island's highest peak. On the top of the hill is an abandoned monastery of 1347.
Beyond Pyrgí the road follows a winding course northward, close to the coast, along the steep slopes of Mt Pantokrátor, with side roads going off to a few small fishing villages and bays with bathing beaches. In 20km/12½ miles it comes to the coastal village of Kassiópi, with the remains of a medieval castle.

Bella Vista

From the road junction at Gouviá the main road descends to the bay of Liapádes on the west coast, and then climbs again. In 10km/6 miles a road goes off on the right to the picturesque village of Lákones (3.5km/2¼ miles) and, 1km/¾ mile beyond this, the viewpoint of Bella Vista.
6km/4 miles: Palaiokastrítsa, a lively and attractive tourist resort, above which, perched on a high crag, stands the monastery of the Panayía Theotokós (views). Near the little town are sea-caves.
From here it is a 1½ hours' climb (with guide; stout footwear required) to the ruined 13th century castle of Angelokástro, from which there are panoramic views. From Kríni, 10km/6 miles north-west of Palaiokastrítsa, it is a shorter climb (30 minutes).

Corinth — G 6

Κόρινθος
Kórinthos

Nomos: Corinth
Altitude: sea level
Population: 22,700

Transport

Station on the Peloponnese Railway: lines to Athens/Piraeus, Patras–Kalamáta, Argos–Kalamáta.
Ferry services from the new harbour to Brindisi in Italy.

Situation

After a severe earthquake Corinth was moved in 1858 from the site of ancient Corinth to its present position, where it was again rebuilt after a further earthquake in 1928 and a great fire in 1933. The site of ancient Corinth, excavated by the American School in Athens from 1896 onwards, lies 7km/4¼ miles south-west in a beautiful setting at the foot of the hill of Acrocorinth (Akrokorinthos). There are extensive remains, mostly dating from the Roman period, dominated by the imposing ruins of the Archaic temple of Apollo.

History

Corinth owed its great importance in ancient times to its situation, with the hill of Acrocorinth providing a strong acropolis. It was said that Acrocorinth and Ithome were the two horns of the Greek bull, and that whoever held them possessed the Peloponnese. Corinth controlled the 6km/4 miles wide Isthmus, the only land route into the Peloponnese, and with its two harbours, Lechaion in the Gulf of Corinth and Kenchreai in the Saronic Gulf, also controlled the movement of goods between the two gulfs.

The area of Corinth (the name of which is pre-Greek) was already occupied in Neolithic times. In historical times the city attributed its foundation to Korinthos, son of Marathon, and to Sisyphos. Around 1000 B.C. Doric settlers established themselves here beside a Phoenician trading post. Under the Bacchiad dynasty (from 747 B.C.) the city enjoyed a period of prosperity, founding colonies on Corfu and at Syracuse. In 657 B.C. (?) the Bacchiads were succeeded by Kypselos, who ruled for 30 years as a tyrant and was succeeded by his more notable son Periandros, as absolute ruler for 40 years, from about 628 B.C. He ranked as one of the Seven Sages, and during his reign the Archaic culture of Corinth reached its apogee, the city's political and economic power being matched by its cultural achievement. Here the Doric temple gained its classical form, and the typical "Corinthian roof" of flat tiles was developed. Corinthian bronzes and pottery were disseminated throughout the Greek world; and during this period, according to Vitruvius, the Corinthian capital was invented by Kallimachos.

In 196 B.C. Corinth became the headquarters of the Achaean League. In 146 it was plundered and destroyed by a Roman general, Mummius, and remained in a state of ruin until it was rebuilt by Caesar in 44 B.C. In A.D. 51–52 the Apostle Paul lived and taught in Corinth. In the 2nd century the city was embellished by the Emperor Hadrian and by Herodes Atticus. In 521 Corinth was destroyed by a severe earthquake, and thereafter only Acrocorinth remained inhabited, until in the 10th century a settlement grew up in the area of the ancient Agora. Neither under the Franks (from 1210) nor under Turkish rule was Corinth able to recover its former importance; nor indeed has it done so in modern times.

★★Ancient Corinth

Precinct of Apollo
★Fountain of Peirene

The best plan is to enter the site from the ancient Lechaion road, on the north side of the excavated area. From here there is a general view of most of the site. Climbing up on an ancient paved road – as travellers arriving in the Lechaion harbour would have done – we come to the propylon at the entrance to the Agora. To the right of the road, here 7.5m/25ft wide, is the Basilica (1st–2nd c. A.D.); on the left there follow in succession the Roman Baths of Eurykles, a 20-seat public latrine (2nd c. A.D.), the Precinct of Apollo and the Fountain of Peirene. The fountain was magnificently rebuilt in marble by Herodes Atticus in the 2nd century A.D., with three apses enclosing a square court, and a new façade with six round-arched openings was erected in front of the old fountain-house, probably dating from the time of Periandros, the old front walls of which can still be seen. (The water is now diverted for the use of the village.)

Agora

A shallow flight of steps leads up to the north propylon of the Agora, a large area (255m/837ft by 127m/417ft) surrounded by colonnades

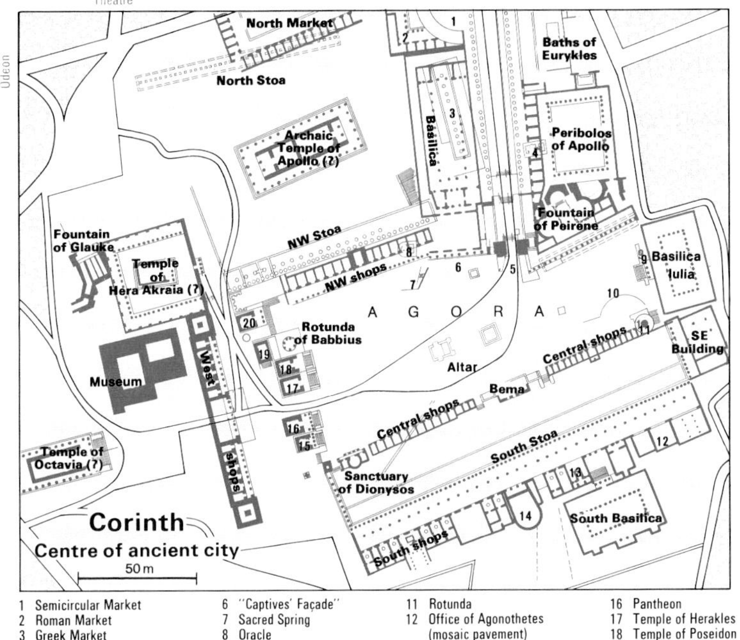

1 Semicircular Market
2 Roman Market
3 Greek Market
4 Greek temple of 4th c. B.C.
5 Propylaia
6 "Captives' Façade"
7 Sacred Spring
8 Oracle
9 Starting-line in Stadion
10 Retaining wall
11 Rotunda
12 Office of Agonothetes (mosaic pavement)
13 Fountain-house
14 Bouleuterion
15 Temple of Venus Fortuna
16 Pantheon
17 Temple of Herakles
18 Temple of Poseidon
19 Temple of Apollo
20 Temple of Hermes

which was the hub of the city's political and economic life. At the lower east end the paving of the Greek period has been preserved, but otherwise the remains are almost entirely Roman. Along the south side runs the South Stoa, 165m/541ft long, with 33 shops. The third room from the east, covered by a protective roof, contains a Roman mosaic pavement and is at present used as a store for the tiled roof structure of a cult building. Behind the South Stoa is the South Basilica, and at its east end are the South-East Building and the Basilica Iulia, built by the Emperor Claudius about A.D. 45.

★ Bema

Parallel to the South Stoa, running from end to end of the Agora, are the "Central Shops", and half way along the row is the Bema from which speakers addressed the people of Corinth. Here in A.D. 52 the Apostle Paul appeared before the Roman governor Gallio, a brother of Seneca's. There is some evidence on the Bema of the Christian church which was later built here.

★ Temples

Along the west end of the Agora are a series of Roman temples set on podia – from south to north the temple of Venus, the Pantheon and the temples of Poseidon, Hercules and Apollo. In front of the temple of Apollo is the Corinthian-style Rotunda of Babbius. To the west of the row of temples are the West Shops, between which is a broad flight of

Ancient Corinth

steps leading up to the higher level on which is Temple E (probably built for Augustus's sister Octavia), by the entrance to the Museum. Recent excavations in the area to the south have revealed a number of different occupation levels and a mosaic pavement dating from about 500 B.C.

★ Sacred Spring

There is also a row of shops along the north side of the Agora, at any rate towards the west end, near the propylon and the "Captives' Façade". In front of the row of shops is the Sacred Spring, in a Greek fountain-house (5th c. B.C.) in the form of a Doric triglyph, with seven steps leading down to the chamber containing the spring.

★ Temple of Apollo

From here we climb the low hill on which stands the conspicuous Temple of Apollo. Of the original temple there survive seven columns with part of the entablature, the rock-cut footings and part of the foundations. There were originally 6 × 15 massive monolithic columns. The naos was divided into two chambers, each of which had two rows of columns. The remains are sufficient to reveal the austere monumentality of the temple, a magnificent example of early Doric architecture, which was built about 540 B.C. on the site of an earlier 7th century temple.

Other notable remains are the Fountain of Glauke (west of the temple of Apollo), the Odeion and Theatre (north-west of the Museum, outside the enclosed area) and the Asklepieion (600m/660yds north of the Museum).

★★ Museum

The Museum provides a comprehensive view of the art of Corinth. Room I contains Neolithic and Helladic material (4th–2nd millennium B.C.). In Room II, opposite Room I, are items ranging in date from the

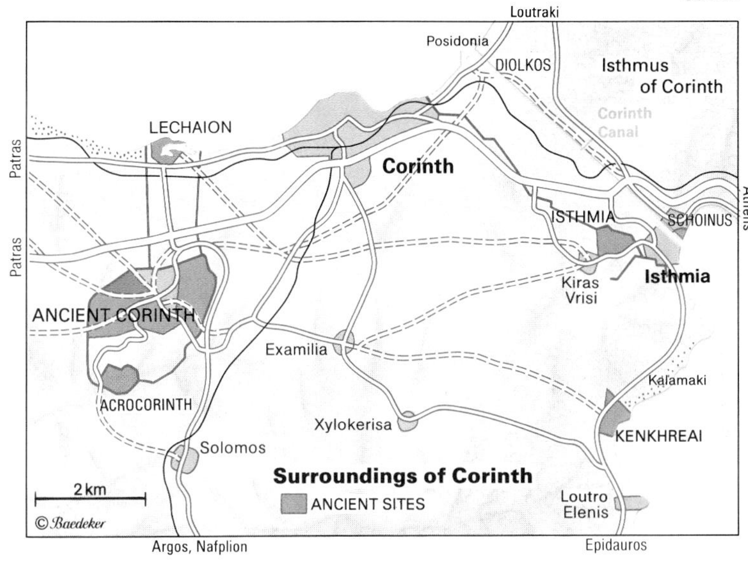

Proto-Geometric period (11th c. B.C.) to Hellenistic times. Of particular interest is the collection of pottery, arranged in chronological order in a clockwise direction, which gives a complete picture of the development of Corinthian pottery from the 11th century onwards. Room III contains Roman, Byzantine and Frankish material, including statues of Augustus and his grandson Lucius Caesar (opposite the entrance) and of other Roman Emperors, a 2nd century mosaic pavement (on the left-hand wall) and figures in Phrygian dress, 2.57m/8½ft high, from the "Captives' Façade".

Acrocorinth

★★ Views

The ascent of Acrocorinth (Akrokórinthos; 575m/1887ft) is made easier by a road which climbs to a point near the lowest gate on the west side. This commanding site was fortified in ancient times, and its defences were maintained and developed during the Byzantine, Frankish, Turkish and Venetian periods. Beyond a moat (alt. 380m/1245ft) constructed by the Venetians we come to the first gate (Frankish, 14th c.) and first wall (15th c.); then follow the second and third walls (Byzantine), with a Hellenistic tower in front of the third gate, to the right. Within the fortress we follow a path running north-east to the remains of a mosque (16th c.), and then turn south until we join a path leading up to the eastern summit, on which there once stood the famous temple of Aphrodite, who was worshipped here after the Eastern fashion. From here there are fine views of the Isthmus and the hills of the Peloponnese.

Lechaion

The old harbour of Lechaion lies north of ancient Corinth, 4km/2½ miles west of the modern town. It is now completely silted up, but the

outlines of the harbour basin can still be distinguished. In 1956–61 Greek archaeologists brought to light on its west side the remains of a 5th century Christian basilica, the largest in Greece (220m/720ft long).

★★Corinth Canal

The Isthmus of Corinth is cut by the Corinth Canal, constructed between 1882 and 1893. Involving an excavation up to 80m/260ft in depth, the canal is 6.3km/4 miles long, 23m/75ft wide and 8m/26ft deep, and can take vessels of up to 10,000 tons. It follows much the same line as a canal planned by the Emperor Nero, but this early project, like other later ones, were never constructed. The best view of the canal is from the bridge which carries the road over it. An interesting feature is the movable bridge at the north-west end, which can be sunk below the surface.

Diolkos

In order to avoid the long passage round the Peloponnese a slipway on which small vessels could be transported across the Isthmus on carts, the Diolkos, was constructed in ancient times. Remains of this can be seen at the west end of the canal.

Crete

H–L 8/9

Κρήτη
Kríti

Nomoi: Khaniá, Réthymnon, Iráklion, Lasíthi
Area of island: 8331 sq.km/3217 sq. miles
Altitude: 0–2456m/0–8058ft
Population: 460,000 (incl. about 12,000 Turks)
Chief town: Iráklion

Air services

Iráklion airport, 5km/3 miles east; Khaniá airport, 12km/7½ miles north-east, at Stérnes on Akrotíri peninsula; Sitía airfield, 5km/3 miles north.
Scheduled flights Athens–Iráklion several times daily; Rhodes or Salonica to Iráklion, several flights weekly; Athens–Khaniá, several flights daily; Rhodes–Sitía via Kárpathos and Kásos, several flights weekly.

Boat services

Athens (Piraeus)–Iráklion and Athens (Piraeus)–Khaniá, twice daily (10–14 hrs; cars carried); sailings, several times weekly, to Cyclades and to Rhodes via Kásos and Kárpathos.

Arrival by sea

Approaching Khaniá, Cape Spátha (on its northern tip, remains of a shrine of the nymph Diktynna) is seen on the right, the peninsula of Akrotíri (ancient Kyamon) on the left. Between the two is the wide sweep of Khaniá Bay (often exposed to storms coming from the north). Ahead can be seen the White Mountains (Lefká Óri). The boats anchor in the open bay, the large ferries beyond the Akrotíri peninsula in Soúda Bay, the only good harbour on the island, which offers a sheltered anchorage for a whole fleet of ships in any weather.
Approaching Iráklion, Cape Stávros, an important landmark, is seen on the right; on the left is the bare island of Día (known to the Venetians as Standia; alt. 265m/869ft; wild goat reserve), a haven of refuge in a northerly storm. Ahead is Iráklion Bay, bounded on the west by Cape Panayía.

◀ *The Corinth Canal*

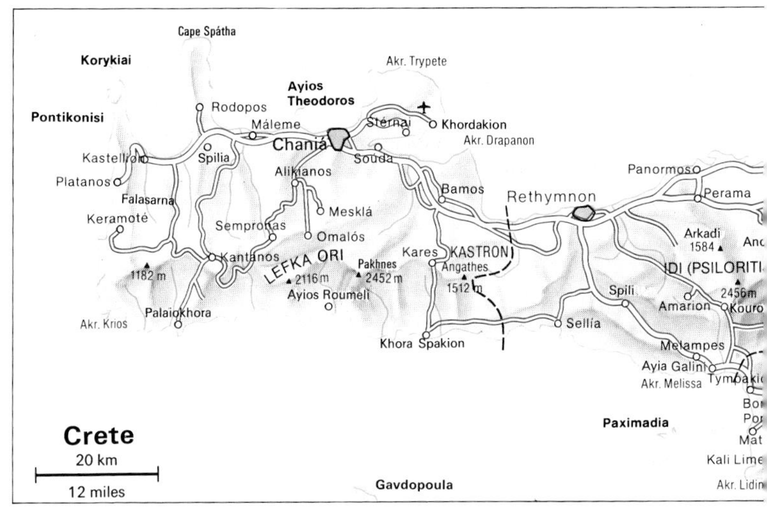

Situation and characteristics

Crete, the largest of the Greek islands and the fifth largest island in the Mediterranean, lies some 100km/60 miles south-east of the Peloponnese at the southern limit of the Aegean Sea. The most southerly outpost of Europe, it is an important link in the chain of islands which forms an arc between southern Greece and Asia Minor. It extends for 260km/160 miles from east to west, varying in width between 12km/7½ miles and 57km/35 miles. It is dominated by three karstic mountain massifs: in the west the Lefká Óri (White Mountains; 2452m/8045ft), which are usually snow-capped; in the centre of the island the Psiloritis range (Ídi Óros, Mount Ida, 2456m/8058ft), which also has a good deal of snow; and in the east the Díkti range (2148m/7048ft). These jagged mountains with their scanty growth of vegetation are the home of the wild goat (*Capra aegagrus*), an ancestor of the domestic goat. Agriculture in this karstic terrain is possible only in the depressions (poljes). Between the mountain ranges are fertile plains (Mesará; Omalós, Lasíthi), with plantations of palms, olives, bananas and oranges and vineyards; in the south early vegetables are grown. While the south coast for the most part falls steeply down to the sea, the north coast is flatter and more indented. On the north coast are Khaniá, the island's capital Iráklion and Réthymnon, its third largest town. The climate is Mediterranean, with relatively mild and wet winters and completely dry summers of subtropical heat (6–7 summer months). The island's main sources of revenue are agriculture and, increasingly, the tourist trade.

History

The earliest traces of human settlement, by incomers from North Africa, date back to the 7th millennium B.C.

From the 3rd millennium B.C. there developed a pre-Greek Bronze Age culture which reached its apogee between 2000 and 1600 B.C. and is known as the Minoan culture, after the legendary King Minos. The cultural and economic influence of Minoan Crete, and also the political authority of this first maritime power in the Mediterranean, were felt as far afield as the Iberian peninsula. Then, around 1400 B.C., for

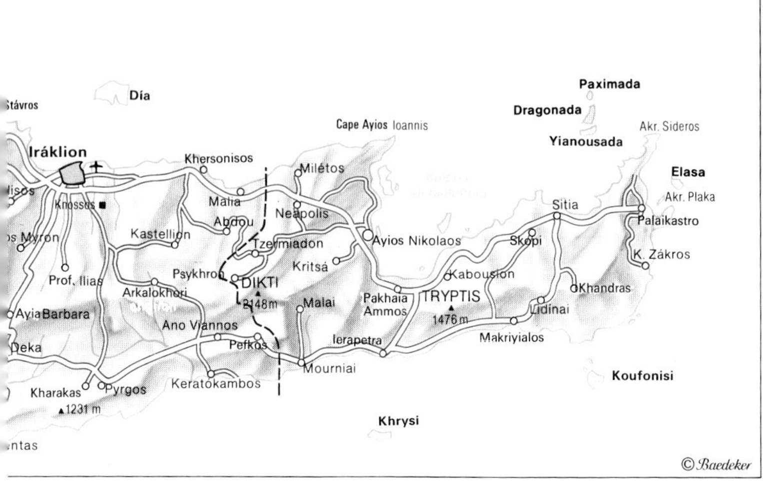

reasons that are not clear, Minoan power collapsed. It may have been a catastrophic earthquake, perhaps following the volcanic explosion on the island of Santorin (see entry), which destroyed the Cretan cities; or the island may have been ravaged by invaders. Whatever the cause, Crete never recovered its former importance.

Towards the end of the 12th century B.C. Dorian Greeks conquered most of the island.

In 66 B.C. Crete – an important base in the Mediterranean – was occupied by Rome. When the Roman Empire was divided in A.D. 395 Crete fell to the Eastern (Byzantine) Empire. In 824 it was occupied by the Saracens, but was recovered by the Empire in 961. From 1204 to 1669 it was ruled by Venice, when the people of Crete fought a long and bitter struggle for independence. Nevertheless the period of Venetian rule saw a considerable cultural flowering on Crete. Among the artists of this period was Domenikos Theotokopoulos, better known as El Greco, who was born in Fódele, near Iráklion, in 1541 (d. Toledo 1614).

In 1669 Crete was captured by the Turks, who did not relinquish it until 1898. After a period of independence the reunion of Crete with Greece was finally proclaimed on October 5th 1912 on the initiative of Elefthérios Venizélos (b. 1864 in Mourniés, near Khaniá), a lawyer and liberal politician who later became prime minister of Greece.

In the spring of 1941 German airborne forces occupied Crete, which, lying between southern Europe and Africa, was of great strategic importance, and remained in occupation until May 1945.

Khaniá

Khanía (pop. 47,000), chief town of its nomos, lies in the south-east corner of Khaniá Bay on the north coast of Crete. The town was founded by the Venetians in the 13th century, under the name of La Canea, on the site of ancient Kydonia. It suffered heavy damage during the Second World War.

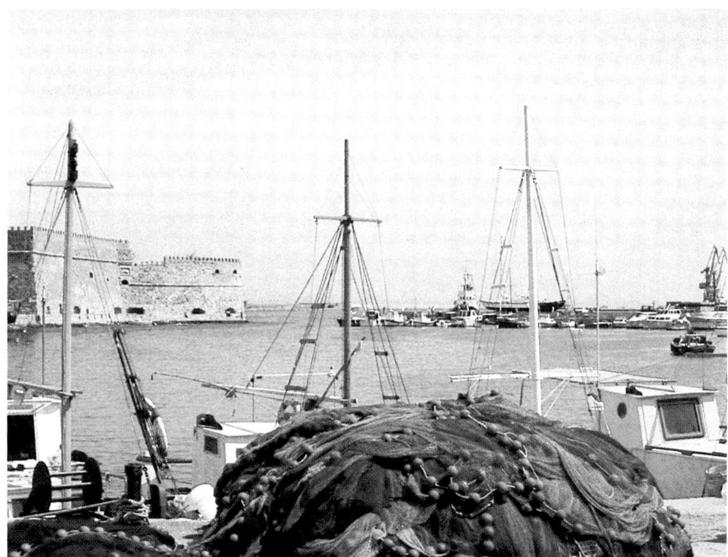

The harbour, Iraklion

Old town

The old town is surrounded by its 16th century walls, with a total length of 3km/2 miles. To the north is the Venetian harbour (boating marina), with a lighthouse at the end of the pier, several Venetian arsenals (*c.* 1500; now used as boat-sheds) and part of the old fortifications.

★ San Francesco Archaeological Museum

The Gothic church of San Francesco now houses the Archaeological Museum. Other features of interest are the church of San Salvatore (16th c.), the Janissaries' Mosque (1645), a number of fine Venetian mansions and the large Market Hall.

Historical Archives

To the south of the old town, at Odós I. Sfakianáki 20, are the Historical Archives, with interesting documents, old weapons and icons.

Khalépa

1.5km/1 mile east of the town is the villa suburb of Khalépa, with the residence of the governor and the foreign consulates.

Soúda Bay

4km/2½ miles south-east of the old town is Soúda Bay, the largest and most sheltered natural harbour on the island (the commercial harbour of Khaniá and a naval base).

Excursions from Khaniá

Profítis Ilías

8km/5 miles east of Khaniá, on Mt Profítis Ilías, are a statue of Liberty and the graves of Sofokles and Eleftherios Venizélos, two Cretan politicians.

Maráthi

6km/4 miles farther east, at Maráthi, are the remains of ancient Minoa.

Akrotíri

17km/10½ miles north-east, on the Akrotíri peninsula, is the monastery of Ayía Triáda (1631), and 4km/2½ miles north of this the monas-

tery of Gouvernéto (1548). Gouvernéto, like Ayía Triáda, has a Renaissance façade showing Venetian influence. An icon in the porch depicts the legend of St John of Gouvernéto, who, fleeing from the Near East, landed on the shore here and, with 98 companions, lived in a cave until a hunter accidentally shot him. The cave can still be seen. From Gouvernéto a broad rocky path (to the right) goes down to some ruined buildings in front of a spacious cave, called the Bear's Cave from the form of a stalagmite in it. The cave is thought to have been a cult site in Minoan times, and in the classical period was dedicated to the cult of Artemis. At the entrance to the cave is the little chapel of the Panayía Arkoudiótissa (Mother of God of the Bear's Cave). From here a narrow path winds its way down to the abandoned monastery of Katholikó, with the cave of St John of Gouvernéto (to the left, shortly before the monastery doorway). The rock-cut church has a Venetian front wall.

Rhodópou

8km/5 miles west of Máleme a road goes off on the right to the village of Kolymbári, with the fortress-like monastery of Goniás and the Oecumenical Academy of the autocephalous (autonomous) Church of Crete. From here the Rhodópou peninsula extends northward. Only 6km/4 miles wide, it rises to a height of 750m/2460ft above sea level. At its north-east end, in Meniés Bay near Cape Scala, can be seen the sanctuary of the nymph Dictynna, excavated by German archaeologists during the Second World War. Dictynna was identical with the Cretan mountain goddess Britomartis and was later equated with Artemis. According to another tradition she was the patroness of fishermen and their nets (*diktyon* = "net"). The best way to reach the site is by boat from Khaniá. From the landing-place a path ascends a small valley with the ruins of an abandoned village and up the southern slope of the hill (to left) to the excavation site. There are the remains of a temple built in the 2nd century A.D. on the site of an earlier temple of the 7th century B.C., together with the altar, cisterns and other buildings.

Kastéli Kisámou

21km/13 miles farther west, on the south side of the Gulf of Kísamos, is the little town of Kastéli Kisámou. From here there are rewarding excursions to the ancient port of Kisamos (2km/1¼ miles north-west); the island of Gramvoúsa (20km/12½ miles) off the Gramvoúsa peninsula, at the north-western tip of Crete, with a 17th century Venetian fort, situated at a height of 135m/445ft above a sheer cliff on the west coast; the ancient port town of Phalasarna (9km/6 miles west), with remains of buildings and harbour installations, tombs and rock carvings; and the remains of the Dorian town of Polyrrhenia (6km/4 miles south).

Kándanos

60km/37 miles south-west of Khaniá lies the village of Kándanos, the inhabitants of which were shot by German forces during the Second World War in reprisal for the activities of the Greek Resistance.

Palaiokhóra

South of Kándanos, on a promontory, is Palaiokhóra (pop. 1000), with a Venetian castle. West of the village extends a long sandy beach.

Lisos

Shortly before Palaiokhóra a road branches off on the left and runs east by way of Rodováni to the bay of Soúyia (ancient Syia). From here a path leads over the hill to the west into the neighbouring bay of Áyios Kýrikos (more easily reached by boat from Palaiokhóra). This was the site of ancient Lisos. The custodian takes visitors to see the temple in the sanctuary of Asklepios, which preserves the walls of the naos, mosaic pavements, the base of the cult image and (to the left of this) a box for offerings. The water of the sacred spring flows under the temple to a fountain. There are also remains of Roman houses and, on the western slope, Hellenistic and Roman tombs. On the shore is the chapel of Áyios Kýrikos, and to the west of the temple a chapel dedicated to the Panayía, both built over the remains of early Christian basilicas.

★★ Samariá Gorge (illustration, p. 219)

42km/26 miles south of Khaniá lies the village of Omalós, on the edge of the fertile Omalós plain. This is the starting-point of the walk (7 hrs) through the Samariá Gorge (Farángi tis Samariás), 18km/11 mile long, up to 600m/2000ft deep and no more than 3–4m/10–14ft wide at its narrowest point, the "Iron Gates" (Síderoportes). The Cretan wild goat (kri kri) still survives in this area.
To undertake the walk through the gorge you need to be fit, to have stout footwear and carry sufficient food and particularly water. At the south end of the gorge is the village of Ayía Rouméli, from which it is 10km/6 miles east (by boat or on foot) to Khóra Sfakíon, with the Venetian fort of Frangokástello or Castelfranco. From there the return to Khaniá (75km/47 miles) is by bus.

Réthymnon

Réthymnon, the third largest town on Crete (pop. 15,000), lies half way along the north coast, at the foot of the Psiloritis range. The periods of Venetian and Turkish occupation have left their mark on the town, which shows a charming mingling of cultures.

Old town

The old town has many Venetian mansions, Turkish houses with enclosed timber balconies, several small mosques (18th c.) and the Fortezza (14th c., extended in 16th c.), within which is a mosque with a massive dome. The Archaeological Museum, opened in 1990 next to the Fortezza, is famous for the superb presentation of its exhibits.

Excursions from Réthymnon

Piyí

10km/6 miles east of Réthymnon, at Piyí, is the largest olive plantation in the Mediterranean area, with 1.5 million trees.

★ Arkádi

23km/14 miles from Réthymnon are the fortress-like monastery buildings of Arkádi, in which, during a rising against the Turks in 1866, the Cretans who had taken refuge here blew themselves up rather than surrender.
Between 30 and 40km (20 and 24 miles) south-east of Réthymnon, around the little town of Amári, are a number of typical Cretan villages (Apóstoli, Méronas, Yerakárion, Vrýses, Áno Méros, Fourfourás, etc.); some of them have interesting old churches. Also in this area is the 17th century monastery of the Asomáton, near which a Mycenaean country house has been excavated.
Farther south-east (62km/39 miles from Réthymnon) is the charming little fishing village of Ayía Galíni, with a beautiful beach.
36km/22 miles south of Réthymnon is Préveli monastery (17th c.), near which is another attractive beach.

Iráklion

Iráklion (Herakleion; pop. 85,000), two-thirds of the way along the north coast of Crete, is the island's largest town, its administrative

The Samariá Gorge ▶

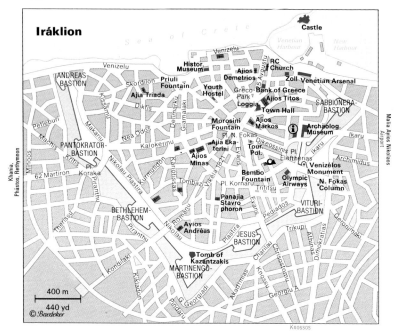

centre and most important commercial port, and the see of an Orthodox archbishop. In ancient times Iráklion was the port of Knossos, but declined in the Roman period and was given a fresh lease of life from A.D. 824 onwards by the Saracens, who called the town Chandak. The Venetians surrounded the town, which they called Candia, with a 5km/3 mile long circuit of massive walls (by Michele Sammicheli, 1538 onwards) and made it the island's capital. In the 16th and 17th centuries Iráklion was the headquarters of an important school of painting, the members of which included the celebrated Greek/Spanish painter El Greco.

★★ Archaeological Museum

Iráklion's principal tourist attraction, and one of the most important sights in the whole of Crete, is the Archaeological Museum (Kretikón Mouseion) in the eastern part of the old town, which displays the magnificent finds from Knossos, Phaistós, Ayía Triáda and other sites on the island, illustrating the splendid pre-Greek cultures which flourished from the 5th millennium B.C. onwards.

Department A, Room 1: Neolithic (5000–2600 B.C.) and Early Minoan (2600–2000 B.C.): stone vessels from the island of Mókhlos (north-east of Crete) and seals.

Department B, Rooms 2 and 3: Middle Minoan (the Proto-Palatial period, 2000–1700 B.C.): vases in Kamáres style (named after the village of Kamáres) from Knossos, Mália and Phaistós.

Department Γ, Rooms 4, 5, 7 and 8: Middle Minoan (Neo-Palatial period, 1700–1450 B.C.): cult vessels, inscribed tablets, statuettes, ivory gaming board, jewellery.

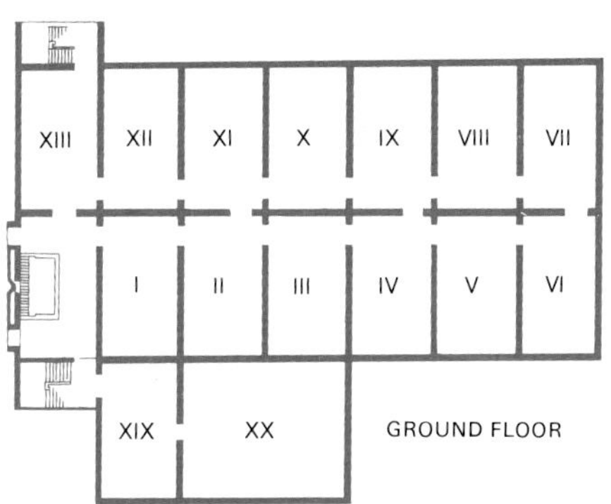

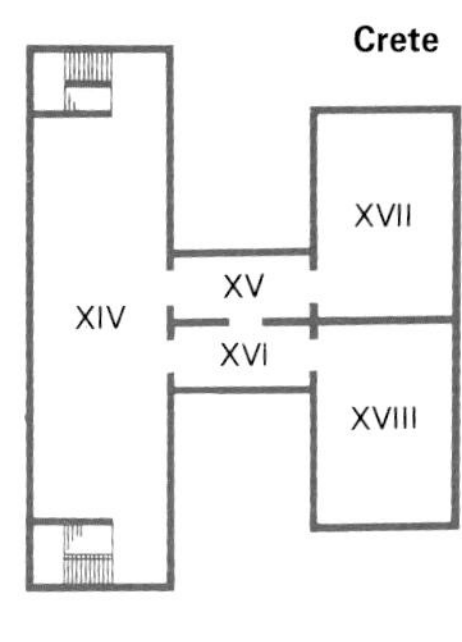

I	Neolithic and Pre-Palatial (2500–2000 B.C.)
II	Proto-Palatial: Knossós, Mália (2000–1700 B.C.)
III	Proto-Palatial: Phaistós (2000–1700 B.C.)
IV	Neo-Palatial: Knossós, Phaistós, Mália (1700–1450 B.C.)
V	Late Neo-Palatial: Knossós (1450–1400 B.C.)
VI	Neo-Palatial and Post-Palatial: Knossós, Phaistós (1400–1350 B.C.)
VII	Neo-Palatial: central Crete
VIII	Neo-Palatial: Káto Zákros (1700–1450 B.C.)
IX	Neo-Palatial: eastern Crete
X	Post-Palatial (1400–1100 B.C.)
XI	Sub-Minoan and Early Geometric (1100–800 B.C.)
XII	Late Geometric and Orientalising (800–650 B.C.)
XIII	Sarcophagi
XIX	Archaic period (7th–6th c. B.C.)
XX	Classical and late (5th c. B.C.–4th c. A.D.)

XIV–XVI	Neo-Palatial: wall paintings
XVII	Giamalakis Collection
XVIII	Archaic to Roman periods: minor arts (7th c. B.C.–4th c. A.D.)

Iráklion Archaeological Museum

Department Δ, Room 6: jewellery and other valuable grave goods of the Late Minoan period (Post-Palatial, 1400–1250 B.C.).
Department E, Room 9: Middle Minoan material from eastern Crete.
Department H, Room 10: Late Minoan/Helladic style (1400–1100 B.C.).
Department Θ, Rooms 11 and 12: Late Minoan/Geometric period (Dorian; 1100–650 B.C.) and later developments.
Department I, Room 13: Minoan sarcophagi from Ayía Triáda, Týlisos, Gourniá and other sites.
Department N, Room 19: Hellenistic period (7th–6th c. B.C.).
Department Ξ, Room 20: Sculpture of the Hellenistic and Roman periods (5th c. B.C.–4th c. A.D.).
Upper floor:
Department K, Rooms 14 (hall)–16: Frescoes and reliefs from Minoan palaces; a magnificent stone sarcophagus from Ayía Triáda.
Department Λ, Room 17: Giamalakis Collection of Dorian sculpture (700–500 B.C.).
Department M, Room 18: Objects of the Hellenistic and Roman periods (700 B.C.–400 A.D.).

★★ Frescoes
★★ Sarcophagus

North of the old town is the charming Venetian Harbour, with a fort commanding the entrance. In Venizélos Square are the Morosini Fountain (1628), with 14th century lions, and St Mark's Church (1303), now a museum of Byzantine painting. In 25th August Street (25 Avgoústou), which runs down from here to the harbour, are the old

★ Morosini Fountain

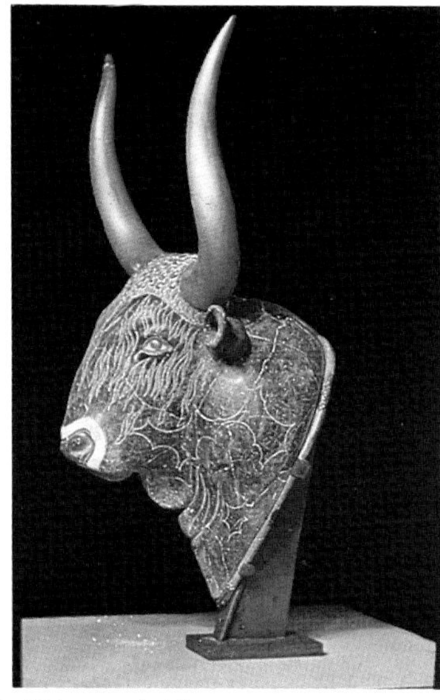

Works of art from Knossos in the Archaeological Museum, Iraklion

Venetian Loggia (1627), now the Town Hall, and just beyond it the church of St Titos (Paul's companion and, according to tradition, the first bishop of Crete), with a reliquary containing the saint's skull.
In St Catherine's Square are the Cathedral of Áyios Minás (19th c.) and the little church of Ayía Ekateríni (St Catherine), now a museum of religious art (16th c. icons by M. Damaskinos).

★ Historical Museum

The Historical Museum, in the northern part of the old town, displays Cretan folk art and relics of the period of Turkish rule. On the second floor is a rich ethnographic collection.

Knossos

★★ Royal Palace (plan, p. 224)

5km/3 miles south-east of Iráklion (5 minutes by bus), near the village of Makritíkhos, is the site of Knossos, once capital of the island, with a royal palace which was excavated and partly reconstructed from 1899 onwards by British archaeologists led by Sir Arthur Evans (1851–1941). The extensive complex laid out on four levels on the hill of Kefála, partly of two and partly of three storeys, was several times destroyed, probably by earthquakes, and subsequently rebuilt. Three phases can therefore be distinguished, the First Palace (*c.* 2000–1800 B.C.), the Second Palace (*c.* 1800–1700) and the Third Palace (*c.* 1700–1400). The remains now visible belong mainly to the Third Palace, built after 1700, which was altered and extended in later centuries but is still substantially in its 16th century state. The complicated layout of the palace suggested that this was the legendary Labyrinth of King Minos, a suggestion supported by the fact that the double axe (*labrys*), the symbol of Minoan Crete, featured in the decoration of the palace.

Tour of palace

The palace is entered from the West Court (on the left, remains of a "theatral area"). Continuing along the Processional Corridor (named

Palace of Knossos (partly reconstructed)

after the frescoes which decorate it), through the monumental South Propylaia and along a long corridor flanked by store-rooms containing large storage jars, we come into the spacious Central Court, in which bull-leaping games (as depicted in representations in the Archaeological Museum, Iráklion) may have been held.

On the west side of the court are the Grand Staircase and the Throne Room (with a stone throne; *c.* 2000 B.C.), and on the east side are domestic offices, workshops and rooms with baths and lavatories (flushed by water). Adjoining the Hall of the Double Axes (after the double-axe symbols on the pillars) are the King's Megaron and Queen's Megaron. The numerous frescoes are copies (originals in the Archaeological Museum in Iráklion).

Around the palace is the site (still largely unexcavated) of the Minoan city of Knossos, which may have had as many as 100,000 inhabitants. Among the remains which have been excavated are a number of villas and the Little Palace (200m/220yds north-west).

Iráklion via Górtys, Phaistós and Ayía Triáda to Mátala

Leave Iráklion on the road which runs west to Réthymnon, and in 2km/1¼ miles take a road on the left, going south.

31km/19 miles: Ayía Varvára, a large village. Beyond this the road climbs to the Askýfou pass (700m/2300ft) and then descends, with magnificent views, into the fertile Mesará plain, with its extensive plantations of olives, oranges, sugar-cane, bananas and other crops.

16km/10 miles: Áyii Déka, with a small archaeological museum (1km/¾ mile south-east).

★ Gortýs

1km/¾ mile beyond this are the remains of ancient Gortýs (Gortyn), once the rival of Knossos and later chief town of the Roman province

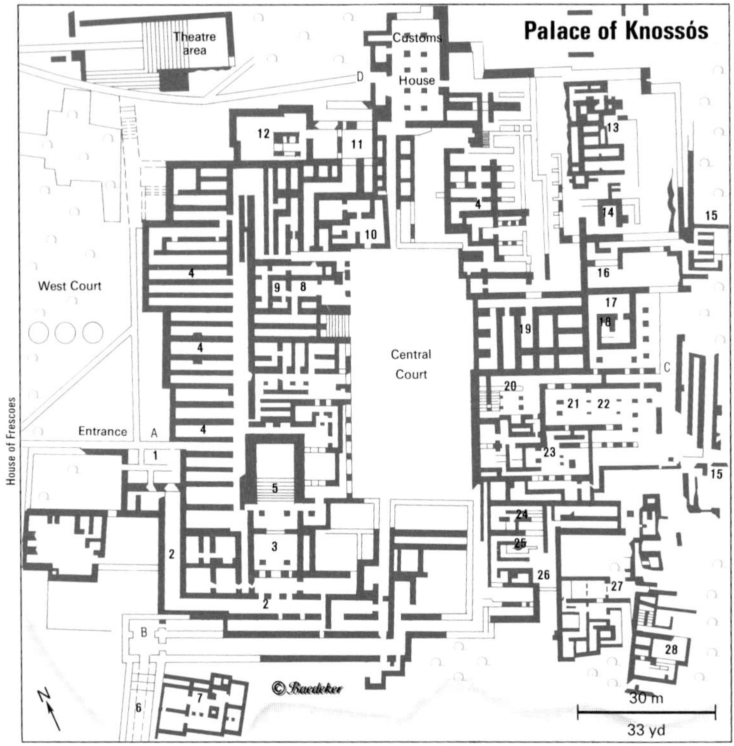

Palace of Knossós

©Baedeker

A West entrance
B South entrance
C East entrance
D North entrance

1 West Propylaia
2 Processional corridor
3 South Propylaia
4 Store-rooms
5 Grand Staircase
6 Stepped Porch
7 South House
8 Throne-Room
9 Inner shrine
10 Prison
11 North-west Portico
12 Lustral basin
13 Pottery stores
14 Store-rooms with giant pithoi
15 Bastions
16 Workshops
17 Potter's workshop
18 Lapidary's workshop
19 Water channel
20 Grand staircase
21 Hall of the Double Axes
22 King's Megaron
23 Queen's Megaron
24 Bathroom
25 Shrine of the Double Axes
26 Lustral basin
27 High altar
28 South-east House

The Hall of the Double Axes in the Palace of Knossós (Reconstruction)

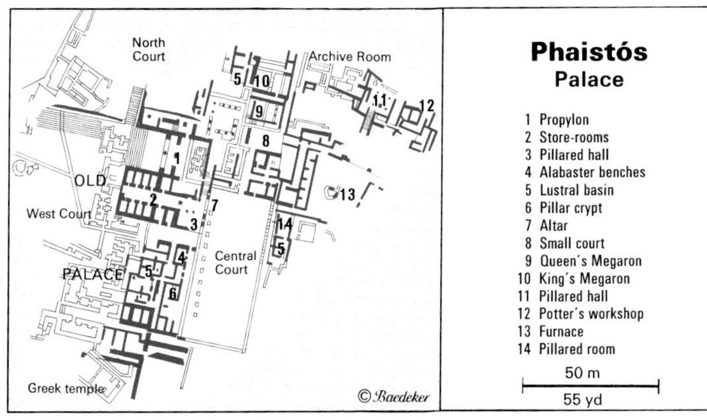

of Creta Cyrenaica, which survived until the coming of the Saracens in A.D. 826. In an olive-grove on the left of the road can be seen the foundations of the temple of Apollo Pythios, the palace of the Roman governor, with a bath-house (2nd c. A.D.), a theatre, an amphitheatre and a 374m/1227ft long circus. 500m/550yds farther on, on the right, at the foot of the acropolis, are the ruins of the 6th century church of Áyios Titos, an ancient theatre and a building, converted into an odeum (concert hall) in Roman times, on which is inscribed the Code of Gortyn, a legal code of around 450 B.C. The code is written "boustrophedon" (i.e. as the ox ploughs, with alternate lines running left to right and right to left).

Platanós

6.5km/4 miles south of the village of Áyii Déka, at Platanós, is the largest tholos tomb on Crete, with an internal diameter of 13m/43ft.

Léntas
Lebéna

The road continues to Léntas (27km/17 miles), on the south coast. Near here, at Lebéna, is a sanctuary of Asklepios founded by Gortýs in the 4th century B.C. round a thermal spring. On a terrace above the village is the temple of Asklepios (4th c. B.C., rebuilt in 2nd c. A.D.), with brick walls faced externally with undressed stone. Two columns are still erect, with the base of the cult image between them. In front of this, to the right, is a room with a mosaic pavement depicting a sea-horse, below which was the temple treasury. From this room a flight of steps and a stoa led east to the fountain-house containing the healing spring, which still survives. Farther east is a chapel of St John (11th c., with frescoes of the 14th and 15th c.), built on the foundations of an earlier three-aisled basilica in which stone from ancient buildings was re-used.

★ Phaistós

14km/8½ miles beyond Gortýs a road goes off on the left, crossing the river Ieropótamos, to the remains of the town of Phaistos (Faistós), founded by King Minos and destroyed in the 2nd millennium B.C. At the east end of the hill ridge on which the town is built is the Palace, laid out on terraces like the palace of Knossos. The present palace was built at some time after 1650 B.C. on the site of an earlier palace built about 1800 and destroyed in an earthquake about 1700, and was itself destroyed in an earthquake about 1450 B.C. (cf. the palace of Knossos). Of the palace, which was built round a central court, there survive only the remains of the north and west wings, the south and east wings having been destroyed in the earthquake. On the west and north sides of the surviving parts of the later palace can be seen remains of the first palace. The palace is entered from the west side by a monumental staircase 13.75m/45ft wide leading to a propylon. Below the steps, to the left, are the tiers of seating of a theatre. From a bastion on the highest terrace there is a magnificent view of the Mesará plain, surrounded by hills.

★ Ayía Triáda

2km/1¼ miles west of Phaistós, on the north edge of the hill ridge, can be seen the remains of the Minoan summer palace of Ayía Triáda, linked with Phaistós by a paved road. The site is named after the Byzantine chapel of Ayía Triáda on a neighbouring hill; its ancient name is not known. Like Phaistós, the palace dates mainly from the 16th century B.C., but was rebuilt after the earthquake of *c.* 1450 and was still occupied in the Dorian period. The frescoes and pottery found here are now mostly in the Archaeological Museum in Iráklion. From the west side of the palace there are fine views of the sea, 3km/2 miles away, and the south coast of Crete. Above the palace is the Venetian chapel of St George (14th c.; frescoes and inscriptions). Lower down, to the north-east, remains of a Late Minoan settlement (14th–11th c. B.C.) have been excavated. At the foot of the hill is a cemetery, with a large tholos tomb.

Vóri

In the village of Vóri (Boroi) a Museum of Cretan Ethnology has recently been opened. (Open: May–Sept. 11am–7pm; at other times 9am–5pm.)

Mátala

10km/6¼ miles beyond Phaistós the road reaches the coast at Mátala, in Minoan times the port of Phaistós, in Roman times the port of Gortýs. In the rock faces around the harbour are rock-cut tombs and dwellings of the early Christian period. Mátala has a beautiful sandy beach.

Other Excursions from Iráklion

Amnisós

7km/4¼ miles east of Iráklion, at Amnisós, are the remains of a two-storey Minoan villa decorated with frescoes and a harbour building, both dating from around 1660 B.C. 3km/2 miles farther east are the well preserved remains of a Minoan villa at the ancient port of Nírou Kháni, with a shrine of the double axe.
There are remains of other Minoan villas at Týlisos (14km/9 miles south-west), Slavókampos (22km/14 miles south-west) and Vathýpetro (20km/12½ miles: see below).

★ Mount Ida

The ascent of Mount Ida (Ídi Óros; Mt Psiloritis, 2456m/8058ft) is a rewarding but strenuous climb (warm clothing and supply of food essential, guide advisable). The starting-point is either Kamáres (with the cave in which the polychrome pottery of the Middle Minoan period known as Kamáres ware was found), from which it is about 9 hours' climb to the summit, or the village of Anóyia (8 hours).
On the north flank of Mount Ida, at a height of 1280m/4200ft, is the Idéon Ántron, a Minoan cult cave.

Arkhánes

15km/9½ miles south of Iráklion lies the little town of Arkhánes (pop. 4000), noted for its *rozakí* table grapes and its wine. Sporadic excavations have shown that this was a place of some importance in Minoan times.

Vathýpetro

4km/2½ miles south of Arkhánes, at Vathýpetro, is a large Minoan villa, the centre of a considerable estate.

Venetian fort, Spinalonga

Áyios Nikólaos

The little town of Áyios Nikólaos (pop. 5200), charmingly situated on the slopes above Mirabello Bay, has developed into a very popular holiday resort, particularly for long-stay holidays, thanks to the beautiful beaches round the town and to its convenience as a centre from which to explore eastern Crete. Linked with the harbour is Lake Voulisméni (fresh water), in which, according to legend, the goddess Athena was accustomed to bathe. ★ Mirabello Bay

The offshore island of Ayii Pántes is a reserve for wild goats.

Excursions from Ayios Nikólaos

★ Eloúnda

6km/4 miles north of Ayios Nikólaos, at the holiday village of Eloúnda, are the remains (partly under the sea) of the Dorian town of Olous.

On the northern tip of the offshore island of Spinalonga (originally a peninsula), which is cut off from the main island by a man-made channel to form the separate island of Kalidóna, stands a Venetian fort of 1571 (enlarged 1585; from 1897 a leper colony).

Psýra

On the island of Psýra, at the east end of Mirabello Bay, are remains of a Middle to Late Minoan settlement.

Mokhlós

Farther east lies the island of Mokhlós, which in ancient times was connected with the mainland. Here were found numerous tombs of the Early Minoan period, the grave goods from which are now in the Archaeological Museum in Iráklion.

Dreros

22km/13½ miles north-west of Áyios Nikólaos (2km/1¼ miles north-east of the village of Neápolis) is the site of the Minoan settlement of Dreros, with a sanctuary of Apollo (8th–7th c.; bronze cult images).

★ Mália

34km/21 miles north-west of Áyios Nikólaos, at the village of Mália (beach), situated in a fertile depression irrigated with the help of windmills, are the remains of a Minoan palace, similar to the palaces of Knossos and Phaistós but smaller, which was built about 1800 B.C. and rebuilt after an earthquake in 1700 B.C. and thereafter fell into ruin. There are also remains of the Minoan town of Mália and of a cemetery.

★ Lasíthi plain

30–40km/20–25 miles west of Áyios Nikólaos is the fertile karstic plateau of Lasíthi (alt. 850m/2790ft), with the 12,000 windmills (now increasingly going out of use) which irrigate the plain and have earned it the name of the Valley of Windmills. On the south-western edge of the plateau, at the village of Psykhró, is the stalactitic Dictaean Cave (Diktaíon Ántron) in which Zeus was believed to have been born.

★ Kritsá

11km/7 miles south-west of Áyios Nikólaos, amid ancient olive-groves, is the picturesque hill village of Kritsá, around which are a number of beautiful Byzantine churches, in particular the chapel of the Panayía tis Kerás (12th–14th c.; frescoes) and the church of Áyios Yeóryios (14th c.). On a hill 4km/2½ miles north-west are the remains, now partly covered by scrub, of the ancient city of Lató, probably built between the 7th and the 4th century B.C. From the terraced site, or from the acropolis above it, there are magnificent views of the surrounding hills and Mirabello Bay.

Máles

30km/19 miles south-west of Áyios Nikólaos, above a valley running south from Mt Diktí, the village of Máles has remains of the Dorian settlement of Malla. 15km/9 miles farther south is Mýrtos (beach), where there are Roman remains.

Ierápetra

36km/22 miles south of Áyios Nikólaos, on the south coast, lies Ierápetra, the most southerly town in Europe, in a fertile vegetable-

Excavations at Gourniá

growing area, which occupies the site of the ancient port of Hierapydna. The harbour is defended by a Venetian fort. In the Town Hall is a small museum of Roman and Venetian material.
Some 18km/11 miles south-west of Ierápetra lies the island of Gaidouronísi. Farther east, 5km/3 miles off Cape Goudoúra, is the island of Koufonísi.

★ Gourniá

20km/12½ miles south-east of Áyios Nikólaos are the remains (only partially excavated) of the Minoan town of Gourniá. With its narrow paved streets, its small houses and its palace and temple on higher ground, it gives a good impression of the aspect of a Late Minoan settlement of between 1600 and 1400 B.C.

Sitía

Sitía (ancient Eteia) is a picturesquely situated little port in eastern Crete, dominated by a Venetian fort. The town, which was destroyed by an earthquake and bombarded by a Turkish fleet commanded by Khaireddin Barbarossa in 1538, is mainly modern; it has a good beach. It was the home of Vintzentinos Kornaros (d. 1677), author of an epic romance, the "Erotokritos", which is still popular. There is an attractive promenade along the harbour (restaurants). In Arkadion Street (parallel to the harbour) is an interesting Folk Museum.

Excursions from Sitía

Ayía Fotiá
Moní Toploú

5km/3 miles east of Sitía, at Ayía Fotiá, can be seen a Minoan necropolis.
16km/10 miles farther east is the fortified monastery of Toploú (17th c.), which was a centre of resistance to the Turks and a place of refuge

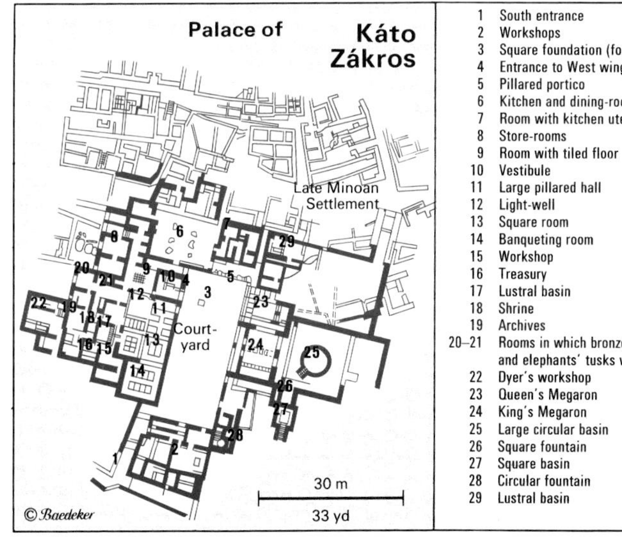

during the German occupation of 1941–44. It has an interesting collection of Bibles and icons.

Palaíkastro

23km/14 miles east of Sitía is the Minoan site of Palaíkastro.

★ Vái Bay (illustration, p. 230)

Around the beautiful sandy bay of Vái, with the modest village of that name, is the only palm-grove on Crete.

Itanos

3km/2 miles north, at Ermoúpolis, are the remains of Minoan Itanos.

★ Káto Zákros

From Sitía a good, and in its final section magnificent, panoramic road runs high above the sea to the partly excavated remains of a Minoan city at Káto Zákros, 46km/29 miles south-east. The town was occupied between 1600 and 1450 B.C. and carried on trade with Egypt and the rest of North Africa.
Some 15km/9 miles south of Sitía is Praisós, with a Minoan villa and a Hellenistic cemetery.
There are numerous other archaeological sites in the neighbourhood of Sitía, including Minoan villas at Piskokéfalon, Zou and Ríza (all south-east of the town) and a Minoan tholos tomb at Akhládia (to the south).

Gávdos

Some 37km/23 miles off the south-west coast of Crete lies the wooded island of Gávdos, Europe's most southerly point. This is thought to be the island of Ogygia, home of Calypso, with whom Odysseus stayed for seven years ("Odyssey", Book 7).

Cyclades

I–L 5–7

Κυκλάδες
Kykládes

The name of Cyclades was given in antiquity to the circle (*kyklos*) of islands, mostly inhabited by Ionians, enclosing the sacred island of Delos (see entry). According to the ancient legend Poseidon struck the mountains with his trident and drove them into the sea, where they took root. The archipelago, consisting of 23 larger and some 200 smaller islands, rises out of a submarine plateau which extends south-eastward and eastward in an arc from Attica and Euboea to the coast of Asia Minor. All the islands are hilly; those in the north consist predominantly of Cretaceous limestones, micaceous schists, gneiss and marble, while the islands to the south consist partly of eruptive rocks. Except on Náxos there are no rivers with a perennial flow; and trees are lacking because of the sharp sea winds which blow throughout the year. Characteristic of the islands are their whitewashed cube-shaped houses and their thatch-roofed windmills with their light-coloured sails.

History and culture

The original inhabitants of the islands are believed to have been Carians belonging to the Cycladic culture of the early Bronze Age (2400–1200 B.C.). The "Cycladic idols" (usually female figures carved from stone) typical of that culture have been found on all the islands. In the late 2nd millennium B.C. the indigenous inhabitants were displaced by Ionians on the northern islands and Dorians on the southern

◀ *Vai Bay, on the east coast of Crete*

islands. Most of the Cycladic islands joined the first and later the second Attic maritime league. In the second half of the 1st millennium B.C. the islands were partly under Macedonian and partly under Ptolemaic rule. They were later occupied by Rome, and when the Roman Empire was divided in A.D. 395 they fell to the East Roman (Byzantine) Empire. During the Middle Ages there were centuries of Venetian and Frankish rule, with a flowering of art and intellectual life. Even after occupation by the Turks in 1579 the islands largely preserved their religious (predominantly Catholic) and cultural identity. They were united with Greece in 1834.
For descriptions of the individual islands see the Index.

The Goulandris Museum of Cycladic Art in Athens (see entry) is devoted to the very individual Cycladic culture of the 4th and 3rd millennia B.C.

Dafní H 5

Δαψνί
Dafní

Region and nomos: Attica

Situation

Dafní, a monastery 10km/6 miles west of central Athens on the road to Eleusis, is famed for its 11th century mosaics.

The monastery of Dafní

History

The name of the monastery refers to a shrine of Apollo, to whom the laurel (*daphne*) was sacred, which once stood on the site. It was succeeded by an Early Christian monastery, which gave place to the present building in 1080. The monastery was dedicated to the Dormition (*koimesis,* modern Greek *kímisis*) of the Mother of God. In 1205, after the Frankish occupation of Athens, it was handed over to Cistercian monks and became the burial-place of the Frankish lords (later dukes) of Athens. From this period date the battlemented defensive walls and a number of sarcophagi. At the beginning of the Turkish period the monastery was reoccupied by Orthodox monks. During the 19th century war of liberation Dafní suffered damage and was abandoned. A thorough restoration in 1955–57 saved the buildings from further decay and ensured the preservation of the structure and the surviving mosaics.

A violent earthquake in 1981 caused severe damage to the buildings and the enclosure wall.

The ★★ monastery

The picturesque and attractive forecourt of the monastery is bounded on the west by one side of the cloister, on the north by the south wall of the church and on the east by other monastic buildings. From the west entrance of the church we pass through the Gothic exonarthex, dating from the period of Cistercian occupation, and the narthex into the church, which ranks with Ósios Loukás near Delphi and the Néa Moní on Chios (see entries) as one of the three finest 11th century churches in Greece. The naos, on a Greek cross plan, is dominated – as in these other two churches – by a large central dome which spans both the central aisle and the two lateral aisles. From the dome the grave and majestic figure of Christ Pantokrátor (Ruler of All) looks down. In the

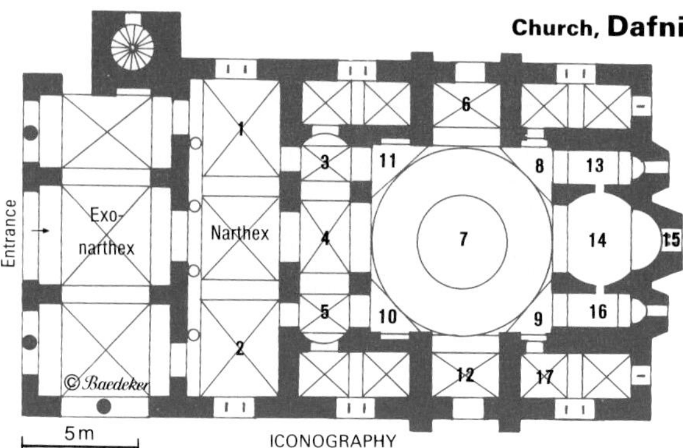

ICONOGRAPHY

1 Betrayal, Washing of the Feet, Last Supper
2 Joachim and Anne, Blessing of the Priests, Presentation of the Virgin
3 Bacchus, Elpidophorus, Aphthonius, Pegasius
4 Dormition
5 Mardarius, Orestes, Auxentius, Sergius
6 Andronicus, Probus, Tarachus, Crucifixion, Nativity of the Virgin, Entry into Jerusalem, Raising of Lazarus
7 Christ Pantokrator, with prophets (Isaiah, Solomon, Elijah, Elisha, Jonas, Habakkuk, Zephaniah, Malachi, Daniel, Micah, Joel, Zechariah, Ezekiel, Jeremiah, Moses, David)
8 Annunciation
9 Nativity
10 Baptism of Christ
11 Transfiguration
12 Incredulity of Thomas, Descent into Hell, Presentation in the Temple, Samonas, Gurias, Abibus
13 Stephen, Sylvester, Aaron, John the Baptist, Zachariah, Anthimus
14 Michael, Preparation of the Throne, Resurrection, Gabriel
15 Mary
16 Lawrence, Eleutherius, Gregory Thaumaturgus, Nicholas, Gregory of Agrigentum, Avercius
17 Magi

pendentives under the dome are four of the major themes of Orthodox iconography – the Annunciation (NE), the Nativity (SE), the Baptism of Christ (SW) and the Transfiguration (NW).

Numerous other mosaics have been preserved in the rest of the church. In the north transept are the Raising of Lazarus and the Entry into Jerusalem (NW), the Nativity of the Virgin and the Crucifixion (NE); in the south transept the Magi and the Descent into Hell (SE), the Presentation in the Temple and the Incredulity of Thomas (SW). In the sanctuary are the Resurrection and the Mother of God, flanked by the Archangels Michael and Gabriel; in the prothesis (to the left) John the Baptist, and in the diakonikon (to the right) St Nicholas. Above the entrance to the naos is the Dormition, in the narthex the prayer of Joachim and Anne, the Washing of the Feet and the Last Supper. All these scenes show the mosaic art of the 11th century at its peak, a fascinating combination of the Greek sense of beauty and Christian spiritualisation.

From July to September the Tourist Pavilion at Dafní is the scene of a Wine Festival, with free wine-tasting, Greek culinary specialities, music and dancing.

Delos K 6

Δῆλος
Dílos

Nomos: Cyclades
Area of island: 3.6 sq.km/1½ sq. miles
Altitude: 0–113m/0–371ft
No towns or villages; no permanent inhabitants

Boat services

Boats from Mýkonos, depending on demand and weather conditions; occasional connections with Tínos, Náxos and Páros.

Situation

Delos, a rocky island 5km/3 miles long and only 1300m/1420yds wide, lies 10km/6 miles south-west of Mýkonos (see entry). Although it is one of the smallest of the Cyclades, and much the smallest of the group formed by Mýkonos, Delos and Rinía, Delos, as the birthplace of Apollo, was a place of such importance in ancient times that the surrounding islands were known as the Cyclades since they lay in a circle (*kyklos*) round the sacred island. The extensive area of remains (excavated by French archaeologists from 1873 onwards) is one of the most important archaeological sites in Greece.
Delos is an island that appeals particularly to those who are interested in Greek antiquity; it has none of the usual tourist facilities.

History

According to the myth it was on Delos that Leto gave birth to Apollo and Artemis, attended by two maidens from the hyperborean regions of the north; and the history of the island was determined by its importance as a pan-Hellenic shrine.
The first settlers, in the 3rd millennium B.C., were Phoenicians and Carians. In the 1st millennium, after the original inhabitants had been driven out by Ionians, the island became the centre of the cult of Apollo. Here the Ionians held splendid annual games, the foundation of which was attributed to Theseus. In 543 B.C. Peisistratos carried out a "purification" (*katharsis*) of the island, with the removal of all tombs from the vicinity of the temples. Under a second purification in 426/425 B.C. births, deaths and burials were prohibited on Delos, and the existing tombs were transferred to the neighbouring island of Rheneia (Rínia). When the Ionian League was founded after the Persian wars its treasury was deposited in the temple of Apollo; but in 454 B.C. the Athenians carried it off to Athens, and thereafter Delos and the other islands remained dependants of Athens until the time of Alexander

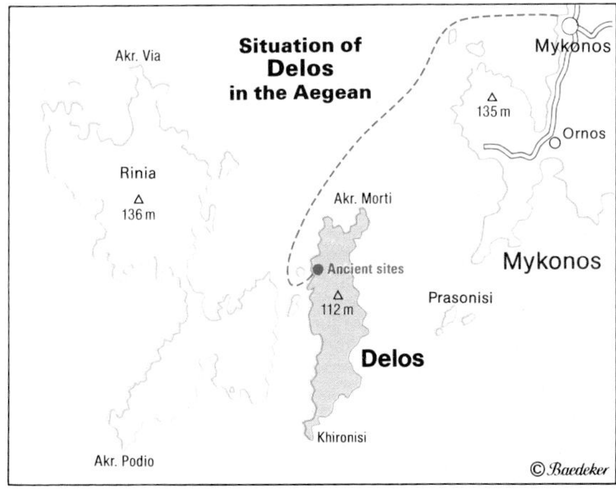

the Great. After breaking away from Athens Delos developed a flourishing trade which made it the economic centre of the archipelago, and foreign trading corporations like the Hermaists (Romans) and Poseidoniasts (Syrians from Berytos/Beirut) had agencies on the island. The Romans, who had established a protectorate over the island in 166 B.C., returned it to Athens. As a result – particularly after the destruction of Corinth (see entry) – Delos enjoyed its greatest period of prosperity, which lasted until the devastation of the island by Mithridates in 88 B.C. initiated its decline. Complete destruction followed in 69 B.C., when the island was sacked by pirates. Thereafter Delos was practically uninhabited. When Pausanias visited it in the 2nd century A.D. he saw only the custodians of the sanctuary. A fresh settlement was established in Christian times, but this did not last.

★★Archaeological Sites

Harbour

On the west side of the island is the Sacred Harbour (landing-stage), now completely silted up, where delegations attending the annual festival used to land. To the south of this is the old commercial harbour. The coast between the Sacred Harbour and Foumi Bay was lined in a later period with quays (completed in 111 B.C.) and warehouses, remains of which can be seen under water.

★ Sacred Precinct

The Sacred Precinct, which was surrounded by walls and stoas, was approached from the south by a broad paved way running between two Doric stoas above the present harbour. The 87m/285ft long Stoa of Philip V (on the left), open on both sides, has an inscription on the architrave recording that it was built by Philip V of Macedon about 210 B.C. On the right of the road is a smaller stoa with eight shops along the far side. Beyond this, to the east, is the almost square South Agora (1st c. B.C.). To the north is an open square, on the east side of which are the South-East Propylaia; on the west side is a passage through the smaller stoa. This whole area, extending north to the Hall of the Bulls, was occupied in the Middle Ages by fortifications erected by the Knights of St John.

From the South Propylaia (2nd c. B.C.), which have Doric columns on each side, on a three-stepped base, the Festival Way ran north, passing over a small esplanade paved with bluish marble and flanked by altars, statues and exedras and then along the west side of three parallel temples of Apollo, finally turning back round the east side of the temples. A shorter route to the east side of the precinct was by way of the long Ionic portico, with narrow open colonnades on each side, just inside the South Propylaia (immediately on right). At its north end is the base of a colossal statue of Apollo, with an inscription (6th c. B.C.) indicating that the statue and its base were carved from a single block of stone; the dedication on the west side ("The Naxians to Apollo") was a later addition.

On the left of the Festival Way, beyond the esplanade, is a precinct containing a stoa and two temples. The larger of the temples, the Keraton, at the south-west corner, was dedicated to Apollo and contained a famous horned altar, regarded as one of the wonders of the world, with rams' horns set round it. The Keraton is believed to be older than the Artemision (shrine of Artemis) in the centre of the precinct, an Ionic temple surrounded by columns built on granite foundations, probably the successor to an earlier temple of the 7th century B.C.

In front of the entrance to the Keraton, which faces south, are a number of bases for equestrian statues, the most northerly and smallest of which bore a statue of Sulla (inscription on rear).

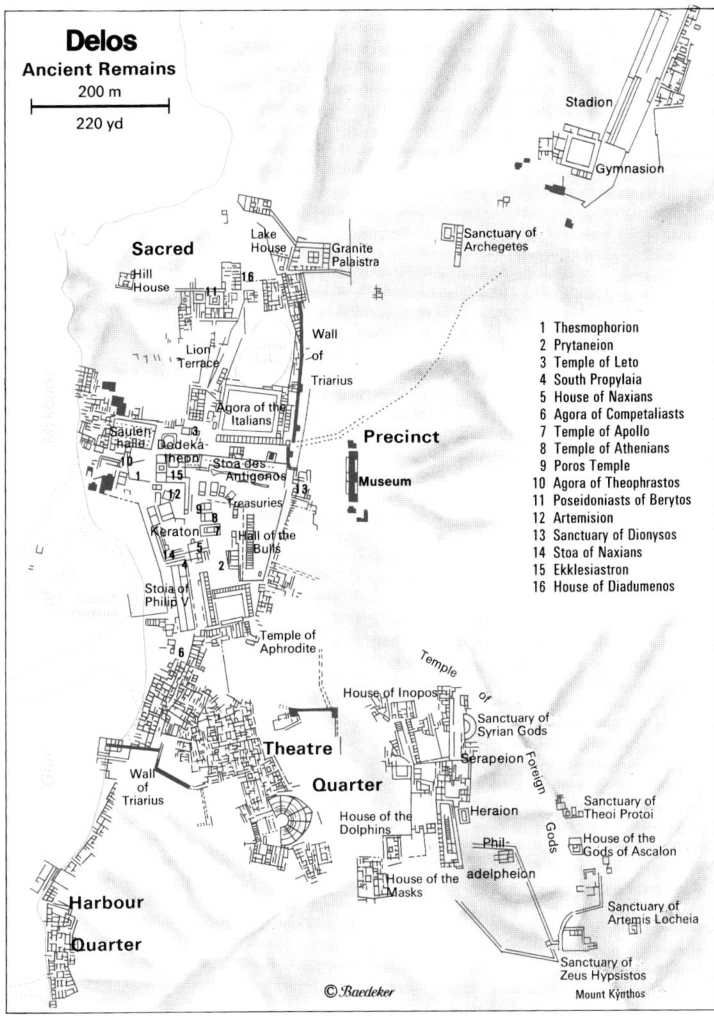

North-west of the precinct of Artemis is the Thesmophorion, which was dedicated to the cult of Demeter.

To the east of the Artemision the Festival Way takes a U-turn round the three parallel temples of Apollo. The most southerly of these (4th–3rd c. B.C.), which resembles the Theseion in Athens (see entry) in layout, is the largest of the three, covering an area of 26.4m/87ft by 13.55m/44ft. The massive foundations, built on a stratum of greyish-blue slate, show that the temple was peripteral, with 6 × 13 columns.

Excavations in harbour area

The pronaos at the east end and opisthodomos at the west end probably had two columns between the antae. The naos measured 11.5m/38ft by 5.6m/18ft. Of the temple itself little is left but the Doric columns and some fragments of the frieze of triglyphs, and of the sculptural decoration only the palmette ornament and the lions' heads from the sima.

Immediately north of this temple are the foundations, built in poros limestone, of the Temple of the Athenians (late 5th c. B.C.; Doric), with a small pronaos and opisthodomos and a naos divided into two parts. Beyond this is the oldest of the temples (first half of 6th c. B.C.), built of poros limestone. In front of this temple is a long statue base on which there were once bronze figures – a monument (3rd c. B.C.) in honour of Proletairos, founder of the royal house of Pergamon.

On the north side of the bend in the Festival Way are five small buildings, four of them facing the three temples. On the basis of their similarity to the corresponding buildings at Olympia and Delphi four of them are believed to be treasuries. The fifth (the most southerly), with a pronaos and opisthodomos, was probably a temple. Facing its entrance is the Prytaneion, seat of the chief magistrate (5th c. B.C.).

★ Hall of the Bulls

East of this is the Hall of the Bulls or Ship Hall, one of the best preserved buildings on Delos, which is dated to the Hellenistic period. Probably designed to house a ship dedicated after a naval victory, it measures 67.2m/220ft from north-east to south-west, with a width of 8.86m/29ft. The building stood on a granite platform approached by three marble steps (still partly preserved), with walls around the sides and the north end; the south end was probably open, with two columns between antae. The interior was in the form of a long gallery with a cavity in the centre. Of the sculptural decoration only a nereid

and a dolphin are left in situ. At the entrance were pillars preceded by Doric half-columns, with capitals depicting recumbent bulls.
The step-like structure south-east of the Hall of the Bulls is part of an altar of Zeus Polieus.
On the east side of the precinct of Apollo was the sanctuary of Dionysos, with several marble phalluses. On one of the bases are carvings of scenes from the cult of Dionysos (*c.* 300 B.C.).
Along the north side of the precinct is the Stoa of Antigonos (3rd c. B.C.), with bull's-head triglyphs. Behind the colonnade were rooms for housing representatives sent to the annual festival. Rather less than half way along this is a semicircular structure dating from Mycenaean times, the tomb of the Hyperborean Maidens who attended Leto at the birth of the divine twins.

Commercial quarter

On the west side of the precinct of Apollo are propylaia leading out of the Sacred Precinct into the commercial quarter of the city. At the near end of the street, which is lined with shops, is the Agora of the Italians (2nd c. B.C.), a large square area surrounded by two-storey colonnaded halls containing shops, workshops and recesses for votive offerings (mosaics). This was the headquarters of the corporation of Roman merchants, who called themselves Hermaists after their patron Hermes. Another similar establishment, the headquarters of the Poseidoniasts of Berytos (Beirut), lay north-west of the Sacred Lake. To the north of the entrance to the Agora of the Italians is the temple of Leto, and farther west is the Stoa of Antigonos (3rd c. B.C.).

Sacred Lake

★Marble lions

The oval Sacred Lake (now dry), on the shores of which Leto was believed to have given birth to Apollo, marks the end of the Sacred Precinct. On a terrace to the west of the lake is a row of nine marble lions of Naxian marble (7th c. B.C.). In this area, to the north of the lake, were the Old and the New Palaistra (courtyards surrounded by colonnades). Farther north-east are the sanctuary of the Heros Archegetes, which only Delians might enter, the Gymnasion and the Stadion, with its north-west side built against the rock.

★Museum

To the east, at some distance from the Sacred Precinct, is the Museum, which contains a good collection of material from the site, although some of the finest items found here are now in the National Archaeological Museum and the Museum of Cycladic Art in Athens.
In the two central rooms are works of Archaic art, including (on the left) a marble tripod base with a ram's head and Gorgons (7th c. B.C.), a sphinx, several kouroi and korai (6th c. B.C.), a hand of the Naxian Apollo (on the right) and three seated figures of women (7th c. B.C.).
The room to the left of the entrance contains fragments (acroteria and figures from the pediment) from the Temple of the Athenians, herms, funerary stelae, small sculpture, terracottas and pottery. In the room to the right are votive offerings from the temple of Artemis, fragments of sculpture and inscriptions.

Theatre Quarter, residential quarter

To the south of the Sacred Precinct is the Agora of the Competaliasts (headquarters of the Roman merchants who practised the cult of the Lares Competales), with statues and a number of small temples.
Farther south, between Mt Kýnthos and the commercial harbour, is the so-called Theatre Quarter (3rd–2nd c. B.C.), which gives an excellent impression of housing conditions in that period. The narrow, winding streets are paved with slate slabs. The houses, many of which stand 4–5m/13–16ft high, had at least one upper storey; the decoration is reminiscent of the First Pompeian style. Particularly notable is the House of the Trident (mosaic pavement).
On the south-east side of the quarter is the Theatre, with a Greek-style auditorium extending round more than a semicircle. The four lowest

The marble lions of Delos

rows have preserved their marble steps, and the seats at the right-hand end of the first row still have their backs. The orchestra was surrounded by a narrow water channel, the stage building by a colonnade, the east side of which served as a proskenion. Below the stage building is a large cistern.

Mt Kýnthos

To climb Mt Kýnthos, follow an ancient road which runs south-east to the dry bed of the river Inopós (which even in antiquity had little water). Immediately west of the gorge is the House of Inopós (2nd c. B.C.), and to the south, farther up the river bed, are the House of the Dolphins (with a dolphin mosaic in the peristyle) and the House of Masks. To the east, on a terrace above the gorge, is the Sanctuary of the Syrian Gods, in which Serapis, Isis, Anubis and Harpokrates were venerated from the 2nd century B.C. From here the ancient road (partly stepped) climbs to the summit of Mt Kýnthos (113m/371ft), once crowned by the temple of Zeus Kýnthos and Athena Kynthia (3rd c. B.C.), successor to an earlier temple of the 7th century B.C.

★ View

From the top of the hill there are extensive views: to the south the hills of Náxos, to the west Sýros with its chief town Ermoúpolis, to the north the mountainous island of Tínos and to the east Mýkonos with its numerous chapels.

On the western slope of the hill is a grotto roofed with massive stone slabs containing the base of a statue.

Rínia

West of Delos is the island of Rínia (also known as Megáli Dílos; area 17 sq.km/6½ sq. miles), the ancient Rheneia. After the second purification it became the burial-place for Delos, but otherwise was of no consequence.

In the 1km/¾ mile wide channel between Delos and the southern half of Rínia are two barren rocks, Mikrós Revmatiáris and Megálos Revmatiáris.

Delphi G 5

Δελφοί
Delfí

Region and nomos: Phocis
Altitude: 520–620m/1705–2035ft
Population: 2500

Transport

Regular bus services from Athens.

Recreation and sport

The Delphi area offers plenty of scope for mountain walks and winter sports, mainly on Mt Parnassus (2457m/8061ft: see entry). There are bathing beaches at Itéa, Kírra and Galaxídi.
The harbour of Itéa has customs clearance facilities.

★★ Situation

Delphi, lying on the slopes of Mount Parnassus high above the Gulf of Corinth, is one of the most famous cult sites in Greece, famed throughout the ancient Greek world and beyond as the sanctuary of Apollo and the shrine of his oracle. The site ranks with the Acropolis in Athens, Olympia and the island of Delos as one of the most important sites of the classical period of Greece; and the wealth of ancient remains combines with its magnificent mountain setting to make Delphi one of the high points of a visit to Greece.

The present little town of Delphi, now a concentration of hotels and shops catering for tourists, was established only in 1892, when the village of Kastrí, which had grown up on the site of the temple of

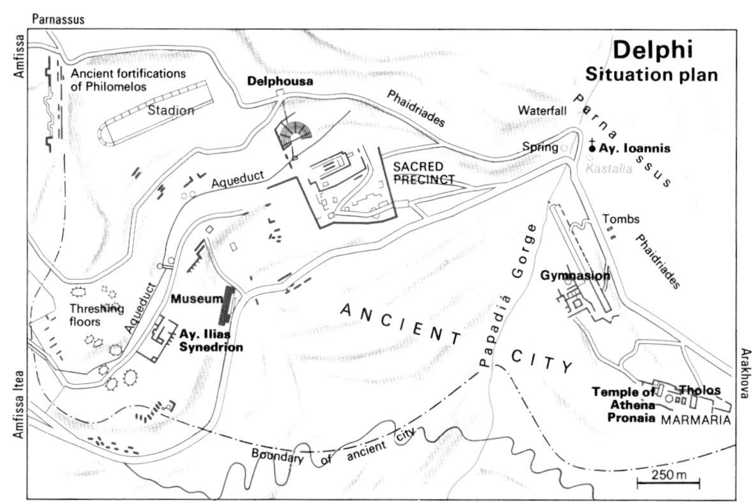

Apollo was moved to a new position 1km/¾ mile west to allow excavation of the ancient site to proceed.

History

The two crags known as the Phaidriades ("Resplendent Ones"), Phlemboúkos ("Flaming") and Rodiní ("Roseate"), enclose a rocky gorge containing the Castalian Spring, from which the ravine of the river Plistos, densely planted with olive-trees, descends to Itéa Bay. At the foot of the Phaidriades, close to the Castalian spring, there was in early times a shrine of the Earth Mother, Ge, guarded by a dragon known as Python. The myth relates that the sun god Apollo killed Python and, after an act of expiation in the vale of Tempe (see entry) in Thessaly, became lord of the sanctuary as Apollo Pythios. The time when this take-over occurred is indicated by the fact that the female idols previously offered at the shrine began to give place to male idols in the 9th century B.C.

But although a male deity had thus displaced the earlier goddess, a woman still played a central role in the cult of the oracle of Delphi, which ranked with Olympia as the principal pan-Hellenic shrine. This was the Pythia, who sat on a tripod in the innermost sanctuary of the temple and whose stammered oracular utterances were conveyed by priests and prophets to those seeking the oracle's advice.

During the three winter months Apollo travelled north to the land of the Hyperboreans and was replaced by Dionysos. The oracle's utterances continued during this period.

Many of the oracle's prophecies are known, dating back to Mycenaean times (2nd millennium B.C.). In those early days Orestes was told by the oracle that he could expiate the murder of his mother by fetching the cult image of Artemis from Tauris in Scythia. In historical times three of the oracle's pronouncements were particularly notable. Around 680 B.C. it directed settlers from Megara to found the city of Byzantion on the Bosporus (the future Constantinople). In 547 B.C. it told Kroisos (Croesus), king of Lydia in Asia Minor, that if he crossed a certain river he would destroy a great kingdom: whereupon Kroisos crossed the river Halys and was defeated by the Persians, so destroying his own kingdom. In 480 B.C. the oracle declared that Athens, then threatened by the Persians, would be invincible behind a wooden rampart – and so it proved when the fleet built by Themistokles (the "wooden rampart") defeated the Persians in the battle of Salamis. As these examples show, the Delphic oracle, which reached the peak of its influence in the 7th and 6th centuries B.C., played a part in directing the establishment of Greek colonies and in reaching political decisions; and no less significant was the influence of Apollo, the god who granted expiation and made laws, on the development of Greek ethics and law.

The recipients of the oracle's advice expressed their thanks in votive offerings, which brought great wealth to Delphi, much of it stored in treasuries built by individual cities. Most of this has been lost, but some important items can still be seen in the Delphi Museum; and the bronze serpent column set up at Delphi in 479 B.C. after the Athenian victory over the Persians at Plataiai still stands in the Hippodrome in Istanbul.

Delphi enjoyed a final period of prosperity in the reign of Hadrian (2nd c. A.D.), but its day was ended by earthquake damage and the edict by Theodosius I in A.D. 392 closing down all pagan shrines. Later the modest little village of Kastrí grew up amid the ruins of the temple. The site was rediscovered by a German archaeologist, Ulrichs, and excavated by French archaeologists from 1892 onwards.

A visit to Delphi falls into three parts: the sanctuary of Apollo, with the Stadion; the Castalian spring and the sanctuary of Athena at Marmariá; and the Museum.

The shrine of the oracle in its magnificent setting

★★Sanctuary of Apollo

The Sanctuary of Apollo lies above the road, and is approached from the Museum on a footpath parallel to the road which runs past the remains of a mosaic pavement belonging to an Early Christian basilica to the main entrance to the site. By way of the Roman Market we come to the south-east gateway of the sacred precinct, which in the classical period was roughly trapezoid in shape, measuring 200m/656ft from north to south and 130m/427ft from east to west, and surrounded by a plain enclosure wall. From the gateway the Sacred Way leads uphill, first going west, then bending sharply north-east and finally bearing north to end in front of the entrance to the temple of Apollo. The Sacred Way was lined with votive monuments erected by various Greek cities, reflecting the diversity of the political pattern of ancient Greece. The monuments themselves have disappeared, but many of their bases have survived. The series begins on the left-hand side of the Sacred Way with the long narrow base of a monument erected by the Athenians in gratitude for their victory over the Persians at Marathon (which had sculpture by Pheidias). Then followed monuments dedicated by Argos – the Seven against Thebes, the Trojan horse and an exedra with figures of the Epigonoi (descendants of the Seven against Thebes) – and others by Taras in southern Italy. On the right-hand side was a bronze bull dedicated by Korkyra (*c.* 480 B.C.), followed by a colonnade built by the Spartans after their defeat of Athens in the naval battle of Aigospotamoi in 405 B.C., standing opposite the Athenian monument in honour of Marathon. In front of the Spartan colonnade was a monument erected by the Arcadians to commemorate their victory over the Spartans at Leuktra in 371 B.C. Beyond it was a semicircular monument erected, like the one on the opposite side of the Sacred Way, by Argos, with figures of kings of Argos.

Sacred Way

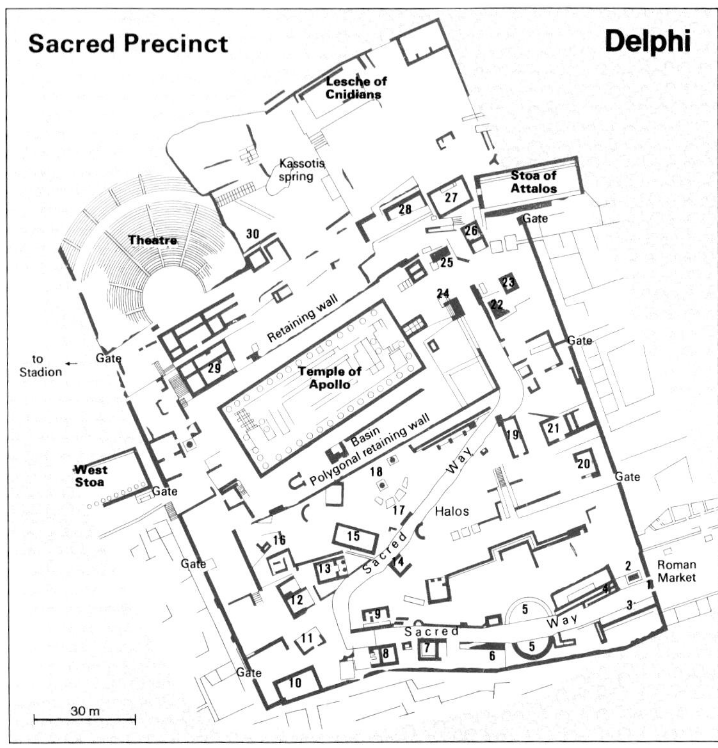

1 Main gate (entrance)
2 Votive monument of Korkyra
3 Votive monument of Athenians
4 Votive monument of Spartans
5 Votive monument of Argos
6 Votive monument of Taras
7 Treasury of Sikyon
8 Treasury of Siphnos
9 Treasury of Megara
10 Treasury of Thebes
11 Treasury of Boeotia
12 Treasury of Potidaia (?)
13 Treasury of Athenians
14 Treasury of Cnidians
15 Bouleuterion
16 Asklepieion
17 Rock of Sibyl
18 Column of Naxians
19 Treasury of Corinthians
20 Treasury of Cyrene
21 Prytaneion
22 Tripod of Plataiai
23 Votive monument of Rhodians
24 Altar of Chios
25 Votive monument of Syracusans
26 Treasury of Akanthians
27 Temenos of Neoptolemos (?)
28 Votive monument of Thessalians
29 Alexander's Lion-Hunt
30 Dionysion

Treasuries

Along the next section of the Sacred Way, on the left, are the first of the more than twenty treasuries in which votive offerings were preserved from the weather and from theft – the Doric treasury of Sikyon (*c.* 500 B.C.), in the foundations of which can be seen an earlier circular structure, and the Ionic treasury of the island of Siphnos (525 B.C.), considerable remains of which can be seen in the Museum. At the point where the Sacred Way bends north-east stands an omphalos stone set up here some years ago, recalling the ancient belief that Delphi was the central point, the navel (omphalos), of the world, established at the place where two eagles sent out by Zeus from the ends of the earth met one another.

Treasury of the Athenians

Castalian Spring

★ Treasury of the Athenians

Then follows the Treasury of the Athenians (built in or shortly after 510 B.C.; re-erected 1903–06), in the form of a Doric temple in antis. The metopes (copies: originals in the Museum) depict themes from the myths of Theseus and Herakles. Immediately beyond the treasury is the retaining wall, with shallow recesses for votive inscriptions, of the Bouleuterion.

We now come to the oldest part of the sacred precinct. Between the Sacred Way, just before it crosses the Halos ("Threshing-Floor"), on which cult ceremonies were performed, and the temple of Apollo stand, side by side, the Rock of the Sibyl, the sanctuary of Ge the Earth Mother and the site of a tall Ionic column bearing the figure of a sphinx erected by the Naxians about 560 B.C. The site selected for this monument, immediately south of the temple, its considerable height (12.5m/40ft) and the significance of the sphinx as a spirit of death support the suggestion by Zschietzschmann and Gross that this sphinx marked the mythical tomb of the god Dionysos.

★ Polygonal wall

To the rear is a polygonal wall of the 6th century B.C., covered with ancient inscriptions, supporting the platform on which the temple stands. Against it is built the 28m/92ft long Stoa of the Athenians (after 479 B.C.). Just before the Sacred Way bears north, on the right, are the remains of the Treasury of the Corinthians, which also contained offerings from king Midas of Phrygia and kings Gyges and Kroisos (Croesus) of Lydia (although these had long since disappeared by the time Pausanias visited Delphi in the 2nd century A.D.).
Alongside the next section of the Sacred Way, which runs north in a series of steps, were other votive monuments. The surviving remains include the circular base of the "Serpent Column" of 479 B.C., formed of three intertwined snakes, and, on the esplanade in front of the

temple of Apollo, the tripods erected by the Deinomids of Syracuse and the pillar which bore an equestrian statue of king Prusias II of Bithynia. The esplanade is dominated by an altar (partly re-erected) dedicated by the island of Chios and by the six re-erected columns of the temple of Apollo, with a ramp leading up to the entrance at the east end.

★ Temple of Apollo
Closed at the present time for restoration purposes

The present temple is the third on the site. The first temple, built in the 7th century B.C., was burned down in 548 B.C. The second was built by the Alcmaeonids in 531 B.C. after their expulsion from Athens by Peisistratos. In Archaic style, with 6 × 15 columns and sculpture depicting Apollo's coming to Delphi on the east pediment, it collapsed in 373, burying the pediment (fragments in Museum). The third temple, built between 346 and 320 B.C., preserved the elongated ground-plan of the Archaic temple and re-used the old column drums, but the detailing has the cool harmony of the late classical period. Of the main structure only the foundations are left, but we know that the pronaos contained inscriptions with the sayings of the Seven Sages (including the famous Apollonian imperative *Gnothi seauton,* "Know thyself") and that at the west end was the adyton, on a lower level, which contained the omphalos stone, a gold statue of Apollo, a laurel tree and (over the aperture for the oracle) the tripod of the Pythia. It is likely, according to Roux, that an area in the right-hand part of the adyton was curtained off for those seeking the oracle's advice.

The water of the Kassotis spring probably played some part in the cult of the oracle: according to Pausanias it "brought the women in the adyton of the god into a condition in which they could prophesy". With this Georges Roux associates the spring chamber on the terrace between the temple and the polygonal wall, to which a flight of twelve steps leads down. From the spring a channel runs into the foundations of the temple, and an outflow hole can be seen in the polygonal wall. This spring belonged to the second temple, but was removed during the building of the third temple in 346 B.C.

On the hillside above the temple stood the figure of the "Charioteer", now in the Museum, which was buried under a mass of earth brought down by an earthquake in 373 B.C. and was thus preserved from later metal-thieves. Close by is a large niche which once housed a sculptured representation of Alexander the Great's lion-hunt.

★ Theatre
Closed at the present time for restoration purposes

A flight of steps leads up to the Theatre (4th c. B.C., with later alterations down to the Roman period), which could accommodate 5000 spectators. It lay within the sacred precinct, as did the Lesche (Assembly Hall) of the Cnidians, built against the north wall of the precinct. From the theatre there is a very fine view of the sacred precinct, extending down to the Marmariá below.

Stadion

50m/165ft higher up, under a vertical rock face, is the Stadion, which received its final form in Roman times. Of this structure there survive the tiers of seating and the seats of honour on the north side, the rounded west end (*sphendone*) and part of the entrance at the east end. The presence of the theatre and the stadion is a reminder that the Pythian Games were held at Delphi from 590 B.C. onwards – musical and athletic contests, which included chariot races in the Hippodrome in the valley below.

★ Castalian spring

To the east of the sacred precinct, in a gorge between the two Phaidriades, is the Castalian spring, with recesses in the rock for votive offerings. Here the faithful purified themselves before making their way to the temple (on a path now barred by the enclosure fence).

Gymnasion

On the opposite side of the road is a path leading down to the Gymnasion, which consisted of a covered running track 180m/200yds long and a palaistra (training area), and a circular bath 10m/33ft in diameter.

★Sanctuary of Athena Pronaia

★★ Tholos

Continuing down the path, we come to the Marmariá precinct, with the sanctuary of Athena Pronaia ("Athena in front of the temple" – i.e. the temple of Apollo). Beyond the later temple of Athena (4th c. B.C.) are the circular Tholos (soon after 400 B.C.; partly re-erected), which had Doric columns on the outside and Corinthian columns in the interior, the Ionic Treasury of Massilia (Marseilles), with a beautifully profiled base (*c.* 530 B.C.), a Doric treasury (5th c. B.C.) and the older temple of Athena, built about 510 B.C. on the site of a still older building of the early 6th century, later destroyed by a rock fall and in 1905 damaged by a further rock fall. The Doric capitals of the earlier building, with their fine echinus mouldings, can still be seen, as can the capitals and columns, still standing, of the late Archaic temple. To the east of this temple – which, like the other Marmariá buildings, is oriented to the south – are a number of altars, extending towards the east gate of the precinct, which can still be identified. Further excavations are now under way in the southern part of the precinct.

★★Museum

The Museum, between the excavated area and the village, contains a fascinating collection of finds from the site, only a selection of which can be mentioned here.

The Tholos, in the precinct of Athena Pronaia

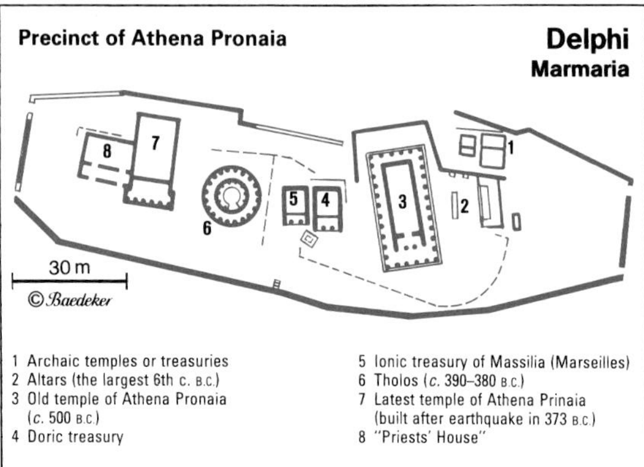

In the vestibule is an omphalos stone of the Roman period, carved with a net-like pattern.

Room 2: three Archaic bronze shields.

Room 3: in the centre the sphinx of the Naxians (*c.* 550 B.C.) and a caryatid from the Treasury of the Siphnians (*c.* 525 B.C.), the friezes from which are displayed on the walls: to the left the pediment (Herakles stealing the Pythia's tripod) and the east frieze (assembly of the gods and Trojan War), to the right the north frieze (Gigantomachia) and the west frieze (Judgment of Paris).

Room 4: Kleobis and Biton, sons of the priestess of Hera at Argos (*c.* 600 B.C.; height 2.16m/7ft high), two massive Archaic figures by a Peloponnesian sculptor.

Room 5: votive offerings of the 7th–5th centuries B.C. found under the Sacred Way north of the Treasury of the Corinthians, including a life-size bull of silver and gold, carved ivories and impressive fragments of chryselephantine statues of Apollo and his sister Artemis. These new finds, offerings from eastern Greece and Asia Minor, are of particular importance, since they include the only examples so far discovered of chryselephantine sculpture. Previously all such figures, including such famous works as those by Pheidias in the Parthenon in Athens and the temple of Zeus at Olympia, had been lost and were known only from literature.

Room 6: metopes from the Treasury of the Athenians, including Theseus and Antiope, Herakles and the Arcadian hind.

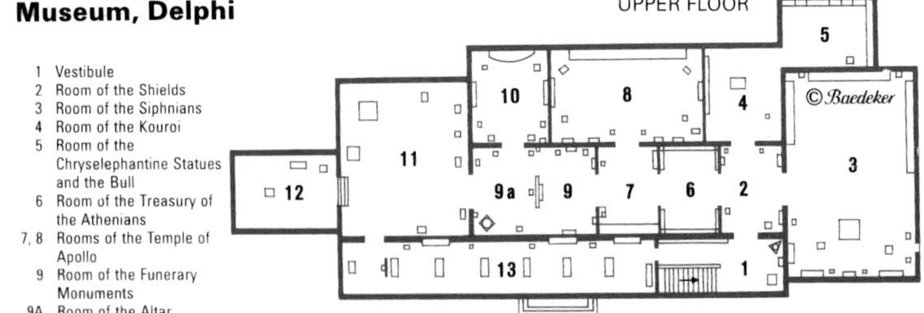

Rooms 7 and 8: remains of the Archaic temple of Apollo; in particular (Room 7) the east pediment, depicting the coming of Apollo to Delphi. To the right of this is an acroterion from the temple in the form of a winged Victory.
Rooms 9 and 9A: stele from Marmariá depicting an athlete and his attendant (460 B.C.); circular altar with the figure of a girl (*c.* 310 B.C.; head of Dionysos (4th c. B.C.).
Room 10 (to the right): architectural fragments from the Tholos in the sanctuary of Athena Pronaia, including part of the entablature, with carved metopes, and semi-columns from the interior with Corinthian capitals (soon after 400 B.C.).
Room 11: statue of Agias (*c.* 350 B.C.; by Lysippos?); acanthus column with three korai or Thyades (*c.* 350 B.C.); head of a philosopher (*c.* 280 B.C.).
Room 12: the Charioteer (illustration, page 63), the famous bronze statue of Sotades of Thespiai, dedicated by the Sicilian tyrant Polyzalos in thanksgiving for a victory in the chariot race at the Pythian Games in 478 or 474 B.C. In adjoining cases are fragments of the chariot and horses.
Room 13: bronzes; marble statue of Antinoos, the Emperor Hadrian's favourite (2nd c. A.D.).

Surroundings of Delphi

★ Arákhova

Arákhova, a mountain village in Phocis, 9km/6 miles east of Delphi, is famed for its magnificent situation in wild country on the southern slopes of Parnassus (winter sports), for its colourful woven fabrics and for its red wine.

From the west end of the village an asphalted road runs up into the Parnassus range (see entry).

Itéa

19km/12 miles south-west of Delphi lies the little port of Itéa (pop. 4400), in a bay on the Gulf of Corinth, with a bauxite works which has been the subject of controversy. East of the town is the site of ancient Kirra.

Galaxídi

17km/10½ miles south-west of Itéa, on the west side of Itéa Bay, is Galaxídi, with a castle, a monastery and a small museum.

Ámfissa

14km/9 miles north-west of Itéa, at the foot of Mount Parnassus, is the country town of Ámfissa (see entry).

Dion G 3

Δίο
Dío

Nomos: Pieria
Altitude: 70m/230ft
Population: 1500

Situation

The village of Dío (formerly known as Malathriá), near which are the excavated remains of the ancient Macedonian city of Dion, lies 16km/10 miles south of Kateríni (chief town of the nomos of Pieria), under the northern foothills of Mount Olympus (see entry). It is 5km/3 miles off the Athens–Salonica expressway (Limáni Litokhórou exit).

History

Ancient Dion, lying in the fertile Pieria plain at the foot of Mount Olympus, on the river Baphyras (then navigable) and near the west coast of the Thermaic Gulf, was a holy city to the Macedonians (its name is derived from Dios, the genitive form of Zeus). In its heyday the town is estimated to have had a population of 15,000. Its strategic situation enabled it to control the coast road between Macedonia and Thessaly, and it was the most southerly frontier stronghold of Macedon. King Archelaos (414–399 B.C.) built a temple of Zeus, a theatre and a stadion and instituted Olympic Games in the town. While Pella was capital of Macedon, Dion became its cultural centre. Alexander the Great made offerings in Dion before setting out on his Persian expedition. The town was destroyed by the Aetolians in 220 B.C. but soon recovered. In the reign of Augustus it was granted Roman citizenship.

The Site

★ Excavations

Excavations by Greek archaeologists in 1928–31, from 1962 and since 1973 have brought to light a considerable part of the ancient town. The remains now visible include sections of the town walls, the main street and several subsidiary streets (fourteen of which have been located),

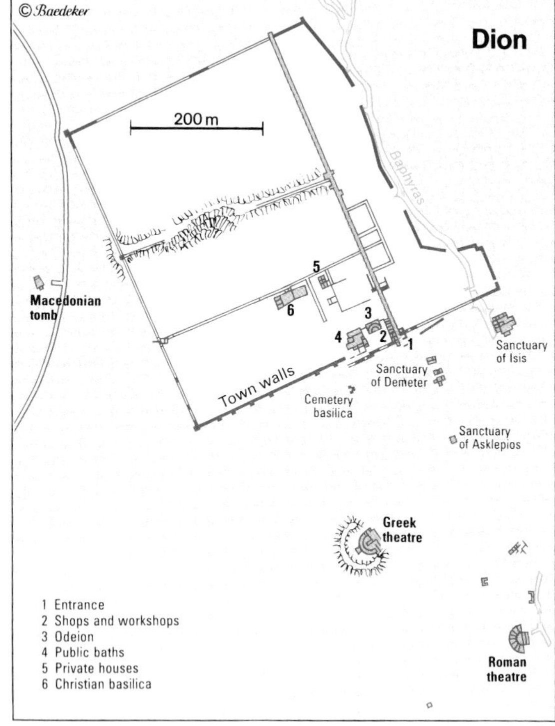

large public baths (4000 sq.m/43,000 sq.ft) with mosaic pavements and good water supply and drainage systems, a small odeion, houses and shops, a Christian basilica and – outside the town walls – temples of Isis, Demeter and Asklepios, a Greek and a Roman theatre and a Macedonian tomb.

Museum

The collections of the Archaeological Museum in Dío (closed Tue.) are excellently displayed. On the ground floor are interesting finds from the Roman baths, the temples and the necropolis of Dion, while the first floor shows material from the Pieria district and Mount Olympus (models of both areas; everyday objects illustrating life in ancient times).

Litókhoron

See entry

Mount Olympus

See entry

Dodecanese L–N 6–8

Δωδεκάνησα
Dodekánisa

The Dodecanese ("Twelve Islands") are a group of islands off the south-west coast of Asia Minor, the most southerly part of the Southern Sporades. The group consists of the fourteen larger islands of Lipsí, Pátmos, Léros, Kálymnos, Kos, Astypálaia, Nísyros, Sými, Tílos, Rhodes, Khalki, Kárpathos, Kásos and Kastellórizo (see entries), together with some 40 smaller islands and islets.

These islands belong geologically to the mainland of Anatolia but culturally and historically to Greece. With the exception of Rhodes

Fisherman on Pátmos in the Dodecanese

they are short of water and for the most part barren. The inhabitants earn their livelihood from agriculture, sponge-diving (headquarters of the Greek sponge-fishing fleet; now declining), silkworm culture, pottery manufacture, tanning, carpet-weaving and now increasingly tourism.

History

Neither in Greek nor in Roman times were the Dodecanese a single political unit. It was only in the 16th century, under Turkish rule, that they gained a common political status, with extensive autonomy in domestic affairs. In 1912 most of the islands were occupied by Italy, which held on to them as security against Turkish-occupied Libya. Under the treaty of Lausanne in 1923 Turkey ceded the whole of the Dodecanese to Italy. After suffering military attack and German occupation during the Second World War the islands were returned to Greece in 1947.
The Dodecanese enjoy certain tax privileges (duty-free alcohol, etc.).

Dodona E 4

Δωδώνη
Dodóni

Region: Epirus
Nomos: Ioánnina

Situation

The sanctuary of Zeus at Dodona, home of a noted ancient oracle, lies in a beautiful setting at the foot of Mt Tómaros in Epirus, 18km/11 miles south-west of Ioánnina (see entry).

Access

The road to Dodona goes off on the right from the Ioánnina–Préveza road 5km/3 miles south of Ioánnina (signposted) and comes in 16km/10 miles to the entrance to the site.

History

The oracle of Dodona developed in a region which was inhabited from around 2000 B.C. by Thesprotians and from 1200 B.C. by Molossians, and was served by priests called *helloi* or *selloi,* believed to have been of pre-Indo-European, Pelasgic origin. After 1200 B.C. the source goddess Naia, who had previously been worshipped here and continued to be honoured under the name of Dione, was joined by the weather god Zeus Naios. The god was worshipped in a sacred oak-tree, his oracle being expressed in the rustling of its leaves, which was then interpreted by the priests. The earliest evidence of votive offerings dates back to the 7th century. The sanctuary, extended by king Pyrrhos of Epirus (297–273 B.C.) and Philip V of Macedon (219 B.C.), was destroyed in A.D. 381. The place continued to exist, however, and in the 5th and 6th centuries Dodona was still the see of a bishop.

Sights

Shrine of the oracle (plan, p. 253)

The shrine of the oracle is marked by an oak-tree planted on the site of the original oak and by the foundations of the precinct of Zeus. Features that can be identified include the precinct wall, the Sacred House beside the oak-tree (early 4th c. B.C.), with various 3rd century additions and alterations, three small temples dedicated to Dione, Herakles and Aphrodite lying to the east of the precinct and a colonnaded hall to the west, all dating from the 3rd century B.C.

★ Theatre

On the way from the entrance to the site to these remains we come to the largest building at Dodona, the theatre (3rd c. B.C.), which was

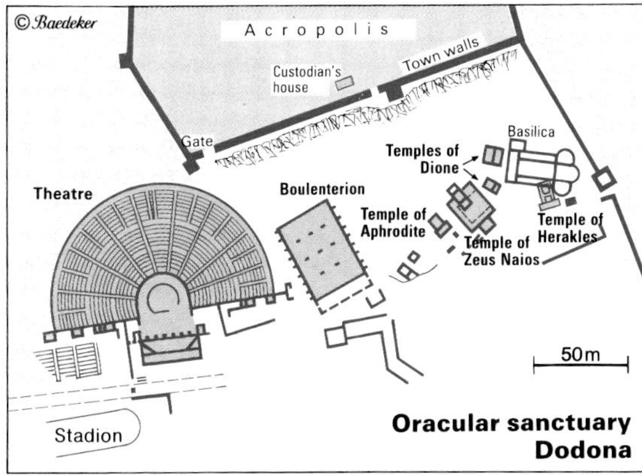

excavated in 1959, with the massive supporting walls of the auditorium. With a diameter of 122m/400ft and 21 tiers of seating in three sections, this is one of the largest theatres in Greece. The orchestra was converted in the Augustan period into an arena for wild beast shows.

Town walls
Stadion

Behind the theatre are the town walls, with towers, and in front of it are the tiers of stone seating of the Stadion. The remains of an episcopal church erected in Early Christian times can be seen to the east of the sacred precinct.

Finds from the site are in the National Archaeological Museum in Athens (small bronzes) and the Archaeological Museum in Ioánnina.

Drama I 2

Δρ άμα
Dráma

Nomos: Dráma
Altitude: 110m/360ft
Population: 36,000

Transport

Station on the Salonica–Alexandroúpolis line.

Situation and characteristics

The town of Dráma, 36km/22 miles north-west of Kavála in eastern Macedonia, lies at the foot of Mt Falakron (2194m/7199ft), on a river which is harnessed to drive oil-mills. The area is well watered and fertile, producing cotton, rice and tobacco which are processed in the town.

Edessa G 3

Έδεσσα
Édessa

Nomos: Pella
Altitude: 450m/1475ft
Population: 16,000

Transport

Édessa is on the Salonica–Flórina road (bus services).

Situation and characteristics

The Macedonian town of Edessa (formerly known as Vódena) lies 70km/43 miles west of Salonica on a terrace in the foothills of Mt Vérmion, above the Macedonian plain. With its abundant supply of water (falls on the river Voda), it is a popular summer resort.
Until the finding of the royal tomb at Vergína (see entry) Édessa was thought to be the ancient city of Aigai, capital of Macedon before the foundation of Pella.

Church of Dormition

Near the Metropolitan's (Archbishop's) Palace, from which there is a magnificent prospect of the plain, stands the church of the Dormition (Kímisis tis Panayías), built on the site of a pagan temple, with frescoes.

Remains of ancient city

Remains of the ancient city were brought to light in 1968 in the Lóngos area, below the town to the east; a signpost on the Salonica road points the way to the site. The remains include a stretch of the town walls, with towers and a gate leading into a colonnaded street (4th c. B.C.).

Surroundings of Édessa

★ Tombs at Lefkádia

Some 30km/19 miles south of Édessa, in the vine- and fruit-growing district of Náousa, three Macedonian tombs – well preserved hypogea of the 3rd–2nd century B.C. – were discovered in 1954.

Ekhinades F 5

Εχινάδες Νησιά
Ekhinádes Nisiá

Nomos: Kefalloniá

Situation

The Ekhinádes are a group of islands lying just off the coast round the mouth of the river Akhelóos, in the Ionian Sea. The principal islands in the group are Dragonéra, Petelá and Oxiá, now partly linked with the mainland as a result of silting up.

Lepanto

In this area was fought, on October 6th 1571, the naval battle of Lepanto (= Náfpaktos), so called because the Turkish fleet was based there, in which the 26-year-old Don John of Austria, with 250 Venetian and Spanish galleys, destroyed almost 200 vessels of the Turkish fleet, which was of similar strength.

Elafonisos G 7

Ελαφονήσι
Elafonísi

Nomos: Laconia
Area of island: 18 sq.km/7 sq. miles

Altitude: 0–277m/0–909ft
Population: 600

Boat services

Weekly services from Athens (Piraeus); local connections with Neápolis (Peloponnese).

Elafonisos (Italian Cervi), known in antiquity as Onougnathos, lies just off the south-eastern "finger" of the Peloponnese (Laconia). The chief place on the island, also called Elafonisos, lies at its northern tip, and it has two sheltered anchorages. Off its west coast are a number of little islets and isolated rocks.
Elafonisos is separated from Kýthira (see entry) to the south by the busy Elafonisos Channel, 10km/6 miles wide.

Eleusis H 5

Ελευσίνα
Elefsína

Region and nomos: Attica
Altitude: 8m/25ft
Population: 20,000

Transport

Station on Athens–Corinth railway line.
Bus connections with Athens.

Situation

Within the present-day industrial town of Elefsína, on the coast 22km/14 miles west of central Athens, is the site of ancient Eleusis, home of the Eleusinian mysteries, an important sanctuary dating back to Mycenaean times.

History

The Eleusinian cult arose out of the myth of the goddess Demeter, who lamented at the Kallichoros well here the loss of her daughter Persephone, abducted by Hades; and no corn grew until Zeus commanded that Persephone should be allowed to return annually in spring. Demeter thereupon established the Eleusinian mysteries, in which she was honoured as the granter of fertility and Persephone (also known as Kore, the Maiden) as an annually returning vegetation goddess.
The initiates of the mysteries, who were admitted in two stages to the Lesser and the Greater Eleusinia, appear to have been given the promise not only of the annual renewal of nature but also of a resurrection.

★Sanctuary of Demeter

From the entrance to the site we walk past remains dating from the Roman period (temple of Artemis, triumphal arch) to the Great Propylaia (2nd c. A.D.), to the left of which is the circular mouth of the Kallichoros well. Beyond this are the older Little Propylaia (54 B.C.), to the right of which, on the hillside, can be seen the Ploutonion, a cave sacred to Pluto.
The central feature of the site is the Telesterion, the hall in which the mysteries were celebrated. The Solonic Telesterion was built around 600 B.C. on the site of a small Mycenaean temple of the 14th century B.C., with an Anaktoron (holy of holies) which remained until Roman times the central element in the structure. Various additions and alterations were carried out in the 6th and 5th centuries B.C., and in its

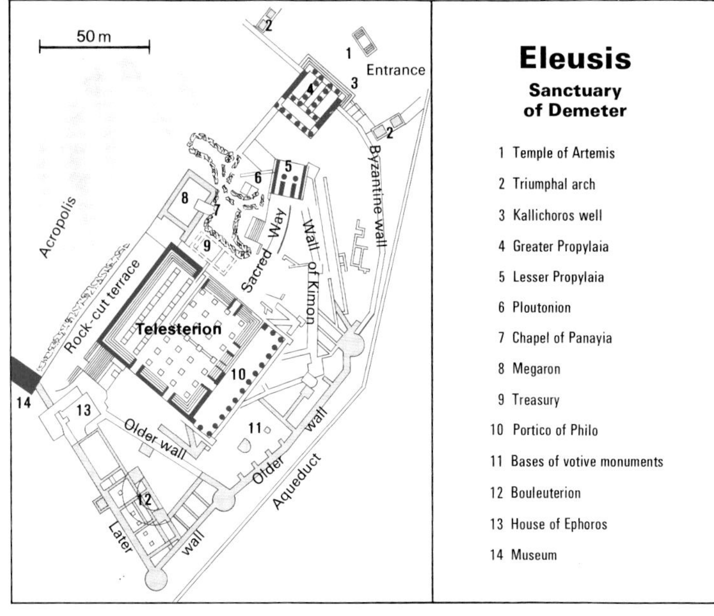

final form the Telesterion measured 54m/177ft by 52m/170ft, with seven rows of six columns. Between 330 and 310 B.C. the Portico of Philo was added. Round the hall ran tiers of seating, those hewn from the rocky hillside being still preserved. Recent Greek excavations have identified the position of the Anaktoron, the focal point of the ceremonies conducted by the hierophants.

Museum

Rock-cut steps lead up to the Museum, in the forecourt of which are statues and a sarcophagus with a representation of the hunt for the Calydonian boar.

In the entrance hall are a Demeter by Agorakritos (*c.* 420 B.C.) and a cast of the Eleusinian votive relief of Demeter, Persephone and the boy Triptolemos (440 B.C.), the original of which is in the National Archaeological Museum in Athens.

Room I: sculpture from the pediment of the Archaic Telesterion; statuette of Persephone (*c.* 480 B.C.); two Archaic kouroi (540 and 530 B.C.); Proto-Attic amphora with the blinded Polyphemos, Perseus and Medusa (7th c. B.C.).

Room II: Archaic kore; Ephebe (4th c. B.C.; by Lysippos?); Asklepios (3rd c. B.C.).

Room III: Statues of the Roman period.

Room IV: caryatid from the Little Propylaia; Corinthian vase with chimaera (7th c. B.C.); terracotta sarcophagus with the skeleton of a child.

Room VI: pottery from Eleusis, bronze vases, etc.

View of Eleusis Bay from the forecourt of the Museum

Epidauros

H 6

Επίδαυρος
Epídavros

Region: Peloponnese
Nomos: Argolid. Altitude: 90m/295ft

Access

Epidauros can be reached from Náfplion (41km/25 miles) or on the new road from Corinth via Néa Epídavros (63km/39 miles).

Situation

Epidauros, the most widely famed sanctuary of the healing god Asklepios, lies in a quietly beautiful setting in the Argolid.

History

In pre-Greek times the god of Maleas (Maleatas) was worshipped on the hill of Kynortion (above the theatre, outside the enclosure), and the Greeks equated this earlier divinity with their god Apollo. Then Apollo was joined by his son Asklepios, who had grown up at Trikka in Thessaly. Every four years games were held in honour of the god, and from 395 B.C. there was also a dramatic festival. From the end of the 5th century B.C. the cult of Asklepios spread widely throughout the ancient world, reaching Athens in 420 B.C. and Rome (under the name of Aesculapius) in 293 B.C. To cater for the great numbers of pilgrims who flocked to Epidauros in quest of healing much new building was carried out at the site in the 4th and 3rd centuries. On the evidence of the votive inscriptions the priest-physicians were already practising psycho-therapeutic methods of treatment. A thermal spring was also used, and surgical instruments have been found on the site. Theatrical performances, which were thought to bring about the purgation or

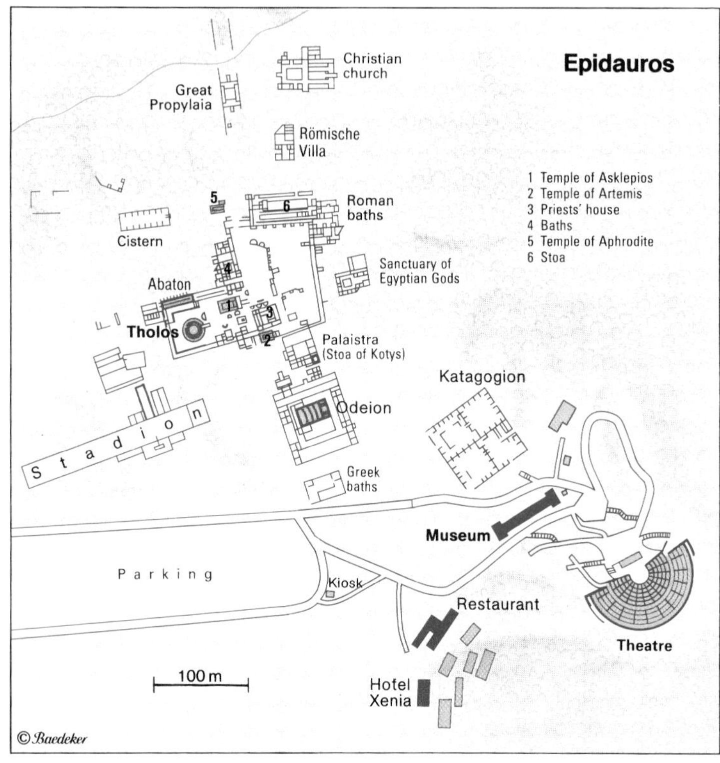

purification (katharsis) of the spectators by inspiring pity and fear, also played a part in treatment.

The sanctuary continued to flourish into the late Roman period, but was closed down about A.D. 400, in the reign of Theodosius I. In the 6th century Justinian built a fortress in the ruins.

The Site

Stadion

Before reaching the entrance to the site we pass the Stadion, with its tiers of stone seating.

★★ Theatre

The theatre, built against the slopes of Mt Kynortion, is remarkable for its excellent state of preservation and for its fine acoustics. A. von Gerkan's investigations have shown that it does not date from the 4th century B.C., as had been supposed on the basis of Pausanias's account. The lower part, up to the semicircular gangway, with its tiers of seats divided by staircases into twelve wedge-shaped sections, was built in the early 3rd century and the upper part added in the 2nd century, giving the theatre a total capacity of 14,000 seats. In the centre is the circular orchestra. Of the stage building (*skene*) only scanty

The ancient theatre, Epidauros

remains survive; on either side were ramps leading up to the roof of the proskenion, which was used as a raised part of the stage. The entrances for the chorus (parodoi), between the stage and the walls of the auditorium, lead into the theatre through ceremonial doorways.

A festival of drama is held annually (July and August) in the ancient theatre, including performances in classical Greek.

From the theatre we walk past the museum to the remains of the Katagogion, a large guesthouse or hostel 76.3m/250ft square, which had 160 rooms on two floors. 100m/110yds west of this are baths and, just to the north, a Gymnasion (76m/249ft square) which was converted into an Odeion in Roman times. In the central square,

Reconstruction of the Asklepieion

approached from the north by a sacred way passing through propylaia, are the principal buildings of the sanctuary, surrounded by stoas in which pilgrims slept while awaiting cure: the Doric temple of Asklepios (380–375 B.C.) and the circular Tholos (360–330 B.C.) by Polykleitos the Younger. Of the Tholos only the foundations survive, with a system of concentric passages in which the snakes sacred to Asklepios may have been kept. A clearer impression of this building, which was notable for its lavish decoration, can be got from a partial reconstruction in the last room of the Museum. The circular cella was surrounded by 26 Doric columns and had 14 Corinthian columns round its internal wall. In the centre of the floor, which was patterned in two colours, was an opening leading down to the basement. The elaborate nature of the decoration can be judged from the coffered ceiling, the high quality of the work by the Corinthian capital carved by Polykleitos himself.

Museum

The other rooms of the museum contain inscriptions, surgical instruments, statues of Asklepios (some of them casts) and architectural fragments from the propylaia and the temple of Asklepios.

Néa Epídavros
Palaiá Epídavros

The little harbour towns of Néa and Palaiá Epídavros, with bathing beaches, can be reached by way of Ligourió (each 19km/12 miles).

Epirus E/F 3–5

Ήπειρος
Ípiros

Situation and characteristics

Epirus (i.e. the "Mainland", as opposed to the offshore islands) covers an area of 9200 sq.km/3550 sq. miles in north-western Greece, between the Albanian frontier and the Ambracian Gulf and between the Ionian Sea and the Pindos mountains. Historically the territory of Epirus extended into southern Albania.

Epirus is a hilly region with an abundance of rain, which favours the development of agriculture and particularly of stock-farming. In ancient times it was regarded as a rather backward area; but the nekromanteion (oracle of the dead) on the river Acheloos was known to Homer, and the oracle of Zeus at Dodona was widely famed. The most notable historical figure produced by Epirus was the Molossian king Pyrrhos (319–272 B.C.), who was praised by Hannibal as the greatest general after Alexander the Great. In later centuries the region was settled by incoming Slavs and Albanians, and in the 13th century it again achieved some importance under the Byzantine Despot of Árta. The Turkish occupation which began in 1449 lasted until 1914, when it was ended by a controversial demarcation of the frontier between Greece and Albania.

The principal ancient sites in Epirus are Dodona, the Nekromanteion of Ephyra and the city of Nikopolis founded by Augustus. The medieval period is represented by the churches of Árta; and evidence of the Turkish occupation is preserved in Ioánnina, which was ruled by Ali Pasha as a semi-independent principality from 1788 to 1822. Párga, with one of the few harbours on this rocky coast, has attractions as a tourist resort. (See the entries for all these places.)

Erimonisia K 6/7

Ερημονήσια
Erimonísia

Nomos: Cyclades

Boat services

No regular services.

Situation

The Erimonísia or Nisídes ("Islets") are a chain of lonely and barren islands in the triangular area between Náxos, Amorgós and Íos. The most northerly are the Voidonísi, a group of small islands. To the south of these are Donoúsa (pop. 200; alt. 0–488m/0–1601ft) and the Makáries, a group of islets between Donoúsa and Náxos. Farther south again are the Koufo islands – Presoúra and Áno Koufónisi (area 8 sq.km/3 sq. miles), to the north, and Káto Koufónisi (5 sq.km/2 sq. miles), to the south; to the east of these are Kéros (14 sq.km/5½ sq. miles), on which an acropolis of the 3rd century B.C. has been excavated, Antikéros and Dríma. To the south-west is Skhinoúsa (10 sq.km/4 sq. miles; pop. 200), with the village of Skhinoúsa in the interior of the island. The most southerly island in the group is Iráklia (18 sq.km/7 sq. miles; pop. 250), with the village of Iráklia above the anchorage in the bay of Áyios Yeóryios.

Euboea G–I 4–6

Εύβοια
Évvia

Nomos: Euboea
Area of island: 3654 sq.km/1411 sq. miles
Altitude: 0–1743m/0–5719ft
Population: 165,000
Chief town: Khalkís

Boat services

Ferry services between Glýfa and Ayiókampos, Arkítsa and Loutrá Aidipsoú, Skála Oropoú and Erétria, Ayía Marína and Néa Stýra; also between Rafína and Néa Stýra and between Marmári and Kárystos.
There is an attractive boat excursion along the Northern Euboean Gulf from Khalkís to Péfki.
Regular services from Vólos via Kými to the Northern Sporades, and to Kavála and Alexandroúpolis.

Access by land

Road connection with the mainland by traversing bridge (toll) at Khalkís; permanent bridge under construction.
Bus services: Athens–Khalkís (1½ hrs; several hourly), continuing to Kými (altogether 3¾ hrs; several daily); to Skála Oropoú (hourly), then ferry to Erétria; Athens–Rafína (several hourly), then ferry to Néa Styra, Marmári and Kárystos; Athens–Loutrá Aidipsoú (3½ hrs; several daily).
By rail: Athens–Khalkís (1¾ hrs; several daily).

Situation and characteristics

Euboea, the second largest Greek island (170km/106 miles long, 5.5km/3½ miles across), lies off the north-east coast of Boetia and Attica, from which it is separated by two enclosed arms of the sea, the Northern and Southern Euboean Gulfs. The two gulfs meet in the narrow strait of Évripos (only 35m/38yds wide and 8.5m/28ft deep), roughly at the mid-point of the island. The principal ports lie on the gentler coast facing the mainland; the rocky north-east coast for the most part falls steeply down to the sea. There are four main ranges of hills, some of them heavily wooded: in the north-west the Teléthri range (Xerón, 991m/3251ft), south-east of this the Kandílio range (highest point 1225m/4019ft); to the east the Dírfys range (Delfí, 1743m/5719ft); and at the south-eastern tip of the island the Ókhi range (1398m/4587ft). Below the hills, particularly on the west coast, are small, fertile alluvial plains. Euboea has minerals (magnesite, lignite) which supply metal-processing industries, particularly around Khalkís. Euboea's principal attraction for visitors lies in its scenic beauty.

History

The earliest inhabitants of Euboea were Ellopians, incomers from Thessaly, in the north-west of the island; Abantes, a Thracian people, in central Euboea; and Dryopians in the south-east. Ionians from Attica mingled with the Abantes and thereafter controlled the whole island, bringing it a period of great prosperity between the 8th and 6th centuries B.C. Their two principal cities, Chalkis and Eretria, established numerous colonies in southern Italy, Sicily and the Thracian Chersonese (Chalcidice).

In 506 B.C. Chalkis was conquered by Athens, for which possession of the fertile island soon became a matter of vital importance. Towards the end of the Peloponnesian War, in 411 B.C., Euboea broke away from Athens, but in subsequent wars was usually on the Athenian side.

After the Latin conquest of Constantinople in A.D. 1204 Euboea was held by three Veronese barons, except the ports, which fell to the Venetians, who after numerous wars with the Frankish princes gained control of the whole island, calling it Negroponte. It became the second most important Venetian stronghold (after Crete) in the eastern Mediterranean, but in 1470 fell into the hands of the Turks. It was finally united with Greece under the Second London Protocol of 1830.

Khalkís

Khalkís (Khalkída; pop. 37,000), chief town and port of the nomos of Euboea (which also includes the Petali Islands and Skýros), is attractively situated on a number of hills around the strait of Évripos, to the west of the ancient city. Its situation at the closest point to the mainland led to the development of a harbour at a very early stage, and by 411 B.C. the town was also linked with the mainland by a timber bridge. At that time too the coastline was extended into the sea by the deposit of soil, thus further securing the vital connection with Boeotia against hostile attack. A rocky islet, on which is the Turkish fort of Karábaba, divides the strait into a western arm, now landlocked, and the broader eastern arm, spanned by a traversing bridge. A new bridge is under construction.

The Évripos is noted for its alternating currents, which change at least four times a day, and sometimes up to twenty times. The phenomenon, which was remarked on in ancient times, is thought to be due to interaction between the tides and areas of stagnant water.

The Latin alphabet is based on the script of ancient Chalkis.

Kástro

At the east end of the bridge, almost surrounded by the sea, is the Kástro, the old Venetian and Turkish town, which still preserves remains of its walls. In the south of the old town is the church of Ayia Paraskeví (originally 5th–6th c.) the principal church in Venetian times, which was rebuilt by the Crusaders in Gothic style (rare in Greece) in the 14th century. Part of aqueduct which brought water to the town from Mt Dírfys can still be traced in the suburban district.

Suburban district

Adjoining the old town is the busy Proasteion (suburban district), with the town's main square, the Archaeological Museum (material from Eretria), the Museum of Medieval Art (in a restored mosque which was converted in 1470 from the church of San Marco di Negroponte) and a beautiful Turkish fountain.

Kastélli

On a projecting spur of rock above Fýlla, 3km/2 miles east of Khalkís, stands the well preserved 13th century Venetian castle of Lílanto, now known as the Kastélli.

Erétria

Eretria, the site of which has been occupied since the 3rd millennium B.C., was in ancient times the island's most important town after Chalkis. In the 8th century B.C., inhabited by Ionian settlers from Attica, it enjoyed a period of great prosperity. When in 500 B.C. the Eretrians, together with the Athenians, gave help to Miletus when it was threatened by the Persians Darius ordered the town to be destroyed and carried off most of the population to Susa as slaves. It seems, however, to have been rapidly rebuilt. Seven Eretrian vessels took part in the naval battles of Artemision and Salamis, and several hundred hoplites from Eretria fought at Plataiai. In 411 B.C. the Eretrians played a major part in liberating Euboea from Athenian rule by destroying the Athenian vessels which sought refuge in their harbour after a naval battle between Athens and Sparta. Later, in 378 B.C., Eretria joined the Attic maritime league and took part in the fight against Macedon. In 198 B.C. the town was captured by the Romans.
Eretria was the birthplace of Menedemos, a pupil of Plato.

The remains of ancient Eretria are the most important on the island. Here and there between the streets of modern houses can be seen the foundations of ancient buildings. The Museum contains finds of Roman material. North-east of the ancient town is the Theatre, built into the plain. Originally it had a stone stage building, with the orchestra on the same level; the seating for the spectators would be on

Excavations, Erétria

Harbour on the Strait of Orei

wooden stands. In the 4th century B.C. a stone theatre was built, with the orchestra on a lower level, an embanked auditorium and a stone stage building. The dramatic action took place on the orchestra in front of a movable wooden proskenion, which in the early Roman period was replaced by a permanent proskenion of white marble.

South-west of the theatre are the remains of a temple of Dionysos and one of the gates in the town walls.

To the east of the theatre is the Gymnasion, with a bath-house at its north-east corner.

At the north-east end of the town are the foundations of a temple of Apollo Daphnephoros (the Laurel-Bearer). Sculpture from the pediments (including Theseus carrying off the Amazon Antiope, 520 B.C.) is in the Khalkís Museum.

1km/¾ mile north-west of the theatre is a tomb with a vaulted roof. The acropolis was surrounded for much of the way by polygonal walls. From a tower on the north side there is a fine view. From the east and west sides of the acropolis walls, traceable for only part of the way, run down towards the shore, where there are other remains of walls.

North-Western Euboea

Khalkís via Artemísion to Loutrá Aidipsoú (151km/94 miles):

The road runs north-east from Khalkís, close to Évripos, passing a number of ancient tombs.

9km/6 miles: Néa Artáky. From here a road on the right leads north-east to Sténi Dírfyos (26km/16 miles), from which it is a 4 hours' climb (with guide) to the summit of Mt Delfí (1743m/5719ft; views), the highest peak in the Dírfys range.

8km/5 miles: Psakhná, 3km/2 miles north of which is the Venetian stronghold of Kástri. The road now runs inland through more rugged

country and goes over a saddle between Mt Kandílion (1209m/3967ft) and Mt Pisariá (1352m/4436ft); from the top there are magnificent views. The road continues through beautiful hill country, passing close to an ancient fort rebuilt by the Venetians, and then descends to the little monastery of Áyios Yeóryios and through the valley of the river Kyreús, amid a luxuriant growth of arbutus and myrtles.
36km/22 miles: Prokópion, a prosperous village and pilgrimage centre, near which is the former Turkish country estate of Akhmet-Aga, amid luxuriant vegetation.

10km/6 miles: Mantoúdi, a small industrial town (magnesite workings). North of the town, at the mouth of the river Kyreús, are the remains of ancient Kerinthos.
8km/5 miles: Strofyliá, from which a road runs south-west to the little port of Límni.
8km: Ayía Ánna, a prosperous village.
32km/20 miles: Agriovótano, just south of Cape Artemísion (also known as Cape Amoni), from which there is an attractive view of the little island of Pontikonísi.

Artemísion

12km/7½ miles: Artemísion, a village on the north coast, famed as the scene of the first naval victory of the Greek fleet over the numerically much superior Persians in 480 B.C. Near the village are remains of a temple of Athena Proseoa. A little way west is the fishing village of Péfki, where the anchovy-fishers gather in summer.

Istiaia

13km/8 miles: Istiaia (pop. 5000), the chief place in the north-west of the island, in a fertile farming area. West of the town is the site of ancient Histiaia, which was conquered by Perikles in 446 B.C. and bound to Athens by the foundation of a colony at nearby Oreí. There is a medieval castle partly built of ancient stones.

★ *Marble Bull*

In the square at Oreí is a massive marble bull (4th c. B.C.) recovered from the sea.

Loutrá Aidipsoú

22km/14 miles: Loutrá Aidipsoú, a popular seaside and thermal resort with hot sulphurous springs (32–82°C/90–180°F) which were already being used in Roman times. The largest of the springs is directly on the shore, with remains of ancient baths.

South-Eastern Euboea

Khalkís via Erétria and Alivéri to Kárystos (128km/80 miles) or Kými (96km/60 miles):
The road runs south-east from Khalkís, at first keeping close to the shore.
2.5km/1½ miles: chapel of Áyios Stéfanos, on the site of ancient Chalkis, with the spring of Arethusa which was famed in antiquity. The bay of Áyios Stéfanos was the harbour of the ancient city.
The road continues over the well cultivated Lelantic Plain, with the village of Vasilikó. Off to the left, on the road to the medieval castle of Fýlla (1.5km/1 mile), are three Venetian watch-towers.
10km/6 miles: Lefkanto, where a temple of the 10th/9th century, measuring 10m/33ft by 40m/130ft, was discovered in 1981; the remains were damaged during excavation work.
19km/12 miles: Néa Psará (officially Erétria), with the remains of ancient Eretria. The marshland in this area, originally an arm of the sea, was drained in antiquity. Beyond Erétria the road runs past several ancient cemetery areas.
9km/6 miles: Amárynthos, a small fishing port. To the north-east is the monastery of Áyios Nikólaos, with a tiled façade (16th c. frescoes; view).

15km/9 miles: Alivéri, a prosperous little industrial town (mining; thermal power station), probably occupying the site of ancient Tamynai. 1km/¾ mile from the town is Skála Alivériou (probably the ancient port of Porthmos).
9km: Lépoura, where a side road branches off on the left to Kými (below).

The main road continues south-east through a marshy depression which is often completely covered with water. To the right is the acropolis hill of ancient Dystos, at the foot of which is the modern village of the same name (with pieces of ancient masonry built into some of the houses). Beyond this the road frequenly passes remains of ancient buildings.
15km/9 miles: Záraka. From here there is a view of a long inlet, at the mouth of which is the island of Kavallianí (probably the ancient Glaukonnesos). The road then climbs a hill, from the top of which there are views of the east coast, extending to Cape Kafareús, and south-west to the bay of Stýra, with the much indented island of Stýra (ancient Aigleia).

Stýra

26km/16 miles: Stýra, where the houses, with the white church of the Panayía, extend up the slopes of a hill with twin peaks. At Néa Stýra, 1km/¾ mile away on the coast, is the site of ancient Stýra, of which there are only scanty remains.

Dragon houses

From Stýra a visit can be paid to the famous "dragon houses". It is a stiff 30 minutes' climb to a saddle above the village, from which it is another 15–20 minutes' walk, passing ancient quarries (partly hewn column shafts, dressed blocks, etc.), to the foot of Mt Áyios Nikólaos, where there are three "dragon houses" (ancient stone huts, probably occupied by quarry workers).

On the top of Mt Áyios Nikólaos are the imposing Frankish castle of Larména and a chapel dedicated to St Nicholas; magnificent views.

Half way between Stýra and Kárystos is the Bey's Spring.

21km/13 miles: road on right to the village of Marmári (on the coast 4km/2½ miles south), now a summer holiday resort. Offshore, to the south-west, are the Nisí Petalií, a group of islands (private property), some with houses on them, others uninhabited.

Kárystos

11km/7 miles: Kárystos (pop. 2000), the chief town of southern Euboea, which was founded after the war of liberation; it is now a holiday resort. The site of the ancient city of the same name, which was renowned in the Roman Imperial period for its whitish-green marble (cipollino), lies a good half hour's walk inland on the slopes of a hill topped by a Venetian castle, the Castel Rosso (views). North-east of Kárystos are the ancient marble quarries of Mýli.
From here it is a rewarding 3½ hours' climb to the summit of Mt Áyios Ilías (1398m/4587ft), the highest peak in the Ókhi range; magnificent views.

On the north-east side of the Ókhi range can be seen some of the buildings known as *arkhampolis* or *kharkhambolis* which are similar to the "dragon houses". Farther north-east is Cape Dóro (Cape Kafireús), which is associated with the story of Nauplios, father of the unfortunate Palamedes, who sought to attract the Greek ships returning from Troy on to the rocks by lighting beacons but threw himself into the sea on discovering that his principal enemies, Odysseus and Agamemnon, had escaped.

9km/6 miles east of Kárystos and 1km/¾ mile from the village of Platanistós (forests of oaks and planes) is the so-called Hellenikon, a terrace supported by massive retaining walls. Beyond this (2 hours' walk), at the sea, is the ancient port of Geraistos, which had a famous temple of Poseidon.

From Lépoura (above) the road to Kými goes north.
1km/¾ mile: road on the right to Avlonári, with the 12th century church of Áyios Dimítrios (ancient column drums built into the walls), and the village of Ayía Thékla, with a church containing 15th century frescoes.
13km/8 miles: Konístres, from which it is a half hour's walk to the ruined castle of Episkopí (remains of ancient and medieval walls).
17km/10½ miles: Kými (pop. 3000), a prosperous little town in a fertile hilly area and the only port on the inhospitable north-east coast. The ancient city was probably on Cape Kými, to the north, or somewhere near the monastery of the Áyios Sotír (north-west of which is a Byzantine castle). North-west of Kými are deposits of lignite (containing fossils of the Tertiary era).

Farmakonisi M 6

Φαρμακονήσι
Farmakonísi

Nomos: Dodecanese
Area of island: 4 sq.km/1½ sq. miles
Altitude: 0–106m/0–348ft
Population: 5

Situation and characteristics

Farmakonísi, an almost uninhabited islet of gentle, partly grass-covered, hills, lies 12km/7½ miles south west of Tekağaç Burun, a cape on the Turkish coast near Didyma. Here in 77 B.C. Caesar was captured by pirates and released only on payment of a ransom of 50 talents.
There are remains of a number of Roman villas and the ancient harbour, now partly under the sea.

Farsala G 4

Φάρσαλα
Fársala

Nomos: Lárisa
Altitude: 180m/590ft
Population: 6500

Transport

Station on the Athens–Salonica railway line (13km/8 miles west).

Situation and characteristics

The Thessalian town of Fársala, on a site which has been continuously occupied since Neolithic times, was destroyed by an earthquake in 1954 and thereafter rebuilt in modern style.
The only evidence of its long past is an ancient tomb on the western outskirts of the town, a circular structure surrounded by large slabs of stone.

History

Fársala is notable mainly as the scene of the battle of Pharsalos in the summer of 48 B.C., in which Caesar defeated Pompey. This was the first of three battles fought in Greece in the 1st century B.C. which had

decisive effects on the history of Rome; the others were Philippi in 42 B.C. (see entry) and Aktion (Actium) in 31 B.C. (see Nikópolis).
From the hill (348m/1142ft) above the town there is a view of the battlefield in the Enipefs valley to the north.

Florina F 3

Φλώρινα
Flórina

Nomos: Flórina
Altitude: 660m/2165ft
Population: 12,000

Flórina lies on a plateau to the north of the Verna hills, 16km/10 miles from the frontier crossing into Yugoslavia (Bitola). Situated in a well cultivated farming region, it has a college of agriculture and a well known fruit market.
There is a trunk road from here via Édessa and Pélla to Salonica (160km/100 miles): see entries.

Folegandros I 7

Φολέγανδρος
Folégandros

Nomos: Cyclades
Area of island: 34 sq.km/13 sq. miles
Altitude: 0–441m/0–1348ft
Population: 700
Chief place: Folégandros (Khóra)

Boat services

Regular service Piraeus–Páros–Santorin–Folégandros–Síkinos–Ios–Náxos–Piraeus.

Situation and characteristics

The long straggling island of Folégandros, between Melos and Santorin (see entries), is still barely touched by the tourist trade. The cliff-fringed eastern part of the island, with its highest hill (411m/1348ft), is bare and arid; the western half is milder, with water from springs, and supports a modest terraced agriculture.

With its poverty and lack of sheltered harbours, Folégandros was never a place of any importance. Its destinies were closely bound up with those of Náxos. In Roman times it was a place of exile.

Features of Interest

From the landing-stage at Karavostásis on the east coast it is an hour's walk (3km/2 miles; mules can be hired) to the chief place on the island, Folégandros (Khóra), a village of typical Cycladic houses with a medieval Kástro. To the east is the hill of Palaiókastro, with scanty remains of the ancient town.
North-west of the Khóra is the island's largest village, Áno Meriá.
On the east coast are the caves of Khrysospiliá and Yeoryítsi (access difficult), with ancient graffiti.

Fourni L 6

Φούρνοι
Foúrni

Nomos: Sámos

Boat services

Motorboats from and to Ikaría and Sámos.

Situation and characteristics

The Foúrni islands are a group of rocky islets with much-indented coasts lying between Sámos, Ikaría and Pátmos. In addition to the main island of Foúrni (area 30 sq.km/11½ sq. miles; alt. 0–486m/0–1595ft; pop. 1000), with the village of Foúrni on its west side, the group includes the smaller islands of Thimena (12 sq.km/4½ sq. miles; 0–483m/0–1585ft) to the west and Áyios Minás (5 sq.km/2 sq. miles; 0–250m/0–820ft) to the east, together with the isolated rocks of Andro, Makronísi and Diapori.

In the Middle Ages the islands were the haunt of pirates, who were able from commanding viewpoints on the hills to keep a lookout for shipping passing between Sámos and Ikaría. The inhabitants now live by farming and fishing.

Fyli H 5

Φυλή
Fylí

Region and nomos: Attica

Situation and characteristics

Although it is only a few kilometres from Athens, Fylí lies in the heart of the countryside of Attica, with an old monastery and one of the ancient Attic frontier fortresses.

Leaving Athens by way of Liosía Street (Liosion), which runs north-west from Lárisa Station, we come to Áno Liosía (13km/8 miles), the village of Fylí (18km/11 miles: bus from Athens to this point) and the lonely monastery of Panayía ton Klistón (22km/14 miles). The name of the monastery (Mother of God of the Gorges) refers to its situation on the rock face above the defile of the river Goúlas, on the slopes of Mt Párnis. The monastery is believed to have been founded in the 14th century, but both the church and the monks' quarters were later rebuilt and enlarged. Higher up the valley is an ancient grotto sacred to the shepherd god Pan, the setting of Menander's comedy "Dyskolos".

A few kilometres farther on the walls of the ancient fortress of Phyle can be seen on the left.

History

After the Peloponnesian War Athens built a ring of frontier fortresses designed to protect Attica against attack from the Megarid and Boeotia to the west. Beginning with the fortified town of Eleusis on the coast, this defensive system continued with the fort of Anakton and the town of Oinoe on Mt Kithairon (north-west of Eleusis) and then east via Phyle, Dekeleia and Aphidna to the coastal stronghold of Rhamnous (see entry).

In response to the construction of Anakton the city of Megara built a counter-fortification at Aigosthena, the most northerly point in its territory (see Pórto Yermenó).

Phyle

Phyle stands on a triangular plateau (alt. 683m/2241ft) at the pass carrying the road from Athens to Tánagra in Boeotia, on the western slopes of Mt Párnis. The site had probably been occupied by an earlier fortress in which Thrasyboulos assembled his supporters in 403 B.C. for an attack on the Thirty Tyrants.

Castle

The western and south-western parts of the 4th century fortress (which was excavated by Skias in 1900) have collapsed into the gorge, but considerable stretches of the walls of dressed stone, with four towers and two gates, have been preserved to the level of the wall-walk. The stones, measuring 2.75m/9ft by 38cm/1ft 3in, stand between six and twenty courses high. At some later period the interior of the fortress was infilled to the height of the walls.

Surroundings of Fylí

Akhárnai

On the way back to Athens a detour can be made from Áno Liosía to the village of Akhárnai, the setting of Aristophanes' "Acharnians" (3km/2 miles along the road to Mt Párnis, to the left). The site was occupied from Mycenaean times, and in the classical period was a place of some consequence.
3km/2 miles before the village, on a hill to the left of the road, near a Mycenaean tholos tomb, are remains of later fortifications.

Geraki G 6/7

Γεράκι
Geráki

Region: Peloponnese
Nomos: Laconia
Population: 2000

Situation

Geráki, a quiet little town occupying the site of ancient Geronthrai, lies in an impressive setting in a high valley in the Párnon range, 41km/25 miles south-east of Sparta.

Sights

From its heyday in Byzantine times, under the rule of the Despots of Mistra, Geráki preserves many churches and chapels, the most notable of which is Áyios Ioánnis. On the way up to the Frankish castle (an hour's walk, first south-east, then to the left beyond the cemetery) are a number of other churches, including the 12th century Ayía Paraskeví.

Crusader castle

Geráki Castle, one of the numerous Crusader castles in the Peloponnese, was built by Guy de Nivellet in 1234 on a commanding hill (500m/1640ft). A vaulted passage leads through the battlemented walls into the castle. The chapel, a three-aisled basilica, is excellently preserved. The altar bears Guy de Nivellet's coat of arms. On the iconostasis is an icon of the church's patron, St George, on whose feast-day a service is still celebrated here.

Leonídi

From Geráki two places of interest on the east coast of the Peloponnese can be visited (on indifferent roads) – the little port of Leonídi

(50km/31 miles north-east) and Monemvasía (67km/42 miles: see entry).

Gla H 5

Γλα
Gla

Region and nomos: Boeotia

Situation

The Mycenaean fortress of Gla lies at the north-east end of the Kopais plain (formerly Lake Kopais).

26km/16 miles from Thebes on the main road to Lamía the hill on which Gla lies can be seen rising out of the plain on the right of the road, 1km/¾ mile away. To reach it, take the turn-off for the village of Kástro. The narrow road encircles the hill, which rises to 70m/230ft on the north side. The massive walls, 5.7m/19ft thick and still standing 3m/10ft high, enclose the whole area of the hill. The walls have a total length of 3km/2 miles (compared with Mycenae's 900m/985yds) and take in an area of 200,000 sq.m/215,000 sq.yds, making this the largest stronghold of its period.
From the north gate we continue up to the highest point on the hill, with the remains of the palace, the two wings of which are set at right angles. To the south, in the direction of the south gate, are the remains of other houses. There was a double gateway on the east side.

Gyaros I 6

Γυάρος
Yiáros

Nomos: Cyclades
Area of island: 37 sq.km/14 sq. miles
Altitude: 0–489m/0–1604ft
Closed area; uninhabited

Boat services

None.

Situation and characteristics

Gyáros, an arid and barren island, lies in the Cyclades north-west of Sýros. After the Second World War, particularly under the military dictatorship, it was a place of internment and a penal colony.

Gythion G 7

Γύθειο
Yíthio

Nomos: Laconia
Altitude: 10m/33ft
Population: 7500

Transport

Boat services from and to Piraeus, Kýthira and Monemvasía. Bus connections with Sparta and Areópolis (Máni).
Yacht supply station.

The harbour, Gýthion

Situation and characteristics

Gýthion is a port on the Gulf of Laconia, 46km/29 miles south of Sparta and 24km/15 miles west of the mouth of the Evrótas.

The island of Marathonísi, connected with the mainland by a causeway, was the ancient Kranai, on which according to tradition Paris spent his first night with Helen, whom he had carried off from Sparta. Near the north end of the town is a Roman theatre.

Surroundings of Gýthion

Gýthion is a good base from which to visit the Máni peninsula (26km/16 miles), Sparta (46km/29 miles), Mistra (51km/32 miles) and Monemvasía (60km/37 miles). See the entries for these places.

Hydra H 6

Ύδρα
Ídra

Nomos: Attica
Area of island: 55 sq.km/21 sq. miles
Altitude: 0–590m/0–1936ft
Population: 2800
Chief town: Hýdra

Boat services

Regular services from Athens (Piraeus) several times daily (3¼ hours). Hydrofoil from Piraeus (Zéa), 1¼ hours.

Local connections with Spetsai and Ermioni.

Situation and characteristics

The island of Hýdra (ancient Hydrea) is a bare limestone ridge, 12km/7½ miles long and up to 5km/3 miles wide, lying off the south-east coast of the Argolid. This arid and infertile island lives mainly on the tourist trade and the sale of its craft products (jewellery, pottery, embroidery; hand-woven cloth, leather goods).
A tempting local speciality is *amygdalotá* (almond cake).

History

The island was occupied from Mycenaean times, but until the 18th century A.D. remained a place of no importance. In the 15th century, and again after 1770, following the rising in the Morea, Albanian refugees settled on the island and through their commercial and seafaring activities, together with a certain amount of piracy, made it a wealthy cultural and social centre. During the war of liberation from the Turks Hýdra converted its merchant fleet into a naval force and also met a considerable proportion of the costs of the war. It has now returned to its former unimportance.

Sights

★ Hýdra town

The island's chief town, Hýdra (pop. 2500), climbs picturesquely up the slopes of the hills around its sheltered harbour on the north coast. It is a favourite resort of artists, particularly painters, and intellectuals, who give the town its special stamp and atmosphere. On the quay is the old monastic church of the Panayía (17th c.), with a beautiful cloister. On both sides of the harbour are the imposing mansions of early 19th century shipowners and merchants, including the houses of Admiral Iakovos Tombazis (now occupied by an outstation of the

Harbour on Hýdra

Athens Academy of Art) and Dimitrios Voulgaris. One such mansion houses a training school for the merchant navy. The plain white and sometimes colour-washed houses of the town on the slopes above the harbour are rather Cycladic in type. Above the town to the west are the ruins of a medieval castle, and lower down are fortifications built during the war of liberation.

Surroundings of Hýdra

West of Hýdra, at the fishing village of Vlykhós, are the remains of ancient Chorisa.
1.5km/1 mile south is Kaló Pigádi (view), with 18th century country houses in the surrounding area.
To the south, in a beautiful hill setting, stands the 15th century monastery of Profítis Ilías (3 hours' walk; or by mule).
At the eastern tip of the island is the 16th century Zoúrvas monastery (3 hours' walk; or by mule).
There are a number of other monasteries, mostly abandoned.

Dokós

North-west of Hýdra is the little grazing island of Dokós (ancient Aperopia), with the village of the same name in a sheltered bay on the north coast.

Hymettos H 6

Υμηττός
Imittós

Region and nomos: Attica

Situation and characteristics

The plain of Attica is bounded on the east by the long ridge of Mt Hymettos (1027m/3370ft), made up of the bluish-grey Hymettian marble, overlying Pentelic marble, which was worked in ancient times. The hills were then covered with forest, and the honey of the region was renowned.

Sights

In recent decades trees have been replanted on the long deforested slopes of the hill, particularly around Kaisarianí monastery. The monastery has an abundant spring, one of the many once found on Hymettos.

On the summit plateau there was a sanctuary of Zeus Ombrios, who was invoked with prayers for rain. Other shrines on Hymettos were the precinct of Apollo Proopsios and, at the southern end of the range, the Grotto of the Nymphs (3km/2 miles north of Vári).

From the suburb of Kaisarianí, on the east side of Athens, a road leads past the monastery of Kaisarianí (see Athens) to Astéri monastery, with a domed cruciform church (frescoes), and on to the summit plateau (military area, closed to the public).

Below the north end of Hymettos is the monastery of Áyios Ioánnis Kynigós, which has a small church of the early 13th century, with later additions. It is reached from the village of Ayía Paraskeví on the Athens–Markópoulo road (2km/1¼ miles before Stavrós).

Igoumenitsa E 4

Ηγουμενίτσα
Igoumenítsa

Nomos: Thesprotia
Altitude: 10m/35ft
Population: 6000

Transport

Ferry connections with Italy, Kérkyra and Patras.

Situation and characteristics

This little town in Epirus is of importance as a ferry terminal and the starting-point of a tour of western Greece or through the Pindos mountains into Thessaly.

Ikaria L 6

Ικαρία
Ikaría

Nomos: Sámos
Area of island: 255 sq.km/98 sq. miles

Harbour, Igoumenítsa

Altitude: 0–1037m/0–3402ft
Population: 8900
Chief town: Áyios Kýrikos

Boat services

The regular service between Athens (Piraeus) and Rhodes, six times weekly in each direction, calls at Áyios Kýrikos. Local connections with Sámos, Foúrni and Pátmos.

Situation and characteristics

Ikaría (Turkish Nikarya), a largely barren island 40km/25 miles long and up to 8km/5 miles wide, lies in the north-eastern Aegean some 18km/11 miles south-west of Sámos. The whole length of the island is occupied by the bare Athéras range (1037m/3402ft), which falls steeply down to the sea on the south coast. The northern slopes of the hills, covered with a macchia of oak and spruce and slashed by fertile valleys with an abundance of water, fall away more gently to the coast, on which there are a number of small unsheltered bays. The inhabitants, mostly concentrated on the north side of the island, live by farming and fishing.
Ikaría has preserved much of its distinctive character.

Myth and history

The name of the island recalls the story of Ikaros, son of Daidalos, the Attic sculptor and inventor of Minoan times, who flew too near the sun with the wings, of feathers bound together with wax, which his father had made for him and plunged to his death in the sea near here. Local legends tell a different tale – that he died when his ship, with great white sails, sank in a storm.
Ikaría was settled from Miletus in the 8th century B.C., when the towns of Oinoe, Histoi, Therma and Drakanon were founded.
In Byzantine times Ikaría was used as a place of exile. Later it was held by various Frankish and Genoese barons; in 1481 it passed to the Knights of St John; and in 1567 it was captured by the Turks.
On July 17th 1912, after a successful rising against Turkish rule, the inhabitants proclaimed the free state of Ikaría, which soon afterwards joined the kingdom of Greece.

Sights

The island's chief town and port, Áyios Kýrikos (pop. 2000), lies near the east end of the south coast. There is an interesting archaeological collection in the Gymnasion.
3km/2 miles north-east is the little spa of Thérma, with hot mineral springs (52.5°C/126.5°F; radioactive, sulphurous). Above the town is the ancient acropolis, which can be climbed from Katafíyi (3km/2 miles north-east) on a path lined by tombs of the 6th century B.C.
7km/4½ miles south-west of Áyios Kýrikos is the monastery of Lefkádos Evangelismós.

On Cape Fanári, the north-eastern tip of the island (1 hour by boat), where according to legend Dionysos was born, are the remains of the Hellenistic fort of Drakanos.

Évdilos

Half way along the north coast is the picturesque village of Évdilos, once the chief place on the island.
2.5km/1½ miles west, at the village of Kámpos, can be seen the remains of the ancient city of Oinoe (small museum). Around the village are a number of beehive tombs (*tholaria*) and small medieval forts (*kastrakia).*
5km/3 miles south of Évdolos, at Kosíkia, is the Byzantine stronghold of Koskinas.

At the north-west end of the island is the little port of Armenistís. 5km/3 miles south-west are the remains of a temple of Artemis (probably 5th c. B.C.).

Inousai Islands F 7

Οινούσαι Νήσοι, Οινούσιδες Νησιά
Inoúsai Nísi, Inoúsides Nisiá

Nomos: Messenia

The Inoúsai Islands, a group notoriously subject to storms, lie off the south coast of Messenia at the south-western tip of the Peloponnese. The group consists of the two larger islands of Sapientza (alt. 0–226m/0–742ft, off Methóni Bay (sheltered anchorage by lighthouse) and Skhiza (or Cabrera; 0–196m/0–643ft), together with a number of rocky islets and isolated rocks.

There are several ancient wrecks on the sea bed around the islands, and they offer excellent opportunities for underwater diving – though here, as elsewhere in Greek waters, the use of breathing apparatus is not permitted.

Ioannina E 4

Ιωάννινα
Ioánnina

View of Ioánnina, looking towards the Ali Pasha Mausoleum

Ioannina

1 Aslan Aga Mosque (Folk Museum)
2 Turkish Library
3 Old Synagogue
4 Church of Ayii Anaryiri
5 Ali Pasha Mausoleum

Nomos: Ioánnina
Altitude: 520m/1705ft
Population: 45,000

Transport

Air connections with Athens and Salonica.
Bus connections with Athens and towns in the surrounding area.

★ Situation

Ioánnina, on the west side of Lake Ioánnina, is the chief town of Epiros and has a university, established in 1965. It is noted for its silversmith's work. The old parts of the town have preserved something of the atmosphere of the Turkish period.

History

Ioánnina grew up in the Middle Ages on the site of a monastery of St John. In 1085 it was fortified by the Normans, and in 1345 became the seat of Serbian princes. From 1430 to 1913 it was in Turkish hands. The town's heyday was between 1788 and 1822, when it was the residence of Ali Pasha (1741–1822), the "Lion of Ioánnina", an Albanian, who was nominally subject to the Sublime Porte but in fact enjoyed almost absolute independence.

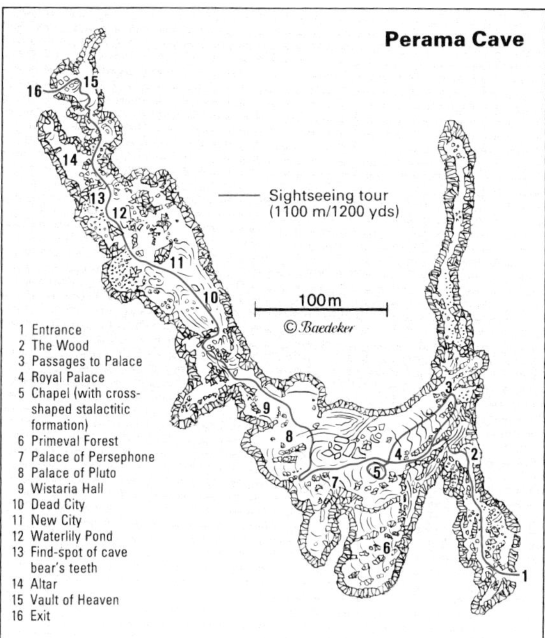

Sights

★ Citadel

The Citadel (Froúrion), with the Aslan Aga Mosque (1619; Folk Museum), has some picturesque nooks and corners, and affords beautiful views of the lake and the Pindos mountains. In the east corner is the Ali Pasha Mausoleum. The Kyrá Frosýni taverna on the lakeside promenade is named after one of a number of Greek women whom Ali Pasha drowned in the lake.

★ Monastery island

An interesting trip is to the island in the lake with its seven monasteries. In one of them, the monastery of St Panteleimon, Ali Pasha was killed by the Turks in 1822 (memorial room).

Archaeological Museum

The Archaeological Museum, in the centre of the town, displays finds from Dodona and the Nekromanteion of Ephyra (see entries).

Surroundings of Ioánnina

Dodóna

23km/14 miles south of Ioánnina is Dodóna, home of the oracle of Zeus (see entry).

Zitsa

30km/19 miles west, to the north of the road to Igoumenítsa, lies Zitsa, with the commandingly situated monastery of the Profítis Ilías, celebrated by Byron in "Childe Harold".

★★ Pérama Cave

4km/2½ miles north-east is the stalactitic cave of Pérama. Discovered by accident in 1940, this has a total area of 14,800 sq.m/17,700 sq.yds. The temperature of the air in the cave is 18°C/64°F.

★ Zagória mountains

A trip northward from Ioánnina in the direction of the Albanian frontier can be recommended for its magnificent scenery. In this area are the Zagokhoriá, the villages in the Zagória mountains which were semi-autonomous even in the Turkish period. 16km/10 miles along the road to Kónitsa a side road branches off on the right to Vítsa and the high village of Monodéndri (37km/23 miles from Ioánnina), with its weavers' workshops. From here a broad path leads to the little monastery of Ayía Paraskeví (1412), above the steep-sided Víkos gorge. The monastery is now abandoned, but the chapel is open to visitors.

★★ Víkos gorge

From here a rocky path, the last section of which is very narrow, leads to a hermit's cave, from which there is a fantastic view down into the Víkos gorge (Farángi Víkou).

In this area are the grazing grounds of the nomadic Sarakatsans, who – unlike the Koutsovlachs and Arromans – believe themselves to be descended from ancient Greek tribes.

Ionian Islands D/E 4–6

Ιόνιδες Νησιά
Iónides Nisiá

Situation and characteristics

The Ionian Islands, also known as the Eptánisos (Seven Islands), are strung out along the west coast of Greece from the Albanian frontier to the Peloponnese. In this westerly situation, with more rain than most other parts of Greece, the islands have a mild climate and a luxuriant growth of vegetation, with the exception of Kýthira, which lies apart from the others off the southern tip of the Peloponnese.

Myth and history

The Ionian Sea, which was equated by ancient authors with the Adriatic and is now seen as its southern continuation, and the Ionian Islands owe their name, according to Aeschylus, to the wanderings of Io or, according to later sources, to the Illyrian hero Ionios (spelt with omicron, the short *o*). They have thus no connection with the Ionian Greeks (derived from Ion, with omega, the long *o*), who left Greece in the 11th and 10th centuries B.C. and settled on the Anatolian coast, giving this eastern Greek territory its name of Ionia.

Evidence of settlement dating back to Mycenaean times has been found on the islands, but their first emergence into the light of history was in 734 B.C., when Corinth founded the city of Korkyra (later Kérkyra). In the 5th century B.C. the islands came under Athenian influence, and in the 2nd century B.C. all of them, including Kýthira, became Roman. Later they came under Byzantine rule, and in A.D. 1085 were conquered by the Normans; then in 1203–04 the Fourth Crusade brought another change of masters. The islands now fell into the hands of Italian barons, and then, one after another, came under Venetian control – Kýthira in 1363, Kérkyra (thereafter known as Corfu) in 1386, Zákynthos in 1479, Kefalloniá in 1500 (after a 21-year period of Turkish rule) and finally Lefkás (which had been Turkish since 1467) in 1684.

Venetian rule lasted until the fall of the Republic of St Mark in 1797. During this period the islands provided a refuge for many Greeks fleeing from the Turks, including artists from Crete who established a school of their own here; and throughout these years they enjoyed a richer cultural life than the rest of Greece.
After an interlude of French rule the young "Republic of the Seven Islands" became a British protectorate in 1815. In 1864 Britain returned the islands to Greece.

For descriptions of the individual islands, consult the Index at the end of the book.

Íos K 7

Ἴος
Íos

Nomos: Cyclades
Area of island: 105 sq.km/41 sq. miles
Altitude: 0–732m/0–2402ft
Population: 1100 (in 19th c. 3500)
Chief place: Íos (Khóra)

Boat services

Íos is served by boats sailing from Athens (Piraeus) to Páros, Íos, Santorin and Iráklion.

Situation and characteristics

Íos is a hilly island, largely fringed by cliffs, lying roughly half way between Páros or Náxos and Santorin. Until quite recently its only source of income was agriculture on the terraced slopes of the Káto Kámpos valley and its side valleys, but in the last few years it has been invaded by large numbers of backpackers and hippies who have destroyed – at any rate during the summer months – the peace and harmony of the island.

According to an ancient tradition Homer's mother Klymene was a native of Íos and he himself was buried on the island.

Harbour, Íos

A church on Íos

Features of Interest

Íos (Khóra)

The little port of Órmos Íou, with the domed church of Ayía Iríni (17th c.), lies in a deeply indented inlet on the west coast of the island. 1km/¾ mile up the fertile Káto Kámpos valley is the chief place on the island, Íos (Khóra; pop. 700). Its white Cycladic houses and twenty or so churches and chapels are enclosed within a dilapidated circuit of medieval walls. (There are some 150 other churches scattered about the island.)

★ Windmills

On the hill above the village, in two rows, are twelve windmills (now out of use).
In a cave on the north side of Mt Pýrgos (732m/2402ft), near the Plakotó monastery, are the remains of a sanctuary (probably Hellenistic) which is said to contain Homer's tomb.
At the north end of the island is a ruined Venetian castle.

Isthmia G 6

Ισθμία
Isthmía

Nomos: Corinth
Altitude: 10m/35ft

Situation and characteristics

Plan: see page 211

The village of Isthmía, to the south of the eastern end of the Corinth Canal, is of interest for the remains of the ancient sanctuary of Poseidon (1km/¾ mile south of the canal), which were excavated by American archaeologists from 1952 onwards. This was the scene of the Isthmian Games, held every second year from 582 B.C. onwards, in which the victor's prize was a wreath of wild celery or spruce.

Sights

Temple of Poseidon

The plan of the temple of Poseidon, built in 460 B.C. as successor to an earlier temple of the 7th century B.C., can be traced on the ground: it was a Doric peripteral temple with the classical proportions of 6 × 13 columns. It was damaged by fire in 394 B.C. and thereafter rebuilt. North-east of the temple was the theatre, to the south-east the stadion, which was rather later (4th c. B.C.).

The ancient buildings were destroyed in the 6th century A.D., during the reign of Justinian, when the stones were used in the construction of a Byzantine fortress (remains east of theatre), part of the defences built across the Isthmus of Corinth, and constantly renewed in later centuries, to protect the Peloponnese from attackers coming from the north. The defensive wall ran roughly parallel to the present canal and was six Roman miles long (1 Roman mile = 1000 paces = 1618yds) – as the name of the village of Examília still indicates.
Remains dating from the Mycenaean period (13th c. B.C.) have been found south and south-east of the temple of Poseidon. There are also substantial remains of a defensive wall built in 480–479 B.C. and restored in 197 B.C. and again in A.D. 253. This was followed by the work carried out in the reign of Justinian (*c.* A.D. 540); and there are references to further repair and strengthening of the wall in late Byzantine times and during the Venetian period.

Surroundings of Isthmía

Kenchreai

2km/1¼ miles south of the temple of Poseidon is the village of Kekhriás, which marks the site of the ancient Corinthian port of Kenchreai, with remains of the old harbour works (partly under water). North of the harbour, near the Kalamaki Beach Hotel, the site of a temple of the classical period has been identified.

2km/1¼ miles south of the harbour of Kenchreai is a spring with an abundant flow of water which has been known since the time of Pausanias as Helen's Bath (Loutró Elénis).

Ithaca E 5

Ιθάκη
Itháki

Nomos: Kefalloniá
Area of island: 93 sq.km/36 sq. miles
Altitude: 0–808m/0–2500ft
Population: 4000
Chief town: Vathý (Itháki)

Boat services

Ferry from Patras via Sámi (Kefalloniá), several times weekly.

Situation and characteristics

Ithaca (popularly called Thiaki) is a rocky island separated from Kefalloniá by a channel 4km/2½ miles wide and almost cut in two by the long Gulf of Mólos on its east side; the isthmus joining the two halves, at Mt Aetós (380m/1247ft), is only 600m/660yds wide. In the north of the island rises the Ani range of hills (Mt Neritos, 808m/2651ft), in the south Mt Stefani (671m/2202ft). Much of the island has been marked by karstic action, but agriculture is possible in a few fertile valleys.

Present-day Ithaca is generally accepted as being Odysseus's island of Ithaca, as described in the "Odyssey", though Wilhelm Dörpfeld located the Homeric Ithaca on the island of Lefkás (see entry).

History

The earliest finds of pottery point to a first settlement of the island towards the end of the 3rd millennium B.C. A number of Mycenaean sites have been identified, though their poverty is difficult to reconcile with the wealthy Homeric Ithaca, which is dated to the Mycenaean period. During the 1st millennium B.C., however, the island seems to have attained a degree of prosperity through an active trade with mainland Greece and Italy.
From Roman times Ithaca shared the destinies of the other Ionian Islands. During the Middle Ages the inhabitants were driven out by pirates, who established their base in what is now Vathý. In the 17th century the island was resettled by peasants from Kefalloniá.
After a long history of devastating raids and earthquakes practically all Ithaca's older buildings have been destroyed.

Sights

Vathý

The chief place on the island is the sheltered port of Vathý or Itháki (pop. 2500), probably founded by the Romans, which is charmingly situated in a bay – generally accepted as being the cove of Phorkys, in which the Phaeacians put the returning Odysseus ashore ("Odyssey", 13, 96 ff.) – defended by two Venetian forts.

Vathý Bay, Ithaca

Cave of the Nymphs

2km/1¼ miles west of Vathý, on the slopes of Mt Áyios Nikólaos, is the Mármaro Spília, a stalactitic cave and ancient cult site which is identified as the Cave of the Nymphs ("Odyssey", 13, 107–108).

Castle of Odysseus

5km/3 miles west of Vathý, on Mt Aetós, is the acropolis of an ancient city (7th c. B.C.), perhaps Strabo's Alalkomenai, which was excavated by Schliemann and is popularly known as the Castle of Odysseus.

Fountain of Arethusa

6km/4 miles south of Vathý on a difficult path is the Fountain of Arethusa, beneath the Ravens' Crag ("Odyssey", 13, 408–409). Farther south is the plateau of Marathiá, with extensive plantations of olive-trees, from which there are good views. Eumaios's farmyard ("Odyssey", 14, 6) is supposed to have been in this area.

Palaiokhorá

3km/2 miles south of Vathý is the site of Palaiokhorá, the island's capital until the 16th century.

Stavrós

The numerous ancient finds made in the vicinity of the village of Stavrós, in the north-west of the island, have suggested this as the most likely site for Odysseus's town and palace.

Pólis Bay

Below Stavrós, to the south-west, is the beautiful Pólis Bay, the only harbour of any size on the west coast of Ithaca. A cave on the west side of the bay was a shrine of Athena and Hera in Mycenaean times. Offshore, near the coast of Kefalloniá, lies the tiny islet of Daskalio, identified as the island of Asteris where the suitors planned to ambush Telemachos ("Odyssey", 14, 6).

1km/¾ mile north, on Mt Pelikata above Pólis Bay, are remains of a settlement dated between 2200 and 1500 B.C.

1km/¾ mile farther north is the chapel of Áyios Athanásios.

West of Stavrós are the picturesque inlets of Fríkes and Kióni.

Panayía Kathará monastery

6km/4 miles south of Stavrós is the monastery of the Panayía Kathará, from which there is a magnificent view; festival celebrated annually on September 8th.

Átokos

10km/6 miles north-east of Ithaca is the rocky and uninhabited island of Átokos.

Kaiafas F 6

Καϊάφας
Kaïáfas

Nomos: Elis
Altitude: 10m/35ft
Population: 1000

Situation

Kaiáfas, 21km/13 miles south of Pýrgos (see entry) on the west coast of the Peloponnese, has been famed since ancient times for its medicinal springs. It has beautiful long sandy beaches.

Surroundings of Kaiáfas

Zákharo

Káto Figalía

5km/3 miles south-east of Kaiáfas is the little coastal town of Zákharo and 8km/5 miles beyond this Tholon, where a road goes off on the left to Káto Figalía (14km/8½ miles). From here there is a road via Petratóna to Andrítsaina and the temple of Apollo at Bassai (see entry).
40km/25 miles south of Kaiáfas is Kyparissía (see entry).

Kalamata G 6

Καλαμάτα
Kalamáta

Nomos: Messenia
Altitude: 25m/80ft
Population: 42,000

Transport

Air services from Athens; bus connections with Athens and local towns; terminus of Peloponnese Railway line Athens–Corinth–Kalamáta.
Yacht supply station.

Situation and characteristics

Kalamáta, lying to the west of Mt Taýgetos, is chief town of the nomos of Messenia and a port for the shipment of the agricultural produce of the region. It occupies the site of Mycenaean Pharai, a town in the kingdom ruled by Menelaos. In 720 B.C., together with the rest of Messenia, it fell into Spartan hands. From 1204, under its present name, it became the residence, along with Andravída, of the Villehardouins. After periods of Byzantine, Turkish and Venetian rule it was sacked by Ibrahim Pasha in 1825. It still bears the marks of the damage caused by a severe earthquake in 1986.

The Town

Above the town is the castle of the Villehardouins. At the foot of the hill stands the convent of Áyios Konstantínos, occupied by nuns who make hand-woven silks. In the Kyriákos House is a museum displaying items of local interest, mainly from the Venetian period and the struggle for liberation.

Surroundings of Kalamáta

Ancient Messene, on Mt Ithómi (30km/19 miles); Pýlos, in Navarino Bay (51km/32 miles); Sparta and Mistra, reached on a beautiful road through the Taýgetos range; the Máni, to the south-east of the town. (See entries for all these places.)

Kalambaka F 4

Καλαμπάκα
Kalambáka

Nomos: Tríkala
Altitude: 220m/720ft
Population: 5700

Transport

Kalambáka is the terminus of the Fársala–Kalambáka railway line.

Situation

Kalambáka is a small country town situated at the point where the river Piniós emerges from the Pindos range into the Thessalian plain. It is a convenient base for a visit to the Metéora monasteries (see entry), or a starting-point for a trip through the Pindos mountains to Ioánnina.

Sights

★ Mitrópolis church

Below a sheer rock face is the Mitrópolis church, dedicated to the Dormition of the Mother of God. A basilica rebuilt by Andronikos Palaiologos in 1309, the original church is traditionally believed to have been founded in the reign of Justinian (6th c.). Some features of the church are consistent with this dating – the basilican plan, the large marble ambo in the nave and the synthronon (a semicircular stone bench for the priests) in the apse. The paintings in the nave date from the period after the rebuilding; they were the work (1573) of Neophytos, son of the Cretan artist Theophanes who was responsible for the paintings in the Áyios Nikólaos monastery in the Metéora.

Kalamos E 5

Κάλαμος
Kálamos

Nomos: Kefalloniá
Area of island: 24 sq.km/9 sq. miles
Altitude: 0–740m/0–2428ft
Population: 1500
Chief place: Kálamos

Kalambáka, at the foot of the Meteora rocks

Boat services

Connections with Astakós and Lefkás.

Situation and characteristics

Kálamos, lying off the coast of Acarnania, is a hilly island of karstic terrain and steep rocky coasts, with some agriculture. The chief place, Kálamos, is on the south-east coast.
To the south of Kálamos lies the island of Kastós, inhabited only by a few fishermen.

Kalavryta G 5

Καλάβρυτα
Kalávryta

Nomos: Achaea
Altitude: 725m/2380ft
Population: 2000

Transport

Terminus of the rack railway from Diákofto on the Gulf of Corinth.

Situation and characteristics

Kalávryta, situated at the foot of Mt Erýmanthos in the northern Peloponnese, is a good base for hill walking and climbing. The town was destroyed and more than 1400 people were murdered by German troops in 1943 in reprisal for partisan activities in the area. There is a memorial on the hill above the town.

Surroundings of Kalávryta

Ayía Lávra

7km/4½ miles south-west of the town is the Ayía Lávra, a monastery founded in 961, where the Greek fight for independence from the Turks was proclaimed in 1821. There is a small museum.

★ Megaspílaion

7km/4½ miles north-east on the road to Diákofto is the monastery of Megaspílaion (the Great Cave). The church has a wax icon of the Mother of God, and there is a small museum (icons).
The monastery can also be reached on an old rack railway, which runs up through the magnificent scenery of the wild Vyraikos gorge.

Kalymnos L/M 6/7

Κάλυμνος
Kálymnos

Nomos: Dodecanese
Area of island: 109 sq.km/42 sq. miles
Altitude: 0–678m/0–2225ft
Population: 13,000
Chief town: Kálymnos (Póthia)

Boat services

Regular services from and to Athens (Piraeus) several times weekly (14–19 hours; cars carried).
Local services in the Dodecanese: Rhodes– Sými – Tílos – Nísyros – Kos – Kálymnos – Léros – Lipsí – Pátmos – Arkí – Agathonísi – Sámos; Rhodes – Kos – Kálymnos – Astypálaia.

Situation and characteristics

Kálymnos is a bare limestone island, slashed by numerous gorges, lying 12km/7½ miles north-west of Kos (see entry) and separated from Léros (see entry), to the north-west, by the narrow Diapori Channel. The coasts are mostly steep and rocky, with numerous coves and inlets.
The inhabitants live partly by farming in the few fertile valleys and depressions, but mainly – as they have done for centuries – by diving for sponges in the south-eastern Mediterranean and processing them for export to America. The departure (April–May) and return (September–October) of the sponge-fishing fleet are celebrated with lively festivities.

History

Finds in various caves round the coasts, particularly at Daskalió, near Vathý, and Ayía Varvára, show that Kálymnos has been continuously inhabited since the Neolithic period. The island never played a prominent part in history.

Sights

Kálymnos

A limestone ridge rising to 678m/2225ft separates the north of the island from the south, in which most of the population has been concentrated since ancient times. From the foot of the hills a fertile plain extends south to the island's chief town and port, Kálymnos (formerly called Póthia; pop. 9500; radioactive springs), its handsome houses, in the neo-classical style popular in the 19th century, rising above the harbour on the gentle slopes fringing the bay. There is a small museum containing Neolithic material and finds from the sanctuary of Delian Apollo (see below).
North-west of the town is the former capital of the island, Khorió (17th c.), with a Byzantine castle.

Christ of Jerusalem church

West of Khorió, in the valley above Linari Bay, can be seen the ruined church of Christ of Jerusalem, an Early Christian basilica (6th c.) built,

◀ *Cross above Kalávryta*

View of the island of Telendos from Kálymnos

re-using ancient stones, on the foundations of a sanctuary of Delian Apollo.

Pánormos Bay

There are also many ancient remains around the sheltered Pánormos Bay on the west coast: remains of fortifications at Xirókampos and Vriokástro, around the little cove of Aryinóntas on the south side of the bay, and the ruined fort of Kástri (probably Carian), high above the cove of Emporió on the north side of the bay.

Télendos

Pánormos Bay is closed on the west by the rocky island of Télendos (alt. 0–458m/0–1503ft). On Mt Áyios Konstantínos is a medieval castle, and at the foot of the hill is the ruined monastery of Áyios Vasílios.

Kamena Vourla G 5

Καμένα Βούρλα
Kaména Voúrla

Nomos: Phthiotis
Altitude: sea level
Population: 2000

Transport

Kaména Voúrla is on the expressway from Athens to Salonica.

Situation

Kaména Voúrla is a small spa (recommended for rheumatism, arthritis and neuritis; sandy beach) on a wooded promontory opposite the island of Euboea.

Surroundings of Kaména Voúrla

7km/4½ miles east of Kaména Voúrla on the road to Athens lies Áyios Konstantínos, a pretty little fishing village.
18km/11 miles beyond Áyios Konstantínos is Arkítsa, from which there is a ferry to Loutrá Aidipsoú on Euboea.
At Livanátes, 4km/2½ miles beyond Arkítsa, where the main road to Athens bears right, a side road goes off to the villages of Atalánti (7km/4½ miles) and Kalápodi (6km/4 miles), where, immediately north of the road, is a site first reported by Wheler, an English traveller, in the 17th century but only recently excavated. The excavations brought to light the foundations of a Doric temple of Artemis measuring 19m/63ft by 46m/151ft (probably 5th c. B.C.), together with an altar which was found intact, complete with votive offerings. This is believed to be the sanctuary of Artemis Elaphebolia of Hyampolis.

Karditsa F 4

Καρδίτσα
Kardítsa

Nomos: Kardítsa
Altitude: 110m/360ft
Population: 27,000

Transport

Station on the branch railway line from Fársala to Kalambáka.

Situation

Kardítsa, founded during the Turkish period, is an agricultural market town in the Thessalian plain, below the east side of the Pindos range.

Surroundings of Kardítsa

Mitrópolis

In the hills, 10km/6 miles west of Kardítsa, is Mitrópolis, with remains of Roman fortifications.

Fanári

15km/9 miles north-west is Fanári (pop. 2000), with a Byzantine castle on a rocky crag.

Karitaina G 6

Καρίταινα
Karítaina

Region: Peloponnese
Nomos: Arcadia
Altitude: 380m/1245ft
Population: 1050

Situation

This Arcadian village is impressively situated in the gorge of the river Alfiós (Alpheios), 16km/10 miles north-west of Megalópolis (see entry) on the road to Andrítsaina (from which a secondary road runs south to Bassai: see entry).

Sights

Above the village towers a Frankish castle (alt. 583m/1969ft) built by Hugues de Bruyère, baron of Karítaina, in the 13th century. A monument on the hillside commemorates Theodoros Kolokotronis, a hero of the war of liberation, who defended the castle against the Turks in 1821. From the castle gate can be seen a medieval bridge spanning the Alfiós below the modern concrete bridge.

Karpathos M 8

Κάρπαθος
Kárpathos

Nomos: Dodecanese
Area of island: 332 sq.km/128 sq. miles
Altitude: 0–1220m/0–4003ft
Population: 6000
Chief town: Kárpathos (Pygádia)

Air services

Airfield 16km/10 miles south of Kárpathos town.
Regular flights Kárpathos–Rhodes, 1–3 daily; Kásos–Kárpathos, daily; Kárpathos–Sitía (Crete).

Boat services

Regular services from and to Athens (Piraeus), weekly (26 hours); also from and to Crete.
Local connections in Dodecanese: Rhodes–Khalkí–Kárpathos–Kásos.

Situation and characteristics

Kárpathos (Italian Scarpanto), a long narrow island in the Dodecanese extending for some 48km/30 miles from north to south, forms, along with its neighbouring island of Kásos, a transition between Rhodes and Crete. A rugged and infertile range of limestone hills, rising to 1220m/4003ft in Kalí Límni, extends along the whole length of the island. The coasts mostly fall steeply down to the sea, with small sandy beaches edged by numerous caves at the south end of the island, on the west coast round Arkása and on the east coast at Pygádia. The inhabitants' main sources of income are stock-farming, cabinet-making, wood-carving and the hand-woven cloth and embroidery produced by the women.

History

The island was originally occupied by settlers from Crete, followed by other settlers from Argos; thereafter it became subject to Rhodes. It had four ancient cities – Arkesia (of which there are scanty traces) at the south end of the west coast, Poseidon at the south end of the east coast, Thoantion on the west coast and Vrykos at the north end – and gave its name to the sea between Crete and Rhodes, the Karpathion Pelagos.

Sights

Kárpathos

The island's chief town and principal port is Kárpathos (pop. 1200), a modern foundation situated in a wide bay near the south end of the east coast, on the site of ancient Poseidion.

★ Ólympos

A rewarding trip from Kárpathos (by bus or taxi) is to the typical old mountain village of Ólympos (beautiful views; windmills, still operating), in the northern half of the island; it can also be reached from Diafáni, near the north end of the east coast. The inhabitants of Ólympos still wear their richly embroidered traditional costumes, and the village's traditional wedding festivities, lasting three days, are famed throughout Greece.
Another interesting village is Apérion, north-west of Kárpathos.

Ancient columns, Pygádia, Kárpathos

Sariá

Off the northern tip of Kárpathos, separated from it by a channel only 100m/110yds wide, is the island of Sariá (area 16 sq.km/6 sq. miles; alt. 0–565m/1855ft), the ancient Saros. On the south side of the island are the remains of a Byzantine town.

Kasos — not on map

Κάσος
Kásos

Nomos: Dodecanese
Area of island: 65 sq.km/25 sq. miles
Altitude: 0–583m/0–1913ft
Population: 1500
Chief place: Frý

Air services

Airfield 1km/¾ mile north-west of Frý. Daily flights Rhodes–Kárpathos–Kásos; also connection with Sitía (Crete).

Boat services

Weekly services from and to Athens (Piraeus) and Rhodes.
Local connections in Dodecanese: Rhodes–Khalkí–Kárpathos–Kásos; also with Crete (Sitía and Áyios Nikólaos).

Features of Interest

The island of Kásos (Italian Caso, Turkish Kasot), south-west of Kárpathos, is rocky (numerous caves), barren and without any sheltered anchorages. Its inhabitants live by farming (in the north) and boatbuilding.

Throughout its history Kásos has shared the destinies of the neighbouring island of Kárpathos. After the war of liberation Albanian sponge-divers settled on the island.

The chief place on Kásos, Frý, in the south of the island, lies above the landing-stage, on the site of the ancient city.

Off the north coast of Kásos is the little island of Armathia, now deserted, which has a sandy beach.

Kastellorizo — not on map

Καστελλόρξο
Kastellórizo

Nomos: Dodecanese
Area of island: 9 sq.km/3½ sq. miles
Altitude: 0–271m/0–889ft
Population: 200
Chief place: Meyísti

Air and boat services

Airfield opened in 1986. Regular flights and sailings once or twice weekly from and to Rhodes; boats to and from Kásos, Khalkí and Tílos. There is no motor traffic on the island.

Situation and characteristics

Kastellórizo (from Italian Castelrosso, the Red Castle; Turkish Meis), also known as Meyísti (the "largest" or "greatest"), is the most east-

Meyísti, Greece's most easterly port

erly outpost of Greece, lying only some 7km/4½ miles off the south coast of Asia Minor (Lycia). The rocky and arid island now has only some 200 inhabitants, mostly elderly (some of them sponge-divers), compared with the population of 15,000 it is said to have had about 1900. There has been a rapid decline in population since then through emigration, particularly to Australia.

Features of Interest

Archaeological evidence has shown that the island was already densely populated in the Neolithic period. Its subsequent destinies were closely linked with Rhodes.

Meyísti

The chief place on the island, Meyísti, a village of brightly painted houses, many of them now abandoned, lies above its sheltered harbour in the north-east of the island, dominated by a castle (13th–16th c.) of the Knights of St John which occupies the site of a fort of the 4th century B.C. At the foot of the castle hill is a domed Lycian tomb (4th c. B.C.). The mosque now houses a small museum.

An excursion which should not be missed is to the Blue Grotto in the south-east of the island.

Ro and Strongylí

5km/3 miles west and 4km/2½ miles south-east of Kastellórizo are the islets of Ro and Strongylí, now uninhabited and used only for the grazing of stock.

Kastoria F 3

Καστοριά
Kastoriá

Nomos: Kastoriá
Altitude: 620–760m/2035–2495ft
Population: 17,000

Transport

Air connection with Athens; bus connections with Athens and with local towns.

★ Situation

The town of Kastoriá in western Macedonia, probably occupying the site of ancient Keletron, is charmingly situated on a peninsula in Lake Kastoriá. It prospered as a centre of the fur trade even during the Turkish period.

The Town

★ Churches

There are no fewer than 72 churches and chapels in the town, many of them with fine wall paintings. In the centre of the town, near the Gymnasion, are the chapel of the Taxiarchs (Archangels; 11th–13th c.) and the church of the Panayía Koumbelidíki (11th c.), the only one of the town's churches on a centralised plan. To the south, in Omónia Square, is the single-aisled chapel of Áyios Nikólaos tou Kasnitzi (*c.* 1000). On the highest point of the former citadel, near the Hôtel du Lac

1 Kursum Mosque
2 Faneromeni church
3 St John Bapt. of Aposari
4 Taxiarchs of Rallis
5 Zapountsis House
6 St Nicholas of Tsotsas
7 Tsiatsapas House
8 St George on the Hill
9 St Nicholas of Kyritses
10 Anaryiri
11 St Nicholas of Thomanos
12 St Andrew
13 Panayia of Kotzopoulos
14 Panayia of Oikonomou
15 St Nicholas of Megeleion
16 Gulas Mosque
17 St Nicholas of Eupraxia
18 Church of Apostles
19 Panayia Eleousa
20 St Stylianus
21 St Stephen
22 St George
23 St Thomas
24 St Nicholas of Mousabiki
25 St George of Mousabiki
26 St Demetrius
27 Panayia Koumbelidiki
28 Gymnasion
29 Taxiarchs
30 St Nicholas
31 St Alypius
32 St Nicholas of Kasnitsis
33 Panayia Raziotissa
34 St Athanasius
35 St Michael the Taxiarch
36 St Nicholas of Dragota
37 St Paraskevi
38 Natsis House
39 St Nicholas of Karibis
40 St John the Theologian

and the Gulas Mosque, stand the church of the Panayía tou Kotzópoulou and the chapel of Áyios Nikólaos tis Efpraxias (11th–12th c.). In the north of the town the most notable churches are the church of the Anáryiri (10th c., with 11th c. wall paintings) and Áyios Stéfanos, an 11th century basilica with numerous wall paintings. There are a number of chapels of the Turkish period belonging to patrician houses, some of which also survive. One such house on the south side of the town, near the lake, is now a Folk Museum.

To the south-east of the town, on the lake, is the monastery of the Panayía Mavriótissa. Built on to the principal church, which has 11th/12th century frescoes, is a chapel of Áyios Ioánnis Theológos, with frescoes of 1552. Both the church and the chapel have also good frescoes on the external walls.

View of Kavála from the harbour

Kavala

I 3

Καβάλα
Kavála

Nomos: Kavála
Altitude: 5–60m/15–195ft
Population: 56,000

Transport

Air service from Athens; bus service from Salonica; ferries to Thásos. Nearest railway station: Dráma (32km/20 miles).

Situation

Kavála, the principal port in eastern Macedonia, is beautifully situated on the slopes of Mt Sýmvolon, rising from the harbour to the Byzantine castle on the acropolis.

History

The town was founded, probably in the 6th century B.C., by settlers from the island of Páros, who called it Neapolis. It owed its rise to prosperity to the gold in the nearby Pángaion hills. In 168 B.C. it became Roman, and in 42 B.C. served as a base for Brutus and Cassius before their defeat at Philippi (see entry). In A.D. 50–51 the Apostle Paul landed here on his first journey into Europe. After the victory of Christianity the town became the seat of a bishopric subordinate to Philippi and took the name of Christopolis. Later the name Kavála came into use.

From 1371 to 1912 the town was in Turkish hands. It was the birthplace of Mehmet Ali (1769–1849), an Albanian who rose to become Pasha of Egypt and founded the royal dynasty which ended with the abdication of Farouk in 1952.

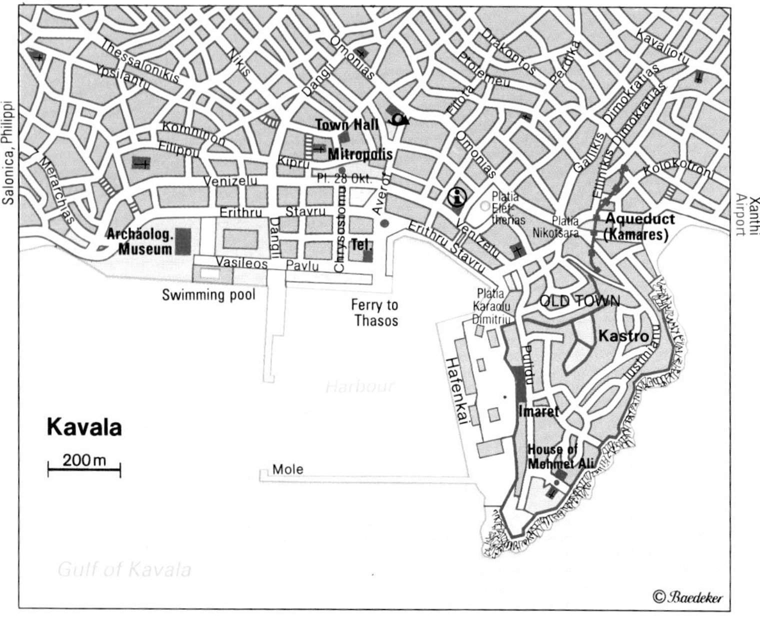

Kavála was occupied by Bulgarian forces in 1916–18 and again in 1942–44. It is now important as a centre of the cotton trade and a port for the shipment of tobacco.

Sights

Harbour
★ Castle
★ Aqueduct

Above the harbour, occupying the site of the ancient acropolis, is the Byzantine castle. Within its walls is the house in which Mehmet Ali was born in 1769. The two-storey aqueduct which supplied the castle with water was built by the Turks in the 16th century. On the way up to the castle we pass an imaret (soup kitchen for the poor) founded by Mehmet Ali. Higher up is a square in which is the birthplace of Mehmet Ali, with an equestrian statue in front of it. The defensive works of the citadel are well preserved; fine panoramic views.

Archaeological Museum

The new Archaeological Museum displays finds from the town and surrounding area (Abdera, Amphipolis, Dráma). On the ground floor, to the left of a corridor, are two rooms. Room I: Ionic columns from the temple of the Parthenos at Neapolis, amphora in early Geometric style, etc. Room II: rich finds from the necropolis of Amphipolis (funerary stelae, including a painted stele, gold jewellery, pottery). In the courtyard are pieces of marble sculpture. On the upper floor: pottery, a mosaic from Abdera (3rd c. B.C.), coins, etc.

Surroundings of Kavála

Within easy reach of Kavála are Philippi (15km/9 miles: see entry), the monastery of Ikosifínissis on the north-eastern slopes of the Pángaion hills (45km/28 miles via Eleftheroúpolis), the ancient site of Amphipolis (see entry), on the road to Salonica (62km/39 miles west), and the island of Thásos (see entry).

Kea I 6

Κέα
Kéa

Nomos: Cyclades
Area of island: 131 sq.km/51 sq. miles
Altitude: 0–560m/0–1837ft
Population: 4000
Chief place: Kéa (Khóra)

Boat services

Regular connections with Rafína and Lávrion (Attica), several times weekly; local connections with Kýthnos and Kárystos (Euboea).

Situation and characteristics

Kéa, the most westerly of the larger Cyclades, lies some 20km/12½ miles south-east of Cape Soúnion (see entry). The island's agriculture and the traditional harvesting of acorns for use in tanning have declined as a result of emigration. There is a certain amount of tourist traffic from mainland Greece.

History

Originally settled by Dryopians from Euboea and later by Ionians, the island was known in antiquity as Keos. It was a "tetrapolis" of four cities – Ioulis, Karthaia, Koressia and Poiessa.

Sights

Kéa (Khóra)

The chief place on the island, Kéa (Khóra; pop. 1700), lies at the foot of Mt Profítis Ilías (560m/1837ft), on the site of ancient Ioulis, of which there are some remains within the medieval Kástro (1210). Ioulis was the home of two notable poets, Simonides and his nephew Bacchylides (6th–5th c. B.C.).

Koríssia

4km/2½ miles north-west of Kéa, on the south side of the bay of Áyios Nikólaos (in the 13th century a pirate stronghold), is the little port of Koríssia (also known as Livádi), on the site of ancient Koressia. There are remains of the ancient town walls and a sanctuary of Apollo. The Kouros of Kéa (530 B.C.) which was found here is now in the National Archaeological Museum in Athens.
1.5km/1 mile north is the seaside resort of Vourkári.

★ Bronze Age settlement

On the little peninsula of Ayía Iríni, opposite Vourkári, is a Bronze Age settlement of about 2500 B.C. which was excavated by American archaeologists from 1960 onwards. The town, which was surrounded by walls around 1900–1800 B.C., traded with the Minoan and Mycenaean worlds, and enjoyed a heyday between 1600 and 1450 B.C. Thereafter there was only sporadic settlement on the site.
The site is entered on a modern flight of steps beside an ancient fountain. The remains are preserved to a considerable height, and the various settlement levels identified by the archaeologists can be distinguished, together with the remains of water and drainage channels. Particularly notable features are a large cellared building (House A), which probably served religious and administrative purposes, the remains of a tumulus tomb and above all the walls of the oldest temple so far found in Greece (15th c. B.C.). Passing an altar, we go through the

The Lion of Kéa

remains of the doorway into the narrow naos, beyond which is a second adyton.

★ Lion of Kéa

On a hillside 1.5km/1 mile north-east of the Khóra is a 9m/30ft long lion carved from the native rock (6th c. B.C.).

Karthaia

Near the south end of the east coast are the massive terrace walls of ancient Karthaia (only accessible on foot; stout shoes recommended). On the lowest terrace are the foundations of a Doric temple of Apollo; on a 6m/20ft long block in the polygonal walls of the terrace above this can be seen an ancient inscription; and on a still higher terrace are the foundations of another temple. Higher still again are the walls of the upper town and remains of buildings.

Poiessa

Above Poísses Bay, on the west coast of the island, are scanty remains of ancient Poiessa. On the way back from here to Kéa is the abandoned monastery of Ayía Marína, near which is a well preserved tower of the 4th century B.C.

On Cape Kefála, on the north coast, are remains of a Neolithic settlement (4000–2800 B.C.). East of this, at Otziás, are the Trypospilies (ancient mine workings).
In the north-east of the island we come to the monastery of the Panayía Kastrianí (18th c.), from which there are fine views.

Kefallonia E 5

Κεφαλλονιά
Kefalloniá

Nomos: Kefalloniá
Area of island: 781 sq.km/302 sq. miles
Altitude: 0–1628m/0–5341ft
Population: 31,000
Chief town: Argostóli

Air services

Airport 9km/5½ miles from Argostóli. Daily flights from and to Athens.

Boat services

Daily services Patras–Sámi (cars carried).

Situation and characteristics

Kefalloniá (or Kefallinía; Italian Cefalonia), the largest of the Ionian Islands, is an island of bare limestone hills rising to 1628m/5341ft in Mt Aínos and slashed by fertile valleys with luxuriant subtropical vegetation. It is generally accepted as being the Homeric island of Same (but for Wilhelm Dörpfeld's divergent view see the entry on Lefkás). The island's main sources of income are agriculture and the tourist trade.

Myth and history

In the "Odyssey" the two islands of Same and Doulichion are described as belonging to the kingdom of Ithaca, but Odysseus's subjects are also called Cephallenians.

In the 6th and 5th centuries B.C. the island, like Corfu, was under the influence of Corinth; then in 456 B.C. Tolmides compelled it to submit to Athens. At that time there were four city states on Kephallenia – Kranioi, Pale, Pronnoi and Same – which Thucydides refers to as a tetrapolis. The cities were members of the Aeolian League, and Cephallenian vessels fought against Philip V of Macedon (220–217 B.C.). They fought, too, against the Romans, but eventually the islands fell into the power of Rome. Thereafter Kephallenia shared the destinies of the other Ionian Islands.

Sights

Argostóli

Kefalloniá's capital, Argostóli (pop. 10,000), lies on a peninsula projecting into the Gulf of Argostóli (or Livádi), which cuts deep into the south-west coast of the island. Once an attractive old town, it was almost completely destroyed by an earthquake in 1953 and has been rebuilt in modern style. The Archaeological Museum contains Mycenaean and Roman material.

Sea-mills

North of the town, at the tip of the peninsula, are the famous sea-mills of Argostóli, now partly buried as a result of the 1953 earthquake. The mills are driven by sea-water surging along a channel cut through the rock and then disappearing into hidden underground passages through the limestone, to emerge on the east side of the island in the Melissáni Cave.

6km/4 miles east of Argostóli are the remains of ancient Kranioi.

★ Áyios Yeóryios Castle

9km/6 miles south-east of Argostóli, at the village of Kástro (once the island's flourishing chief town), stands the 13th century castle of Áyios Yeóryios (alt. 320m/1050ft; view). The 17th century monastery of Áyios Andreas has fine frescoes (12th c.) and icons. The site of ancient Kephallenia is believed to have been in this area. To the south, at the foot of Mt Áyios Yeóryios, extends the fertile upland region of Liváto. Byron stayed at Metaxáta in 1823. In the neighbourhood are three Mycenaean rock-cut tombs.

Sámi

24km/15 miles east of Argostóli is Sámi (pop. 1200), with the island's principal harbour. Ancient Same, the island's capital, which prospered particularly in the time of the Diadochoi, lay to the south of the

The little port of Fiskárdo on Kefallonia

modern town on the slopes of the double-topped hill which rises above it (remains of town walls; Roman villa of 2nd c. A.D.).

★ Stalactitic caves

In the vicinity of Sámi are the stalactitic caves of Frongaráti (south-west) and Melissáni (north-west; underground lake).

Near the village of Ayía Effimía on the Erisso peninsula, on the north side of the Gulf of Sámi, can be seen remains of the walls of ancient Same.

At Ássos is a ruined Venetian castle (1595; views).

Fiskárdo

At the north-eastern tip of the island lies the little port of Fiskárdo (ancient Panormos), named after the Norman leader Robert Guiscard, who died here in 1085. Some of the old houses in the village have been converted for use as holiday homes.

Lixoúri

North-west of Argostóli, on the Palikí peninsula on the far side of the gulf, is the port of Lixoúri (pop. 6000), which is connected with Argostóli by ferry and by road. North of the town are scanty remains of ancient Pale.

Kimolos

I 7

Κίμωλος
Kímolos

Nomos: Cyclades
Area of island: 35 sq.km/14 sq. miles

Altitude: 0–398m/0–1306ft
Population: 1500
Chief place: Kímolos

Boat services

Regular services Piraeus–Kýthnos–Sérifos–Melos–Santorin (passengers brought ashore in small boats).
Local connection with Melos.

Situation and characteristics

Kímolos is an arid and inhospitable island of volcanic origin, covered with a low growth of vegetation, lying north-east of Melos. It was known in antiquity for its *terra kimolia* (cimolith), used both as a detergent and in medicinal baths. The inhabitants make a sparse living from agriculture.

Features of Interest

The chief place on the island, Kímolos, lies near the sheltered anchorage of Psáthi (beach), around the remains of the late medieval settlement of Kástro.

On the highest point on the island is the ruined medieval castle of Palaiókastro (access difficult: rough track).

Áyios Andréas

Off the south-west coast of Kímolos lies the little islet of Áyios Andréas, which in ancient times was connected with the main island by a narrow spit of land. On it was the oldest organised settlement on Kímolos, Ellenikon (100 B.C. onwards; remains of walls under water).

Polýaigos

2km/1¼ miles east of Kímolos is the uninhabited islet of Polýaigos.

Komotini K 2

Κομοτηνή
Komotiní

Nomos: Rhodope
Altitude: 45m/150ft
Population: 34,000

Transport

Komotiní lies on the Kavála–Alexandroúpolis road and the Salonica–Alexandroúpolis railway line.

Komotiní, chief town of Thrace, is an agricultural market centre (tobacco, grain, livestock). It has a population of Greeks, Turks and a few Bulgarian-speaking Muslim Pomaks.

Archaeological Museum

The Archaeological Museum (Odós N. Zoidou), opened in 1976, displays in topographical order finds from all over Thrace from the 4th millennium B.C. onwards. Particularly notable items are a Klazomenian sarcophagus from Abdera (found in 1975), sculpture of the

6th–4th centuries B.C. (including a small marble lion), gold jewellery from Orestis, bronzes from Didymotikho and a golden head of the Emperor Marcus Aurelius, also from Didymotikho.

Koroni F 7

Κορώνη
Koróni

Nomos: Laconia
Altitude: 10m/35ft
Population: 2300

Situation and characteristics

The little port of Koróni, 42km/26 miles south-west of Kalamáta on the west side of the Gulf of Messenia, is particularly noted for its castle. It occupies the site of ancient Asine, but in late antiquity it was re-settled by the inhabitants of Korone (25km/16 miles north; now called Petalídi) and took over the name of that town.

After the 4th Crusade the town was taken by Geoffroy de Villehardouin, but was made over by him in 1206, together with Methóni (see entry) to the Venetians, who enlarged and strengthened the old Byzantine fortress on the peninsula. From 1560 to 1686 and again from 1715 to 1828 Koróni was held by the Turks, who built further fortifications. Outside the walls on the east side of the town is a monastery dedicated to St John the Baptist.

Kos L/M 7

Κως
Kos

Nomos: Dodecanese
Area of island: 295 sq.km/114 sq. miles
Altitude: 0–846m/0–2776ft
Population: 12,000
Chief town: Kos

Air services

Airfield at Antimákhia, 27km/17 miles south-west. Regular flights Athens–Kos, daily; Rhodes–Kos and Léros–Kos, several times weekly.

Boat services

Regular services from and to Athens (Piraeus), six times weekly (21 hours; cars carried).
Local connections in the Dodecanese: Rhodes – Sými – Tílos – Nísyros – Kos – Kálymnos – Léros – Lipsí – Pátmos – Arkí – Agathonísi – Sámos and Rhodes – Kos – Kálymnos – Astypálaia.
Excursions from Bodrum in Turkey.

Situation and characteristics

Kos (Italian Coo, Turkish Istanköy) lies at the mouth of the Gulf of Kos, which cuts deep into the coast of Asia Minor. It was separated from the Bodrum (Halikarnassos) peninsula, 5km/3 miles north-east, by the collapse of a rift valley in the Pliocene period. It is the largest island in the Dodecanese after Rhodes.
A range of limestone hills, rising to 846m/2776ft in Mt Díkaios (ancient Oromedon), traverses the island for almost its entire length from west to east. Unlike most other Aegean islands, Kos has a population that is

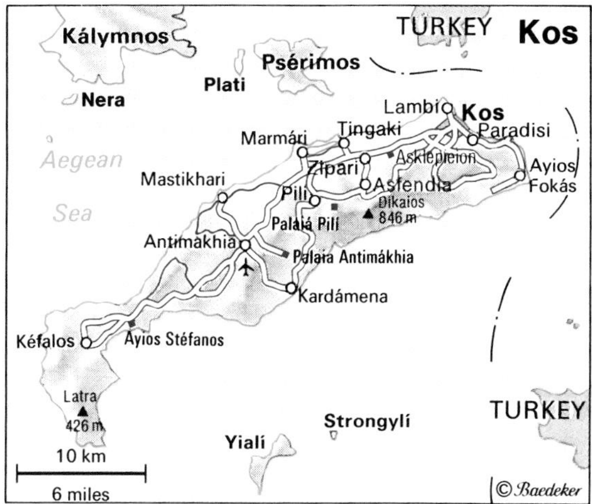

increasing in numbers. Their main sources of income are agriculture and horticulture, the rearing of small livestock, fishing, crafts (particularly pottery and weaving) and, increasingly, the tourist trade.

History

Kos has been well populated since Neolithic times. About 700 B.C., together with the other five cities of the Hexapolis (Knidos, Halikarnassos, Lindos, Ialysos and Kameiros), Kos was an outpost of the Dorian League of cities on the Carian coast and the neighbouring islands. The earliest capital of the island, Astypálaia, was situated in the wide bay at the south-west end; another important place, Halasama, lay half way along the south coast. The island was celebrated for the oldest cult site of the healing god Asklepios and for a medical school of which the most famous representative was Hippokrates (5th C. B.C.). The sanctuary of Asklepios was destroyed by an earthquake in A.D. 554, and on its ruins was built the monastery of the Panayía tou Alsoús (Our Lady of the Grove – recalling the ancient sacred grove).

The Byzantines were succeeded as rulers of the island by the Knights of St John (1309–1523), who in the 14th century established the headquarters of their Order in the island's capital, Narangia (now the town of Kos).

Kos was captured by the Turks some years earlier than Rhodes. The island was occupied by Italy in 1912, during the Balkan War, but was returned to Greece in 1948.

Sights

Kos Town

The chief town, Kos (pop. 6000), rebuilt after an earthquake in 1933, lies in a deep bay, now silted up, on the north-east coast, at the east end of the plain which extends along the north coast – the only plain of any size on the island. On the east side of the sheltered harbour stands the Castle of the Knights (1450–80), with pieces of ancient sculpture and inscribed stones built into its walls.

★★ Hippokrates' Plane-Tree

On the south side of the castle is Hippokrates' Plane-Tree, under which Hippokrates is traditionally believed to have taught his disciples. In

The hill village of Kefalos

In the Asklepieion

fact, however, the mighty tree, with a girth of 12m/40ft, is only some 500 years old. To the south of the tree is the ancient Agora, on the west side of which are the charming Defterdar Mosque (18th c.), with Hellenistic and Byzantine columns, and the Archaeological Museum, which, among much else, displays the most recent finds from the Asklepieion.

★ Archaeological Museum

South-west of the harbour are the remains of Hellenistic and Roman baths.

To the south and south-west of the town are remains of a temple of Dionysos, the Gymnasion and Stadion (Hellenistic), the Roman Odeion, the Hellenistic and Roman Theatre and a reconstructed Roman villa of the 3rd century A.D., the Casa Romana, with fine mosaics.

8km/5 miles south-east of Kos is the little spa of Áyios Fokás.

★ Asklepieion

4km/2½ miles south-west of the town, magnificently situated 100m/330ft above the sea, is the Asklepieion, the sanctuary of Asklepios (Aesculapius), famed for its medical school. Laid out on three terraces, it was built in the early 3rd century B.C. on the site of an earlier (5th c.) temple of Apollo. On the lowest terrace, to the north, is a rectangular precinct some 90m/300ft long by 45m/150ft across surrounded on three sides by Doric colonnades, to the rear of which were a series of rooms. On the north side, to the left of the entrance, can be seen the remains of three houses of the Roman or late Hellenistic period. At the north-east corner of the precinct a bath-house was later inserted, subsequently converted into the church of the Panayía tou Alsoús. Adjoining this is a small museum. Along the south side of the terrace is the retaining wall of the next terrace. To the left, between the second and third buttresses, is the sacred spring. To the right, in front

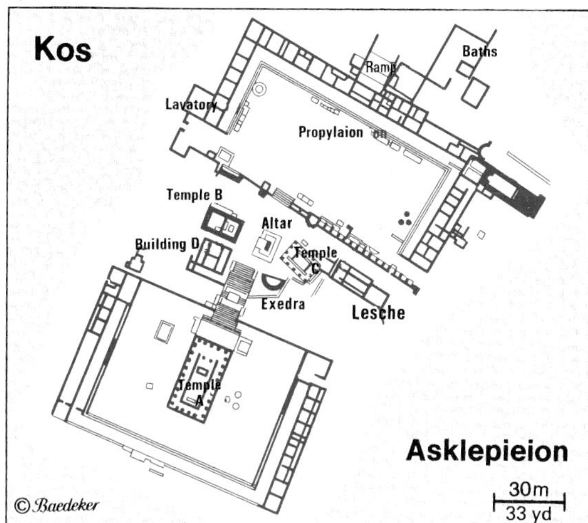

of a stretch of wall without buttresses, is a naiskos (small temple) dedicated to Nero, the "new Asklepios", by C. Stertinius Xenophon. From here steps lead up to the second terrace, the oldest part of the sanctuary. At the top of the steps is an altar, which in its present form is later than the small temple of Asklepios (*c.* 400 B.C.) to the west; of the earlier temple on this site only scanty traces have survived. To the east of the altar is an Ionic peripteral temple of 6 × 9 columns, possibly dedicated to Apollo. To the south-west was a semicircular exedra, and facing this, behind the old temple, a Roman building on earlier foundations.

Between these two buildings a monumental staircase 11m/36ft wide leads up to the third terrace, 12m/39ft higher up, with the later (2nd c. B.C.) temple of Asklepios, a Doric peripteral temple of 6 × 11 columns. The black marble sill-stone has been preserved.

Higher up the hill (a 45 minutes' climb) is the Vourinna spring, which supplied the ancient city with water.

From Kos Town to the Western Tip of the Island

The road first runs along the northern slopes of the hills.

10km/6 miles: Zipári, with the Early Christian basilica of Áyios Pávlos, which has a fine baptistery and mosaics. 4km/2½ miles south is the charming mountain village of Asfendíou, in a fertile vegetable-growing area. From here Mt Díkaios can be climbed (beautiful panoramic views).

5km/3 miles: side road to Palaiá Pylí (4km/2½ miles south), with a castle of the Knights of St John. In the deserted village at the foot of the castle hill is a church with Byzantine frescoes.

13km/8 miles: Antimákhia. 5km/3 miles south is another castle of the Knights, prominently situated on a hill at Palaiá Antimákhia, which was rebuilt after an earthquake in 1493 (coats of arms of knights). Within its walls is another deserted village.

1km/¾ mile: Kos Airport. 6km/4 miles south is the fishing village of Kardámena (fruit-growing, particularly melons; pottery).

Remains of the sanctuary of Asklepios

17km/10½ miles: Kéfalos, a mountain village perched high above the sea, with an ancient theatre. It is the principal place in the western part of the island. Important prehistoric remains were found in the caves at the entrance to the village. Nearby is the ruined Early Christian basilica of Áyios Stéfanos. In the bay are the striking St Nicholas's Rock, with a small chapel, and St Stephen's Rock.

Psérimos

Off the north coast of Kos lies the island of Psérimos (area 17 sq.km/6½ sq. miles; alt. 0–268m/0–879ft; pop. 100), which has a beautiful sandy beach.

Kozani F 3

Κοζάνη
Kozáni

Nomos: Kozáni
Altitude: 720m/2360ft
Population: 25,000

Situation and characteristics

Kozáni, chief town of a nomos in western Macedonia, is an important regional centre and traffic junction (airfield; terminus of railway from Salonica and Flórina), where the main roads from Salonica (140km/87 miles) to Ioánnina and from Flórina (and Bitola in the Republic of Macedonia) to Lárisa cross at right angles. It lies in a wide and fertile basin and has expanded considerably in recent years. It is the seat of a Greek Orthodox metropolitan and during the centuries of Ottoman rule was an important centre of Greek culture.

Features of Interest

Old town

Although Kozáni is not generally regarded as a place of great tourist interest, it is worth taking a stroll through the irregular streets and lanes in the town centre with their old houses, part stone-built and part half-timbered, set round inner courtyards and gardens. The best starting-point is the town's central square, Platía Níkis (Victory Square; partly pedestrianised), with a clock-tower of 1855. This was formerly the point from which main roads radiated in all directions.

Áyios Nikókaos

The metropolitan church of Áyios Nikólaos (1664–1721), a low squat church partly built of wood, has fine carving on the iconostasis and choir-stalls.

Museums

Two museums are worth visiting: the small Archaeological Museum and the well arranged Regional Folk Museum (Laografikó Mousío; closed Tue.), housed in a carefully restored old mansion (follow the signposts to "Museum").

Municipal Library

The Municipal Library has more than 50,000 old manuscripts, including rare items from the Kozáni scribes' school, famed in the Middle Ages.

Metamórfosis church

Prominently situated on a hill on the north-western outskirts of the town stands the church of the Metamórfosis tou Sotíros, from which there are views over the town into the wide river valley to the south-east, with a large artificial lake formed on the river Aliakmon.

Surroundings of Kozáni

Lake Aliakmon

20km/12½ miles south-east of Kozáni extends the long artificial lake formed by the damming of the Aliakmon. There is an attractive trip (70km/45 miles) round the lake. Leave Kozáni on the Lárisa road (No. 3), which runs south-east by way of Petraná and Vathýlakkos, crosses the lake on a curving bridge over 2km/1¼ miles long and bears south-west at Sérvia (see entry). Soon after this turn off the main road, which continues into the hills, into a side road on the right which leads along the south side of the lake to the village of Rýmnio, beyond which it again crosses the lake (narrower at this point) and comes to Aianí (several churches, with 15th and 16th c. frescoes). Just outside the village, above the left bank of the Aliakmon, is the Zavorda monastery, founded in the 16th century. The return to Kozáni is by way of Lefkopyrgí.

Kyllini — F 6

Κυλλήνη
Kyllíni

Region: Peloponnese
Nomos: Elis
Population: 600

Transport

The nearest railway station is Gastoúni, on the Patras–Pýrgos line. Ferry between Kyllíni and Zákynthos 2–3 times daily.

Situation and characteristics

The Kyllíni peninsula – not to be confused with the hill of the same name in the northern Peloponnese – is the most westerly point in the Peloponnese. It ends in a ridge of hills which rises commandingly out of the wide coastal plain and is crowned by Khlemoutsí Castle. To the north of the hills is the little port of Kyllíni (known in the Middle Ages as Glaréntsa); in the middle is the village of Kástro; and to the south is the spa of Loutrá Kyllínis, with long sandy beaches which have made it a popular holiday centre.

History

The area of alluvial land, partly flat and partly rolling, between the Kyllíni peninsula and Mt Erýmanthos was known in antiquity as Elis. Then as now it was a productive farming region, whose abundance of livestock is referred to by Homer ("Iliad", 11, 671 ff.; "Odyssey", 4, 635 ff.). In this region too were the Augean stables which Herakles had to cleanse. By conquering the territory of Pisatis, on the river Alpheios, and Triphylia, to the south of the river, Elis gained control of Olympia and the conduct of the Olympic Games. Its capital was the city of Elis, founded in 471 B.C.

After the 4th Crusade (1203–04) the territory fell into the hands of the Villehardouins, who built the town of Andréville (now Andravída) as their capital. Communications with Europe were maintained through the port of Glaréntsa, 15 km/9 miles west on the north side of the Kyllíni peninsula, on which Geoffrey II de Villehardouin built in 1223 the mighty castle of Clairmont (now garbled into Khlemoutsí).

Sights

Elis

On the site of the ancient city of Elis, at the present-day village of Boukhóti, Austrian and Greek excavations have brought to light a theatre and the Hellenistic agora. The site, 15 km/9 miles east of the village of Gastoúni, which lies on the Patras-Pýgros road, is reached on a field track.

Andravída

In Andravída the only relic of the medieval Frankish capital is the 13th century cathedral of St Sophia, which has fine Gothic vaulting. In the chancel is the carved tombstone of Agnès, daughter of Geoffrey de Villehardouin.

★ Khlemoutsí Castle

Khlemoutsí Castle has recently been thoroughly restored. The main entrance, on the north-west side, leads into the spacious outer ward,

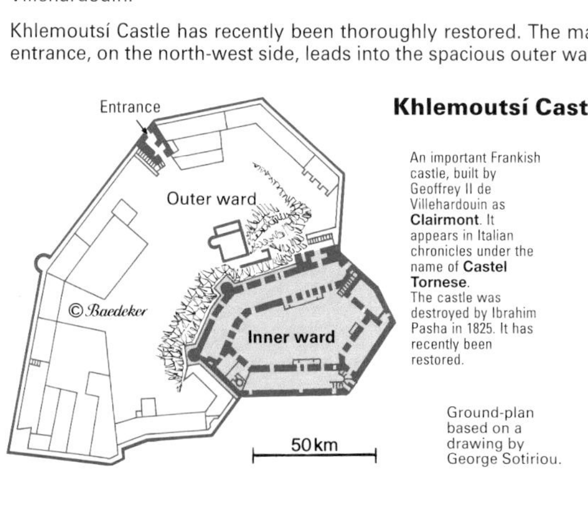

Khlemoutsí Castle

An important Frankish castle, built by Geoffrey II de Villehardouin as **Clairmont**. It appears in Italian chronicles under the name of **Castel Tornese**.
The castle was destroyed by Ibrahim Pasha in 1825. It has recently been restored.

Ground-plan based on a drawing by George Sotiriou.

beyond which is the inner ward, roughly elliptical in plan, with a series of rooms and galleries, including a chapel, built against its high outer walls. From the upper platform there are views extending as far as the island of Zákynthos.

Kyparissia F 6

Κυπαρισσία
Kyparissía

Region: Peloponnese
Nomos: Messenia
Altitude: 160m/525ft
Population: 4000

Situation

The Messenian town of Kyparissía, chief town of the district of Trifylia, lies near the west coast of the Peloponnese on the slopes of Mt Psykhró (218m/715ft).

Features of Interest

In antiquity this was the port of Messene. During the Middle Ages it was known as Arkadiá, having provided a home for refugees from Slav-occupied Arcadia. Its castle has a history going back to ancient times, and in later centuries was enlarged and strengthened by the Byzantines and the Crusaders, who captured it in 1204; it is commandingly situated, with extensive views. The town was destroyed by Ibrahim Pasha in 1825 during a punitive expedition against the rebellious Greeks.

Surroundings of Kyparissía

14km/9 miles south on the coast road is Filiátra. The road then turns inland to Gargalianí (5km/3 miles) and continues via Khóra to Pýlos (see entry), 69km/43 miles from Kyparissía.

Kythira G/H 7

Κύθηρα
Kýthira

Nomos: Attica
Area of island: 285 sq.km/110 sq. miles
Altitude: 0–506m/0–1660ft
Population: 5000
Chief place: Kýthira (Khóra)

Air services

Airfield 10km/6 miles north of Kýthira. Daily services from Athens.

Boat services

Regular services between Athens (Piraeus) and Ayía Pelayía, several times weekly (10 hours); Athens (Piraeus)–Kapsáli, weekly (5 hours); Athens (Piraeus)–Antikýthira, weekly (22 hours).
Local connections with Pórto Káyio, Gýthion, Néapoli, Monemvasía, Elafónisos, Antikýthira and Kísamos (Crete).

Kapsali, Kýthira

Situation and characteristics

Kýthira (the ancient Kythera, Cythera) is the most southerly of the Ionian Islands (Eptánisos), lying 15km/9 miles off the southern tip of Laconia, with rugged karstic hills slashed by numerous gorges and sheer coastal cliffs. The meagre yields of the island's agriculture have led many of the younger people to emigrate, particularly to Australia.

History

Kýthira's abundance of murex shellfish (producing a much valued purple dye) led to an early Phoenician settlement on the island. Later it belonged to Sparta, and the Phoenician cult of the goddess Astarte gave rise to the Greek cult of Aphrodite, who was believed to have emerged from the sea in a large shell off the coast of Kýthira. As a military stronghold off the coast of Lacedaemon the island was of great strategic importance in ancient times.

Under Venetian rule (from 1207) Kýthira was known as Cerigo. Thereafter, as a late addition to the Eptánisos, it shared the destinies of the Ionian Islands. It was reunited with Greece in 1864, and on occasion served as a place of exile for opponents of the government.

Sights

★ Kýthira (Khóra)

At the southern tip of the island, high above the bay and harbour of Kapsáli, lies the charming village of Kýthira (Khóra; pop. 750), the chief place on the island. Above the village is a massive Venetian castle (16th c.).

Palaiókhora

Magnificently situated above the north-east coast are the ruins of the island's former capital, Palaiókhora, with a medieval castle; the town was destroyed by the Turks in 1536.

Ayía Pelayía

North of Palaiókhora, in a wide bay of the north-east coast, is the island's second port, Ayía Pelayía, where during the military dictatorship (1967–74) political opponents of the regime lived in exile.

Milopótamos

Above a bay on the west coast stands the medieval castle of Milopótamos. Nearby is a stalactitic cave.

Panayía Myrtidiótissa

10km/6 miles north-west of Kapsáli is the 17th century monastery of the Panayía Myrtidiótissa, with an icon which is revered as wonderworking.

Avlémona

On the east coast lies the bay of Avlémona (or Áyios Nikólaos), where the yacht "Mentor", carrying some of the Elgin marbles, ran aground in 1802; the marbles were subsequently recovered and sent on to Britain.

Islets

There are numerous rocky islets off the coasts of Kýthira: to the south Avgó, with the Blue Grotto, to the east the two Dragonéra islands (with some cultivated land).

Antikýthira

South-east of Kýthira, roughly half way to Crete, lies the little limestone island of Antikýthira (Italian Cerigotto; area 22 sq.km/8½ sq. miles; alt. 0–360m/0–1180ft), the ancient Aigila or Aigilla. The inhabitants live mainly by farming and fishing. In the channel between the two islands the wreck of a Roman ship was discovered in 1900; its cargo of bronze and marble statues of the 5th–2nd centuries B.C., including the "Ephebe of Antikýthira", together with pottery, glass and an astronomical clock, is now in the National Archaeological Museum in Athens.

Kýthnos I 6

Κύθνος
Kýthnos

Nomos: Cyclades
Area of island: 101 sq.km/39 sq. miles
Altitude: 0–326m/0–1070ft
Population: 630
Chief place: Kýthnos (Khóra, Mesariá)

Boat services

Regular service from and to Athens (Piraeus), 5 times weekly (4 hours; cars carried).
Local connections with Kéa and Sérifos.

Situation and characteristics

Kýthnos, a rocky and barren island of karstic limestone, lies south-east of Kéa. The coast is much indented and for the most part falls steeply down to the sea. The inhabitants live by farming and fishing. In antiquity iron was mined on the island.

History

The first settlers were Dryopians from Euboea, who have left their mark in the name of the village of Dryopís. Later they were driven out by Ionians. Kýthnos never played an important part in history.

Sights

Kýthnos (Khóra)

The chief place on the island, Kýthnos (Khóra, Mesariá), lies on the north-east coast, 6km/4 miles south of the harbour of Ayía Iríni.

Mérikhas, Kýthnos

Thermal springs

On the north side of the bay are the hot mineral springs (40–55°C/104–131°F) of Loutrá, which were already frequented in the Roman Imperial period. During the period of Venetian rule the island was known, after the springs, as Thermiá (Italian Fermenia). The present bathing establishment was built in the reign of Otto I.

Kástro Oriás

Farther north, high above the sea, lies Kástro Oriás.

Near Kýthnos is a modern installation, built with German help, for harnessing wind-power.

Mérikhas

7km/4½ miles south-west of Kýthnos is the island's principal port, Mérikhas. To the north, on a high crag (150m/490ft) above the bays of Apókrousis and Episkopí, are the remains of the island's old capital,

Vryókastro

Vryókastro (Evraiokastro). On a rocky offshore islet traces of an ancient agora and a number of tombs can still be identified.

Dryopís

6km/4 miles south of Kýthnos, on both sides of a rocky gorge, is the lively little village of Dryopís (also called Syllakas or Khorió), which preserves the name of the island's original settlers. Around the village are numerous windmills. Nearby is the Katafaki gorge, which served in the past as a place of refuge.

Kanála

In the south-east of the island is Kanála, with the church of the Panayía, which contains a wonderworking icon.

Lamia G 5

Λαμία
Lamía

Nomos: Phthiotis
Altitude: 100m/330ft
Population: 42,000

Transport

Lamía lies on the Athens–Salonica expressway.

Situation and characteristics

Lamía, chief town of the nomos of Phthiotis, which was believed in ancient times to be the home of Achilles, lies at the foot of Mt Óthrys. The site of the acropolis is now occupied by a medieval castle.

Surroundings of Lamía

A number of places on the coast near Lamía are now rising tourist resorts. 4km/2½ miles north-east of the town is Karavómylos.

25km/16 miles west, in the Sperkhiós valley, is the spa of Ypáti (recommended for cardiac conditions and circulatory disorders); it has a 14th century castle.

14km/9 miles south-east is the pass of Thermopylai (see entry).

Gorgopotamos

Historic railway viaduct: see page 102.

Lárisa G 4

Λάρισα
Lárisa

Nomos: Lárisa
Altitude: 75m/245ft
Population: 72,500

Transport

Air services from Athens; on Athens–Salonica and Lárisa–Vólos railway lines.

Situation and characteristics

Lárisa, chief town of Thessaly (see entry) and an agricultural market town, lies at a bend in the river Piniós (Peneios) in the Thessalian plain, to the south of Mount Olympus (see entry).

History

Human settlement in this area dates back to the Palaeolithic period. In the 2nd millennium B.C. Lárisa (the "Citadel") was founded by Pelasgians. They were followed by Achaeans and later by Dorians, who established a number of principalities, including that of the Aleuadai at Lárisa. Among those whom they attracted to their court was the physician Hippokrates of Kos, who died here in 370 B.C. In 344 B.C. the town was captured by Macedon. During the Middle Ages it was a staging point for incomers and invaders (Goths, Slavs, Bulgars). In the 13th century it came under the authority of the Despotate of Árta, and in 1389 fell into the hands of the Turks, who held it until 1881.

Sights

★ Archaeological Museum

In a square in the centre of the town, housed in a former mosque, is the Archaeological Museum, with material ranging in date from the Palaeolithic (implements from the Piniós valley) through the Mesolithic (Magoula of Gremmos) and Neolithic to the classical and Christian periods. The classical material includes funerary stelae, while Early Christian art is represented by sculpture and altar screens.

Surroundings of Lárisa

25km/16 miles north lies the Vale of Tempe (see entry).

Ayía

Ayía (39km/24 miles east; alt. 200m/655ft) is a good base from which to climb Mt Ossa (1978m/6490ft): see Mount Olympus.
Round Lárisa are a number of *magoulas* (settlement mounds), among them the Magoula of Gremmos (11km/7 miles north-west), which was occupied from the Neolithic period into Roman Imperial times.

At the village of Gonni Greek archaeologists have brought to light the remains of a sanctuary of Asklepios of the 4th century B.C.

Lefkas E 5

Λευκάς, Λευκάδα
Lefkás, Lefkáda

Nomos: Lefkás
Area of island: 302 sq.km/117 sq. miles
Altitude: 0–1158m/0–3799ft
Population: 25,000
Chief town: Lefkás

Air services

Airport at Áktion, 18km/11 miles north, on the mainland. Daily flights from Athens.

Bus services

Athens–Lefkás, several times daily.

Situation and characteristics

Lefkás or Lefkáda (Ancient Leukas; Italian Santa Maura) is a hilly island, marked by karstic action, lying off the Playiá peninsula in Acarnania, from which it is separated by a shallow lagoon varying in width between 600m/650yds and 5km/3 miles. It is now linked with the mainland by a causeway and a bascule bridge.

Most of the island is occupied by a range of hills rising to 1158m/3799ft in Mt Stavrotás and running south-west to end at Cape Doukáto or Lefkádas (72m/236ft; lighthouse), at the tip of the Lefkás peninsula. It was from this Leucadian Rock of gleaming white limestone that Sappho was supposed to have thrown herself for love of the handsome Phaon.

The main sources of income of the inhabitants are farming on the island's thin soil, fishing, the recovery of salt from the lagoon and various crafts, particularly lace and knitwear.

Lefkás never had any permanent natural connection with the mainland. The shingle spit at the northern tip of the island was pierced in ancient times by the Corinthians to provide a channel for shipping, and, like the spit to the south of Lefkás town which came into being in the Middle Ages as a result of the establishment of salt-pans, allowed vessels of some size to pass through.

History and archaeology

The earliest evidence of human settlement on the island dates from the Neolithic period.
In the 7th century B.C. the town of Leukas was founded by settlers from Corinth, who closed off the south end of the lagoon, opposite the fort of Áyios Yeóryios, by a 600m/650yd long mole, remains of which are

Kiato harbour, Lefkás

still visible under water. They cut a channel through the spit of shingle at the north end of the lagoon, opposite the fort of Santa Maura (Ayía Mávra) – though by the time of the Peloponnesian War, in which Leukas was allied with Sparta, the channel had silted up. In the time of the Achaean League Leukas was the capital of Acarnania. It supported Philip II of Macedon against Rome, but was conquered in 197 B.C. by the Romans, who later built a bridge linking Leukas with the mainland.

In the Middle Ages the island belonged to the barons of Cefalonia and Zante and other Frankish dynasts. In 1479 it was taken by the Turks – the only one of the Ionian Islands to fall into Turkish hands – but was recovered for Venice by Morosini in 1684. After a brief interlude of French rule during the Napoleonic wars it was assigned in 1815 to Britain, which returned it to Greece, together with the other Ionian Islands, in 1864.

As a result of the vicissitudes of its history and of a series of earthquakes Lefkás has preserved very few old buildings.

Dörpfeld's theory

The German archaeologist Wilhelm Dörpfeld (1853–1940), who worked on Lefkás and made his home there, believed that this island, and not the one now called Ithaca, was the Homeric Ithaca, the home of Odysseus. He based his theory mainly on topographical similarities between Lefkás and the Ithaca described in the "Odyssey", but this was contested by other archaeologists, and Dörpfeld's excavations failed to produce convincing evidence in support of his theory.
According to Dörpfeld Homer's Zakynthos was the present-day island of that name, Doulichion was present-day Kefallónia, Same present-day Ithaca and Ithaca itself the island now known as Lefkás. He believed that Odysseus's city was in the western part of the Nýdri

plain; and excavations at many points in this area did in fact yield house walls and sherds of pottery (monochrome, with scratched decoration) at depths of between 4m/13ft and 6m/20ft which might be held to support Dörpfeld's theory.

In the south of the island are two inlets, Skýdi Bay to the south-west and the narrow Sýbota Bay to the south-east, with caves in the hillside along its shores. The latter, in Dörpfeld's view, was the cove of Phorkys, the Old Man of the Sea, where Odysseus was put ashore by the Phaeacians and hid his treasures in the Cave of the Nymphs ("Odyssey", 13, 345 ff.). From there he made his way up through the hills to the farm of the swineherd Eumaos, situated "far from the city" at the Spring of Arethusa, which Dörpfeld would identify as the spring at the village of Évyiros ("Odyssey", 13, 404 ff.; 14, 6 and 399; 24, 150). Skýdi Bay would then be the place where Telemachos landed ("Odyssey", 15, 495). On his return voyage from Pylos, warned by Athena, he escaped the ambush prepared for him by the suitors on the islet of Asteris – perhaps Arkoúdi (alt. 0–135m/0–445ft), south of Lefkás.

Sights

Lefkáda

At the north end of the island is its chief town, Lefkáda (pop. 6500). The unusual structure of the houses, with supporting timber posts and beams and lightly built upper floors, is designed for protection against earthquakes.

Santa Maura

3km/2 miles north of the town, on the shingle spit, stands the Venetian fort of Santa Maura (Ayía Mávra; 13th c.).

3km/2 miles west is the Faneroméni monastery, from which there are magnificent panoramic views.

Vlykho Bay

On a hill 3km/2 miles south are the remains of ancient Leukas, with the acropolis, an aqueduct, stretches of the town walls and a theatre.

Leukas

14km/9 miles south of Lefkás, reaching far inland, is Nýdri Bay. On Cape Kyriáki, opposite the little port of Nýdri on the east side of the bay, are Dörpfeld's house and his grave.
Off Nýdri Bay, to the east, lie the picturesque little islands of Spárti (sea-caves), Madourí, home of the 19th century poet Aristotelis Valaoritis, and Skorpiós, which belongs to the Onassis family.

Nýdri

Meganísi

Off the south-east coast of Lefkás lies the attractive island of Meganísi (area 18 sq.km/7 sq. miles; alt. 0–267m/0–876ft; pop. 2500), the ancient city of Thaphos, with sandy beaches and sea-caves. There is some farming land in the flatter western part of the island; the eastern part is occupied by a range of wooded hills (quarries). The chief place on the island is the little port of Vathý (regular service from Lefkás). To the west is the harbour of the village of Spartokhóri.

Lemnos

K 3/4

Λήμνος
Límnos

Nomos: Lesbos
Area of island: 476 sq.km/184 sq. miles
Altitude: 0–470m/0–1540ft
Population: 16,000
Chief town: Mýrina

Air services

Airfield 25km/15 miles north-east of Mýrina. Flights from Athens several times daily, from Salonica daily, from Mytilíni (Lesbos) several times weekly.

Boat services

Regular service Athens (Piraeus)–Lemnos–Samothrace–Alexandroúpolis.

Situation and characteristics

Lemnos is a hilly island rising to 470m/1540ft at its highest point. Fertile and almost treeless, it produces corn and, increasingly, cotton. The coast is much indented, with two inlets, Pourniás Bay in the north and Moúdros Bay in the south, cutting so deep inland that the eastern and western parts of the island are joined by a strip of land only 4km/2½ miles wide. The volcanic rock in the east recalls the ancient tradition that after his fall from Olympus Hephaistos set up his smithy and married Aphrodite here. The people of Lemnos were notorious for their "wicked deeds", as reported by Herodotus, which provided the Athenian general Miltiades with a pretext for his conquest of the island.

History

The walled city of Poliokhni, dated to the beginning of the 3rd millennium B.C., belonged to the same pre-Greek culture as Troy and Thermoi (on Lésbos). The first Greeks came to Lemnos about 800 B.C., but a century later gave place to the Tyrsenoi from Asia Minor, whose language, on the evidence of inscriptions found at Kamínia, was related to Etruscan. This provides some support for the theory, first put forward by Herodotus, that the Etruscans originally came from the

region of Lydia in Asia Minor. The island was resettled by Greeks after the Athenian conquest at the end of the 6th century B.C. It was celebrated for the cult of Hephaistos, centred on an "earth fire" near the city of Hephaisteia in the north of the island.
In the 4th century A.D. Hephaisteia became the see of a bishop, but the bishopric was later transferred to Mýrina on the west coast.
After the 4th Crusade the island was occupied by the Venetians. A hundred years later it was recovered by the Byzantines, and was then granted to the Gattelusi family of Lésbos as a fief. It was held by the Turks from 1479 to 1912. During the Orlov rising of 1770 it became a Russian naval base. In the First World War Moúdros Bay was the Royal Navy's base during the Gallipoli campaign.

Sights

Mýrina

The island's chief town and principal port is Mýrina (pop. 3400), usually called Kástro, which lies on the west coast on the site of ancient Myrina, below a crag crowned by a Venetian castle occupying the site of the ancient acropolis. The crag, from which there are fine views of the town and surrounding area, and a prospect extending on a clear afternoon as far as Mount Athos (some 60km/40 miles away), separates two bays; the one to the south is the harbour, while the one to the north has a long and beautiful sandy beach.

★ Museum

In the bay to the north is a well arranged Museum displaying material from the prehistoric settlement of Polióknhi, the site of ancient Hephaisteia and the sanctuary of the Kabeiroi at Khlói (Chloe).

Kontiás

Kontiás, 10km/6 miles east of Mýrina, is beautifully situated in a bay with a sandy beach.

Moúdros

The island's second port, Moúdros (pop. 1200), lies on the east side of Moúdros Bay, 28km/17 miles east of Mýrina. From here a road runs via Kamínia, near which were found the Tyrsenian inscriptions mentioned above (see History), to Polióknhi (34km/21 miles), where Italian archaeologists found remains of a settlement dating back to the 3rd and 4th millennia B.C. (town walls, houses and a gate approached by a ramp similar to that of Troy II).

Hephaisteia

In the north-east of the island, reached by way of Kontopoúli (30km/19 miles; pop. 1100), are the site of ancient Hephaisteia, on Pourniás Bay (necropolis of 8th–6th c. B.C.; Hellenistic theatre), and the ancient port of Chloe (Khlói), where excavations by Italian archaeologists (not yet complete) have brought to light a sanctuary of the Kabeiroi (non-Hellenic divinities whose cult was centred on the island of Samothrace). The visible remains include two cult buildings of the 6th and 5th–4th centuries B.C.

Leros L 6

Λέρος
Léros

Nomos: Dodecanese
Area of island: 53 sq.km/ 20 sq. miles
Altitude: 0–327m/0–1073ft
Population: 6000
Chief town: Ayía Marína

Air services

Athens–Léros daily; Kos–Léros several times weekly.

Boat services

Regular service from and to Athens (Piraeus), several times weekly (11–12 hours; cars carried); from and to Kavála, weekly. Local services in Dodecanese: Rhodes – Sými – Tílos – Kos – Kálymnos – Léros – Lipsí – Pátmos – Arkí – Agathonísi – Sámos.

Characteristics

Léros is a hilly and fertile island with an abundance of water and a much indented coast. The inhabitants live by farming and fishing.

History

In antiquity Léros was dependent on Miletus in Asia Minor. Although continuously inhabited since then, it has never played a part of any importance in history. In the 14th century the Knights of St John established themselves on the island and held it against the Turks until the 16th century. In recent years it has had a rather mixed fate: for many years a leper colony, it was a German naval base during the Second World War, a re-education centre for the children of Communist partisans from 1947 onwards, a notorious psychiatric institution from 1957 onwards and a concentration camp for opponents of the military dictatorship from 1967 to 1974.

Features of Interest

Ayía Marína

The island's chief town, Ayía Marína (pop. 2500), lies on the south side of Álinda Bay, on the south coast. Above the little town, on the ridge of hills between Álinda Bay to the north and Plátanos Bay to the south, is the Kástro (14th c.), a castle of the Knights of St John, on the site of the ancient acropolis.

Lakkí

To the south of Ayía Marína, in a sheltered bay which cuts deep into the west coast, is Lakkí (pop. 1500), with a British military cemetery. The village has a medieval church of St John.

Castle of the Knights of St John above Ayía Marina

Palaiokastro

In the plain south-east of Lakkí is the village of Xerókambos, above which are the remains of ancient Palaiokastro, a stronghold of the 4th century B.C.
In the north of the island is Parthéni Bay (closed military area), closed on the north-west by the little island of Arkhángelos.

Lesbos K/L 4/5

Λέσβος
Lésbos

Nomos: Lésbos
Area of island: 1630 sq.km/629 sq. miles
Altitude: 0–967m/0–3173ft
Population: 97,000
Chief town: Mytilíni

Air services

Airport 8km/5 miles south-east of Mytilíni. Regular flights from Athens, 5 times daily; from Salonica, daily; from Lemnos, several times weekly.

Boat services

Regular service from and to Athens and from and to Kavála, several times weekly (cars carried); from and to Salonica, Rhodes and Kými, weekly in each case.
Ferry connection with Dikili (Turkey).

Situation and characteristics

Lésbos (popularly called Mytilíni; Turkish Midilli, Italian Metellino), the third largest of the Greek islands (after Crete and Euboea), lies in an angle formed by the Anatolian coast, which is only 10km/6 miles away on the north side of the island and 15km/9 miles away on the east

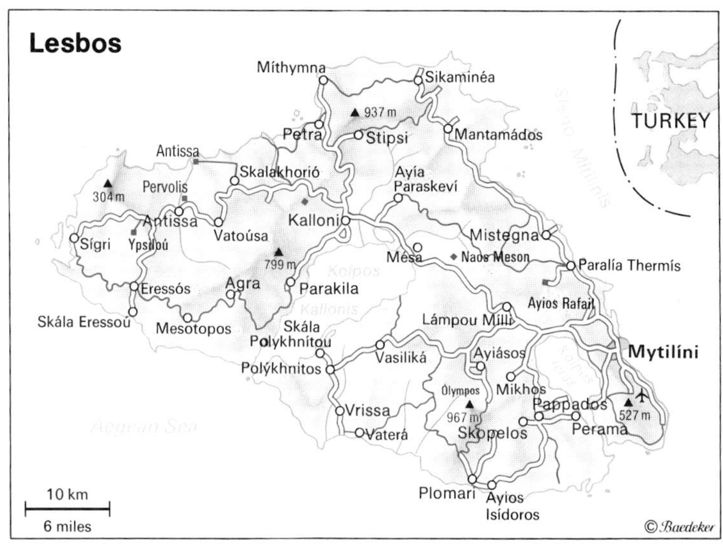

side. An island of great scenic beauty, Lésbos is also one of the most fertile parts of Greece. It is broken up by the gulfs of Kalloní and Iéra, which cut deep inland on the south-west and south-east sides of the island. The island's proximity to the mainland of Asia Minor was a major factor in the vicissitudes of its history.

History

At Thermí, 12km/7½ miles north of Mytilíni, excavation has brought to light a pre-Greek settlement established about 2700 B.C. which belonged to a cultural group embracing also the Troad and the offshore islands as far away as Lemnos. Around 1000 B.C. Aeolian Greeks from Thessaly arrived on the island and founded the cities of Mytilene and Methymna, ruled by aristocratic families who were constantly at odds with one another. About 600 B.C. the tyrant (sole ruler) Pittakos put an end to faction and arbitrary government, retired voluntarily after ten years and thereafter was accounted one of the Seven Sages. From 546 to 479 B.C. Lésbos was under Persian rule, and after its liberation became a member of the Attic maritime league. Throughout this period, however, and in Hellenistic and Roman times, it was able, like Chios, to maintain its independence.

Sappho

Lésbos was the home of the poet Terpandros (7th c. B.C.), who was credited with the invention of the seven-stringed lyre; and about 600 B.C. the singer Arion was born in Methymna, the poet Alkaios was born in Mytilene and Sappho, the greatest Greek poetess, was born in Eressos. Sappho instructed young girls in the arts – with no suggestion of the later meaning of the word "Lesbian". Another native of Lésbos was the philosopher Theophrastos (322–287 B.C.), who became head of Aristotle's Lykeion (Lyceum) in Athens.

In 1355 a Genoese nobleman named Francesco Gattelusi married a daughter of the Byzantine Emperor, who received Lesbos as her dowry. Thereafter the Gattelusi family ruled the island as a Byzantine fief until 1462, when Lésbos was captured by the Turks. During the period of Turkish rule, which lasted until 1913, many of the inhabitants moved to the mainland, particularly to the nearby town of Kydonia (now Ayvalık in Turkey). After the catastrophe of 1922–23 their descendants returned to the island, the economy of which was badly hit by the loss of its Anatolian hinterland.

Mytilíni

The island's chief town, Mytilíni (or Kástro; pop. 24,000), lies in a bay on the east coast, on the site of ancient Mytilene. A breakwater, which is also a popular promenade, protects the harbour, on which the commercial activity of the town is centred. Above the tiled roofs of the low houses, some of them fronted by colonnades, rises the characteristic dome of the church of Áyios Therapón (late 19th c.), the architecture of which betrays western influence. Between the present south harbour and the ancient harbour to the north is an area of low ground, once traversed by a canal, which separates the main part of the town from the massive Gattelusi castle, built on a crag projecting eastwards into the sea. A path runs up through a pinewood to the entrance, on the strongly fortified south-east side. Fragments of ancient masonry built into the walls and towers are a reminder that the extensive castle ward occupies the site of the ancient acropolis. Canadian archaeologists who recently carried out the first excavations in this area found remains of buildings which on the basis of the Aeolian pottery recovered from the site they interpreted as a sanctuary of Demeter of the Archaic period (7th–6th c. B.C.).

Gattelusi castle

Panoramic view of Mytilíni

There are a number of mosques dating from the Turkish period. Over a side gate in the north-west wall can be seen the double coat of arms of Francesco I Gattelusi (1355–85) and his Byzantine princess, with an inscription of 1377. From the north end of the castle there is a fine view of the ancient north harbour, with the remains of its breakwater.

Ancient theatre

Above the north harbour, to the west, is the ancient theatre (3rd c. B.C.), which gave Pompey the idea of building the first stone theatre in Rome.

Monument

At the south end of the castle hill is a monument to those who died during the fighting with the Turks between 1821 and 1923.

★ Archaeological Museum

The small Archaeological Museum contains, among other things, a number of capitals of the rare Aeolian type and mosaics dating from late antiquity.

Vária

In the Vária district on the southern outskirts of the town are two interesting museums. The first, devoted to the naïve painter Theofilos, was founded by Stratis Eleftheriadis (1897–1983), a native of Mytilíni who worked in Paris as an art writer, publisher and patron under the name of Tériade. He also founded in 1979 the neighbouring Tériade Museum, which contains works by modern artists, including Marc Chagall, Fernand Léger and Pablo Picasso.

North of the Island (circuit, 125km/78 miles)

12km/7½ miles north-west of Mytilíni is the little spa of Paralía Thermís, near which is the prehistoric settlement of Thermí, dating back to 2700 B.C.

Míthimna

The road continues to Mantamádos (38km/24 miles), with an icon of the Mother of God which is venerated as wonderworking (pilgrimage on November 8th), and Sikaminéa (50km/31 miles), birthplace of the contemporary writer Stratis Mirivillis, and then, following the coast for part of the way (some stretches in poor condition), to Míthimna (63km/39 miles; pop. 1800), also known as Mólyvos, on the site of ancient Methymna. Above this little port is a Gattelusi castle, from which there is a view extending to Asia Minor. As H. G. Buchholz explains in his monograph on Methymna, the first settlement was established here in the 3rd millennium B.C. in the area known as Palaiá Míthimna, to the east; in the latter part of the 2nd millennium it was moved to the present site, and in the 1st millennium the city developed extensive trading connections, reaching in the Hellenistic period as far afield as Egypt.

Kalloní

Continuing south from Míthimna, we pass the little port of Petrá (72km/45 miles), lying at the foot of a high crag topped by the interesting church of the Panayía (approached by a stepped path), and come to Kalloní (87km/54 miles; pop. 2000), 4km/2½ miles north of the Gulf of Kalloní, which reaches 21km/13 miles inland.

★ Límonos monastery

Near here is Límonos monastery, with a church containing a richly carved iconostasis and completely preserved wall paintings. Only men may enter the church; women are admitted only to the outer monastic buildings. The monastery's large library, its archives and a museum are housed in new buildings.

Lámpou Mílli

The road now turns south-east, leaving the Gulf of Kalloní at Mésa (94km/58 miles). Near here are the remains of a temple, within which a church was later built. At Lámpou Mílli (also called Mória; 109km/68 miles) are remains of a Roman aqueduct.

From here we return to Mytilíni (125km/78 miles).

West of the Island (circuit, 177km/110 miles)

Antissa

Going west from Mytilíni, we come to Skalakhorió (54km/34 miles), just beyond which a poor road goes off to the remains of ancient Antissa (about 8km/5 miles).

Perivólis monastery

Beyond Vatoúsa (61km/38 miles), to the right of the road, is Perivólis monastery (17th c. frescoes). Beyond the new village of Ántissa (69km/43 miles), on Mt Ordímnos, is Ypsiloú monastery (museum containing 12th c. manuscripts and vestments of former patriarchs; magnificent views).

Sígri

The road reaches the sea at Sígri (84km/52 miles; pop. 550), a little seaside resort on the west coast with a beautiful sandy beach in a sheltered bay. In the village itself (in the main square) and to the south-east (shortly before Ypsiloú monastery, on the right; 1½ hours walk) are petrified trees, buried under volcanic ash at least 700,000 years ago.

★ Petrified trees

Eressós

From Eressós (98km/61 miles; museum) it is worth making a detour to Skála Eressoú (101km/63 miles), on the south coast, which has a beautiful sandy beach. This is the site of ancient Eressos, birthplace of Sappho and Theophrastos. To the west, near the beach, are the ruins of an Early Christian basilica known as the Skholí Theofrástou, the School of Theophrastos.

Also in the village are remains of another three-aisled basilica dedicated to St Andrew, with a large mosaic pavement, much of which has been preserved. Behind it is a small museum containing local finds.

From Eressós an unsurfaced road runs via Mesotopos (fine church; pilgrimage, led by Patriarch, on August 15th) to Ágra (118km/73 miles) and Kalloní (147km/91 miles), and so back to Mytilíni (177km/110 miles).

South of the Island

Ayiássos

An interesting trip in the south of the island is to Ayiássos (30km/19 miles; pop. 5000), on the northern slopes of Mt Ólympos (967m/3173ft). Its central feature, the church of the Dormition (last restored in 1816), attracts thousands of pilgrims on the feast of the Dormition (August 15th). In the monastic buildings is a small but very interesting museum (good icons, liturgical vestments and utensils; folk art). Fine pottery and homespun cloth can be bought in the shops of the little town.

Polýkhnitos

From Ayiássos it is worth continuing to Polýkhnitos (24km/15 miles; pop. 5100), its port of Skála Polykhnítou and the Damándri monastery (frescoes of 1580). Beyond Polýkhnitos, to the south, is Vaterá, with a good beach.

Plomárion

For another excursion to the south coast, leave Mytilíni on the road which runs along the north end of the Gulf of Iéra and down its west side to the beach of Áyios Isídoros and the little town of Plomárion (42km/26 miles; pop. 5200).

Lipsi L 6

Λειψοί
Lipsí

Nomos: Lipsí
Area of island: 18 sq.km/7 sq. miles
Altitude: 0–275m/0–900ft
Population: 500
Chief place: Lipsí

Boat services

Local connections with Pátmos and Léros.

Situation and characteristics

Lipsí, formerly called Lepsia, is a small island in the Southern Sporades, 12km/7½ miles east of Pátmos, which was resettled in the 19th century. On the south coast is the modest little village of Lipsí, the chief place on the island and its principal port. It was a Greek naval base during the war of liberation from the Turks. The few inhabitants live by farming and fishing.

Litokhoron G 3

Λιτόχωρον
Litókhoron

Nomos: Piéria
Altitude: 240m/790ft
Population: 6000

Situation and characteristics

Litókhoron, 5km/3 miles west of the Salonica–Lárisa road, is the best starting-point for an ascent of Mount Olympus (see entry).

From Litókhoron a road (unsurfaced, but negotiable by cars) climbs to a height of some 1200m/3900ft, from which it is three hours on foot to a mountain hut (skiing area) at 2100m/6900ft. From there it is another three hours to the summit of Mitikás, the highest peak (2917m/9571ft). From Litókhoron there is also a gentle walk through the beautiful Enippeas valley; the route follows the covered watercourse.

Dion

See entry

Livadia **G 5**

Λειβαδειά
Livadiá

Nomos: Boeotia
Altitude: 200m/655ft. Population: 17,000

Transport

Bus connections with Athens and Delphi.

Situation

Livadiá, capital of Boeotia, is a busy town on the south-western edge of the fertile Kopais plain. On the main road through the town is a spacious square laid out in gardens, with tavernas.

History

In antiquity Livadiá was famed for the oracle of Trophonios, which continued to flourish into the Roman Imperial period and was described by Pausanias in the 2nd century A.D. In the Middle Ages the town was occupied by Catalan mercenaries, who built a castle on the hill (now called Áyios Ilías) on which the sanctuary of the oracle once stood. In 1460 Livadiá fell into Turkish hands and became the chief town in Boeotia.

Sights

★ Cold Spring

In the Erkyna gorge at the west end of the town is the Cold Spring (Kria), probably the ancient Spring of Mnemosyne. The Springs of Memory (Mnemosyne) and Forgetfulness (Lethe) played a part in the process of consulting the oracle. Cut in the rock are recesses for votive offerings.

Surroundings of Livadiá

Chaironeia (14km/8½ miles), Orkhomenós (12km/7½ miles), Ósios Loukás (37km/23 miles): see entries.

Loutraki **G 6**

Λουτράκι
Loutráki

Nomos: Corinth. Altitude: 10m/35ft

Transport

Bus service from Athens.

Situation and characteristics

Loutráki is a popular seaside resort and spa (recommended for disorders of the urinary tract, gravel and stones in the kidneys and gallstones) at the east end of the Gulf of Corinth. To the north-west is the beautiful peninsula of Perakhóra (see entry), with the sanctuary of Hera.

Macedonia

Μακεδονία
Makedonía

Situation and characteristics

Extending from the Albanian frontier in the west to the river Néstos in the east and from the Yugoslav frontier in the north to Mount Olympus in the south, Macedonia is the largest region in Greece, with an area of 30,000 sq.km/11,600 sq. miles. Its extensive plains, including considerable areas brought into cultivation by the drainage of marshland, make it Greece's most productive agricultural region.
Macedonia's industrial and commercial centre is Salonica (see entry), its capital. An industrial zone has also developed round Ptolemáis.

History

In early times Macedonia lay on the margin of the Greek world. Then in the 4th century B.C., after achieving internal unity, it rose under Philip II to become the dominant power in Greece and the basis of the world empire of Alexander the Great (356–323 B.C.). Aristotle, Alexander's teacher, came from Stageira (Stayíra) in Macedonia.

Features of Interest

Although Macedonia did not become part of Greece until 1913, it has few remains of the Turkish period. It has, however, important ancient sites such as Pella, once its capital, and Vergína, and numerous monuments of the Christian period – the basilicas of Philippi, the monasteries of Athos, the churches of Salonica and Kastoriá (see entries for all these places).
In the past Macedonia was little visited by tourists except as an area of passage to somewhere else, but in recent years the Chalcidice peninsula (see entry) has developed into a large and well equipped holiday region.

Makronisi I 6

Μακρονήσι
Makronísi

Nomos: Cyclades
Area of island: 18 sq.km/7 sq. miles
Altitude: 0–281m/0–922ft

Situation and characteristics

Makronísi, the "Long Island", lies 5km/3 miles off the coast of Attica to the east of Cape Soúnion. In antiquity it bore the name of Helen, who according to Pausanias rested here.

Archaeological evidence points to a modest degree of settlement from the Neolithic period onwards. In more recent times the island has been used as an internment camp for opponents of the government. It is now inhabited only by a few shepherds.

Gýthion – gateway of the Máni peninsula ▶

SHELL

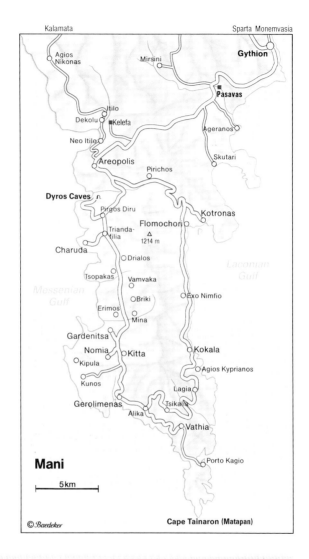

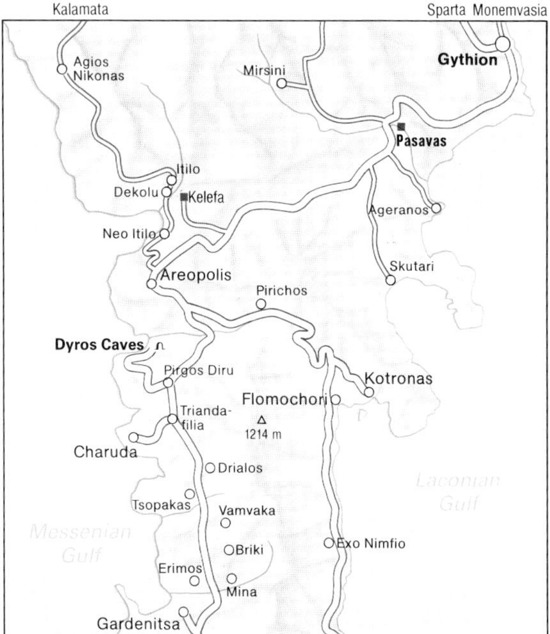

Máni

G 7

Μάνη
Máni

Region: Peloponnese. Nomos: Laconia

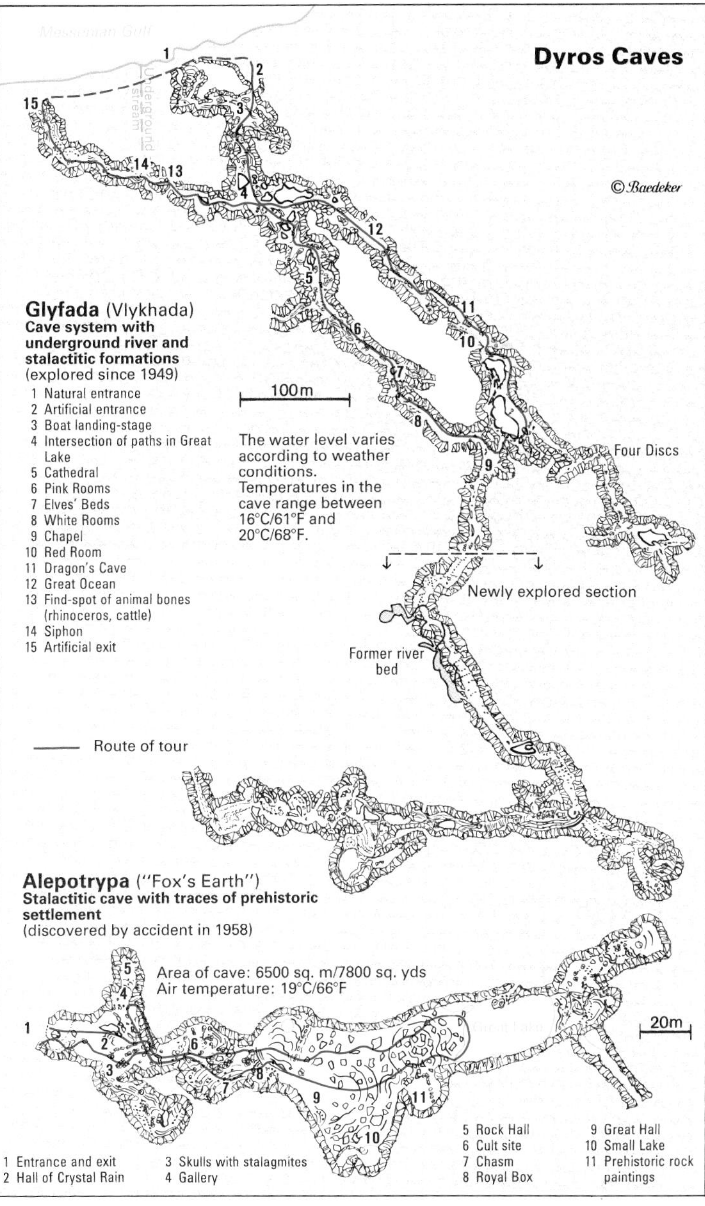

Dyros Caves
© Baedeker
Underground stream
Glyfada (Vlykhada)
Cave system with underground river and stalactitic formations
(explored since 1949)
1 Natural entrance
2 Artificial entrance
3 Boat landing-stage
4 Intersection of paths in Great Lake
5 Cathedral
6 Pink Rooms
7 Elves' Beds
8 White Rooms
9 Chapel
10 Red Room
11 Dragon's Cave
12 Great Ocean
13 Find-spot of animal bones (rhinoceros, cattle)
14 Siphon
15 Artificial exit
100m
The water level varies according to weather conditions.
Temperatures in the cave range between 16°C/61°F and 20°C/68°F.
Four Discs
Newly explored section
Former river bed
Route of tour
Alepotrypa ("Fox's Earth")
Stalactitic cave with traces of prehistoric settlement
(discovered by accident in 1958)
Area of cave: 6500 sq. m/7800 sq. yds
Air temperature: 19°C/66°F
20m
1 Entrance and exit
2 Hall of Crystal Rain
3 Skulls with stalagmites
4 Gallery
5 Rock Hall
6 Cult site
7 Chasm
8 Royal Box
9 Great Hall
10 Small Lake
11 Prehistoric rock paintings

The tower houses of the Máni

Situation and characteristics

The Máni is the middle one of the three peninsulas which reach out from the south of the Peloponnese. It is traversed by the tail of the Taýgetos range. This remote, hilly and barren region was able, throughout all Greece's periods of foreign rule, to preserve a degree of independence. For centuries the Máni was racked by feuds between different clans, who built the defensive towers still to be seen in many of the little towns and villages.

Landscape

This unproductive land is now increasingly being abandoned by its inhabitants. Its great attraction lies in its beautiful mountain scenery, at heights of up to 1215m/3985ft, its picturesque villages and its numerous old chapels, many of them in a state of ruin but still of interest for their wall paintings. Much of the Máni can be reached only on foot or from the sea.

Sights

Areópolis

★ Kardamyli

Going south-west from Gýthion (see entry) or south from Sparta (see entry), we pass the ruined Frankish castle of Passava (10km/6 miles) and cut across the peninsula to Areópolis (26km/16 miles; pop. 610), on the west coast. From there a road runs north along the coast to Kalamáta (82km/51 miles), passing Ítylos, with the Turkish fortress of Kélefa, Áyios Nikólaos, with the Frankish castle of Léfktron, and Kardamyli, which Patrick Leigh Fermor calls "Byzantium restored".

Pýrgos Dýrou

★ Stalactitic caves

8km/5 miles south of Areópolis is Pýrgos Dýrou, with the stalactitic caves of Dyros (5km/3 miles west; restaurant, bathing). Farther south is Kitta (tower houses). The road continues to Yerolimín, beyond which are the villages of Alíka and Kyparissós.

At the southernmost tip of the peninsula is Cape Taínaron (Matapán). In ancient times this was thought to be one of the entrances to the underworld, where Herakles descended in quest of the dog Kerberos (Cerberus). More recently, Cape Matapán is remembered as the scene of a naval action in the Second World War.

Cape Taínaron (Matapán)

On the east coast of the peninsula, 5km/3 miles north of the cape, is the 16th century Turkish fortress of Pórto Káyio.

Mantineia G 6

Μαντίνεια
Mandínia

Region: Peloponnese
Nomos: Arcadia

Situation

The ancient city of Mantineia, formed in 500 B.C. by the amalgamation of five villages, lies 15km/9 miles north of Trípoli in the Peloponnese. The site is reached by taking the road which runs north from Trípoli and in 8km/5 miles, where the main road bears north-west towards Vytína and Olympia, turning right into a side road signposted to Kakoúri.

History

Mantineia was destroyed by Sparta in 385 B.C. but rebuilt in 371 after a Theban victory over Sparta. The battle of Mantineia in 362 B.C. put an end to Theban predominance in the Peloponnese.

Excavations

The surviving remains date from the rebuilding around 370 B.C. There are considerable remains, particularly on the north and east sides, of the elliptical circuit of town walls, which had a total length of almost 4km/2½ miles. The walls, faced inside and outside with dressed stone, are 4.2–4.7m/14–15ft thick, with ten gates and 120 towers. The river Ophis was diverted to encircle the walls.

Within the town French excavations between 1869 and 1898 brought to light the agora, with the bouleuterion on the south side, a theatre on the west side and scanty remains of temples.

Marathon H/I 5

Μαραθώνας
Marathónas

Region and nomos: Attica
Altitude: 52m/171ft

Transport

Bus services from Athens.
Local boats from Rafína to the islands of Euboea, Ándros, Tínos and Kéa.

Situation and characteristics

Marathon was celebrated in antiquity as the place where Theseus killed the bull of Marathon and the scene of the first great battle between Greeks and Persians in 490 B.C. It was the birthplace of Herodes Atticus (A.D. 101–177), famous in his day as a rhetor but better known for his munificence in financing such buildings as the Odeion

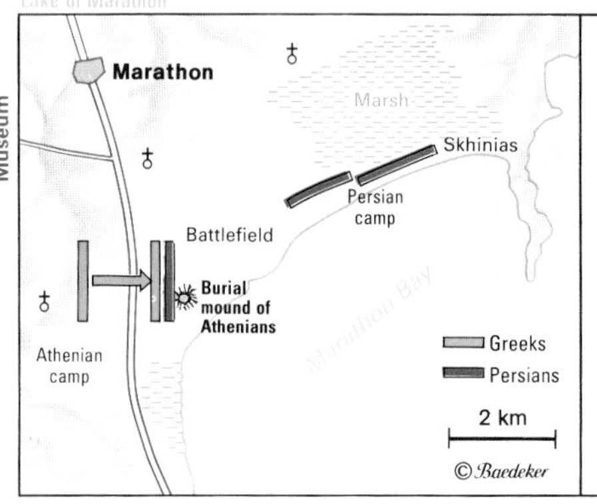

Battle of Marathon
September 490 B.C.

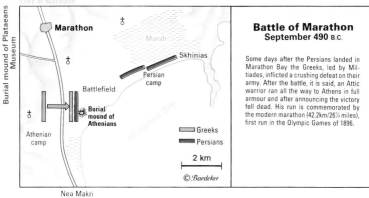

Some days after the Persians landed in Marathon Bay the Greeks, led by Miltiades, inflicted a crushing defeat on their army. After the battle, it is said, an Attic warrior ran all the way to Athens in full armour and after announcing the victory fell dead. His run is commemorated by the modern marathon (42.2km/26¼ miles), first run in the Olympic Games of 1896.

and Stadion in Athens, the Stadion at Delphi and the Nymphaeum at Olympia.

Sights

Burial mound

The large modern village of Marathon (Marathónas) lies near the east coast of Attica, 5km/3 miles north of the battlefield of Marathon, on which is the 12m/40ft high burial mound (*sorós*) raised over the remains of the 192 Athenians who fell in the battle. At the foot of the mound is a replica of the funerary stele of Aristion (*c.* 510 B.C.; original in National Archaeological Museum, Athens). From the top of the mound there is a view of the battlefield, with the wide arc of the bay in which the Persians landed to the north-east and the site of the Athenian camp to the west, at the foot of Mt Agrielíki.

Burial mound of Plataeans
Museum

3km/2 miles north of the burial mound on the road to the village of Marathónas a side road goes off on the left to the hamlet of Vranás, with the burial mound of the Plataeans, a prehistoric necropolis (under a protective roof) and a museum.

Surroundings of Marathon

★ Lake Marathon

8km/5 miles west of the village is Lake Marathon, an artificial lake which supplies Athens with water, now a favourite weekend resort.

Bathing beaches

The extensive beaches south of Marathon offer excellent bathing and recreational facilities.

Megalopolis G 6

Μεγαλόπολη
Megalópoli

Region: Peloponnese. Nomos: Arcadia
Altitude: 427m/1401ft. Population: 3000

Transport

Megalópolis is a station on the Peloponnese Railway (Corinth–Kalamáta).

Situation

The little mining town of Megalópolis lies south of the river Elisson in the centre of the Peloponnese. It has suffered severe earthquake damage on several occasions.

History

Megalopolis was founded after the Theban general Epameinondas's victory over Sparta at Leuktra (371 B.C.), and was intended, together with Mantineia and Messene (see entries), to prevent any resurgence of Spartan power. In 353, 331 and 234 B.C. the town, peopled by settlers from the surrounding area, successfully withstood attacks from Sparta, but in 223 B.C. it was conquered and destroyed. Although it was rebuilt in 194 B.C., Pausanias, visiting the site in the 2nd century A.D., found only ruins. Megalopolis was the birthplace of the historian Polybios (208–120 B.C.).
The site of the ancient city, which lies astride the river Elisson, a tributary of the Alfiós (Alpheios), was excavated by British archaeologists.

Sights

Theatre

The remains of the ancient city, which was surrounded by walls with a total extent of almost 9km/6 miles, lie near the present-day town on the road to Pýrgos. Immediately south of the river is the theatre, which could accommodate 50,000 spectators. The 59 tiers of seating in the semicircular auditorium are divided into wedges by two horizontal gangways and ten staircases. The stage buildings were of wood, and could be stored in the *skenotheke* or property room on the west side of the stage; only in the Roman period were they replaced by stone structures.

★ Skenotheke

Thersileion

Immediately north of the theatre is the Thersileion (so named after the donor), a huge rectangular hall measuring 66m/217ft by 52m/171ft in which Arcadian federal assembly met. The interior probably had the form of an odeion, with radially disposed Doric columns supporting the roof. On either side of the Thersileion were altars. To the west was the stadion, to the east a sanctuary of Asklepios.

On the far side of the river, opposite the Thersileion, was a large sanctuary of Zeus Soter, and beyond this the agora, bounded on the north by a stoa erected by Philip II of Macedon.

Surroundings of Megalópolis

Karítaina, 16km/10 miles north-east, in the Alfiós gorge. Temple of Apollo at Bassai, 60km/37 miles west. See entries.

Lykosoúra

12km/7½ miles south-west of Megalópolis on a country road is the lonely sanctuary of the Despoina (Mistress) at Lykosoúra, with remains of a temple of the 4th century B.C. In the naos can be seen the large base of the cult image. In front of the foundations of a Doric stoa are altars dedicated to the Despoina, Demeter and Ge. In the small site museum are cult statues of the three goddesses by Damophon.

Melos 17

Μήλος
Mílos

Nomos: Cyclades
Area of island: 147 sq.km/57 sq. miles
Altitude: 0–751m/0–2464ft
Population: 4500
Chief place: Mílos

Air services

Airport 5km/3 miles from Mílos. Daily flights Athens–Melos.

Boat services

Regular service from and to Athens (Piraeus), several times weekly. Local connections with neighbouring islands.

Situation and characteristics

The island of Melos or Mílos (from the Greek word for "apple": Italian Milo), the most westerly of the larger Cyclades (see entry), owes its distinctive topography and the pattern of its economy to its origin as the caldera of a volcano of the Pliocene period – an origin to which the sulphurous springs in the north-east and south-east of the island still bear witness. It has one of the best harbours in the Mediterranean, formed when the sea broke into the crater through a gap on its north-west side. The north-eastern half of the island is flatter and more fertile than the hilly south-west, which rises to 751m/2464ft in Mt Profítis Ilías. The island's main economic resources are its rich deposits of minerals, including pumice, alum, sulphur and clay. The tourist trade now also makes a contribution to the economy.

History

The island was already densely populated in the 3rd millennium B.C., when the inhabitants made implements and weapons from the large local deposits of obsidian and exported them all over the Aegean and as far afield as Asia Minor and Egypt.

About 1200 B.C. Dorian incomers settled on the island and founded the city of Melos, defended by walls and towers, on a hill on the north side of Mílos Bay, on the site of present-day Kástro, with its harbour at what is now the hamlet of Klíma. They prospered through the export of sulphur, pumice, clay and alum, as well as oil, wine and honey.

Melos reached the peak of its artistic achievement in Roman and Early Christian times. Its best known work is the Aphrodite of Melos or Venus de Milo (2nd c. B.C.), now in the Louvre.

Venus de Milo

After the fall of the Roman Empire Melos became Byzantine; in the Middle Ages it belonged to the Venetian duchy of Náxos; and after centuries of Turkish rule it became part of the newly established kingdom of Greece in 1832.

Sights

Adámas

The port of Adámas (pop. 750), on the north side of Mílos Bay, is a typical little Cycladic town of whitewashed cube-shaped houses.

★ Mílos (Pláka)

4km/2½ miles north-west of Adámas is the chief place on the island, Mílos or Pláka (alt. 200m/655ft; pop. 900), which has an interesting little museum. On the way up to the Venetian fortress on top of the hill is the notable church of the Panayía Thalassítras.

★ Catacombs

1km/¾ mile below Pláka is the village of Trypití (the name means "riddled with holes"), from which a concrete road leads to the Early

Adámas

Christian catacombs (2nd c.), with the tomb of a saint in the principal chamber and some 2000 burial recesses. The catacombs are unique in Greece.

Melos

A side road which branches off the concrete road leads to the remains of the ancient Dorian city of Melos. A sign (on the left) marks the spot where the Aphrodite of Melos (Venus de Milo), a Hellenistic work of about 150 B.C., was found in 1820. To the right can be seen part of the town walls and a tower. A short distance away, beautifully situated on the hillside overlooking the bay, is a small Roman theatre.

Phylakope

East of Trypití, above the precipitous north coast, is the site of ancient Phylakope, with the foundations of houses of the 3rd and 2nd millennia B.C. and Mycenaean walls of about 1500 B.C.

Apollónia

Beyond this is the pretty little port of Apollónia (11km/7 miles), with a sandy beach.

Zefyriá
Palaiokhóra

South-east of Adámas are Zefyriá (6km/4 miles) and the ruins of Palaiokhóra, founded in the 8th century and abandoned in 1793.

Antímilos

North-west of Melos lies the small rocky island of Antímilos (area 8 sq.km/3 sq. miles; alt. 0–643m/0–2110ft), which is inhabited only by wild goats.

Glaronísia

Off the north coast of Melos are the Glaronísia ("Seagull Islands"), four bizarrely shaped basalt stacks, with the Sykia Caves.

Mesolongi F 5

Μεσολόγγι
Mesolóngi

Nomos: Aetolia and Acarnania
Population: 10,200

Situation and characteristics

Mesolóngi (Italian Missolunghi), chief town of the nomos of Aetolia and Acarnania, lies – as its name indicates – "amid the lagoons" on the north side of the Gulf of Patras. The poet Kostis Palamas (1843–1943), who grew up here, depicts the character and history of the town in his poem "Lament of the Lagoon".

History

Mesolóngi's main claim to fame is its heroic defence against the Turks during the war of liberation. The town, in which Alexander Mavrokordatos, President elect of Greece, had set up his headquarters in 1821, was defended by the Souliot leader Markos Botsaris. On January 5th 1824 Byron landed at Mesolóngi, but died of fever on April 19th. The Greek defenders tried to break through the Turkish lines in April 1826, but only 1800 out of 9000 were successful in doing so; those left in the town thereupon set fire to the powder magazines and blew themselves up.

Sights

★ Heroon

Entering the town through a gate in the town walls, we bear right to reach the Heroon (modern Greek Iróon), a worthy tomb and memorial for those who fell between 1821 and 1826. Beside it is a burial mound

Monument to Byron, Mesolóngi

containing their remains, and also Byron's heart. To the right, on the axis of the main hall of the Heroon, is a statue of Byron. Note also the tomb of Botsaris and the monuments to Philhellenes from Britain, America, France, Germany, Italy, Poland and Scandinavia who died for the cause of Greek independence.

★ Museum

There is a museum with mementoes of the war of liberation in the Dimarkhíon (Town Hall).

Surroundings of Mesolóngi

From the Theoxenia Hotel a causeway runs far out into the lagoons.

Pleuron

4km/2½ miles north of Mesolóngi on the new road to Agrínion (on the right) are the remains of the Hellenistic town of Pleuron (small theatre, cistern, walls).

Aitolikón

6km/4 miles beyond this a causeway on the left leads to the little island town of Aitolikón, where visitors can sample a local delicacy, **avgotárakho** (fish roe wrapped in wax).

Oiniadai

Continuing west by way of Neokhorió, where the broad river Akhelóos is crossed, and Katókhi, we come to the overgrown remains of ancient Oiniadai, situated on a low ridge of hills. The town was founded by Alkmaion, son of Amphiaraos, and named after his son Oineus. To the north, on what was once the shore of Lake Melite, are remains of the harbour; to the south-east is the acropolis, with a polygonal wall of the 6th century B.C.

Oxia Islands

To the south of the Akhelóos estuary are the Oxia Islands, scene of the battle of Lepanto in 1571, in which the western fleet commanded by Don John of Austria, a natural son of the Emperor Charles V, defeated the Turkish fleet.

Here and there in the country round Mesolóngi the reed huts of the nomadic Sarakatsans can still be seen.

Messene F 6

Μεσσήνη
Messíni

Region: Peloponnese
Nomos: Messenia

Situation

Ancient Messene lies on the slopes of Mt Ithómi (798m/2618ft), 30km/19 miles north-west of Kalamáta (see entry), which dominates the landscape of Messenia.
The site of the ancient city, at the village of Mavrommáti, is reached from Kalamáta by way of the modern town of Messíni (30km/19 miles). Visitors coming from the north should turn off the main road from Megalópolis at Tsoukalaíika into a road on the right which leads via Lamvaína to Mavrommáti (19km/12 miles from Tsoukalaíika).

History

In the three wars (740–720, 660 and 464–459 B.C.) in which Sparta, Messene's powerful neighbour to the east of the Taýgetos range, sought to gain control of Messenia Mt Ithómi was the last refuge of the Messenians. In 455 B.C. Athens offered the last defenders of the hill a

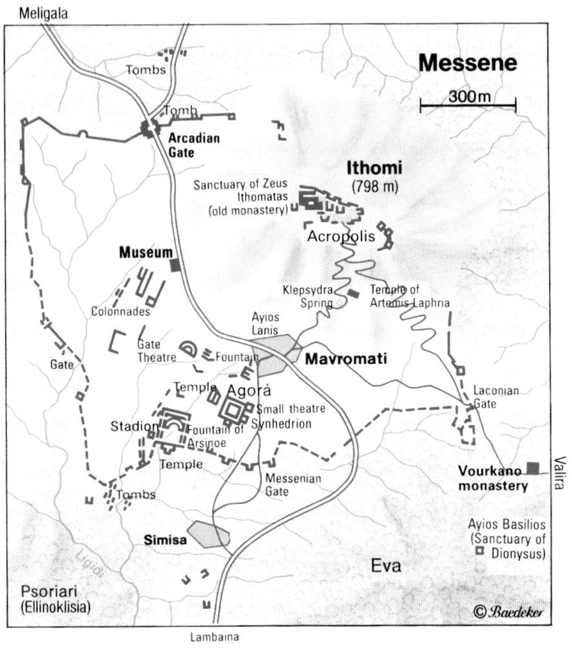

new home in the port of Náfpaktos (see entry) on the Gulf of Corinth. Two years after his victory over Sparta at Leuktra, in 369 B.C., the Theban leader Epameinondas founded the city of Messene on the western and southern slopes of Mt Ithómi. The new foundation was intended, along with Mantineia and Megalópolis (see entries), to prevent any resurgence of Spartan power. The city and its immediate territory were surrounded by a wall 9km/6 miles long. In the centre of the site is the little village of Mavrommáti.

Sights

Voúrkano monastery

From Mavrommáti a road runs east to a saddle in the hills, beyond which stands the fortress-like Voúrkano monastery (17th c.). From the saddle a track winds its way up to the summit of Mt Ithómi, with a ruined monastery occupying the site of the acropolis; the climb takes an hour.

Temple of Asklepios

From the east end of the village a path descends to a rectangular area which was formerly thought to be the agora. Recent excavations have brought to light, in the centre of the area, a Doric temple of Asklepios of the Hellenistic period, with 6 × 12 columns. Adjoining it on the east are a small theatre (assembly room), a propylon and a hall; to the west are several cult chambers, including one dedicated to Artemis Orthia.

Arcadian Gate

From the west end of this sanctuary a path runs up to the north, past the site of the theatre, to join the road from Mavrommáti to the

Ancient Messene

Arcadian Gate at the small local museum. Of this monumental north gate of the ancient city there still survive nine courses of dressed stone. On the outer side of the gate are two square towers flanking a forecourt, and inside it is a circular outer ward with a diameter of 19.7m/65ft. On either side of the gate, but particularly on the west side, the course of the walls, with their towers and wall-walks, can be traced in the hilly surrounding country.

Meteora F 4

Μετέωρα
Metéora

Region: Thessaly
Nomos: Tríkala

Situation

In north-western Thessaly there rears up out of the plain of the Peneios (Piniós) a group of conglomerate rock formations up to 300m/985ft high which have been weathered by erosion into a variety of bizarre forms. Vertical rock faces, sharply pointed pinnacles and massive crags tower up above Kalambáka (see entry) and the village of Kastráki, separated by deeply slashed defiles. Perched on these rocks are the monasteries of Metéora, which take their name from their situation – *ta metéora monastíria,* the monasteries hanging in the air.

Originally accessible only by bridle tracks, ladders and windlasses, the monasteries have now been brought within the reach of visitors by the construction of modern roads and flights of steps and by signposting; but it should not be forgotten that these are places of peace and prayer and meditation, and visitors should conduct themselves accordingly.

★★ Landscape

To get the most out of a visit to this awe-inspiring landscape visitors should avoid merely driving quickly from one sight to the next. The best plan is to allow time to explore the area on foot and to see some of the remoter monasteries, now abandoned, as well as those that are shown to tourists.

History

In the 9th century the first hermits settled in caves beneath the rocks of Metéora, and a church of the Panayía was built at Doupianí. The place became known as "stous Ayious" ("at the saints' place"), which was corrupted into Stágoi. In 1340 Thessaly came under Serbian control, and Simeon, an uncle of the young king Stephen Uroš V, was crowned as king of the Serbs and Greeks at Tríkala. During this troubled period the hermits sought safety and tranquillity on the summits of the rocks. Then monasteries were built, beginning with the Great Metéoron, founded by Athanasios the Meteorite between 1356 and 1372 on the Broad Rock (Platýs Lithós) and enlarged from 1388 onwards by his disciple and successor Joasaph, a son of King Simeon. In the heyday of Metéora there were 24 monasteries; but decline set in during the 16th century, and only six monasteries are now still occupied. Together with the monasteries of Athos, they make an important contribution to our knowledge of the post-Byzantine painting of the 16th century.

The Monasteries

The road climbs up from Kalambáka to the rocks of Metéora by way of the village of Kastráki. At various points in the rock faces on the way up can be seen the caves in which the early hermits lived.

Áyios Nikólaos Anapafsás

After passing the little church of the Mitrópolis at Doupianí we come (on the left) to the steep ascent leading up to the monastery of Áyios

Rousanoú monastery

Varlaám monastery

Ayía Triáda monastery

Nikólaos Anapafsás, founded in 1368 and enlarged in 1628, with paintings of 1527 by the Cretan artist Theophanes.

★ Rousanoú

Beyond the monastery of Rousanoú, perched on a slender pinnacle of rock – the most boldly sited of all the monasteries – the road to the Great Metéoron and Varlaám monasteries branches off on the left.

★ Great Metéoron

Standing below the Great Metéoron monastery, we can see on the rock faces the traces of the earlier ladders, and at the top the little tower-like building with a timber roof which still houses the windlass once used to haul visitors up in a net but now serving only to hoist up supplies. As a result of the increasing numbers of visitors considerable parts of the monastery have been closed to the public.
Visitors are admitted to the principal church (open 9am–1pm, 3–6pm), dedicated to the Metamórfosis (Transfiguration). The chapel built by the founder, Athanasios, is now the sanctuary of the larger church erected by Joasaph. The tombs of the two founders are in the spacious narthex, which, like the body of the church (16th c.) and the apse (1438), has preserved its wall paintings intact.
There is an interesting collection of icons and books in the former refectory (trápeza). Particularly notable is an icon of the Incredulity of Thomas (14th c.), which shows Christ and the Apostles together with the cruel Thomas Preljubović of Ioánnina and his pious wife Angelina Comnena.

Varlaám

The nearby monastery of Varlaám (open 9am–1pm, 3.30–6pm), founded in 1517, has some lively paintings by Frangos Kastellanos of Thebes in the church of All Saints (Áyion Pánton), including an impressive Crucifixion (1548). In the narthex is a fine Last Judgment (1566). The monastery also has an interesting museum and library.

Ayía Triáda
Áyios Stéfanos

On the way back we take the left-hand road at the fork, pass the monastery of Ayía Triáda (founded 1438, open 10am–noon, 4–6pm) on the right, and come to the attractive convent of Áyios Stéfanos, occupied by nuns (open Tue–Sun.). It was founded in 1367 by a Serbian prince, Antony Cantacuzene, and has frescoes of 1400 in its chapel. The principal church (Áyios Kharalambos) dates only from 1798.
From the open space behind the church, on the edge of the crag, there are magnificent views of the plain of Thessaly, traversed by the river Peneios (Piniós).

Methoni F 7

Μεθώνη
Methóni

Region: Peloponnese
Nomos: Messenia
Altitude: 10m/35ft. Population: 1300

Transport

Bus service from Pýlos.

Situation

Methóni is a small village in a sandy bay 12km/7½ miles south of Pýlos, dominated by a large Venetian fortress.

History

Methóni was held for a brief period after the 4th Crusade by the Villehardouins, who ceded it to Venice in 1206. The Venetians developed it, under the name of Modon, into a powerful stronghold and naval station on the route between the Adriatic and Crete. In 1500 it was captured by the Turks, but in 1686 it was retaken by Morosini and held by Venice until 1715. During the war of Greek liberation (1825–28) there was violent fighting here between Ibrahim Pasha and a Greek force led by Admiral Miaoulis, supported by a French contingent.

The ★Castle

The castle is entered on a bridge built by French troops in 1828 over the deep castle moat. To the right of the first gate are two strong Venetian bastions of the 15th and early 18th centuries. Inside the gate we turn left through a long outer ward, pass through two further gates and enter the spacious inner ward, in which is the granite Morosini Column, with a Byzantine capital. To the right is a gate leading into the Citadel, with the remains of Turkish buildings. The wall on the west

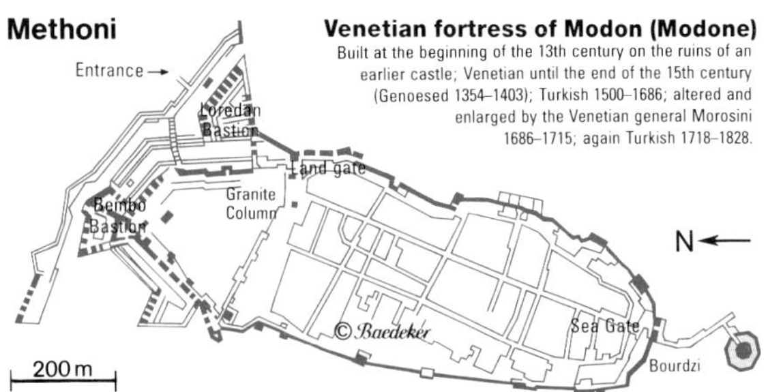
Methoni
Venetian fortress of Modon (Modone)
Built at the beginning of the 13th century on the ruins of an earlier castle; Venetian until the end of the 15th century (Genoesed 1354–1403); Turkish 1500–1686; altered and enlarged by the Venetian general Morosini 1686–1715; again Turkish 1718–1828.
Entrance
Loredan Bastion
Land gate
Granite Column
Bembo Bastion
N
Sea Gate
Bourdzi
© Baedeker
200 m

Land Gate and Morosini Column

View to the south

Bourdzi

(seaward) side rises directly above the edge of the rock. At the south end of the fortress we pass through a gate flanked by towers and along a causeway to an octagonal structure of the Turkish period, the Bourdzi (16th c.), from which there is a view of the islands of Sapiéntza and Skhíza.

★ Bourdzi

Returning along the wall-walk on the east side of the chapel, we see the remains of an imposing building abutting the walls and, beyond this, a gate (now walled up) opening on to the bay, with coats of arms on the outside.

Metsovo F 4

Μέτσοβο
Métsovo

Nomos: Ioánnina
Altitude: 1160m/3806ft
Population: 2700

Transport

Métsovo lies 2km/1¼ miles below the Ioánnina–Kalambáka road.

★ Situation and characteristics

The mountain village of Métsovo, situated in a wooded region in the Pindos range below the Katára pass, is popular both with summer holiday visitors and winter sports enthusiasts (ski-lift). During the Turkish period well known families like the Averofs and Tositsas built themselves houses in this inaccessible spot. Features of interest are the Folk Museum in the Tositsa House, the church of Ayía Paraskeví and the monastery of Áyios Nikólaos at the lower end of the village.
The nearby village of Mília is famed for its trout and its yogurt.
The planned new section of the road from Igoumenítsa via Ioánnina and Kozáni to Salonica will pass just to the south of Métsovo (in a tunnel for part of the way).

Mistra G 6

Μυστράς
Mystrás

Nomos: Laconia
Altitude: 380–620m/1245–2035ft
Population: 610

Situation and characteristics

The village of Mistra, 7km/4½ miles from Sparta (see entry), lies below the ruins of the medieval town of Mistra, built on an outlying hill of the Taýgetos range, which provides the most complete picture we have of a town of the late Byzantine period (13th–15th c.).

History

The castle of Mistra was built in 1249 by Guillaume II de Villehardouin, but in 1263, having been taken prisoner by the Byzantine Emperor Michael VIII, he was compelled to yield it up to the Emperor, together with the castles of Maina and Monemvasía. Thereafter, until the Turkish conquest in 1460, Mistra was ruled by Byzantine princes, who bore the title of Despot, the second highest rank in the Empire (after the Basileus but above Sebastokrator and Caesar).
Below the Frankish castle on the summit of the hill there grew up first the upper and then the lower town. The Despot's palace became the centre of a splendid court and an active intellectual life, particularly

when George Gemisthos Plethon developed his neo-Platonic philosophy here in the 15th century, contributing a significant impulse to the Renaissance in Florence. This, combined with the marriage of one of the Despots to a Malatesta princess, was the motive which led Sigismondo Malatesta in 1464 to thrust down through Turkish-occupied territory to Mistra in order to bring back Plethon's remains to Rimini, where they were deposited in the church of San Francesco, the "Tempio Malatestiano".
After the Turkish conquest of the town in 1460 Mistra declined, particularly after Turkish reprisals in response to the Orlov rising of 1770;

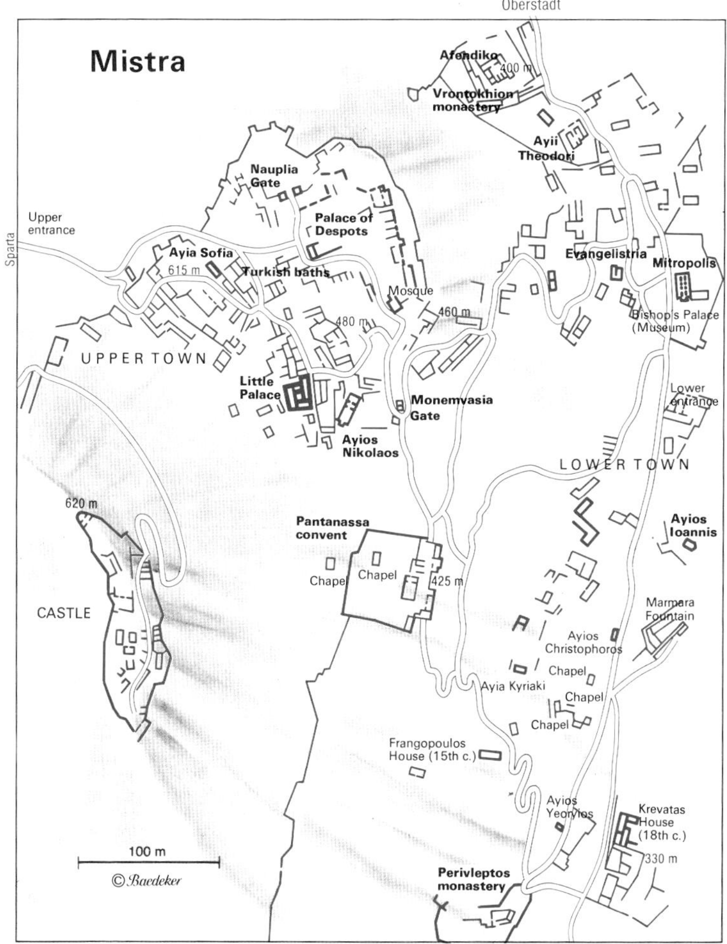

and when, following the liberation of Greece, the population moved in 1834 to the newly founded town of Sparta, Mistra shrank to a small village below the town walls. The houses and churches fell into decay: a process which was halted only by the considerable work of restoration and conservation carried out by Orlandos and others in the present century. Thanks to their work we are now able to get an impression of the life of this town, ruled by Greek princes married to wives from western Europe, which became a meeting-place between Byzantine and western culture.

★★Mistra, the City of Ruins

★ Mitrópolis

Bearing right from the lower entrance to the site, we come to the Mitrópolis, Mistra's metropolitan or episcopal church, a three-aisled basilica erected in 1309. In the 15th century, following the model of other churches subsequently built in the town, the Mitrópolis was given a new upper storey on a cruciform plan. Most of the vigorous paintings and the interior furnishings have been preserved. On the floor in front of the iconostasis is a carving of the Byzantine double eagle, traditionally believed to mark the spot on which Constantine XI Dragases stood to be crowned as Emperor on January 6th 1449, relinquishing his authority as ruler of the Peloponnese; after which he made his way to the beleaguered city of Constantinople to rule it as the last Christian monarch and to die fighting on the land walls when the Turks captured the city on May 29th 1453.
In the forecourt, which is flanked on two sides by arcades, with its open side towards the plain, is an ancient sarcophagus carved with Dionysiac scenes. The former bishop's palace, which incorporates some fragments of ancient masonry, now houses a small museum. A

Ruins of Mistra

grille on the outer wall of the church marks the spot where the Turks killed the Metropolitan after the Orlov rising of 1770.

★ Vrontókhion monastery
Áyii Theódori

Farther north is the Vrontókhion monastery, with the oldest church in Mistra, Áyii Theódori (1296). This has a large central dome like that of Dafní spanning all three aisles, fine stone and brick masonry in the east end, and the tomb of a Despot in the north-eastern chapel.

★ Afendikó church

The Vrontókhion monastery also has the largest church in Mistra, the Afendikó, built shortly before 1311, which has impressive frescoes (recently restored). This was the first example of a type of church characteristic of Mistra, with a basilican lower storey and an upper storey in the form of a domed cruciform church – a synthesis of the Early Christian and Byzantine basilica with later Byzantine traditions.

★ Palace

Retracing our steps, we now walk up past the Evangelistria, a mortuary chapel of around 1400, towards the upper town, pass through the Monemvasía Gate and come to the Palace (13th–15th c.), with its great hall (10m/33ft by 36m/118ft), its beautiful loggia looking out on to the Evrotas plain and its imposing façade, on which the projecting throne recess and remains of Flamboyant window decoration can still be seen.

To the west of the Palace is the fortified Nauplia Gate, and higher up the church of Ayía Sofía (1350), from which the castle can be reached (fine views). Near Ayía Sofía is the upper entrance to the site.

Pantánassa convent
★ Wall paintings

Returning to the Monemvasía Gate and keeping straight ahead, we come to the Pantánassa convent (dedicated to the Mother of God as "Mistress of All"), occupied by a few nuns – the only monastic house in Mistra which is still occupied. The Pantánassa church, the last major building to be erected in Mistra (1428), contains notable paintings.

Byzantine church

Fresco in church

Perívleptos monastery

★ Wall paintings

Continuing down the hill, towards the south, we come to the Perívleptos monastery (second half of 14th c.), built against the rock face, which has very fine paintings of the "Palaeologue Renaissance" – masterpieces of this late Byzantine style, full of vigour, life and expressive force.

From here it is a short distance north to the exit.

Monemvasia H 7

Μονεμβασία
Monemvasía

Nomos: Laconia
Altitude: 5–300m/15–985ft
Population: 5000

Transport

Boat services from Athens (Piraeus), Kýthira and Gýthion. Yacht supply station.

By road, Monemvasía is 98km/61 miles from Sparta and 64km/40 miles from Gýthion.

★★ Situation and characteristics

This little walled town situated at the foot of a 300m/985ft high crag projecting into the sea on the east side of the Peloponnese takes its name from its single entrance (*móni émvasis*). For centuries an almost impregnable stronghold, it is now almost deserted, most of its inhabitants having moved to the new village on the mainland. But even in its abandonment it preserves its magnificent situation.

In recent years the local people have increasingly been returning to the old part of the town, giving it a new lease of life and making it a busy and attractive tourist centre.

The Rock of Monemvasía

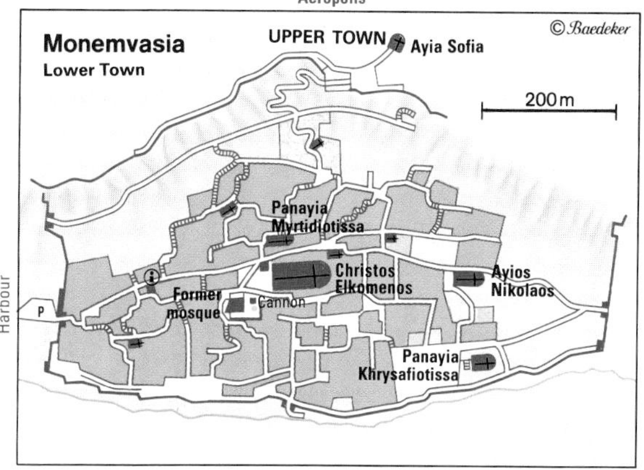

History

The ancient name of the town, Minoa, points to a Cretan settlement. 6km/4 miles north are the remains (town walls and temples of the 1st millennium B.C.) of the Mycenaean town of Epidauros Limera. Monemvasía first appears on the stage of history, however, in the 8th century, when it became a place of refuge for Greeks fleeing before the Slav invasion of Laconia. It soon developed into a flourishing port, which was able to repel a Norman attack in 1149 and was taken by Guillaume de Villehardouin in 1249 only after a three year siege. Only fourteen years later, however, in 1263, he was compelled to return Monemvasía, together with Mistra and Maina, to the Byzantine emperor, by whom he had been taken prisoner. In 1460, faced with the threat of Turkish attack, the town submitted to the authority of the Pope. Later it passed under Venetian rule, but in 1540 fell into the hands of the Turks, who held it (with another Venetian interlude between 1690 and 1715) until 1821.

Monemvasía gave its name, in garbled form, to the wine called Malmsey, which was originally produced here and exported in large quantities.

★Lower Town

The lower town is entered on its south side through the only gate in the walls, built by the Turks in the 16th century on earlier Byzantine foundations. Through picturesque lanes we come to the main square, in which stands a Turkish cannon.

Elkómenos church

In the square stands the Elkómenos church (14th c.; rebuilt 1697). Over the doorway is a broken carved panel depicting two peacocks, evidently from the templon of an earlier church. The church originally possessed a celebrated icon of Christ Elkómenos (led to the Cross) and a fine icon of the Crucifixion.

Higher up is the domed church of the Panayía Myrtidiótissa, in severer style (14th c.; iconostasis).

Áyios Nikólaos

At the east end of the town is the chapel of Áyios Nikólaos (1703).

Khrysafiótissa church

In a square on the south side of the town is the 17th century church of the Panayía Khrysafiótissa, with a large dome. Beyond this stretches the sea wall with its gun embrasures.

The picturesque lower town of Monemvasía

★Upper Town

Ayía Sofía

A paved lane zigzags its way up to the upper town, which in earlier days was strongly fortified. Here, on the edge of a precipitous crag, is the church of Ayía Sofía, built in the time of Andronikos II (1287–1328), which, like the church at Dafní (see entry), has a large central dome spanning both the nave and the lateral aisles. Notable features of the exterior are the fine capitals and a carving of Salome's dance.

Castle
★★ View

The summit of the crag is crowned by the curtain walls of the old castle, from which there is a fantastic view.

Mycenae G 6

Μυκήνες
Mykínes

Region: Peloponnese
Nomos: Argolid
Altitude: 120–278m/394–912ft
Population: 440

Transport

The village of Mykínes is a station on the Corinth–Trípoli railway line. Bus services from Corinth and Árgos.

The fortified city of Mycenae and the Mycenaean civilisation to which it gave its name were first introduced to the world by Heinrich Schlie-

Lion Gate ▶

mann's excavations from 1874 onwards, which carried the history of Europe far back into the Bronze Age of the 2nd millennium B.C.; and although many other strongholds and settlements of the same period have since been discovered Mycenae still retains its pre-eminence.

History

When the first Greeks came to this region around 2000 B.C. they would no doubt establish themselves on the 278m/912ft high hill "in the farthest corner of Argolis, nourisher of horses". Thereafter they mingled with the indigenous population and a hybrid culture evolved. In religion Greek and pre-Greek elements interpenetrated one another; linguistically the newcomers soon established their predominance, but the pre-Indo-European name of Mycenae was retained. Shaft graves dating from the 17th century B.C. give evidence of this period. Then, around 1580 B.C., a radical change began to take place, as influences from Egypt and the refined Minoan culture of Crete made themselves felt. The Early Mycenaean period which now began (1580–1500 B.C.) is notable for the wealth of gold found in the shaft graves, including the famous gold mask laid over the face of some dead prince and wrongly identified by Schliemann as belonging to Agamemnon (who lived at a later period). From the Middle Mycenaean period (1500–1425 B.C.) date the first known defensive walls and the early tholos tombs. The Late Mycenaean period (1425–1100 B.C.) also yielded a rich harvest of finds. The 14th century saw the construction of the later tholos tombs, including the so-called Treasury of Atreus; the older Megaron on the acropolis (*c.* 1350 B.C.), the first palace of some pretension; and the cyclopean walls enclosing the site. The later Megaron, the Lion Gate and the extension at the east end were built about 1250 B.C. After 1230 B.C., when the threat from new invaders coming from the north was felt to be pressing, five different phases of work on strengthening the defences have been identified; and the history of Mycenae finally came to an end about 1100 B.C. as a result of an attack by the "Sea Peoples" who are referred to in Egyptian sources or by the Dorians who followed them.

★ Treasury of Atreus

On the left of the road which runs up from the village of Mykínes to the site is the famous tholos tomb known (without any historical warrant) as the "Treasury of Atreus" or the "Tomb of Agamemnon".
A dromos 36m/118ft long leads to a doorway 10.5m/34ft high, with a massive lintel 8.5m/28ft long, 5m/16ft wide and 1.2m/4ft thick which is estimated to weigh 120 tons. On either side of the doorway were half-columns of greenish stone, remains of which are now in the National Archaeological Museum in Athens; traces of the column bases and sockets for fixing them in place can still be seen. Above the doorway is a relieving triangle, originally covered with a carved stone slab. The interior is circular, with a diameter of 14.5m/48ft and a height of 13.2m/43ft. It is roofed with a false vault formed of overlapping courses of stone and originally decorated with bronze rosettes. The main chamber was designed for cult purposes; the actual tomb chamber is to the right. The tomb is an impressive example of Mycenaean architectural skill: its dimensions were exceeded only by the Pantheon in Rome, built in the 2nd century A.D.

The Site

N.B.

In walking about the site beware of slippery stone.

On the way to the Citadel a number of Mycenaean houses can be seen on the right of the road. Just inside the enclosure are Grave Circle B, discovered in 1951, and a number of tholos tombs.

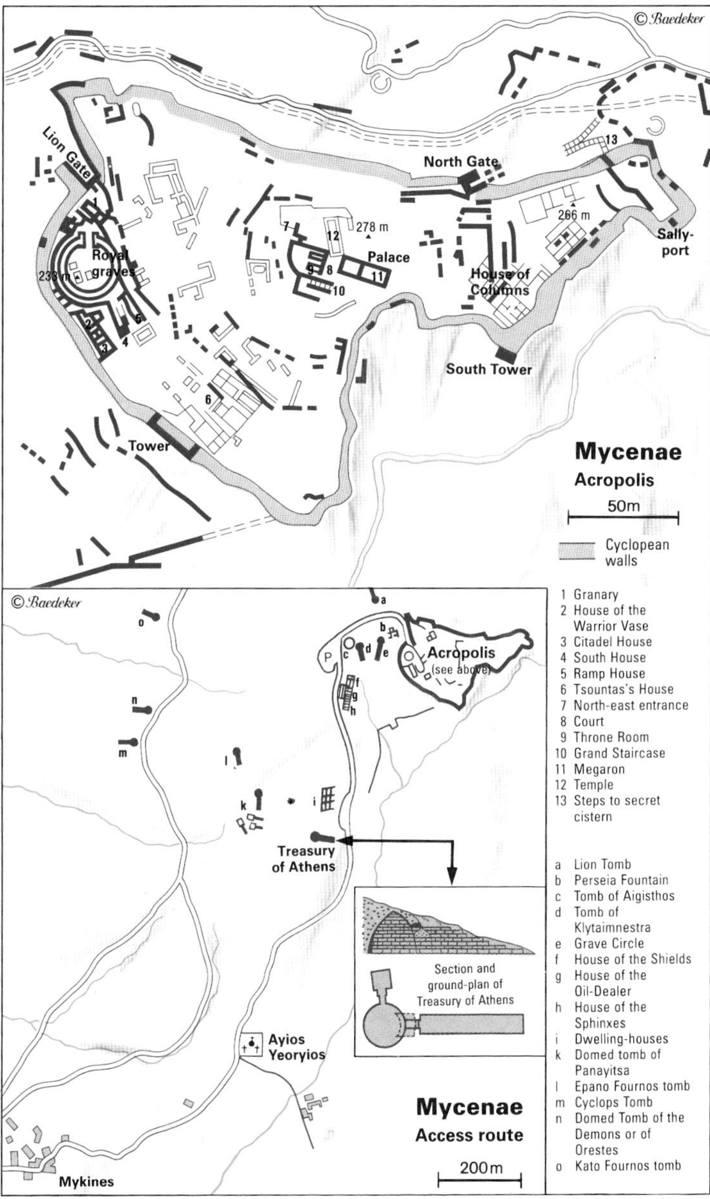
© Baedeker
Lion Gate
North Gate
13
278 m
266 m
Sally-port
Palace
Royal graves
233 m
House of Columns
South Tower
Tower
Mycenae
Acropolis
50m
Cyclopean walls
1 Granary
2 House of the Warrior Vase
3 Citadel House
4 South House
5 Ramp House
6 Tsountas's House
7 North-east entrance
8 Court
9 Throne Room
10 Grand Staircase
11 Megaron
12 Temple
13 Steps to secret cistern
© Baedeker
Acropolis (see above)
Treasury of Athens
Section and ground-plan of Treasury of Athens
Ayios Yeoryios
Mykines
Mycenae
Access route
200m
a Lion Tomb
b Perseia Fountain
c Tomb of Aigisthos
d Tomb of Klytaimnestra
e Grave Circle
f House of the Shields
g House of the Oil-Dealer
h House of the Sphinxes
i Dwelling-houses
k Domed tomb of Panayitsa
l Epano Fournos tomb
m Cyclops Tomb
n Domed Tomb of the Demons or of Orestes
o Kato Fournos tomb

★★ Lion Gate
(illustration, p. 353)

We then enter the Citadel through the Lion Gate, flanked by bastions on either side. In the relieving triangle is the famous carving of two lions, one on either side of a central column; the heads, which were carved separately and attached with the aid of dowels, are missing. This symbol of religiously based royal authority is a theme found on Cretan seals, here enlarged to monumental proportions.

★ Royal graves

Inside the gateway is the Grave Circle found by Schliemann, which originally lay outside the walls. It was only during the extension of the walls in the 13th century B.C. that the tombs were enclosed within a double ring of stone slabs; the funerary stelae were then set up on a higher level, and the grave circle became a shrine devoted to the cult of the dead. In the six shaft graves to be seen in the excavated area there were found the remains of nine men, eight women and two children, accompanied by numerous gold grave goods. The recently discovered Grave Çircle B is dated to the late 17th century B.C.; this Grave Circle A found by Schliemann dates from some time after 1580 B.C. The fact that no more shaft graves were constructed and that tholos tombs then came into favour points to a change of dynasty; and indeed ancient traditions spoke of the descendants of the original founder, Perseus (the Perseids), being succeeded by the descendants of Pelops (the Pelopids or Atreids).

Beyond Grave Circle A are a number of other buildings, including the South House, the House of the Warrior Vase and Tsountas's House (named after the Greek archaeologist who excavated it).

Palace

From the ramp beyond the Lion Gate a path runs uphill on the left to the badly ruined Palace, over which a Greek temple of Athena was

Grave Circle A

built in the 7th century B.C. The most important parts of the palace lie on the south side – a courtyard approached by a stone staircase of Mycenaean date which has been preserved, and the throne-room and megaron of the rulers of Mycenae. In the centre of the megaron is the circular sacred hearth. From here there are fine views of the Argolid.

Going downhill towards the east, we see on the right, built against the citadel walls, the House of Columns. Beyond this is the east bastion, with a sally-port and the entrance to a secret underground cistern. This area of the citadel is part of the extensions carried out in the 13th century B.C.
Returning to the entrance along the north side of the walls, we pass the North Gate. Lower down the hill can be seen a number of store-rooms with pottery jars for provisions.

Mykonos K 6

Μύκονος
Mýkonos

Nomos: Cyclades
Area of island: 75 sq.km/29 sq. miles
Altitude: 0–364m/0–1194ft
Population: 4000
Chief place: Mýkonos (Khóra)

Air services

Airfield 3km/2 miles from Mýkonos. Flights from Athens, several times daily; also from Chios. Iráklion (Crete), Sámos and Santorin.

Mýkonos Town

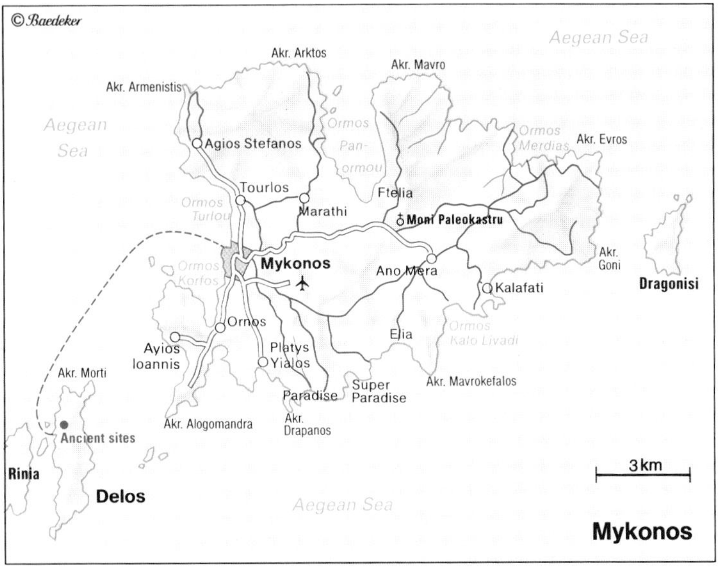

Windmills on Mýkonos

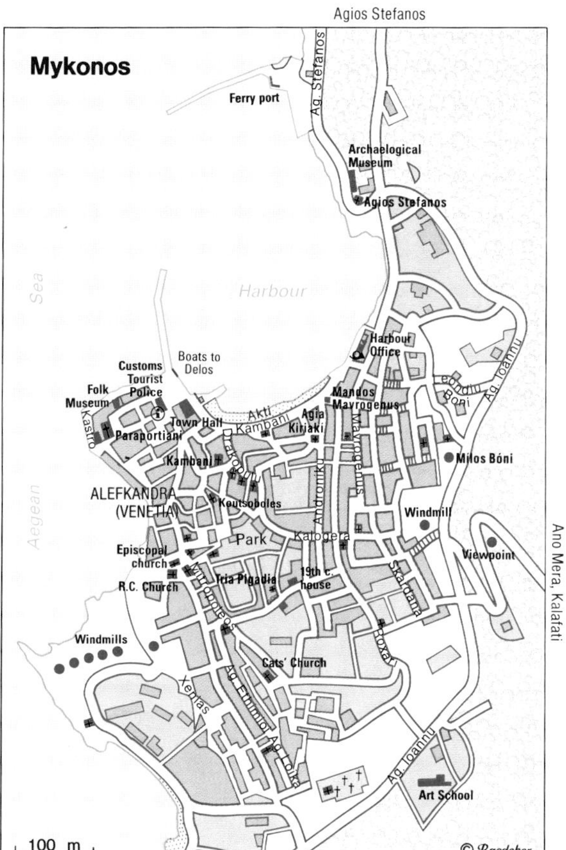

Boat services

Regular service from and to Athens (Piraeus), several times daily (6–7 hours; cars carried). Local connections with Delos, depending on weather conditions, and with other neighbouring islands.

Situation and characteristics

The bare rocky island of Mýkonos, the most easterly of the northern Cyclades, was once one of the most important trading centres in the western Aegean. Its arid and only moderately fertile soil permits only a modest development of agriculture, but its beautiful beaches have made it one of the most popular holiday islands in the Aegean. Mýkonos is also a good base from which to visit the neighbouring islands of Delos (see entry) and Rínia.

Myth and history

According to legend Mýkonos was the rock with which Poseidon slew the giants. The island's history was closely bound up with that of

Tínos. Unlike Tínos, however, it was occupied by the Turks for almost three hundred years, though it contrived to maintain a considerable degree of independence under Turkish rule.

Sights

★ Mýkonos (Khóra)

The chief place on the island, Mýkonos or Khóra (pop. 2500), is a charming little town of whitewashed cube-shaped houses, with numerous churches and several windmills, extending in a semicircle round a bay on the west coast. It occupies the site of the ancient city of the same name.

Museum
Paraportianí church

There is a small museum with archaeological material from Rínia and Delos. The most interesting of the churches is the Paraportianí, which is built on four levels.

Young pelican

The mascot of Mýkonos for more than thirty years was a tame pelican called Petros. After his universally lamented death in December 1985 he was stuffed and can now be seen in the museum. The town now has a number of younger pelicans.

10km/6 miles east of Mýkonos town, in the quiet little village of Áno Merá, is Tourlianí monastery. A little way north of this, at Palaiokástro, is a ruined Venetian castle, built on the remains of an ancient settlement.

From the two summits of Mt Profítis Ilías, to the north-west (364m/1194ft) and to the east (351m/1152ft; closed military area), there are superb views.

Dragonísi

Some 2km/1¼ miles east of Mýkonos lies the rocky island of Dragonísi, with sea-caves frequented by seals.

Nafpaktos F 5

Ναύπακτος
Náfpaktos

Nomos: Aetolia and Acarnania
Altitude: 10m/35ft. Population: 9000

Transport

Bus service from Antírrion.
Yacht supply station.

Situation and characteristics

Náfpaktos (Naupaktos) is a charming little port on the north side of the Gulf of Corinth, 9km/6 miles east of the Strait of Ríon. It was known to the Venetians as Lepanto, and became famous as the scene of the naval battle of Lepanto in 1571.

History

The ancient town of Naupaktos in western Lokris was captured by Athens in 455 B.C. and was used by the Athenians to house the Messenians who had been expelled from their city by Sparta. At the end of the Peloponnesian War, however, the Messenians were once again expelled. During that war, in which Naupaktos played an important

part as a base for the Athenian expedition to Sicily, Phormion defeated a numerically superior Spartan fleet (429 B.C. – the year in which Perikles died).
From 1407 to 1499 and from 1687 to 1700 Náfpaktos was a Venetian naval base, which along with the fortresses of Ríon (see entry) and Antírrion controlled the entrance to the Gulf of Corinth. From 1499 to 1687 and from 1700 to 1821 the town was held by the Turks, whose fleet sailed from here to fight the battle of Lepanto, the first naval victory by the allied European powers over the hitherto undefeated Turks (October 6th 1571). This historic battle took place off the Oxia Islands to the west. The commander of the "Holy League" formed by the Pope, Spain, Venice, Genoa and the Order of St John was Don John of Austria, a natural son of the Emperor Charles V. Among those who fought in the battle was Cervantes, author of "Don Quixote", who lost an arm in the encounter.

The Town

The harbour is protected by a Venetian wall, in which many fragments of ancient masonry can be seen. From the harbour the town's powerful fortifications climb in several successive rings to the castle on top of the hill. A walk through the town, passing the main square just off the harbour with its coffee-houses and tavernas, will give some impression of the skill displayed by the military engineers in taking full advantage of the town's excellent strategic situation.

Surroundings of Náfpaktos

Immediately east of the town the river Mórnos, which rises on Mt Iti (2152m/7061ft), flows into the Gulf of Corinth. A dam on the upper course of the river has formed an artificial lake which supplies water to Athens.

40km/25 miles from here, at the village of Kállion, is the partly excavated site of ancient Kallipolis. The remains so far brought to light include 3km/2 miles of the town walls, baths and a statue of Artemis. The town is thought to have been the capital of the region of Callieis mentioned in the writings of Thucydides (III, 96, 3).

Nafplion (Nauplia) G 6

Ναύπλιον
Náfplion

Nomos: Argolid
Altitude: 5–85m/15–280ft. Population: 10,600

Transport

Bus services from Árgos, Corinth and Athens.
Boats to the island of Boúrdzi.
Yacht supply station.

Situation and characteristics

Náfplion (Nauplia) has a magnificent situation in the Argolic Gulf below the rocky promontory of Akrónafplia (85m/280ft) and the fortified hill of Palamídi (216m/709ft). The beauty of its situation, the many places of archaeological interest in the surrounding area and the town's numerous hotels have made Náfplion a popular tourist centre.

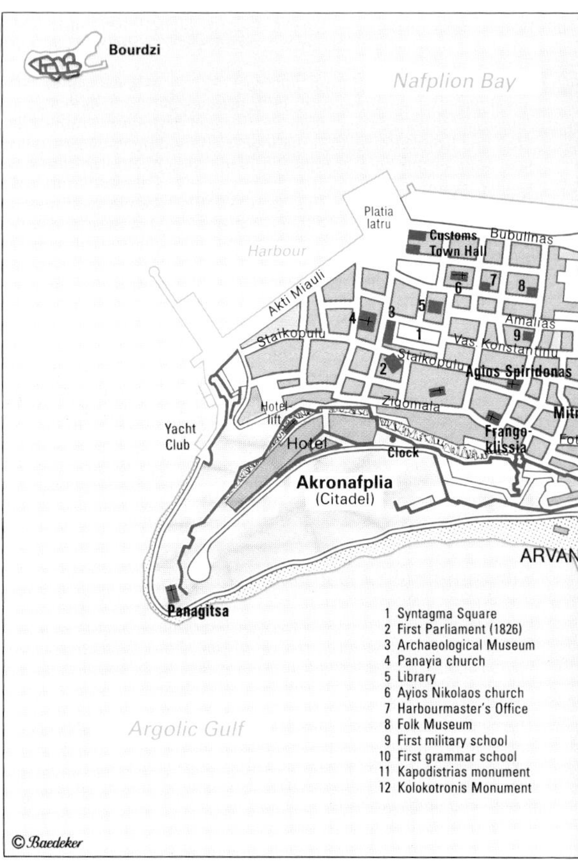

History

According to an ancient tradition Nauplia was founded by Nauplios, son of the sea god Poseidon, and his son Palamedes. From 628 B.C. it was the port of Árgos.

After the 4th Crusade (1203–04) Leon Sgouros, who had used the town as a base for his conquest of Corinth in 1202, held it against the Crusaders, who were unable to take it until 1246. In 1387 it fell into the hands of the Venetians, who made it one of the most powerful strongholds of the day under the name of Napoli di Levante. The town withstood two Turkish sieges, but was ceded to the Turks by treaty in 1540. It was further strengthened by the Turks, who held it from 1540 to 1686 and from 1715 to 1822. Between 1686 and 1715 it was briefly held by the Venetians under Francesco Morosini, who built the fortress of Palamídi.

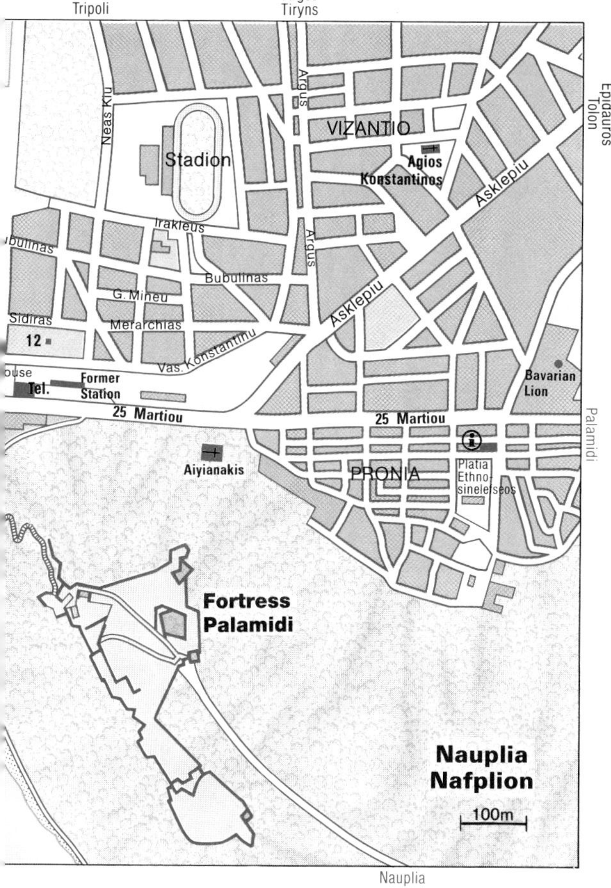

The town was captured by the Greeks in 1822, and in 1828 became capital of Greece. The first President of Greece, Count Kapodistrias, was murdered in an act of private revenge outside the church of St Spyridon on November 8th 1831.

On January 25th 1833 the 18-year-old King Otto, son of Ludwig I of Bavaria, landed here to take up his new kingdom. In 1834 the king transferred his capital from Náfplion to Athens.

Sights

★ Townscape

The town has remained largely unspoiled, in spite of land reclamation from the sea to the north and east of Akrónafplia and much recent building. It preserves a number of Venetian buildings, one or two

Náfplion: view from the Citadel

churches and neo-classical houses dating from the reign of King Otto. In Sýntagma (Constitution) Square is a former mosque now known as the Vouleftikó from its use as the meeting-place of the Greek Parliament (Vouli).

Museum

The Museum, housed in a Venetian building in Sýntagma Square, contains archaeological material from Náfplion and the surrounding area. The oldest items are pieces of Neolithic pottery from Asini and Berbati, while the Mycenaean period is represented by fragments of frescoes and terracotta idols from Mycenae, a suit of armour from Dendra (15th c. B.C.) and a helmet of the same period.

Prónia

In the district of Prónia is the square in which the Greek National Assembly approved the selection of King Otto in 1832. Here too, on a rock on the right-hand side of the road to Epidauros, is a carved figure of a recumbent lion (by a German sculptor, Siegel) commemorating the Bavarians killed in 1833–34. Also in Prónia is the Ayía Moní, a nunnery with a church dating from 1149 and a luxuriant garden containing the spring of Kanathos in which the goddess Hera annually renewed her virginity.

★ Akrónafplia

Venetian Lion

The town's fortifications are still impressive – for example the entrance to Akrónafplia, on the east side, with a gate built of Roman bricks, a Byzantine gatehouse containing fine frescoes of 1291 and Venetian bastions. Akrónafplia itself, with a history going back to the 4th century B.C., is now a luxury hotel.

★ Palamídi

The mightiest of Náfplion's fortifications is the Venetian stronghold of Palamídi (1711–14). It can be reached from the saddle between the two hills on a flight of 857 steps (partly roofed over) or, less strenuously, on

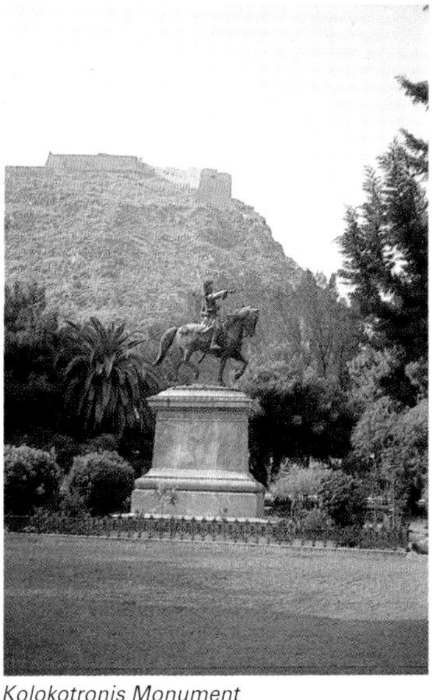
Kolokotronis Monument

Within the fort of Palamidi

the 3km/2 mile long motor road which runs through Prónia. From the top there are magnificent panoramic views of the town and the Argolic Gulf.

★★ Views

Boúrdzi

The little offshore island of Boúrdzi is also fortified.

Surroundings of Náfplion

Within easy reach of Náfplion are the Mycenaean stronghold of Tiryns (see entry) and other sites in the Argolid (see entry); ancient Asine, near the village of Tolón (see entry); and the sanctuary of Asklepios at Epidauros (see entry).

Naxos K 6/7

Νάξος
Náxos

Nomos: Cyclades
Area of island: 445 sq.km/172 sq. miles
Altitude: 0–1003m/0–3291ft
Population: 14,000
Chief town: Náxos

Boat services

Regular service from Athens (Piraeus), several times daily (8 hours; cars carried). Local connections with the larger neighbouring islands.

Situation and characteristics

Náxos, the largest and most beautiful of the Cyclades, is traversed from north to south by a range of hills which fall away steeply on the

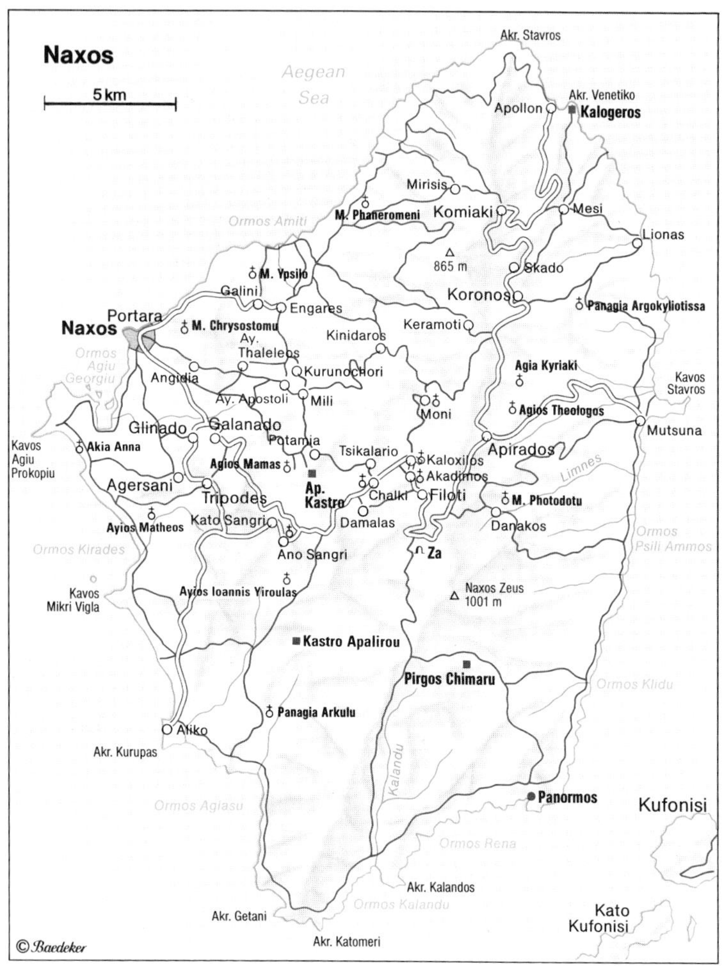

east but slope down gradually on the west into fertile rolling country and well-watered plains. The hills rise to a height of 1003m/3291ft in Mt Zas (ancient Drios) and are cut by two passes. The economy of the island has depended since ancient times on agriculture, marble-quarrying, emery-mining and the recovery of salt from the sea, which have brought it a considerable degree of prosperity. With its limited hotel resources, the island is not yet equipped to cope with mass tourism, but it has much to offer visitors – an equable climate, a wide variety of scenery and monuments of antiquity and the Middle Ages.

Myth and history

Náxos was a centre of the cult of Dionysos. It was here, according to the legend, that Theseus abandoned Ariadne.

There is much archaeological evidence to show that the island was first settled by Carians and Cretans and developed a flourishing Cycladic culture in the 3rd and 2nd millennia B.C. In the 1st millennium these first settlers were followed by Ionian Greeks, who in the 6th century B.C. extended their rule over Páros, Ándros and other neighbouring islands. During this period there was a celebrated school of sculptors on Náxos, notable for such works as the colossal statue of Apollo on Delos (see entry). A member of the first Attic maritime league, Náxos became subject to Athens after an unsuccessful rising and was compelled to accept the redistribution of land on the island to Athenian citizens. In spite of this it became a member of the second Attic maritime league. After being held by Macedon it passed under Egyptian rule, was briefly assigned to Rhodes by Mark Antony and thereafter became part of the Byzantine Empire.

In 1207 Náxos was occupied by a Venetian nobleman, Marco Sanudo, who made it capital of the duchy of the Twelve Islands (duchy of Náxos), which flourished until 1566. It was taken by the Turks in 1579 and was under Russian rule from 1770 to 1774, but, like the other Cyclades, retained a measure of independence. In 1830 it joined the newly established kingdom of Greece.

Náxos Town

The island's capital, Náxos (pop. 2500), in a fertile district in which vines, fruit and vegetables are grown, is picturesquely situated on the slopes of a rocky hill crowned by a ruined Venetian castle, the Kástro (1260; panoramic views), which now houses a school run by Ursuline nuns. Other features of interest in the town are a number of dilapidated Venetian palaces (in particular the Barozzi and Sommaripa palaces), the Roman Catholic church of St Mary (13th c.) and the 15th century chapel of Áyios Antónios on the harbour. Excavations beside the principal Orthodox church have brought to light Hellenistic stoas and evidence of Cycladic culture.

★ Museum

There is an interesting museum with archaeological material from all periods of the island's history, including a fine collection of stone vessels and Cycladic idols of the 3rd millennium B.C., pottery of the Geometric, Archaic and later periods, statues and capitals. In the courtyard are stones carved with Venetian coats of arms and a large mosaic of Europa and the bull.

★ *Marble doorway*

Náxos Town occupies the site of the ancient capital of the island, the main visible relics of which are a 6m/20ft high marble doorway and the foundations of an unfinished temple of Apollo or Dionysos (6th c. B.C.) on the rocky islet of Sto Paláti, which is connected with the main island by a stone causeway.

North-east of the town is the old fortified monastery of St John Chrysostom.
10km/6 miles north-east of Náxos is the white Faneroméni monastery, with a church of 1603.

Excursion to the Marble Quarries

Above Apollónia Bay, to the south-east of Cape Stávros, the northernmost tip of the island (40km/25 miles from Náxos Town), are a number of ancient quarries of the Naxian marble which was used in sculpture and architecture and also as a roof cladding.

★ Ston Apollona

In the Ston Apollona quarry is the 10.4m/34ft long figure of a kouros, left unfinished because of a defect in the marble. Above the quarry is the Venetian castle of Kalóyero.
The characteristic coarse-grained Naxian marble also outcrops between Mélanes and Potamiá, farther south, where there are other unfinished kouroi and a door-jamb (which was presumably destined for the Sto Paláti castle).
On the slopes of the Vóthri valley can be seen large emery mines which were already being worked in ancient times.

Other Features of Interest

Kimáro Tower

Below the south-east side of Mt Zas is the marble tower of Kimáro (Hellenistic). On the west side of the hill is the Cave of Zeus, an ancient cult site.

Venetian castles

Also worth visiting are the Venetian castles of Ápano Kástro (2km/1¼ miles from Khalkí; 13th c.), Áno Potamiá (south-east of Náxos town; guide needed), Apaliros (in the south-west of the island) and Cape Panerimos (south-east of the island).

Tower houses

Characteristic of the Venetian and Turkish periods on Náxos are the fortified tower houses (*pyryi*) to be seen, for example, at Khalkí (15km/9 miles east of Náxos town) and in the Drimália valley.

Churches

Many churches on the island have Byzantine wall paintings, notably Áyios Kýriakos at Apíranthos (where there is a small museum with Cycladic material of the 3rd millennium B.C.) and Áyios Artemios at Sangrí (9th c. frescoes).

Nekromanteion of Ephyra E 4

Νεκρομαντείον Εφύρας
Nekromandíon Efýras

Region: Epirus
Nomos: Préveza

Situation

The only oracle of the dead (nekromanteion) so far discovered lies just outside the village of Mesopótamos, near the west coast of Epirus.
The village can be reached on the new road which runs south from Igoumenítsa (51km/32 miles: see entry) or from the port of Párga (24km/14 miles: see entry).

★Nekromanteion

The road to the Nekromanteion branches off on the left just before the entrance to the village. The land now occupied by rice-fields was formerly Lake Akherousia, which has been drained and taken into cultivation. Through the lake flowed Acheron, the river of the dead, which rises in the Tomaris hills and flows into the sea to the west. The Acheron and the Kokytos, flowing down from the north, formed a right angle, in which the ancients saw the entrance to the underworld; and the existence of an oracle of the dead here is referred to as early as Homer.
This cult site, situated on a conical hill under a chapel of St John, was excavated by Sotir Dakaris between 1958 and 1964. It belonged to the

city of Ephyra, a short distance away to the north. According to Herodotus this was the setting of the myth of Orpheus and Eurydice. Material found here and at Ephyra dates back to the Mycenaean period (14th–13th c. B.C.), but nothing is known of the early period of the oracular cult: the buildings excavated date only from about 300 B.C., and were destroyed in 198 B.C. They do, however, agree with the description given by Homer much earlier (8th c. B.C.) of Odysseus consulting the dead ("Odyssey", 10, 516 ff., and 11, 24 ff.). The excavator stresses the accuracy of Homer's topographical information (though his reference to the Cimmerians is an error for the Cheimerioi, a local Thesprotian people).
A late satirical description of the consultation of the dead is given by Lucian in his "Menippos".

Approaching the site from the west, we enter a courtyard surrounded by the remains of later (3rd c. B.C.) buildings, at the south end of which, near a medieval tower house, is a Mycenaean cist tomb. The way into the inner shrine, which was probably windowless, leads along a succession of corridors (originally roofed) at right angles to one another. To the left of the north corridor are a number of rooms in which those who wanted to consult the oracle prepared themselves by a period of meditation and the use of some kind of stimulant. Beyond this are the east corridor and the south corridor, which is broken up by internal walls into a kind of labyrinth or maze. Turning right again, we come into the inmost shrine, which measures 21.8m/71½ft by 21.65m/71ft. Its polygonal walls, fitted together with great accuracy, are 3.3m/11ft thick and still stand 3.25m/10½ft high. It consists of a central aisle and two lateral aisles, each divided into three parts, which contained pithoi (storage jars) for corn and honey and clay figures of Persephone. Through an opening in the floor of the central aisle offerings of food for the shades were deposited in the vaulted crypt below, which was held to be the uppermost part of the underground palace of Hades and Persephone. Wheels found here by the excavators pointed to some kind of mechanism by which the priest could cause figures of the dead to appear before worshippers consulting the oracle.

By climbing up on to the walls of the sanctuary it is possible to look into the chapel of St John, which is supported on concrete piers inserted by the excavators, and to enjoy an extensive view over the Acherousian plain and the sea, with the Paxí group of islands (see entry) lying offshore.

Nemea E 4

Νεμέα
Neméa

Region: Peloponnese
Nomos: Corinth
Altitude: 320m/1050ft

Transport

The ancient site lies 4km/2½ miles west of the Neméa station on the Corinth–Árgos railway line and the main road which runs parallel with the railway.

Situation and characteristics

The name of Nemea, near the modern village of Iráklion in the north-western Argolid, is linked with one of the labours of Herakles, the killing of the Nemean lion, and with a sanctuary of Zeus. It is also the place where, according to an ancient tradition, the seer Amphiaraos founded the Nemean Games in 1251 B.C., during the expedition of the Seven against Thebes. This took place on the occasion of the funeral ceremony for the king's infant son Opheltes, who was left unattended by his nurse when she went to show the Seven a spring and was fatally bitten by a snake. The Nemean Games were revived in 573 B.C. and thereafter were held in alternate years until the 2nd century B.C., when they were transferred to Árgos.

The Site

★ Temple

The main feature of the site is a Doric temple, originally with 6 × 12 very slender columns, three of which still stand, forming a prominent landmark. The temple was built in the 4th century B.C. on the site of an earlier Archaic temple (of which the crypt survives). Outside the east end can be seen the tufa substructure of an altar. To the south of the temple were a long guest-house or hostel (20m/66ft by 86m/282ft), over which a three-aisled Christian basilica was built in the 5th century, a palaistra and baths of the Hellenistic period, near the remains of which is a museum.

Stadion

Recent American excavations have revealed the Stadion.

Surroundings of Nemea

Dervenáki pass

Beyond the turning for Nemea the Corinth–Árgos road reaches the Dervenáki pass. In a gorge near here Greek forces led by Kolokotronis defeated a much larger Turkish army under Dramali Pasha in August 1822.

Phlious
Kaliáni

Going west from the site of Nemea, we come in 15km/9 miles to the site of ancient Phlious (remains of polygonal wall of acropolis on the right of the road). 26km/16 miles beyond this is Kaliáni, on the north side of the Stymphalian Lake, the scene of one of the labours of Herakles.

Nikopolis E 4

Νικόπολη
Nikópoli

Region: Epirus
Nomos: Préveza

Situation

The extensive remains of ancient Nikopolis, the "Victory City" founded by Octavian, the future Emperor Augustus, after his victory at Actium (Áktion) in 31 B.C., lie 6km/4 miles north of the port of Préveza (see entry) on the road to Árta (see entry), on the peninsula between the Ionian Sea and the Ambracian Gulf.

History

After the defeat of Caesar's murderers, Brutus and Cassius, by Octavian and Antony at Philippi in 42 B.C. Antony contrived, with the help of the Egyptian queen, Cleopatra, to make himself master of the eastern half of the Roman Empire. The decisive engagement in the conflict between Octavian and Antony took place on September 2nd 31 B.C., when Octavian's fleet, under the command of Agrippa, annihilated Antony and Cleopatra's fleet as it attempted to break out of the Ambra-

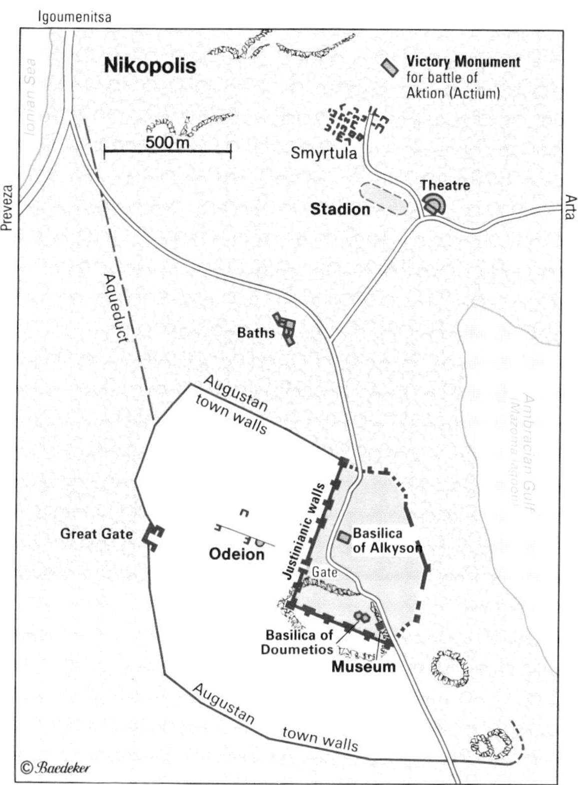

cian Gulf. Octavian thus became sole ruler of the Empire, and four years later adopted the style of Augustus. The town of Nikopolis was founded on the site of his camp and populated with settlers from the surrounding area, from as far afield as Árta. The 13th Pope, Eleutherius (174–189), was a native of Nikopolis. After being destroyed by the Visigoths in 397 and the Vandals in 474 the town was rebuilt, on a smaller scale, by Justinian.

The ★Site

Coming from Árta, we first see, on the right of the road, the massive Roman theatre and, some distance farther on, the Stadion, overgrown by scrub. We then cross the (barely visible) line of the Augustan town walls and see on the right, running parallel with the road, the inner side of Justinian's walls, which are reminiscent of the land walls of Constantinople with their towers and gates and their alternation of stone and brick in the masonry. Then come, immediately to the left of the road, the considerable remains of the Basilica of Alkyson, named after Bishop Alkyson (d. 516).

Town walls

Basilica of Alkyson

Remains of Justinian's walls

Odeion
Basilica of Doumetios

After a bend in the road, where a path goes off on the right to the Roman Odeion (recently completely restored), we see on the right, on rather higher ground, the three-aisled Basilica of Doumetios, with fine mosaics and inscriptions in the name of Bishop Doumetios (= Demetrius) dating from about 540. Just beyond this is the Museum: notable among the exhibits are a good portrait head of Agrippa and a circular base of the Roman period, with a relief of Amazons partly covered by Christian mosaics, which was re-used as an ambo in the Basilica of Alkyson.

Museum

Surroundings of Nikopolis

6km/4 miles south is the port of Préveza (see entry), with Áktion opposite it on the south side of the Ambracian Gulf.
29km/18 miles from Nikopolis, on the right of the road to Árta (44km/27 miles), the fortress of Rógi (13th c.), built on ancient foundations by the Despots of Árta, rears out of the plain.

Kassope

18km/11 miles from Nikopolis on the road to Igoumenítsa is Kamarina, with remains of ancient Kassope (small theatre, stoa). From here it is possible to continue to the Nekromanteion of Ephyra, near Mesopótamos, and the seaside resort of Párga (see entries).

Nisyros M 7

Νίσυρος
Nísyros

Nomos: Dodecanese
Area of island: 41 sq.km/16 sq. miles
Altitude: 0–698m/0–2290ft
Population: 2000
Chief place: Mandráki

Boat services

Regular weekly service from and to Athens (Piraeus) and Rhodes. Local connections in Dodecanese: Rhodes– Sými – Tílos – Nísyros – Kos – Kálymnos – Léros – Lipsí – Pátmos – Arkí – Agathonísi – Sámos.

Situation and characteristics

The island of Nísyros, lying half way between Kos and Tílos, 18km/11 miles south-west of the Reşadiye (Knidos) peninsula in Asia Minor, is formed by an extinct volcano, Mt Diabates, which was still occasionally active in the Middle Ages and erupted in 1522, but now manifests itself only in the form of solfataras (sulphureous vapours). It is a green and well watered island, with fertile pumice soil which is cultivated on laboriously constructed terraces on seaward-facing slopes. Pumice is exported.

A biological research station is in course of being established.

History

Nísyros was originally settled by Dorians from Kos and Kameiros. In 1312 it was occupied by the Knights of St John, and later became a fief of the Assanti family. It was taken by the Turks in 1533.

Sights

Mandráki

The island's capital and principal port, Mandráki (pop. 1200; thermal springs), lies on the north coast. Above the little town, to the west, is the castle of the Knights of St John, now a monastery. Within the precincts of the castle is the Late Byzantine cave church of the Panayía Spilianí. To the south is the Palaiokástro, with impressive and well preserved remains of walls and flights of steps belonging to the Hellenistic city (4th–3rd c. B.C.).

Páli

Emporió

3km/2 miles east of Mandráki is the little port of Páli or Thérma, with hot sulphurous springs (remains of ancient baths). From here it is an hour's climb to the hilltop village of Emporió, with a medieval castle (fine views), and a further hour's walk along the rim of a volcanic crater (alt. 410–570m/1345–1870ft; diameter 2700–3800m/2950–4150yds) to Nikiá (see below).

Caldera

In the caldera of the volcano is the little plain of Lakkí (alt. 139m/456ft), the northern part of which is cultivated, while the southern half is covered with bubbling hot springs and mud pools, brightly coloured concretions and steaming fumaroles. On the west side is a small crater which is the highest point on the island (698m/2290ft).

Nikiá

An hour's walk south of the crater is the beautifully situated village of Nikiá, with a medieval castle.

Other medieval castles are Sto Stavró, in the south of the island, and Parkettiá, in the south-east.

Yialí

Off the north coast of Nísyros in the direction of Kos is the little obsidian island of Yialí (Gyalí; area 6 sq.km/2¼ sq. miles; alt. 0–177m/0–581ft; pumice quarry). To the west are the islets of Pasikiá

Palaiokástro

and Peroúsa, both with ancient watch-towers, and Kandelioúsa (area 2 sq.km/¾ sq. mile; alt. 0–103m/0–338ft; lighthouse).

Northern and Eastern Aegean Islands I–L 3–5

The islands of Chios, Lésbos, Lemnos, Samothrace and Thásos, scattered in the northern and eastern Aegean, do not form a group in any real sense. Each has an individuality of its own.

History

The history of this region reaches far back into the past. The site of Thermí on Lésbos was occupied about 2700 B.C., and Polióknni on Lemnos is older than its neighbour Troy. During the Greek colonising movement Aeolians came to Lésbos about 1100 B.C., Ionians to Chios about 1000 and to Lemnos about 800. Around 700 B.C. colonies were established on Thásos (from Páros) and Samothrace. The islands enjoyed a period of prosperity in the 7th and 6th centuries, when Lésbos produced the singers Terpandros and Arion and the poets Sappho and Alkaios, and Chios a fine school of sculptors. After a period of Persian rule (546–479 B.C.) the islands became members of the first Attic maritime league; then from the 4th century onwards they came successively under Macedonian, Ptolemaic and Roman influence.

After the 4th Crusade (1204) the islands belonged to Venice and later to Genoa. Then came the Turkish period, which lasted until 1912. In 1922–23 Lésbos and Chios took in many refugees from Asia Minor, and after the Second World War many Greeks from Egypt settled on Lemnos.

In recent years Turkey has put forward claims to the Anatolian continental shelf, of which Chios and Lésbos form part.

Olympia F 6

Ολυμπία
Olymbía

Region: Peloponnese
Nomos: Elis
Altitude: 60m/195ft
Population: 1100

Transport

Branch railway line Pýrgos–Olympia.

Situation and characteristics

Olympia, lying in the angle between the rivers Alpheios and Kladeos, was a great Panhellenic sanctuary, the venue of the Olympic Games. German excavations from 1875 onwards, which led to the establishment of the present village of Olympia, brought to light the sacred precinct which was known in antiquity as the Altis (the sacred grove) and is now again planted with trees. Situated at the foot of the wooded Mt Kronos in an area of gentle hills, the site of ancient Olympia – one of the great achievements of archaeological excavation – makes an impact on the present-day visitor which is fully commensurate with its importance in ancient times. A direct consequence of the excavation was the revival of the Olympic Games by Baron Pierre de Coubertin, the first Games of modern times being held in Athens in 1896.

History

Potsherds of the 3rd millennium B.C. and apsidal houses of the 2nd millennium bear witness to the early settlement of the site. Later the houses gave place to a sanctuary of Zeus which was associated with the older cult of Hera. Olympia lay within the territory of King Oinomaos of Pisa, who was succeeded by Pelops after his victory in a chariot race and his marriage to Oinomaos's daughter Hippodameia. A column from the palace of Oinomaos and the grave mound of Pelops (who gave his name to the Peloponnese) were still being shown to visitors when Pausanias visited the site in the 2nd century A.D.

The Olympic Games probably began as a local funerary celebration in honour of Pelops. The Greeks believed that Herakles had laid down the regulations for the Games and had specified the length of the stadion as 600 feet (192 m). The first historical reference to the Games is in 776 B.C., when a treaty between kings Iphitos of Elis and Lykourgos of Sparta provided for an Olympic truce (*ekecheiria*) during the summer Games.

From 776 B.C. onwards lists were kept of the winners in the foot race round the Stadion, giving rise to the Greek system of chronological reckoning by olympiads (i.e. periods of four years). Other events were added later – in the 8th century the two-stade race, the long-distance race and the pentathlon, in the 7th century boxing, chariot-racing and the pankration, in the 6th century a race with weapons. The winners received a branch from the sacred olive-tree, but could also expect substantial material rewards (for example meals at public expense) on their return to their native city. The finishing line of the race round the Stadion was originally near the temple of Zeus, in front of which, facing the runners, was Paionios's statue of Nike (Victory) – underlining the religious significance of the race, victory in which was granted by Zeus, the supreme god of the Greek pantheon. Only in the 4th century B.C. was the Stadion moved 80m/88yds east and separated from the Altis.

After their heyday in the 5th century B.C. the Games gradually declined; the religious element became steadily less prominent, and

eventually the Games were contested by professional athletes. They were finally banned by the Emperor Theodosius, and came to an end in A.D. 393 after an existence of more than a thousand years.

The ★★Site

The road from the village of Olympia crosses the Kladeos on a modern bridge and comes to the large car park.
Entering the site, we see on the left the Prytaneion, in which the victors were entertained with a banquet, and on the right the Gymnasion, with a propylon at the south-east corner (2nd c. B.C.; only east end preserved), and the Palaistra (3rd c. B.C.), the columns of which have been re-erected. Beyond this, on a site originally occupied by 5th century baths, is the Workshop of Pheidias, which was later converted into a church. In this workshop, which was exactly the same size as the naos of the temple of Zeus, Pheidias created (438 B.C. onwards) the huge chryselephantine cult statue of Zeus. Continuing south, we come to the Leonidaion, at the south-west corner of the excavated area. Originally built by Leonidas of Naxos in the second half of the 4th century B.C. as a large hostel for the accommodation of visitors to the sanctuary, this was altered in Roman times to a new layout in which the living quarters were set round an inner court with a garden and fountains and surrounded externally by Ionic colonnades. To the east are the Southern Baths (2nd c. A.D.), the South Stoa (4th c. B.C.) and the Bouleuterion with its two apses (6th–5th c. B.C.). All these buildings lie outside the walls of the Altis.

Sacred Precinct (Altis)

★ Triangular pillar

We now enter the Sacred Precinct through a Roman gateway on the south side and see, beyond the triangular pillar which bore Paionios's figure of Victory (*c.* 425 B.C.) and the bases of numerous votive monuments, the temple of Zeus, built by Libon of Elis between 470 and 456 B.C., which has been called "the finest expression of the Doric canon" (Gruben). A ramp leads up to the entrance.

★★Temple of Zeus

Although the temple collapsed in an earthquake in the 6th century A.D. the massive remains still allow us to gain some idea of what it was like. On the three-stepped crepidoma (27.7m/91ft by 64.1m/210ft; completely preserved), supported on foundations 3m/10ft high, stood 6 × 13 columns, each 10.53m/34½ft high and 2.23m/7ft 4in in diameter at the base. The total height of the temple was about 20m/65ft. While the main structure was of muschelkalk limestone faced with stucco, Parian marble was used for the roof with its 102 lion's-head water-spouts and for the sculpture on the metopes and pediments. The sculpture (*c.* 460 B.C.) is masterly work in the Severe style (finds in Museum).

★ East pediment

On the east pediment Zeus stands in the middle, flanked by King Oinomaos, his wife Sterope, his daughter Hippodameia and Hippodameia's future husband Pelops, before the chariot race in which Oinomaos lost both his throne and his life.

★ West pediment

The west pediment shows Zeus's son Apollo in the middle, intervening imperiously in the battle between Lapiths and Centaurs which

◄ *Ancient remains in a beautiful park-like setting*

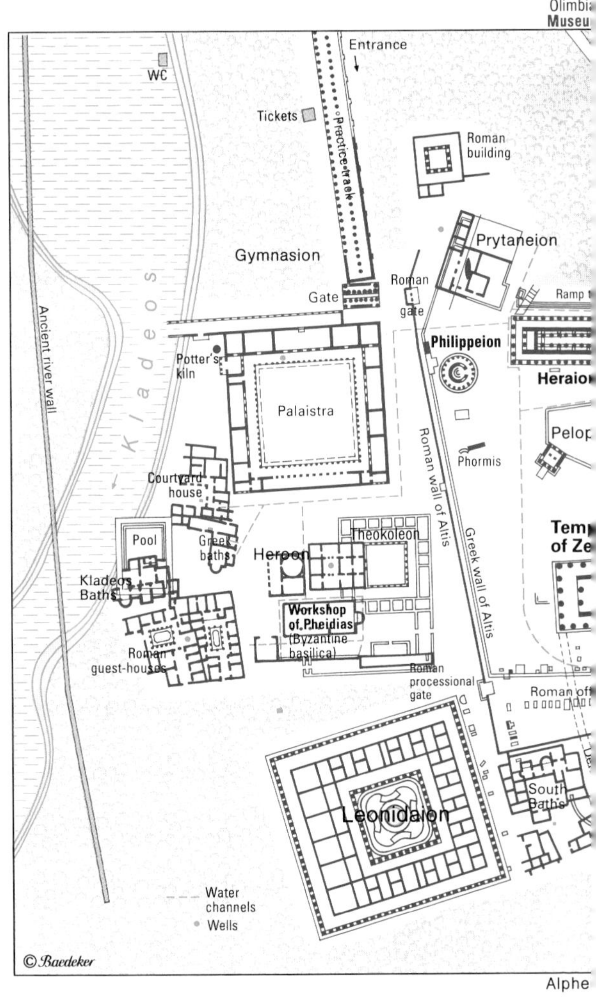

flared up at the marriage of Theseus's friend Peirithoos with Deidameia. Here the sculptor has broken the scene up into groups of two and three, whose violent movement is in sharp contrast to the tense tranquillity of the east pediment.

★ Metopes

The metopes above the pronaos and opisthodomos depict the twelve labours of Herakles. Particularly fine are the metopes of Atlas and Augeias; some of the others are heavily restored or are casts of

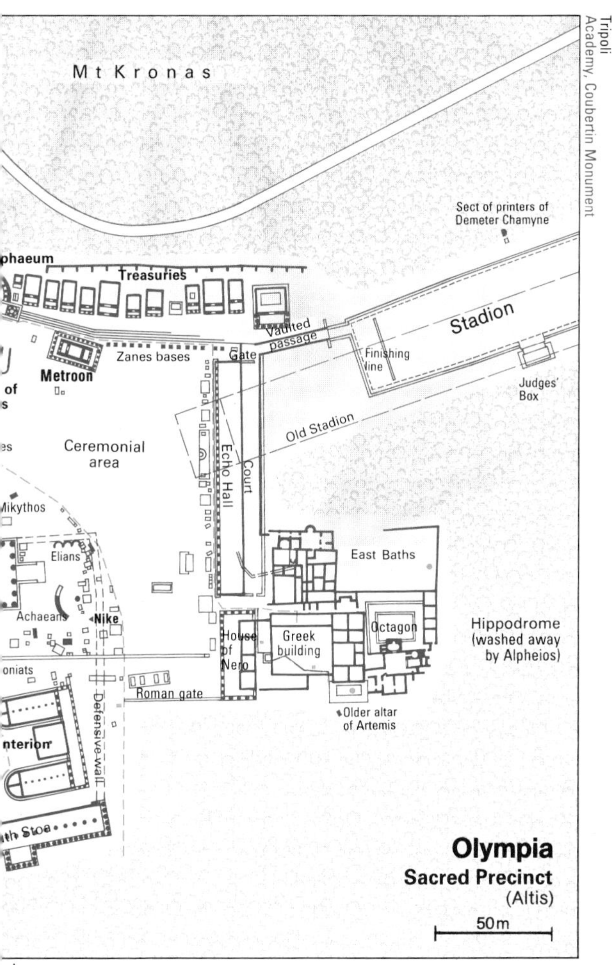

the originals (which were carried off by the French Expédition de Morée and are now in the Louvre).

The naos of the temple, in the pronaos of which is a mosaic of the 4th or 3rd century B.C., had two rows of columns and housed the cult image of Zeus (after 438 B.C.). This huge chryselephantine statue, which depicted Zeus sitting on a richly decorated throne, was counted among the seven wonders of the world. (See suggested reconstruction, page 65.)

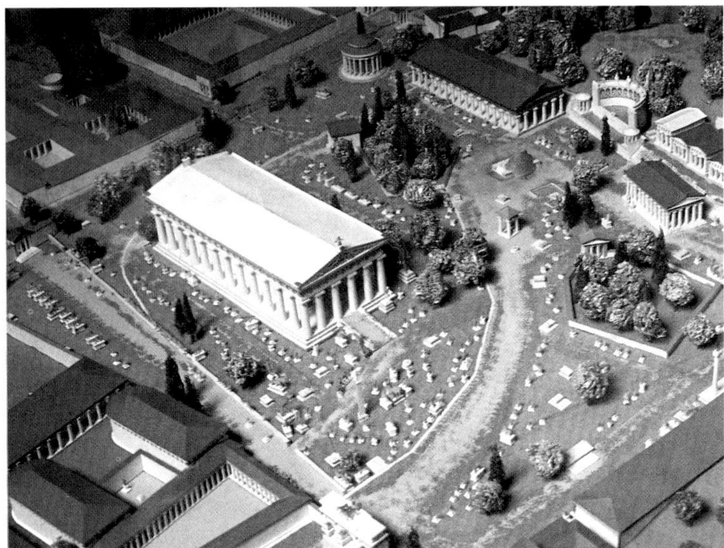

Model of the Sacred Precinct (Altis)

★Heraion

North of the temple of Zeus was the supposed tomb of Pelops, the Pelopion (foundations of propylon preserved). Beyond this, parallel to the temple of Zeus, is the oldest temple of Olympia, the Heraion (*c.* 600 B.C.). This Doric temple of Hera had 6 × 16 columns 5.2m/17ft high, four of which have been re-erected. The shafts and capitals of the columns show considerable variety, since the original wooden columns were replaced by stone columns at different times as the need arose, so that the luxuriant Archaic types of echinus can be seen side by side with the severer forms of a later period. The naos walls were built of the limestone orthostats which have been preserved, with upper courses of mud brick. Along each side were four short cross-walls or buttresses, with columns between them. In one of the recesses so formed, on the north side, the Hermes of Praxiteles was found.

Nymphaeum

Going east from the Heraion, we pass on the left the Nymphaeum (fountain-house) built by Herodes Atticus about A.D. 160 in memory of his wife Regilla, a priestess of Demeter, and in honour of the Imperial house. Beyond this is a terrace at the foot of Mt Kronos with a row of treasuries, mostly in the form of small temples in antis, built by various Greek cities between the early 6th and the 5th century to house their votive offerings. Pausanias mentions ten. It is a striking fact that of the ten only two (those of Sikyon and Megara) were built by cities in Greece proper. Six belonged to cities of western Greece – Syracuse, Selinus and Gela in Sicily, Sybaris and Metapontion in southern Italy and Epidamnos (Durrës) in Albania – and the remaining two to Kyrene in North Africa and Byzantium.

★Treasuries

At the west end of the terrace, immediately adjoining the Nymphaeum of Herodes Atticus, is a small naiskos (3.9m/13ft by 3.5m/11½ft), with an altar in front of it. Then follow the treasuries, beginning with that of Sikyon, the last to be built (first half of 5th c. B.C.), which has recently been partly rebuilt. Beyond this are the treasuries of Syracuse, Epidamnos, Byzantium, Sybaris and Kyrene, a structure which is thought to be an altar of Herakles, and finally the treasuries of Selinus, Metapontion, Megara and Gela.

Metroon

Immediately below the terrace with the treasuries is the site of the badly ruined Metroon (*c.* 300 B.C.), a shrine of the Mother of the Gods which in Roman times was re-dedicated to the Imperial cult. Beside it are a series of bases for the "Zanes" – statues of Zeus which were financed out of fines levied for offences against the rules of the Games. Immediately beyond them is the entrance to the Stadion (*c.* 200 B.C.), the vaulting of which, still visible, was originally concealed by a propylon.

Stadion

The Stadion, which after the erection of the Echo Hall (330–320 B.C.) was separated from the Sacred Precinct, was completely excavated by German archaeologists in 1958–62 and restored to its 4th century form. On the track can be seen the starting-lines for the two-stade race (to the west) and the Stadion race (to the east). The spectators sat on earth embankments: there were no tiers of stone seating, and only the judges had their tribune on the south side and the priestess of Demeter – the only woman who was allowed to be present at the Games – on the north side.

Philippeion

On the way back we can see, near the west wall of the Altis, the Philippeion, a circular structure begun by Philip II of Macedon in 338 B.C. and completed by his son Alexander, for which Leochares carved five chryselephantine statues of the Macedonian royal family.

★★Museum

The Museum contains a large collection of bronzes, pottery and sculpture. The excavations in the Stadion in recent decades have proved extraordinarily productive, yielding many works which had originally been set up along the embankments. The forecourt of the museum, surrounded by concrete colonnades, gives a foretaste of what is to be seen inside.

The rooms are laid out round a central hall containing the pediment sculpture and metopes from the temple of Zeus. In the entrance hall (sale of tickets, literature, postcards and slides) is an interesting model of ancient Olympia.

The rooms are arranged clockwise, starting from the left. Room I contains bronzes of the Geometric and Archaic periods (9th–6th c. B.C.), including elements from tripods, figures of horses, weapons and small bronzes.

Room II contains more bronzes – helmets and weapons, griffins' heads (*c.* 600 B.C.), a relief of a female griffin suckling a young one (*c.* 620 B.C.), a relief depicting the Lapith Kaineus between two Centaurs (*c.* 630 B.C.) and a bronze breastplate with figures of Zeus and Apollo (*c.* 650 B.C.). This last piece was originally set up as a trophy on the south side of the Stadion. It was published by Adolf Furtwängler in 1890 but later disappeared; then in 1969 it turned up in Basle and was bought by Marinatos for 200,000 francs. Other interesting items in this room are a limestone head of the goddess Hera (?) of around 600 B.C. and a terracotta acroterion from the pediment of the Heraion.

In Room III are the treasuries of Gela, with the painted terracotta facing of the geison (*c.* 560 B.C.), and Megara (*c.* 510 B.C.).

Striking items in Room IV are a terracotta group of Zeus and Ganymede (*c.* 470 B.C.), an early classical bronze horse from a four-horse chariot and two helmets, one with an inscription recording that it was dedicated at Olympia in 490 B.C. by Miltiades, the victor of Marathon, the other a trophy of the Persian wars.

In Room V is a statue of Hermes with the boy Dionysos which is generally agreed to be an original work by Praxiteles (*c.* 350 B.C.).

Room VI contains the bull of Regilla, priestess of Demeter and wife of Herodes Atticus, which originally stood in the Nymphaeum of Herodes Atticus.

Among exhibits in the last room are items of sporting equipment (jumpers' weights, strigils, etc.).

Mount Olympus G 3

Όλυμπος
Ólymbos

Region: Thessaly/Macedonia
Nomos: Lárisa
Altitude: 2917m/9571ft

View, looking towards Olympus, in spring

The highest mountain in Greece, lying near the sea on the borders of Macedonia and Thessaly, is the most famous of a number of mountains bearing the pre-Greek name of Olympus in Greece, Asia Minor and Cyprus. It already features in Homer ("Iliad", 5, 361) as the home of the gods, who were accordingly known as the Olympians.

★ Landscape

This mighty massif, covering an area some 20km/12½ miles across, climbs steeply up towards the summit, reaching its highest point in Mítikas (2917m/9571ft). The highest ridges are difficult to climb: more easily accessible is the most northerly peak (2787m/9144ft), on which there is a chapel of Profítis Ilías (Elijah). On the Áyios Antónios peak (2817m/9243ft), to the south of Mítikas, a shrine of Zeus has been excavated, yielding remains of sacrifices, pottery, inscriptions and coins. A shrine of Apollo was found on the west side of the mountain at an altitude of 700m/2300ft.
The best starting-point for the ascent of Olympus is Lítókhoron (see entry), under its east side.

Ossa

Separated from Mount Olympus by the Vale of Tempe (see entry) rises Mt Ossa (1978m/6490ft), part of the range which cuts Thessaly off from the sea. There is a mountain hut on the summit. The best starting-points for the ascent of Ossa are the mountain villages of Ambelákia, above the west end of the Vale of Tempe (on the north-west side of the hill) and Ayiá (on the south-east side).

Olynthos H 3

Όλυνθος
Ólynthos

Region and nomos: Chalcidice

Situation

The ancient city of Olynthos lay on the south coast of Chalcidice at the head of the long gulf between the Kassándra and Sithoniá peninsulas. The remains can be seen 8km/5 miles west of the seaside resort of Yerakíni.

History

Evidence of human occupation in this area dates back to around 2500 B.C. Later, about 800 B.C., the site was occupied by Macedonians. After the destruction of the town in the Persian wars (480 B.C.) it was repopulated by settlers from Khalkís on Euboea and developed into the most important city in Chalcidice. In 348 B.C. Olynthos, then allied with Athens, was totally destroyed by Philip II of Macedon, and the site has remained uninhabited ever since.

The site

American excavations in 1928–34 revealed a rectangular street layout, public buildings and houses and produced valuable evidence of regular Greek town planning before 348 B.C. The site is now largely overgrown.

Pebble mosaics

Notable among the finds made here were early pebble mosaics (5th c. B.C.).

Orkhomenos G/H 5

Ορχομενός
Orkhomenós

Nomos: Boeotia
Altitude: 360m/1180ft
Population: 1800

Situation and characteristics

The little town of Orkhomenós, situated at the north end of a rocky ridge known in antiquity as Akontion and now called Dourdouvana, on the north-western margin of the Kopais plain in Boeotia, is of interest for its ancient remains and for the 9th century church of Skrípou (a village now incorporated in the town).
6km/4 miles north-west of Livadiá on the road to Lamía a side road branches off on the right to Orkhomenós, continuing to Kástro, on the Athens–Salonica expressway.

History

The site of ancient Orkhomenos was already occupied in Neolithic times. Later it became the capital of a Minyan principality which belonged to the Mycenaean cultural sphere. Homer refers to the wealth of the Minyans, and evidence of this is provided by a large tholos tomb dating from the heyday of the city (14th c. B.C.). In the 7th century Orkhomenos was overshadowed and finally conquered by Thebes. The site was refortified during the Macedonian period and was occupied into Byzantine times, when it was abandoned.

Sights

★ Tholos tomb

From the village of Skrípou a road runs north to the site of ancient Orkhomenos, at the east end of the Akontion ridge. In the lower part of the site, near the modern cemetery, the excavators found early circular structures, the tholos tomb already mentioned and two temples. The long triangular area of the site is divided up by two cross walls. At the western tip is the acropolis (alt. 228m/748ft).

Panayía church

Immediately east of the ancient site is the church of the Panayía of Skrípou, which according to an inscription in the apse was built by a high Imperial official called Leon in 873/874 on the site of an earlier 5th century church. This church is important as being the earliest example of a domed cruciform church in Greece. The walls contain many architectural fragments from ancient buildings.

Áyios Nikólaos

5km/3 miles north-east of Skrípou is another old church, Áyios Nikólaos sta Kámpia (St Nicholas in the Fields). Built about 1040 by the architect of the principal church at Ósios Loukás (see entry), it has a simplified version of the same ground-plan.

Osios Loukas G/H 5

Όσιος Λουκάς
Ósios Loukás

Region and nomos: Boeotia

Situation

The monastery of Ósios Loukás occupies an isolated situation in the Helikon range near the Gulf of Corinth. It is reached on a road (13km/8 miles) which runs south from the Livadiá–Delphi road by way of the village of Dístomo (rebuilt after its destruction during the Second World War). Its mosaics rank along with those of Dafní (see entry), near Athens, and the Néa Moní on Chios as the finest examples of 11th century mosaic art.

History

This St Luke – Ósios Loukás, as distinct from Áyios Loukás, the Evangelist – was born about 898 in Kastoriá, the village now known as

Monastery of Ósios Loukás

Kastrí on the site of Delphi, and lived from about 910 as a hermit in Phocis, where he died, much revered, on February 7th 953. Between 941 and 944 the Byzantine governor of the region built a chapel dedicated to St Barbara at his hermitage. Round this developed the monastery which now dominates its lonely surroundings with its two magnificent churches standing side by side.

The ★Monastery

St Barbara's Chapel

The chapel of St Barbara (Ayía Varvára) has been preserved as the crypt of the principal church. It contains the sarcophagus of St Luke and two other sarcophagi, traditionally believed to contain the remains of the Byzantine Emperor Romanos II (959–963) and Empress Theophano. There are a number of wall paintings, including a Last Supper (on the south side of the east wing).

Principal church
Church of Theotókos

The two churches, the principal church dedicated to St Luke and the other to the Theotókos (Mother of God), both follow the Middle Byzantine pattern of the domed cruciform church. The deep narthex (*lití*) of the church of the Theotókos is characteristic of a monastic church.
The monastery was damaged during the Second World War and was thoroughly restored between 1953 and 1962, particular attention being given to the splendid mosaics dating from the first half of the 11th century. In the course of the restoration work a number of windows which had previously been walled up were reopened, making the principal church lighter and enhancing the spatial effect.
Three factors contribute to the powerful effect of the principal church. As at Dafní and the Néa Moní, the large central dome, borne on eight piers, spans both the central and the lateral aisles; the marble facing of

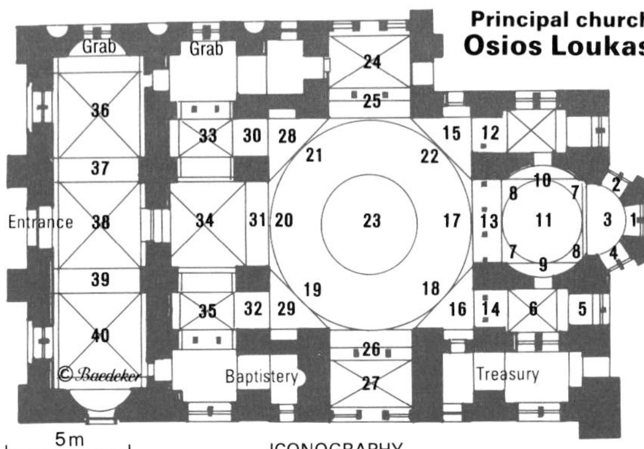

ICONOGRAPHY

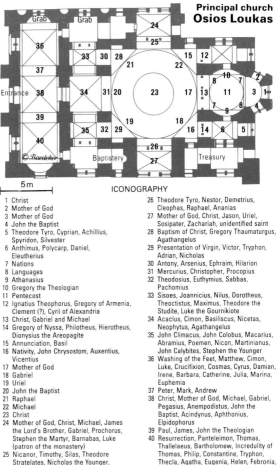

1 Christ
2 Mother of God
3 Mother of God
4 John the Baptist
5 Theodore Tyro, Cyprian, Achillius, Spyridon, Silvester
6 Anthimus, Polycarp, Daniel, Eleutherius
7 Nations
8 Languages
9 Athanasius
10 Gregory the Theologian
11 Pentecost
12 Ignatius Theophorus, Gregory of Armenia, Clement (?), Cyril of Alexandria
13 Christ, Gabriel and Michael
14 Gregory of Nyssa, Philotheus, Hierotheus, Dionysius the Areopagite
15 Annunciation, Basil
16 Nativity, John Chrysostom, Auxentius, Vicentius
17 Mother of God
18 Gabriel
19 Uriel
20 John the Baptist
21 Raphael
22 Michael
23 Christ
24 Mother of God, Christ, Michael, James the Lord's Brother, Gabriel, Prochorus, Stephen the Martyr, Barnabas, Luke (patron of the monastery)
25 Nicanor, Timothy, Silas, Theodore Stratelates, Nicholas the Younger, George
26 Theodore Tyro, Nestor, Demetrius, Cleophas, Raphael, Ananias
27 Mother of God, Christ, Jason, Uriel, Sosipater, Zachariah, unidentified saint
28 Baptism of Christ, Gregory Thaumaturgus, Agathangelus
29 Presentation of Virgin, Victor, Tryphon, Adrian, Nicholas
30 Antony, Arsenius, Ephraim, Hilarion
31 Mercurius, Christopher, Procopius
32 Theodosius, Euthymius, Sabbas, Pachomius
33 Sisoes, Joannicius, Nilus, Dorotheus, Theoctistus, Maximus, Theodore the Studite, Luke the Gournikiote
34 Acacius, Cimon, Basiliscus, Nicetas, Neophytus, Agathangelus
35 John Climacus, John Colobus, Macarius, Abramius, Poemen, Nicon, Martinianus, John Calybites, Stephen the Younger
36 Washing of the Feet, Matthew, Cimon, Luke, Crucifixion, Cosmas, Cyrus, Damian, Irene, Barbara, Catherine, Julia, Marina, Euphemia
37 Peter, Mark, Andrew
38 Christ, Mother of God, Michael, Gabriel, Pegasius, Anempodistus, John the Baptist, Acindynus, Aphthonius, Elpidophorus
39 Paul, James, John the Theologian
40 Resurrection, Panteleimon, Thomas, Thallelaeus, Bartholomew, Incredulity of Thomas, Philip, Constantine, Tryphon, Thecla, Agatha, Eugenia, Helen, Febronia, Anastasia

the walls – missing at Dafní – has been preserved; and most of the mosaics, which were the work of artists from Constantinople and are of the highest quality, have been preserved or restored.

★★ Mosaics

The subjects of the mosaics, which are notable for their dramatic vigour, are arranged according to the hierarchical rules which had been established by the 9th century. In the narthex are scenes from the Passion, together with figures of angels, saints and the Evangelists. Over the doorway into the church is a figure of Christ as the Light of the

World. The mosaic of Christ in the central dome was destroyed when the dome collapsed in 1593.
In the squinches under the dome are the Nativity (SE), the Presentation in the Temple (SW) and the Baptism of Christ (NW). In the dome over the sanctuary are the Etimasia (the Preparation of the Throne) and the Descent of the Holy Ghost (Pentecost), in the apse the Mother of God as Panayía Platytéra.
In the north aisle, on the left, is a portrait-like figure of Ósios Loukás, who is given the style of saint, though he was never officially canonised. Opposite is the shrine containing the saint's relics, directly above his sarcophagus in the crypt.
In addition to St Luke other saints of the period of only local importance are included in the iconographic scheme, among them St Nikon Metanoeite, who evangelised Sparta (west end of south aisle) and St Luke the Gournikiote (west end of north aisle).

In the monastic buildings, which include the monks' refectory (trápeza), there is a small café (near the entrance, on the left).

Othonian Islands D 4

Nomos: Kérkyra

Situation

The Othonian Islands are an archipelago in the northern Ionian Sea, north-west of Corfu (Kérkyra), consisting of a number of islets which are either uninhabited or only occasionally inhabited – Othoni (Italian Faro; lighthouse), Erikousa (Italian Merlera), Mathraki and Diaplo. The island of Calypso was believed to be one of the islands in this group.

Parga

Parga E 4

Πάργα
Párga

Nomos: Préveza
Altitude: 10m/35ft
Population: 1700

Transport

Bus services from Athens, Préveza and Igoumenítsa. Yacht supply station.

★ Situation and characteristics

Beautifully situated at the foot of a 16th century Venetian castle in a bay on the west coast of Greece between Igoumenítsa and Préveza – a stretch of coast with few harbours – Párga is an ideal place for a seaside holiday. There are sandy beaches along the bay and beyond the crag on which the castle stands, and rocky coasts on the little offshore islands.
Párga, 50km/31 miles from Igoumenítsa, is reached from the Igoumenítsa–Préveza road, turning off at Morfí (38km/24 miles).

Surroundings of Párga

24km/15 miles south-east, rising out of the Akheron plain, is the Nekromanteion of Ephyra (see entry).

14km/8½ miles north of Morfí lies the village of Paramythiá, dominated by a Turkish fortress.

At the foot of Parnassus, near Arákhova

Mount Parnassus

G 5

Παρνασσός
Parnassós

Region and nomos: Phocis
Altitude: 2457m/8061ft

Situation and characteristics

Mount Parnassus, a limestone massif near Delphi rising to a height of 2457m/8061ft, was sacred to Apollo and Dionysos, and in Roman times was regarded as the home of the Muses.
The area, with extensive coniferous forests, is still largely rugged and inhospitable.

From the village of Arákhova (see Delphi, Surroundings) an asphalted road winds its way up into the hills. At the end of the road is a chair-lift to a mountain hut at 1900m/6235ft, from which there is a further lift to the skiing area below the summit plateau.

Mount Parnis

H 5

Πάρνηθα
Párnitha

Region and nomos: Attica
Altitude: 1413m/4636ft

Situation and characteristics

Mount Párnis is a limestone hill (1413m/4636ft) in Attica, north of Athens, with large areas of coniferous forest, which is frequently snow-capped well into spring. On the summit there was an ancient shrine of Zeus, the Rain-Bringer. The hill attracts many visitors, both for the sake of its climate and for the extensive views it affords.
There is a casino in the Hotel Mont Parnis.

Mount Parnon

G 6

Πάρνωνας
Párnonas

Region: Peloponnese
Nomoi: Laconia and Arcadia

Situation and characteristics

The Párnon range extends along the east side of the Peloponnese for a distance of some 90km/56 miles from north to south, separating the Laconian plain around Sparta from the Argolic Gulf. The northern part of the range consists of schists, the southern part of limestone and marble. Only at Ástros is there a small alluvial plain (the plain of Kynouriá) between the high ground and the sea. The range ends at Cape Maléa in the south-east.

This isolated region is still occupied by Tzakonians, who preserve some remnants of the old Dorian dialect. Along the east coast are a number of small places, beginning in the north with Kivéri, where some years ago a freshwater spring was discovered in the sea. Then follow Ástros, with the coastal resort of Paralía Týrou 4km/2½ miles away; the little ports of Leonídi and Kyparíssi; and finally the little town of Monemvasía (see entry) with its castle. The coastal boats sailing between Piraeus and Gýthion call at Kyparíssi and Monemvasía.

Paros K 6/7

Πάρος
Páros

Nomos: Cyclades
Area of island: 186 sq.km/72 sq. miles
Altitude: 0–771m/0–2530ft
Population: 8500
Chief place: Páros (Parikía)

Air services

Regular flights from Athens, several times daily; also from Iráklion (Crete) and Rhodes.

Boat services

Regular service from and to Athens (Piraeus), several times daily (cars carried).
Local connections, daily, with the neighbouring islands of Náxos, Ios, Santorin, Sýros and Antíparos.

Situation and characteristics

Páros, lying some 8km/5 miles west of Náxos, is occupied by a range of hills of gently rounded contours, rising to 771m/2530ft in Mt Profítis Ilías (rewarding climb, with guide; magnificent panoramic views). Three bays cut deep inland – in the west the sheltered Parikía Bay, with the island's capital; in the north an even more sheltered bay with the little town of Naoúsa (pop. 1400), which in Roman times was the island's main port for the shipment of the island's Lychnites marble; and in the east the shallow Mármare Bay. The whole island is covered with a layer of coarse-grained crystalline limestone, in which lie rich beds of pure white marble.

The island's considerable prosperity has depended since ancient times on agriculture, favoured by fertile soil and an abundance of water, and on the working of marble, which is still quarried on a small scale. In recent years the rapid development of the tourist trade has brought changes in the island's landscape, economy and social structure.

History

Excavations on the islet of Saliangos, which was once joined to Páros, have yielded evidence of settlement in the late Neolithic period (5th–4th millennium B.C.).
The island, which has preserved its ancient name, was already well populated in the age of the Cycladic culture (3rd millennium B.C.). In the 1st millennium B.C. Ionian Greeks settled on Paros and made it a considerable sea power, minting its own coins, and in the 7th century B.C. Paros founded colonies on Thasos and in Thrace. In the 6th and 5th centuries Paros was celebrated for its school of sculptors. It was a member of the first Attic maritime league, and its unusually large contributions to the league (30 talents in 425 B.C.) are evidence of its wealth in the 5th century B.C.
In Hellenistic, Roman and Byzantine times Paros was of no importance. In the 9th century A.D. it was depopulated as a result of raids by Arab pirates who ravaged and plundered the island. From 1207 to 1389 it belonged to the duchy of Náxos, and thereafter was ruled by various dynasts until its conquest by the Turks in 1537. It was reunited with Greece in 1832, after the establishment of the new Greek kingdom.

Windmill, Parikía

Sights

Páros town (Parikía)

The island's chief town, Páros or Parikía (pop. 3000), lies on the west coast, on the site of the ancient capital. The central feature of the town was (and is) a 15m/50ft high gneiss crag on the south-east side of the bay, now occupied by the Kástro, a ruined Frankish castle of about 1260, with stonework from an ancient Ionic temple, the Hekatompedon (the "hundred-footer") built into its walls. The tower incorporates a circular building of the 4th century B.C., walled in during the Frankish period, part of which serves as the apse of the castle chapel. To the west, on the highest point of the Kástro, are the foundations of an unfinished temple of about 530 B.C., below which are remains of prehistoric houses (3rd millennium B.C.). The marble wall of the temple was incorporated in the church of Áyios Konstantínos.
In ancient times there was another harbour on the east side of the hill, some remains of which can be seen under water.

★ Cathedral

At the west end of the modern lower town stands the Cathedral, the Ekatontapylianí ("hundred-gated") church, which was built in three stages between the 5th and 7th centuries. The name is a corruption of Katapolianí ("in the lower town"). The principal church (built in the second phase, about 600, re-using ancient stones) is a two-storey domed cruciform church with a barrel-vaulted gallery for women (the oldest part, belonging to a 5th century basilica). The high altar is borne on two Doric column drums and has egg-and-dart moulding of the 6th century B.C. In the semicircular apse are three tiers of stone benches for the clergy, with the bishop's throne in the middle. To the right is the baptistery (a domed basilica of the 7th century), with a cruciform font set into the floor.

Fishing boats in Parikía harbour

To the left of the church can be seen a number of Hellenistic sarcophagi, re-used in Byzantine times.

★ Museum

In the adjoining building is the Museum, with inscriptions (including one referring to the poet Archilochos, who lived on Paros in the 7th century B.C.), funerary reliefs, small works of sculpture, Cycladic idols and a fragment (relating to the years 336–229 B.C.) of the "Marmor Parium", a record of events in Greek history, which was found here in 1627. The major part of it is in the Ashmolean Museum in Oxford.

To the east, beyond the rear wall of the Cathedral, is a well preserved Hellenistic tomb.

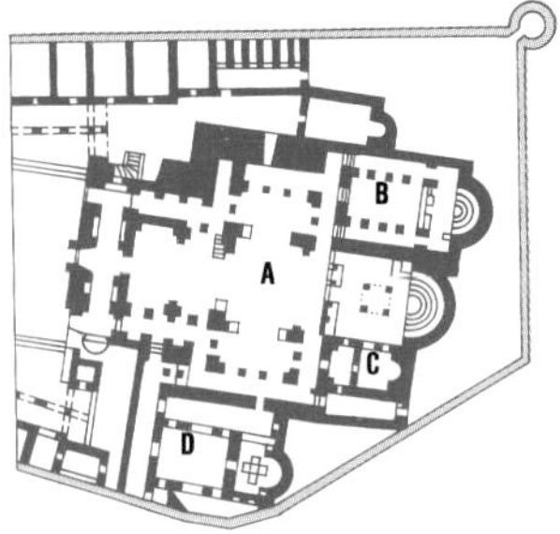

Páros

Katapolianí Church (Cathedral)

A Principal church
B Church of St Nicholas
C Church of Anaryiri (diakonikon/sacristy)
D Baptistery

20 m
22 yd
© Baedeker

On the hills outside the ancient city, which covered a larger area than the modern town (some sections of the walls brought to light by excavation), were a number of other temples.

Asklepieion

North-west of the town, near the sea, on a terrace below the hill with the windmills, is the Doric Asklepieion (4th c. B.C.), with some remains of walls and a fountain basin (6th c. B.C.). A building laid out around a square courtyard, with a central altar, dates from a later period. Beyond this is the new fountain basin. On the terrace above the Asklepieion stood the Pythion, the sanctuary of Apollo Pythios and of Asklepios, who was associated with him. The square building on the lower level was used for the treatment of those who came to seek healing at this sanctuary.

Sanctuary of Aphrodite

On Mt Kounados, to the east of the town, was the sacred precinct of Aphrodite, with a rock-cut altar in the centre. 40m/130ft lower down, on the south side of the hill, is the Cave of Eileithyia, which contains a spring.

Delion

On the highest point (the south-westerly peak; view of the semicircle of the Cyclades) of Mt Taxiarkhis, beyond Parikía Bay in the north-west of the island (about 45 minutes from Páros town), was the walled sanctuary of the three Delian divinities Apollo, Leto and Artemis, the Delion.

At Tris Ekklisies, 1.5km/1 mile east of Parikía, on the site of the Heroon of Archilochos, the foundations of an aisled basilica of the 7th century A.D. have been brought to light.

★ Marble quarries

A little way north of the monastery of Áyios Minás in the Maráthi valley (1 hour north-east of Parikía) are the quarries which produced the

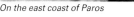

On the east coast of Paros

famous Parian marble, worked from the time of the Cycladic culture (3rd–2nd millennium B.C.; vases, idols) to the 15th century A.D. The marble, called Lychnites ("lamp-lit") because it was hewn in underground shafts, was purer and more translucent (up to a thickness of 3.5mm, or just under one-seventh of an inch) than all other types of marble, and was highly prized in antiquity, being used on Delos, at Epidauros and Delphi and in Imperial Rome. The old mine shafts have been preserved. On the west side is the so-called Cave of Pan, one of the entrances to the quarry face, with a figure of a nymph carved from the rock.

Antíparos

South-west of Páros, separated from it by a channel varying in width between 1km/¾ mile and 8km/5 miles, is the island of Antíparos (area 46 sq.km/18 sq. miles; alt. 0–299m/0–981ft; pop. 600), ancient Oliaros. The chief place, also called Antíparos, clusters round a Venetian castle. There is a beautiful stalactitic cave on the island.

Off the northern tip of Antíparos are two islets of volcanic origin, Diplo and Kavoura.

Some 500m/550yds south-west of Antíparos lies the little island of Despotiki (area 8 sq.km/3 sq. miles), with a sheltered harbour. Farther to the south-west is the islet of Strongylí.

Patmos L 6

Πάτμος
Pátmos

Nomos: Dodecanese
Area of island: 34 sq.km/13 sq. miles
Altitude: 0–269m/0–883ft
Population: 2500
Chief place: Pátmos (Khóra)

Boat services

Regular service from and to Athens (Piraeus), several times weekly (10 hours; cars carried); from and to Salonica and Rhodes, weekly. Local connections in Dodecanese and with Ikaría and Arkí.

Situation and characteristics

Pátmos lies in the eastern Aegean, south of Sámos and south-east of Ikaría. The most northerly of the Dodecanese, it is a rugged island of volcanic origin – perhaps the rim of the crater of an extinct volcano – with a much indented coastline. It has been celebrated since the Middle Ages as the island of St John the Divine, who is said to have written the Book of Revelation while living in exile on Pátmos.

History

Pátmos was originally settled by Dorians and later by Ionians, and had a sanctuary of Artemis. The early history of the island – a place of no political or economic importance – is unknown. Like its barren neighbouring islands, Pátmos was used as a place of exile in Roman times. During the early Middle Ages it seems to have been abandoned and desolate.
The island was given a new lease of life as an intellectual and religious centre when Abbot Christodoulos fled from Asia Minor and transferred his monastery from Mount Latmos, near Miletus, to Pátmos in

1088. The monastic island, receiving rich donations and granted extensive privileges, grew wealthy and influential. Living under its own strict Rule (Typikon), it survived 250 years of Turkish rule unscathed, subject only to the annual payment of tribute.
Since 1946 the whole island has been under statutory protection as an ancient monument. The acquisition of land by foreigners and the export of antiquities are prohibited save in exceptional circumstances.

Sights

Pátmos town (Khóra)

The island consists of three parts joined by narrow isthmuses. At the head of the longest inlet on the east side is the busy port of Skála, from which it is an hour's climb (3km/2 miles; bus service) to the quiet little town of Pátmos or Khóra (130m/425ft; pop. 1000) with its whitewashed houses and its monasteries, churches and chapels. The most notable of these is the monastery of St John the Theologian (Áyios Ioánnis Theológos; St John the Divine), towering over the town with its massive 15th century walls topped by 17th century battlements. The monastery is directly subordinate to the Oecumenical Patriarchate in Istanbul.

★★ Monastery of St John

A ramp leads up through the entrance gateway into a courtyard surrounded by loggias. On the left is the principal church (Katholikón), with an open exonarthex containing four ancient columns and some mediocre 18th and 19th century paintings. The church itself was decorated and furnished in the 19th century at the expense of the Tsars of Russia (iconostasis of 1820, with rich carving). The paintings include many representations of St John and his apocalyptic visions. In the first chapel on the right is the silver-plated sarcophagus of the foun-

The fortified monastery of St John

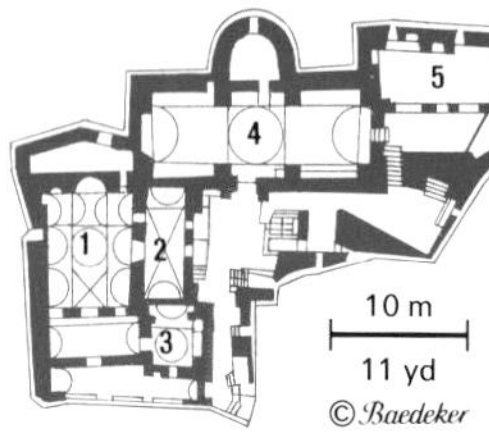

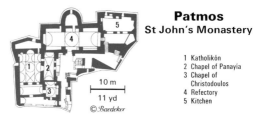

Patmos
St John's Monastery

1 Katholikón
2 Chapel of Panayía
3 Chapel of Christodoulos
4 Refectory
5 Kitchen

der, Ósios (Blessed) Christodoulos. In the second chapel, dedicated to the Panayía, are frescoes of 1745, under which older paintings were discovered, including the Mother of God enthroned, Abraham entertaining the three angels and the Woman of Samaria (12th c.). Frescoes of the 14th century have been preserved in the refectory (trápeza).

Treasury, Library

The Treasury contains mitres, vestments, chalices, crosses, etc., as well as a number of valuable icons. There is a rich Library, with 890 manuscript codices and 35 parchment rolls, 2000 early printed books and the monastic archives, containing over 13,000 documents. Some of the finest items are displayed, including the charter of 1088 (1.42m/5ft long) granting the island of Pátmos to Christodoulos, 33 pages of a 6th century manuscript of St Mark's Gospel, an 8th century manuscript of the Book of Job, with 42 miniatures, and a manuscript of 941 containing a book of sermons by St Gregory of Nazianzus. Of the rich collection of ancient literature once possessed by the monastery there remains a manuscript of the "History" of Diodorus Siculus.

Mother of God Eleousa

Ósios Christodoulos

Together, the Treasury and the Library constitute what is surely the richest collection of its kind outside the monasteries of Athos.

From the roof terraces of the monastery (now unfortunately closed to visitors) there are superb views of Pátmos and the surrounding islands.

Monastery of the Apocalypse

Half way up the road from the port of Skála to Pátmos town, on the left, is the monastery of the Apocalypse (Moní Apokalýpseos), with the cave in which, according to tradition, John wrote the Book of Revelation. The iconostasis in the right-hand chapel, which is built into the cave, depicts John's visions, and on the floor and on the wall are marked the places where he rested, where he heard "a great voice, as of a trumpet", and where he wrote down his visions. Immediately above the monastery can be seen the ruins of the 18th century Patmiás School, and above this again the terraced buildings of the modern Theological College which continues the old tradition.

★ Iconostasis

Patras

F 5

Πάτρα
Pátra

Nomos: Achaea
Altitude: 5–103m/16–338ft
Population: 140,000

Transport

Ferry services from Ancona and Brindisi in Italy. Boat connections with the islands of Kefalloniá, Paxí and Corfu.
Station on the Athens–Corinth–Pýrgos railway line.
Bus connections with Athens and Pýrgos.

Situation

Patras is the largest town and principal port of the Peloponnese, chief town of the nomos of Achaea, the see of an archbishop and a university town.

History

The town was founded about 1100 B.C., but became of importance as a port only in Roman times.
After the 4th Crusade it became the see of a Roman Catholic archbishop. In 1408 it came under the control of Venice and in 1430 of Mistra. In 1460 it fell into the hands of the Turks, by whom it was destroyed in 1821, at the beginning of the war of liberation. Thereafter it was rebuilt in neo-classical style on a rectangular street layout.

Sights

Harbour
Acropolis

The main part of the town lies between the harbour in the west and the acropolis in the east. On the acropolis (alt. 103m/338ft) is the Kástro, originally built by the Byzantines in the 6th century and rebuilt by the Crusaders in the 13th century. South-west of the Kástro is a Roman odeion.

Odeion

In the central square is the Municipal Theatre, and to the north of this the interesting Folk Museum.

Folk Museum

At the south-west end of the harbour, on the site of an ancient sanctuary of Demeter, is the large church of Áyios Andréas (1836), with a reliquary containing the skull of St Andrew, who is traditionally believed to have been martyred at Patras in A.D. 60.

Áyios Andréas

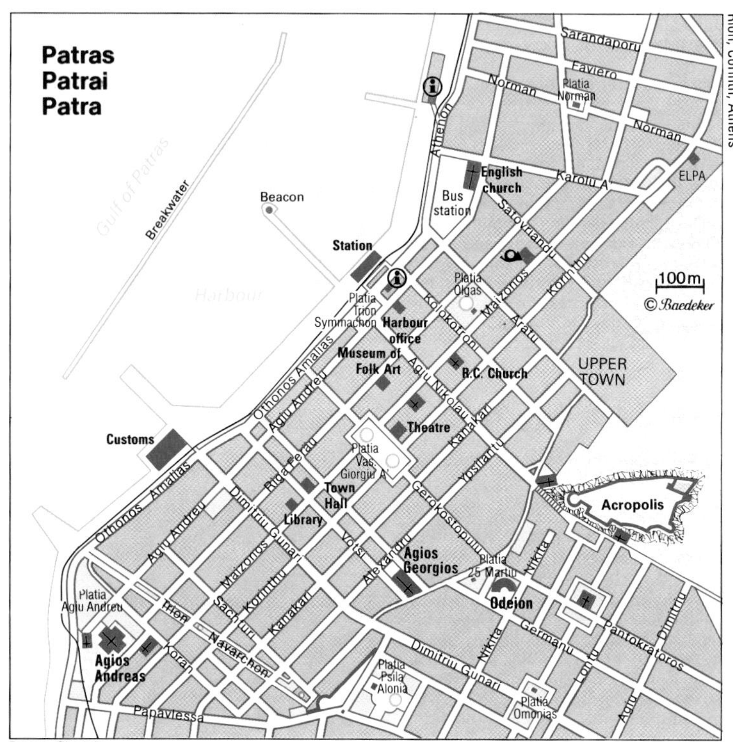

Surroundings of Patras

Káto Akhaía

20km/12½ miles south-west of Patras, on a road running close to the coast, is Káto Akhaía, on the site of ancient Dyme. Beyond this the road turns away from the coast and comes to Áraxos, at the south end of a long coastal lagoon. On a hill which rises above the lagoon at this point are the remains of massive walls belonging to the Early Helladic settlement of Kalogria. At the north end of the lagoon is Cape Áraxos.

Kalogria
Cape Áraxos

Paxi — E 4

Παζοί
Paxí

Nomos: Corfu (Kérkyra)
Area of island: 19 sq.km/7½ sq. miles
Altitude: 0–247m/0–810ft
Population: 2700
Chief place: Paxí (Gáios)

Boat services

Regular weekly service from and to Patras (cars carried); from and to Corfu (Kérkyra), several times daily (2½ hours).

Situation and characteristics

Paxí is a charming little island to the south of Corfu covered with subtropical vegetation, with beautiful beaches and good diving grounds.

The inhabitants live mainly by farming (the local olive oil is highly esteemed) and fishing.

On two islets lying off the principal port, Paxí or Gáios (pop. 500), are a Venetian fort and the former monastery of the Panayía (pilgrimage on August 15th).

On the south coast is the Ypapantí sea-cave (seals).

Off the south-east coast of Paxí are the islets of Mongonísi (causeway) and Kaltsonísi.

Antípaxi

South-east of Paxí is its rocky little sister island of Antípaxi (area 6 sq.km/2¼ sq. miles; alt. 0–107m/0–351ft), which has beautiful lonely beaches. Its hundred or so inhabitants live by sheep-farming and fishing.

There are boats from Paxí to Antípaxi in summer; but the island has no accommodation for visitors.

Gaios, Paxí

Mount Pelion G/H 4

Πήλιον
Pílion

Region: Thessaly
Nomos: Magnesia
Altitude: 1618m/5309ft

Situation and characteristics

The Pelion range extends to the south of Mt Ossa along the east coast of Thessaly as far as the Magnesia peninsula, which encloses the Gulf of Vólos. Rising to a height of 1054m/3458ft in the peak of Mavrovoúni, to the north, and to 1618m/5309ft in Mt Pelion itself, above Vólos, it falls steeply down to the east coast, a rugged stretch with no natural harbours.

Pelion was renowned in antiquity for its healing herbs and as the home of the Centaurs, one of whom, the wise Chiron, noted for his skill in medicine, was the teacher of Asklepios and Achilles. Beneath the peak of Pliasídi (1548m/5079ft), which can be climbed from Portariá in 3½ hours, are the Cave of Chiron and a sanctuary of Zeus Akraios.

There are large tracts of deciduous forest in this region. The 24 villages which grew up here, well supplied with wood and water, prospered and during the Turkish period were able to retain a measure of independence. Some of these villages can be seen in a round trip from Vólos, which in addition to the charm of the villages themselves and

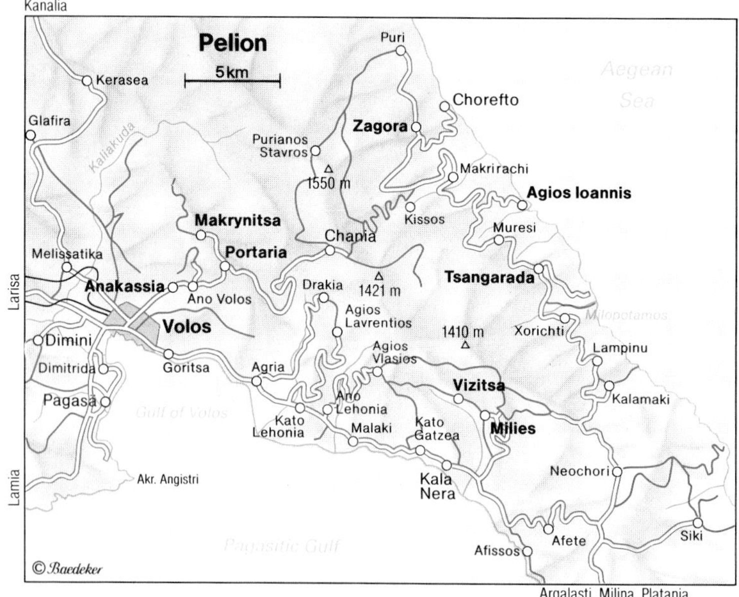

the magnificent hill scenery takes in the beautiful sandy bays on the east coast.

★Circuit of Mount Pelion

Going north-east from Vólos (see entry), we come in 14km/9 miles to Portariá (alt. 600m/1970ft), from which we can take a road on the left to Makrýnitsa (2km/1¼ miles; alt. 600m/1950ft), with a folk museum. From Portariá we continue to Khaniá (12km/7½ miles; alt. 1100m/3610ft) and Zagorá (21km/13 miles; alt. 500m/1640ft), from which it is 3km/2 miles to the beach at Khoreftó. Going south from Zagorá, we come to the villages of Áyios loánnis (22km/13½ miles), on the coast, and Tsangaráda (11km/7 miles; alt. 420m/1380ft), and then return via Neokhóri (15km/9 miles), Kala Nerá (14km/8½ miles) and Agriá (15km/9 miles) to Vólos. From Áfyssos a road goes down to Milína and Plataniá (29km/18 miles), at the southern tip of the Magnesia peninsula.

Pella G 3

Πέλλα
Pélla

Region: Macedonia
Nomos: Pélla

Situation

Pélla, once capital of the kingdom of Macedon, lies 40km/25 miles west of Salonica on the road to Édessa.

History

About 410 B.C. King Achelaos of Macedon transferred his capital from Aigai (see Édessa and Vérgina) to what was then the north coast of the Thermaic Gulf and founded the city of Pella, in which the Attic tragedian Euripides spent the last years of his life and Alexander the Great was born in 356 B.C. The city seems to have had two acropolises, one on the site of the present-day village of Palaiá Pélla (1km/¾ mile north of the main road) and the other to the west of this, where walls probably belonging to the palace were found (Site II). From there the town extended south as far as the former island of Phakos, to the south of the road. Following the destruction of the town by the Romans after the battle of Pydna (196 B.C.), of which Pliny gives an account, Pella disappeared from sight and was rediscovered only in 1957 by Makaronas and Petsas. The excavations carried out since then have been highly productive.

The ★Site

Coming from Salonica, we see on the right of the road, immediately after the turning for Palaiá Pélla (bus stop), the remains of a number of large buildings, between which are streets intersecting at right angles. Dating from about 300 B.C., they are laid out round colonnaded courtyards and apparently served some public function. Particularly notable is one on the right (Block 1), with an Ionic peristyle and fine mosaics, which have been left in situ. Numbers of such mosaics, composed of black, white and yellow pebbles, were found on the site. One of them, the Lion Hunt, shows Alexander the Great being saved by Krateros; two other major compositions are Dionysos riding on a panther and another hunting scene; and other scenes depict Theseus

The remains of Pélla

carrying off Helen while Deianeira flees, a fight with Amazons, a pair of Centaurs, etc.

★ Museum

Some of these mosaics are still in situ; others can be seen in the Museum, on the opposite side of the road, which also contains various architectural fragments and sculpture.

Palace

On the hill at the present-day village of Pélla considerable remains of a large palace dated to between 370 and 300 B.C. have recently been excavated.

Burial mounds

Parallel to the Salonica road is a series of burial mounds of the Hellenistic period.

Peloponnese F–H 5–7

Πελοπόννησος
Pelopónnisos

Situation and characteristics

The most southerly part of the Greek mainland, linked with the rest of the country only by the Isthmus of Corinth, is a peninsula, but it has been regarded since ancient times as an island – the island of Pelops or Peloponnese.

The myth tells us that Pelops, a descendant of Tantalos, came into this land, defeated King Oinomaos of Pisa in a chariot race, married his daughter Hippodameia and took over his kingdom. In the course of his funeral ceremonies the Olympic Games were founded to honour his memory. His descendants, the Pelopids or Atreids, ruled in Mycenae and Sparta.

The peninsula, with an area of 21,440 sq.km/8280 sq. miles, is much broken up by hills and the sea and shows great variety of landscape pattern. In the centre is the thinly populated upland region of Arcadia (see entry), bordered on the north by a mountain range, with Erýmanthos (2223m/7294ft), Khelmós (2355m/7727ft) and Kyllíni (2376m/7796ft) as its highest peaks. Beyond this the region of Achaea extends north to the Gulf of Corinth. On the east side of the peninsula is the Argolid (see entry), with the Argolic Gulf, Náfplion and the strongholds of Mycenae and Tiryns (see entries). To the south of Arcadia is Laconia with its capital Sparta (see entry), open to the sea in the south and separated from Messenia to the west by the Taýgetos range (see entry), which ends in the Máni peninsula (see entry). Finally there is the low-lying region of Elis in the north-west of the Peloponnese, with Olympia (see entry) as its best known sight.

History

Originally occupied by a pre-Greek population, in the 2nd millennium B.C. the centre of the Mycenaean world and in the 1st millennium largely under the domination of the Doric state of Sparta, the Peloponnese is a region rich in both myth and history; and later centuries have also made their contribution to its story. During the Middle Ages there was an influx of Slavs, though the towns remained entirely Greek. After the 4th Crusade (1204) the whole of the Peloponnese passed into the hands of Frankish knights; but Mistra (see entry) soon became the starting-point of the Byzantine reconquest. In 1453 the Turks arrived; and after more than three and a half centuries of Turkish rule it was in the Peloponnese that the war of liberation began.

Sights

All the various phases of this long history have left their mark on the Peloponnese, from the strongholds of the Mycenaeans and Greek

Coast of the Peloponnese near Neapolis

sites like Olympia, Messene and Neméa to the castles of the Crusaders and Byzantine Mistra. In addition the long sandy beaches on the west coast, on the Gulf of Corinth, at Náfplion and on the peninsula to the east make the Peloponnese a popular holiday region which offers every facility for relaxation and recreation, ideally combined with an encounter with the past. (See entries on these various places.)

Mount Pentelikon H 5

Πεντέλη
Pendéli

Region and nomos: Attica
Altitude: 1109m/3639ft

Situation and characteristics

The Pentélikon or Pénteli range bounds the plain of Attica on the north-east. Pentelic marble was the material used in the great classical buildings on the Acropolis in Athens.

Sights

Pentéli monastery

In a hollow below the summit of Pentélikon, surrounded by poplars, is the Pentéli monastery (alt. 430m/1410ft), founded in 1578. It can be reached from Athens by way of the suburb of Khalándri (8km/5 miles beyond Khalándri). The road continues to just below the summit.

Marble quarries

From the monastery the ancient marble quarries can be reached (alt. 700m/2300ft).

★ Daou Pentéli monastery

On the eastern slopes of Pentélikon, above the road from Athens to Stavrós and Marathón, is the Daou Pentéli monastery, founded in the 12th century and rebuilt in the 16th, which has been called "the only example of a large monastic establishment in Greece outside Athos" (Kirsten-Kraiker).

Dionysós

On the north side of Pentélikon, on the road from Athens via Kifissiá and Drosiá to Néa Mákri on the east coast, is the little town of Dionysós (alt. 460m/1510ft), whose tavernas are popular with the citizens of Athens. Near here is a sanctuary of Dionysos, which belonged to Ikaría (see entry), home of Thespis, who produced the first tragedy in Athens in 534 B.C.

Perakhora G 5

Περαχώρα
Perakhóra

Region: Megarid
Nomos: Corinth

Situation and characteristics

The ancient shrine of Hera at Perakhóra lies on the shores of a sharply pointed peninsula between the Halcyonic Gulf and the Gulf of Corinth. The road from Corinth, running north-west via Loutráki, passes (on the right) the village of Perakhóra, which was badly damaged in an earthquake in 1981, skirts a lake (bathing beach, taverna) and ends near a lighthouse (20km/12½ miles). Below, to the left, is the little bay with the remains of the ancient sanctuary; straight ahead, on the south side of the gulf, is the prominent bulk of Acrocorinth.

It is well worth while making the trip to Perakhóra both for the historical importance of the scanty remains, dating from the early period of Greek temple-building, and for the magnificent setting; and there is, too, the additional attraction of a swim in the ancient harbour.

History

In the Mycenaean period the sanctuary belonged to Megara, later to Corinth. The oracle here, sacred to the goddess Hera, flourished particularly in the Geometric period (9th and 8th c.), although nothing is known of the cult practices. In 390 the sanctuary was seized by the Spartan Agesilaos. During the Roman period the site was abandoned. It was excavated by British archaeologists in 1930–33.

The Site

On the shores of the bay is an altar with Doric triglyphs (*c.* 500 B.C.), and to the north of this are traces of the temple of Hera Akraia. A stretch of wall 6.8m/22ft long running from east to west, with an apse at the west end, is all that remains of a temple of the Geometric period (*c.* 850 B.C.), which was only 5–6m/16–20ft wide and 8m/26ft long. About 530 B.C. a considerably larger Archaic temple (9.5m/31ft by 30m/98ft), the west end of which has been preserved, was built to the west of the first one. This temple was flanked by an L-shaped stoa (5th–4th c. B.C.) and the Agora (*c.* 500 B.C.).

Higher up, in a small valley to the east, are other ancient buildings, which were approached by a stepped path. The most striking feature is a large Hellenistic cistern. Nearby, facing south, is the temple of Hera Limenaia, which dates from about 750 B.C. (i.e. the time of Homer). Measuring 5.6m/18ft by 9.5m/31ft, it contains a number of stone slabs which formed part of the sacrificial altar. While the normal Greek temple was merely designed to house the cult image, and the cult ceremonies took place outside the temple, this temple was an assembly hall in which the sacred ceremonies were performed. It thus marks the beginning of a development which ended in the Telesterion of the Eleusinian mystery cult (see Eleusis).

Near the temple were found a sacrificial pit with many thousands of votive potsherds and a sacred lake where the pronouncements of the oracle are thought to have been made.

Philippi

I 2/3

Φίλιπποι
Fílippi

Region: Macedonia
Nomos: Kavála

Situation and characteristics

Although the Apostle Paul first set foot in Europe at Neapolis (Kavála) on his first missionary journey, it was at Philippi, 15km/9 miles northwest of Kavála on the road to Dráma, that he established the first Christian community in Europe.

History

The rich deposits of gold in the Pangaion hills led settlers from the island of Thasos to establish a town here which they called Krenides after the springs (*krenai*) in the area. The old name is perpetuated in the present-day village of Krínides. In 361 B.C. new settlers established themselves on the site, but only five years later the town was taken by Philip II of Macedon, who renamed it Philippoi. The place is best known for the battle of Philippi in 42 B.C., in which Octavian (later the Emperor Augustus) and Antony defeated Caesar's murderers, Brutus and Cassius. The victors then established a colony of veterans in the town. Philippi grew in importance as a result of its situation on the Via

Via Egnatia

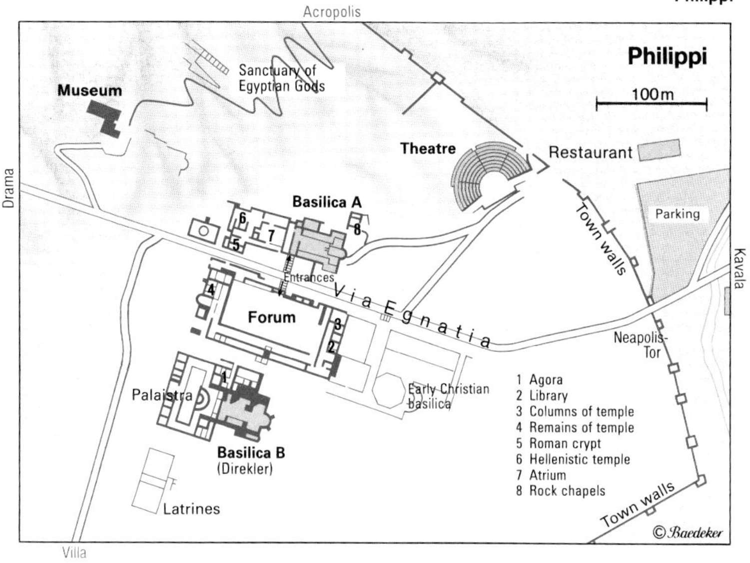

Philippi

100m

Acropolis
Sanctuary of Egyptian Gods
Museum
Theatre
Restaurant
Parking
Basilica A
Entrances
Via Egnatia
Forum
Town walls
Neapolis-Tor
Early Christian Basilica
Palaistra
Basilica B (Direkler)
Latrines
Drama
Kavala
Villa

1 Agora
2 Library
3 Columns of temple
4 Remains of temple
5 Roman crypt
6 Hellenistic temple
7 Atrium
8 Rock chapels

Egnatia, which ran from the Adriatic to Constantinople, and at the beginning of the 4th century it became the see of a bishop. The town's decline began with the Slav and Bulgar invasions of the 9th century.

The ★ Site

★ Theatre

Town walls

Approaching the site from Kavála, we see on the hillside on the right the Theatre (4th c. B.C.), which was altered by the Romans in the 3rd century A.D. to make it suitable for wild beast shows. It is now used for dramatic performances in summer. Following the line of the old town walls (well preserved for most of their length) up the hill, we come to the site of the acropolis, on which there are remains dating from Macedonian, Roman and Byzantine times.

Basilica A

From the theatre there is a view of the extensive plain below, with the excavations carried out by French and Greek archaeologists on both sides of the modern road, which here follows the line of the Via Egnatia. On the near side of the road, to the right, is Basilica A (*c.* A.D. 500), a three-aisled building with a flight of steps leading up to the atrium and a synthronon in the apse. To the west of Basilica A another three-aisled basilica of the same period has recently been excavated. Higher up the hill is the sanctuary of the Egyptian Gods.

Museum

Above the road is a new Museum displaying finds from the area.

Forum

Most of the excavated area lies to the south of the road. Immediately flanking the road is the large rectangular Roman Forum (70m/230ft by 148m/485ft), dating from the time of Marcus Aurelius (A.D. 161–180),

◀ *Philippi: view of the lower part of the site*

which had colonnades round three sides and a temple at each end. A Roman cistern between the western temple and Basilica A is identified by local tradition as the prison in which the Apostle Paul was confined. At the south-west corner of the forum is a marble table marked with standard measures.

Basilica B

Immediately south of the forum is the largest church in Philippi, Basilica B, also known by its Turkish name of Direkler ("Pillars") from the massive masonry piers which are a prominent landmark. Built about 560 by an architect from Constantinople over an ancient palaistra (remains of which can be seen to the west), it was designed as a domed basilica on the model of St Sophia in Constantinople, but the dome collapsed and the church was never completed. In addition to the massive piers there are extensive remains of the building, including some fine Early Byzantine capitals.

South-west of Basilica B are well preserved latrines. To the east of the basilica, approached by a colonnaded road, is the oldest church in Philippi, an octagonal structure built about 400.

North-west of the excavated area, beyond a rest-house on the left of the road, stands a new church dedicated to St Paul and Lydia. Nearby, in the river, is a place of baptism.

Pindos E–G 3–5

Πίνδος
Píndos

Situation and characteristics

This massive mountain range traverses Greece from north to south, extending in a series of chains, for the most part over 2000m/6560ft, from Mts Grámmos (2529m/8298ft) and Smólikas (2637m/8652ft) on the Albanian frontier to Mts Vardoúsia (2437m/7996ft), Gióna (2510m/8235ft) and Parnassus (2457m/8061ft), near the Gulf of Corinth. This region of forest-covered heights, with summer grazings above the tree line, is thinly populated, much of its occupied only by shepherds, and with only two roads of any consequence passing through it – between Ioánnina and Kalambáka and between Karpenísi and Lamía. The Píndos range forms the watershed between the rivers flowing into the Ionian Sea (Thyámis, Ákheron, Árakhthos and Akhelóos) and those flowing into the Aegean (Piniós and Sperkhiós).

Piraeus H 6

Πειραιάς
Piraiás

Nomos: Attica
Altitude: 0–15m/0–50ft
Population: 500,000

Town map see p. 410/411

Piraeus, now part of the Athens conurbation, is Greece's largest port and a major factor in the country's economy. From here ships sail to ports all over Europe and the Near East, and this is also the starting-

Zea harbour, Piraeus

point of most domestic shipping routes, including services to the numerous islands which now attract so many visitors.

History

Piraeus was developed by Themistokles from 482 B.C. onwards as a commercial harbour and naval base for Athens. It was connected with Athens by the "Long Walls" and laid out in the time of Perikles on a regular street pattern in accordance with the system evolved by Hippodamos of Miletus. The town was destroyed by Sulla in 86 B.C. and thereafter was a place of no importance. In the Middle Ages it was known as Porto Leone, after an ancient marble figure of a lion which stood at the entrance to the harbour but was removed to Venice in 1682 and now stands outside the Arsenal there.
Piraeus recovered its importance after the liberation of Greece in the 19th century, when the modern town was laid out on a regular plan as the ancient one had been.

Sights

Harbour

In addition to the principal harbour, Kántharos, the smaller ancient harbours to the east are still in use – Pasalimáni (ancient Zea), Tourkolímano and recently also Mikrolímano (ancient Mounychia). New port installations to relieve the pressure on the main harbour are under construction at Fáliron, where the original harbour of Athens, before Piraeus, had been.
The most characteristic parts of the modern town, which combines the atmosphere of a large port with the amenities of a city, are around the principal harbour, around Mikrolímano with its tavernas, and in Korais Square, on the hill between the two harbours.

Ancient remains

The remains of ancient boat-sheds can be seen under water on the east side of Pasalimáni harbour. To the west, near the Archaeological Museum, is the Hellenistic theatre (2nd c. B.C.). Round the west and south sides of the peninsula between the Kántharos and Pasalimáni harbours are remains of Konon's town walls (394–339 B.C.).

★ Shipping Museum

At the south end of Zéa harbour, by the new marina, a semicircular building houses an interesting Shipping Museum, which covers the history of shipping from antiquity to modern times.

Plataiai

H 5

Πλαταιές
Plataiés

Region and nomos: Boeotia

Situation

Plataiai is reached from Thebes (see entry) on the old road to Athens. 2km/1¼ miles beyond Thebes a road goes off on the left to the site of

the battle of Leuktra, in which Epameinondas defeated the Spartans in 371 B.C. (fragments of a trophy erected by the Thebans at km16). 11km/7 miles from Thebes is Erythrai, where the road to Plataiai (5km/3 miles) branches off on the right.

History

Plataiai (Plataea) was the scene of the last battle on Greek soil during the Persian wars. The battle, in which the Persian commander Mardonios was killed, finally ended the Persian threat to Greece. To commemorate the victory the allied Greek cities set up in the sanctuary of Apollo at Delphi the bronze column of intertwined snakes, originally bearing a tripod, which now stands in the Hippodrome in Istanbul, and established the Eleutheria (Freedom Games) which were held every four years.

The Site

The ancient city lay on the northern slopes of Mt Kithairon, at the present-day village of Kókla. Excavations by an American expedition (1890) and by the Greek archaeologist Skias (1899) established the line of the walls round the oval acropolis on the level top of the hill and of other associated walls. To the south of this central area were the agora and a temple.
Plataiai sent 1000 men to take part in the battle of Marathon. Destroyed and rebuilt on a number of occasions, the town survived into Roman and Byzantine times.
The battle of Plataiai took place to the north-east of the town in the plain of the river Asopos.

Poros H 6

Πόρος
Póros

Nomos: Attica
Altitude: 0–345m/0–1130ft
Population: 4000
Chief place: Póros

Boat services

Regular service from and to Athens (Piraeus), 6–10 times daily (2½ hours). Hydrofoil from Piraeus (Zéa), several times daily (65 minutes). Regular shuttle service to Galatás, on the mainland.
Local connections with Hýdra/Spetsai, Aegina and the Methana peninsula.

Situation and characteristics

The island of Póros, ancient Kalaureia, lies south-west of the Methana peninsula (Peloponnese), separated from the north coast of the Argolid by a strait between 250m/275yds and 1000m/1100yds wide, 1.5km/1 mile long and up to 4m/13ft deep. Most of the island is covered by thin woodland and macchia. The inhabitants, many of whom are of Albanian descent, live by farming the fertile coastal areas on the mainland which belong to Póros and, increasingly, by the tourist trade.

History

In Mycenaean times there was a settlement on the site later occupied by the sanctuary of Poseidon. The ancient city was abandoned after the Roman period, and the modern town was established only in the late Middle Ages.

The town of Póros

Sights

Póros

The island's capital, Póros (pop. 4300; naval training school) is beautifully situated on ancient Sphairia, a promontory of volcanic origin on the south side of the island, linked with it by the narrow Bísti isthmus. In the 18th and 19th centuries this was the principal naval harbour on the south-east coast of Greece.

5km/3 miles north-east of the town can be seen the scanty remains of the sanctuary of Poseidon (5th c. B.C.), the centre of the Kalaurian amphictyony (religious league) of the maritime cities on the Saronic and Argolic Gulfs. It was here that Demosthenes, fleeing from the henchmen of the Macedonian governor Antipatros, poisoned himself in 322 B.C. The numerous remains of buildings in the surrounding area suggest that this was the site of ancient Kalaureia.

Monastery of Zoodókhos Piyí

4km/2½ miles east of Póros is the 18th century monastery of the Zoodókhos Piyí (the Life-Giving Spring).

★ Lemon-grove

On the mainland opposite the island lies the large lemon-grove of Lemonodásos (30,000 trees), which belongs to Póros.
10km/6 miles west, at the village of Damalás, are the scanty remains of ancient Troizen, the setting of the legend of Hippolytos and Phaidra.

Porto Kheli — H 6

Πόρτο Χέλι
Pórto Khéli

Region: Peloponnese
Nomos: Argolid
Population: 750

Transport

Air services from Athens. Boats from Piraeus; hydrofoil service from Marina Zéa.

Situation and characteristics

The little port of Pórto Khéli lies in a large seaside holiday area near the southern tip of the Argolid peninsula, opposite the island of Spétsai (see entry). The holiday area begins at Sáladi, to the north-west, continues with Pórto Khéli, Kósta, Petrothálassa, Ermióni and Plépi, opposite the island of Hýdra (see entry) and extends round to Galatás on the north coast, opposite the island of Póros.

Porto Rafti **I 6**

Πόρτο Ράφτη
Pórto Ráfti

Nomos: Attica
Altitude: 5m/15ft

Situation and characteristics

Pórto Ráfti, a picturesque little port in a bay on the east coast of Attica, takes its name from a large marble statue of the Roman period, popularly known as the "Tailor" (*raftis*), on a rocky islet which shelters the harbour.

History

The predecessor of the present town in ancient times was Prasiai, on the hill of Koroni at the south end of the bay, which played an important part in the shipping trade between Attica and the islands during the 7th and 6th centuries B.C. The ancient town walls which can still be seen, however, date only from the 3rd century B.C.

Surroundings of Pórto Ráfti

There are a number of other ancient sites along the neighbouring coast. To the north of Pórto Ráfti bay was Steiria, to which a necropolis of the Mycenaean period in the Perati district belonged. Finds from this site are in the museum at Brauron (see entry), 9km/6 miles north of Pórto Ráfti.

Merénda

Inland, at Merénda, a later cemetery (8th–4th c. B.C.) was found, together with a kouros and kore which are now in the National Archaeological Museum in Athens.

Loútsa

9km/6 miles farther north is Loútsa, where, behind the dunes, a Doric temple of the 4th century B.C. was discovered. It was probably the temple of Artemis Tauropolos which according to Euripides was erected by Orestes after returning from Tauris with his sister Iphigeneia and landing at Brauron. Loútsa occupies the site of ancient Halai Araphenides, which is known from inscriptions to have been the scene of a festival of Artemis (the Tauropolia) and a festival of Dionysos.

Rafína

9km/6 miles north of Loútsa is the port of Rafína, which preserves the name of ancient Araphen. Rafína is connected by local boat services with Marmári and Kárystos on Euboea and with the islands of Ándros, Tínos, Kéa, Mýkonos and Sýros.

Keratéa
Thorikós

25km/16 miles south of Pórto Ráfti is Keratéa or Kakí Thálassa. Beyond this, to the left of the road to Lávrion, is the site of ancient Thorikos (28km/17 miles), on a hill on the north side of Lávrion Bay which was fortified in 490 B.C., during the Persian wars. There are remains of two tholos tombs (between the two summits of the hill and on its eastern slope) belonging to the Mycenaean settlement.

★ Theatre

The most striking feature of the site is the theatre (5th–4th c. B.C.), which was associated with a sanctuary of Dionysos. It has a rather archaic air, since the orchestra is neither circular nor semicircular but almost rectangular and the auditorium also departs from the usual semicircular form. In front of the auditorium, to the left, is the site of a small temple of Dionysos; to the right are two earlier rock-cut chambers.

Porto Yermeno H 5

Πόρτο Γερμενό
Pórto Yermenó

Nomos: Attica
Altitude: 10m/35ft

Transport

Bus service from Athens.

Situation and characteristics

Pórto Yermenó is a village on the southern slopes of the Kithairon range at the north-east corner of the Gulf of Corinth, with a broad sandy beach. It occupies the site of ancient Aigosthena, with fortifications which are a magnificent example of Greek defensive architecture of around 300 B.C.

Pórto Yermenó is reached from the Eleusis–Thebes road. 3km/2 miles beyond Inón, at the ancient fortress of Panakton (after 346 B.C.) on the frontier of Attica – whose walls of dressed stone, still standing to the height of the wall-walk, with towers and seven gates, are impressive even when seen from the road, some distance away – a side road branches off on the left and leads via Vília to Pórto Yermenó (23km/14 miles).

The Site

There are substantial remains of ancient Aigosthena, which was founded by Megara to counter the Attic frontier fortress of Panakton, to the east of the village. The acropolis is surrounded by a double wall with towers at intervals of 48m/160ft, and a long stretch of defensive wall extends down from the north-west corner to the sea. Within this wall are the remains of a five-aisled Early Christian basilica, over which a monastic church was later built. The walls are mostly constructed of polygonal blocks. The gateway of the acropolis stands on the west side. Diagonally uphill from this, to the right, stands the imposing south-east tower.

Preveza E 5

Πρέβεζα
Préveza

Nomos: Préveza
Altitude: 10m/35ft
Population: 12,700

Situation and characteristics

The port of Préveza is attractively situated on the north side of the entrance, only 350m/380yds wide, to the Gulf of Árta (Ambracian Gulf).

History

A town was founded on this site about 290 B.C. by King Pyrrhos of Epirus, who named it Berenikia after his mother-in-law Berenike, wife of the Egyptian ruler Ptolemy I. In 31 B.C. the battle of Actium (Aktion) was fought in the waters south of the town, and Octavian founded the town of Nikópolis (see entry) to commemorate his victory.
In the late medieval period a new town was founded under the present name of Préveza, and in 1499 this town passed into the hands of Venice. From this period dates the castle which is the only substantial remnant of the town's former fortifications, and which affords an excellent general view of the gulf. In 1797, under the treaty of Campo Formio, the town passed from the Venetians to the French, but in the following year the French forces were driven out by Ali Pasha of Ioánnina. Préveza became part of Greece in 1912.

Surroundings of Préveza

Nikópolis, 6km/4 miles north; Vónitsa, on the south side of the gulf (15km/9 miles); the island of Lefkás (20km/12½ miles). See entries for these places.

Psara K 5

Ψαρά
Psará

Harbour, Psará

Nomos: Chios
Area of island: 40 sq.km/15½ sq. miles
Altitude: 0–564m/0–1850ft
Population: 500
Chief place: Psará

Boat services

Local connections with Chios.

Situation and characteristics

The bare rocky island of Psará, ancient Psyra (Mycenaean tombs found), lies 18km/11 miles north-west of Chios. The chief place, also called Psará, is on the south coast, below a medieval castle. To the north-east is the monastery of the Dormition (Kímisis Theotókou).

Now poor and depopulated, Psará had a period of considerable prosperity in the 18th century, when the descendants of Albanians who had settled on the island in the 16th and 17th centuries made it the third naval power in the Aegean, after Hýdra and Spétsai. The island's dilapidated old mansions and the stumps of windmills on the hills bear witness to this period, when Psará had a population of 20,000. Then, in reprisal for the islanders' stubborn resistance to the Turks, a Turkish force landed on the island and slaughtered the inhabitants. After Psará became part of the new kingdom of Greece in the 19th century it was resettled from Chios. The population lives by farming and seafaring.

Antipsara

South-west of Psará is the smaller island of Antipsara.

Pylos F 7

Πύλος
Pylos

Nomos: Messenia
Altitude: 20m/65ft
Population: 2100

Transport

Buses from Kalamáta and Athens.

★★ Situation

The name of Pýlos conjures up memories of the Mycenaean hero Nestor and the more recent naval battle of Navarino; but it also offers the attraction of one of the most beautiful spots in Greece, Navarino Bay.

Navarino Bay – the name is a corruption of the Byzantine name Ton Avarinon ("of the Avars" – referring to the Slav invaders of Greece) – is the only large natural harbour on the west coast of the Peloponnese. It is enclosed on the seaward side by the island of Sfaktiría (see entry), a huge rocky barrier 4.6km/3 miles long rising to a height of 135m/443ft. The main entrance to the bay, at the south end, is wide, but is constricted by the islet of Pýlos and a number of small reefs. The entrance at the north end is the strait of Sykia, only 100m/110yds wide and much silted up, which runs between Sfaktiría and the 250m/820ft high hill of Koryfásion, below which is the Osman Aga lagoon.

History

The Mycenaean kingdom of Pylos was conquered by Neleus, and thereafter was ruled by his youngest son, Nestor. In 1939 Carl Blegen discovered at Epáno Englianós a site belonging to that period.
In the 7th–6th century B.C. a Dorian settlement named Pýlos was established on Mt Koryfásion, at the north end of the bay. In 425 B.C.,

Pýlos, in Navarino Bay

during the Peloponnesian War, the town was occupied by the Athenians, who also captured the island of Sphakteria (Sfaktiría) and took its Spartan defenders prisoner.

In the 13th century A.D. a Crusading knight, Nicolas de Saint-Omer, built a castle here (Palaiókastro, the "Old Castle"), which was later successively held by Venetians and Turks. In 1573 the Turks built a new castle (Neókastro) on the hill of Áyios Nikólaos at the south end of the bay, and in 1825, during the war of Greek independence, Ibrahim Pasha made this his headquarters during his Peloponnesian campaign.

The Town

The present-day town of Pýlos grew up at the foot of the hill of Áyios Nikólaos, on a site which had not been occupied in ancient times. Its most notable features are the arcaded houses in the main square and the wide-spreading old plane-tree which gives shade to the square and the patrons of its coffee-houses and tavernas. The square is called the Platía ton Trión Navárkhon (Square of the Three Admirals) after the three commanders of the victorious allied fleet in the battle of Navarino – the British Admiral Sir Edward Codrington, the French Admiral de Rigny and the Russian Count von Heyden – who are also commemorated by a monument on one side of the square. There are relics of the battle in the small Museum (on the way up to the castle), which also contains some very fine antiquities (pottery, gold jewellery).

The battle of Navarino

The allied fleet sailed into Navarino Bay on October 20th 1827 to make a show of strength, but a shot fired by the Turkish and Egyptian fleet sparked off a battle which had not been intended by the allied governments and which ended in the destruction of 58 out of the 87 Turkish vessels. Their remains can be seen lying on the bottom of the bay when the sea is calm. The battle gave a decisive new impulse to the Greek war of liberation.

There are three monuments to those who fell in the battle – a British one on Khelonáki ("Tortoise Island") in the middle of the bay, a Russian one on the island of Sfaktiría and a French one on the islet of Pýlos, to the south.

Surroundings of Pýlos

Sfaktiría

A motorboat can be taken to the island of Sfaktiría (see entry). Above the landing-stage at Panagoúla is the monument to the Russian sailors who died in the battle of Navarino, with a chapel which was restored some years ago by the Soviet Union.

Methóni

12km/7½ miles south of Pýlos is the Venetian fortress of Methóni (see entry).

Mt Koryfásion

9km/6 miles north-west is Mt Koryfásion (30 minutes' climb; view), with the ruins of a medieval castle built on ancient foundations. On the north side of the hill is the "Cave of Neleus"; at the foot is the site of the Mycenaean harbour.

★ Palace of Nestor

The Mycenaean palace at Epáno Englianós (18km/11 miles north) is not so imposing as Mycenae or Tiryns, since it lacks their massive cyclopean walls (it is the only unfortified Mycenaean palace); but the layout is so clear and easy to follow that the site is a very rewarding one to visit. The whereabouts of Nestor's stronghold were the subject of dispute even in ancient times; but the American excavations in 1939 and since 1952 have suggested very strongly that the palace found here was indeed the home of the Homeric hero. The excavations brought to light some early remains dating from before 1300 B.C., an Old Palace (1280 B.C.) and a New Palace (1250 B.C.): dates which fit in

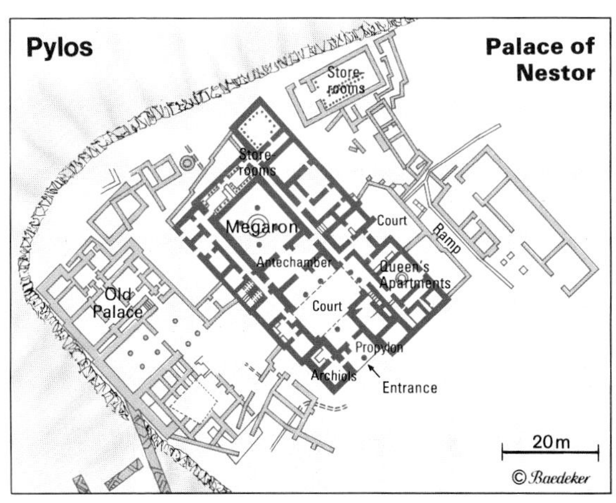

with the traditions about Neleus's conquest of the land, his palace and the palace of his son Nestor.

Parts of the Old Palace can be seen on the west side of the site. The plan of the New Palace is completely preserved, and the rooms are now covered with a protective roof and labelled. The propylon, beside which were archive rooms, leads into a court, beyond which is the central element in the palace, the Megaron, with two antechambers preceding the main hall (11.2m/37ft by 12.9m/42ft). In the centre of the hall is a circular hearth 4m/13ft in diameter, with painted stucco decoration. On the right-hand wall the position of the throne can be identified; a depression in the floor beside the throne was probably for libations.

On the right-hand side of the court a propylon gives access to a corridor, in which are a staircase leading to the upper floor and apartments for the queen or for guests. In one of the rooms is a small circular hearth, in the next one a terracotta bath-tub. Other rooms alongside or beyond the Megaron served as store-rooms (with pithoi for oil still in situ).

North-east of the palace is a tholos tomb. At the foot of the hill on which the palace stands the excavators found remains of the lower town and numbers of tombs. From in front of the palace there is a good view of the gentle green countryside extending to Navarino Bay.

Museum

In the village of Khóra, 3km/2 miles north, is a museum displaying finds from the Palace of Nestor (tablets with inscriptions in Linear B, gold jewellery, fragments of fine wall paintings, pottery, etc.).

Pyrgos F 6

Πύργος
Pýrgos

Nomos: Elis
Altitude: 23m/75ft
Population: 23,000

Transport

Pýrgos is on the Peloponnese Railway line from Athens to Patras and Kalamáta and on the branch lines to Olympia and Katákolo. Buses from Athens and Patras.

Situation

The busy commercial town of Pýrgos in Elis (western Peloponnese) is believed to occupy the site of ancient Letrinoi. Most visitors see it only on the way to Olympia (see entry), 21km/13 miles east.

Katákolo

The port of Pýrgos is Katákolo, 13km/8 miles west (sand and shingle beach), on the site of ancient Pheia. On the acropolis of Pheia is the Póndiko Kástro, a castle built by the Villehardouins in the 13th century. There are good bathing beaches north of Katákolo in the direction of Kyllíni (see entry).

Rhamnous I 5

Ραμνούς
Ramnoús

Region and nomos: Attica

Situation

Rhamnoús is an ancient city and coastal stronghold on the north-east coast of Attica, opposite the island of Euboea. It is reached from Marathón (see entry) by way of Káto Soúli (8km/5 miles), continuing

Temple of Nemesis, Rhamnoús

past the turning for Ayía Marína (on the right, 5km/3 miles) for another 2km/1¼ miles.

The Site

Approaching from the south, we come first to the terrace of the sanctuary of Themis and Nemesis, the goddesses of order and retribution. Immediately adjoining a temple in antis dedicated to Themis and built of polygonal limestone masonry (*c.* 500 B.C.), which housed a cult statue by Agorakritos, is the larger temple of Nemesis, built in marble. This is a Doric peripteral temple with 6 × 12 columns which was begun about 430 B.C. but – as can be seen from the unfinished state of some of the columns – never completed. In front of the temple is an altar.

From the temple terrace there are beautiful far-ranging views over the site of the ancient town, now largely overgrown by macchia, and across the gulf to the hills of Euboea.

A footpath flanked by tombs leads down to the sea, above which rises the acropolis hill. Remains of walls can be seen on the east side, of a theatre on the seaward side.

Rhodes — M/N 7/8

Ρόδος
Ródos

Nomos: Dodecanese
Area of island: 1398 sq.km/540 sq. miles
Altitude: 0–1215m/0–3985ft
Population: 91,000
Chief town: Rhodes

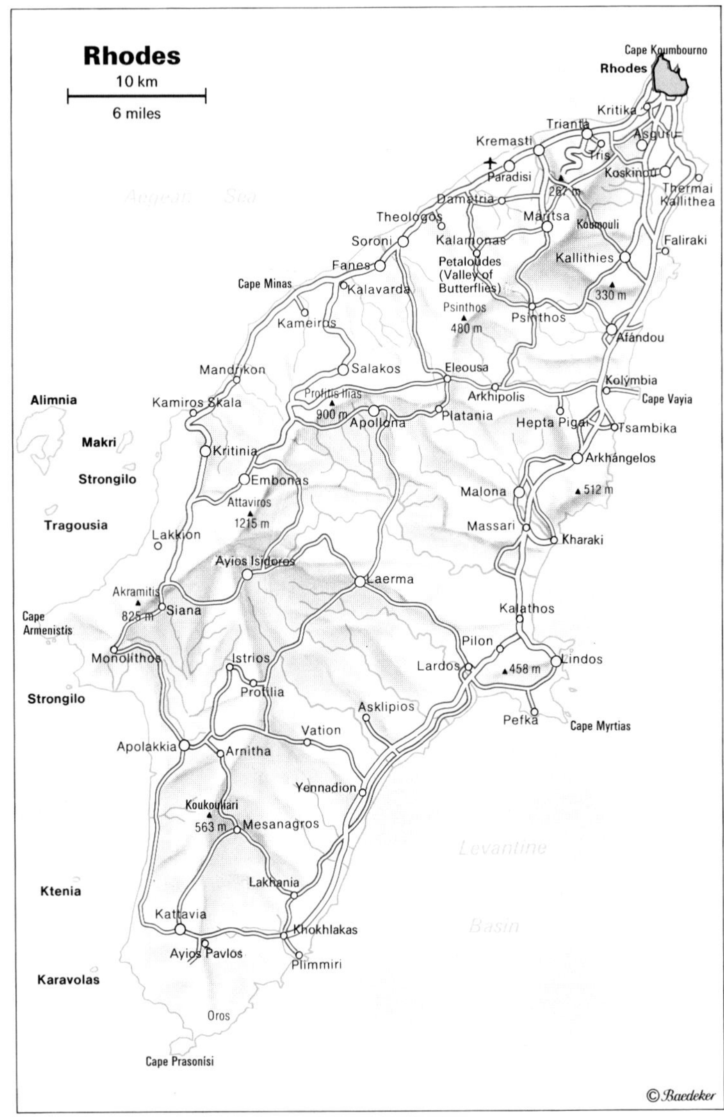
Rhodes
10 km
6 miles
Cape Koumbourno
Rhodes
Kritika
Trianta
Asguru
Kremasti
Tris
Paradisi
Koskinou
267 m
Thermai Kallithea
Aegean Sea
Damatria
Theologos
Maritsa
Koumouli
Soroni
Kalamonas
Faliraki
Fanes
Petaloudes (Valley of Butterflies)
Kallithies
Cape Minas
Kalavarda
330 m
Kameiros
Psinthos
480 m
Psinthos
Afándou
Mandrikon
Salakos
Eleousa
Kolýmbia
Alimnia
Kamiros Skala
Profitis Ilias
900 m
Arkhipolis
Cape Vayia
Apollona
Platania
Hepta Pigai
Tsambika
Makri
Kritinia
Arkhángelos
Strongilo
Embonas
Malona
512 m
Attaviros
1215 m
Massari
Tragousia
Lakkion
Kharaki
Ayios Isidoros
Laerma
Akramitis
825 m
Siana
Kalathos
Cape Armenistís
Pilon
Monolithos
Istrios
Lardos
458 m
Lindos
Strongilo
Profilia
Asklipios
Pefka
Cape Myrtias
Vation
Apolakkia
Arnitha
Yennadion
Koukouliari
563 m
Mesanagros
Levantine Basin
Ktenia
Lakhania
Kattavia
Khokhlakas
Ayios Pavlos
Plimmiri
Karavolas
Oros
Cape Prasonísi
© Baedeker

Air services

Airport 16km/10 miles south-west of Rhodes town.
Regular flights from and to Athens, several times daily (55 minutes); Salonica, twice weekly (70 minutes); Crete (Iráklion and Sitía), several times weekly (40 minutes); Kárpathos, twice weekly (45 minutes); Kásos, daily (80 minutes); Kos, several times weekly (30 minutes); Kastellórizo, several times weekly (45 minutes).

Boat services

Regular service from and to Athens (Piraeus), several times daily (16–22 hours; cars carried); also from Venice or Ancona via Brindisi (less frequently Dubrovnik), Corfu, Patras (less frequently) and Athens (Piraeus).
Local connections in the Dodecanese: Rhodes – Sými – Tílos – Nísyros – Kos – Kálymnos – Léros – Lipsí – Pátmos – Arkí – Agathonísi – Sámos; Rhodes – Kos – Kálymnos – Astypálaia; Rhodes – Kastellórizo; Rhodes – Khálki – Diáfani – Kárpathos – Kásos.

Situation and characteristics

Rhodes, the "Island of Roses" (actually of hibiscus), the largest of the Dodecanese and the fourth largest Greek island (after Crete, Euboea and Lésbos), is one element in the island bridge which extends from the Peloponnese by way of Crete and Kárpathos to Asia Minor, from which it is only 18km/11 miles distant. 78km/48 miles long and up to 30km/19 miles wide, Rhodes is traversed from end to end by a long mountain ridge rising to 1215m/3986ft in Mt Atáviros. The land falls away gradually towards the coasts, well watered and well wooded, affording good soil for agriculture, particularly near the coast.

★★ Tourist attractions

With its beautiful scenery, its excellent beaches and the fine old buildings erected by the Knights of St John, now well restored, Rhodes holds a wealth of attraction for visitors and has long been a major tourist centre. In and around Rhodes town is one of the largest concentrations of hotels in Greece, but elsewhere, particularly in the south, the island is still relatively unspoiled.

History

The island of Rhodes was already occupied in the Neolithic period, but its great cultural flowering came only with its settlement by Dorian Greeks. Their three cities of Lindos, Ialysos and Kameiros were members of the Hexapolis, the league of six Dorian cities, which became subject to the Persians in the 6th century B.C.

In the 5th century B.C. Rhodes became a member of the first Attic maritime league, the Confederacy of Delos. About 408 B.C. the new capital city of Rhodes was laid out on a regular plan by the famous Greek town-planner Hippodamos of Miletus, and in the 4th century it overshadowed Athens itself in commercial importance. Its great landmark, one of the seven wonders of the world, was the celebrated Colossus of Rhodes, a 32m/105ft high statue of the sun god Helios standing on a stone base 10m/35ft high. Cast between 304 and 292 B.C., it stood at the entrance to the harbour and probably served as a lighthouse. It collapsed in an earthquake about 225 B.C. A block of stone found in the sea in 1987 which was at first thought to be a fragment of the statue turned out not to be so.

With the extension of Roman control in the East the island's trade declined, but the city of Rhodes remained an important cultural centre, with a well known school of rhetoric which was attended by Cicero and Caesar and a major school of sculptors which produced the famous Laocoon group (*c.* 50 B.C.) now in the Vatican Museums.

During the Middle Ages Rhodes was the subject of dispute between the Arabs, the Byzantines, the Venetians and the Genoese. In 1309 it

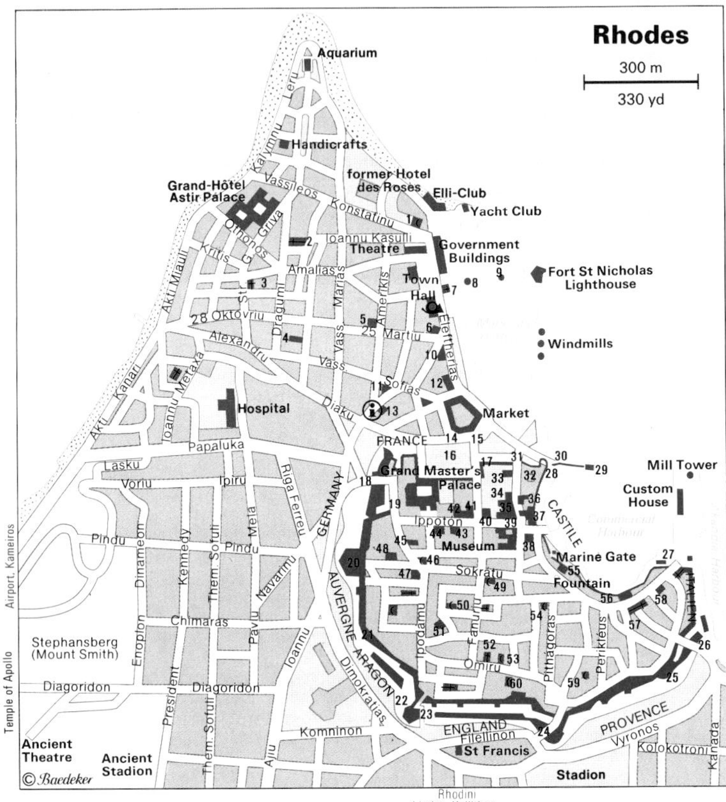

1 Murad Reis Mosque
2 Church of Our Lady (RC)
3 Church of Assumption
4 German Consulate
5 Telephone and Telegraph Office
6 Harbour Office
7 Evangelismós Church
8 Stag
9 Hind
10 Law Courts
11 National Bank of Greece
12 Bank of Greece
13 EOT, Tourist Police
14 Bus Station
15 Taxi stance
16 Son et Lumière
17 St Peter's Tower
18 Amboise Gate
19 Artillery Gate
20 St George's Tower
21 Tower of Spain
22 St Mary's Tower
23 St Athanasius' Gate
24 Koskinou (St John's) Tower
25 Tower of Italy
26 Gate of Italy
27 St Catherine's Gate
28 Arsenal Gate
29 Naillac (Arab) Tower
30 St Paul's Gate
31 Freedom Gate

OLD TOWN

32 Temple of Aphrodite
33 Municipal Picture Gallery
34 Archaeological Institute
35 Museum of Decorative Art
36 Inn of Auvergne
37 Church of the Order of St John (museum)
38 Inn of England
39 Inn of Italy
40 Palace of Villiers de l'Isle-Adam
41 Inn of France
42 Inn of Provence
43 Inn of Spain
44 Loggia (Turkish school)
45 Clock-Tower
46 Süleiman Mosque
47 Turkish Library
48 Medresse Mosque
49 Aga Mosque
50 Sultan Mustapha Mosque
51 Süleiman Baths
52 Church of Ayios Fanoúrios
53 Redjeb Pasha Mosque
54 Ibrahim Pasha Mosque
55 Commercial Tribunal
56 Archbishop's Palace
57 Church of Our Lady of the City
58 Hospice of St Catherine
59 Dolapli Mosque
60 Bourouzan Mosque

was occupied by the Knights of St John, who developed the town into a powerful stronghold and in the 15th century defended it and the rest of the island against Egyptian and Turkish attack, but were compelled to surrender it to Suleiman the Magnificent in 1522. After almost 400 years of Turkish rule the island was occupied by Italy in 1912. In 1947, after the Second World War, it was returned to Greece.

Rhodes Town

The town of Rhodes (Ródos; pop. 33,000), situated at the northern tip of the island, has been capital of the island since its foundation in 408 B.C., and is now the administrative centre of the nomos of the Dodecanese. Laid out on a rectangular grid in accordance with the principles of Hippodamos of Miletus, the ancient city extended from the acropolis hill in the west to the east coast of the island. Some of the streets in the considerably smaller medieval town (Street of the Knights, Homer Street, Hippodamos Street and Pythagoras Street) still follow the ancient grid. The Knights' town, the Collachium, occupied the northern part of the walled town, with its streets running roughly at right angles. The larger southern part was occupied by Greeks, while the west part became the Turkish quarter and the smaller east part the Jewish quarter, which existed until the Second World War.

★★ Town walls

The old town, within which no Christian was allowed to live during the Turkish period (1523–1912), is surrounded by a magnificent 4km/2½ mile long circuit of 15th and 16th century walls, with towers, bastions and a moat – one of the finest examples of the medieval art of fortification. Particularly impressive are the Amboise Gate (with gardens and a deer-park adjoining) built by Grand Master Aimeri d'Amboise in

★ Amboise Gate

Colossus of Rhodes: an impression

Stag and hind, Mandráki harbour

★ Marine Gate

1512, on the north-west side of the town, and the Marine Gate (1468; relief of the Virgin) on the north-east side, by the Commercial Harbour. Visitors can take a fascinating walk round the old town on the walls, starting from the square in front of the Grand Master's Palace (entrance at Artillery Gate; open only for brief periods on certain days). A walk round the town outside the walls is also full of interest.

Commercial Harbour

Mandráki Harbour

The Commercial Harbour (Emborikó Limáni), the town's principal harbour, used by the ships sailing to and from Piraeus, and the old Mandráki Harbour to the north, which has been in continuous use since 408 B.C. and is now mainly used by pleasure craft (boating marina) and excursion boats, are protected by long breakwaters. On the Mandráki breakwater are three disused windmills, and at its northern tip are the circular Fort St Nicholas (built about 1400 and strengthened in 1460) and a lighthouse. Flanking the entrance to the harbour are stone columns topped by figures of a stag and a hind, the town's heraldic animals. (Accordingly red deer are a protected species on Rhodes, and surplus animals are given away to zoos throughout the world.)

Stag and hind

On the east side of the old town is the Akándia Harbour, with a boatyard.

★ Old town

The Freedom Gate, at the south end of the Mandráki breakwater, leads into the busy old town with its maze of narrow streets and lanes, its domes and minarets set amid palms and plane-trees. In Sými Square are the remains of a temple of Aphrodite (3rd c. B.C.) and the Municipal Art Gallery (modern art). Immediately south of this lies picturesque Aryirokástro Square, in the centre of which is a small fountain constructed from fragments of a Byzantine baptistery. On the west side of the square is the former Arsenal (14th c.), now housing the Archaeological Institute and the Museum of Decorative Art. A passage leads through to the former church of the Order of St John (on the left), now the Museum of Early Christian and Byzantine Art.

★ Hospital of the Knights (Archaeological Museum)

Diagonally opposite the church is the massive Hospital of the Knights (15th c.; restored), now occupied by the Archaeological Museum.

From the inner courtyard a staircase leads up to the Infirmary on the upper floor (small chapel in a recess opposite the entrance; gravestones of knights). A passage on the right leads to the rooms displaying finds from Ialysos, Kameiros and other sites, including two Archaic kouroi (6th c. B.C.) and, in the same room, the funerary stele of Krito and Tamariste (end of 5th c. B.C.). In other rooms are a life-size figure of Aphrodite and an expressive Hellenistic head of Helios, and a small crouching figure of Aphrodite known as the Venus of Rhodes (1st c. B.C.). Also of interest is the rich collection of vases opening off the gallery round the courtyard, which covers all periods from Mycenaean times onwards and includes some particularly fine examples of Rhodian ware.

★ Street of the Knights

From the north side of the Hospital the Street of the Knights (Odós Ippotón) runs west. In this street, which still conveys an excellent impression of a street of the 15th and 16th centuries, were most of the Inns of the various nations in the Order of St John. The finest of these is the Auberge de France (on the right), built between 1492 and 1503.

★ Grand Master's Palace

At the west end of the street, on the highest point in the town, is the Grand Master's Palace, a massive stronghold which was defended by a triple circuit of walls. It suffered heavy destruction during the Turkish siege, and was almost completely destroyed by an explosion in 1856, but during the period of Italian occupation (1912–43) was rebuilt on the basis of old plans (commemorative tablet at entrance). The in-

Grand Master's Palace

Street of the Knights

ternal arrangement does not, however, follow the original pattern. Notable features of the interior are the many pebble mosaic pavements from the island of Kos.
On the north-east side of the palace are beautiful gardens (entrance in Papagós Street; *son et lumière* shows in summer). At its southwest corner is the Artillery Gate (St Antony's Gate), which gives access to the town walls.

Suleiman Mosque

To the south of the Grand Master's Palace is a striking 19th century clock-tower. Still farther south stands the Suleiman Mosque, the largest mosque on the island, with a beautiful Renaissance doorway. Facing this, to the south, is the Turkish Library (1794), with valuable manuscripts of the Koran.

From here Sokrates Street, flanked by bazaars and always bustling with activity, runs east through the centre of the old town towards the Commercial Harbour. South-east of the Marine Gate are the Commercial Tribunal (1507) and the Archbishop's Palace (15th c.), on the north side of Archbishop's Square, in which can be seen the beautiful Seahorse Fountain.

South of Sokrates Street is a picturesque maze of lanes around Fanoúrios Street, Homer Street (Odós Omírou), both spanned by flying buttresses, and Pythagoras Street, with numerous mosques, including the Ibrahim Pasha Mosque, the oldest in the town (1531), and, opposite the magnificent Suleiman Baths with their many domes (open to visitors as well as bathers), the Sultan Mustafa Mosque (1765). In Fanoúrios Street is the little Orthodox church of Áyios Fanoúrios, partly underground (founded 1335; used as a mosque during the Turkish period).

On the west side of the old town, near St George's Tower, stands the Hurmale Medrese, originally the Byzantine church of the Redeemer, with a picturesque inner courtyard.

New town

The new town, with government offices and many hotels and restaurants, extends to the north of the old town, reaching almost to the sandy northernmost tip of the island. At Mandráki Harbour is the massive New Market (Néa Agorá), with a large inner courtyard. From here Freedom Avenue (Eleftherías) runs north, past the Law Courts and the Post Office, to the Evangelismós church (originally Roman Catholic, now Orthodox), a reproduction (1925) of the old monastic church of St John, which originally stood beside the Grand Master's Palace and was destroyed in the 1856 explosion. Farther north are the Venetian-style Government Buildings (Nomarkhía), the Town Hall and the Theatre. Beyond these is the charming Murat Reis Mosque, surrounded by the old Turkish cemetery, with the tombs of Muslim dignitaries who died in exile here.

At the northern tip of the new town, which is fringed by beaches, is an Aquarium, with a small museum of natural history. 500m/550yds south is the Casino.

2km/1¼ miles south of the old town, on the road to Kallithéa, are a large Orthodox cemetery, Catholic and Jewish cemeteries and a new Turkish cemetery.

Rodíni valley

Farther south, outside the town, lies the beautiful Rodíni valley, with a park, a small zoo, a folk theatre and a variety of attractive footpaths.

3km/2 miles south of the new town, on Mt Áyios Stéfanos (Mount Smith; 111m/364ft; view), are the remains of the ancient acropolis, with fragments of temples. On the slopes of the hill are a stadion and a theatre (restored).

Ialysos

15km/9 miles south of Rhodes Town (bus service) rises Mt Filérimos (267m/876ft; view), with the remains of the acropolis of Ialysos, one of the three ancient cities on the island. The hill was occupied by a series of strongholds from Mycenaean times (*c.* 1400 B.C.) onwards. In 1308 it was a base for the Knights of St John during their siege of Rhodes, and in 1522 it served a similar purpose for the Turks. The ancient acropolis was approached by a handsome wide stepped road. On the plateau can be seen the foundations of a temple of Athena, built in the 3rd century B.C. on the site of an earlier temple and replaced in Early Christian times by a church (cruciform font set in the floor). There are also a small chapel with 15th century frescoes and the church and cloister (rebuilt during the Italian occupation) of the Filérimos monastery. Lower down the hill, reached by a difficult stepped path, is a Doric fountain-house of the 4th century B.C.

Rhodes via Kameiros to Lindos (111km/69 miles or 131km/81 miles)

★ Valley of Butterflies

The road runs south-west along the coast. In 16km/10 miles, beyond the airport, a side road (7km/4½ miles) branches off on the left and leads via Kalamónas to the Valley of Butterflies (Petaloúdes), which in the height of summer is the haunt of thousands of brownish-red butterflies.

12km/7½ miles: minor road to Émbonas, offering an attractive alternative route.

Kameiros

4km/2½ miles: side road (1.5km/1 mile) to the site, partly excavated, of ancient Kameiros (6th c. B.C.–6th c. A.D.). The remains include the temple precinct, the agora, cisterns, baths and houses.

Monólithos

The route continues on a beautiful panoramic road above the coast to Monólithos (32km/20 miles; alt. 280m/920ft), with an imposing castle of the Knights of St John south-west of the village.
From here a road crosses the island to Lindos (47km/29 miles): see below.

The road to Émbonas mentioned above comes in 16km/10 miles to a side road on the left leading to Mt Profítis Ilías (798m/2618ft), from which there are superb panoramic views.

Rhodes via Arkhángelos to Lindos (62km/39 miles)

The trip to Lindos is an essential excursion for every visitor to Rhodes. The road runs south from Rhodes, at some distance from the east coast for much of the way.

Kallithéa

7km/4½ miles: side road on the left (3km/2 miles) to the seaside resort and former spa of Kallithéa, beautifully situated amid magnificent gardens. The thermal springs, known and frequented since ancient times, have quite recently dried up. The handsome bath-houses and spa establishments, now abandoned and dilapidated, were built by the Italians in the 1930s.
2km/1¼ miles: Koskinoú, picturesquely situated on a hill, with colour-washed houses which are regularly repainted at Christmas or Easter.
7km/4½ miles: road on the left (3km/2 miles) to Faliráki (beautiful sandy beach; ceramic factory).
9km/6 miles: Afándou (sandy beach; large carpet factory).
6km/4 miles: Kolýmbia (bathing beach in beautiful cove).

Arkhángelos

6km/4 miles: Arkhángelos, a picturesque place with a ruined castle on a hill to the south.
7km/4½ miles: Malóna, a modest little village surrounded by beautiful orange and lemon groves.
18km/11 miles: Lindos.

★★ Lindos

Lindos is one of the three ancient cities on the island (the others being Ialysos and Kameiros) and, with its magnificent situation between two bays, its combination of sandy beaches and bizarrely shaped lime-

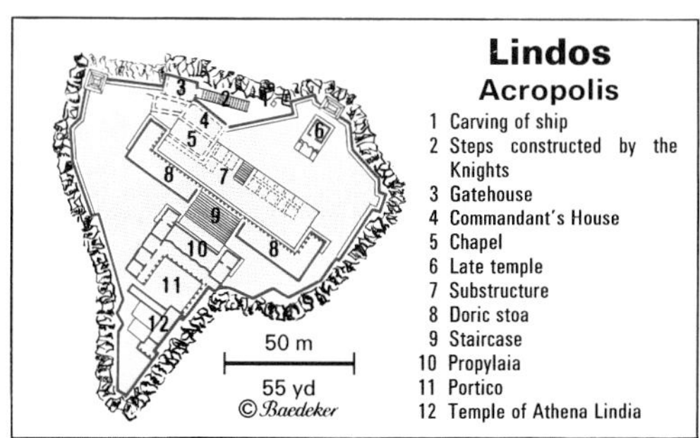

stone crags, its whitewashed houses, its medieval castle and ancient acropolis, the most striking and impressive of the three.

History

Remains of the Neolithic period and finds in Mycenaean cemeteries bear witness to the occupation of this site, on the only natural harbour on the island, from the earliest times. During the Dorian period Lindos – a city mentioned in Homer – owned more than half the island. About 700 B.C. it founded a colony at Gela in Sicily. Its heyday was in the 7th and 6th centuries under the tyrant (sole ruler) Kleoboulos, one of the Seven Sages, who built a temple to the goddess of Lindos on the acropolis. Important historical sources found here were the "Temple Chronicle of Lindos" and a list of priests for the years 375–327 B.C. The city continued to be occupied and developed during the Hellenistic period and into Late Roman times. A Byzantine castle was built on the acropolis, and in the 15th century the Knights of St John built this up into a mighty stronghold. During the 15th, 16th and 17th centuries the ship-owners and sea-captains of Lindos grew wealthy, leaving handsome mansions to bear witness to their prosperity.

Just before Lindos the road from Rhodes crosses a low pass, beyond which there is a fascinating view of the bay, the town and the acropolis. Cars must park at the entrance to the town, which is closed to all but pedestrian and donkey-borne traffic.

Walking through the narrow lanes of the town, visitors will see – in addition to the innumerable shops and stalls selling needlework and pottery – the typical whitewashed cube-shaped houses of the inhabitants and some of the handsome mansions of wealthy sea-captains, built in stone with characteristic relief decoration. To the left of the road up to the acropolis, in a courtyard behind high walls, is the

Lindos: the acropolis . . .

. . . and the steps to the citadel

beautiful church of the Panayía, built for the Orthodox population by Pierre d'Aubusson, Grand Master of the Order of St John from 1476 to 1503. It has a richly decorated iconostasis and one of the pebble mosaic pavements which were much favoured in Lindos. On the barrel-vaulted roof and the dome are ceiling paintings of 1779.

★ Church of Panayía

Below the town is the sheltered harbour, now lined with tavernas and bathing huts.

Tomb of Kleoboulos

On the way up to the acropolis (on foot or by donkey) there is a fine view of the harbour and the large circular tomb (6th c. B.C.) known as the Tomb of Kleoboulos.

★ Acropolis

Within the acropolis there are both ancient and medieval buildings. Beyond the outer entrance is a small square built over underground cisterns, below a sheer rock face with a carving of a ship, commemorating a Rhodian naval victory in 180 B.C. A steep flight of steps leads up to the gatehouse, which together with the adjoining buildings (the commandant's house and the castle chapel) was built by the Knights of St John and was left undisturbed by the excavators of the ancient site.

★ Temple of Athena Lindia

At the top of the steps is a large terrace dominated by an 80m/260ft long stoa with projecting wings (partly re-erected), built about 200 B.C. in front of the 4th century structures on the acropolis – a monumental staircase 21m/70ft wide, the propylaia (with five openings, like the Propylaia on the Acropolis in Athens) and the temple terrace. This highest terrace was surrounded on all four sides by stoas, the foundations of which have survived. At the far left-hand corner of the terrace is the temple of Athena Lindia, a small shrine in a grandiose setting, built after 300 B.C. on the site of Kleoboulos's 6th century temple. It is 23m/75ft long by 8m/25ft across, with four Doric columns at the east end (the type technically known as prostyle tetrastyle). The unusual situation of the temple, on the very edge of the precipitous crag, suggests that the goddess was originally worshipped in the cave below the temple.

From the farthest tip of the crag, beyond the temple, there are views of this cave (which can also be seen from the east end of the large stoa) and of the small and almost exactly circular harbour, the only natural harbour on the island of Rhodes. In antiquity it was the base of the Lindian fleet, and according to local tradition the Apostle Paul sought shelter from a storm here during his voyage from Ephesus to Syria in A.D. 51. There is a small chapel dedicated to St Paul.

From the acropolis there is also a view of a Hellenistic tomb in the rock face beyond the town.

Alimniá and Khalkí

To the west of Rhodes, at distances of up to 65km/40 miles, are the islands of Alimniá (pop. 25), with a ruined Genoese castle, and Khalkí (pop. 3000; chief place Nimborió), a rocky island with a medieval castle and the remains of a temple of Apollo.

Rion — F 5

Ρίο
Río

Region: Peloponnese. Nomos: Achaea

Situation and characteristics

Ríon, 6km/4 miles north-east of Patras (see entry), owes its importance to its situation at the narrowest point of the Gulf of Corinth, the "Little Dardanelles", opposite Antírrion, only 2km/1¼ miles away on the north side of the gulf. It is a busy ferry station linking the Peloponnese with mainland Greece (many crossings daily).

Beside the landing-stage is the Kástro Moréas (16th c.), which along with the Kástro Roumélis at Antírrion controlled the entrance to the gulf.

Salamis H 6

Σαλαμίνα
Salamína

Nomos: Attica
Area of island: 93 sq.km/36 sq. miles
Altitude: 0–365m/0–1200ft
Population: 20,500
Chief town: Salamína (Koulоúri)

Boat services

Ferry (cars carried) from Pérama (5km/3 miles west of Piraeus) and from Megálo Péfko (Mégara).

Situation and characteristics

Salamis (modern Greek Salamína), the largest island in the Saronic Gulf, with a much indented coast, closes off the entrance to the Bay of Eleusis. Its limestone hills, much eroded by karstic action, bear a scanty growth of trees; but the island's modest agriculture, combined with some tourist trade, particularly in the south-east and north-west of the island, is no longer sufficient to support the population (mostly descendants of Albanian immigrants), who now find employment in the industrial installations (refineries, shipyards) which have been established around the naval base in the north-east of the island and on the east side of the Bay of Eleusis (see entry).

History

The island owes its name (from *shalam,* "rest, peace") to Phoenician settlers from Cyprus. For long the subject of contention between Athens and Mégara, it was finally won for Athens by Solon and Peisistratos in 598 B.C. The ancient capital lay on a tongue of land between the bays of Kamateró and Ambeláki on the east coast; then in the 6th century B.C. it was moved south-west to Ambeláki (remains of acropolis and of harbour, visible under water).

Battle of Salamis

Salamis is celebrated as the scene of the great naval battle in 480 B.C. in which the Athenians, their resources depleted by war, inflicted a devastating defeat with their force of 378 triremes on a much larger Persian fleet and thus finally frustrated Xerxes' plans to expand westward into Europe. The battle – which Aeschylus, an eye-witness, took as the theme of his tragedy "The Persians" – was fought in the waters to the east of Salamis, between the island of Áyios Yeóryios to the north and the island of Psyttaleia and the Kynosoura ("Dog's Tail") peninsula to the south. Xerxes is said to have watched the battle from Mt Aigaleos, above Pérama.

Sights

Salamína

The island's capital, Salamína or Koulоúri (pop. 17,000), lies on the north side of Salamína Bay; it has a local museum. 3km/2 miles east is the principal port, Paloúkia (shipyards).

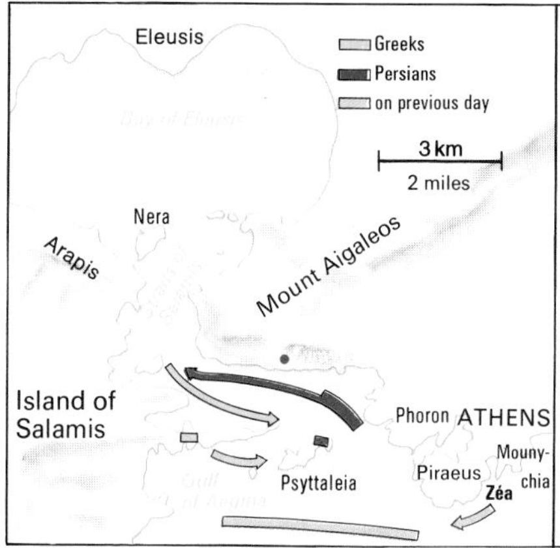

Battle of Salamís

27–28 September 480 B.C.

With only 378 triremes against a Persian force of over 1200 vessels, the Athenian fleet was able to inflict a decisive defeat on the Persians thanks to the manœuvrability of their ships, the local knowledge of their commanders and their skill in fighting at close quarters and to the Persian warships' inability to navigate in these narrow waters. The battle was watched by the Persian King Xerxes, seated on a golden throne on a hill near the coast. Cf. the account given by Aeschylus, who had himself taken part in the battle, in his drama "The Persians" (472 B.C.).

Faneroméni monastery

6km/4 miles west of Salamína on a scenically beautiful road is the Faneroméni monastery, which is revered as the scene of various apparitions of the Mother of the God and has fine frescoes. The monastery was founded in 1661 on the site of an ancient sanctuary, re-using architectural elements from the older buildings. To the south are the remains of the small fort of Boudorón (6th c. B.C.). At the foot of the hill on which the monastery stands is the landing-stage used by the ferry from Megálo Péfko (Mégara).

6km/4 miles south of Salamína lies the village of Agántio or Moúlki, with two churches of the 12th and 13th centuries. Farther south-west is the 18th century monastery of Áyios Nikólaos.

There are scanty remains of Mycenaean settlements at many points on the island.

Salonica G/H 3

Θεσσαλονίκη
Thessaloníki

Nomos: Salonica
Altitude: 0–150m/0–490ft
Population: 450,000 (Greater Salonica 750,000)

General

Situation and climate

Salonica (officially Thessaloníki), Greece's second largest city and capital of Greek Macedonia (see entry), lies at the head of the Thermaic Gulf (Gulf of Salonica), the most north-westerly gulf in the Aegean, near the mouth of the important river Axiós (Vardar) and on the foothills of the Khortiátis range (1200m/3900ft). The city's harbour is threatened by the steadily advancing delta of the Axiós.
During the winter months north winds blowing down the Vardar valley can bring very low temperatures. In summer the weather is not

infrequently oppressively hot, since the area of water in the Gulf of Salonica is too small to exert a moderating influence.

Economy

Salonica's economic importance depends on its role as a busy seaport (the largest in Greece after Piraeus) and a developing industrial centre. Its industries – predominantly on the western outskirts of the town – include a steelworks, an oil refinery, factories producing artificial fertilisers, cement, animal feeds, sugar, vegetable oils and other foodstuffs, engineering and shipbuilding. Old-established local industries are the processing of tobacco (from the tobacco-growing areas in eastern Macedonia), leather goods and textiles.
With excellent communications – shipping services, trunk roads, main-line rail services, an international airport – Salonica has developed an active trade both within Greece and with other countries. The Salonica Trade Fair, held annually in autumn, is an event of international importance.

Culture
European City of Culture 1997

Salonica is the principal cultural centre in northern Greece, with a major University (founded 1925), the National Theatre of Northern Greece (founded 1961), which is also an opera house, and the Salonica National Orchestra (KOTh); it is the see of a Greek Orthodox metropolitan (archbishop); and it has an important Archaeological Museum, numerous Byzantine churches, some notable Roman remains and a number of buildings of the Turkish period.

The town

The old town of Salonica, rising from the shores of the gulf on the slopes of a western outlier of the Khortiátis range, roughly in the form of a large square, is bounded on the landward side by a massive battlemented Byzantine wall, reinforced by towers, above which is a citadel dating in its present form from the Venetian period. The rest of the walls, on the south-east side and along the seafront, were demolished in the 19th century except for the White Tower at the south-east corner and the Vardar Fort at the south-west corner. On both sides of the walled town there were formerly large cemetery areas – on the north-west for Christians and Muslims, on the south-east for the Jews who made up a large proportion of the population; the site of the Jewish cemetery is now occupied by the Trade Fair grounds and the University campus.
The lower (southern) part of the old town is relatively flat and is traversed by wide boulevard-like streets. This area was rebuilt on a spacious scale after a devastating fire in 1917, leaving such ancient monuments as survived or were restored to form small cultural oases among the modern buildings.
Above this the older part of the town reaches up the hill to the ancient walls – a maze of irregular streets out of which rise the domes of old churches. The minarets of the Turkish period were destroyed after the First World War with the exception of a few remnants.
In recent times the city has expanded far beyond its old limits. The growth began with the development of a large residential area in the south-eastern suburb of Kalamaria, while industry established itself mainly on the north-west side of the town.
The city's life centres on the seafront promenade which extends east to the White Tower, the elongated Aristotle Square (Platía Aristotelous) half way along and Aristotle Street (Odós Aristotelous), with its attractive gardens, which runs north-east from there to the market quarter and its numerous tavernas. At right angles to Aristotle Street are Mitropolis Street and Tzimiskis Street, with Salonica's most fashionable shops.

Seafront promenade and White Tower

History

Origins

Numerous prehistoric mounds and remains of settlements in the vicinity of Salonica show that this area was settled by man in the Iron Age (*c.* 1000 B.C.). It is generally agreed, however, that the town first enters the historical record in 315 B.C., when King Kassandros of Macedon combined a number of existing small communities in a new town on the site of the earlier settlement of Thermai (which has given its name to the Thermaic Gulf), situated at the village of Sedes, 12km/7½ miles south-east of the present city. Kassandra named his new foundation Thessalonikeia after his wife Thessalonike, a half-sister of Alexander the Great.

Salonica as a Roman provincial centre

Under the Romans Salonica (Thessalonica) became capital of the province of Macedonia Prima (148 B.C.), and thanks to its situation on the sea and on the Via Egnatia, the great highway which ran from Dyrrhachium (Italian Durazzo, Albanian Durrës) on the Adriatic to Constantinople, developed into the leading city in the southern Balkans.

In 58 B.C. Cicero spent some time in Thessalonica during his exile from Rome. The Apostle Paul visited the town twice (in A.D. 50 and 56) and founded one of the first Christian communities on European soil (cf. his Epistles to the Thessalonians).

Late Roman period

In 253 and 269 the town repelled attacks by the Goths.

At the beginning of the 4th century it became the residence of the Emperor Galerius, a ruthless persecutor of the Christians. St Demetrius, a Roman officer of Greek origin, was martyred for his faith in 306, and the church of St Demetrius was built over his grave.

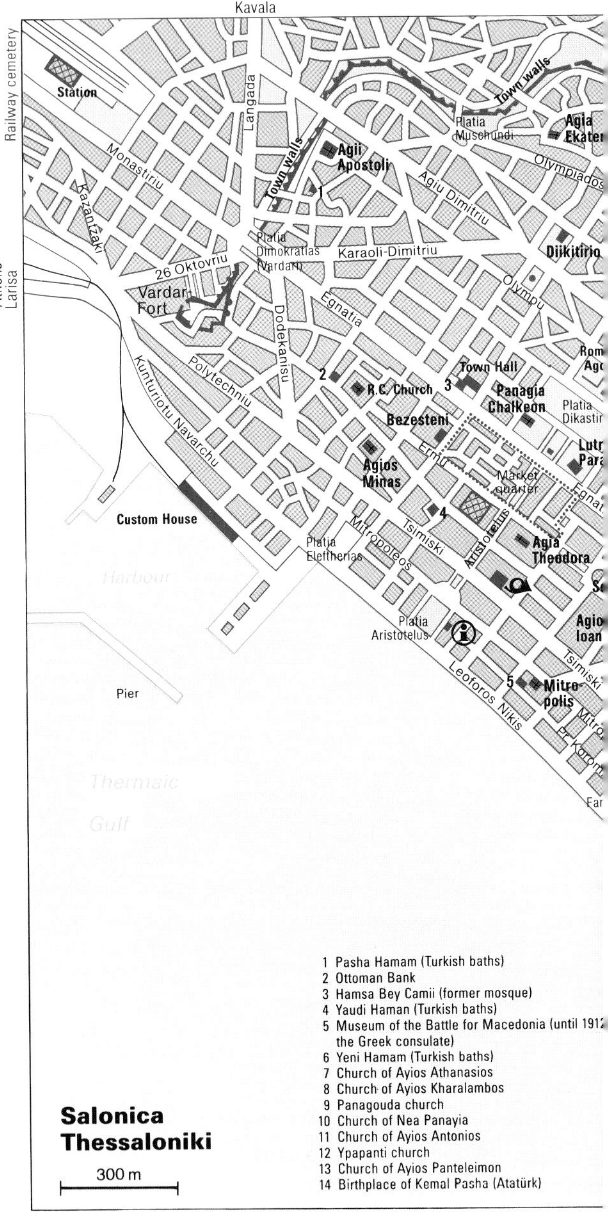
Kavala
Railway cemetery
Athens
Larisa
Station
Monastiriu
Kazantzaki
Langada
Town walls
Agii Apostoli
Platia Muschundi
Agia Ekater
Olympiados
Agiu Dimitriu
Platia Dimokratias (Vardari)
Karaoli-Dimitriu
Diikitirio
26 Oktovriu
Vardar Fort
Olympu
Egnatia
Dodekanisu
Polytechniu
Kunturiotu Navarchu
R.C. Church
Town Hall
Panagia Chalkeon
Platia Dikastir
Bezesteni
Ermu
Agios Minas
Market quarter
Custom House
Platia Eleftherias
Mitropoleos
Tsimiski
Aristotelus
Agia Theodora
Platia Aristotelus
Leoforos Nikis
Mitropolis
Harbour
Pier
Thermaic Gulf
Salonica Thessaloniki
300 m
1 Pasha Hamam (Turkish baths)
2 Ottoman Bank
3 Hamsa Bey Camii (former mosque)
4 Yaudi Haman (Turkish baths)
5 Museum of the Battle for Macedonia (until 191
the Greek consulate)
6 Yeni Hamam (Turkish baths)
7 Church of Ayios Athanasios
8 Church of Ayios Kharalambos
9 Panagouda church
10 Church of Nea Panayia
11 Church of Ayios Antonios
12 Ypapanti church
13 Church of Ayios Panteleimon
14 Birthplace of Kemal Pasha (Atatürk)

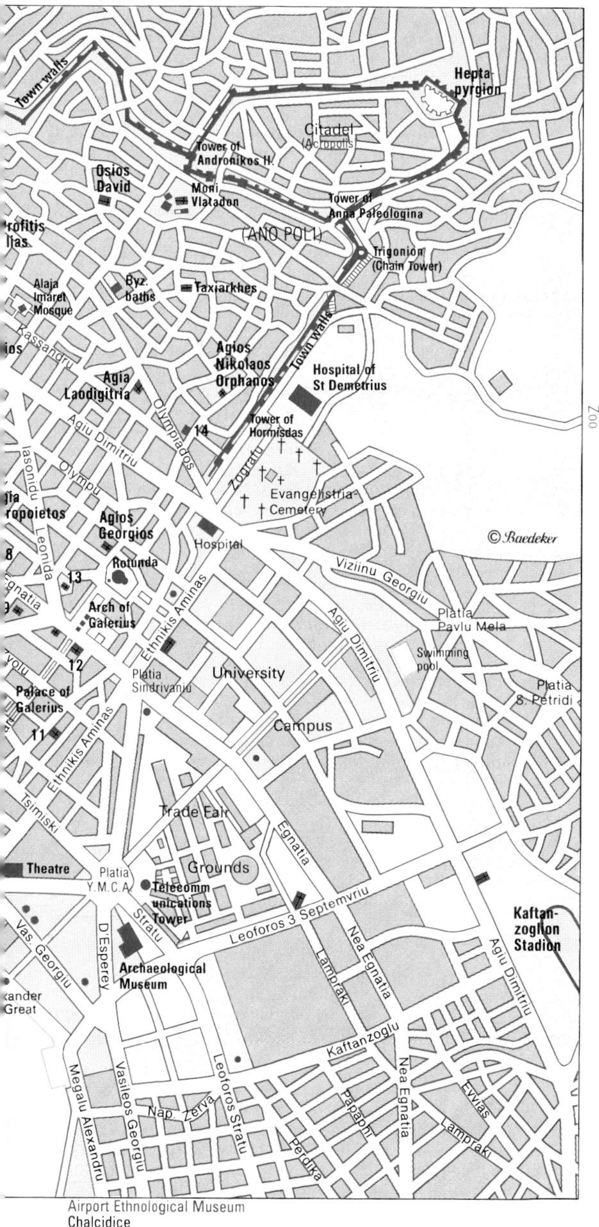
Town walls
Hepta-
pyrgion
Citadel
(Acropolis)
Tower of
Andronikos II.
Osios
David
Moni
Vlatadon
Tower of
Anna Paleologina
(ANO POLI)
Trigonion
(Chain Tower)
Byz.
baths
Taxiarkhes
Alaja
Imaret
Mosque
Kassandru
Agios
Nikolaos
Orphanos
Hospital of
St Demetrius
Agia
Laodigitria
Olympiados
Agiu Dimitriu
14
Tower of
Hormisdas
Zografu
Evangelistria-
Cemetery
Iasonidu
Olympu
Leonida
Agios
Georgios
Hospital
© Baedeker
Zoo
Rotunda
13
Arch of
Galerius
Viziinu Georgiu
Ethnikis Aminas
Platia
Pavlu Mela
12
Swimming
pool
Platia
Sindrivaniu
University
Platia
S. Petridi
Palace of
Galerius
Campus
11
Tsimiski
Trade Fair
Egnatia
Theatre
Platia
Y.M.C.A.
Grounds
Telecommunications
Tower
Leoforos 3 Septemvriu
Kaftanzoglion
Stadion
Vas. Georgiu
D'Esperey
Stratu
Archaeological
Museum
Lampraki
Nea Egnatia
Agiu Dimitriu
Great
Kaftanzoglu
Megalu Alexandru
Vasileos Georgiu
Nap. Zerva
Leoforos Stratu
Papaphi
Perdika
Evvias
Lampraki
Airport Ethnological Museum
Chalcidice

Although Theodosius the Great (379–395) made Christianity the state religion, he nevertheless ordered 7000 citizens of Thessalonica to be killed in 391 in reprisal for the murder of one of his generals.
When the Roman Empire was divided into two in 395 Thessalonica became part of the Eastern (Byzantine) Empire.

Byzantine period

Under the Byzantine Emperors Salonica remained the most important city in the Empire after Constantinople and the leading commercial city in south-eastern Europe. This was Salonica's heyday, during which many fine churches were built.
In the 6th and 7th century suffered siege and occupation by Slavs, Avars and Bulgars (578–732).
St Cyril (826/827–869) and St Methodius (before 820–885), the Apostles of the Slavs, came from Salonica, which was then bilingual in Greek and Southern Slavonic. For the writing of Church Slavonic they created the Glagolitic alphabet, which was later developed into Cyrillic.
The town was sacked by Saracen pirates in 904 and by Norman raiders in 1185.
At the beginning of the 13th century, after the capture of Constantinople by the Crusaders in 1204, Marquis Boniface de Montferrat established a Frankish kingdom and bishopric in Salonica, but in 1223 it was captured by the Despot of Epirus. In the 14th century the town was threatened by Catalans, Serbs and Turks, and the fortifications on the seaward side were strengthened. From 1342 Salonica was controlled by the Zealots in a kind of people's republic, until Byzantine authority was restored in 1349. Thereafter the town was held by various petty Byzantine rulers, and from 1423 to 1430 by Venice.

Under Turkish rule

In 1430 the town was captured by Sultan Murad II, and it remained Turkish for almost 500 years, until 1912, under the name of Selanik. The Turks expelled many of the Greek inhabitants and turned most of the churches into mosques. It was finally liberated in 1912.

Salonica's Jewish community

The population of the town was considerably increased by an influx of some 20,000 Jews expelled from Spain in 1492 (Sephardim) and smaller numbers from Germany and Hungary (Ashkenazim). Specialising in the cutting of precious stones and the manufacture of woollens and silks, they soon developed into an active commercial community trading with all parts of Europe. Between the 17th and 20th centuries these Jews, speaking Ladino (a hybrid dialect of Spanish and Hebrew), made up more than half the population. They were active in all trades and professions and played a predominant part in commerce and industry. In the second half of the 17th century the Dönme sect split off from the Jewish community and became converts to Islam. Some of the town's many Christian churches (most of which, as noted above, were converted into mosques) were used by the Jews as synagogues.

18th century

As the power of the Ottoman Empire declined Turkish rule in the Balkans, and particularly in Macedonia, grew steadily harsher, and the inhabitants of Salonica, suffering ever greater hardship and privation, several times rose in revolt (1720, 1753, 1758, 1789).

19th century

In the course of time large numbers of Greeks moved into the town, which was granted a degree of autonomy by the Turkish authorities. Many Salonicans took part in the struggle for Greek liberation; and when Emmanuel Pappas declared open rebellion on the Chalcidice peninsula in March 1821 the Turks killed at least 3000 people in Salonica, including leading figures in the Greek community, and imprisoned hundreds of others in the White Tower.

By the year 1865 the population of Salonica had risen to around 50,000. Towards the end of the 19th century the town enjoyed an economic upswing: in 1888 a railway link with the rest of Europe was established, in 1893 the first horse-drawn tramway system began operating, and between 1897 and 1903 a new commercial harbour was built. By 1895 the town had a population of 120,000. More than half of them were Jews, and the city had some thirty synagogues.

20th century

At the beginning of the 20th century Salonica became the headquarters of the "Young Turks", who deposed Sultan Abdul Hamid II (and exiled him to Salonica). One of the Young Turks was Mustafa Kemal Pasha (1881–1938), a native of Salonica, who in 1923, under the name of Atatürk ("Father of the Turks"), became the first President of the Turkish Republic.
In 1908 electric lighting and electric trams were introduced in Salonica.

Balkan Wars

Soon after the outbreak of the first Balkan War the 25,000 strong Turkish garrison, after some skirmishes with a Bulgarian unit, surrendered the town to Greek forces advancing from the west.
In March 1913 King George I was assassinated in Salonica.

Reunion with Greece

Under the treaty of Bucharest (August 1913), which ended the second Balkan War, Salonica and much of Macedonia were returned to Greece. In 1914 the town had a population of 180,000, half of them Jews, and newspapers were published in French, Greek, Turkish and Ladino.

First World War

During the First World War – in spite of Greece's neutrality – the headquarters of the Allied Eastern Command were in Salonica (1915–18). Here too (in the former Greek consulate, now a museum, near the Mitrópolis church) were the headquarters of Venizelos's government of national defence.
In 1916 the railway line from Salonica via Lárisa to Athens was opened.

Great fire, 1917

Of the many great fires in Salonica's history (1890, 1894, 1898, 1910, etc.) the most devastating was the one in 1917, which destroyed large areas of the city (including a number of old churches and mosques) and left 80,000 people homeless. The exchange of population between Turkey and Greece in 1923 meant that Salonica had to provide a home for more than 115,000 refugees, putting a further strain on its housing resources. Between 1925 and 1935 the city was rebuilt in modern style, largely to the design of the French architect and town planner Hébrard.
At the end of September 1918 an armistice between Bulgaria and the Allied powers was signed in Salonica.

Second World War

In April 1941 Salonica was occupied by German armoured forces thrusting down the Vardar valley from Yugoslavia. During the ensuing German occupation almost the whole Jewish population of Salonica (estimated at over 60,000) was deported to Nazi death camps and killed. The large Jewish cemetery on the east side of the old town was destroyed and its site occupied after the war by the Trade Fair grounds and the University campus.

Present-day Salonica

The development of the city after the war was delayed by the bloody Greek civil war, and a severe earthquake in 1978 brought a further setback. Nevertheless Salonica has continued to prosper and now presents the aspect of a busy modern city.

Sights

Visitors arriving in Salonica by car and finding their way, after a long drive through the city's extensive suburbs, into the heavy traffic of the city centre will be well advised to find a parking place – itself no easy task – and do their sightseeing as pedestrians. Distances in the lower town are not particularly great, and the main sights can easily be seen on foot. Alternatively, it is easy, and not expensive, to hire a taxi.

A convenient and easily identifiable starting-point for a sightseeing tour is the seafront promenade on the south-west side of the town.

★ Seafront promenade

The seafront promenade (Leofóros Níkis, Avenue of Victory), laid out on the line of the old walls which were pulled down in 1866, extends from the Central Harbour (Kentrikí Limáni) to the White Tower. In spite of the busy traffic the pedestrian strip along the water's edge is still a favourite promenade for both local people and visitors, not least because of the beautiful view over the gulf, extending in clear weather as far as Mount Olympus (see entry).

Aristotle Square

Half way between the long building of the Custom House, on the harbour, and the White Tower (see page 443), extending north into the town, is the rectangular Platía Aristotélous (Aristotle Square). The many cafés and restaurants in the arcades around the square make this a popular rendezvous, particularly in the evening, but the traffic-free area in the centre of the square is also a good place for rest and relaxation durting the day.
On the east side of the square (No. 8) can be found the office of the National Tourist Organisation (EOT).

City Centre

Aristotle Street
Mitropóleos
Tsimíski
Egnatía

From Aristotle Square Aristotle Street (Odós Aristotélous) runs north-east into the city centre. After crossing Odós Mitropóleos and Odós Tsimíski, two long streets lined with luxury shops, boutiques and other shops, it joins the broad Odós Egnatía, the city's main east–west street. (In spite of its name this is probably not the Roman Via Egnatia, which is believed to have bypassed the city.)

Market quarter

Here the picturesque Central Market area (Kentrikí Agorá) extends on either side of Aristotle Street, with numerous shops supplying every-day domestic needs as well as many tavernas.

Bezesteni

At the west end of the market area is the old Turkish Bezesteni, which in the 16th century ranked as the finest bazaar in the whole of the Balkans. To the south of this, between Ermoú and Tsimíski, is a Turkish

Yaudi Hamam

bath-house, the Yaudi Hamam.

Hamsa Bey Mosque

On the north side of Egnatia Street, between Venizelou and Dragoumi Streets, stands another monument of the Turkish period, the Hamsa Bey Mosque (now known as the Alkazar), which is thought to have been built about 1468.

Platía Dikastiríou

In the centre of the ancient city was the Agora, now a large square, Platía Dikastiríou (Lawcourt Square), laid out after the great fire in 1917. In the lower part of the square, on Egnatia Street, are two notable buildings.

Panayía Khalkéon

At the south-west corner of the square is the church of the Panayía Khalkéon (Mother of God of the Coppersmiths), so called because of its situation in the old coppersmiths' quarter. Built in 1028 as the

Áyios Dimitrios

church of the Theotókos and converted into a mosque during the Turkish period, it is a typical example of Byzantine church architecture.

Paradise Baths

To the south-east, opposite the Panayía Khalkéon, is a large Turkish bath-house, the Tsifte Hamam (= "Double Baths") or Hamam Bey, built in 1444 by Sultan Murad II, which later became known as the Paradise Baths (Loutrá Paradisou). The baths are still in use.

Roman Agora

At the north end of the square considerable remains of buildings of the Roman period have been brought to light in recent years, suggesting

The Bezesteni, the old Turkish bazaar

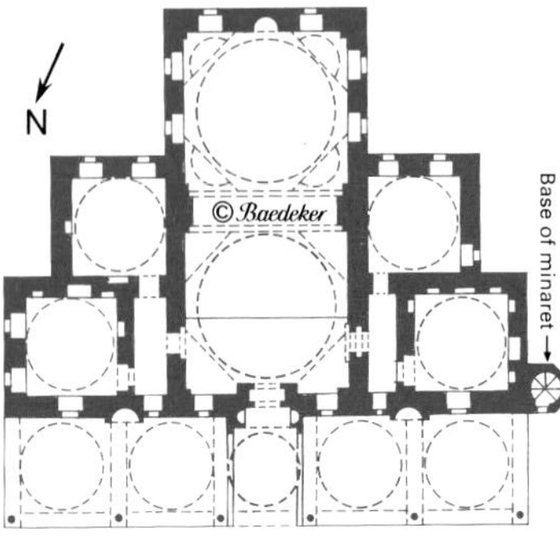

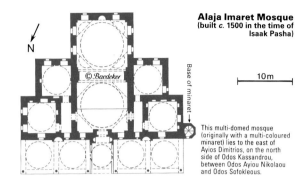

Alaja Imaret Mosque
(built *c.* 1500 in the time of Isaak Pasha)

10 m

This multi-domed mosque (originally with a multi-coloured minaret) lies to the east of Ayios Dimitrios, on the north side of Odos Kassandrou, between Odos Ayiou Nikolaou and Odos Sofokleous.

that this was the Roman Forum. The site is now known as the Roman Agora (Romaïkí Agorá).

Panayía Acheiropoietos

Two blocks south-east of the Paradise Baths along Egnatia Street lies a small public garden (on the left), on the east side of which, sunk below the level of the surrounding buildings, is the Early Christian church of the Panayía Acheiropoietos (Mother of God Made without Hands), later also known as Ayía Paraskeví (St Parasceva). Originally built in the 5th century, it was converted into a mosque in 1430, at the cost of some damage to its structure, and restored in the 20th century. (See plan on page 83).

Notable features of the interior, apart from the fine spatial effect, are the remains of mosaics and an Arabic inscription on a marble column recording that "Sultan Murad conquered Thessalonica in the year 833 (A.D. 1430)".

★★ Áyios Dimitrios

To the north of the Roman Agora is the city's principal church, Áyios Dimítrios (St Demetrius). This five-aisled basilica was built over a Roman bath-house (remains of which can be seen on the north side of the church) and a Roman road (seen from the crypt, which contains a small lapidarium). Until the 9th century it was known as the "church by the Stadion". Investigations after 1917 confirmed the tradition that the Emperor Galerius caused a Roman officer named Demetrius to be imprisoned and executed here in the year 306. Thereafter Demetrius became the town's principal saint and patron, and pilgrims came from all over the Byzantine Empire to visit his tomb.

The church was originally built in the 5th century, and its main features were preserved in a 7th century rebuilding made necessary by a fire and in the reconstruction of the church after its destruction in the great fire of 1917. During the Turkish period it was converted into a mosque, the Kasimiye Cami.

Notable features of the interior of the church, the largest in Greece (43m/141ft long), are the finely carved capitals of the antique columns in varicoloured marble, the huge wheel chandelier in the central aisle, the small mosaics on pillars in the apse and the large marble tomb of Loukas Spantounis (d. 1481) on the north wall of the narthex.

In 1980 the relics of St Demetrius were brought back to Salonica from the Italian town of San Lorenzo in Campo; they are now preserved in a sarcophagus in front of the iconostasis.

Yeni Hamam

North of Áyios Dimítrios, at the junction of Kassándrou and Ayíou Nikoláou Streets, is another Turkish bath-house, the Yeni Hamam (New Baths), also built on Roman foundations.

To the east of Áyios Dimítrios, on the north side of Odós Kassándrou between Odós Ayíou Nikoláou amd Odós Sofokleous, is the Alaja Imaret Mosque with its seven domes. Of its multi-coloured minaret there remains only the base.

Alaja Imaret Mosque

Another important Early Christian church is Ayía Sofía, at the east end of Hermes Street (Odós Ermoú). This three-aisled domed cruciform church on an almost exactly square plan dates from the 8th century. In the 9th and 10th centuries, after the end of the iconoclastic conflict, it was decorated with new figural mosaics, including the Mother of God in the apse (replacing the earlier Cross) and a magnificent representation of the Ascension in the dome. Also notable are the capitals of the columns, which are believed to have come from a 5th century building.

★ Ayía Sofía

From 1204 to 1430 the church of Ayía Sofía was the town's metropolitan church or cathedral (now the Mitrópolis, to the south, in the street of that name). During the Turkish period it became a mosque, the Aya Sofya Camii. It was restored after a fire in 1890 and survived the great fire of 1917 unscathed. A graceful Turkish porch was destroyed in an Italian air raid in 1941, and the church was badly damaged in the 1978 earthquake.

In a small public garden at the south-east end of the seafront promenade – the southern tip of the city centre – is the city's best-known landmark, the White Tower (Lefkós Pýrgos). This was a major element in the system of walls and fortifications which originally surrounded the whole town, and is the only relic of the seaward defences which were demolished from 1869 onwards.

★ White Tower

The present round tower was built by the Turks about 1430 on the site of an earlier defensive tower, and was used mainly as a prison. After a rebellion by the janissaries against Sultan Mahmud II in 1826 they were imprisoned and killed in the tower, which then became known as the Bloody Tower. Thereupon the Turkish authorities whitewashed the tower and renamed it Beyaz Kule, the White Tower.

The massive 35m/115ft high tower (from the top of which there are fine views of the city and the harbour) now houses a museum on the history and art of Byzantine Salonica from around A.D. 300 to its capture by the Turks in 1430 (Early Christian coins from the town mint, gravestones and grave goods, vases, mosaics, fragments of wall paintings, capitals, liturgical objects, etc.).

Museum

From the White Tower a broad avenue, Leofóros Ethnikís Amínas, runs north-east along the line of the former town walls to a large square, Platía Syntrivaníou, which is crossed by Egnatia Street. In the centre of the square is an obelisk fountain, set up here by the Turks in the late 19th century and re-erected in its original form in 1977.

Syntrivani Square

Going along Egnatia Street towards the city centre, we come to the Arch of Galerius (Apsída Galeríou or Kamára), the town's most important Roman monument, which is believed to have been erected in A.D. 297. Of the original structure, a double gateway with four brick piers on each side situated at the intersection of the city's two principal streets, there remain three piers on the west side. The four central piers originally supported a dome. Two of the surviving piers, linked by an arch, have a marble facing decorated with four bands of reliefs separated by garlands. The reliefs, depicting scenes from the Emperor's Persian, Mesopotamian and Armenian campaigns (292–311), are among the finest of the kind (note particularly the lively scenes on the south pier). Although badly weathered, these reliefs, both in the individual figures and the grouping, retain much more of their original

★ Arch of Galerius

★★ Reliefs

Arch of Galerius and Rotunda

Reliefs on Arch of Galerius

vigour than the almost contemporary reliefs on the Arch of Constantine in Rome (A.D. 315).

Palace of Galerius

From the Arch of Galerius Gounari Street runs south-west to a large square, Platía Navarínou, with remains of the Palace of Galerius (Anáktora Galeríou) which were excavated in the 1970s. On the south side of the site is an octagonal structure, the function of which has not been determined.

Hippodrome

To the east of the Palace of Galerius extended the Roman Hippodrome (Circus), which was some 500m/550yds long. Although it has been located by archaeological investigation, it has not been excavated because of the modern buildings which cover the site. Here in A.D. 391 the Emperor Theodosius the Great ordered the massacre of 7000 citizens of Thessalonica, for which he was taken to task by St Ambrose, bishop of Milan.

★ Rotunda

From the Arch of Galerius a colonnaded street originally ran north for some 100m/110yds to the Rotunda, which is believed to have been built as a Pantheon or a mausoleum for Galerius (though he was not buried here) and is now known as St George's Church (Áyios Yeóryios). This circular structure with thick, inward-corbelled walls and an interior diameter of 24m/80ft, preserves the remains of fine mosaics in the dome and the vaulted recesses round the walls (one of which was later extended to form the choir of the church). The mosaic in the centre of the dome is missing, but below it can be seen the figures of angels, and below these again architectural façades on a gold ground.

On the west side of the building is a minaret, badly damaged but still standing – a relic of the time when the church was converted into a mosque (the Hortaci Suleiman Effendi Camii).
The Rotunda is now open to the public as a museum (lapidarium).

★ Church of the Holy Apostles

At the opposite end of the old town, close to the Byzantine walls, stands the handsome church of the Holy Apostles (Áyii Apóstoli; 1312–15), on a cruciform ground-plan, with five domes and richly patterned brickwork (blind arcades reaching up into the roof). During the Turkish period it was used as a mosque, the Soğuk Su Camii ("Mosque of the Cold Spring"). The main dome rises high above the barrel-vaulted arms of the cross, with four subsidiary domes over the corners of the portico – a Late Byzantine innovation – which surrounds the church on three sides.

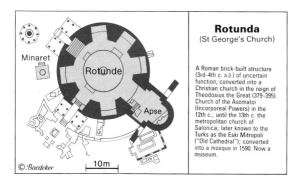

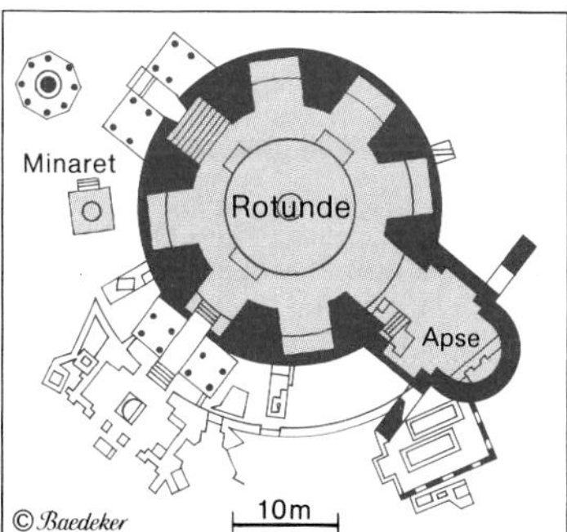

Rotunda
(St George's Church)

A Roman brick-built structure (3rd–4th c. A.D.) of uncertain function, converted into a Christian church in the reign of Theodosius the Great (379–395). Church of the Asomatoi (Incorporeal Powers) in the 12th c.; until the 13th c. the metropolitan church of Salonica; later known to the Turks as the Eski Mitropoli ("Old Cathedral"); converted into a mosque in 1590. Now a museum.

Church of the Holy Apostles

The church contains fine wall paintings and mosaics of the Palaeologue period which were discovered during restoration work in 1940. On the north side of the church is a cistern belonging to the former monastery of the Holy Apostles.

Pasha Hamam

South of the church of the Holy Apostles, at the junction of Karátsa, Kálvou Andréa and Zefirón Streets, is a Turkish bath, the Pasha Hamam (now known as the Phoinix).

Diikitírion (Dioiketerion)

In the north-west of the old town, on the north side of the broad Odós Ayíou Dimitríou at its intersection with Odós Dragoúmi Filímonos, is an imposing building now known as the Diikitíron (Dioiketerion; Government House) which houses the Ministry of Northern Greece. It was originally built in 1891 by the Italian architect Vitaliano Poselli on the site of the old Turkish Konak to house the Turkish governor's offices.

Upper Town

★ Áno Polí

The upper town (Áno Polí), an area of steep and irregular little streets and lanes which was formerly occupied mainly by Turks and still has something of an Oriental aspect, rises up the hill from Odós Olympíados, the curving street which bounds the lower town on the north, to the old town walls and citadel.
In this part of the town there are several fountains of the Turkish period as well as a number of notable churches, some of which deserve particular mention.

Ósios David

On a steep site half way up the upper town, surrounded by modest little houses, is the little square church of Ósios Davíd, which was originally built in the 5th/6th century and later served as the church of the Latómou monastery (now disappeared).

★ Mosaic

Externally unpretentious, it has a fine mosaic in the apse depicting the prophet Ezekiel's vision (a beardless figure of Christ between Ezekiel and Habakkuk). The mosaic dates from the time of the church's foundation but remained hidden for many centuries. It was first concealed behind an ox-skin to protect it from the iconoclasts, came to light again by accident in the 9th century and was later covered with whitewash by the Turks, to be finally rediscovered in 1921.

Vlatádon monastery

To the east of Ósios Davíd, immediately below the west end of the citadel, is the Vlatádon monastery (Moní Vlatádon), founded between 1351 and 1371, which now houses the Patriarchal Academy. In the principal church (Katholikon), which was extensively rebuilt in 1801, 11th century wall paintings were found during restoration work in 1983, showing that the church must have been in existence well before the foundation of the monastery.

Church of the Taxiarchs

In the south-eastern part of the upper town is the three-aisled church of the Taxiarchs (Archangels), dedicated to SS Michael and Gabriel, which is dated to the 14th century; the outer wall of the apse has fine patterned brickwork. Much altered, the church was used as a mosque (Iki Şerefe Camii, the "Mosque with Two Minaret Galleries") during the Turkish period.

Áyios Nikólaos

At the south-eastern corner of the upper town stands the little 14th century church of Áyios Nikólaos Orfanós (St Nicholas the Orphan), which is surrounded by an arcaded portico. It contains some well preserved 14th century frescoes, particularly in the apse.

★ Ayía Ekateríni

In the north-west part of the upper town is the 13th century church of Ayía Ekateríni (St Catherine), with unusually rich decorative brickwork, some of it coloured. A harmoniously proportioned building on a square ground-plan, it is a fine example of the Macedonian school of architecture. It contains notable 13th century mosaics and frescoes.

★ Profítis Ilías

The church of Profítis Ilías (the Prophet Elijah) stands on a raised site in a large square on the southern fringe of the upper town (on the south side of Odós Olympiádos). This cruciform 14th century church was probably the Katholikon of the lost Néa Moní, a monastery built on the ruins of the Byzantine palace which is believed to have stood here. It was known in Turkish times, when it was converted into a mosque, as the Eski Saray Camii, the Old Palace Mosque.

The church is notable both for its gracefully articulated exterior and the fine monolithic columns in the transepts.

Atatürk's Birthplace

Near the south corner of the upper town, adjoining the reddish Turkish Consulate in Odós Apóstolou Pávlou, is the house in which Mustafa Kemal Pasha (Atatürk), first President of the Turkish Republic, was born in 1881.

Town Walls

Origins

It is certain that the town of Thessalonikeia founded by Kassandros in 315 B.C. was very soon afterwards surrounded by defensive walls, for it was able to withstand attacks by King Pyrrhos of Epirus in 285 and by the Celts in 279. In Roman times no substantial alterations were made to the old Greek walls, but they were extensively developed and strengthened by Constantine the Great, particularly on the seaward

Walls of the Citadel

side. Under the Byzantine Empire the town's defences were frequently reinforced, as many inscriptions on the wall record. The final phase of construction was in the 14th and 15th centuries, when the Turkish authorities built further defensive structures (particularly towers), sometimes employing Venetian military engineers.

Present condition

Until the second half of the 19th century the old town was still surrounded by a complete circuit of walls, with bastions, forts, towers and gates. From 1869 onwards, however, with the declared intention of "modernising" and "beautifying" the town, the Turkish authorities pulled down the walls along the seafront between the Vardar Fort and the White Tower. Later the stretch of walls between the White Tower and the south-east corner of the upper town was demolished to make way for a new street, originally called the Boulevard Hamidiye, later Queen Olga Avenue and now Leofóros Ethnikís Amínas. The rest of the walls, including the citadel, have been preserved and in recent years have been restored section by section.

Dimensions and materials

The walls, which originally had a total length of 8km/5 miles and enclosed a large square area, consist mainly of alternating courses of stone and brick and incorporate considerable numbers of ancient remains (fragments of statues, columns, altars, gravestones, etc.). They range in thickness between 3m/10ft and 4.6m/15ft and stand to a height of 10–12m/33–39ft.

★ Tour of the walls

A good starting-point for a tour of the walls is the Evangelistria cemetery to the north of the University campus. From here we can walk up outside the walls to the massive 15th century round tower known as the Trigonion (or Alysos Tower; Turkish Zincirli Kule, Chain Tower). Beyond this is the Tower of Anna Palaiologina, with a gateway

through which we enter the Citadel, on the site of the ancient acropolis. The interior of the citadel is fully built up, and on the highest point is a fortress, the Heptapyrgion ("Seven Towers"; Turkish Yedi Kule), formerly used as a prison. At the south corner of the acropolis stands the Tower of Andronikos II, with numerous inscriptions relating to the different phases of construction built into the walls.
From the Citadel it is possible to continue westward following the walls, either inside or outside, to the position of the old Letaia Gate (Turkish Yeni Kapu, "New Gate"), near the church of the Holy Apostles, and then down to the spacious Democracy Square (Platía Dimokratías), formerly Vardar Square, on the site of the former Golden Gate or Vardar Gate. From there the walls continue down towards the harbour, ending at the Vardar Fort.

Outside the Old Town

★★ Archaeological Museum

Facing the south side of the extensive Trade Fair grounds, set in gardens, is the low modern building which houses the new Archaeological Museum opened in 1963 (Arkhaioloyikó Mousío; closed Tue.), with an important collection of material from Salonica itself, Macedonia and Thrace.
The main hall has a variety of interesting exhibits illustrating the story of the city from prehistoric times to the Early Christian period. The Museum's star attraction, however – displayed in a special wing of the building – is the unique collection of finds from the Macedonian royal tombs at Vergína (see entry), including two richly decorated chests of solid gold and other masterpieces of Macedonian metalworking.
The prehistoric collection includes material from the middle Neolithic to the early Chalcolithic.
Also of great interest are the objects of the Archaic and early classical period (silver, gold and iron articles, weapons, pottery, idols, etc.) found in the Sindos necropolis and the grave goods of the 4th century B.C. from Derveni, just north of Salonica (gold jewellery, silver and bronze vases, including a large mixing jar of gilded bronze).
Other exhibits include finds from Olynthos (see entry), Roman mosaics and glassware, much sculpture of the Archaic, classical and Roman periods (including Roman copies of classical Greek works) and a door arch from the octagonal structure in the Palace of Galerius.

Statue of Alexander the Great

South-west of the Archaeological Museum on the seafront promenade, reached by walking through the gardens, can be seen a modern equestrian statue of Alexander the Great.

Ethnological Museum

The Ethnological Museum (Ethnoloyikó Mousío; closed Tue.) is housed in a handsome 19th century building in Queen Olga Street (Vasilíssis Ólgas 68), formerly the fashionable Rue des Campagnes, which runs south-west from the town. The collection displays folk art and life of the last two and a half centuries – costumes from all over northern Greece, jewellery, weapons and everyday objects.

Patrician houses

In the south-western suburb of Kalamaria are numbers of fine 19th century villas and mansions, many of them designed by Italian architects in neo-classical style.
One such house of some historical interest is the Villa Allatini (designed by the Italian architect Vitaliano Poselli, 1896), in which the deposed Sultan Abdul Hamid II was confined from 1909 to 1912. From 1926 it was occupied by the newly founded University.

Yeni Cami

The Yeni Cami (New Mosque), also designed by Poselli, was built in 1902 for the Dönme sect (Jews converted to Islam). From 1917 to 1962 it housed the Archaeological Museum.

Railway cemetery

An attraction of a rather different nature is the large "railway cemetery" in the old railway depot (much overgrown: beware of snakes!) on the western outskirts of the city, with numbers of old and frequently rusting locomotives (the oldest dating from 1887) and rolling-stock from many European countries. The "cemetery" can be visited only with special permission from the railway authorities; but it is possible to get some impression of it from outside by following the railway line westward from the town, passing between warehouses and workshops.

Excursions from Salonica

Bathing beach

The nearest bathing beach is at Ayía Triáda, on the south side of the Gulf of Salonica (leave the city on the airport road; boat service to beach at weekends).

Hill villages

A popular excursion from Salonica is to the villages in the Khortiátis range (Oraiokastro 10km/6 miles, Panorama 12km/7½ miles, Khortiatis 22km/14 miles).

Chalcidice and Mount Athos

Salonica is a good base from which to visit the Chalcidice peninsula (see entry), with its beautiful beaches, and the monastic republic of Athos (see entry).

Ancient sites

Within convenient reach of Salonica are the ancient sites of Pella (40km/25 miles north-west) and Vergína (80km/50 miles south-west; expressway to Véria). See entries for these places.

Samos L/M 6

Σάμος
Sámos

Nomos: Sámos
Area of island: 476 sq.km/184 sq. miles
Altitude: 0–1440m/0–4725ft
Population: 33,000. Chief town: Sámos

Air services

Airfield 5km/3 miles south-west of Sámos. Flights from Athens twice daily; also to Chios, Lésbos and Mýkonos.

Boat services

Regular services from Athens (Piraeus) and Rhodes, several times weekly (cars carried).
Ferry service to Kuşadası (Turkey).

Situation and characteristics

The island of Sámos (Turkish Sisam) has other attractions as well as the wine for which it is famed. It is a green, well wooded island which has only recently become a target for mass tourism, with the site of one of the most important sanctuaries and cultural centres of the ancient world, the Heraion.
Geographically an outpost of Asia Minor, from which it is separated by a strait only 1.9km/1¼ miles wide, it rises in the centre to 1140m/3740ft in Mt Ampelos and in the west to 1440m/4725ft in Mt Kerkis.
The island's main sources of income from time immemorial have been farming, boatbuilding and fishing.

History

The first inhabitants of Sámos, probably Carians, were displaced at an early stage by Ionians, who used the island as a base for the conquest

and settlement of the nearby coast of Asia Minor. In the second half of the 6th century B.C., under the tyrant (sole ruler) Polykrates, the island grew wealthy and powerful. Like other tyrants of the period, Polykrates erected magnificent buildings and fostered the arts. Although allied with Persia, he was executed by the Persian satrap Oroites about 522 B.C. and succeeded by his brother Syloson, ruling subject to Persian overlordship, and then by other tyrants. The island took part in the Ionian rebellion, achieved independence and became a privileged member of the first Attic maritime league, the Confederacy of Delos. After a rising in 440 B.C. Sámos was conquered by Perikles, and until the end of the Peloponnesian War became a base for the Athenian fleet. Thereafter it was alternately under Spartan, Athenian and Persian influence. It did not join the second Attic maritime league. Its history in the period after Alexander the Great is obscure, though it seems to have belonged to the empire of the Ptolemies in the 3rd century B.C. Hostile to Rome but forced to submit to it, the island achieved independence in the reign of Tiberius (A.D. 17).

In subsequent centuries Sámos was held by Byzantines, Arabs (from 824), Venetians and Genoese. After being plundered by the Turks at the end of the 15th century the island – then depopulated and devastated – came under Turkish rule in 1509. In 1562 it was resettled, and thereafter was granted considerable privileges. During the war of Greek independence, in 1821, the islanders held out against the Turks, and under the London Protocol of 1832 Sámos was declared a principality required to pay tribute to the Ottoman Empire, ruled by a prince who was to be appointed by the Sultan but who must be a Christian. Its flag was to bear a Greek cross.

During the Tripolitanian war of 1912 Italian troops drove out the Turkish occupying forces, and after further military action the island was reunited with Greece later in that year. In the great fire of 1990 the south-eastern part of the island lost as much as 80% of its trees.

Sámos was the home of the Greek mathematician and philosopher Pythagoras.

Sights

Sámos town

Since 1832 the island's capital has been the little town of Sámos (pop. 8000), which was founded in that year. It lies in a semicircle round the sheltered inner harbour of Vathý, climbing picturesquely up the hill with its vineyards and olive groves to the upper town of Apáno Vathý. It has an attractive square and picturesque little streets and alleys.

Mountain village on Sámos

★ Museum

The Museum, housed in the former residence of the Prince of Sámos and a new building opposite it financed by the Volkswagen Foundation and opened in 1987, displays material recovered in the German excavations of the Heraion from 1910 onwards.

The main hall of the museum had to be specially enlarged to accommodate the most sensational find made in the Heraion, the colossal marble figure, 4.8m/15½ft high, of an Archaic kouros (*c.* 580–570 B.C.), possibly a votive statue from the Sacred Way. The torso was found in 1980 and the head (70cm/27½ inches high) in 1984 in a vineyard near the Heraion; the knee had been found 70 years earlier, in 1912. Also displayed in the hall is an Archaic over-lifesize female figure (*c.* 570 B.C.) excavated in 1984, a counterpart to the famous Hera of Cheramyes, found in the Heraion in 1879, which is now one of the treasures of the Louvre.

In the room to the left are the base and three of the original six figures in a group by Geneleos, a sculptor of the Archaic period (*c.* 560 B.C.). The room to the right contains Hellenistic and Roman sculpture. On the upper floor is prehistoric material (pottery, ivories, bronzes).

Pythagórion (Tigáni)
Town walls

The friendly little port of Pythagórion or Tigáni, 11km/7 miles southwest of Sámos town on the south coast of the island, occupies the site of the ancient city of Samos. There are remains of town walls (4th c. B.C.) and the foundations of a breakwater. On the acropolis hill, near the cemetery, are the church of the Transfiguration (Metamórfosis) and a castle built by Lykourgos Logothetis (1822–24). Close by is the site of a Hellenistic villa, on which a Christian basilica was built in the 5th century. A small museum contains Archaic and Hellenistic funerary stelae, portraits of Roman Emperors and a seated figure of Aiakos, father of Polykrates. No structures belonging to the ancient acropolis have been found.

In the eastern part of the site of the ancient city is the monastery of the Panayía Spilianí, below which, reached on a signposted path, is a depression marking the site of a theatre.

★ Aqueduct of Eupalinos

Farther west is the entrance to an underground aqueduct, 1km/¾ mile long, constructed by Eupalinos in the 6th century B.C. 1.75m/5ft 9in high and wide, it has been made passable for visitors. 425m/465yds from the entrance can be seen the point where the two shafts, one driven from each end, met one another, making an almost perfect join.

★ Heraion

8km/5 miles west of Pythagórion (19km/12 miles from Sámos town) is the Heraion, the sanctuary of the goddess Hera. Here, at the mouth of the river Imbrasos, according to an ancient tradition, the Ionian settlers led by Prokles found a wooden image caught in the branches of a willow tree. Recognising it as a cult image of Hera, they set up an altar beside the tree.

Along the processional way between the town of Sámos and the Heraion stood a variety of votive statues, including the group by Geneleos to be seen in the museum in Sámos town. Its place is now taken by a replica.

★ Altar of Rhoikos

The original altar by the willow tree was followed by others. The seventh was the altar by the sculptor Rhoikos (*c.* 550 B.C.; partly rebuilt), which in size and magnificence was surpassed only by the great altar of Zeus at Pergamon.

Temple of Hera

To the west of the altar is the temple of Hera. The modest wooden Temple I (first half of 8th c. B.C.) and Temple II (after 670 B.C.) were succeeded by a colossal stone structure, Temple III, built by Rhoikos and Theodoros in 570–550 B.C. This covered an area 105m/345ft by 52.5m/172ft and had a double peristyle of Ionic columns 18m/60ft high, 104 in all. Soon afterwards this temple was destroyed, and

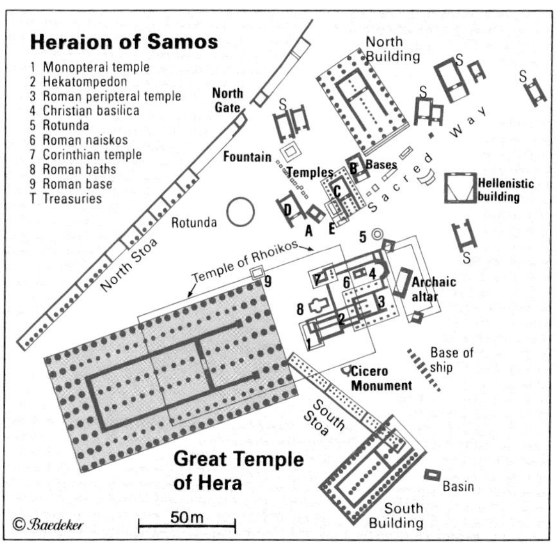

Polykrates thereupon commissioned a replacement, Temple IV. Covering an area 112.2m/368ft by 55.16m/181ft, this was the largest temple ever designed by Greek architects, but – like other gigantic Ionic temples – it remained unfinished. Nothing of this temple now survives but its massive foundations and a single column. Finally a small peripteral temple of 4 × 6 columns was built close to the altar to house the cult image.

The high water table made excavation difficult, but the work of E. Buschor and his successors has made it possible to follow the development of the sanctuary in detail. In 1963 the excavators even brought to light the remains of the ancient willow tree. Near the site of the temples is the apse of an Early Christian church. To see some of the other remains in the area – including the basin in which the image of Hera was annually bathed – it is necessary to have either a knowledgeable guide or a good plan of the site.

The return to Sámos town is either via Pythagórion or by way of the island's medieval capital, Khóra (7.5km/4½ miles from the Heraion) and Mytilíni (10.5km/6½ miles; pop. 5000).

Circuit of the Island

The scenery along the north coast is particularly attractive with narrow valleys and terraced slopes. The road from Sámos town along the north coast, which is mostly fringed by cliffs, comes in 10.5km/6½ miles to the little port of Kokkári. About half way there, near a chapel of Ayía Paraskeví on the right of the road, is a modest Early Christian baptistery. Beyond Avlákia (20km/12½ miles) a road goes off on the left to Vourliótes (3km/2 miles), from which it is 2km/1¼ miles to the Vrontianí monastery (founded 1566), on the northern slopes of Mt Ampelos.

The coast road continues to Áyios Konstantínos (26km/16 miles) and Karlovási (32km/20 miles), a port of call for the regular boats. The remote west coast is picturesque but can only be reached on foot by means of steep and tortuous paths.

From here there is an attractive return route to Sámos through the beautiful hilly country in the interior of the island, passing through Pýrgos, Koumaradéi and Khóra.

There are a number of other monasteries on the island, including Zoodókhos Piyí (founded 1756; extensive views), 8km/5 miles east of Sámos, Profítis Ilías (founded 1625), 4km/2½ miles south of Karlovási, and Stavrós (founded 1586), 3km/2 miles east of Khóra.

Samothrace K 3

Σαμοθράκη
Samothráki

Nomos: Évros. Area of island: 178 sq.km/69 sq. miles
Altitude: 0–1640m/0–5380ft. Population: 3000
Chief place: Samothráki (Khóra)

Boat services

Samos is on the shipping route from Athens (Piraeus) to Lemnos, Samothrace and Alexandroúpolis.
Daily ferry service from and to Alexandroúpolis.

Situation and characteristics

Samothrace, lying 40km/25 miles off the Thracian coast, is the most north-easterly outpost of the Greek island world. From its highest peak, Mt Fengári (1640m/5380ft), according to Homer, Poseidon watched the fighting at Troy. Lying by itself in a sea without any neighbouring islands, it is an island of great scenic beauty with a regular coastline but no sheltered anchorages. The inhabitants live by arable farming, growing fruit and vegetables (particularly onions).

History

As its name ("Thracian Samos") indicates, Samothrace was originally populated by Thracians, who founded the sanctuary of the Great Gods. About 700 B.C. the first Greeks arrived on the island, and thereafter the sanctuary grew and developed; until the 1st century B.C., however, Thracian remained the cult language. In the 4th century B.C. Philip II of Macedon was initiated into the mysteries, and it is said that he met his wife Olympias here. From the early 3rd century, when Ptolemy II and his sister Arsinoe erected splendid new buildings in the sanctuary, the cult spread widely through the Hellenistic world. Under the Romans (from 168 B.C.) the cult of Kybele, which had originated in Asia Minor, became associated with that of the Great Gods. Only the spread of Christianity put an end to the cult, about A.D. 400, but the town of Palaiopolis, immediately west of the sanctuary, was inhabited until the 15th century.
Excavations by French and Austrian archaeologists in the 19th century and more recent American investigations (Karl and Phyllis Lehmann, 1939 and 1948 onwards) have thoroughly explored the site and thrown some light on the mysteries practised there, but our knowledge of the cult remains imperfect, partly because of the secrecy maintained by the adepts and partly because the remains have been overlaid by the deposits of many subsequent centuries.

The Kabeiroi, to whom the sanctuary was formerly thought to be dedicated, were not the only objects of worship there. A central position among the Great Gods who are referred to in inscriptions was

Ancient columns on Samothrace

occupied by the Thracian mother goddess Axieros as mistress of nature. Associated with her were Axiersos and Axiersa, two divinities of the underworld who were identified by the Greeks with Pluto and Persephone, the youthful vegetation god Kadmilos and the two Kabeiroi. They were revered as the protectors of nature, and later increasingly as the patrons of seafarers and rescuers of those in peril on the sea. Initiation into the mysteries, which took place in two stages, was open to both Greeks and non-Greeks, men and women, free men and slaves – a factor which no doubt promoted the later spread of the cult.

After the fall of the Roman Empire Samothrace alternated between Byzantine, Venetian and Genoese rule until it fell to the Turks in 1457. It was reunited with Greece in 1912 after the Balkan War.
During the Second World War the island was occupied by Bulgarian troops.

Sights

Samothráki (Khóra)

The chief place on the island, the picturesque little medieval town of Samothráki (Khóra; pop. 1500), lies in the hills 3km/2 miles east of the tiny port of Kamariótissa (ruined castle).

★ Sanctuary of Kabeiroi

6km/4 miles north-east, above the site of ancient Palaiopolis, are the remains of the sanctuary of the Great Gods or of the Kabeiroi, which have only recently been completely exposed. A chapel dedicated to Ayía Paraskeví and the ruins of a castle of the Gattelusi family on the slopes of the hill mark the site of the ancient port (shingle beach). In spite of repeated destruction by pirates, war and earthquakes the sanctuary continued in existence until the 4th century A.D. During the Middle Ages the ruins of the ancient buildings served as a quarry of dressed stone for the construction of the castle.

Anaktoron

The excavations lie 500m/550yds inland. From the museum (behind the Xenia hotel and restaurant) a signposted path runs south-east,

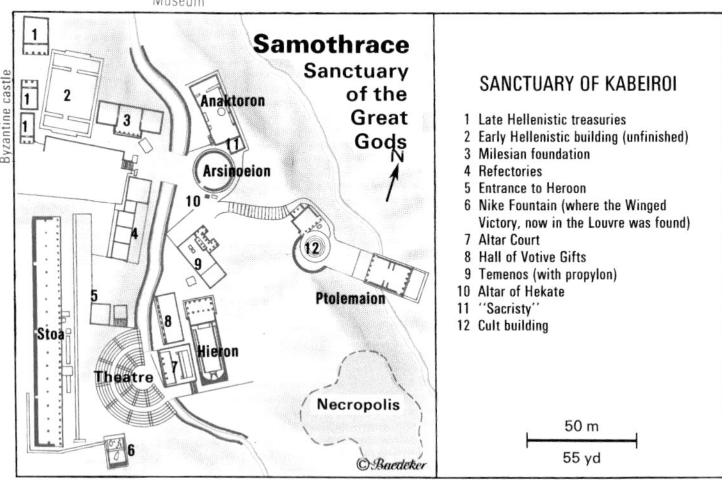

passes through an iron gate, crosses the middle one of the three streams which flow down through the hilly terrain and, after passing a viewpoint, reaches the first large structure on the site, the Anaktoron (House of the Masters or House of the Gods; *c.* 550 B.C.), in which the worshippers underwent the first degree of initiation (*myesis*). The northern part of the building, the holy of holies, was closed off; in the south-east corner is a libation pit.

"Sacristy"

Immediately south, on a higher level, is the "Sacristy", in which registers of the initiate were maintained.

Arsinoeion

Beyond this stood the Arsinoeion, the largest roofed rotunda of Greek antiquity (diameter over 20m/65ft), built by Arsinoe (later Queen Arsinoe II of Egypt) between 289 and 281 B.C. It occupies the site of an earlier cult building, now represented by walls and a rock-cut altar brought to light by the excavators within the Arsinoeion.

On the hillside above the Arsinoeion are remains of an ancient road and a circular building.

Temenos

Other altars dating from the early period of the cult lie between the Arsinoeion and the next building to the south, the Temenos. Built between 350 and 340 B.C., this was the first marble structure on the site, with an Ionic propylon which had a frieze of female dancers in Archaicising style (fragments in museum).

Hieron

Going along the middle terrace past an Archaic altar, we come to the re-erected façade of the Hieron, built in the late 4th century B.C., with a portico added in the 2nd century. At the south end is an apse (under which a crypt was built in Roman times), giving the building a plan reminiscent of a Christian church. Here the adepts were admitted to the second degree of initiation (*epopteia),* probably, as Lehmann suggests, after confessing their sins at two marble blocks outside the east side of the building.

Parallel to the Hieron are the Hall of Votive Gifts (6th century B.C.) and the Altar Court (340–330 B.C.), the colonnade of which probably served as the stage wall of the (badly ruined) theatre built about 200 B.C.

★ Archaeological Museum

South-east of the sanctuary are an ancient necropolis (7th–2nd c. B.C.) and the Archaeological Museum.

Palaiopolis

North-east of the sacred precinct is the site of ancient Palaiopolis, founded by Aeolian Greeks in the 7th century B.C. The massive town walls of the 6th century B.C. extend high up the slopes of the hill. Little is left within the walls. On the site of the ancient acropolis are the ruins of a castle (1431–44) of the Gattelusi family.

At Therma, to the east of Palaiopolis, a hot spring (55°C/131°F) emerges from a 10m/35ft high cone of silica deposits.

Mt Fengári

Mt Fengári or Fengan (1640m/5380ft), the island's highest peak, offers a rewarding climb. The ascent (guide advisable) takes about six hours.

Santorin/Thera K 7

Σαντορίνη
Santoríni

Nomos: Cyclades. Area of island: 73 sq.km/28 sq. miles
Altitude: 0–584m/0–1916ft. Population: 6000
Chief place: Thíra (Firá)

Air services

Airfield 6km/4 miles south-east of Firá. Daily flights from and to Athens; also connections with Iráklion (Crete), Mýkonos and Rhodes.

Boat services

Regular services from and to Athens (Piraeus; 12 hours; cars carried) and Crete (7 hours), several times weekly.

★★ Situation and characteristics

Santorin or Thíra (Thera, the Wild Island; Italian Santorino or Santorini, after the island's patron saint, St Irene), the most southerly of the larger Cyclades, and the smaller islands of Thirasía (9 sq.km/3¼ sq. miles; 0–295m/0–970ft) and Aspronísi (2 sq.km/¾ sq. mile; 0–71m/0–233ft) are remnants of a volcanic crater which has been engulfed by the sea. The rim of the caldera emerges from the sea in a ring, open to the north-west and south-west, enclosing a basin up to 400m/1300ft deep, in the centre of which are the two Kaiméni islands, the peaks of a later volcano which came into being in historical times. Hot springs and emissions of gas bear witness to continuing volcanic activity.

The dense volcanic deposits lie on top of a massif of argillaceous schists and greywacke overlaid by semi-crystalline limestones. The highest point on the island is Mt Profítis Ilías (584m/1916ft), in the south-east; at the northern tip is Megálo Voúno, on the east side Monólithos. The inner wall of the crater falls down to the sea in sheer cliffs, ranging in height between 200m/650ft and 400m/1300ft, of greyish-black lava with bands of white pumice and reddish tufa. On

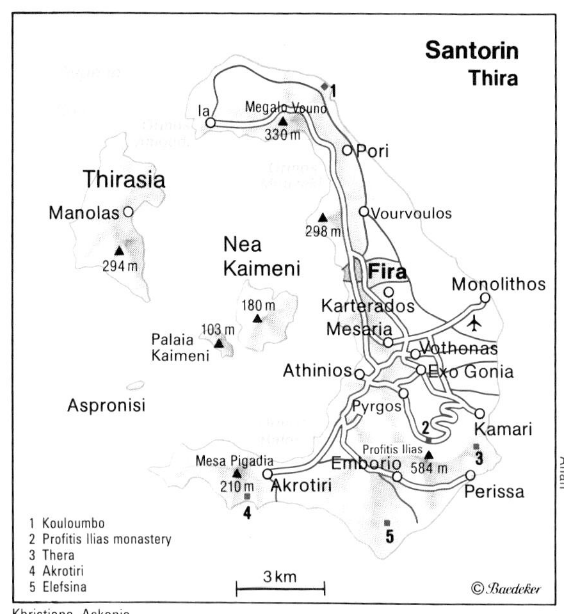

Khristiana, Askania

the outside the land slopes gradually down to the sea in fertile slopes of pumice soil covered with vines. Owing to lack of water the island is treeless. The inhabitants achieve a modest degree of prosperity through the export of wine, pulses, pistachios and tomato purée, and also Santorin earth (pozzolana), a natural hydraulic cement used in structures exposed to water (harbour works, the Suez Canal).
In recent years large numbers of visitors have been attracted to the island by its extraordinary natural structure and its archaeological sites, which are among the most important in Greece, and the tourist trade has made an increasing contribution to the economy. But this is not an island for an ordinary seaside holiday, particularly for visitors with children.

History

In antiquity Thera was known as Kalliste (the "fairest" island) or Strongyle (the "round" island).
Thera was inhabited, probably by Carians, in the 3rd millennium B.C. (Cycladic culture). Achaean Greeks settled on the island about 1900 B.C., but were later driven out by the Phoenicians. The excavations at Akrotíri have shown that Santorin was a flourishing and prosperous island in the first half of the 2nd millennium B.C. It was in contact with Minoan Crete but had developed a distinctive culture of its own. It seems likely that at least the city of Akrotíri was ruled not by some central authority but by a plutocracy of merchants and shipowners who had trading links reaching as far afield as Libya. This trade, and perhaps also an ethnic connection with North Africa, can be deduced from the wall paintings, of astonishingly high quality, which are at present in the National Archaeological Museum in Athens.
The golden age ended with the eruption of the volcano around 1510 B.C., which turned the centre of the island into a gigantic crater. The suggestion by Spyridon Marinatos that this catastrophe also brought about the end of the Minoan cities on Crete has not been generally accepted.
It has been speculated that the legend of the disappearance of the island kingdom of Atlantis under the sea might be associated with the eruption.
After the eruption the island remained uninhabited for 500 years, until the beginning of the 1st millennium B.C., when it was resettled by Dorian (Minoan) incomers from Crete, who established themselves on a limestone ridge south-east of Mt Profítis Ilías. In 630 their king, Grinos, founded a colony at Kyrene – the largest Greek colony in North Africa. Allied with Sparta at the beginning of the Peloponnesian War, Thera was obliged to pay tribute to Athens from 427/426 B.C. onwards. It enjoyed a measure of prosperity under the Ptolemies, when an Egyptian garrison was stationed on the island. Thereafter it came under Roman rule.

In 1207, after the 4th Crusade, Santorin was conquered by Marco Sanudo, Duke of Náxos, and remained in Italian hands for three centuries, until its capture by the Turks in 1539. It was reunited with Greece in 1830.

The volcanic force which originally built up the island round the older limestone cone of Mt Profítis Ilías and later destroyed it continued to manifest itself in later centuries. The last violent volcanic phenomena, combined with earth tremors which caused considerable damage, occurred in 1956.

Sights

★ Approach by sea

Although many visitors now come to Santorin by air, the approach by sea, entering the crater from the north-west, is an experience which

Ía, on the rim of the crater

should not be missed. After passing the gentle green slopes on the outside of the island the boat enters the huge central basin, almost totally enclosed by sheer rock walls.

Ía

At the northern tip of the main island, clinging to the rim of the crater, is Ía (Oia), a trim little town of whitewashed houses which until the Second World War was the island's economic and commercial centre. Steep paths zigzag up the wall of the crater to the town from Ammoúdi Bay, to the west, and the little harbour of Áyios Nikólaos, to the south. As the boat sails on the basin is closed off by the island of Thirasía (on the right) and the south-western tip of Thíra, visible in the distance beyond the Kaiméni islands.

★ Firá

From the landing-place in the little port of Skala, where passengers are landed in small boats, the island's chief town Firá (or Thíra; pop. 1500) is reached either by walking or riding (by mule or donkey) up the steep and winding stepped path (587 steps) or by taking the new cableway. Large passenger ships now regularly put in at the new port of Athiniós, to the south, from which there is a road (17km/10½ miles) to Firá.

With its whitewashed houses, many of them built into the rim of the crater, its winding lanes and little squares, which continually open up new views, and the turquoise-blue domes of its churches and chapels, Firá is a charming little town. With the development of the tourist trade numbers of new shops of all kinds have been established, including several jewellers. The Archaeological Museum at the north end of the town displays material of the Cycladic and Minoan periods (before the eruption of the volcano) and also later material of Dorian, Hellenistic and Roman date.
A new museum to house the finds from Akrotíri is under construction beside the modern Mitrópolis church (1956).

The new cableway, an alternative to the donkey

★ Profitis Ilías monastery

From Firá a road runs south by way of the village of Pýrgos (6km/4 miles) to the summit of Mt Profítis Ilías (584m/1916ft), the highest point on the island, from which there are far-ranging views. The principal church has a richly carved iconostasis and a Cretan "crown of St Elijah" (15th c.). In the museum can be seen the mitre and crozier of Patriarch Gregory V, who was hanged in Constantinople by the Turks in 1821. Also of interest are the library, the monastic archives

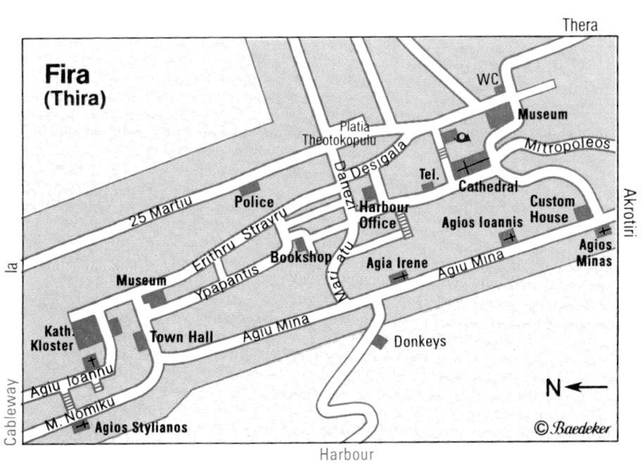

and the kitchen. The monastery ran one of the many "secret schools" which operated during the Turkish period.

From Mt Profítis Ilías a road descends eastward to the Selláda (a saddle between two hills), on either side of which are the necropolises of ancient Thera. From here a road on the left runs down to Kamári on the east coast, on the site of ancient Oia, and a road on the right leads south to Períssa. Straight ahead the road winds its way up to Mt Mésa Vounó, passing the church of Áyios Stéfanos, built on the site of a 5th century basilica and incorporating ancient masonry, and continuing to the Evangelismós chapel (alt. 297m/974ft), adjoining which is a heroon of the 2nd century B.C.

★ Thera

The remains of Thera, the ancient capital of the island, extend from the Selláda over the rocky ridge of Mésa Vounó, which slopes down steeply on three sides. The town, which continued in existence into Byzantine times, has preserved its original Hellenistic layout.

From the Evangelismós chapel a path winds its way southwards up the hillside to the retaining wall of a terrace on which are the remains of the temple of Apollo Karneios (6th c. B.C.). The temple has a pronaos, naos and two rooms built against the south-west wall of the naos. The terrace (also 6th c.) to the south of the temple, built up to make it larger, was used for ceremonies in honour of the god. Between the temple and the corner of the wall are the foundations of a rectangular building, within which, cut in the rock, are the names of various gods (north-west side; some dating from 8th c. B.C.) and of citizens of Thera (south-east side).
At the south-east end of the ridge is the Gymnasion of the Ephebes (2nd c. B.C.). On the north-east side of a large courtyard is the Grotto of Hermes and Herakles; at the east end are a rectangular hall and a round building. Above are rock-cut inscriptions, some of them erotic in content.

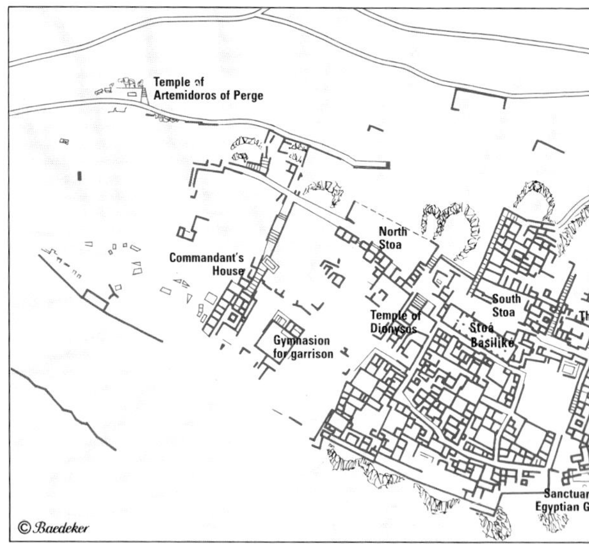

Flanking the main street are the foundations of a number of Hellenistic houses with ground-plans of Delian type and the Theatre, with a Roman stage building, under which are traces of the Ptolemaic proskenion. At the entrance to the theatre a side street branches off and runs up to the rock sanctuary of the Egyptian deities Isis, Serapis and Anubis.

Farther along the main street is a colonnade with shops, and beyond this are Roman baths. Then comes the Agora, a long irregularly shaped area with a number of streets opening off it. On its east side is the Stoa Basilike (1st c. B.C.), with two inscriptions in the name of Kleitosthenes opposite the entrance. The inner hall is divided into two aisles by a row of Doric columns. The pilasters along the walls and the building at the north end (a tribunal?) were later additions.

Farther left, above the north end of the Agora, is a terrace with a temple of Dionysos, converted in the 2nd century B.C. to the cult of the Ptolemies and in the Roman Imperial period to the cult of the Emperors. Opposite it is a temple of the goddess Tyche (Fortune).

The main street continues north beyond the Agora. A side road leads west up the hill to the barracks and the gymnasion (to the south) of the Ptolemaic garrison, on the highest point of Mésa Vounó.

At the lower end of the main street, near the Selláda, is the temple of Artemidoros of Perge (3rd c. B.C.), with rock-cut reliefs.

From the Selláda it takes half an hour to reach the picturesque 19th century church of Períssa. South-west of the church, to the right of the churchyard, are the foundations of a round building of the early Empire, with inscriptions relating to the ownership of land (2nd–4th c. A.D.).

From Períssa the return to Firá is by way of Emborió and the temple of Thea Basileia (1st c. B.C.), excellently preserved, with the ancient roof,

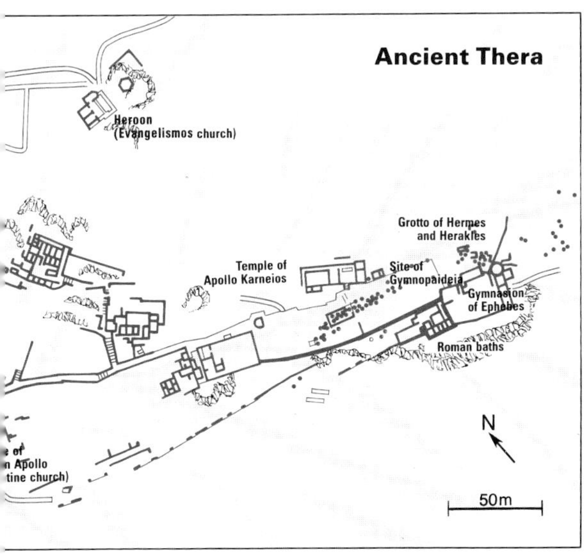

A typical island church

Youth with fish, from Akrotíri

Excavated remains, Akrotíri

View of the Kaimeni islands from Ía

a handsome door-frame and a niche in the interior, as a result of its conversion into the church of Áyios Nikólaos Marmarítis.

★★ Akrotíri

Near the village of Akrotíri, 12km/7½ miles south-west of Firá, the Greek archaeologist Spyridon Marinatos brought to light between 1967 and his death in 1974 considerable areas of a large town destroyed in the great eruption. The buildings date from the 16th century B.C. and show evidence of the earthquake damage which preceded the final catastrophe (e.g. displaced walls which were held in place by the pumice sand deposited by the erupting volcano). Combined with the fact that some of the buildings were of two or three storeys, this created great problems of excavation and conservation. Indeed Marinatos himself was killed during the excavation work and is buried in a building opposite the spot where the accident occurred.

Entering the site (which is roofed over for protection from the weather) on the south side, we pass between houses which have been preserved to first- and second-floor level. Going north along Odós Telkhinon, we come to a triangular space, on the far side of which is the West House. This contained many frescoes (at present in the National Archaeological Museum in Athens), including a representation of a naval expedition and a well preserved painting of a naked youth carrying bunches of fish (see illustration, page 464). In the northernmost house are a number of jars for the storage of food. Returning south, we pass a house with a staircase leading up to the first floor, with steps broken by an earth tremor, and a large complex with a small room (No. 2) in which the "Spring Fresco" was found.

On the principal buildings in this second Pompeii, which is 1600 years older than the Italian Pompeii and will keep the archaeologists busy for years to come, are plans and explanations for the benefit of visitors.

On the way back from Akrotíri to Firá a detour can be made (turning right at a junction 2km/1¼ miles from Akrotíri) to the chapel of Áyios Stéfanos, set amid trees on the site of an ancient temple, and beyond this to the little seaside resort of Períssa (bathing beach).

Kaiméni islands

The Kaiméni islands (reached by boat from Skála) are the cone – still active – of the volcano. A visit to the islands is fairly strenuous and not particularly spectacular.
There are records of the emergence and disappearance of small islands in this area in 197 B.C. and between A.D. 19 and 46; volcanic changes took place in the year 726, probably on Palaiá Kaiméni (to the south-west), and in 1457 there was a non-volcanic rock-fall. Mikrá Kaiméni (to the north-east) came into being in 1570–73; in 1650 there was an eruption north-east of Thera (Koloumbos Bank); in 1707–11 Néa Kaiméni emerged from the sea; and between 1866 and 1870 there were further violent eruptions, when the island of Afroéssa, south-west of Néa Kaiméni (and later joined to it), was formed by masses of boiling lava. The George Crater (alt. 128m/420ft) on the south-east coast of Néa Kaiméni, named after King George I of Greece, which still occasionally emits sulphurous vapours (most recently in 1956), can be climbed on its north side from the bay between Néa and Makrá Kaiméni; the climb takes about half an hour.

Boat-owners like to put in at Néa Kaiméni for a day or two in order to expose the hull of their boat to the warm sulphurous water and thus cleanse it of seaweed and barnacles, etc.

Idyll on the Saronic Gulf

Some 18km/11 miles south-west of Santorin are the islets of Khristiana (alt. 0–279m/915ft) and Askania (0–143m/0–469ft), the most southerly of the Cyclades.

Saronic Gulf H 6

Σαρωνικός Κόλπος
Saronikós Kólpos

The Saronic Gulf, on the east side of the Isthmus of Corinth, separates Attica from the Peloponnese. It is named after Saron, an otherwise unknown king of Troizen (see entry), who was drowned in these waters.

Round the coasts of the gulf are a series of tourist resorts – Méthana, Palaiá and Néa Epídavros (see Epidauros) on the south side of the gulf, Loutró Elénis and Isthmía (see entry) at its west end, and the resorts on the Attic Riviera (see Attica) on its north-east side.

Saronic Islands H 6

Σαρωνικές Νησιά
Saronikés Nisiá

The collective name of Saronic Islands covers all the islands in the Saronic Gulf – Salamis (see entry), Aegina and Angístri (see Aegina) and Póros (see entry), together with numerous other islets and isolated rocks. The Argolic Islands (see entry) are also included in this general designation.

Serifos I 6

Σέριψος
Sérifos

Nomos: Cyclades
Area of island: 66 sq.km/25 sq. miles
Altitude: 0–486m/0–1595ft
Population: 1800
Chief place: Sérifos (Khóra)

Boat services

Regular daily service from and to Athens (Piraeus; 5–6 hours; cars carried).

Situation and characteristics

Sérifos, north-west of Sífnos (see entry), is a bare and rocky island, its hills slashed by gorges; its highest point is Mt Toúrlos (486m/1585ft). The island's main sources of income are its modest agriculture and its opencast iron-mines, which have been worked since ancient times. The ore is shipped from Koutalás, on the south coast.

History

Originally settled by Ionian Greeks, the island shared the fortunes of the other Cyclades. In Greek mythology it was the island on which Danaë and the young Perseus were washed ashore.

Sights

Sérifos (Khóra)

At Sérifos, the island's capital, above the sheltered harbour of Livádi, are the ruins of a Venetian castle (view).

Monastery of the Taxiarchs

★ Church of Panayia

At the north end of the island is the monastery of the Taxiarchs (Archangels), founded in 1600, which has a fine library. North-west of the monastery is the pretty village of Panayía, with the church of Xyló Panayía (950).

Serrai H 2

Σέρρες
Sérres

Nomos: Serrai
Altitude: 50m/165ft
Population: 40,000

Transport

Station on the Salonica–Alexandroúpolis railway line.

Situation and characteristics

Sérrai, 100km/62 miles north-east of Salonica, is a commercial town which was rebuilt in modern style after its destruction by the Bulgarians in 1913.

Sights

Its main features of interest are the Mitrópolis church, a three-aisled basilica with a synthronon and remains of mosaics, and the ruined castle which crowns the hill formerly occupied by the acropolis (view).

Servia F/G 3

Σέρβια
Sérvia

Nomos: Kozáni
Altitude: 430m/1410ft
Population: 4000

Situation and characteristics

The Macedonian town of Sérvia lies on a pass between two ranges of hills to the west of Mount Olympus (see entry). As its name indicates, it was founded by Serbs during the Middle Ages.

Sights

The town's main tourist attraction is not so much its ruined 11th century episcopal church as Lake Aliakmón, an artificial lake 6km/4 miles north-west.

20km/12½ miles north-west of Sérvia is Kozáni (see entry), and 28km/17 miles beyond this is the industrial town of Ptolemáis (pop. 21,000).

Sfaktiria F 7

Σφακτηρία
Sfaktiría

Nomos: Messenia
Area of island: 5 sq.km/2 sq. miles
Altitude: 0–137m/0–449ft

Situation and characteristics

Sfaktiría, the ancient Sphagia, is a cliff-fringed island lying off the south-western Peloponnese, separated from it by the narrow Sikiá Channel, which is only 200m/220yds wide. The island, 4.6km/2¾ miles long and between 500m/550yds and 1000m/1100yds across, forms a protective barrier on the west side of Navarino Bay (see Pýlos), in which on October 20th 1827 a Turkish fleet of 82 warships suffered an annihilating defeat at the hands of a numerically inferior British, French and Russian fleet. The sea bed is still littered with wrecks.

Memorials

On the saddle between the two highest points on the island is a spring, to the east of which are the Panagoúla chapel (annual consecration festival) and a monument to the Russian sailors who fell in the battle.

On the east coast, to the south of the little Panagoúla Bay, are the Tsamados Cave and the grave of the Piedmontese general and philhellene Count Santa Rosa, who fell here in 1825, along with a Greek captain named Tsamados, in a battle with Ibrahim Pasha's Egyptian forces.

On the southern hill can be seen the tomb of Prince Paul-Marie Bonaparte, killed off Spétsai in 1825. Opposite this, on the mainland, is the Venetian and Turkish fort of Néo Kástro (1573).

Off Cape Kípri, on the south coast, is the islet of Pýlos (lighthouse), with a monument to the French sailors killed in the battle of Navarino.

In the north-east of Navarino Bay, on the flat rocky islet of Khelonáki (Marathonísi), is a memorial to the British sailors who fell in the battle.

Sifnos/Siphnos — I 6/7

Σίφνος
Sífnos

Nomos: Cyclades
Area of island: 73 sq.km/28 sq. miles
Altitude: 0–680m/0–2230ft
Population: 2000
Chief place: Apollonía

Boat services

Regular service from and to Athens (Piraeus), several times daily (5½ hours; cars carried).
Local connections with Sérifos, Kímolos and other neighbouring islands.

Situation and characteristics

Sífnos, one of the southern Cyclades, lies roughly in the centre of the triangle formed by Melos, Sérifos and Páros. The north and north-west of the island are occupied by barren ranges of hills, the east and south by gentler uplands. The coast is much indented, and lined by cliffs for much of its length.

Agriculture (particularly onion-growing) on the island's fertile soil, the manufacture of pottery of traditional type and weaving bring the inhabitants a modest degree of prosperity.

History

Already well populated in the period of the Cycladic culture (3rd and 2nd millennia B.C.), the island grew so wealthy in classical times from the produce of its silver-mines that the Siphnians built a treasury in the sanctuary of Apollo at Delphi. When the flooding of the mines made it impossible to work the silver the island declined into insignificance.

Entrances to the silver workings can be seen in the sea at Áyios Sóstis and Áyios Minás.

Sights

Kamáres
Apollonía

From the principal port, Kamáres (beach; pottery workshops), on the west coast, a road goes up to the island's capital, Apollonía. The church of Áyios Sózon has fine wall paintings, as have the church of the Panayía Gourniá in Artemón (to the north) and the church of the Panayía in Katavatí (to the south).

Kástro

5km/3 miles east, above a sheltered bay, lies the picturesque little town of Kástro, with a medieval castle. On the evidence of Herodotus this was the site of the island's ancient capital, Asty; there are still some remains of walls of the 4th century B.C.

Watch-towers

Around the coasts of the island there are numerous Hellenistic, Roman and medieval watch-towers.

Pre-Greek remains

On the hill of Áyios Andréas, south-west of Apollonía, are the remains of a pre-Greek settlement. There are tombs of the same period at Vathý and Mávro Khorió.

★ Monasteries

There are a number of interesting monasteries on Sífnos, some of which have accommodation for visitors. Particularly notable is the fortified monastery on Mt Profítis Ilías (680m/2230ft; pilgrimages). Others are Áyios Khrysóstomos (with a lilac tree and a palm dating back to 1653), the Panayía tis Vrýsis (library) at the south-eastern tip of the island, the monastery of the Taxiarchs (Archangels) above Vathý

Khrysopiyí monastery

Bay, the Panayía tou Vounoú (view) and the Panayía Khrysopiyí, on the south coast, with a 17th century icon which is revered as wonderworking.

Dovecots

All over the island, but particularly in the east, can be seen Venetian dovecots.

Kitrianí

To the south-east of Cape Kontoú, the southernmost tip of the island, lies the little island of Kitrianí, which consists mainly of marble. There is a chapel on the island.

Sikinos K 7

Σίκινος
Síkinos

Nomos: Cyclades
Area of island: 41 sq.km/16 sq. miles
Altitude: 0–600m/0–1970ft
Population: 350
Chief place: Síkinos

Boat services

Regular service from and to Athens (Piraeus), three times a week (10 hours).
Local connections with Íos and other neighbouring islands.

Situation and characteristics

Síkinos, 6km/4 miles south-west of Íos, is a bare and rocky island fringed by sheer cliffs, with rugged hills in the north and north-west and gentler terrain in the south-east (terraced cultivation).

History

With its inhospitable soil and lack of sheltered anchorages, Síkinos was never of any great political or cultural importance in antiquity. Its fortunes were closely linked with those of Naxos. In Roman times it was used as a place of exile.

Sights

Síkinos town

From the anchorage of Aloprónia (sandy bay), on the south-east coast, it is an hour's climb (2.5km/1½ miles; mules can be hired) up a wooded gorge to the chief place on the island, Síkinos (pop. 350), a typical Cycladic village, with the picturesque Kástro quarter within the walls of its medieval castle. On the hillside above this is the main village, Khorió.

Higher up are the ruins of the Zoodókhos Piyí monastery.

1½ hours' walk west is the chapel of the Panayía, which belonged to the Episkopi monastery, built on the site of an ancient sanctuary of the 2nd century B.C.

On the steep hill beside the little church of Ayía Marína are scanty remains of the ancient city.

Skiathos H 4

Σκίαθος
Skíathos

Nomos: Magnesia
Area of island: 48 sq.km/18½ sq. miles
Altitude: 0–438m/0–1437ft
Population: 4100
Chief place: Skíathos

Air services

Airport 4km/2½ miles north-east of Skíathos. Daily flights from and to Athens in summer (55 minutes).

Boat services

Regular service from Áyios Konstantínos, most days; from Vólos, two to five times daily (3–3½ hours); from Kými (Euboea), three times weekly (5 hours).
Connections with neighbouring islands.

Situation and characteristics

Skíathos, a gently rolling wooded island in the Northern Sporades, lies 4km/2½ miles east of the Magnesia peninsula. With its equable climate and beautiful sandy bays, it is a popular holiday island, particularly favoured by Greeks. Its main source of income apart from the tourist trade is its 600,000 olive trees.

History

Skíathos was never a place of any importance in ancient times. Herodotus mentions the island in connection with the naval battle off Cape Artemision in 480 B.C., reporting that the men of Skiathos conveyed information about Persian naval movements by means of fire signals.

Sights

Skíathos town

The chief place on the island, and indeed its only town, is Skíathos (pop. 3000), on the south-east coast. Founded in 1830, it occupies the site of the ancient city, on two low hill ridges flanking a small sheltered bay. From the church of Áyios Fanoúrios, north-west of the town, there is a fine view. Skíathos was the home of the short-story writer A. Papadiamantis (1851–1911), whose house is now a museum.

Kástro

2½ hours' walk north of the town (also accessible by boat), on an impregnable crag (view) are the ruins of the island's medieval capital, Kástro. Of interest are stretches of the town walls, with a drawbridge, Turkish baths and three of the 22 churches the town once possessed, including the church of Christós sto Kástro (17th c.; frescoes).

Evangelistria monastery

Half way between Skíathos and Kástro is the Evangelistria monastery (18th c.), with a Byzantine chapel, which was a refuge for Greek rebels during the struggle for liberation.

Abandoned monasteries

There are pleasant walks from Skíathos to the abandoned monasteries of Áyios Kharalámbos (8km/5 miles north), Kekhriá (7km/4½ miles north-west; 18th c. frescoes), Panayía Kounístria (9km/5½ miles west; 17th c.) and Ayía Sofía at Toúrlos.

Koukinariés

9km/5½ miles west of Skíathos (bus, motorboat) is the beautiful sandy bay of Koukinariés, one of the finest bathing beaches in the Aegean, with a fringe of umbrella pines to give shade. There are also interesting sea-caves.

Tsoúngrias

South-east of Skíathos are nine smaller islands. The largest of these, Tsoúngrias (area 6 sq.km/2¼ sq. miles; some cultivated land), and the islets of Tsoungriáki, Daskalonísi (lighthouse), Myrmingonísi (Ant Island) and Marangós lie off the harbour bay; farther north, off the east coast, are the isolated rocks of Répi, Arkí and Aspronísi; to the south is Prasonísi.

Skopelos H 4

Σκόπελος
Skópelos

Nomos: Magnesia
Area of island: 96 sq.km/37 sq. miles
Altitude: 0–680m/0–2230ft
Population: 10,000
Chief place: Skópelos

Boat services

Regular services from Áyios Konstantínos and Vólos, several times daily (4½ hours in each case); also from Kými (Euboea), three times weekly (3½ hours).

Situation and characteristics

Skópelos, known in antiquity, down to the 3rd century A.D., as Peparethos, is a hilly and well wooded island in the Northern Sporades. The steep north-east coast is unwelcoming, and, apart from the wide bay of Skópelos near the east end, without inlets or irregularities of any consequence, and the gentler south-east coast is also relatively featureless. The fertile areas on the island are mainly devoted to the growing of almonds and fruit (particularly plums; dried fruit packing station in Skópelos town). In many convents the nuns make woven goods and other craft products for sale. The tourist trade also makes a contribution to the island's economy.

Myth and history

The oldest traces of human settlement date from the Neolithic period. The ancient city of Peparethos was said to have been founded by the Cretan hero Staphylos, son of Dionysos and Ariadne. In the so-called Tomb of Staphylos gold jewellery, idols, a variety of implements and

Harbour, Skópelos Town

utensils and Minoan double axes were found; they are now in the museum in Vólos (see entry). The archaeological evidence indicates, however, that from an early stage the inhabitants of the island were influenced by Mycenaean rather than Minoan culture.
After the 7th century Skópelos prospered, and the tribute it paid as a member of the first Attic maritime league was substantial. The Peloponnesian War, however, quickly and finally put an end to its prosperity. Thereafter it had a succession of different masters – Macedonians, Romans, Byzantines, Venetians and finally Turks – who allowed this remote and economically unimportant community a considerable measure of autonomy. In 1830 it was reunited with Greece.

Sights

Skópelos town

The chief place on the island, Skópelos (pop. 3000), lies in a wide unsheltered bay on the site of the ancient and the Byzantine capital. Its narrow lanes and whitewashed slate-roofed houses climb the slopes of the hill above the harbour, on which are the ruins of a Venetian castle and the foundations of a temple of Asklepios (5th–4th c. B.C.). The flanks of the hill are covered with beautiful olive groves. The town is said to have some 120 churches and chapels, some of them dating from Byzantine times. The most notable are the churches of Áyios Athanásios (9th–11th c.), built on the foundations of an ancient temple, and the Archangel Michael, with fine carved woodwork, icons and ancient gravestones.
There are scanty remains of settlements at Pánormos on the south coast and round Glóssa, the site of ancient Selinous, on the north-west coast.

★ Churches and monasteries

Of the 360 churches, chapels and monasteries on the island the most interesting are the Evangelístria monastery (1712; view), above Skópelos town to the west, which has a 10th century icon of the Mother of God framed in silver; the 16th century Metamorfósis monastery south-east of Skópelos, the oldest on the island; the Áyios Taxiárkhos monastery, with an early Christian church (A.D. 672) in the forecourt; the monastery of the Panayía Livadiótissa (17th c.), on the east side of the island, with an icon of 1671 by the Cretan painter A. Agorastos; the Pródromos monastery (1721), also on the east side; the abandoned monastery of Ayía Varvára (1648); the ruined Episkopí monastery, south-west of Skópelos, with a church of 1078; the church of Áyios Reyínos, the island's first bishop and patron saint, to the south of the town (mid 4th c.); and the church of the Zoodókhos Piyí, with a wonderworking icon said to have been painted by St Luke himself.

On the north-western tip of the island are four old watch-towers.

In Agnóntas Bay, on the south coast, is the Trypití sea-cave.

Skyros I 4/5

Σκύρος
Skýros

Nomos: Euboea
Area of island: 209 sq.km/81 sq. miles
Altitude: 0–814m/0–2671ft
Population: 2900
Chief place: Skýros (Khóra)

Air services

Flights from Athens several times weekly (50 minutes).

Boat services

Regular service from and to Kymi (Euboea), four times weekly (2 hours); from and to Vólos, twice weekly (12 hours).

Situation and characteristics

Skýros, the largest and most easterly of the Northern Sporades, is a rugged island, partly covered by a sparse growth of trees, with a much indented coastline. It is divided into two distinct parts by a strip of sandy low-lying land between Kalamítsa Bay on the west and Akhílli Bay on the east. The south-eastern half of the island is occupied by the steep and arid massif of Mt Kókhilas (814m/2671ft). In this area are the quarries of the coarse-grained variegated marble which was much prized in Roman times. The north-western half, rising to 403m/1322ft in Mt Ólympos, is a region of gentler contours, with more water and a more fertile soil. Here are the Mármara quarries, which have been worked from antiquity into modern times. The coasts of the island are steep and inhospitable, but there are beautiful sandy bays at the foot of the cliffs.

In recent years the traditional terraced agriculture, practised since ancient times, has been giving place to the rearing of goats. The small pony-like horses which used to live wild on the island, particularly in the barren south-east, are now much reduced in numbers. The island's main sources of revenue, in addition to farming, are a limited tourist trade and the sale of its high-quality craft goods (embroidery, carved furniture, pottery, copperware).

Myth and history

According to legend Thetis disguised her son Achilles as a girl on Skýros in an attempt to prevent him from fighting in the Trojan War. Traces of Neolithic occupation (5th millennium B.C.) have been found north-east of the Venetian castle. In the 2nd millennium B.C. Carian and Pelasgian farmers and seafarers settled on the island, which then became known as Pelasgia. In the 1st millennium B.C. they were displaced by Dolopians, a Dorian people, who made the island, now called Dolopia, a base for plundering raids in the Aegean. In 469 B.C. Athens drove out the pirates and settled farmers from Attica on the land. In Roman times the islanders achieved a modest degree of prosperity through the export of their much sought-after marble, but their remote island remained of no political importance.
Skýros was reunited with Greece after 1821.

Sights

Skýros (Khóra)

The chief place on the island, Skyros (Khóra; pop. 2400), lies on the east coast. This little town of typically Cycladic whitewashed cube-shaped houses, finely decorated and furnished, nestles on the slopes of a hill, the rocky summit of which was occupied by the ancient acropolis (4th c. B.C.; remains of walls) and is now crowned by a Venetian castle (originally Byzantine), the Kástro (view). From this crag, it is said, Theseus was cast down to his death; according to the legend his remains were later found here and deposited in the Theseion in Athens. In the Kástro is the former monastic church of Áyios Yeóryios (museum).
In Platía Kýprou can be seen a monument to the poet Rupert Brooke, who died on his way to the Dardanelles in 1915 and is buried in the bay of Tris Boúkes (below).

Linariá

10km/6 miles south of Skýros town, in the more westerly of the two inlets opening off Linariá Bay, which is sheltered on the north-west by the island of Baláxa, is Linariá, the principal port of Skýros.

At the south end of the west coast lies the sheltered bay of Tris Boúkes, almost completely shut off from the open sea by the islands of Platý and Sarakíniko.

Off the west coast of Skýros are the uninhabited islets of Rínia and Skýropoula.

Sounion H/I 6

Σούνιον
Soúnion

Region and nomos: Attica
Altitude: 60m/200ft

Transport

Buses from Athens (60km/37 miles).

Situation

Cape Soúnion, at the south-eastern tip of Attica, is famed for the magnificent situation of its temple of Poseidon, perched on the edge of a precipitous crag.

History

Homer refers in the "Odyssey" (3, 278) to the "sacred cape" of Soúnion. In the 7th century B.C. there was probably a simple altar here; about 600 B.C. the large figures of kouroi now in the National Archaeological Museum in Athens were set up beside it; and around 500 B.C. work began on the construction of a temple in poros limestone which was still unfinished when the Persians destroyed it in 480 B.C.

★★Temple of Poseidon

On the substructure of the earlier temple destroyed by the Persians the architect responsible for the temple of Hephaistos in Athens

Cape Soúnion, the south-eastern tip of Attica

erected in 449 B.C. the present marble temple of Poseidon, with 6 × 13 exceptionally slender Doric columns. It stands on a terrace, artificially enlarged, to which a propylon gave access. In the bay below were boat-houses, some remains of which can still be seen.

Sanctuary of Athena

On a flat-topped hill north-east of the temple (beyond the modern road) is a sanctuary of Athena of the 6th century B.C. Beside a small building measuring only 5m/16½ft by 6.8m/22ft, of which the lower courses of the walls and the base of a cult statue are preserved, are the foundations of a similar but larger temple (11.6m/38ft by 16.4m/54ft), with the base of a cult statue. The roof was borne on four columns, in the fashion of a Mycenaean megaron. After suffering damage during the Persian wars the temple was rebuilt with two colonnades, not at the east and west ends as was the normal arrangement but at the east end and along the south side. The reasons for this departure are unknown.

Surroundings of Soúnion

Lávrion
Thorikós

9km/6 miles north is Lávrion, noted in antiquity for its silver mines. 2km/1¼ miles farther on is Thorikós, with a theatre of rather archaic type.

Sparta G 6

Σπάρτη
Spárti

Nomos: Laconia
Altitude: 211m/692ft
Population: 12,000

Situation and characteristics

Sparta, chief town of Laconia, lies in the fertile Evrótas plain, which is enclosed between the Taýgetos range (2404m/7888ft) and Mt Párnon (1937m/6355ft) and bounded on the south by the sea. The street was re-founded on the ancient site in 1834 by King Otto, with streets laid out at right angles around a large central square.

History

The subjugation of the original pre-Greek population of this area by Mycenaean Greeks is reflected in the myth of Hyakinthos, who was killed by Apollo during a discus-throwing contest. The story of the Mycenaean period (2nd millennium B.C.) also finds expression in the myths of Leda, the Dioskouroi (Kastor and Polydeukes/Pollux), and Menelaos and Helen. King Menelaos, who like his brother Agamemnon belonged to the Trojan War generation, was later revered in the Menelaion. The last Mycenaean king was Tisamenos, son of Orestes.

A new epoch began when the Dorians arrived, established the four villages of Pitane, Limnai, Mesoa and Kynosoura about 950 B.C. and divided up the conquered territory among the Spartiates. When Amyklai, which had remained a Mycenaean stronghold, also fell to Sparta about 800 B.C. the characteristic Spartan dual monarchy came into being, with one king continuing the line of Dorian tribal leaders, the other that of the kings of Amyklai. In addition to the two kings Sparta had a Council of Elders (Gerousia) and five ephors, who were elected annually. It developed into a military state, in which art was not entirely disregarded (as the finds made at Olympia and Dodóna

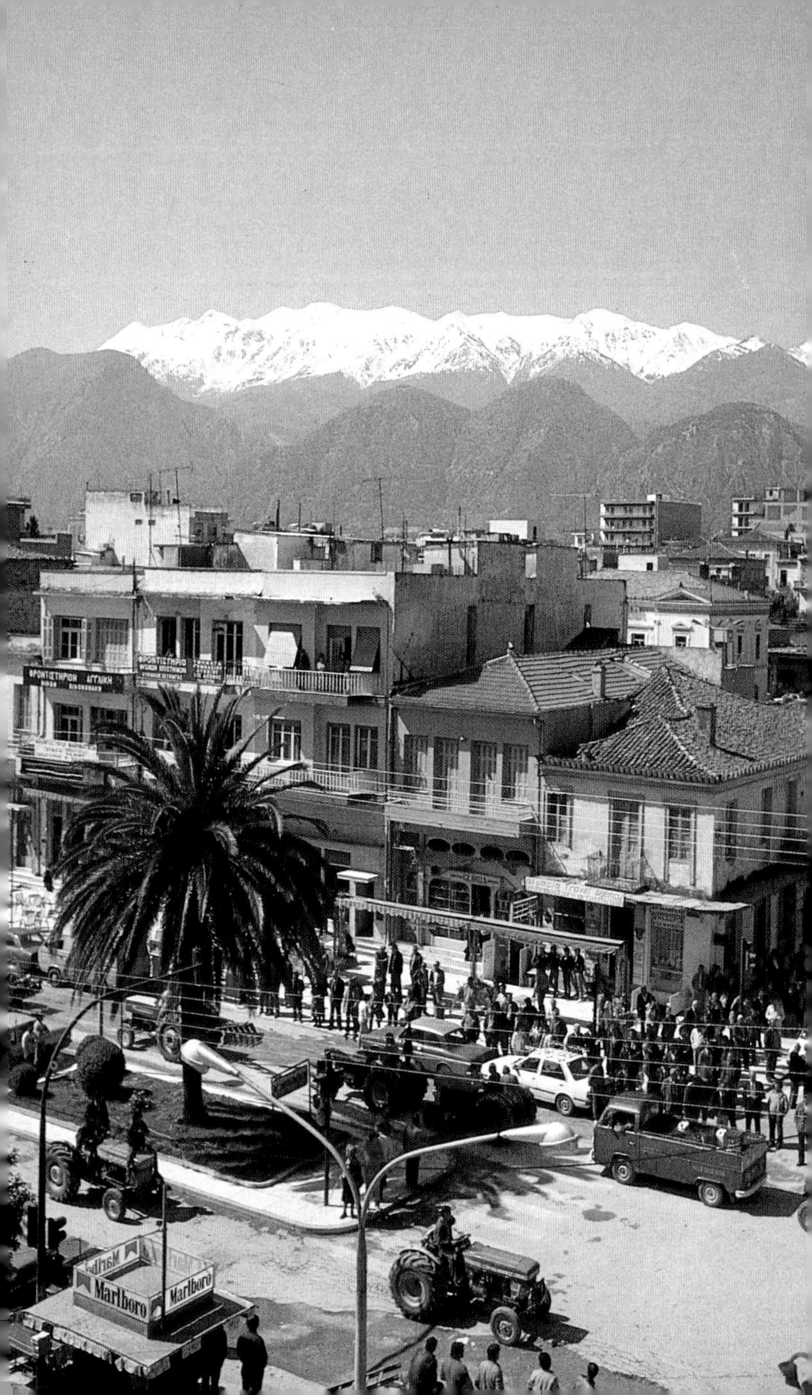
ΦΡΟΝΤΙΣΤΗΡΙΟΝ ΑΓΓΛΙΚΗ
ΦΡΟΝΤΙΣΤΗΡΙΟ
Marlboro
Marlboro

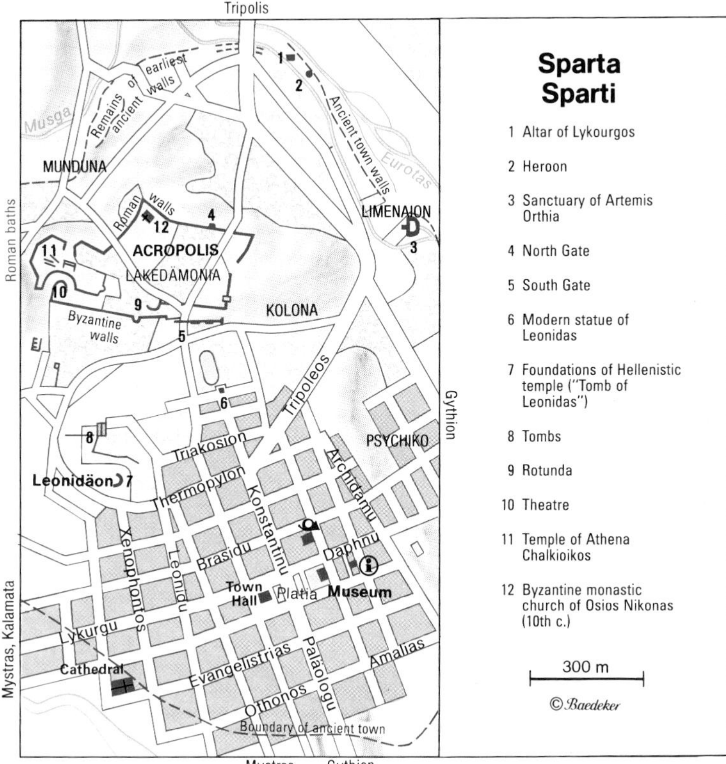

show) but played a less important role than in Athens. Thus Thucydides could write: "If Sparta became desolate and only the temples and the foundations of its public buildings were left, posterity would be unable to accept its fame as the true measure of its power." The Spartan ideal was incorporated in the lawgiver Lykourgos (8th c. B.C.) and in Leonidas and his 300 Spartans who fell at Thermopylai (see entry) in 480 B.C.

In a succession of wars (740–720, 660, 464–459 B.C.) Sparta subjugated Messenia, to the west of Taýgetos. Its decline began with a severe earthquake in 464 B.C. which killed all its young men, and it received a further blow in the defeat of a Spartan army by the Thebans under Epameinondas at Leuktra in 371 B.C. The first defensive walls were built round the town about 200 B.C. Under the Roman Empire Sparta enjoyed a revival of prosperity, but it was devastated by the Herulians in A.D. 267 and by Alaric's Visigoths in 395. In the 7th century Slavs established themselves in the region. In the 10th century it was evan-

◀ *Sparta, with Taýgetos as backdrop*

gelised by St Nikon Metanoeite, who was buried on the acropolis hill at Sparta.
In the 13th century Sparta was replaced by the newly founded town of Mistra (see entry).

Sights

★ Archaeological Museum

In Evrótas Street, to the east of the central square, is the Archaeological Museum (1975–76), set in attractive gardens. In the entrance hall are sickle stelae associated with the cult of Artemis. In the rooms to the right of the entrance can be seen an Archaic stele depicting Helen and Menelaos, finds from the Menelaion and the "Throne of Apollo" at Amyklai, figures of the Dioskouroi and an early classical torso of a warrior (Leonidas?) of remarkable vigour and power. Notable items in the rooms to the left are lead figurines and terracotta masks from the sanctuary of Artemis.

Leonidaion

Just off Leonidas Street, on the north side of the town, is the so-called Leonidaion, a building of unknown function: the tomb of Leonidas was elsewhere, to the west of the acropolis.

Acropolis

500m/550yds north of this building is the low acropolis hill, on the south side of which is the Hellenistic theatre, rebuilt in Roman times, which had a movable stage building. On the summit of the hill are the foundations of a temple of Athena built by Gitiadas in the 6th century B.C. This was a timber-framed mud-brick building on a stone base, known as the Chalkioikos from its facing of bronze plates. To the east is the 10th century three-aisled basilica of Áyios Nikon, in which St Nikon was buried.
The Agora, which lay to the south of the acropolis, has not been excavated, and most of the buildings mentioned by Pausanias cannot be identified.

Sanctuary of Artemis

Between the road to Trípoli and the Evrótas, just outside the town (on right), is the sanctuary of Artemis Orthía, so named because the cult image was found standing upright. According to Pausanias the image was brought from Tauris by Iphigeneia and Orestes. In this sanctuary Spartan boys were flogged as part of their initiation into manhood. There was a 6th century temple (foundations preserved) built over an earlier 8th century structure, with altars for burnt offerings. During the Roman period tiers of seats were built round the sanctuary to accommodate spectators of the ritual flogging.

Surroundings of Sparta

7km/4½ miles west is the ruined medieval town of Mistra (see entry).

★ Menelaion

To reach the Menelaion, leave Sparta on the Geráki road, which crosses the Evrótas; then in 4.5km/3 miles turn into a footpath which runs past a chapel of the Profítis Ilías and up Mt Therapne (500m/1640ft). On top of the hill are the remains of the Menelaion, a heroon built in honour of Menelaos in the 5th century B.C. It stands on the site of a complex of Mycenaean buildings, excavated in 1973, which it has been suggested was the palace of Menelaos.

Amyklai

11km/7 miles south of Sparta, on the hill of Ayía Paraskeví, is the site of Amyklai, with the sanctuary of Apollo Amyklaios and the 13m/43ft high "Throne of Apollo" built over the grave of Hyakinthos.

48km/30 miles south-east is Geráki (see entry) with its Crusader castle.

Khrýsafa

18km/11 miles east of Sparta we come to Khrýsafa, with four churches containing frescoes – Khrysafiótissa (1290), Áyii Pántes (All Saints; 1367), the Dormition (Kímisis) and Áyios Dimítrios (17th c.) – and the monastery of the Pródromos (St John the Baptist), which has a church of 1625.

North-west of Sparta is a Mycenaean tholos tomb (1500–1300 B.C.) discovered in 1982.

Spetsai H 6

Σπέτσες
Spétses

Nomos: Attica
Area of island: 22 sq.km/8½ sq. miles
Altitude: 0–244m/0–801ft
Population: 3500
Chief place: Spétses

Boat services

Regular service from and to Athens (Piraeus), several times daily (4½ hours).
Hydrofoils from Piraeus and Zéa (1½ hours).
Local connection with Kósta (20 minutes).

Situation and characteristics

Spetsai (modern Greek Spétses; Italian Spezzia), the ancient Pityousa (Island of Pines), is a hilly and well wooded island off the south-east coast of the Argolid. The income of the inhabitants, who are mostly of Albanian descent, comes from farming and now, to an even greater extent, from the tourist trade, for the island's mild climate attracts large numbers of holidaymakers. No motor vehicles except public service vehicles are allowed on Spetsai.

History

In antiquity Spetsai was an island of no importance. In 1770, after the Orlov rising, a rebellion against the Turks supported by Catherine the Great of Russia, the population was expelled from the island and Spétses town was laid waste. The inhabitants soon returned to their island, however, and their trading and seafaring activities brought them prosperity. In 1821 Spetsai was the first island to take part in the war of independence: an event commemorated every year by ceremonies in the Panayía Armata chapel near Ayía Marína.

Spétses town

The island's capital, Spétses (pop. 3000), is built on the gentle slopes above the wide bay containing its harbour. The present town, with a number of handsome mansions and three interesting churches in Kastélli, the upper town, dates from the 19th century.

Museum

The Mexis House, a fine late 19th century mansion, houses a local museum, with relics of the war of liberation in 1821, including a casket containing the remains of Bouboulina, a local heroine of the resistance.

★Circuit of the Island

The circuit of the island (12km/7½ miles) is a pleasant day's walk, or it can be done in a horse-drawn carriage. From Spétses the route runs

Boats in Spétses harbour

south-east by way of the monastery of Áyios Nikólaos (19th c.) to Ayía Marína, where there are scanty traces of a prehistoric settlement.

Off Cape Bísti, at the south-east end of the island, lies the islet of Spetsipoúla, which is owned by the shipowner Stavros Niarchos.

The road goes west to Cape Kouzouna, where there are remains of an Early Christian basilica (5th c.), and then turns north.
In the bay of Áyii Anáryiri (good bathing) is the Bekiri Cave, with remains of rock-cut sculpture.

From here it is possible to return direct to Spétses, or alternatively to continue round the island by way of Ayía Paraskeví (pilgrimage church) to Breloú, in a wooded region. Then either by way of the highest point on the island, Mt Profítis Ilías (244m/801ft), and the monastery of Áyii Pántes to Ayía Marína, or on the beautiful coast road back to Spétses.

Sporades

Σποράδες
Sporádes

Northern Sporades

In antiquity all the islands around the Cyclades were known as the Sporades (the "Scattered Islands"). Nowadays a distinction is made between the Northern Sporades or Magnesian Islands, lying north-east of Euboea – Skópelos, Skíathos, Alónissos, Skýros (see entries) and some 75 smaller islands and islets – and the Southern Sporades, off the south-west coast of Asia Minor, including Pátmos, Lipsí, Léros,

Southern Sporades

Kálymnos, Kos, Nísyros, Tílos, Sými, Foúrni, Ikaría (see entries) and Khalkí. The islands of Lésbos, Chios and Sámos (see entries) are sometimes also regarded as belonging to the Southern Sporades.

Symi M 7

Σύμη
Sými

Nomos: Dodecanese
Area of island: 64 sq.km/25 sq. miles
Altitude: 0–616m/0–2021ft
Population: 2500
Chief place: Sými (Yialós)

Boat services

Regular service from and to Athens (Piraeus), twice weekly (27 hours). Local connections with Rhodes and Tílos.

Situation and characteristics

The island of Sými (Italian Simi, Turkish Sömbeki), in the Dodecanese, lies 44km/27 miles north-west of Rhodes at the mouth of Sými Bay (Sömbeki Körfesi), which is bounded on the north by the Reşadiye (Knidos) peninsula and on the east by the Daraçya peninsula. It has a much indented coast, and according to Homer it possessed eight harbours. The inhabitants live, as they have lived since ancient times, by sponge-fishing and boatbuilding. There is an experimental plant for the desalination of sea-water.

History

From ancient times the fortunes of Sými were closely linked with those of Rhodes. The island was occupied by the Turks in 1523, and

Sými, beautifully situated chief town of its island

after the Balkan War (1912) was held by Italy. It was reunited with Greece in 1947.

Sights

Sými (Yialós)

The island's capital, Sými or Yialós (pop. 2200), with its handsome 18th and 19th century mansions, lies on the north coast, in a bay sheltered by the little island of Nimos (alt. 0–360m/0–1180ft). In the upper part of the town is a small museum.
This was also the site of ancient Syme, the acropolis of which was on the jagged crag now occupied by the medieval Kástro (reached by a flight of more than 500 steps). From the top there is an extensive view over Pédi Bay to the south.
1km/¾ mile east is a massive ancient tumulus.

Panormítis monastery

On a long inlet in the south of the island stands the massive Panormítis monastery, dedicated to the Archangel Michael, the protector of inlets of the sea; it has a charming bell-tower and a beautiful 12th century church (pilgrimage centre).

Nimborió

North-west of Sými, in Nimborió Bay, are the remains of an Early Christian basilica with beautiful mosaic pavements. To the south of the church are catacombs, said to have housed a school of icon-painters and sculptors in the 5th century A.D.

Sými has more than a hundred churches, chapels and monasteries, as well as numerous windmills, mostly dismantled.

Off the southern tip of the island lies the islet of Sesklia, with a lighthouse.

Syros I 6

Σύρος
Sýros

Nomos: Cyclades
Area of island: 82 sq.km/32 sq. miles
Altitude: 0–415m/0–1360ft
Population: 30,000
Chief town: Ermoúpolis (Néa Sýros)

Boat services

Regular service from and to Athens (Piraeus) several times daily (4½ hours; cars carried).
Local connections with neighbouring islands in the Cyclades.

Situation and characteristics

The hilly island of Sýros lies half way between Kýthnos and Mýkonos (see entries). Its central situation makes it the principal centre of administration, commerce and fisheries in the Cyclades and a focal point of the shipping routes in the central Aegean. Agriculture provides the major contribution to the island's economy, supplemented in recent years by a rapidly developing tourist trade.

History

From the time of the 4th Crusade, at the beginning of the 13th century, until 1568 Sýros belonged to the Venetian duchy of Náxos, and since then it has had a substantial Roman Catholic minority, which during the Turkish period was under the protection of France. During the war of Greek independence Sýros remained neutral, and those who escap-

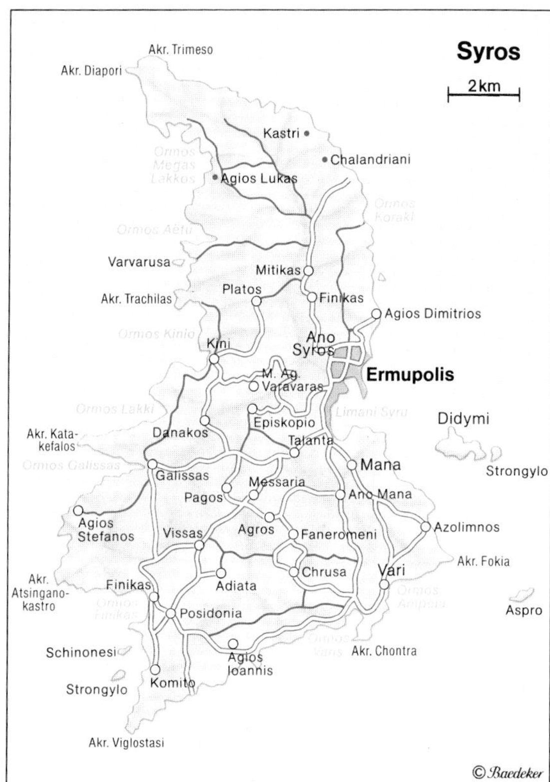

ed the massacres of Chios and Psará were able to find refuge here. Close to the town of Áno Sýros, which was founded in the 13th century and has remained predominantly Catholic, these new settlers established the town of Ermoúpolis (City of Hermes) by the harbour, and during the 19th century this developed into the largest Greek port, before being overtaken by Piraeus.

Sights

Ermoúpolis

The island's capital, Ermoúpolis or Nea Sýros (pop. 14,000), named after Hermes, the Greek god of trade, occupies the site of an ancient settlement of which no trace remains. It is the seat of the Prefect (governor) of the Cyclades, a Roman Catholic bishop and an Orthodox archbishop. The town owes its present extent to the influx of Greek refugees from Chios, Psará, Crete, Hýdra and other islands, who settled here in 1821 after the Greek war of liberation and built the town up into a major port on the sea routes between Asia Minor and western Europe. Towards the end of the 19th century, however, the economy of the town began to suffer from the competition of Piraeus.

Ermoupolis, Sýros

Taýgetos

The town, with its handsome houses in neo-classical style, extends from the harbour quarter, which is also the administrative and business centre, with the town hall and theatre, on the slopes of two hills. Its central feature is the large marble-paved Miaoulis Square, with a bandstand and a monument to Admiral Miaoulis, commander of the Greek fleet in the war of liberation. The neo-classical Town Hall (designed by Ernst Ziller) contains a small but interesting museum. Beyond the Town Hall is the Apollo Theatre (a copy of La Scala, Milan), which once enjoyed a considerable reputation.

The backdrop of the town is formed by its two hills: to the right Vrontado (105m/345ft), with the principal Orthodox church (Anástasis, the church of the Resurrection), and to the left Áno Sýros (180m/590ft), crowned by the Roman Catholic cathedral of St George (19th c.; view).

On Vrontado is the Greek Orthodox quarter, built from 1834 onwards, which is dominated by the 19th century domed church of Áyios Nikólaos.

Áno Sýros

On the northern hill is the Roman Catholic quarter of Áno Sýros, established during the Venetian period (13th c.), with a number of monasteries as well as St George's Cathedral.

Pýrgos

Mt Pýrgos, the island's highest peak (415m/1362ft), can be climbed from Áno Sýros. From the summit there are beautiful views in all directions.

Posidonía

15km/9 miles south-west of Ermoúpolis lies the popular seaside resort of Posidonía (formerly known as Santa Maria della Grazia). Near the town is an ancient necropolis.

Kastrí
Grammatá Bay

12km/7½ miles north of Ermoúpolis, at the village of Khalandrianí, is the fortified Cycladic settlement of Kastrí (*c.* 1800 B.C.). Farther west lies Grammatá Bay, in earlier times a welcome harbour of refuge, with Roman and medieval inscriptions (expressions of thanksgiving, prayers).

Taygetos G 6/7

Ταΰγετος
Taíyetos

Region: Peloponnese
Nomoi: Messenia and Laconia

Situation and characteristics

The Taýgetos range, fully 100km/60 miles long and rising to a height of 2407m/7897ft in Mt Profítis Ilías, traverses the Peloponnese from north to south, separating the regions of Laconia and Messenia. The range, built up of limestones and marbles, ends in Cape Tainaron or Matapán in the Máni peninsula. The main ridge, 18km/11 miles long and 2100m/6890ft high, is snow-capped for most of the year. The only route through the range is the well engineered road, largely following the old bridle path through the Langáda gorge, which links Sparta with Kalamáta (see entries).

Tegea G 6

Τεγέα
Teyéa

Region: Peloponnese
Nomos: Arcadia

Situation

At the little village of Tegéa, 8km/5 miles south-east of Trípoli (see entry), is a sanctuary of Athena Alea.

History

Tegéa, until 560 B.C. a centre of resistance to Sparta, was described by Pausanias in the 2nd century A.D. as a flourishing city, but in A.D. 395 was destroyed by Alaric. Later the Crusaders built the town of Nikli nearby.
According to the myth Tegéa was founded by Aleos, whose daughter Auge conceived Telephos after being raped by Herakles. Telephos travelled to Mysia in Asia, defeated the Trojans at the river Kaikos before the Trojan War and was later revered by the royal house of Pergamon as their ancestor (frieze on Pergamon Altar).
Tegéa was the birthplace of Atalanta, who received the skin of the Calydonian boar from Meleagros.

★Temple of Athena

On the site of an earlier Archaic building, destroyed by fire in 395 B.C., Skopas erected between 350 and 340 B.C. a new temple, which was decorated with his own sculpture. In this temple, the first in the Peloponnese entirely built of marble, Skopas retained the older elongated ground-plan with 6 × 14 columns. In the naos he departed from the regular practice of dividing it into three aisles by two rows of columns and instead set Corinthian half-columns against the interior walls so as to achieve an effect of space and magnificence. He thus carried a stage further the trend towards giving increased emphasis to the interior which Iktinos had begun in the Parthenon and continued at Bassai (see entry).

On the east pediment was a representation of the hunt for the Calydonian boar, whose skin was preserved in the temple; the west pediment showed Telephos in the battle on the river Kaikos.

Ramps at the east end and on the north side show that the temple could be entered either from the east or the north. The only surviving remains of the temple are the foundations and a few columns and capitals.

Museum

The Museum nearby exhibits finds from the site. In the entrance hall is a marble throne from the ancient theatre, in the left-hand room are elements from the temple and sculpture by Skopas, in the right-hand room a statue of Demeter, a head of Asklepios, a funerary stele and a Roman sarcophagus with a representation of Achilles and Hector at Troy; in the rear room are finds from Tegéa and Assia (bronzes, pottery, etc.).

Tempe Valley — G 4

Τέμπη
Témbi

Region: Thessaly. Nomos: Lárisa

Situation and characteristics

The river Piniós (Peneios), coming from Thessaly, flows through the 8km/5 mile long gorge-like Vale of Tempe to reach the sea. Celebrated in antiquity for its abundance of water and luxuriant vegetation, and as the place where Apollo came to purify himself after slaying Python, the valley – the principal route into central Greece from the north – has lost much of its original character through the construction of a modern road.

Platamónas Castle

12km/7½ miles north of the entrance to the Vale of Tempe is the mighty Crusader castle of Platamónas (begun 1204).

The ★Vale

Visitors travelling through the Vale of Tempe should spare the time to pause at a parking place, visit the Spring of Daphne in its shady setting and cross a suspension bridge to the much frequented cave chapel of Ayía Paraskeví. Just beyond this, going south, is the narrowest point in the gorge, Lykóstomo, the Wolf's Jaws. At the south end of the Vale, opposite the village of Témpi, is the site of the fortress of Gonnos, built by Philip II of Macedon to control the valley (Greek excavations). Beyond Témpi a road goes off on the left and climbs, with many sharp bends, to Ambelákia (5km/3 miles; alt. 600m/1970ft; pop. 1500), on Mount Ossa.

Thasos — I 3

Θάσος
Thásos

Nomos: Kavála. Area of island: 379 sq.km/146 sq. miles
Altitude: 0–1203m/0–3947ft. Population: 16,000
Chief town: Thásos (Liménas)

Boat services

Ferry Kavála–Thásos, 15 times daily (1¾ hours); Keramotí–Thásos, 12 times daily (40 minutes).

Situation and characteristics

Thásos, an attractive and fertile island, well watered in the north and east, lies just off the eastern Macedonian coast in the northern Aegean, here called the Sea of Thrace (where deposits of oil have recently been found). It is occupied by a range of wooded hills rising to 1203m/3947ft in Mt Ypsári and slashed by deep valleys. The northern and eastern slopes fall steeply down to the sea; on the south and west sides the hills slope down more gradually, forming numerous deep sandy bays along the coasts. The island's income comes from farming, mining (copper, zinc) and increasingly from the tourist trade.

History

The earliest traces of human settlement on Thásos date from the late Neolithic period. About the middle of the 2nd millennium B.C. Phoenicians settled on the island, but were later displaced by Thracians. In the 7th century B.C. Ionian Greeks from Páros captured Thásos from the Thracians and thereafter grew prosperous through gold- and silver-mining and trade. Between 464 and 404 B.C. the island was occupied, after fierce resistance, by Athens, and later became subject to Philip II of Macedon.

After periods of Roman, Byzantine, Venetian and Bulgarian rule Thásos was occupied by the Turks in 1455. Between 1841 and 1902 it was an appanage of the Khedive of Egypt. It was occupied by Greek forces in 1912, during the first Balkan War.

Thásos town (Liménas)

The island's capital and port, Thásos or Liménas (pop. 2000), occupies the western half of ancient Thásos, the size of which is evidenced by the walls enclosing the ancient naval harbour (now the fishing harbour), stretches of the old town walls, originally 3515m/3845yds long, and the foundations of houses and temples which extend in a semicircle, rising south-eastward from the shore up the slopes of the ancient acropolis, now crowned by a ruined medieval castle, the Kástro. At the south-western end of the castle can be seen an ancient relief of a funeral banquet.

Kástro

★ Museum
★ Agora

At the north gate, south-east of the ancient naval harbour, are the Museum, with a fine collection of Greek and Roman finds, and the Agora (4th c. B.C.), flanked by stoas. At its east corner is the Thereon, the residence of the city's chief dignitary. To the south-east is the sanctuary of Artemis Polo (6th c. B.C.).

Odeion

Outside the south corner of the Agora are the Odeion (2nd c. A.D.) and, beyond the Roman road, a paved courtyard. South-west of this can be seen the remains of a triumphal arch erected in honour of the Emperors Caracalla and Septimius Severus in A.D. 213–217 and a temple of Herakles (6th c. B.C.).

Temples

In the northern part of the ancient city are sanctuaries of Poseidon and Dionysos (both 4th c. B.C.), a theatre (3rd–2nd c. B.C.), a sanctuary devoted to foreign divinities and, at the northern tip of the city, a sanctuary of the Patrooi Theoi (6th c. B.C.). Farther north, in the sea, can be seen remains of the breakwater of the ancient commercial harbour.

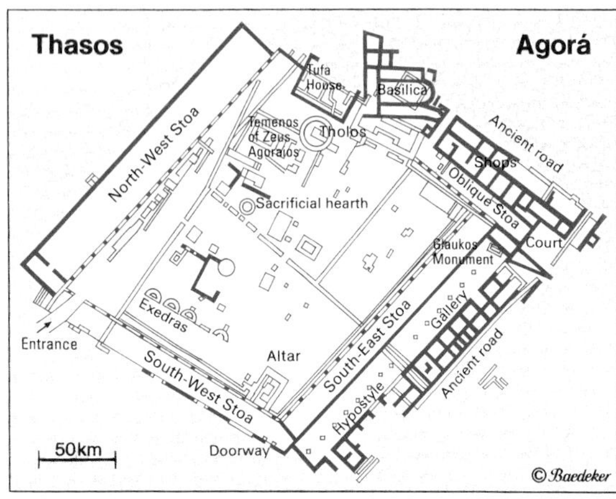

On another hill south-west of the Kástro are the foundations of a temple of Athena (5th c. B.C.; panoramic views), and on the rocky slopes of a third hill a niche belonging to a sanctuary of Pan.

Circuit of the Island

There is an attractive drive round the island (92km/57 miles) on a good road which keeps close to the coast all the way.

From Thásos town the road runs south to Panayía (9km/5½ miles) and Potamiá (12km/7½ miles), on the eastern slopes of Mt Ypsári, with beautiful views over the wooded valley to the sea and the 4km/2½ mile long beach of Khrysi Ammoudiá, on which is the little port of Potamiá Skála (14km/8½ miles).

The road continues via Kínyra (23km/14 miles) and the Alikí peninsula (ancient marble quarries, remains of a sanctuary of the Dioskouroi, two Early Christian basilicas) to Potós (45km/28 miles), where a road goes off on the right and ascends through a romantic valley to the hill village of Theológos (8km/5 miles; alt. 240m/785ft).

Then on to the little mining town of Limenariá (50km/31 miles; pop. 2000), with an office building above the harbour which belonged to the German firm of Krupp, and via Prínos (78km/48 miles) and Rakhóni (82km/51 miles) back to Thásos (92km/57 miles).

Thebes H 5

Θήβα
Thíva

Nomos: Boeotia
Altitude: 218m/715ft
Population: 18,700

Transport

Station on the Salonica–Athens railway line; bus services from Athens. Access to Salonica–Athens expressway 5km/3 miles north of the town.

Situation

Thebes (modern Greek Thíva), chief town of the nomos of Boeotia in central Greece, occupies the site of the ancient city of the same name.

History

Over a stone apsidal building of the Early Helladic period (second half of 3rd millennium B.C.) similar to the building of the same date at Lérna (see Argos, Lérna) a Mycenaean stronghold was built on the site of "seven-gated Thebes".

The myth relates that Kadmos came from Phoenicia to Boeotia in search of his sister Europa, who had been carried off by Zeus, and about 1500 B.C. founded the fortress which was named Kadmeia after him. Around his royal dynasty there grew up the great cycle of tragic myths centred on such figures as Oidipous (Oedipus), his mother Iokaste (Jocasta), their daughters Antigone and Ismene and their sons Eteokles and Polyneikes, whose rights the Seven against Thebes sought to establish.

The site of Kadmos's palace, which was destroyed in the 13th century B.C., was later occupied by the Agora of Thebes and, according to Pausanias, a sanctuary of Demeter Thesmophoros. In the 4th century B.C. Thebes, under the leadership of Pelopidas and Epameinondas, became for a brief period the dominant power in Greece; but after a rising against Macedonian rule it was razed to the ground in 335 B.C. by Alexander the Great, who spared only the house of the great lyric poet Pindar (*c.* 520–445 B.C.). Thereafter Thebes, which was destroyed on a number of later occasions, was a place of no importance until the 19th century, when it began to recover a measure of prosperity.

The Town

Acropolis

The ancient acropolis is now covered with modern building, which inevitably hampers archaeological investigation. Recent excavations, however, have brought to light walls belonging to the Mycenaean Kadmeia. In buildings on the south side of the excavated area were found not only jewellery, ivory and tablets written in Linear B but also cuneiform texts which provided support for the ancient tradition of connections between Kadmos's city and the Near East. Tombs were found on the hill of Kastélla, to the east of the town, and a sanctuary of Apollo Ismenios near the cemetery, to the south-east. The positions of the city's seven gates are known, but the only visible remains are the foundations of a round tower at the Elektra Gate on the south-east side of the ancient city.

★ Museum

In the north of the town, beside a 13th century Frankish tower built when Thebes was ruled by the de la Roche family, then masters of Athens, is the Museum.

Room I: kouros (No. 3; *c.* 550 B.C.) from the sanctuary of Ptoan Apollo, the Ptoion.

Room II: lapis lazuli seals from the East; Mycenaean amphoras with inscriptions in Linear B (13th c. B.C.), found in Kadmos's palace.

Room III: painted funerary stelae from Thespiai and Tanagra.

Room IV: Mycenaean sarcophagi from Tanagra (13th c. B.C.).

Surroundings of Thebes

20km/12½ miles south is the site of the battle of Plataiai (see entry) in 479 B.C., which ended the Persian wars. 19km/12 miles south-west is the battlefield of Leuktra, where Thebes broke the power of Sparta in 371 B.C.

★ Kabeirion

The Kabeirion (sanctuary of the Kabeiroi) of Thebes is reached by taking the road to Livadiá and in 4km/2½ miles, just after a bridge, turning left into the Thespiai road and then bearing right towards a hill on which is the site (enclosed by a fence). The remains include parts of the temple and the theatre.

Thermaic Gulf G/H 3

Θερμαϊκός Κόλπος
Thermaïkós Kólpos

Situation

The Thermaic Gulf – named after the ancient city of Thermai near present-day Salonica – lies between the mainland of Macedonia and the Chalcidice peninsula (see entry).

The present coastline has been formed by alluvial deposits from three rivers, the Axiós (Vardar), the Loúdias and the Aliakmón, flowing respectively from the north, the north-west and the south-west. As a result the inlet giving access to the port of Salonica is now only 6km/4 miles wide. Originally the gulf extended far to the west, reaching almost to Édessa (see entry) in the north-west and to Véria (see entry), the ancient Beroia, in the south, joining up with the present coastline at Methóni (see entry). When the Macedonian capital of Pella (see entry) was established about 400 B.C. it lay on the north shore of the gulf: it is now 30km/19 miles from the sea. In the lowest-lying part of this area the lake of Yianitsá (now drained) survived into modern times. The new alluvial land is now under cultivation.

Around the Thermaic Gulf is a string of holiday and seaside resorts.

Thermopylai G 5

Θερμοπύλες
Thermopýles

Nomos: Phthiotis

Situation and characteristics

Thermopylai ("Warm Gates") takes its name from the hot sulphurous springs around which a small spa has grown up.

Here the mountains approach so close to the sea that in ancient times there was only the breadth of a single wagon at the narrowest point in the pass. The extension of the land area by alluvial deposition has completely altered its character, and the modern highway now approximately follows the ancient coastline. In the little museum on the east side of the hill is a model showing the lie of the land in antiquity.

History

Here Leonidas and his 300 Spartans sacrificed themselves in 480 B.C. in order to cover the retreat of the Greek army after the treachery of Ephialtes had revealed to the Persians the alternative route by a mountain track called the Anopaia.

There is a modern monument on the hill on which the Spartans made their last stand, and also a tablet with the famous epitaph by Simonides, "Go tell the Spartans, thou who passest by,/That here, obedient to their laws, we lie".

Water from a hot spring, Thermopylai

Surroundings of Thermopylai

Gorgopotamos railway viaduct: see page 102.

Thessaly

F–H 4

Θεσσαλία
Thessalía

Situation

Thessaly is a region in central Greece, bounded on the west by the Pindos range, on the north by Macedonia, on the east by the Aegean and on the south by Boeotia.

Topography

Thessaly, with an area of 14,000 sq.km/5400 sq. miles, is a fertile agricultural region which was famed in ancient times for its horses and is now important for agricultural produce such as cotton and sugar-beet. The wide expanses of cultivable land available here, in contrast to the regions farther south, led in classical and Turkish times to the development of large estates and in more recent times has favoured the establishment of agricultural cooperatives. The mountains which enclose the region – Pindos, Olympus, Ossa, Pelion, Othrys – give it a continental climate, with hot summers and cold winters. As a result the olive does not flourish in Thessaly.

The chief town of Thessaly is Lárisa (see entry), near which recent excavations have brought to light traces of very early settlement.

From the 4th millennium B.C. onwards the land around the Gulf of Vólos saw a continuous succession of settlements – Sesklo (4th millennium), Dimini (3rd millennium), Iolkos (2nd millennium), in the 1st millennium B.C. Pherai, Pagasai and Demetrias, and finally Vólos, the only port in Thessaly, most of which is cut off from the sea by Mt Pelion.

Myth and history

The importance of this region in Mycenaean times is reflected in the numerous myths which have Thessaly as their setting. This was the home of the Centaurs, including the wise Cheiron who initiated Asklepios into the art of healing and brought up Peleus and his son Achilles; Admetos and Alkestis lived in Pherai; and the Argonauts set out from Iolkos in quest of the Golden Fleece.

Apart from the monasteries of Metéora (see entry), the tourist interest of Thessaly is confined to the mountain villages in the Pélion massif (see entry) and the coastal resorts on the Magnesia peninsula.

Thrace

Θράκη
Thráki

Situation and characteristics

Thrace, the most north-easterly province of Greece, of which it became part only in 1913, is named after the Thracians who settled here from the 2nd millennium B.C. onwards. It extends in a long narrow strip, between the northern Aegean and Bulgaria, from Néstos in the west to the river Évros in the east, which forms the frontier with Turkey. Like Macedonia, Thrace is a land of fertile plains, an agricultural region which in addition to corn, wine and in recent years rice also produces tobacco. The chief town is Komotiní (see entry).

Tilos/Telos M 7

Τήλος
Tílos

Nomos: Dodecanese
Area of island: 60 sq.km/23 sq. miles
Altitude: 0–651m/0–2136ft
Population: 800
Chief place: Megalokhorió

Boat services

Regular service from and to Athens (Piraeus), twice weekly (25 hours). Local connections in Dodecanese: Rhodes– Sými – Tílos – Nísyros – Kos – Kálymnos – Léros – Lipsí – Pátmos – Arkí – Agathonísi – Sámos.

Situation and characteristics

Tílos (Italian Piscopi) is a bare and rugged island in the Dodecanese (Southern Sporades), lying half way between Rhodes and Kos. The inhabitants make a modest living from farming, on terraces which have been laboriously built up over the centuries, and fishing. Throughout the island's history its fortunes were closely linked with those of Rhodes.

Sights

Megalokhorió

The chief place on the island, Megalokhorió (pop. 350), lies above the bay of Áyios Antónios on the north coast. It occupies the site of ancient

Telos (some remains of walls). On the hill of Áyios Stéfanos, to the north of the village, is the medieval Kástro, built on ancient foundations, with a handsome church (16th c. frescoes).

Livádia

South of Megalokhorió, on the road to Livádia, the island's port, are the ruins of the Venetian castle of Mesariá. Nearby is the Kharkadió Cave, in which the bones of prehistoric dwarf elephants were found.

Mikrokhorió

In the centre of the island lies the deserted village of Mikrokhorió.

Áyios Panteleímon monastery

At the north-western tip of the island is the early 18th century monastery of Áyios Panteleímon.

Tílos also has a number of other ruined castles and some 25 churches, chapels and monasteries of the 13th–18th centuries, most of them in a dilapidated condition.

1.5km/1 mile north-west of Tílos lies the little island of Gaidouronísi (lighthouse). 3km/2 miles south-east is the island of Antítilos.

Tinos/Tenos I/K 6

Τήνος
Tínos

Nomos: Cyclades
Area of island: 195 sq.km/75 sq. miles
Altitude: 0–713m/0–2339ft
Population: 3500
Chief place: Tínos

Boat services

Regular service from and to Athens (Piraeus), several times daily (5 hours; cars carried); also from and to Rafína, twice daily (5 hours). Local connections with neighbouring Cycladic islands.

Situation and characteristics

Tínos is the south-eastern continuation of the mountain massif which extends from Euboea by way of Ándros. Its highest peak is Mt Tsikniás (713m/2339ft), at the east end of the island. The inhabitants live by farming (terraced fields). Characteristic features of the landscape are the Venetian-style tower-like dovecots, of which there are some 1300. There are also numerous windmills.

History

In ancient times, from the 3rd century B.C. onwards, the sanctuary of Poseidon and Amphitrite on Tenos was a major religious centre, and in more recent times, since the early 19th century, the island has possessed a leading shrine of the Orthodox church. Held by Venice from 1207 to 1712, Tínos had the longest period of Frankish occupation of any part of Greece, and in consequence its population includes a considerable proportion of Roman Catholics. The Orthodox population began to increase from 1822, when – during the war of liberation from the Turks – a nun named Pelagia, guided by a vision, found a wonderworking icon of the Panayía, which soon became the object of annual pilgrimages on the feasts of the Annunciation (March 25th) and Dormition (August 15th), so that Tínos developed into a kind of Greek Lourdes.

Dovecote tower

The island came into international prominence when on August 15th 1940, two months before Mussolini's declaration of war, an Italian submarine torpedoed the Greek cruiser "Elli", which was lying in Tínos harbour for the feast of the Dormition.

Sights

Tínos

The island's capital, Tínos (pop. 3000), a little town of whitewashed cube-shaped Cycladic houses, is a conspicuous sight above an open bay on the south coast. Originally a modest coastal village, it became the chief place on the island after the Turks destroyed the original capital on Mt Exómbourgo (below).

★ Panayia Evangelístria

From the harbour a broad processional way leads up (15 minutes) to the Orthodox pilgrimage church of the Panayía Evangelístria, an imposing structure built between 1823 and 1830, using stone from the sanctuary of Poseidon and the temple of Delian Apollo. The interior is richly furnished, its principal treasure being the wonderworking icon of the Panayía Megalokhóri. From the marble terrace there is a magnificent view.

★ Archaeological Museum

Below the church is the Archaeological Museum, which contains finds from the sanctuary of Poseidon and Amphitrite, including architectural elements (in the courtyard) and, on the upper floor, large pottery vessels, among them a pithos with relief decoration depicting the birth of Aphrodite from the head of a winged Zeus (7th century B.C.).

Asty

The present town occupies the site of the island's ancient capital, Asty (5th c. B.C.).

Poseidonion

At Kiónia, 4km/2½ miles west in Stavrós Bay (ancient harbour works) are the remains of the Poseidonion, the sanctuary of Poseidon and Amphitrite, the Hellenistic or later rebuilding of an earlier (5th c.) sanctuary, with a marble exedra at the east end and a sundial made by Andronikos.

Mt Exómbourgo

13km/8 miles north of Tínos town, on the southern and eastern slopes of Mt Exómbourgo, a steep-sided granite cone 553m/1814ft high (ruined Venetian castle; panoramic views), are the surviving remains – three churches and a fountain-house – of the island's medieval capital, which was devastated by the Turks.

Marble quarries

In the north-west of the island, to the south of Pánormos Bay (beach), are a number of marble quarries. The marble is widely used in the building of houses.

In the village of Pánormos is the house once occupied by the sculptor Yiannolis Khalepas, now a museum. The neighbouring village of Pýrgos has a school of sculpture.
South of Pýrgos is Istérnia, which has a church with tile-clad domes.

Tiryns G 6

Τίρυνθα
Tíryntha

Region: Peloponnese
Nomos: Argolid

Situation and characteristics

The mighty Mycenaean citadel of Tiryns stands on a rocky hill which is only 25m/80ft high but commands the coastal plain on the Argolic Gulf. The site was occupied from the 3rd millennium B.C., and excavation has revealed the remains of a large circular structure dating from

◄ *Church of the Panayià Evangelistria, Tínos*

Interior of the Mycenaean stronghold of Tiryns

that early period. The site was excavated by Schliemann and Dörpfeld from 1884 onwards, and some sections of the massive cyclopean walls were re-erected.

History

Tiryns was associated in ancient legend with Perseus and with Eurystheus, in whose service Herakles performed his twelve labours. It shows many parallels with Mycenae (see entry). The first fortress was built in the 16th century B.C.; then in the 14th and 13th centuries the walls and bastions on the south and east sides were built in their present form, and the old eastern gate was buried under the new propylaia. The ramp on the east side, the flight of steps on the west side and the new palace also date from this Late Mycenaean period, when there was evidently a threat from bands of invaders. Recent excavations have shown that the lower part of the citadel to the north was not, as had long been supposed, merely a place of refuge for the population of the surrounding area but was densely built up and remained inhabited after the fall of Tiryns (*c.* 1125 B.C.) and into the 11th century B.C.

The ★★Mycenaean Citadel

Partially closed off for safety reasons

The entrance to the site is at the south-east corner. The ramp on the east side leads up to the entrance gate, guarded by two towers. Turning left, we pass through another gate, which was originally of the same size as the Lion Gate at Mycenae, turn right and pass through the propylaia into the large forecourt. From here we can descend to the east bastion; the passage, which was originally roofed in Mycenaean style, has been preserved, but the six chambers in the thickness of the outer wall are badly ruined.

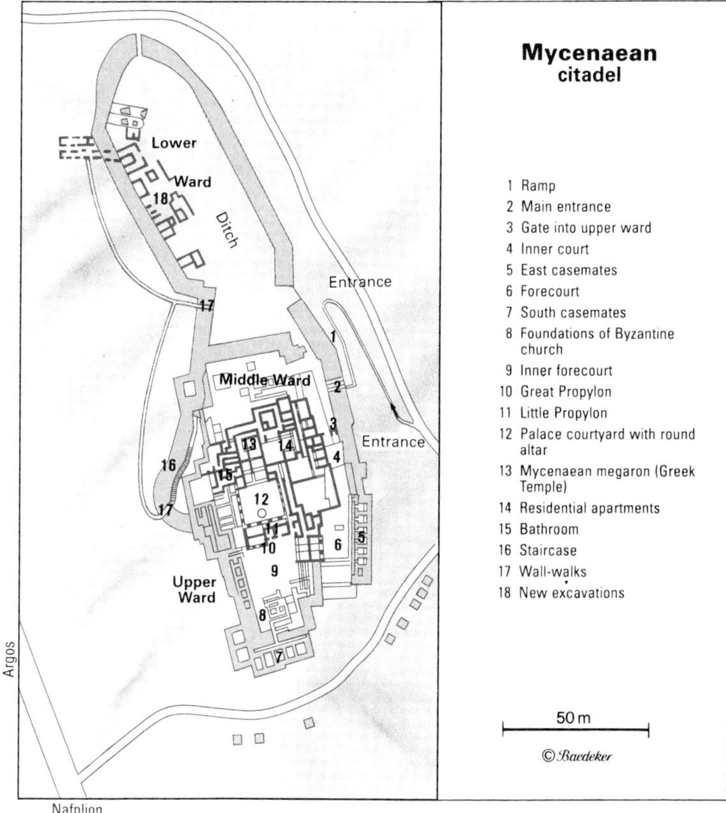

From the forecourt we enter the inner court, in which, immediately on the right, is an altar. The far side of the court was occupied by the dominating bulk of the principal megaron (with remains of a 7th century temple of Hera built over its ruins). Adjoining it on the right is a smaller megaron. These two rooms were the central elements of the palace, with a series of smaller rooms grouped round them. To the west can be seen a large stone slab which was the floor of a bathroom (with drain) – recalling the story that on his return from Troy (not to Tiryns but to Mycenae) Agamenon was killed by his wife Klytaimnestra in his bath. Near this is the massive west bastion, a 13th century addition to the citadel's defences. Within this bastion is a staircase leading down to a postern gate. Outside this is a recently excavated part of the town.

Staircase, Tiryns

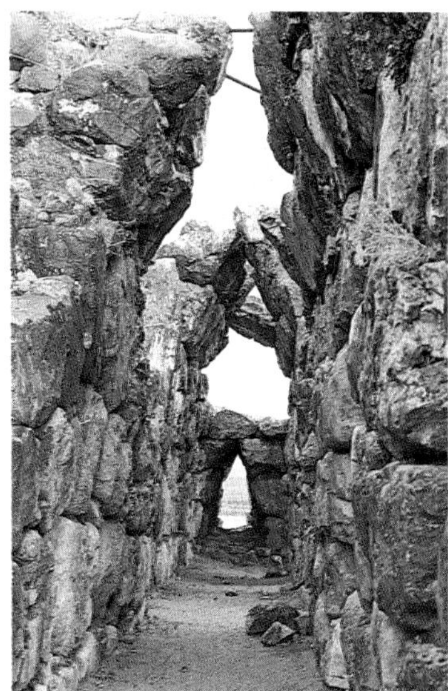
Vaulted passage

Tolon G 6

Τολό
Toló

Region: Peloponnese. Nomos: Argolid
Altitude: 0–15m/0–50ft. Population: 1200

Situation and characteristics

Tolón, formerly a small fishing village in a bay on the Argolic Gulf, 12km/7½ miles south-east of Náfplion (see entry), has developed in recent years into a popular holiday resort, thanks to its beautiful situation and its sandy beach.

Surroundings of Tolón

Asine

Near the village of Asíni, north-west of the town, are the remains of ancient Asine, on a site which was occupied from the 3rd millennium onwards. The remains include the massive walls of the acropolis, on which there are traces of other buildings.

Trikala F 4

Τρίκαλα
Tríkala

Nomos: Tríkala
Altitude: 115m/375ft
Population: 40,800

Transport

Station on Palaiofársalos–Kalambáka railway line; bus connections with Athens, Kalambáka and Lárisa.

Situation and characteristics

Tríkala, on the western edge of the plain of Thessaly, famed in ancient times for its horses, is the market town and centre of this agricultural region.

Sights

Ancient Trikka was the home of Asklepios, the god of healing. In the Middle Ages it was the capital of a Serbian principality. It has a lively bazaar, with excellent tavernas, and pleasant walks along the banks of the river Lithaios. There are fine views from the Byzantine castle which occupies the site of the ancient acropolis.

Surroundings of Tríkala

Piyí

A road runs south-west from Tríkala by way of Piyí (7km/4½ miles) to the Pórta pass (21km/13 miles), with the church of the Panayía Pórtas, founded in 1283 (mosaics of that period and 15th c. frescoes).

Pelinnaion

On a hill 14km/8½ miles east, to the left of the road to Lárisa, are the walls of ancient Pelinnaion, on a site later occupied by the Byzantine episcopal town of Gardiki.

Tripoli G 6

Τρίπολι
Trípoli

Region: Peloponnese
Nomos: Arcadia
Altitude: 660m/2165ft
Population: 21,300

Transport

Station on the Corinth–Kalamáta railway line; bus connections with Athens, Corinth and Sparta.

Situation and characteristics

Trípoli, capital of Arcadia (see entry), on the central Arcadian plateau, was founded in the 14th century by settlers from Albania. During the Turkish period, under the name of Tripolitsa, it was the seat of the Pasha of the Morea. The town was captured by Kolokotronis in 1821, but was destroyed by Ibrahim Pasha in 1828.

Trípoli, situated at the intersection of the principal roads through the Peloponnese, is now the centre of the surrounding agricultural region.

Surroundings of Trípoli

Within easy reach of Trípoli are the sites of three ancient cities – Mantineia (15km/9 miles north), Tegea (8km/5 miles south-east) and Megalopolis (34km/21 miles south-west).

35km/22 miles north of Tripoli (leave on the road to Olympia and at Kandila take a road on the right) is the village of Orkhomenós (not to be confused with Orkhomenós in Boeotia), where in 1914 French archaeologists brought to light a sanctuary of Artemis Mesopolitis in the upper town and remains of a Doric temple of Apollo or Aphrodite (6th c. B.C.) in the lower town.

Troizen H 6

Τροιζήνα
Trizína

Region: Peloponnese
Nomos: Argolid

Situation and characteristics

The ancient city of Troizen, on the north coast of the Argolid peninsula opposite the island of Póros, was closely linked with Athens.

History

Troizen was believed to be the birthplace of the Attic hero Theseus. Here too Hippolytos, son of Theseus and the Amazon Hippolyte, was dragged to death by his horses when he rejected the love of his stepmother Phaidra (cf. the "Hippolytos" of Euripides). When Athens was evacuated in 480 B.C. in face of the Persian threat many refugees, particularly women, fled to Troizen. The town continued to exist into Christian times.
The site was excavated by French archaeologists in 1890 and by a German team in 1932.

The village of Trizína (commonly known as Damalá) can be reached from Náfplion (see entry) via Ligourió, Trakhiá and the coastal villages of Fanári and Kalóni, turning right 9km/6 miles beyond Kalóni into a side road (3km/2 miles); or from Galatás (opposite Póros), going 7km/4½ miles west and then taking a side road on the left (3km/2 miles).

Sights

From the village a footpath leads in 25 minutes to the scattered ancient remains. After crossing the line of the town walls and passing through the much overgrown town centre, with the remains of a temple of Athena Soteira and a number of churches, we come to a road fork, with a large stone known as the "Stone of Theseus". This, it is said, is the stone under which Theseus's father hid his weapons, and which the young Theseus was able to raise so as to recover the weapons. The road to the right leads to the sanctuary of Hippolytos, with the remains of buildings of the 4th and 3rd centuries B.C. The temple of Hippolytos (late 4th c. B.C.) had 6 × 11 columns. To the north-west are a peristyle building of some size which is interpreted as an Asklepieion or a sacred refectory, a small temple of Aphrodite Kataskopia (?) and a Byzantine episcopal church (11th c.), with the bishop's palace adjoining. To the south-west are some foundations which may belong to the tomb of Phaidra.

The road to the left at the fork leads to a Roman vaulted building and, after a left-hand bend, a Hellenistic tower which was rebuilt in the Frankish period. The road continues to the "Devil's Bridge" over an ancient aqueduct, which no doubt originally drew water from the spring on the other side.

Vergina G 3

Βεργίνα
Veryína

Region: Macedonia
Nomos: Imathia

Situation and characteristics

The village of Vergína, 80km/50 miles south-west of Salonica on the southern edge of the Aliakmón plain, has long been known for the palace and tombs of Palátitsa, but has recently come into the news again with the sensational finds made there by Manolis Andronikos, an archaeologist who has made a special study of this region.

Palátitsa

★ Chamber tomb

Palátitsa, situated on a terrace above the river Aliakmón, was settled about 1000 B.C., but its rise to importance did not begin until the 4th century. The discovery of a domed tomb of the Hellenistic period in 1855 was followed after a long interval by the excavation in 1939 of a chamber tomb with four Ionic half-columns and a temple-like pediment on the façade and a marble throne in the tomb chamber (*c.* 250 B.C.). The tomb lies 500m/550yds from the east end of Vergína, on the right of the road. The occupant of this tomb must have been a member of the same aristocratic caste to which the palace situated above the village must be ascribed.

★ Palace

From the east end of the palace, which is rectangular in plan, an entrance corridor 10m/33ft wide leads into a large central courtyard, 44.8m/147ft square, surrounded by four colonnades of 16 columns each, off which the various rooms of the palace open. A circular room on the left, beyond the entrance corridor, was probably a heroon for the cult of ancestors. At a subsidiary entrance on the south side are two rooms with mosaic pavements, probably used for the reception of guests. At the west end are large banqueting rooms, on the north side a hall 104m/341ft long. The living quarters were no doubt on the upper floor, of which no trace remains.

Royal tomb

Both the palace and the chamber tomb date from the first half of the 3rd century B.C. In the autumn of 1977, however, Manolis Andronikos discovered a completely intact royal tomb which was dated by the coins and pottery it contained to the 4th century (350–320 B.C.).
Under a burial mound 12m/39ft high and 100m/330ft in diameter was found a stone-built tomb chamber with a sealed marble door, over which was a painting of a lion-hunt (5.5m/18ft by 1.2m/4ft) – the first original Greek painting of this period so far discovered. In the antechamber was a marble sarcophagus, within which was a casket of solid gold weighing 8.5kg/19lb containing human remains and fragments of a cloak of deep blue material embroidered with gold. In the main chamber was a larger casket (11kg/24lb) with the Macedonian royal emblem of a 16-pointed star on the lid, containing human remains, a diadem and sceptre, and parts of a costly suit of armour.

King's Tomb

The excavator concluded from the contents of the tomb that it was the tomb of King Philip II of Macedon (383–336 B.C.), father of Alexander the Great. The armour found in the main tomb chamber included two greaves of unequal length, and it is known from the literary sources that Philip had a limp. Five small ivory heads found in the tomb were identified by Andronikos as Philip, his parents, his last wife Kleopatra and his son Alexander. All this suggests that the Macedonian capital of Aigai, where members of the royal family would be buried, lay not at Édessa (see entry), as had been supposed, but at Vergína. At any rate it is certain that the tomb was a royal one, and its furnishings – first shown to the public at Salonica in 1978 and now among the principal treasures of the Archaeological Museum there – were of astonishing quality.

In August 1978 Andronikos found a second richly furnished tomb, also intact, in the same mound, only a few metres away from the first. Further finds and further additions to knowledge are to be anticipated.

Veria G 3

Βέροια
Véria

Nomos: Imathia
Altitude: 180m/590ft
Population: 37,100

Situation

The pleasant Macedonian town of Véria, ancient Veroia, lies on a terrace to the north of the river Aliakmón, 75km/47 miles south-west of Salonica on the road to Kozáni.

History

Beroia, first recorded in 500 B.C., belonged to the kingdom of Macedon, and in 168 B.C. became Roman together with the rest of Macedonia. In A.D. 64 the Apostle Paul preached the new faith to the Jewish community of the town (Acts 17, 10–13 and 20, 4). In the 14th century the town was occupied by the Serbs, in the 15th by the Turks.

Sights

Véria has a number of churches, the most notable of which are Áyios Christós (with paintings of 1315), Ayía Fotiní (also with paintings) and Áyios Kýrikos, all in Odós Makaritissa. In the main square are remains of the ancient town walls and a Turkish mosque, and there are other ancient remains, including a town gate excavated in 1960, at the junction of the roads from Salonica and Naoúsa.

Museum

The Museum (on the north side of the road to Vergína) contains local finds of the Hellenistic and Roman periods.

Surroundings of Véria

The excavations at Vergína (see entry) are 15km/9 miles east.

Mt Vermíon

Within easy reach of Véria is Mt Vermíon (2016m/6614ft), a popular winter sports area (ski-lifts).

Volos G 4

Βόλος
Vólos

Nomos: Magnesia
Altitude: 10–30m/35–100ft
Population: 71,400

Transport

Buses from Athens. Boat connections with the Sporades and Kými (Euboea). Station on the Vólos–Lárisa and Vólos–Palaiofársalos railway lines.

Situation and characteristics

Vólos, in the much indented Gulf of Vólos (modern Greek Pagasitikós Kólpos), rebuilt after a severe earthquake in 1955, is Greece's third largest port and the principal port for the shipment of the agricultural produce of Thessaly. It has weaving mills, cement works and tobacco factories.

History

The town was founded only in the 14th century, although it lies in an area which has been occupied by man since the Neolithic era. The oldest settlements were found at the villages of Sésklo (4th millennium) and Dímini (3rd millennium), to the west of the town. The 2nd millennium saw the establishment, within the area of the present-day town, of the Mycenaean city of Iolkos, seat of King Pelias and home of his nephew Jason, who sailed from Iolkos with the Argonauts. To the same period belongs Pherai, situated near Lake Karla (ancient Lake Boibeis), now almost completely drained, the seat of Admetos and Alkestis; the site is at Velestinó, 20km/12½ miles north-west of Vólos, to the right of the Vólos–Lárisa road. The port of Pherai was Pagasai, from which the gulf takes its name. Immediately north of Pagasai is the site of Demetrias, founded by Demetrios Poliorketes in 193 B.C.

Sights

On the way up from the busy new town around the harbour to the eastern outskirts on the slopes of Mt Pelion an extensive view opens up. On the north-west side of the town, to the right of the Lárisa road, remains of Mycenaean buildings have been brought to light between the railway and the river. Here an earlier palace built about 1400 B.C. was succeeded by a later one, which was destroyed by fire about 1200 B.C.

★ Archaeological Museum

There is an interesting Archaeological Museum in the west of the town. Reorganised in 1976, it presents the exhibits in the most modern way. The material begins with the Neolithic period (Sésklo, Dímini, Pýrasos), but the great feature of the museum is its unique collection of more than 300 funerary stelae of the 3rd century B.C. from Demetrias. Other items of interest are a torso of Aphrodite from Skópelos and a Hellenistic head of Asklepios from Tríkka.

Surroundings of Vólos

Sésklo
Dímini

Sésklo (18km/11 miles west) and Dímini (6km/4 miles west) are recommended only for those with a special interest in the prehistoric and early historical periods.

Demetrias
Pagasai

3km/2 miles south of Vólos the road crosses the sites of Demetrias and the older town of Pagasai. To the right of the road can be seen the theatre (restored 1960) and the hill (84m/276ft) once occupied by the palace of Demetrios Poliorketes. The chapel of Áyios Ilías on a hill to the left of the road marks the most southerly point of the walls of Demetrias and the most easterly point of Pagasai (some remains of walls still to be seen).

Néa Ankhialós

The road continues to Néa Ankhialós (22km/14 miles), founded by refugees from the Black Sea coast of Anatolia in 1907. It lies on the site of ancient Pyrasos, which was occupied by man from Neolithic times onwards. Four Early Christian basilicas have been found here. The small museum contains material from Pyrasos, which was the port of the ancient city of Thebai Phthiotides.

Within easy reach of Vólos is the beautiful scenery of Mt Pelion (see entry).

Vonitsa E 5

Βόνιτσα
Vónitsa

Nomos: Aetolia and Acarnania
Altitude: 10m/35ft
Population: 3600

Transport

Bus connections with Amfilokhía and Lefkás.

Situation and characteristics

Vónitsa lies on the south side of the Ambracian Gulf, dominated by a massive castle.
The town can be reached either from the fishing village of Amfilokhía at the south-east corner of the gulf (tavernas on the shore; fish a speciality) on a narrow asphalted road running through beautiful hilly country (40km/25 miles) or by taking the ferry from Préveza (see entry) and driving 15km/9 miles east.

History

The castle was originally built in the Byzantine period, and in 1084 withstood an attack by Robert Guiscard. From 1362 it was held by Leonardo Tocco and his successors, who gloried in the titles of Duke of Leucadia, Count of Cefalonia and Lord of Vónitsa. They developed the castle into such a formidable fortress that it was able to hold out until 1479, although surrounded by Turkish territory.

The Castle

The castle has well preserved walls, bastions and gates, and contains within the ramparts several towers, a chapel, a cistern and other buildings. It is approached by a path on the east side.

Surroundings of Vónitsa

From Vónitsa a road runs south-west, passing the airfield, to the island of Lefkás (19km/12 miles): see entry.

Páleros
Mítikas
Astakós

A recently improved road leads south to the three fishing villages of Páleros (15km/9 miles), Mítikas (18km/11 miles; boats to the offshore island of Kálamos: see entry) and Astakós (33km/21 miles), continuing to Aitolikón (38km/24 miles) and Mesolóngi (10km/6½ miles: see entry).

Xanthi I 2

Ξάνθη
Xánthi

Nomos: Xánthi
Altitude: 80m/260ft
Population: 26,000

Transport

Station on the Salonica–Alexandroúpolis railway line.

Situation and characteristics

Xánthi, dominated by the remains of a Byzantine castle, lies on the southern slopes of Mt Karaóglou, in the tobacco-growing region of Thrace.

Surroundings of Xánthi

Abdera

27km/17 miles south of Xánthi is Avdíra, the site of the ancient port of Abdera, founded in 656 B.C. by settlers from Klazomenai in Asia Minor (near Izmir). It owed its prosperity in the 6th and 5th centuries B.C. to its fertile soil and its trade with the hinterland. It was the birthplace of Protagoras (*c.* 485–*c.* 415 B.C.), the first of the sophists, and Demokritos (*c.* 460–*c.* 380 B.C.), who developed an atomic theory.
From 1950 onwards D. Lazarides excavated part of the ancient city on a promontory flanking a sheltered bay, bringing to light the foundations of houses, a stretch of town walls on the landward side of the site and remains of a theatre.

The delta of the river Nestos with its many lagoons is a favoured, but now endangered, port of call for a great variety of migrant birds.

Xylokastron G 5

Ξυλόκαστρο
Xylókastro

Nomos: Corinth
Altitude: 10m/35ft
Population: 4900

Transport

On the highway and railway between Corinth and Patras; bus connections with both towns.

Situation

Xylókastron is a popular holiday resort on the south side of the Gulf of Corinth, 33km/21 miles west of Corinth.

Surroundings of Xylókastron

Sikyon

From Kiáton, 13km/8 miles south-east of Xylókastron, a road branches off on the right to the village of Vasilikó (6km/4 miles), and the site of ancient Sikyon, birthplace of the sculptor Lysippos. To the left of the access road are the foundations of a temple of Apollo or Artemis. South of this can be seen the remains of a stoa, a bouleuterion and a gymnasion. On the slopes of the acropolis is a theatre.
There is a small museum in a Roman bath-house (pavement mosaics, sculpture, etc.).

Stymphalian Lake

From Kiáton a road runs 35km/22 miles south-west to the village of Stymfalía, on the Stymphalian Lake (alt. 740m/2430ft), the scene of one of the labours of Herakles, the killing of the man-eating Stymphalian birds. Strabo believed that the spring at Kefalári, south of Argos, was an outflow from the Stymphalian Lake.

Tríkala
Mt Kyllíni

31km/19 miles south-west of Xylókastron lies the village of Tríkala (alt. 1100m/3610ft), from which Mt Kyllíni (2376m/7796ft) can be climbed.

Zakynthos E 6

Ζάκυνθος
Zákynthos

Nomos: Zákynthos
Area of island: 406 sq.km/157 sq. miles
Altitude: 0–758m/0–2487ft
Population: 30,000
Chief town: Zákynthos

Air services

Airport 6km/4 miles south of Zákynthos town. Daily flights from Athens and Kefallónia.

Boat services

Ferry Kyllíni–Zákynthos, several times daily (1¼ hours).

Situation and characteristics

Zákynthos (Italian Zante), one of the Ionian Islands (see entry), lies in the Ionian Sea only 16km/10 miles off the west coast of the Peloponnese. The western half of the island is occupied by a karstic plateau rising to 758m/2487ft, the eastern half by a fertile and intensively cultivated alluvial plain with a luxuriant growth of vegetation. With its beautiful scenery and good bathing beaches, Zákynthos is a very popular holiday island.

History

The island has been known since the time of Homer by the name it still bears, said to be derived from the wild hyacinth (*Hyacinthus orientalis*

Harbour, Zákynthos Town

L.). Settled at an early period by Achaeans and Arcadians, it soon developed into a trading and seafaring town the influence of which extended as far as the Iberian peninsula, where it founded the colony of Zakantha, later known as Saguntum. In 455 B.C. the Athenian admiral Tolmides made the island a dependency of Athens. After the Peloponnesian War it became a member of the Attic maritime league. In 217 B.C. it was conquered by the Macedonians, in 191 B.C. by the Romans.
After being devastated by the Vandals it was captured by the Normans, and later was ruled by Frankish dynasts. It was occupied by the Turks in 1479 but recovered two years later by the Venetians, who held it until 1797. Thereafter it shared the fortunes of the other Ionian Islands.

From its long period of association with Venice the island has preserved an Italian and Venetian stamp. It was the birthplace of the Italian poet Ugo Foscolo (1778–1827) and the Greek poets Dionysios Solomos (1798–1857), author of the Greek national anthem, and Andreas Kalvos (1792–1869).

As a result of the devastations suffered in the course of an eventful history and of severe earthquake damage (particularly in 1515 and 1953) Zákynthos has preserved few old buildings.

Sights

Zákynthos town

The island's capital, Zákynthos (pop. 12,000), on the same site as its ancient predecessor, extends in a wide arc along the gently sloping shores of a bay in the south-east of the island. Above the town are the ruins of a Venetian castle (view), which is believed to have collapsed in the 1515 earthquake.
The only one of the town's magnificent Venetian mansions to survive the 1953 earthquake is the residence of the Roma family, with the charming chapel of Kyra ton Angelon. Other notable churches are Áyios Nikólaos, on the harbour, and Áyios Dionysios, with the relics of the town's patron saint.

★ Museums

The Municipal Museum has a fine collection of Byzantine painting and religious art (icons, iconostases). The Solomos Museum contains the tombs of Dionysios Solomos and Andreas Kalvos and relics of the island's history and culture.

Pitch springs

14km/8½ miles south-west of Zákynthos, at the village of Kerí, are the famous pitch springs mentioned by Herodotus. The pitch has been used since ancient times for the caulking of boats. The springs are now much less productive.

Laganás Bay

In the south-east of the island, 8km/5 miles south of Zákynthos town, is the wide bay of Laganás, with beautiful sandy beaches which are much frequented (and during the main holiday season overcrowded) by holidaymakers.
This bay has been since time immemorial the most important breeding site of the loggerhead turtle in the whole of the Mediterranean. Only a few years ago more than 1300 of these turtles, which are over a metre long and weigh anything up to 150kg/330lb, were still laying their tennis-ball-sized eggs in the sand of the beaches every year; but recently, as a result of the rapidly developing tourist trade, their numbers have declined sharply and the young turtles' chances of survival are being steadily reduced.

In order to protect this endangered species, therefore, the Greek Ministry of the Environment has announced a plan to establish closed breeding areas; but the plan has come up against strong resistance from local people, who fear that it will lead to a decline in the tourist trade. The establishment of a fully protected national park is being strongly urged by those concerned for the protection of nature, but this seems unlikely to be achieved in the near future.

Church of Ayía Mávra

11km/7 miles west of Zákynthos, in the village of Makhaiadron, stands the church of Ayía Mávra, with a typical (though much reconstructed) interior and a beautiful peal of bells.

Anafonítria monastery

35km/22 miles north-west of Zákynthos is the 15th century Anafonítria monastery (15th c. icons, 17th c. frescoes), in which the island's patron saint, Dionysios, was a monk.

Blue Grotto

At the northern tip of the island, accessible only by boat, is the Blue Grotto.

A hospitable Greek lane ▶

Practical Information from A to Z

Warning

It is strictly forbidden, subject to heavy penalties, to take away anything – even the smallest sherd of pottery or fragment of building stone – from an ancient site, and the export of antiquities without proper authorisation is similarly prohibited.

Accommodation

See Bungalow Villages, Camping and Caravanning, Hotels, Private Accommodation, Self-Catering, Youth Hostels.

Airlines

Olympic Airways

The national airline of Greece is Olympic Airways.

In Greece:

Head office:
Leofóros Syngroú 96
11741 Athens
Tel. (01) 9 26 91 11

Office in central Athens:
Othonos 6 (Sýntagma Square)
Athens
Tel. (01) 9 26 75 55 (international services)
and 9 26 74 44 (domestic services)

Athens/Ellinikón Airport, West Terminal (domestic services)
Tel. (01) 93 69 111 and 401
East Terminal (international services)
Tel. (01) 9 66 63 17

Desks at all commercial airports in Greece.

In Great Britain:

164–165 Piccadilly
London W1
Tel. (0171) 493 3965

In the United States:

645 Fifth Avenue
New York
Tel. (212) 735 0200 and 735 0292

In Canada:

1200 McGill College Avenue
Montreal
Tel. (514) 878 9691 and 878 3891

80 Bloor Street West
Toronto
Tel. (416) 920 2452 and 964 7137

British Airways

Othonos 10 (Sýntagma Square)
10557 Athens
Tel. (01) 3 25 06 01

Greek Skies
Kapodistriou 20A
Corfu
Tel. (0661) 3 99 10 and 3 91 60

Plotin of Crete SA
Iráklion
Tel. (081) 28 68 81

Periegetis Travel and Tourism Bureau
Kourna 27
Lárisa
Tel. (041) 22 12 45

W. Morphy and Son
Vitsi 2
Patras
Tel. (061) 27 73 29 and 27 70 79

Windsor Tours Ltd
11 Lerou Lochou Street
Rhodes
Tel. (0241) 2 77 56

Nikis 13
Salonica
Tel. (031) 23 83 26

Air Travel

International flights

Greece is linked with the international network by the national airline, Olympic Airways, and many foreign airlines.

The country's principal airport is Athens–Ellinikón. There are also international flights to and from Salonica, and Kavála airport in eastern Macedonia has recently attained international status.

A new airport in Sparta (about 20km/12 miles east of Athens) is being planned to come into operation in 1997; Athens–Ellinikón will then be closed.

Domestic services (see map, page 590)

Greece has a dense network of domestic air services flown by Olympic Airways, with daily flights from Athens to all the major towns in the Greek islands.
For information about services and fares (including various reductions) apply to any Olympic Airways office (see Airlines).

There are also flights from other Greek airports, including Aktion/Preveza, Alexandroúpolis, Ioánnina, Kalamáta, Kastoriá, Kavála, Kozáni and Salonica.

It should be noted that Greek domestic air timetables cannot always be implicitly relied on: it is advisable, therefore, to check in advance that your particular flight will actually be operating at the time shown in the published timetables.

Services from Athens

To Chios, Corfu Town, Iráklion (Crete), Kárpathos, Kásos, Kastellórizo, Kefalloniá, Khaniá (Crete), Kos, Kýthira, Lemnos, Léros, Melos, Mýkonos, Mytilíni (Lesbos), Páros, Rhodes, Sámos, Sitía (Crete), Skíathos, Skýros, Thíra (Santorin) and Zákynthos.

Services from Iráklion (Crete)

To Rhodes and Salonica.

Services from Salonica

To Athens and Ioánnina as well as to the islands of Chios, Crete, Lemnos, Lésbos and Rhodes.

For detailed information about these and other services consult the timetables of Olympic Airways, which are published twice a year.

Charter flights

There are numerous charter flights to Greece, particularly during the main holiday season. Information from travel agents.

Antiquities

Export prohibited

The export of antiquities and works of art (e.g. icons) is strictly prohibited. In exceptional cases an authorisation to export such items may be granted by the State Archaeological Service (Aristidoú 14, Athens). There are heavy penalties for contravention of the regulations.

Bathing Beaches

Greece is well supplied with sandy beaches and beautiful bays and coves, both on the coasts of the Greek mainland and on the islands. The bathing season lasts from April to November. Between June and September average water temperatures range betwen 19°C/64°F and 23°C/73°F, varying from north to south.
Since the breezes blowing in from the sea in the evening can be decidedly cool, it is advisable to take some warm clothing.

Open beaches

Open beaches (i.e. beaches left in their natural state) have no facilities or safety installations (warning notices, boundary buoys, nets, etc.) of any kind.

EOT bathing stations

The Greek National Tourist Organisation (Ellinikos Organismos Tourismou, EOT) maintains a series of excellently equipped bathing beaches, which in addition to the usual facilities such as changing cabins, kiosks and play areas have a range of sports facilities, restaurants, discothèques, etc. Most of these are situated in and around the larger towns and concentrations of population and are mainly designed to cater for Greek holidaymakers.

Hotel beaches

Beaches belonging to hotels are subject to strict government control and are therefore well maintained and serviced. Not all of them, however, are supervised and provided with first aid facilities.

Water quality

Many stretches of the Mediterranean coast are no longer so clean and unspoiled as they were only a few decades ago. This applies mainly to beaches in the neighbourhood of the larger concentrations of population, particularly those of the Attic Riviera on the Saronic Gulf, where

the quality of the water has suffered from the heavy shipping traffic and the disposal of sewage from the Athens conurbation into the sea. Bathing should therefore be avoided in the immediate vicinity of the city.
Apart from ecological damage to the water regard must be had to other possible hazards. At some points on the coasts of Attica there are dangerous currents, and bathers in the northern Aegean may have to beware of stinging jellyfish. Occasionally, too, a lookout may have to be kept for sharks, sting-rays, sea urchins, poisonous dragon-fishes (*drakena*) and other unattractive marine fauna.

The entries in the A to Z section of this guide include recommendations on particularly good facilities for bathing.

Sandy beaches

Islands with good sandy beaches include Thásos, Lemnos, Lésbos, Kálymnos, Rhodes, Crete (north coast), Kefalloniá and Corfu.

Shingle beaches

There are shingle beaches on Thásos, Lésbos, Chios, Sámos and Santorin.

Rocky coasts

There are rocky coasts, sometimes with bays and coves offering good bathing, in the Cyclades and on Santorin, Crete (south coast) and Corfu (north coast).

Popular beaches

Among popular beaches on the Attic Riviera (the Coast of Apollo) are Glyfáda (a very popular and well equipped beach near Ellinikón Airport), Kavoúri, Voúla, Vouliagméni, Varkitsa, Lagonísi (exclusive recreation facilities) and Soúnion.
There are other popular and less crowded beaches at Vravrona (Brauron), Loutsa, Marathón, Néa Makir and Rhamnous.
Also popular is the beach at Kinetta, between Athens and Corinth, where there are a number of luxury hotels.

On the islands of Aegina, Póros, Hýdra and Spetsai it is still possible to find beautiful and uncrowded bathing beaches.

There are also good bathing facilities on the Chalcidice peninsula, on the island of Kos, at Lindos on Rhodes, on Elounda Beach in Crete, at Pérama and Benítses on Corfu and on Kefalloniá.

Naturist Bathing

See entry

Bungalow Villages

Holidays in bungalow villages, with half board, are becoming increasingly popular. Villages of this kind are to be found on the Attic Riviera (Coast of Apollo), in the Peloponnese, on the Chalcidice peninsula and on several of the Greek islands.
For information on bungalow villages, apply to the Greek National Tourist Organisation (see Information).

See also Self-Catering.

Bus Services

Greece has a dense network of bus services centred on Athens, with two bus stations from which it is possible to travel to all parts of the country at very reasonable rates.

Bus station at Kifissou 100

Kifissou Street can be reached by Bus 051, which leaves from the corner of Vilara and Menandrou Streets.
From here buses go to Patras, Pýrgos (Olympia), Náfplion (Mycenae), Andrítsaina (Bassai), Kalamáta, Sparta (Mistra), Gýthion (Dýros), Trípoli, Mesolóngi, Igoumenítsa, Préveza, Ioánnina, Corfu, Zákynthos, Kefalloniá, Lefkás, Kozáni, Kilkis, Kavála, Kastoriá, Komotiní, Corinth, Salonica, Édessa, Dráma, Grevená, Flórina, Véria, Serrai, Naoúsa, Kranídi, Xylókastron, Argos, Agrínion and Arta.

Bus station at Liosion 260

The other bus station in Liosion Street is reached by Bus 024, which leaves from Leofóros Amalias, in front of the National Garden (Sýntagma Square).
From here buses go to Khalkís, Aidipsós, Kými, Delphi, Ámfissa, Kaména Voúrla, Lárisa, Livadiá, Thebes and Tríkala (Metéora).

Information about bus services can be obtained from the local offices of the Greek National Tourist Organisation or from the bus company.

Bus Tours

Various tour operators in Athens run organised bus tours (often with an English-speaking guide) of Athens and the surrounding area, mainland Greece and some of the Greek islands (including flight). Information about such tours can be obtained from tourist information offices, travel agencies and hotel reception desks. The following is merely a short selection indicating some of the possibilities:

Half-day (morning) sightseeing tour of Athens
Athens by night
Son et lumière, Greek folk dancing
"Night highlights"
Excursion to Cape Soúnion
Day trip to Delphi; also two- and three-day trips including the monasteries of Metéora
Day trip to Corinth, Mycenae and Epidauros; also two-day tours
Classical tour of Greece (three or four days)
Classical tour, including Metéora monasteries (five days)
Mistra (five days)
Eight days in Crete
Northern Greece (six days)
Fifteen-day tour of the Peloponnese
Nine-day tour of Greece
Four-day tour of north Greece–Macedonia

Business Hours

Banks

See Currency

Chemists

See entry

Flea market

Every Sunday morning in Monastiraki (Athens).

Exchange offices at frontier crossings

See Currency

Hairdressers

Summer: Mon. 2–8pm; Tue., Thu. and Fri. 9am–6pm; Wed. 9am–3pm; Sat. 8am–4pm.
Winter: Mon. and Wed. 9am–2.30pm; Tue., Thu. and Fri. 9 a.m–6pm; Sat. 9am–5pm.

Greek Hotel Chamber

See Hotels

Museums

See entry

Post offices

See entry

Public holidays

See entry

Souvenir shops

Mon.–Sat. 8am–9pm, Sun. and pub. hols. 9am–3pm.

Shops

There are no official opening times for shops in Greece. The shopkeeper can decide how long to keep open. He can open 24 hours a day on weekdays as well as on Sundays and public holidays if the shop is in a tourist area.
In the larger towns many foodshops are open Mon. to Fri. 8.30am–3.30pm; Sat. 8am–3pm; other shops Mon. and Wed. 8.30am–3.30pm, Tue., Thur. and Fri. 8.30am–2pm and 5–8pm.

Camping and Caravanning

Information

Greek Camping Association
102 Solonos Street
Athens
Tel. (01) 3 62 15 60

Classification of camping sites

The great majority of camping sites in Greece are subject to supervision by the tourist authorities. They are classified in categories according to the standard of facilities and amenities provided:
Category A: first-class facilities
Category B: good facilities
Category C: satisfactory facilities.
In addition to the sites managed by the Greek National Tourist Organisation there are others run by the Greek Touring Club or privately owned. Some of the sites have small chalets which can be hired.

"Sunshine" Camping Club Greece

This organisation at present operates 26 camping sites throughout Greece. Information: Sunshine, 251 Mesogion Ave., Athens. Tel. (01) 6 47 65 66.

Trailer caravans

Trailer caravans are subject to the following limits on size and weight: maximum height 3.8m/12ft 6in; maximum width 2.5m/8ft 3in; maximum length 12m/39ft; maximum axle weight 9 tons; maximum length of car and trailer 15m/49ft.

Hire of motor caravans

Motor caravans can be hired from the following agencies in Athens:

Motor Caravan Club of Greece
Athinon 251, Haidari
Tel. (01) 5 81 21 03 and 5 81 21 05

Camper Caravans SA
38 Voulis Street
Tel. (00301) 3 23 05 52–5

"Wild" camping

Camping outside authorised sites – by the roadside, in parking places and in the open country – is officially prohibited.

Camping guide

"Camp in Greece", a guide listing camping sites in Greece, is published by Maria Papayianopoulou (Leoforos Posidonos/Parthenonos 1, Palaion Faliron, Athens) in association with the Greek Automobile and Touring Club (ELPA) and the Greek National Tourist Organisation (EOT).
A list of camping sites can also be obtained from the Greek National Tourist Organisation (see Information). Other sources of information are the local Tourist Police and the ELPA office in Athens (Odos Mesoyion 2; tel. 7 79 16 19).

Car Ferries

Warning

Ferry companies often change their schedules according to demand and weather conditions. It is therefore essential that prospective passengers check that the particular ferry on which they wish to travel is actually sailing and also confirm the time of departure.

International Car Ferries to and from Greece

SERVICE Port	SHIPPING COMPANY Frequency	BOOKING AGENT
Italy–Greece		
Ancona–Iráklion	Minoan Lines Weekly (in season)	Seetours
Ancona–Igoumenitsa/Patras–Iráklion	Marlines Weekly	Euronautic Tours
Ancona–Igoumenitsa–Corfu–Kefallonia–Patras	Marlines Daily (in season)	Euronautic Tours
Ancona–Corfu/Igoumenitsa/Patras	Anek Lines 5 times a week (in season)	Ikon Travel
Ancona–Corfu/Igoumenitsa/Patras	Strintzis Lines 4 times a week (in season)	DERTRAFFIC; Viamare
	Minoan Lines 6 to 10 times a week	Seetours
Ancona–Patras	Karageorgis Lines 4 times weekly	Karageorgis Lines
Bari–Corfu/Igoumenitsa	Ventouris Ferries Arkadia and Poseidon Lines Daily (July to Sept.)	Ikon Travel Viamare
Bari–Patras	Adriatica 3 times a month (Mar. to Jan.)	Seetours
Bari–Corfu/Igoumenitsa–Patras	Ventouris Ferries and Poseidon Lines nearly every day (in season)	Ikon Travel Viamare
Bari–Kefallonia–Patras	Ventouris Ferries 3 times a week (1 to 16.7)	Ikon Travel

SERVICE Port	FREQUENCY Frequency	COMPANY
Brindisi–Igoumenitsa	Hellenic Med. Lines Daily (in season)	DERTRAFFIC; Neptunia; Viamare
Brindisi–Kefallonia (continuing to Ithica; Lefkas; Zákynthos with connection to/from Kefallonia	Hellenic Med. Lines Daily (in season)	DERTRAFFIC; Neptunia; Viamare
Brindisi–Corfu/ Igoumenitsa	Marlines Daily (in season)	Euronautic Tours
Brindisi–Corfu/ Igoumenitsa/ Patras	European Seaways and Fragline Daily (in season)	Viamare
	Adriatica 3 times a week to daily (all year)	Seetours
Brindisi–Corfu–Igoumenitsa–Paxi–Kefallonia–Patras	European Seaways Daily (25.6–14.9)	Viamare
Brindisi–-Patras	Hellenic Med. Lines Daily (in season)	DERTRAFFIC; Neptunia
	Hellenic Med. Lines Daily	Viamare
Brindisi–Paxi	Hellenic Med. Lines Every 2 days (in season)	DERTRAFFIC
Venice–Iráklion	Adriatica 3 times a month	Seetours
Venice–Patras	Adriatica 3 times a month (Mar. to Jan.)	Seetours
Trieste–Corfu–Igoumenitsa–Patras	Anek Lines Twice a week (in season)	Ikon Travel

Greece–Italy

Patras–Ancona	Karageorgis Lines 4 times a week	Karageorgis Lines
Patras–Brindisi	Adriatica About 3 times a week	Seetours
	Hellenic Med. Lines Daily (in season)	DERTRAFFIC
Patras–Igoumenitsa–Corfu–Ancona	Strintzis Lines Minoan Lines Anex Lines Several times a day Ikon several times a week	DERTRAFFIC; Seetours Ikon Travel
Patras–Kefallonia–Igoumenitsa–Corfu–Ancona	Marlines Several times a day (in season)	Euronautic Tours

SERVICE Port	FREQUENCY Frequency	COMPANY
Patras–Kefallonia–Paxi–Igoumenitsa–Corfu–Brindisi	European Seaways Daily (in high season)	Viamare
Patras–Igoumenitsa–Corfu–Bari	Venturis Ferries; Poseidon Lines Daily (in season)	Ikon Travel; Viamare
Patras–Igoumenitsa–Corfu–Brindisi	Marlines Fragline Several times a week Marlines daily (in season)	Euronautic tours Viamare
Patras–Corfu–Igoumenitsa–Trieste	Anek Lines Twice a week (in season)	Ikon Travel
Paxi–Brindisi	Hellenic Med. Lines Every 2 days (in season)	DERTRAFFIC
Piraeus–Bari	Adriatica 3 times a month (17.3–17.10)	Seetours
Piraeus–Venice	Adriatica 3 times a month (17.3–17.1)	Seetours

Greece to Greece

Piraeus–Khaniá	Anek Lines Daily	Ikon Travel
	Minoan Lines 3–5 times a week	Seetours
Piraeus–Iráklion	Anek Lines Daily	Ikon Travel
	Minoan Lines Daily	Seetours

Greece to Turkey

Patras–Kuşadasi	Minoan Lines Weekly (in season)	Seetours

Turkey–Greece

Kuşadası–Iráklion	Minoan Lines Weekly (1.6–12.10)	Seetours
Kuşadası–Patras	Minoan Lines Weekly (1.6–12.10)	Seetours

Greece–Egypt

Piraeus/Iráklion–Alexandria	Adriatica 3 times a month	Seetours

SERVICE Port	FREQUENCY Frequency	COMPANY
Greece–Israel		
Piraeus–Rhodes/ Limassol/Haifa	Stability Lines Arkadia Lines and Poseidon Lines Weekly	Viamare
Greece–Cyprus		
Piraeus–Rhodes– Limassol	Stability Lines Arkadia Lines and Poseidon Lines Weekly	Viamare
Piraeus/Iráklion– Limassol	Stability Lines Weekly (June–Sept.)	Viamare

Since the shipping companies accept no responsibility for losses, no objects of value should be left in your car during the crossing. It is advisable to take out insurance covering loss or theft during transport by sea.

Owners of trailer and motor caravans should check with the shipping line or with a travel agent that their vehicle is within the permitted limits of size.

For ferry connections to and between individual islands, see entries in the A to Z section of this guide.

Car Rental

Car rental facilities are widely available in Greece. In addition to the well known and efficient international car rental organisations there are numerous local firms, particularly in Athens, Piraeus, Salonica and the main tourist centres, both on the mainland and the islands. The rates charged by these local firms tend to be lower; so also, very often, is the standard of cars provided.

The main car rental companies have desks at Greek international airports. Arrangements for car hire can also be made through hotel reception desks.

The minimum age for hiring a car is 21. National driving licences are usually accepted, though it may sometimes help to have an international driving licence.

Tariffs vary according to size of car, duration of hire and time of year.

Fly-drive

Many tour operators offer fly-drive holidays covering the flight to Greece and the hire of a car (or in some cases a motor caravan).

Casinos

Gaming casinos operate in Greece throughout the year. Among them are the following:

Casino Mont Parnis

The Casino Mont Parnis, on Mount Parnis (1413m/4636ft), north of Athens, is housed in the luxury Hotel Mont Parnis (see Hotels), at the upper station of a cableway which operates 24 hours a day. Baccarat, blackjack, chemin de fer and American and French roulette are played here.

Casino Porto Karras

The Porto Karras casino is on the Sithonia peninsula (Chalcidice), to the south of Neos Marmaras.

Corfu

During the summer there is a casino in the Villa Achillion, 10km/6 miles from Corfu Town (shuttle bus service from town centre); in winter there is gaming in the luxury Corfu Palace Hotel (see Hotels). Here the patrons can play blackjack, chemin de fer and roulette or try their luck on the gaming machines.

Rhodes

There is a casino in the Grand Hotel in Rhodes Town (see Hotels). Associated with it is a night club. Blackjack, chemin de fer, roulette; gaming machines.

Caves

The Greek Speleological Association has a record of more than 7500 karstic caves on the Greek mainland and the islands. Several thousand of them have already been explored and mapped, and many of them are open to visitors.

The best known caves open to the public in Greece (mostly stalactitic caves) are shown on the map on page 523.

Chemists

Chemists' shops are identified by a round sign with a cross over the entrance and the name ΦΑΠΝΑΛΕΙΟΞ (Pharmakeion).

Opening times

Mon. and Wed. 8.30am–3.30pm; Tue., Thu. and Fri. 8.30am–2pm and 5–8pm.

Out-of-hours service

Every chemist's shop displays a notice giving the address of the nearest pharmacy which is open outside the normal hours.

The "Athens News" also lists, under the heading "Chemists/Pharmacies", pharmacies which are open at night and on Sundays and public holidays.

Emergency telephone

Tel. 107 (nights and Sundays) or
Tel. 100 (Police who will pass on emergency calls)

Cruises

The principal base of the cruise ships operating in the Mediterranean is the port of Piraeus.

There are very popular half-day cruises, combined with land excursions, to the celebrated archaeological sites of Delphi, Olympia, Vergína and Metéora.

There are also day trips from Piraeus to the islands of Aegina, Póros and Hýdra in the Saronic Gulf and longer trips, lasting several days, to the Aegean (including Rhodes), Crete, the Cyclades, Katakolon in the Peloponnese, the island of Corfu, the Gulf of Corinth, Asia Minor (e.g. Bodrum, Kuşadası) and Cyprus (e.g. Limassol), as well as throughout the Mediterranean and in the Black Sea.
A list of the shipping companies which run cruises can be obtained from the Greek National Tourist Organisation (see Information).

Caves in Greece

Show Caves
(mostly stalactitic; a selection)

1 Cave of the Cyclops, Maronia (Komotini)
2 Maara underground river, Drama
3 Cave with sinter formations, Alistrati (Serrai)
4 Petralona Cave (Chalcidice; red rock)
5 Ayios Yeoryios Cave, Kilkis
6 Caves on Great Lake, Prespa
7 Perama Cave, Ioannina (plan p. 000)
8 Anemotrypa Cave, Pramanta (Ioannina)
9 Sea-caves at Graves (Paxi)
10 Sea-cave at Papanikolis (Lefkas)
11 Cave of the Nymphs, Ithaca
12 On Kefallonia: Katavothren, Argostoli; Drongorati Cave; underground lake, Melissani
13 Korykion or Sarantavli Cave on Mt Parnassus
14 Koutouki Cave on Mt Hymettos
15 Dyros Caves (Mani; plans, p. 000)
16 Ayia Sofia Cave, Kythira
17 Sea-caves on Melos
18 Cave on Antiparos
19 Ayios Ioannis Cave on Iraklia
20 Cave of Zeus on Naxos
21 Five caves on Samos
22 Kefalas Cave on Kalymnos
23 Gouverneto Cave, nr Khania
24 Yerani Cave, nr Rethymnon Yerontospilios (Old Man's Cave), Melidoni
25 Ayia Paraskevi Cave, Skoteino; Eileithyia Cave, nr Iraklion; Milatos Cave, on Mirabello Bay
26 Dictaean Cave, Psykhro (Lasithi)

Fares

The fare for day trips usually includes pick-up from and return to the visitor's hotel and a buffet lunch. For longer trips it includes full board (with reductions for children).

Hydrofoils

The hydrofoils known as "Flying Dolphins" ply from the harbour of Zéa (Piraeus) to Hýdra, Kea, Kýthnos, Póros, Spétsai, to the Agolic Islands, the Sporades and to the Chalcidice Peninsula.

Information

Further information about cruises can be obtained from the offices of the Greek National Tourist Organisation (see Information).

Currency

Unit of currency

The Greek unit of currency is the drachma (dr.), which is divided into 100 lepta. There are banknotes for 50, 100, 500, 1000, 5000 and 10,000 dr. and coins in denominations of 1, 2, 5, 10, 20 and 50 dr. and 5, 10, 20 and 50 lepta (now disappearing from use).

Exchange rates

Exchange rates are subject to considerable fluctuation. Current rates are published in national newspapers and can also be obtained from banks and tourist offices.

Import of currency

Visitors may take into Greece a maximum of 100,000 dr. in Greek currency. There are no restrictions on the import of foreign currency in the form of travellers' cheques. Foreign currency amounting to more than US $1000 per head should be declared on entry into Greece so that any unspent amount can be taken out again.

Export of currency

Visitors may take out up to 20,000 dr. in Greek currency, in notes of no higher value than 1000 dr. Foreign currency to a value of US $1000 may be taken out, or a higher amount if declared on entry.

Opening hours of banks

Mon.–Thur. 8am–2 p.m; Fri. 8am–1.30pm; closed Sat. and Sun.

Athens:
Some of the large banks in Sýntagma Square (which are also open on Sundays and public holidays) and in Piraeus stay open until 8 and sometimes 9pm, as do the banks in the Central (Lárisa) Station in Athens.
Banks in both the East and West Terminals of Athens/Ellinikón Airport are open 24 hours a day.

Patras:
Odós Ermou and Odós Othonos/Amalias, Mon.–Sat. 8am–1pm and 5.30–9.30pm, Sun. and pub. hols. 10am–1pm.
Platía Trion Symmakhon, Mon.–Fri. 6–8pm.

Salonica:
Odós Tsimiski 11, Mon.–Fri. 3.30–8pm, Sat. 8am–2.30pm, Sun. 9.30am–2pm.
Mikra Airport, daily noon–7pm.
Central Station, Mon.–Fri. 5–8pm.

Changing money

As is usual in countries with weak currencies, it is best to change money in Greece rather than outside it.
When money is changed in a bank or other official institution the receipts should be kept, since you may be asked to produce them when leaving the country.

Changing money in hotels

Some hotels will change money at the reception desk, though the rate of exchange is likely to be less favourable than in a bank.

Exchange offices in post offices

Some post offices also change money.

Credit cards

The principal credit cards are widely accepted in larger towns. Cash cards do not operate in Greece.

Eurocheques, travellers' cheques

It is advisable to take money in the form of travellers' cheques or to use Eurocheques. Eurocheques may be drawn for sums of up to 25,000 dr., and can be cashed, on production of the drawer's Eurocard, at many banks in the larger towns and in tourist centres, as can travellers' cheques.
Ordinary cheques will be honoured only after reference back to the drawer's home bank, a process which may take some days.

In the event of loss or theft of credit cards, Eurocheques or travellers' cheques the company or bank which issued them should be informed at once by telephone, with confirmation in writing.

Customs Regulations

Customs allowances in European Union countries

In theory there are no limits to the amount of goods imported from one EU country to another, *provided they have been purchased tax paid in an EU country and are for personal use.* However the customs authorites have issued a list of maximum amounts of alcoholic drinks and tobacco considered reasonable for persons over 17 years of age. These are: spirits or strong liqueurs over 22% volume–10 litres; fortified wine (port, sherry, etc.) 20 litres; table wine–90 litres (of which not more than 60 litres may be sparkling wine): beer–110 litres; cigarettes–800 or cigarillos 400 or cigars 200 or pipe tobacco 1kg.
There is no limit on perfume, toilet water, coffee, tea or other goods. Personal use includes gifts, but if a traveller is receiving any payment in return for buying alcohol and tobacco (such as help with expenses) the transaction will be dutiable and the duty must be paid to the Customs authorities.

Visitors from non-EU countries

For those travelling direct from a country outside the EU or who have arrived from another EU country without having passed through customs control with all their baggage, the allowance for goods obtained anywhere outside the EU are (for persons over 17): spirits–1 litre or fortified wine–2 litres or table wine–3 litres plus a further 2 litres of table wine. Perfume 50 cc; toilet water 250cc. 200 cigarettes or 100 cigarillos or 50 cigars or 250g of tobacco; (for those over 15 years of age) coffee–500g, coffee extract–100g, tea–500g, tea extract–40g. All other goods, including gifts, 10,000 drs (children under 15: 5500 drs).

The import of radio equipment and weapons of any kind is strictly prohibited.

Private cars (and trailers, motorcycles, sidecars and mopeds) may be taken into Greece without payment of duty for up to six months (with the possibility of extension for another six months), but must be entered in the owner's passport.

Similar regulations apply to small motorboats and sailing boats brought in by road. Yachts (i.e. boats with cabin, galley, lavatory, etc.) must, on arrival in Greece, put in at a port with customs facilities and obtain a transit log (valid for six months, with the possibility of unlimited extension) entitling them to free passage in Greek waters (see entry on Sailing).

Further information can be obtained from local customs offices or from the Customs Investigation Department, Odós Amvrosiou Fratzi 14, Neos Kosmos, Athens, tel. (01) 9 22 73 07 and 9 22 73 15.
Yacht-owners may take in one Very pistol and one flare pistol.

Export

Visitors may take out provisions for their journey up to a value of US $50 and souvenirs up to a value of $150. The export of antiquities and works of art is prohibited save, exceptionally, with an authorisation from the State Archaeological Service. There is no difficulty about taking out replicas of antiquities or works of art.

Written-off cars

If a foreign car has an accident in Greece and becomes a write-off the customs authorities must be informed before the car can be scrapped.

Travel documents

See entry

Electricity

Electricity is normally 220 volts AC; on ships it is frequently 110 volts AC.
Power sockets are of normal European type. Adaptors are necessary for British or North American plugs. Adaptors can sometimes be borrowed in hotels, but this cannot be relied on.

Embassies and Consulates

United Kingdom

Embassy:
Odos Ploutarkhou 1
10675 Athens. Tel. (01) 7 23 62 11

Consulates:
Leoforos Alexandras 2
49100 Kerkyra, Corfu. Tel. (0661) 3 00 55 and 3 79 95

Odos Papa Alexandrou 16
71202 Iráklion, Crete. Tel. (081) 22 40 12

Odos Votsi 2
26221 Patras. Tel. (061) 27 73 29

Odos 25 Martiou 23
85100 Rhodes. Tel. (0241) 2 72 47 and 2 73 06

Odos Venizelou 8, Platia Eleftherias
54110 Salonica. Tel. (031) 27 80 06 and 26 99 84

Odos Themistokli Sofouli 15
83100 Vathý, Sámos. Tel. (0273) 2 73 14

Akti P. Ralli 8
84100 Ermoupolis, Sýros. Tel. (0281) 2 22 32 and 2 89 22

Odos Iolkou 4
38221 Volos. Tel. (0421) 2 46 42

United States

Embassy:
Leoforos Vasilissis Sofias 91
11521 Athens. Tel. (01) 7 21 29 51 and 7 21 84 01

Consulate:
Leoforos Nikis 59
54622 Salonica. Tel. (031) 26 61 21

Canada

Embassy:
Odos Ioannou Yennadiou 4
11521 Athens. Tel. (01) 7 23 95 11

Emergencies

Tourist Police

The most useful source of assistance for visitors is the Tourist Police (Astynomía Allodapón), which has offices in many towns of tourist interest.

Telephone in Athens; 171 (24 hours a day)

Traffic police

Athens: Tel. 9 22 94 21
Kerkyra (Corfu Town): Tel. 3 02 65
Patras: Tel. 22 09 02
Piraeus: Tel. 4 11 38 32
Salonica: Tel. (031) 52 28 21

National police

Telephone in Athens suburban area, Piraeus, Salonica, Patras and Corfu; 109

Telephone in Athens; 100

First aid

Telephone in Athens–Piraeus area; 166

Red Cross (ambulance)

Telephone in Athens; 150

Fire Service

Telephone throughout Greece; 199

Forest Fires

Telephone throughout Greece; 191

Coastguard

Telephone throughout Greece; 108

Warnings for yachtsmen

Special weather reports and warnings (advance warning of wind strengths of 6–7 or more on Beaufort scale) for yachtsmen, in Greek and English, are broadcast by Hellas Radio on VHF channel 16 daily at 7.03, 9.03 and 11.33am and 11.03pm (Greek time).

European Union Emergency numbers

The EU hopes to introduce uniform emergency numbers in all member countries for police, fire brigade, medical aid, ambulance service and other emergency services.

Breakdown assistance

See Motoring

Events

Calendar of Events

The following is a selection of events, but the calendar can change quite considerably from year to year.

Events

January 1st	New Year's Day; St Basil's Day; cutting of the *vasilopitta* (New Year cake; often containing a coin, which brings luck to the person who finds it). Children (and sometimes adults) go round the houses singing *kalanda* (carols) and are given money and/or cakes (see also December 31st).
On Ándros and at Plateos (Véria)	Popular festivals.
January 6th Many places	Three Kings' Day (Epiphany); Blessing of the Water, with immersion of cross in sea, lake or river (celebrated with particular ceremony in Piraeus).
Kozáni	Bourbousaria festival.
January 8th Kilkis, Komotiní, Monoklisia (Serrai)	"Women's Day". The women have a good time in the coffee-houses and tavernas, which they normally never go to; the men get back to their usual haunts only in the evening.
February Many places	Carnival celebrations, particularly in Patras (celebrated with particular enthusiasm), Athens (Plaka), Salonica, Kozáni, Véria, Zákynthos, Xánthi, Lamía, Kefalloniá, Vólos, Ámfissa, Réthymnon, Kárpathos, Iráklion, Messíni, Sokho (near Salonica), Serrai, Galaxídi, Thebes, Sparta, Poliyíros (Chalcidice), Salonica, Kalambáka, Skyros, Pournos and Ayía Ánna (Euboea), Ayiassos (Lésbos), Mesta, Olymbi and Thimiana (Chios) and Naoúsa.
February/March Meliki (Véria)	Mock peasant wedding.
March Kastoria	Fur Fair.
Beginning of March Kozáni	Fanos festival (folk dances of the Pontos region).
Sunday before Lent Athens	Carnival procession through city centre (Omonia Square to Zappion).
Katharí Deftéra (Monday before Lent) Everywhere	Kite-flying on hills, preparation for Lent with unleavened bread, fish, seafood and wine.
2nd half of March Salonica	Philoxenia (International Tourism Fair).
March 25th Independence Day	Military parades.
April 15th and 21st Corfu	Feast of St Spyridon, the island's patron saint.
Holy Week Everywhere	Procession with lighted candles on Good Friday, midnight celebration of the liturgy on Easter Saturday.
Easter (usually on different date from Western church) 1995: Apr. 23rd 1996: Apr. 14th	The most important Greek religious festival. The liturgy is celebrated on the night of Easter Saturday/Sunday, culminating in the cry "Christos anesti!" ("Christ is risen!"). Ringing of bells, firing of cannon, fireworks; *mayiritsa* (Easter soup); egg-rolling; exchange of gifts. Feast, with lamb on the spit; *tsoureki* (Easter cake, decorated with a red egg). Particularly picturesque celebrations: Ía, Trípoli, Livadiá, Trápeza (near Patras), Olympos (Kárpathos; on Tuesday after Easter).

St George's Day. Particular celebrations on Lemnos and Kos (horse-races; folk-singing and dancing), at Asi-Gonia (Khaniá; sheep-shearing competition) and at Arakhova (where the celebrations last three days).	**April 23rd** Many places
Son et lumière shows every evening on the Acropolis in Athens and in the gardens of the Grand Master's Palace in Rhodes.	**April–October** Athens and Rhodes
Greek folk dancing in the old Municipal Theatre and other events in Grand Master's Palace and elsewhere.	**Beginning of May to October** Rhodes
Departure of the sponge-divers.	**May** Kálymnos
Labour Day, with parades, flower festivals and a general exodus into the country. Particular celebrations at Néa Filadelfia, Néa Khalkidona, Néa Smyrni, Kifissiá and Karyes (near Flórina).	**May 1st** Everywhere
Son et lumière shows in Citadel, Corfu Town.	**Mid May to end September**
Anniversary of reunion with Greece.	**May 21st** Corfu
Anastenaria: barefoot dancing on glowing embers with icons of SS Constantine and Helen in the villages of Ayía Eleni and Áyios Petros (nomos of Serrai) and at Langada (nomos of Salonica).	**May 21st–23rd** Northern Greece
Dance festival, commemorating the battle for Crete.	**May 27th–29th** Khaniá
Palaioloyia festival.	**May 29th** Mistra
Karaiskakia festival.	**End of May** Kardítsa
Cherry Festival.	**End of May** Kolindron
Acropolis Rally in Athens.	**End May/ beginning of June**
Bull Fair, with sacrifice of calf, equestrian events and folk songs and dances.	**End May/ beginning of June** Ayía Paraskeví (Lésbos)
Papastratia festival of cultural and sporting events.	**June** Agrinion
Kalafonon: midsummer bonfires.	**June 21st** Rhodes
Klydona: folk festival in villages of Piskokefalo and Krousta.	**End of June** Lasithi (Crete)
Navy Week (in alternate years: enquire locally about exact dates); at Vólos a re-enactment of the sailing of the Argonauts.	**June/July** Coastal towns
Papakharalambia: festival of artistic and sporting events.	**July** Náfpaktos

Events

Beginning of July Lefkimmi (Corfu)	Fair, with folk dancing.
Mid July Crete	Wine Festival at Dafnes (Iráklion) and in municipal park, Réthymnon (lasting a week); Raisin Festival in Sitía.
Mid July to September Dafní, Alexandroúpolis, Rodini	Wine Festivals, with wine-tasting, at Dafní (11km/7 miles from central Athens; bus service), Alexandroúpolis (mid July to mid August) and Rodini (Rhodes).
July 26th Langadia (Tripoli)	Feast of Ayía Paraskeví, with folk-song contest.
July/August Préveza	Nikopolia festival.
July/August Many places	Various festivals, e.g. Olympus festival in Platamónas castle; festivals at Katerini, Litokhoron, Dion and Makriyialo; festival of music and drama, Ithaca; festival of literature and art, loánnina.
August Lefkás	Festival of literature and art.
August Kos	Ippokratia: theatrical performances, evening concerts, flower show, folk art, presentation of the Hippocratic Oath.
August Vólos	Artistic events (concerts, drama, folk dancing); exhibition in gardens of Municipal Theatre.
August 6th Anoyia (Crete)	Fair, with folk events.
Mid August Zákynthos	International Festival of Medieval and Popular Drama.
Mid August Zakýnthos	Ancient tragedies.
August 15th Many places	Feast of the Dormition of the Mother of God, celebrated with particular pomp on Tínos, Corfu and Lésbos, at Neapolis (Crete) and Kými (Euboea), on Páros (Fish and Wine Festival), and at Siatista (equestrian events) and Vlastis (Kozáni).
2nd half of August Portaria (Pelion), Ithaca, Kritsá	Mock wedding in local style at Portaria; festival of drama, Ithaca; Cretan Wedding at Kritsá (Lasithi).
August 24th Zákynthos	Feast of St Dionysios, the island's patron saint.
August/September Eleusis (Attica)	Aiskhylia, with ancient dramas on the archaeological site.
End August/ beginning of September	Chalcidice Rally.
September Corfu	Cricket Week, with visiting foreign sides.
September Salonica	International Trade Fair, with Song Festival and Film Festival.
September Zákynthos	Festival of Art.

September
Mesolóngi
Vyronia (Byron Festival of literature and art).

September 1st–15th
Ankhialos (Salonica)
Wine Festival.

September 1st–20th
Patras
Wine Festival.

September 8th–9th
Spétsai
Naval Festival, commemorating the defeat of the Turks.

Mid September
Nikiti (Chalcidice)
Folk Festival.

End September
Kythira
Fair at Myrtidiótissa monastery.

End September
Elos Kisamou (Khaniá)
Chestnut Festival.

October 28th
Everywhere
National Day (Okhi Day, "No" Day), with military parades.

November 4th
Corfu
Feast of St Spyridon.

November 8th
Réthymnon (Crete)
Commemoration of Arkadi monastery.

December 24th
Everywhere
Christmas Eve: children (and in many parts of the country adults as well) go round singing *kalanda* (carols).

December 31st
Chios
The island's seamen carry model ships (2–3m/6–10ft long, with lamps and flags) round the town, singing carols.

December 31st
Everywhere
Kalanda singing, as on January 1st and December 24th.

Seasonal Events

The Greek National Tourist Organisation organises every year, particularly during the summer, a series of events of tourist interest:

Athens Festival (June/July–September): performances of ancient dramas, operas, music and dancing in the Odeion of Herodes Atticus.

Performances of (mainly modern) music in the open-air theatre on Lykabettos, Athens (June–September), and operatic performances by the Lyric Theatre, given in the Odeion of Herodes Atticus in summer and in the Olympia Theatre in winter.

Epidauros Festival (beginning of July to beginning of September): performances of classical drama in the ancient theatre.

Festivals of music, drama and dance (during the summer) in other ancient theatres – Dodona, Patras, Philippi, Thásos.

Performances in Patras amphitheatre (end June to mid September): drama, music, ballet.

Greek Film Festival in Salonica (during Trade Fair in September).

Demetria festival, Salonica: artistic and cultural events in honour of the city's patron saint.

Greek Song Festival (October) in Salonica.

Festival of Short Films (September) in Asteria Cinema, Dráma.

Various artistic events during the summer in the Theatron Dasous (Forest Theatre) in Salonica.

Performances of folk dances in Philopappos Theatre, Athens (May to September), and in the theatre in the old town of Rhodes (May to October).

Performances in the National Theatre in Athens, the State Theatre of Northern Greece in Salonica, and operatic performances in the Olympia Theatre, Athens.

Wine Festival: see under Calendar of Events, above.

Sporting Events

Information about sporting events like car rallies and marathon races (and the Spartathlon, a 150-mile race from Athens to Sparta) can be obtained from:

SEGAS
Leoforos Syngrou 137, Athens
Tel. (01) 9 34 10 10

Sailing Championships

For information about international sailing championships, apply to:

Greek Yachting Association
Akti Navarkhou Kountourioti 7
Piraeus
Tel. (061) 4 13 73 51

Food and Drink

Food

Hotel restaurants usually offer the standard international cuisine, with some Greek dishes to add an extra touch of colour. In restaurants the national cuisine predominates, showing strong Eastern (mainly Turkish) influence and making much use of olive oil, garlic and herbs. Fruit and vegetables feature prominently on the menu. Fish and meat are almost always grilled.
Visitors requiring special diets should discuss this with the hotel management. Those with stomach or liver conditions should wherever possible ask for meat or fish to be grilled without salt. Caution should be used in drinking iced water.
Essential items in the table setting are bread (*psomí*), salt (*aláti*), pepper (*pipéri*) and sugar (*zákhari*).

Times of meals — See Restaurants

Hors d'œuvres (orektiká)

There is a wide choice of hors d'œuvres. In addition to the appetisers (*mese*) which are served with the aperitif the range includes prawns, seafood, vine-leaves stuffed with rice (*dolmádes*) and salads (*salátes*).

Soups (soúpes)

Greek soups are usually very substantial, and are often made with eggs and lemon juice. *Fasolada* is a popular thick bean soup; other favourite soups are pepper soup (*pipéri soúpa*), with the addition of vegetables and meat, and clear bouillon (*somós kréatos*). There are also excellent fish soups (*psárosoupes*).

Meat (kréas)

The favourite kind of meat is lamb (*arnáki* or *arní*), usually roasted or grilled. Also popular are *souvlákia* (kebabs) and *gyros* (meat grilled on a vertical spit). *Kokorétsi* are lamb entrails roasted on the spit.

Vegetables and salads (lakhaniká, salátes)

Typical Greek vegetables are artichokes (*angináres*), aubergines (*melitsánes*), courgettes (*kolokithákia*) and peppers (*piperiés*), usually stuffed or cooked in oil. Salads include lettuce (*maroúli*), tomato salad (*tomáto saláta*), asparagus salad (*sparángia saláta*) and "country salad" (*khoriátiki*).

Fish (psári)

Fish and seafood feature prominently on Greek menus. The commonest species are sea-bream (*sinagrída, tsipoúra*), sole (*glóssa*), red mullet (*barboúni*) and tunny (*tónnos*), together with lobsters (*astakós*), mussels (*mydia*), squid (*kalamária*), octopuses (*oktapódes*), and others.

Desserts (dessér)

The commonest desserts are fruit (*froúta*) or an ice (*pagotó*). There is a wide variety of fruit, depending on the time of year: water melons (*karpoúsia*), musk melons (*pepónia*), peaches (*rodákina*), pears (*akhládia*), apples (*míla*), oranges (*portokália*), grapes (*stafylia*), figs (*syka*).

Cheese (tyrí)

Most Greek cheeses are made from ewe's milk or goat's milk, which are also used to make yogurt (*yaoúrti*).

The Coffee-House

An important role is played in the daily life of the Greeks by the coffee-house or café (*kafeníon*), which is not merely for drinking coffee but performs a social function (like the ancient Greek agora) as a place for meeting friends, for conversation, for playing cards or other games and for doing business. Coffee is served with the accompaniment of a glass of water (*neró*); *ouzo,* the aniseed-flavoured national aperitif, is accompanied by *mese* (small pieces of cheese, olives, etc.).

In towns there are also patisseries (*zakharoplastía*), which serve pastries and sweets (which are usually very sweet) together with French coffee and other beverages.

Drinks

Wine

The commonest drink is wine (*krasí*), either white (*áspro*) or red (*mávro*). There are both dry and sweet wines.

Retsína

Greek country wines are resinated to improve their keeping quality (*retsína, krasí retsináto*). This gives them a characteristic sharp taste

which may not appeal to everyone at first; but resinated wines, once the taste has been acquired, are very palatable and stimulating to the appetite.
The Greek liking for resinated wines dates back to ancient times, as is shown by the remains of resin found in some of the earliest amphoras. The resin is added to the wine during fermentation.

There are also unresinated wines, both white and red, which meet European Community regulations; they are identified by the letters VQPRD on the label.

Wine-Growing Regions

Attica

The country around Athens is the home of retsina. It also produces a rosé wine (*kokkinéli*).

Peloponnese

Something like a third of all Greek wine is produced in the Peloponnese. Its speciality is sweet wine. The finest wine of this type is Mavrodaphne, a heavy, dark, sweetish wine.

The islands

The dry white wines produced in the Greek islands are usually not particularly notable. The wines of Kefalloniá (Rombola), Zákynthos

(Verdea) and Rhodes (Lindos) are among the best. The white muscatel wine of Samos is excellent.

The Language of the Wine Label

Sparkling wine	Afródes krasí
Bottling	Emfiálosis
Table wine	Epitrapézio krasí
Wine-making establishment	Inoplion
Wine	Ínos
Red wine	Ínos érythros
White wine	Ínos lefkós
Sparkling wine	Kambanítis
Wine	Krasí
Red wine	Mávro krasí
Production	Paragoyí
To be drunk chilled	Pinetaí droseró
Retsina (resinated wine)	Retsína
Rosé	Rozé
Champagne	Sampánia
Dry	Xerós

Beer

The brewing of beer (*bíra*) in Greece dates from the reign of King Otto I, a native of Bavaria, and the popular Fix brand is still made to a Bavarian recipe. There are also various international brands of beer brewed under licence.

Spirits (pnevmatódi potá)

The commonest aperitif is *ouzo,* an aniseed-flavoured schnaps, usually diluted with water, which turns it milky. *Ráki* is similar but stronger. Mastikha is a liqueur made from the bark of the mastic tree. Greek brandy (*koniák*) is fruity and fairly sweet.

Soft drinks

In addition to water (*neró*) and mineral water (*metallikó neró, sóda*), the most popular soft drinks are orangeade (*portokaláda*), lemonade (*lemonáda*) and freshly pressed fruit juices (*portokaláda fréska,* orange juice).

Coffee (kafés)

Coffee comes in different strengths and degrees of sweetness – e.g. *kafés glykís vrastos* made with plenty of sugar, *varýs glykós* strong and sweet, *elafrós* light. A popular version is *métrios* medium strong and medium sweet.

Tea (tsái)

Tea is of different kinds – *mávro tsái* black tea, *tsái ménda* peppermint tea, *kamoumillo* camomile tea, *tsái tou vounoú* an infusion of mountain herbs.

Getting to Greece

Visitors travelling to Greece from northern Europe have the choice between a direct flight to Athens, Salonica, Corfu or Iráklion (Crete) and a drive (or rail journey) down through Italy followed by a ferry (see Car Ferries) to Corfu, Igoumenítsa, Athens (Piraeus) or Crete.

For travel from mainland Greece to the islands and between the islands see Island-Hopping and Cruises.

By car

It is possible to drive from the Channel ports through France, Switzerland and down through Italy, then cross to Greece by one of the many car ferries from the Italian Adriatic ports (see Car Ferries). This is a tiring journey and several days should be allowed. The amount of driving can be reduced by using one of the European Motorail services (e.g. Paris–Munich and Munich–Athens) but this adds considerably to the cost.

By bus

An economical way to travel to Greece is by bus. Eurolines (address below) run a bus from London (Victoria Coach Station) on Fridays in Summer (July 1st–September 30th), travelling via Dover, Paris, Rimini and Ancona to Corfu, Igoumenítsa, Patras and Athens.

Information and reservations

Eurolines (UK) Ltd
23 Crawley Road,
Luton, Beds LU1 1HX; tel. (01582) 404511

Frontier crossing points

The frontier crossing points into Greece, which are open 24 hours a day, are as follows:

From Bulgaria:
Kulata/Promakhon (660km/410 miles to Athens)

From Turkey:
Edirne/Kastanea (1000km/620 miles to Athens)
Ipsala/Kipi (910km/565 miles to Athens)

By rail

This is quicker and less tiring than by car, although possibly more expensive than a charter flight. The route would be through France to Milan and south to the Italian Adriatic ports and by ferry to Greece, or to connect with through trains from Dortmund and Munich in Germany. The Hellas Express from Dortmund travels to Salonica in 43 hours and Athens in 52 hours; the Acropolis Express from Munich takes 32 hours to Salonica and 40 hours to Athens.

By air

Greece is linked with the international network of air services by the national airline, Olympic Airways, and by many foreign airlines. There are direct flights from London to Athens, Salonica and Corfu.
There are also many charter flights, mainly during the summer to various destinations in Greece from London and other UK airports.

It is advisable to enquire of a travel agency in advance about the availability of reduced fares for scheduled flights (Apex, Super Apex, stand-by, etc.) and to compare these with the fares for charter flights (which are not always cheaper than the cheapest scheduled fares).

Travel to Athos

There are strict controls on access to Athos which is open to men only. The number of visitors is restricted to ten per day, and the maximum period of stay is four days. Visitors must be properly dressed and long hair is banned. For obtaining permission to visit Athos see Travel Documents.

The only access to Athos is by boat from Ouranópolis (which can be reached from Salonica by bus) to the port of Dafní; the crossing takes about 3 hours. From there a bus runs twice daily to Karyes, the administrative centre of Athos (see entry).

Guides

Only qualified Greek guides are permitted to lead conducted tours in Greece.

Information from:

Association of Greek Guides
(Syndesmos Xenagon)
Apollonos 9A
Athens
Tel. (01) 3 22 97 05

P.O. Box 163
Salonica
Tel. (031) 54 60 37

Hotels

Greece has some 5700 hotels affiliated to the Greek Chamber of Hotels (see below).

Reservation

When travelling in Greece at Easter or during the main holiday season it is advisable to book rooms in advance.

Information and reservations:

Greek Chamber of Hotels
(Xenodokhiako Epimelitirio)
Stadiou 24
Athens
Tel. (01) 3 23 66 41, 3 22 35 01

Branch office in Sýntagma Square (National Bank):
Stadiou 2/Karayeoryi Servias 2
Tel. (01) 3 23 71 93
Open: Mon.–Fri. 8.30am–8pm, Sat. 8am–2pm.

Tariffs

During the main holiday season hotel prices in Greece are little below the level of hotels in western European countries; out of season they are substantially lower.

Categories

Greek hotels are officially classified in six categories – L (luxury), A, B, C, D and E – and most visitors will look for accommodation in one of the first four categories.

The following list is based on the official list published by the Greek Chamber of Hotels, with a Baedeker star (★) for hotels of particular quality. b. = beds, r. = rooms.

Hotels in Adamas (Melos)	Adamas, 2 Griara, B, 22 b.; Popi, B, 12 b.; Venus Village, B, 173 b.; Chronis (bungalows), C, 32 b.; Corali, C, 31 b.; Meltemi, C, 24 b.; Milos, C, 67 b.; Santa Maria, C, 46 b.
Aegina	See Aiyina
Afantou (Rhodes)	Oasis Holidays (hotel and bungalows), A, 70 b.; Xenia Golf, B, 52 b.
Afyssos (Pelion)	Alexandros, 7 Pigis, 18 b.; Galini, B, 58 b.; Faros, C, 21 b.; Katia, C, 47 b.
Agria	Barbara, C, 17 b.
Agrinion	Esperia, 31 H. Trikoupi, B, 42 b.; Galaxy, 19 G. Kazatzi, B, 51 b.; Soumelis (motel), 3 Ethniki Odos, B, 36 b.; Acropole, 1 Ilia Iliou, C, 41 b.; Alice, 2 Papastratou, C, 50 b.; Leto, Platia Dimokratias, C, 63 b.; Tourist, 51 Papastratou, C. 64 b.
Aidipsos	See Loutra Aidipsou
Aiyina	Danae, B, 100 b.; Nausika (Nafsika; bungalows), 55 N. Kazantzaki Ave, B, 66 b.; Pavlou, 21 P. Eginitou, B, 17 b.; Areti, 4 N. Kazantzaki Paralia, C, 39 b.; Avra, 2 N. Kazantzaki, Paralia, C, 57 b.; Brown, 4 Toti Hatzi Paralia, C, 48 b.; Faros, Paralia, C, 77 b.; Klonos, C, 84 b.; To Petrino Spiti, C, 20 b.
Aiyion	Galini, 35 Vas. Yeoryiou, B, 59 b.; Telis, 98 Korinthou, C, 56 b.
Akrotiri (Santorin)	Akrotiri, C, 30 b.
Akharavi	Aharavi Beach, B, 82 b.; Ionian Princess (Pringipissa Ioniou), B, 98 b.; Marie, C, 46 b.
Akharnes	Acharnis, km 20 on Parnithos Ave, C, 77 b.; Belle Vue, km 19 on Parnithos Ave, C, 38 b.; Dekelia, C, 60 b.
Alexandroupolis	Motel Astir, 280 Komotinis, A, 99 b.; Alexander Beach (2km/1¼ miles along road to Komotini), Ethnikis Odou, B, 194 b.; Egnatia (motel), Leoforos Makris, B, 180 b.; Alkyon, 1 Moudanion Apolonias, C, 52 b.; Alex, 294 Vas. Yeoryiou B, C, 60 b.; Aphroditi, Ethniki Odos Alexandroupoleos, C, 36 b.; Dionyssos, Leoforos Makris, C, 66 b.; Galaxias, 159 Vas. Yeoryiou B, C, 97 b.; Hera, 179 Dimokratias Ave & M. Yefiras, C, 60 b.; Oceanis, 20 C. Paleologou, C, 45 b.; Olympion, Vas. Yeoryiou/12 Malgaron, C, 26 b.; Park, 458 Vas. Yeoryiou B, C, 42 b.; Plaza (2km/1¼ miles along road to Komotini), C, 36 b.
Alinda	See Leros (town)
Almyron	Messinian Bay, B, 86 b.
Almyropotamos	Galazio Delfini, D, 20 b.
Alonnisos (town)	Alkyon, B, 30 b.; Alonnissos Beach, C, 90 b.; Galaxy, Patitiri (harbour), C, 98 b.; Marpounda (bungalows), Marpounda, C, 200 b.
Alykes (Corfu)	Kerkyra Golf, A, 444 b.; Alykes Beach, C, 39 b.; Salina, C, 31 b.; Sunset, C, 101 b.
Alykes (Zákynthos)	Asteria, C, 37 b.; Astoria, C, 60 b.; Galini, C, 14 b.; Ionian Star, C, 42 b.; Montreal, C, 56 b.

Alyki (Paros)
Afroditi, B, 40 b.; Angeliki, C, 26 b.

Amalias
Amalia, Othonos & Amalias, C, 28 b.; Hellinis, 9 Othonos & Amalias, C, 27 b.; Korivos, Amalias & Othonos, C, 21 b.; Olympic Inn, 10 Filellinon, C, 77 b.

Amaroussion
Alsos, 27 Alsous Paradisos, D, 17 b.; Neon, 2 Ermou, D, 34 b.

Amarynthos (Euboea)
Olymbiakos Asteras, B, 399 b.; Stefania, B, 152 b.; Flisvos, C, 43 b.; Artemis, D, 54 b.

Ámfissa
Amfissaeum, 18 Gidogiannou, C, 78 b.; Stallion, 3 Thoandos, C, 45 b.

Ammoudi (Crete)
Polydoros, B, 11 b.; Delfini, D, 24 b.

Amorgos (town)
Mike, C, 19 b.

Amoudara (Iráklia)
Agapi Beach, A, 391 b.; Dolphin Bay, A, 498 b.; Agapi Village, B, 141 b.; Marilena, B, 116 b.; Agia Eleni, C, 70 b.; Minoas, C, 67 b.; Tsangarakis Beach, C, 83 b.; Violetta, C, 33 b.

Amoudares
Virginia (apartments), Listi Spilio, B, 38 b.

Anavyssos (Attic Riviera)
Saronic Gate, km 46, A, 195 b., Akti Apollon, km 51, B, 168 b., Motel Calypso, km 49, B, 85 b., and Eden Beach, km 47, all on road from Athens to Cape Sounion; Xenia Ilios, B, 568 b.; Silver Beach, km 51 on road from Athens to Cape Sounion, C, 54 b.

Andritsaina
Theoxenia, B, 58 b.; Pan, D, 12 b.

Andros (town)
Paradissos, B, 76 b.; Xenia, B, 44 b.; Aegli, C, 27 b.

Anemomylos (Corfu)
Arion, 5 Emm. Theotoki, B, 199 b.; Marina, B, 192 b.

Angistri
Alcyon, D, 27 b.; Andreas, D, 42 b.; Dina, D, 28 b.; Galini, D, 42 b.; Manaras, D, 48 b.; Mylos, D, 23 b.; Saronis, D, 34 b.

Ano Mera (Mýkonos)
Ano Mera, A, 124 b.; Kalo Livadi, D, 20 b.

Antimakhia
See Mastikhari

Antissa (Lésbos)
Athina, E, 8 b.

Anyfanta (Lésbos)
Silver Bay (hotel and bungalows), B, 150 b.

Apikia (Andros)
Pigi, C, 79 b.

Apollonia (Sifnos)
Apollonia, B, 18 b.; Flora, Khrysopiyi, B, 24 b.; Anthoussa, C, 12 b.; Sifnos, Katarati, C, 19 b.; Sofia, C, 22 b.

Aptera
Aptera Beach (bungalows), Paralia Ayion Apostolon, C, 92 b.

Arakhova
Anemolia, B, 78 b.; Xenia, B, 86 b.

Hotels

Arakhovitika	Patra's Bay (hotel and bungalows), B, 150 b.
Areopolis	Pýrgos Kapetanakou, A, 16 b.; Mani, C, 30 b.
Argassion (Zákynthos)	Akti Zakantha, A, 227 b.; Chryssi Akti, B, 146 b.; Levante, B, 120 b.; Lokanda, B, 40 b.; Mimoza Beach (bungalows), B, 84 b.; Yliessa, B, 118 b.; Argassi Beach, C, 64 b.; Captain's, C, 69 b.; Family Inn, C, 31 b.
Argos	Mycenae, 12 Platia Ayiou Petrou, C, 42 b.; Telessila, 2 Danaou & Vas. Olgas, C, 60 b.
Argostolion	Xenia, Platia Rizospastron, B, 44 b.; Aegli, 3, 21 Maiou, 17 b.; Aenos, 11, 21 Maiou & Platia Metaxa, C, 74 b.; Aghios Gerassimos, 6 Ayiou Yerasimou, C, 28 b.; Argostoli, 21 Vironos, C, 39 b.; Armonia, 1 Yeroulanou, C, 24 b.; Castello, Platia Metaxa, C, 22 b.; Cephalonia Star, 50 I. Metaxa, C, 73 b.; Galaxias, C, 20 b.; Mouïkis, 3 Vironos, C, 70 b.; Phokas, 3 Yeroulanou, C, 80 b.; Regina, 24 Vergoti, C, 40 b.; Tourist, 94 I. Metaxa, C, 38 b.
Arilas (Corfu)	Arilla Beach, C, 68 b.; Marina, C, 32 b.
Arkhanes (Crete)	Dias, B, 55 b.
Arkhangelos	Arkhangelos, 184, 7 Martiou, D, 37 b.; Filia, D, 39 b.; Fivos, D, 26 b.
Arkitsa	Faros, B, 10 b.; Kalypso Club (bungalows), B, 506 b.
Árta	Xenia, Frourion, B, 40 b.; Amvrakia, 13 N. Priovolou, C, 110 b.; Anessis, 7 Mitropolitou Xenopoulou, C, 48 b.; Cronos, Platia Kilkis, C, 102 b.
Artemon (Sifnos)	Artemonas, 3 Ayiou Konstantinou, C, 44 b.
Asprovalta	Strymonikon, 49 Egnatia, D, 26 b.
Assyrmatos Potamos (Corfu)	Gefyraki, C, 54 b.
Astros Kynurias	Georgakakis, C, 35 b.
Astypálaia (town)	Aegeon, D, 31 b.; Astynea, 21 M. Karayeoryi, D, 39 b.; Paradissos, 24 M. Karayeoryi, D, 42 b.
Atalanti	Anessis, C, 29 b.
Athens	Around Sýntagma Square: ★ Astir Palace Athens, Leoforos Vas. Sofias & Panepistimiou, L, 148 b.; ★ Athenaeum Inter-Continental, 89–93 Leoforos Syngrou, L, 1178 b.; ★ Athens Chandris, 385 Leoforos Syngrou, L, 720 b.; ★ Athens Hilton, 46 Vas. Sofias, L, 862 b.; ★ Caravel, 2 Vas. Alexandrou, L, 841 b.; ★ Grande Bretagne, Platia Syntagmatos, L, 668 b.; ★ Holiday Inn, 50 Mikhalakopoulou, L, 338 b.; ★ Ledra Marriott, 113–115 Leoforos Syngrou, L, 477 b.; ★ N. J. V. Méridien Athens, Voukourestiou/Stadiou/Vas. Yeoryiou A, L, 336 b.; ★ Royal Olympic, 28–34 Diakou, L, 554 b.; ★ St George Lycabettus, 2 Kleomenous & Platia Dexamenis, L, 278 b.; Amalia, 10 Leoforos Amalias, A, 188 b.; Astor, 16 Karayeoryi Servias, A, 234 b.; Electra, 5 Ermou, A, 180 b.; Elektra Palace, 18 Nikodimou, A,

196 b.; Esperia Palace, 22 Stadiou, A, 338 b.; Olympic Palace, 16 Filellinon, A, 144 b.; Aretousa, 6–8 Mitropoleos & 12 Nikis, B, 158 b.; Athens Gate, 10 Leoforos Syngrou, B, 259 b.; Athinais, 99 Vas. Sofias & Platia Mavili, B, 162 b.; Christina, 15 Petmeza & Kallirois, B, 173 b.; Lycabette, 6 Valaoritou, B, 63 b.; Minerva, 3 Stadiou, B, 86 b.; Omiros, 15 Apollonos, B, 60 b.; Palladion, 54 Panepistimiou, B, 115 b.; Pan, 11 Mitropoleos, B, 92 b.; Plaka, 7 Kapnikareas & Mitropoleos, B, 123 b.; Titania, 52 Panepistimiou, B, 754 b.; Aphrodite, 21 Apollonos, C, 162 b.; Carolina, 55 Kolokotroni, C, 57 b.; Hermes, 19 Apollonos, C, 85 b.; etc.

Around Omonia Square:
King Minos, 1 Pireos, A, 287 b.; Acadimos, 50 Akademias, B, 227 b.; Alpha, 17 Khalkokondyli, B, 167 b.; Arcadia, 46 Marni, B, 154 b.; Athens Center, 26 Sofokleous & 2 Klisthenous, B, 259 b.; Cairo City, 42 Marni, B, 140 b.; Candia (Heraklion), 40 Th. Diliyiani, B, 254 b.; Dorian Inn, 15–19 Pireos, B, 287 b.; El Greco, 65 Athinas, B, 167 b.; Grand Hotel, 10 Veranzerou, B, 190 b.; Ilion, 7 Ayiou Konstantinou, B, 166 b.; Ionis, 41 Khalkokondyli, B, 194 b.; Marathon, 23 Karolou, B, 174 b.; Minoa, 12 Karolou, B, 81 b.; Alcestis (Alkistis), 18 Platia Theatrou, C, 224 b.; Amaryllis, 45 Veranzerou, C, 98 b.; Ares (Aris), 7 Pireos, C, 71 b.; Arias, 20 Karolou, C, 79 b.; Aristides, 50 Sokratous, C, 158 b.; Artemission, 20 Veranzerou, C, 76 b.; Aspasia, 20 Satovriandou, C, 65 b.; Astra, 46 Diliyiani, C, 49 b.; Asty, 2 Pireos, C, 224 b.; Atlas, 30 Sofokleous, C, 33 b.; Attalos, 29 Athinas, C, 155 b.; Banghion, 18B Platia Omonias, C, 93 b.; Capitol, 11 Marikas Kotopouli & Platia Omonias, C, 168 b.; Carlton, 7 Platia Omonias, C, 60 b.; Diros, 21 Ayiou Konstantinou, C, 84 b.; Elite, 23 Pireos, C, 80 b.; Europa, 7 Satovriandou, C, 67 b.; Evripides, 79 Evripidou, C, 119 b.; Mediterranean, 28 Veranzerou, C, 82 b.; Nausika (Nafsika), 21 Karolou, C, 73 b.; Nestor, 38 Ayiou Konstantinou, C, 95 b.; Odeon, 42 Pireos, C, 98 b.; Olympia, 25 Pireos, C, 66 b.; Orpheus, 58 Khalkokondyli, C, 71 b.; Parnon, 20 Tritis Septemvriou & 21 Khalkokondyli, C, 79 b.; Pythagorion, 28 Ayiou Konstantinou, C, 106 b.; Vienna, 20 Pireos, C, 114 b.; etc.

Near National Archaeological Museum:
★Acropole Palace, 51, 28 Oktovriou, L, 173 b.; ★Park, 10 Leoforos Alexandras, Pedion Areos, L, 275 b.; Divani–Zafolia Alexandras, 87–89 Leoforos Alexandras, A, 350 b.; Plaza, 78 Akharnon & 1 Katrivanou, B, 239 b.; Xenophon, 340 Akharnon, B, 350 b.; Aristoteles, 15 Akharnon, C, 102 b.; Morpheus, 3 Aristotelous, C, 35 b.; Museum, 16 Bouboulinas & Tositsa, C, 109 b.; etc.

Aviakia (Sámos)

Avlakia, C, 28 b.

Ayia Ánna

Kyma, E, 19 b.

Ayia Effimia

Pylaros, C, 19 b.

Ayia Galini (Crete)

Rea, B, 35 b.; Stella, B, 19 b.; Acropolis, 1 Bizaniou, C, 32 b.; Adonis, C, 39 b.; Adonis II, C, 52 b.; Ariadni, C, 12 b.; Astoria, Bizaniou, C, 42 b.; Athina, C, 33 b.; Candia, 15 Arkadiou, C, 22 b.; Dedalos, Arkadiou, C, 24 b.; Galini Mare, C, 48 b.; Ghioma, C, 33 b.; Iro, C, 21 b.; Miramare, 12 Bizaniou, C, 13 b.; Petra, C, 52 b.; Phaestos, C, 16 b.; Selena, 1 Zaboudaki, C, 15 b.; Soulia, E. Venizelou, C, 22 b.

Ayia Marina (Aegina)

Apollo, B, 203 b.; Argo, B, 116 b.; Motel Aegli, 199 Afeas, C, 14 b.; Akti, C, 44 b.; Ammoudia, C, 26 b.; Aphaea, C, 46 b.; Blue Horizon, C, 28 b.; Galini, C, 120 b.; Hermes, C, 25 b.; Isidora, C, 40 b.; Kalliopi, C, 25 b.;

Karras, C, 52 b.; Karyatides, C, 56 b.; Kyriakakis, C, 57 b.; Liberty, C, 40 b.; Magda, C, 40 b.; Marina, C, 55 b.; Nektarios (formerly Nyremvergi), C, 24 b.; Oassis, C, 37 b.; Panorama, C, 49 b.; Pantelaros, C, 106 b.; Possidon, C, 48 b.; Saronis, C, 20 b.; Ta Tria Adelfia, C, 32 b.

Ayia Marina (Crete)
Santa Marina, B, 120 b.; Amalthia (hotel and bungalows), C, 76 b.; Santa Marina II, C, 90 b.; Ta Thodorou, Kato Ayia Marina, C, 14 b.

Ayia Paraskevi (Nr Athens)
Park, 9 Efkalipton, C, 75 b.; Hellas, 12 Ydras, D, 40 b.; Hill, 6 Dimitras, D, 42 b.

Ayia Paraskevi (Crete)
Zorbas, 1 Navarkhou Nearkhou, C, 40 b.

Ayia Paraskevi (Kassandra)
Aphrodite, Loutra, B, 46 b.

Ayia Pelayia (Crete)
Capsis Beach (hotel and bungalows), A, 1250 b.; Peninsula (hotel and bungalows), Psaromoura, A, 367 b.; Panorama, B, 156 b.

Ayia Pelayia (Kefallonia)
Irina, B, 325 b.

Ayia Pelayia (Kythira)
Kytheria, B, 15 b.

Ayia Roumeli
Agia Roumeli, B, 13 b.

Ayiassos (Lésbos)
Aghia Sion, B, 24 b.

Ayii Theodori
Hanikian Beach, A, 516 b.; Margarita, B, 22 b.; Siagas Beach, km 62 on Athens–Corinth road, B, 190 b.

Ayios Avgoustinos
Club Aquarius San Agostino Beach (hotel and bungalows), B, 633 b.

Ayios Fokas (Cos)
Dimitra Beach, Palaioskala, A, 261 b.

Ayios Gordios (Corfu)
Agios Gordios, A, 388 b.; Alonakia, B, 30 b.; Chrysses Folies, C, 40 b.

Ayios Ioannis (Corfu)
Sidari Beach (Karoussadon), C, 55 b.

Ayios Ioannis (Triklianou)
Merida (Triklianou), A, 26 b.; Vladimir, C, 40 b.

Ayios Ioannis (Pelion)
Aloe, B, 84 b.; Maro, B, 88 b.; Sevilli, B, 40 b.; Galini, C, 29 b.; Kelly, C, 28 b.; Kentrikon (hotel and bungalows), C, 34 b.; Sofoklis, C, 38 b.; Zephyros, C, 77 b.

Ayios Kyrikos
See Therma Lefkados

Ayios Nikolaos (Crete)
★Minos Beach (bungalows), Akti Ilia Sotirou Amoudi, L, 233 b.; ★Minos Palace, L, 276 b.; ★Mirabello Village (hotel and bungalows), L, 251 b.; Hermes, Akti Koundourou, A, 379 b.; Mirabello, A, 322 b.; Amalthia, 13 Prinkipos Yeoryiou, B, 38 b.; Ariadni Beach (bungalows), Gargadoros, B, 142 b.; Artemis Beach, Mandri, B, 30 b.; Athina, 34A Prinkipos Yeoryiou, B, 33 b.; Castle, B, 10 b.; Coral, Akti Koundourou, B, 323 b.; Cri-Cri, Ayia Paraskevi, B, 39 b.; Diana, 28 Ethnikis Anti-

staseos, B, 31 b.; El Greco, Akti Kitroplatias Milos, B, 70 b.; Eva, 20 Stratigou Koraka, B, 12 b.; Ikaros, 11 Alexomanoli, B, 35 b.; Iris, K. Loukareos-Minoos, B, 41 b.; Leventis, 15 M. Sfakianaki, B, 17 b.; Lida, 3 Salaminos, B, 40 b.; Magda, 13 Gournon, B, 47 b.; Marigo, Palaiologou-Katehaki, B, 24 b.; Miramare, B, 100 b.; Niki, 16 Idomeneos, B, 20 b.; Odysseas, B, 35 b.; Olga, 20 Ergatikis Estias, B, 54 b.; Ormos, B, 86 b.; Rhea (Rea), 10 Marathonas & Milatou, B, 220 b.; St Nicolas Bay, B, 102 b.; Sun Rise, 1 Idomeneos, B, 34 b.; Victoria, 34 Akti Koundourou, B, 28 b.; Zina (Pension), 47 Pr Georgiou, B, 33 b.; Acratos, 19, 28 Oktovriou, C, 59 b.; Acropole, C, 15 b.; Alcestis (Alkistis), 30 Akti Koundourou, C, 45 b.; Alfa, 23 Tselepi, C, 75 b.; Alymyros Beach, C, 87 b.; Apollon, 9 Minoos, C, 114 b.; Argyro, 1 Solonos, C, 19 b.; Arion, 14 Minoos, C, 31 b.; Atlantis, C, 18 b.; Caravel, 18 Ergatikis Estias, C, 28 b.; Castello Maris, Amoudi, C, 36 b.; Creta, Kitroplatia, C, 50 b.; Cronos, 4 N. Plastira, C, 68 b.; Crystal, C, 56 b.; Delta, Akti Kitroplatias, C, 19 b.; Dias, 2 Latous, C, 25 b.; Domenico, 3 Argyropolou, C, 46 b.; Doxa, 3 Idomeneos, C, 36 b.; Du Lac, 17, 28 Oktovriou, C, 74 b.; Europa, 12 Ayiou Athanasiou, C, 64 b.; Helena, 15 Minoos, C, 77 b.; Istron, 4 Sarolidi, C, 16 b.; Kamara, 8 Minoos, C, 51 b.; Kera, 34 Kontoyiani, C, 24 b.; Knossos, C, 24 b.; Kouros, 17 Ethnikis Anastaseos, C, 45 b.; Lato, 12 Iosif Koundourou Limin, C, 48 b.; Lito, C, 71 b.; Mavroforos, Khortatson, C, 21 b.; Myrsini, 35 Akti Koundourou, C, 60 b.; New York, 21A Kontoyiani, C, 16 b.; Nikos, C, 71 b.; Panorama, Akti Koundourou & 2 Sarolidi, C, 50 b.; Pergola, 20 Sarolidou, C, 50 b.; Perla, C, 12 b.; Possidonas, C, 54 b.; Sgouros, N. Pangalou Kitroplatia, C, 48 b.; Vlassis, C, 90 b.; Zephyros, C, 48 b.

Ayios Nikolaos (Euboea)

Ayios Nikolaos, B, 39 b.; Chryssi Ammoudia, B, 30 b.; Kastoria, B, 57 b.; Park, B, 36 b.

Ayios Nikolaos (Mani)

Mani, E, 13 b.

Ayios Stefanos (Corfu)

Nafsika, C, 31 b.; Saint Stefanos, C, 16 b.

Ayios Stefanos (Mýkonos)

Alkistis (bungalows), B, 182 b.; Artemis, C, 39 b.; Panorama, C, 51 b.

Ayios Yeoryios (Euboea)

Alexandros, B, 54 b.; Vachos, B, 36 b.

Barbati (Corfu)

Alexiou, B, 104 b.; Barbati, C, 54 b.; Poseidon, C, 114 b.

Batsi (Andros)

Lykion, B, 28 b.; Chryssi Akti, C, 118 b.; Karnassos, C, 44 b.; Skouna, C, 38 b.

Benitses (Corfu)

San Stefano, A, 470 b.; Belvedere, B, 342 b.; Eugenia, B, 36 b.; Potomaki, B, 270 b.; Bavaria, C, 35 b.; Bella Vista, C, 42 b.; Corfu Maris, C, 48 b.; Kamares Benitson, C, 56 b.; Le Mirage, C, 44 b.; Loutrouvia, C, 44 b.

Bokhali (Zákynthos)

Akrotiri, Akrotiri, B, 31 b.; Varres, B, 67 b.

Bouros (Euboea)

Karystos Beach Club, B, 163 b.; Amalia, C, 162 b.

Brauron

Vraona Bay (hotel and bungalows), A, 670 b.

Chios (town)
Chios Chandris, Prokimea, B, 294 b.; Perivoli, Kambos, B, 24 b.; Xenia, Bella Vista, B, 50 b.; Diana, 92 E. Venizelou, C, 98 b.; Kyma, C, 82 b.

Corfu (town)
★Corfu Palace, Leoforos Dimokratias, L, 195 b.; Cavalieri, 4 Kapodistriou, A, 91 b.; Anthis, Kefalomandouko, B, 86 b.; Astron, 15 Donzelotou, B, 63 b.; King Alkinoos, 29 Dimarkhou Panou Zafiropoulou, B, 102 b.; Olympic, 4 Doukissis Marias, B, 90 b.; Phoenix (Finix), 2 Khr. Smyrnis, B, 34 b.; Arcadion, 44 Kapodistriou, C, 95 b.; Atlantis, Xen. Stratigou, C, 112 b.; Bretagne, 27 Yeorgaki, C, 84 b.; Calypso, 4 Vraïla, C, 34 b.; Dalia, 9 Platia Ethnikou Stadiou, Garitsa, C, 32 b.; Hermes, 14 G. Markora, C, 62 b.; Ionion, 46 Xen. Stratigou, Neos Limin, C, 144 b.

Corinth
Acropolis, 25. Vas. Yeoryiou, C, 50 b.; Belle Vue, 41 Damaskinou, C, 31 b.; Ephira, 52 Vas. Konstantinou, C, 85 b.; Korinthos, 26 Damaskinou, C, 64 b.

In ancient Corinth:
Xenia (pavilion), A, 3 b.

Dafni
Dafni, 4 Ieras Monis, D, 23 b.

Dafnila (Corfu)
Eva Palace, Kato Korakiana, A, 323 b.; Grecotel Dafnila Bay (hotel and bungalows), A, 481 b.

Dassia (Corfu)
Corfu Chandris (hotel, bungalows and villas), A, 558 b.; Dassia Chandris, A, 467 b.; Elaea Beach, A, 366 b.; Margarona Corfu, A, 219 b.; Paloma Bianca (Asproperistera), B, 64 b.; Sofia, Kato Korakiana, B, 15 b.; Amalia, C, 48 b.; Dassia, C, 102 b.; Dassia Margarita, C, 50 b.; Galini, C, 20 b.; Laskaris, C, 42 b.; Primavera, Kato Korakiana, C, 59 b.; San Remo, C, 52 b.; Tina, Krevatsoula, C, 35 b.

Delos
Xenia, B, 7 b.

Delphi
Amalia, Apollonos, A, 334 b.; Vouzas, 1 Pavlou & Friderikis, A, 111 b.; Xenia, A, 82 b.; Europa, B, 92 b.; Kastalia, 13 Vas. Pavlou & Friderikis, B, 52 b.; King Iniohos, B, 70 b.; Orfeas, B, 17 b.; Zeus, 10 D. Fragou, B, 53 b.; Acropole, 9 Filellinon, C, 51 b.; Aeolos, C, 48 b.; Greca, 8 Vas. Pavlou & Friderikis, C, 26 b.; Hermes, 29 Vas. Pavlou & Friderikis, C, 51 b.; Iniohos, 27 Vas. Pavlou & Friderikis, C, 32 b.; Kastri, 23 Syngrou, C, 47 b.; Leto, 25 Apollonos, C, 42 b.; Maniatis, 2 Isaïa, C, 11 b.; Odysseus, 1 Filellinon, C, 15 b.; Oracle (Mantion), 14 Vas. Pavlou & Friderikis, C, 24 b.; Pan, 53 Vas. Pavlou & Friderikis, C, 25 b.; Parnassos, 30 Vas. Pavlou & Friderikis, C, 44 b.; Phaethon, Syngrou & Ionos, C, 35 b.; Pythia, 6 Vas. Pavlou & Friderikis, C, 50 b.; Stadion, 21 Apollonos, C, 45 b.; Varonos, 27 Vas. Pavlou & Friderikis, C, 18 b.

Diafani (Karpathos)
Chryssi Akti, 10 Diafani, E, 19 b.

Diakofto
Chris-Paul, C, 50 b.; Acropole, D, 10 b.; Chelmos, D, 15 b.; Lemonies, D, 18 b.; Panorea, D, 14 b.; Panorama, D, 34 b.

Dodona
Andromachi, B, 9 b.

Drama
Xenia, 10 Ethnikis Aminis, B, 88 b.; Anessis, 9 Ayion Anaryiron, C, 25 b.; Apollo, 20 Lambrianidou, C, 75 b.; Marianna, 3 G. Vorazani, C, 66 b.

Drossia
Dionyssos, 4 Argonafton & Komninou, C, 26 b.; Pefkakia, 4 Argonafton, C, 93 b.; Zorbas, 5 Leoforos Marathonas, Platia Drossias, C, 23 b.

Annezina, C, 26 b.; Avra, C, 18 b.; Chryssi Akti, C, 52 b.; Julia, C, 23 b.; Ivi (Hebe), C, 23 b.

Dryos (Paros)

Gabriel, C, 34 b.

Eantion

Katarraktes, 4 Karanou, B, 83 b.; Xenia, 41 Pilippou Paradisos, B, 40 b.

Edessa

Neon Ariadne, 3–7 Fassideri, C, 33 b.

Ekali

Asteri tis Elafonnisou, B, 21 b.; Elafonnisos, B, 21 b.

Elafonnisos

Melissa, 21 Persefonis, C, 31 b.

Eleusis

Ikaros, 17 Vas. Yeoryiou, D, 32 b.

Elliniko

★Astir Palace Elounda (hotels and bungalows), L, 551 b.; ★Elounda Beach (hotel and bungalows), L, 578 b.; ★Elounda Mare (hotel and bungalows), L, 184 b.; Elounda Marmin, A, 247 b.; Armos, B, 41 b.; Driros Beach, B, 32 b.; Korfos Beach, B, 29 b.; Sophia, B, 26 b.; Akti Olous, Shisma, C, 95 b.; Aristea, Shisma, C, 70 b.; Calypso, Shisma, C, 30 b.; Krini, Shisma, C, 61 b.; Selena Village, C, 80 b.

Elounda (Crete)

Agia Irini, C, 23 b.; Archaea Elefsina, D, 28 b.; Marianna, D, 20 b.

Emborion (Santorin)

Xenia II (bungalows), B, 48 b.

Epidauros

In Nea Epidavros: Epidaurus, C, 13 b.

In Palaia Epidavros:
Stratos, B, 22 b.; Aegeon, C, 15 b.; Aktis, Paralia, C, 16 b.; Apollon, C, 72 b.; Christina, C, 26 b.; Hellas, C, 36 b.; Koronis, 166 Maniadaki, C, 14 b.; Maik, C, 25 b.; Maronika, Paralia, C, 35 b.; Paola Beach, C, 52 b.; Plaza, Paralia, C, 17 b.; Possidon, C, 18 b.; Rena, C, 13 b.; Saronis, C, 72 b.

Xenon Galini, B, 39 b.; Sappho the Eressia, 12 Theofrastou Skala, C, 33 b.

Eressos (Lésbos)

Chryssi Akti, B, 247 b.; Perighiali Eretrias, B, 71 b.; Delfis, C, 168 b.; Xenia, Pezonisi, C, 180 b.

Erétria (Euboea)

Costa Perla (hotel and bungalows), B, 362 b.; Lena-Mary, B, 228 b.

Ermioni

Ermones Beach (bungalows), A, 504 b.; Athina Ermones Golf, C, 39 b.

Ermones (Corfu)

Vourlis, A, 14 b.; Ypatia, A, 21 b.; Ghiannis, 2 Emm. Roidou, B, 12 b.; Hermes, Platia Kanari, B, 47 b.; Syrii, B, 16 b.; Europe, 74 Stam. Proiou; Nissaki, 2 E. Papadam, C, 78 b.

Ermoupolis (Sýros)

Evdoxia, B, 12 b.; Georgios, E, 13 b.

Evdilos (Ikaria)

Makarios, C, 54 b.

Exo Gonia

Xenia, Mesaras, D, 11 b.

Faistos

Apollo Beach, A, 539 b.; Blue Sea, A, 548 b.; Calypso, A, 495 b.; Colossos Beach, A, 1533 b.; Columbia, A, 222 b.; Esperides, P.O. Box

Faliraki (Rhodes)

	202, A, 1016 b.; Esperos Palace, A, 285 b.; Faliraki Beach, P.O. Box 104, A, 586 b.; Ladiko Bungalows, A, 84 b.; Pighassos Beach, A, 438 b.; Rodos Beach (hotel and bungalows), A, 429 b.; Sun Palace, A, 300 b.; Erato, B, 70 b.; Muses (hotel and bungalows), B, 58 b.; Tsambika, B, 56 b.; Argo, C, 84 b.; Dimitra, C, 73 b.; Edelweiss, C, 102 b.; Evi, C, 110 b.; Gondola, C, 75 b.; Liberia, C, 71 b.; Lido, P.O. Box 363, C, 38 b.; Sophia, C, 56 b.
Fanari	Vosporos, B, 38 b.; Fanari, C, 60 b.
Farsala	Achillion, 4 N. Koukoufli, D, 28 b.; Emborikon, 28, 28 Oktovriou, E, 17 b.
Ferma (Crete)	Coriva Village (hotel and bungalows), B, 69 b.; Porto Belissario, B, 63 b.
Finix	Olympia, C, 78 b.; Finikas, C, 25 b.
Fira	See Thira
Firostefano (Santorin)	Galini, C, 13 b.; Galini II, C, 13 b.; Kafieris, C, 20 b.
Fiskardo	Panormos, B, 10 b.
Florina	King Alexander, 68 Nikis Ave, B, 108 b.; Lyngos, 3 Tagmatarkhou Naoum, B, 76 b.; Tottis, B, 108 b.; Antigone, 1 Arianou, C, 152 b.
Folegandros	Fani-Vevis, B, 49 b.; Aeolos, C, 22 b.
Gaena (Corfu)	Achilleus, B, 138 b.
Galatas (Crete)	Vachos, C, 44 b.
Galatas (Poros)	Stella Maris Nautic Holiday Center (hotel and bungalows), B, 176 b.; Galatia, C, 51 b.; Papassotiriou, 41, 25 Martiou, C, 61 b.
Galaxidi	Ta Adelfia, B, 11 b.; Ganymede, E. Vlami, C, 15 b.
Galissas (Sýros)	Françoise, C, 64 b.
Gastouri (Corfu)	El Greco, 3 Vas. Konstantinou, B, 63 b.; Montaniola, B, 93 b.; Argo, C, 30 b.; Gefyra Kaizer, C, 50 b.
Gavrion (Andros)	Aphrodite, B, 43 b.; Perrakis, B, 57 b.; Gavrion Beach, C, 41 b.
Gennadi (Rhodes)	Panorama Genadi, C, 37 b.
Glossa (Skopelos)	Avra, C, 51 b.
Glyfada (Attic Riviera)	★Astir (bungalows), 58 Posidonos, L, 256 b.; Atrium, 10 Posidonos, A, 104 b.; Congo Palace, 75 Posidonos, A, 157 b.; Emmantina, 33 Posidonos, A, 144 b.; Palace, 4 Posidonos, A, 140 b.; Palmyra Beach, 70 Posidonos, A, 95 b.; Antonopoulos, 1 Lambraki, B, 84 b.; Delfini, 5 Xanthou, B, 73 b.; Fenix, 1 Artemidos, B, 265 b.; Florida, 33 Metaxa

Ave, B, 159 b.; Four Seasons, 49 Posidonos, B, 146 b.; Golden Sun (Chryssos Ilios), 72 Metaxa Ave, B, 112 b.; Gripsholm, 4 Saki Karayiorga, B, 107 b.; Ideal, 47 Lazaraki & Zissimopoulou, B, 74 b.; John's, 3 Pandoras-Lazaraki, B, 128 b.; Kreoli, 17 Posidonos, B, 92 b.; Leto, Evriali-2 Menipis & Veli, B, 11 b.; London, 38 Posidonos, B, 142 b.; Miranda, 11 Meropis & Posidonos, B, 64 b.; Regina Maris, 11 Diadokhou Pavlou & Platia Fleming, B, 137 b.; Riviera, Posidonos & 2 Fivis, B, 151 b.; Sea View, 4 Xanthou, B, 141 b.; Stergios, 31 Ilias, Ano Glyfada, B, 84 b.; Triton, 106 Posidonos, B, 71 b.; Adonis, 20 Nikiforou, C, 85 b.; Arion, 13 Lazaraki, C, 57 b.; Avra, 5 Lambraki, C, 81 b.; Beau Rivage, 87 Posidonos, C, 156 b.; Blue Sky, 26 Eleftherias & Zamanou, C, 37 b.; Glyfada, 40 Posidonos & Nafsikas, C, 100 b.; Ilion, 4 G. Kondyli, C, 56 b.; Oceanis, 23 Lambraki, C, 135 b.; Perla (Margaritari), 7 Khrysiidas, C, 112 b.; Rial, 7 Posidonos, C, 67 b.; Themis, 5 Posidonos & E. Venizelou, C, 84 b.

Glyfada (Corfu)

Grand Hotel Glifada Beach, A, 465 b.; Glyfada Beach, B, 66 b.

Glyfada (Thasos)

Glifada, C, 102 b.

Gournes (Crete)

Erato, B, 46 b.; Royal, 42, 25 Martiou, B, 126 b.

Gouves (Crete)

Creta Sun (formerly Candia Beach), P.O. Box 106, A, 568 b.; Marina, P.O. Box 81, A, 728 b.; Aphrodite Beach, B, 446 b.; Apollo, B, 56 b.; Astir Beach, B, 161 b.; Despo, C, 67 b.; Ederi, C, 52 b.; Gouves Sea, C, 31 b.; Kouros, C, 78 b.; Mon Repos, C, 70 b.; Sonia, C, 35 b.; Studios Lida, C, 41 b.; Villa Calypso, C, 68 b.

Gouvia (Corfu)

Grecotel Corcyra Beach (hotel and bungalows), A, 487 b.; Angela, B, 38 b.; Aspa, B, 33 b.; Molfetta Beach, B, 49 b.; Park, B, 338 b.; Artemis, Skliri Gouvion, C, 53 b.; Constantinos, C, 23 b.; Elizabeth, C, 39 b.; Galaxias, C, 67 b.; Gouvia, C, 40 b.; Iliada, C, 100 b.; Maltezos, C, 40 b.; Pheacion, C, 70 b.; Sun Flower, C, 23 b.

Grikos (Patmos)

Artemis, B, 45 b.; Grikos, B, 36 b.; Xenia, B, 62 b.

Gýthion

Githion, A, 20 b.; Laconis (bungalows), 3 Skalas, A, 148 b.; Cavo Grosso (bungalows), Mavrovouni, B, 54 b.; Laryssion, 7 I. Grigoraki, C, 150 b.; Milton, Mavrovouni, C, 30 b.; Pantheon, 33 Vas. Pavlou, C, 99 b.

Heraion (Samos)

Venetia, B, 26 b.; Adamantia, C, 60 b.

Heraklion

See Iráklion

Hýdra

Miramare, Mandraki, A, 50 b.; Miranda, A, 26 b.; Amaryllis, 15 Tombazi, B, 22 b.; Delfini, Paralia, B, 20 b.; Greco, B, 36 b.; Hydroussa (formerly Xenia), B, 72 b.; Kamini, B, 16 b.; Orlof, B, 25 b.; Hydra, 8 Voulgari, C, 23 b.; Leto, C, 74 b.

Ía

See Oia

Ialysos

Blue Horizon, A, 412 b.; Ialyssos Bay, A, 282 b.; Sun Beach II, A, 111 b.; Eleni, 37 Ierou Lokhou, B, 24 b.; Lisa, Kandili, B, 53 b.; Green View, 5 Leoforos Kremastis, C, 62 b.

Ierapetra (Crete)

Ferma Beach (hotel and bungalows), A, 289 b.; Kritika Spitia, A, 70 b.; Petra-Mare, A, 405 b.; Blue Sky, Peristera, B, 45 b.; Minoan Prince, B,

105 b.; Achlia, C, 51 b.; Atlantis, Ayios Andreas, C, 134 b.; Camiros, 17 M. Kothri, C, 75 b.; Creta, Platia E. Venizelou, C, 47 b.; El Greco, 40 M. Kothri, C, 62 b.; Ersi, C, 25 b.; Kyrva, 45 Emm. Lambraki Manoliana, C, 31 b.; Lygia, Parodos Kirba, C, 29 b.; Zakros, C, 88 b.

Ierissos Marcos, D, 40 b.

Igoumenitsa Xenia, 2 Vas. Pavlou, B, 72 b.; Astoria, 147 Ayion Apostolon, C, 25 b.; El Greco, 86 Ethnikis Antistaseos, C, 84 b.; Epirus, 20 Pargas, C, 11 b.; Jolly, 20 Vas. Pavlou, C, 51 b.; Oscar, 149 Ayion Apostolon, C, 68 b.; Tourist, 22 Vas. Pavlou, C, 40 b.
Outside town, to south: Robinson Club Nea Sivota, 250 b.

Inousai Prassonissia, D, 11 b.; Thalassopolos, D, 23 b.

Ioannina Palladion, 1 Pan. Skoumbourdi & 28 Oktovriou, B, 242 b.; Xenia, 33 Vas. Yeoryiou B, B, 112 b.; Acropole, 3 Vas. Yeoryiou A, C, 58 b.; Alexios, 14 Poukevil, C, 160 b.; Astoria, 2A Paraskevopoulou, C, 30 b.; Bretannia, 11 Kentriki Platia, C, 43 b.; Dioni, 10 Tsirigoti, C, 74 b.; Egnatia, 2 Dagli & Aravandinou, C, 96 b.; El Greco, 8 Tsirigoti, C, 68 b.; Esperia, 3 Kaplani, C, 59 b.; Galaxy, Platia Pirou, C, 72 b.; King Pyrros, 1 I. Gounari, C, 40 b.; Metropolis, 2 C. Kristali & Averof, C, 33 b.; Olympic, 2 G. Melanidi, C, 84 b.; Tourist, 18 Koleti, C, 55 b.; Vyzantion, Dodonis Ave, C, 200 b.; Zakas, Ziakas, Perama, C, 75 b.

Íos Chryssi Akti, B, 19 b.; Ios (hotel and bungalows), Milopotas, B, 86 b.; Akti Iou, C, 42 b.; Armadoros, C, 50 b.; Corali, C, 25 b.; Delfini, Milopotas, C, 33 b.; Flisvos, C, 25 b.; Giorgos-Irini, C, 44 b.; Fragakis, C, 27 b.; Homer's Inn, C, 34 b.; Mare-Monte, Ormos, C, 52 b.; Philippou, C, 22 b.; Sea Breeze (Thalassia Avra), Limin, C, 28 b.

Iráklion (Crete) Astoria, 5 Platía Eleftherias, A, 273 b.; Atlantis, 2 Meramvelou & Iyias, A, 296 b.; Creta Beach, Amoudara, A, 262 b.; Galaxy, 67 Leof. Dimokratias, A, 264 b.; Xenia, S. Venizelou, A, 156 b.; Anna-Bella, Talon & Kourmoulidon, B, 14 b.; Ares, 5 Ayisilaou, B, 30 b.; Atrion, 9 K. Palaiologou, B, 117 b.; Diamantis, B, 6 b.; Esperia, 20 Idomeneos, B, 92 b.; Ilaira, Epimenidou & 1 Ariadnis, B, 32 b.; Kastro, 22 Theotokopoulou, B, 63 b.; Kreta, 3 Anopoleos, B, 18 b.; Kris, 2 Doukos Beaufort, B, 17 b.; Mediterranean, 1 Smyrnis & Platia Daskaloyiani, B, 105 b.; Petra, 55 Dikaiosynis, B, 59 b.; Phaedra, 11 Satha Kamaraki, B, 41 b.; Xenon Georgiades, 17 Kandanoleon, B, 19 b.; Apollon, 63 Minoos & Anogion, C, 96 b.; Asterion, 50 Ikarou & Irodotou, Nea Alikarnassos, C, 108 b.; Athinaikon, 89 Ethnikis Anastaseos, C, 77 b.; Atlas, 6 Kandanoleon, C, 35 b.; Blue Sky, 105, 62 Martyron, C, 50 b.; Castello, 1, 62 Martyron & Platia Koraka, C, 124 b.; Daedalos, 15 Daidalou, C, 115 b.; Domenico, 14 Almyrou, C, 73 b.; El Greco, 4 Odos 1821, C, 165 b.; Evans, 14B Ayiou Fanouriou, Nea Alikarnassos, C, 48 b.; Gortis, 4 Akrotiriou, C, 20 b.; Gloria, 15 Aiyeou Poros, C, 95 b.; Grabelles, 26 Skordylon, C, 80 b.; Heracleion, 128 Kalokerinou & Delimarkou, C, 72 b.; Irene, C, 105 b.; Kirki, 157 Leoforos Kalokerinou, C, 30 b.; Knossos, 43, 25 Avgoustou, C, 46 b.; Kronos, 3 Platia Kalergon, C, 28 b.; Lato, 15 Epimenidou & Lavyrinthou, C, 99 b.; Marin, 12 Beaufort, C, 83 b.; Metropole, 48 Karterou, C, 75 b.; Mirabello, 18 Theotokopoulou, C, 42 b.; Olympic, Platia Kornarou, C, 135 b.; Santa Elena, 372, 62 Martyron, C, 105 b.; Selena, 7 Androyeo, C, 52 b.; Sofia, Nea Alikarnassos, C, 48 b.
South-east of the town: Robinson Club Lythos Beach, 600 b.

Isthmia King Saron, A, 301 b.

Istiaia (Euboea) Neon, 7 Angeli Goviou, E, 19 b.

Itea

Galini, 57 Akti Posidonos, B, 60 b.; Kalafati, Paralia, B, 62 b.; Nafsika, Iroon & Kapodistriou, B, 144 b.; Panorama, 153 Akti Posidonos, Paralia, B, 49 b.; Xenia (motel), B, 36 b.; Akti, 81 Akti Posidonos, C, 40 b.

Ithaca

Mendor, Paralia, B, 68 b.; Odysseus, Vathy, B, 17 b.; Nostos, Frikies, C, 51 b.

Ixia (Rhodes)

★Miramare Beach (hotel and bungalows), L, 330 b.; ★Olympic Palace, Leoforos lalysou, L, 591 b.; ★Rodos Palace (hotel apartments and bungalows), Leoforos lalysou, L, 1220 b.; Avra Beach (hotel and bungalows), Leoforos lalysou, A, 353 b.; Bel Air, Leoforos lalysou, A, 293 b.; Blue Bay (hotel and apartments), Leoforos lalysou, A, 410 b.; Cosmopolitan, A, 484 b.; Dionysos, Ippoton, A, 523 b.; Electra Palace, Paralia lalysou, A, 513 b.; Elina, Paralia lalysou, A, 277 b.; Golden Beach (bungalotel), Akto lalysou, 536 b.; Metropolitan Capsis, Leoforos lalysou, A, 1198 b.; Oceanis, Leoforos Triandon, A, 459b.; Rodos Bay (hotel and bungalows), A, 611 b.; Leto, Leoforos lalysou, B, 184 b.; Solemar, 66 Sotiros, B, 194 b.; Mihalis, C, 26 b.; Natalia, C, 74 b.; Pefka, C, 18 b.; Roma, C, 80 b.; Vellois, Leoforos Triandon, C, 92 b.

Kaiafas

Jenny, B, 16 b.; Anemoni, Geranion, C, 12 b.; Archaea Sami, C, 46 b.; Geranion, C, 77 b.; Lapitha, C, 22 b.

Kalafati (Mýkonos)

Anastassia (bungalows), Ayia Anna, B, 56 b.; Aphroditi (bungalows), B, 256 b.

Kalamaki (Attic Riviera)

Saronis, 13 Posidonos, A, 74 b.; Albatros, 77 Posidonos, B, 152 b.; Imperial, 83 Thoukydidou & Kondyli, B, 31 b.; Rex, 40 Posidonos, B, 63 b.; La Maison, 14 Vas. Konstantinou, B, 22 b.; Venus, 9 Meyistis, B, 54 b.; Alkyon, 2 K. Kotzia & Posidonos, C, 26 b.; Attica, 18 P. Tsaldari, C, 62 b.; Galaxy, 39 Posidonos, C, 83 b.; Hellinikon, 76 Posidonos, C, 96 b.; Nefeli, 5 Fan Vaïk & Posidonos, C, 70 b.; Tropical, 74 Posidonos, C, 88 b.

Kalamaki (Zákynthos)

Kalamaki Beach, B, 55 b.; Crystal Beach, C, 105 b.

Kalamata

Elite, 2 Navarinou, Fare, Paralia, A, 94 b.; Filoxenia, Navarinou, Paralia, B, 254 b.; Nedon, 153 Navarinou, Paralia, B, 20 b.; Rex, 26 Aristomenous, B, 96 b.; America, 37 Navarinou, Paralia, C, 38 b.; Avra, 10 Santaroza, Paralia, C, 16 b.; Flisvos, 135 Navarinou, Paralia, C, 75 b.; Galaxias (Galaxy), 14 Kolokotroni, C, 52 b.; Haicos, 115 Navarinou, Paralia, C, 112 b.; Valassis, 95 Navarinou, Paralia, C, 70 b.; Byzantion, 14 latropoulou, C, 49 b.

Kalambaka

Motel Divani, A, 315 b.; Xenia (motel), A, 44 b.; Aeolikos Astir, 4 Ath. Diakou, C, 31 b.; Atlantic, C, 50 b.; Galaxias, 31 Khatzipetrou, C, 38 b.; Helvetia, 45 Kastrakiou, C, 22 b.; Odyssion, Kastrakiou, C, 42 b.; Olympia, 97 Trikalon, C, 42 b.; Rex, 11A Kastrakiou, C, 62 b.

Kalami (Sámos)

Fenix, B, 26 b.; Kirki Beach, B, 36 b.; Myrini, B, 42 b.; Notis, Roditses, B, 12 b.; Panthea, B, 23 b.; Andromeda, 107A Kallistratou, C, 65 b.; Pythagoras, 12 Kallistratou, C, 31 b.

Kalandra

Mendi, A, 311 b.

Kala Nera (Pelion)

Alcyon, B, 22 b.; Rodia, B, 33 b.; Izela, C, 62 b.

Kalathas (Crete)

Tzanakaki Beach, C, 68 b.

Kalathos (Rhodes)
Mouratis, E, 15 b.

Kalavryta
Chelmos, Platia Eleftherias, B, 45 b.; Filoxenia, B, 110 b.; Maria, 2 Syngrou, C, 23 b.

Kallithea (Chalcidice)
Athos Palace (hotel and bungalows), A, 1130 b.; Pallini Beach (hotel and bungalows), A, 938 b.; Ammon Zeus, B, 208 b.; Belvedere, C, 116 b.; Delfini, C, 23 b.

Kallithea (Rhodes)
Sunwing, A, 738 b.

Kalloni (Lesbos)
Kalloni, C, 23 b.

Kalo Khorio (Crete)
★Istron Bay, Pylos, L, 199 b.; Elpida, C, 145 b.; Golden Bay, C, 94 b.

Kalymnos (town)
Aris, B, 33 b.; Drossos, Kantouni Beach, Panormos, C, 97 b.; Evanik, C, 39 b.; Olympic, Ayiou Nikolaou, C, 81 b.; Thermae, Platia Kharalambous, C, 30 b.

Kamares (Sifnos)
Kamari, B, 35 b.; Boulis, C, 85 b.; Stavros, C, 28 b.

Kamari (Santorin)
Sunshine (Iliaktida), B, 68 b.; Akis, C, 29 b.; Artemis Beach, C, 54 b.; Astro, C, 68 b.; Kamari, C, 104 b.; Kasteli, C, 20 b.; Orion, C, 40 b.; Poseidon, C, 60 b.; Zephyros, C, 44 b.

Kamariotissa (Samothrace)
Aeolos, B, 100 b.; Niki Beach, C, 72 b.

Kamena Vourla
Galini, A, 231 b.; Agamemnon, B, 18 b.; Anessis, Platia Plastira, B, 22 b.; Angela, 5, 28 Oktovriou, B, 35 b.; Antonios, 59 Ermou, B, 29 b.; Aphrodite, B, 23 b.; Artemis, Nea Ethniki Odos, B, 26 b.; Athina, 31, 28 Oktovriou & I. Metaxa, B, 36 b.; Atlantis, B, 25 b.; Avra, 33 G. Vasiliadi, B, 46 b.; Christina, 4 Knimidos, B, 28 b.; Dellis, 1 Thermopylon, B, 28 b.; Dimitra, B, 24 b.; Dionyssos, B, 12 b.; Drossia, 20 Ermou, B, 17 b.; Efstathiou, B, 22 b.; Fotini, 1 Palama, B, 25 b.; Fouli, 19 Androutsou, B, 14 b.; Galaxy, 19, 28 Oktovriou, B, 30 b.; Haravghi, 7 E. Venizelou, Atiki, B, 28 b.; Hermes, G. Vasiliadi, Plataneïka, B, 26 b.; Ilion, G. Vasiliadi, B, 16 b.; Iphigenia, 2 Knimidos, B, 30 b.; Ion, 5 Ath. Diakou, B, 25 b.; Leonidas, Ayiou Nikolaou, Atiki, B, 20 b.; Leto, B, 46 b.; Loucy, 12 Ayiou Nikolaou, B, 33 b.; Loula, 8, 28 Oktovriou, B, 39 b.; Morfi, 23 Ermou, B, 22 b.; Nadia, 3 Ar. Kakouri, B, 31 b.; Nana, 19 Ath. Diakou, Akti, B, 22 b.; Natassa, 13, 28 Oktovriou, B, 28 b.; Noufara, 28, 28 Oktovriou, B, 26 b.; Oassis, B, 36 b.; Pantheon, 17 Ayiou Nikolaou, B, 53 b.; Parnassos, B, 24 b.; Persephoni, B, 34 b.; Possidon, B, 176 b.; Possidonion, B, 24 b.; Radion, B, 94 b.; Ritsa, B, 38 b.; Sissy, B, 190 b.; Sonia, B, 35 b.; Thronion, B, 78 b.; Violetta, 81 G. Vasiliadi, B, 70 b.; Acropole, 85 G. Vasiliadi, C, 52 b.; Akti, G. Vasiliadi, C, 35 b.; Alexandros, 16 A' Odos, C, 14 b.; Alma, 141 G. Vasiliadi, Platania, C, 53 b.; Amaryllis, C, 16 b.; Anastassia, 1 Ermou, C, 26 b.; Angelika, 6 Knimidos, C, 28 b.; Apollonion, 3 Ayiou Nikolaou, C, 20 b.; Argo, 51 G. Vasiliadi, C, 41 b.; Armonia, 5 Ipokrati, C, 43 b.; Asteria, C, 25 b.; Astir, 10, 25 Martiou, C, 64 b.; Athinea, C, 32 b.; Attiki, C, 51 b.; Boucas, 18 E. Venizelou, C, 38 b.; Caterina, C, 49 b.; Cavo d'Oro, Asproneri, C, 32 b.;

Cecil, 6 Ar. Kakouri, Platia Plastira, C, 35 b.; Chloe, 4 Dim. Karaoli, C, 40 b.; Cleo, 10 Ath. Diakou, C, 14 b.; Dafni, C, 21 b.; Delphi, 9 Piyis Sotiros, C, 26 b.; Delfini, G. Vasiliadi & Karaoli, C, 42 b.; Diana, C, 34 b.; Diktaeon, 2 Riga Fereou, C, 27 b.; Dodoni, C, 29 b.; Elite, G. Vasiliadi C, 24 b.; Elpida, 12 Ath. Diakou, C, 15 b.; Esperia, 31 G. Vasiliadi, , Atiki, C, 26 b.; Estia, 10 Karias, C, 15 b.; Gardenia, 11 Ayiou Nikolaou, C, 17 b.; Georgia, C, 23 b.; Heleana, C, 16 b.; Helena, C, 32 b.; Hellinis, 10 G. Vasiliadi, C, 24 b.; Iniohos, C, 19 b.; Irene, 30 G. Vasiliadi, C, 16 b.; Ismini, 4 Ath. Diakou, C, 20 b.; Kallidromon, 3, 28 Oktovriou, C, 32 b.; Kallithea, 58 Ayiou Nikolaou, C, 25 b.; Kamelia, 11 A' Odos, C, 16 b.; Knimis, C, 16 b.; Kymata, C, 23 b.; Kypreos, 6 G. Vasiliadi, C, 20 b.; Laconis, C, 30 b.; Lemonia, 4 B' Odos, C, 16 b.; Lilia, 4 E. Venizelou, C, 16 b.; Martha, C, 15 b.; Matina, C, 24 b.; Messinia, 1 Piyis Sotiros, C, 13 b.; Nefeli, C, 17 b.; Neon Astron, 14 Ayiou Nikolaou, C, 41 b.; Niki, 18, 28 Oktovriou, C, 38 b.; Niobe (Niovi), 3 G. Vasiliadi, C, 19 b.; Oceanis, C, 52 b.; Orpheus (Orphefs), 6 B' Odos, C, 15 b.; Pagonion, 21 Ermou, C, 28 b.; Paris, 10 A' Odos, C, 16 b.; Penelope, C, 14 b.; Pringhipikon, 75 G. Vasiliadi, C, 49 b.; Rania, C, 23 b.; Regina, C, 29 b.; Rizos, C, 20 b.; Silia, C, 23 b.; Stroghyli, 16–18 Knimidos, C, 38 b.; Ta Kymata, C, 23 b.; Thalia, 12 A' Odos, C, 32 b.; Thermae, 4 Ath. Diakou, C, 28 b.; Timos, 18 Kakouri, C, 23 b.; Trikala, C, 25 b.; Tselios, 20 Kakouri, C, 22 b.; Tymphristos, 14, 28 Oktovriou, C, 36 b.; Velouhi, C, 13 b.; Vicky, 28, 25 Martiou, C, 19 b.

Kanoni (Corfu)

★ Corfu Hilton International (hotel and bungalows), Nafsikas, P.O. Box 124, L, 515 b.; Ariti, 40 Nafsikas, A, 312 b.; Corfu Divani Palace, 20 Nafsikas, A, 306 b.; Royal (Vassilikon), 110 Figareto, C, 232 b.; Salvos, 108 Figareto, C, 176 b.

Karavomylos

Stylis Beach, C, 297 b.

Kardamena (Kos)

Norida Beach, A, 747 b.; Alma, B, 40 b.; Carda Beach (bungalows), B, 127 b.; Christina Beach, B, 19 b.; Marigo, B, 13 b.; Silver Beach, B, 80 b.; Villa Pantarota, B, 18 b.; Mikartzi, C, 61 b.; Kardamena, C, 30 b.; Panorama, C, 40 b.; Stelios, C, 24 b.; Valinakis Beach, C, 141 b.

Kardamyla (Chios)

Kardamyla, B, 60 b.

Kardamyli (Peloponnese)

Dioscouri, D, 12 b.

Karditsa

Arni, 4 Karaiskaki, C, 62 b.; Astron, 97 Iezekiil, C, 78 b.; Avra, 42 Karaiskaki & Averof, C, 41 b.

Karlovasi (Samos)

Aegeon, B, 109 b.; Aspassia, B, 82 b.; Merope, Kentriki Odos Pefkakia–Alsos, B, 152 b.; Samena Bay, B, 142 b.

Karpathos (town)

Romantica, B, 61 b.; Seven Stars, B, 62 b.; Atlantis, C, 73 b.; Panorama, C, 50 b.; Porfyris, C, 41 b.

Karteros (Crete)

Minoa Palace, Paralia Amnisou, A, 230 b.; Amnissos (bungalows), B, 108 b.; Karteros, Amnisos, B, 104 b.; Motel Xenia, B, 84 b.

Karystos (Euboea)

Apollon Resort, Psili Ammos, B, 150 b.; Galaxy, C, 136 b.; Karystion, Kriezotou, C, 75 b.; Plaza, 9 Ioannou Kotsika, C, 68 b.

Kasos

Anagenissis, C, 18 b.; Anessis, 9 G. Mavrikaki, C, 14 b.

Kassiopi (Corfu)

Oasis, D, 25 b.

Kastelli Kisamou (Crete)	Helena Beach, B, 75 b.; Castle (Kastron), Platia Kastelliou, C, 21 b.; Kissamos, C, 29 b.
Kastellorizo	Xenon Dimou Meyistis, B, 32 b.
Kastoria	Xenia du Lac, Platia Dexaminis, A, 49 b.; Maria (motel), B, 88 b.; Tsamis, Dispilio (3km/2 miles from Kastoria), B, 153 b.; Acropolis, 16 Gramou, C, 41 b.; Anessis, 10 Gramou, C, 38 b.; Europa, C, 68 b.; Kastoria, 122 Leoforis Nikis, C, 25 b.; Keletron, 52, 11 Noemvriou, C, 41 b.; Lazos, Petra, C, 25 b.; Orestion, 1 Platia Davaki, C, 33 b.
Kastraki	Kastraki, E, 14 b.
Kastro Kyllinis	Robinson Club Hotel Kyllini Beach, A, 624 b.; Chryssi Avgi, 9 Loutropoleos, C, 20 b.
Katakolon	Ionio, C, 19 b.
Katapola	Minoa, C, 19 b.
Katerini	Lido, 16 P. Tsaldari, C, 43 b.; Olympion, 15 Vas. Yeoryiou B, C, 72 b.; Park, Ethniki Odos Katerinis–Thessalonikis, C, 38 b.
Kavala	Tosca Beach (bungalows), A, 199 b.; Blue Bay (hotel and bungalows), Nea Iraklitsa, B, 64 b.; Egnatia, 139, 7 Merarkhias, B, 70 b.; Filoxenia, Ayios Silas, B, 60 b.; Galaxy, 51 E. Venizelou, B, 283 b.; Lucy, Kalamitsa, B, 391 b.; Oceanis, 32 Leoforos Erythrou Stavrou, B, 318 b.; Vournelis, B, 23 b.; Acropolis, 53C E. Venizelou, C, 28 b.; Esperia, 42 Leoforos Erythrou Stavrou, C, 200 b.; Europa, 29 Irinis Athineas Viron, C, 21 b.; Nefeli, 50 Leoforos Erythrou Stavrou, C, 179 b.; Panorama, 32C E. Venizelou, C, 99 b.
Kavos Lefkimmis (Corfu)	Roussos, B, 34 b.; Saint Marina, B, 58 b.; Alexandra Beach, C, 46 b.; Cavos, C, 39 b.; Morfeas, Kokinia, C, 84 b.
Kavouri (Attic Riviera)	Amarilia, A, 185 b.; Pine Hill, 22 Kronou, B, 158 b.; Sunrise, 11 Ayiou Nikolaou, B, 112 b.; Maro, 2 Kivelis & Vas. Pavlou, C, 15 b.
Kea	Ioulis, B, 21 b.; I Tzia Mas (motel), Korissia, B, 48 b.; Kea Beach (hotel and bungalows), Koundouros, B, 150 b.; Carthea, Korissia, C, 67 b.
Kefalos (Kos)	Kokalakis Beach, C, 44 b.; Sidney, D, 40 b.
Khalkis (Euboea)	Lucy, 10 Leoforos Voudouri, A, 156 b.; John's, 9 Angeli Goviou, B, 98 b.; Paliria, 32 Leoforos Voudouri & E. Venizelou, B, 200 b.; Hara, C, 80 b.; Kentrikon, 5 Angeli Goviou, C, 35 b.; Manica, Leoforos Panayitsa-Artakis, C, 48 b.
Khania (Crete)	Amfora, 20 Parodos Theotokopoulou, A, 30 b.; Captain Vassilis, 12 Theotokopoulou, A, 13 b.; Contessa, 15 Theophanous, A, 14 b.; Kydon, Platia Agoras, A, 191 b.; Panorama, P.O. Box 73, A, 309 b.; Porto del Colombo, A, 15 b.; Akrotiri, Profitis Ilias, B, 26 b.; Arcadi, Platia 1866, B, 109 b.; Ariadni, Kalamaki, B, 17 b.; Artemis, B, 10 b.; Doma, 124 E. Venizelou, B, 56 b.; Domenico, 71 Zabeliou, B, 10 b.; El Greco, 47–49 Theotokopoulou, B, 25 b.; Faliro, B, 17 b.; Ghiannis, B, 5 b.; Lissos, 68 Dimokratias, B, 68 b.; Nostos, 46 Zambeliou, B, 10 b.; Pasiphae, 36 Koundourioti, B, 15 b.; Porto Veneziano (Enetikos Limin),

Enoseos, B, 120 b.; Samaria, Kidonias & Zimvrakakidon, B, 110 b.; Xenia, Theotokopoulou, B, 88 b.; Afroditi, 18 Ayion Deka, C, 20 b.; Amphitriti, C, 27 b.; Aptera Beach (bungalows), Paralia Ayion Apostolon, Aptera, C, 92 b.; Astor, 2 Verovits Pasa, C, 28 b.; Candia, C, 29 b.; Canea, 16 Platia 1866, C, 94 b.; Diktynna, 1 Betolo, C, 66 b.; Hellinis, 68 Tzanakaki, C, 28 b.; Kriti, 10 N. Foka & Kyprou, C, 189 b.; Kydonia, C, 68 b.; Kypros, 17 Tzanakaki, C, 36 b.; Lato, 8 Ionias, C, 51 b.; Lucia, Akti Koundourioti, Palaio Limani, C, 72 b.; Manos, 17 Koundourioti, C, 19 b.; Mary Poppins, C, 20 b.; Omalos, 71 Leoforos Kydonias, C, 58 b.; Plaza, 1 Tombazi, C, 17 b.; Theofilos, 76 Papanastasiou, C, 19 b.

Khani Kokkini (Crete)

Arina Sand (hotel and bungalows), A, 452 b.; Knossos Beach (hotel and bungalows), A, 207 b.; Themis Beach, A, 229 b.; Prima, B, 24 b.; Akti, km 13 on Iraklion–Ayios Nikolaos road, C, 37 b.; Armilides, C, 29 b.; Danae, C, 34 b.; Kamari, 1 Platia 18 Angion, C, 62 b.

Khaniotis

Pella, B, 342 b.; Soussouras (bungalows), B, 144 b.; Ermis (Hermes), C, 49 b.; Hanioti, C, 58 b.; Plaza, C, 32 b.; Strand, C, 85 b.

Khersonisos (Limin Khersonisou; Crete)

★Creta Maris (hotel and bungalows), L, 1014 b.; ★Belvedere (hotel and bungalows), A, 547 b.; Cretan Village, A, 178 b.; King Minos Palace (hotel and bungalows), A, 253 b.; Lyttos, Ayissaras, P.O. Box 295, A, 601 b.; Nana Beach (hotel and bungalows), A, 296 b.; Adonis, 55 Venizelou, B, 18 b.; Angelos, 4 Venizelou, B, 23 b.; Chryssi Amoudia, B, 179 b.; Glaros, 5 Bouboulinas, B, 270 b.; Hersonissos, Zotou, B, 168 b.; Hersonissos Maris, B, 102 b.; Lena-Mary, B, 20 b.; Maragakis, B, 92 b.; Mastorakis, B, 19 b.; Nora, B, 344 b.; Oceanis, B, 62 b.; Sergios, B, 149 b.; Silva Maris, B, 472 b.; Stella, 5, 28 Oktovriou, B, 19 b.; Villes Esperides, B, 54 b.; Virginia, 12 Makhis Kritis, B, 18 b.; Voula, B, 26 b.; Vrito, B, 29 b.; Adamakis, C, 32 b.; Albatros, Parodos Dimokratias, C, 143 b.; Anna, 144 E. Venizelou, C, 76 b.; Armava, Gourgouthia, C, 76 b.; Averinos, C, 58 b.; Avra, 131 Ayias Paraskevis, C, 32 b.; Blue Sky, C, 44 b.; Bizantium, C, 50 b.; Charalambakis-Georgalis, C, 26 b.; Diktina, C, 72 b.; Dimitra, C, 60 b.; Eva, 1 Yianboudaki, C, 62 b.; Flisvos, C, 18 b.; Floral, C, 33 b.; Heleana, C, 34 b.; Helena, 12 Ayias Paraskevis, C, 24 b.; Ilios, 1 E. Venizelou, C, 139 b.; Iro, 72 Evangelistrias, C, 94 b.; Maistrali, C, 27 b.; Marie-George, C, 25 b.; Marianna, C, 94 b.; Marie-Christine, C, 78 b.; Melpo, C, 77 b.; Memory, 7, 28 Oktovriou, C, 58 b.; Miramare, C, 67 b.; Nancy, 15 Ayias Paraskevis, C, 49 b.; Nefeli, C, 53 b.; Niki, C, 57 b.; Palmera Beach, C, 123 b.; Pela-Maria, C, 168 b.; Psarros, 5 Ethnikis Anastaseos, C, 33 b.; Rea, 1 E. Venizelou, C, 29 b.; Regina, C, 22 b.; Thalia, C, 69 b.; Vasso, C, 59 b.; Velissarios, C, 41 b.; Zorbas, 1 Navarkhou Nearkhou, Ayia Paraskevi, C, 40 b.

Kiaton

Triton, 2 Metamorfoseos Sotiros, B, 56 b.; Galini, 3 Mavroulia, C, 45 b.; Pappas, 31 Sikyonos, C, 76 b.; Pefkias, Neapolis, C, 22 b.

Kifissia

★Pentelikon, 66 Deliyanni Kefalari, L, 90 b.; Costis Dimitracopoulos, Deliyanni & Khar. Trikoupi, Kefalari, A, 54 b.; Grand Chalet, 38 Kokinara, A, 36 b.; Semiramis, 36 Khar. Trikoupi & Filadelfeos, Kefalari, A, 78 b.; Theoxenia, 2 Filadelfeos & Kolokotroni, Kefalari, A, 120 b.; Nafsika (Nazika), 6 Pelis & 2 Epidavrou, B, 32 b.; Acropolis, 32 Kolokotroni, Kefalari, C, 53 b.; Aegli, Platia Platanou, C, 54 b.; Des Roses, 4 Miltiadou, C, 71 b.; Katerina, 3 Mykonou, Kefalari, C, 88 b.; Roussos, 18 P. Tsaldari, C, 18 b.

Kinetta

Kineta Beach Club (hotel and bungalows), at km 57, A, 361 b.; Sun, at km 54, B, 96 b.; Boussoulas, at km 56, C, 48 b.; Hotel 50, at km 50, C, 38 b. – all on the old Athens–Corinth road (Palaia Odos).

Hotels

Kionia (Tinos)	Tinos Beach (hotel and bungalows), A, 339 b.
Kokkarion (Samos)	Galini, B, 14 b.; Olympia Beach, B, 20 b.; Asterias, B, 18 b.; Hatziandreou, C, 25 b.; Kokkari Beach, C, 84 b.; Niki, C, 27 b.; Tsamadou, C, 34 b.; Lemos, C, 23 b.; Venus (Afroditi), Osos Kokkariou, C, 72 b.
Kokkinos Pyrgos (Crete)	Libyan Sea, B, 42 b.; Ta Adelfia, C, 20 b.
Kokoni	Angela, Paralia, C, 260 b.; Eva-Giorgos, C, 36 b.; Kokoni Beach, C, 60 b.
Kolymbia (Rhodes)	Kolimbia Sun, C, 75 b.; Relax, C, 90 b.
Komeno (Corfu)	★ Astir Palace Corfu (hotel and bungalows), L, 590 b.; Radovas (hotel and bungalows), A, 221 b.
Komotini	Archontiko Christou-Evis, km 3 on Komotini–Alexandroupolis road, B, 153 b.; Olympos, 37 Orfeos, B, 51 b.; Orpheus, 48 Platia Vas. Konstantinou, B, 150 b.; Xenia, 43 Sismanoglou, B, 46 b.; Anatolia, 53 Ankhialou, C, 108 b.; Astoria, 28 Platia Vas. Konstantinou, C, 27 b.; Democritus, 8 Platia Viziinou, C, 96 b.
Kontokali (Corfu)	★ Kontokali Palace, L, 467 b.; Pyrros, C, 49 b.; Telessila, C, 63 b.
Korakies (Crete)	Corakies Village, B, 34 b.
Korissia	See Kea
Koroni	Auberge de la Plage, B, 54 b; Flisvos, P. Ralli, D, 16 b.; Panorama, D, 18 b.
Korthion (Andros)	Korthion, C, 27 b.
Kos (town)	Continental Palace (Epirotikon Melathron), A, 393 b.; Dimitra Beach (hotel and bungalows), Ayios Fokas, Palioskala, A, 261 b.; Aegeon, 30 M. Alexandrou, B, 76 b.; Agios Constantinos, B, 232 b.; Alcyon, B, 42 b.; Alexandra, 1, 25 Martiou, B, 150 b.; Alexis Place, B, 29 b.; Aliki, 23 Themistokleous, B, 37 b.; Amerikana, Ayia Marina, B, 26 b.; Anne, 65 E. Venizelou, B, 34 b.; Arion, Ayia Marina, B, 32 b.; Artemis, 93 Kanari, B, 108 b.; Astron, Akti Koundouriotou, B, 136 b.; Atlanta Beach, B, 80 b.; Australia, 39 G. Averof, B, 16 b.; Constantia, Artemisias, B, 32 b.; Costis, Artemisias & Fenaretis, B, 22 b.; Fotini, 3 Veriopoulou, B, 23 b.; Galazios Ouranos, 3 G. Ioannidi & Kouroukli, Ayios Nikolaos, B, 20 b.; Gallia, B, 39 b.; Georgia, 63 E. Venizelou, B, 18 b.; Golden City, B, 26 b.; Hellas, 23 Parodos Amerikis, B, 36 b.; Ippoton, Vas. Yeoryiou, B, 78 b.; Kos, 31 Vas. Yeoryiou, B, 262 b.; Marina, B, 104 b.; Marmari Beach, B, 207 b.; Meropis, B, 36 b.; Mersini, Parodos Amerikis, Ayios Pavlos, B, 20 b.; Olympia, Veriopoulou, B, 41 b.; Oscar Sevasti, E. Venizelou, B, 42 b.; Paritsa, Spetson & 39 Kanari, B, 100 b.; Sophia, 81 Kleovoulou, B, 17 b.; Theodorou Beach, B, 103 b.; Theoxenia, 4 Vas. Yeoryiou, B, 78 b.; Acropole, 4 P. Tsaldari, C, 10 b.; Agios Georgios, C, 77 b.; Anastasia, Panayia Faneromeni, C, 77 b.; Anneta, Kharmilou, C, 42 b.; Bahames, Parodos B' Amerikis, C, 56 b.; Bristol, C, 71 b.; Captain's, C, 52 b.; Costel, C, 71 b.; Delfini, Kanari, C, 34 b.; Diethnes, 2 Ayios Foka, C, 121 b.; Dimitris-Paritsa, C, 80 b.; Ekaterini (Catherine), 8 P. Tsaldari,

C, 48 b.; Elisabeth, 9 E. Venizelou, C, 32 b.; Elli, 10 Themistokleous, C, 150 b.; Elma, 11 Akti Koundouriotou, C, 92 b.; Galaxias, 143 Kharmilou, C, 42 b.; Galini, C, 60 b.; George, C, 59 b.; Ibiscus (Iviskos), 2 Akti Miaouli, C, 25 b.; Imperial, C, 134 b.; Ippokratis, 4 Ayiou Nikolaou, C, 48 b.; Kamelia, 3 Artemisias, C, 42 b.; Karis, C, 54 b.; Koala, Kharmilou, C, 81 b.; Kondia Beach, C, 101 b.; Koni, 25 Themistokleous, C, 37 b.; Manos, 11 Artemisias, C, 29 b.; Marie, 24 Themistokleous, C, 39 b.; Martina, C, 132 b.; Messoghios, C, 67 b.; Milva, Platia Konitsis & Meropidos, C, 99 b.; Niriides Beach (hotel and bungalows), C, 147 b.; Olga, 1 Platia 3 Septemvriou, C, 57 b.; Oscar, 59 E. Venizelou, C, 308 b.; Paradissos, C, 100 b.; Pavlos, C, 121 b.; Phaethon, C, 48 b.; Possidon, 143 Kharmilou, C, 67 b.; Theonia, Amerikis, C, 89 b.; Titania, C, 109 b.; Veroniki, 2 P. Tsaldari, C, 36 b.; Virginia, 1B Korai, C, 42 b.; Zephyros, 34 Vas. Yeoryiou, C, 93 b.; Zikas, C, 36 b.

Kosta

Cap d'Or (hotel and bungalows), B, 284 b.; Lido, B, 72 b.

Kounoupidiana (Crete)

Pyrgos, B, 33 b.

Kountouroudia (Lesbos)

Kountouroudia, B, 17 b.

Kourna (Crete)

Happy Days Beach, Kavros, C, 69 b.; Kavros Beach, C, 43 b.; Manos Beach, C, 29 b.

Kratigos (Lesbos)

Katia (bungalows), Akti Katia Agrilia, B, 76 b.

Kremasti (Rhodes)

Blue Bay Kremasti, B, 94 b.; Iliotropio, B, 141 b.

Kritika (Rhodes)

Sirene Beach, A, 156 b.; Poseidon, B, 63 b.

Kyllini (Loutra Kyllinis)

Xenia, A, 160 b.; Glarentza, C, 58 b.; Ionion, C, 45 b.; Xenia, C, 150 b.; Robinson Club Kyllini Beach.

Kymi (Euboea)

Beis, Paralia, C, 73 b.; Aktaeon, Paralia, D, 22 b.; Halkidis, 15 Leoforos Athinon, D, 22 b.; Kymi, 20 Leoforos Athinon, D, 23 b.

Kyparissia

Artemis, 6 Doufa, Paralia, C, 41 b.; Ionion, 1 Kalantzakou, C, 57 b.; Vassilikon, 7 Alexopoulou, C, 45 b.

Kythira (town)

Keti, 28 Melpomenis Livanou, B, 16 b.

Laganas (Zákynthos)

Esperia, B, 62 b.; Galaxy, B, 152 b.; Laganas, B, 91 b.; Megas Alexandros, B, 245 b.; Zante Beach (hotel and bungalows), B, 494 b.; Alkyonis, C, 37 b.; Asteria, C, 23 b.; Atlantis, C, 20 b.; Australia, C, 33 b.; Blue Coast, C, 20 b.; Eugenia, C, 28 b.; Hellinis, C, 17 b.; Ilios, C, 16 b.; Ionis, P.O. Box 21, C, 91 b.; Margarita, C, 58 b.; Medikas, C, 20 b.; Olympia, C, 32 b.; Panorama, C, 26 b.; Selini, C, 24 b.; Sirene, C, 54 b.; Vezal, C, 16 b.; Victoria, C, 18 b.; Vyzantion, C, 16 b.

Lagonisi (Attic Riviera)

★ Xenia Lagonissi (hotel and bungalows), L, 711 b.; Var (bungalows), Leoforos Souniou, B, 38 b.; Kinoussis (bungalows), Kherones Kalivion, C, 14 b.

Lakki (Leros)

Xenon Angelou, B, 16 b.; Athena, Krithoni, C, 27 b.; Artemis, C, 14 b.; Leros, C, 35 b.; Panteli, C, 48 b.

Lambi (Kos) — Atlantis (hotel and bungalows), A, 576 b.; Athina, B, 98 b.; Calypso, B, 84 b.; Cosmopolitan, B, 148 b.; Alice Springs, C, 40 b.; Argo, C, 100 b.; Atlantis 2, C, 153 b.; Columbia Beach, C, 108 b.; Frossyni, C, 97 b.; Irene, C, 70 b.; Laura, C, 43 b.

Lambiri — Avra, C, 27 b.; Galini, C, 23 b.

Lamia — Apollonion, 25 Khatzopoulou, Platia Parkou, C, 66 b.; Delta, 41 Kapodistriou, C, 75 b.; Helena, 6 Thermopylon, C, 85 b.; Leonideon, 8 Platia Eleftherias, C, 53 b.; Samaras, 24 Diakou, C, 128 b.; Sonia, 10 Eslin, C, 38 b.

Larisa — Divani Palace, 19 Vas. Sofias, A, 144 b.; Astoria, 4 Protopapadaki, B, 150 b.; Edelweiss, km 12 on Larisa–Athens road, Nea Lefki, B, 150 b.; Grand Hotel, 16 Papakyriazi, B, 173 b.; Metropole, 8 Roosevelt, B, 177 b.; Motel Xenia, 135 Farsalon, B, 60 b.; Achillion, 10 Kendavron, C, 80 b.; Acropole, 142 E. Venizelou, C, 88 b.; Adonis, 8 Vas. Konstantinou, C, 62 b.; Ambassadeur, 65 Papakyriazi, C, 160 b.; Anessis, 25 Megalou Alexandrou, C, 104 b.; Atlantic, Vas. Konstantinou & 1 Kyprou, C, 108 b.; Dionyssos, 33 Vas. Yeoryiou B, C, 156 b.; Doma (previously Pella), 1 Anthimou Gazi-Kiprou, C, 56 b.; Esperia, 4 Amalias, C, 34 b.; Galaxy, 23 Panagouli, C, 55 b.; Helena, 13, 28 Oktovriou, C, 85 b.; I Ennea Mousses, Ambelakia, C, 16 b.; Kentrikon, 17 Roosevelt, C, 29 b.; Melathron, 20 Kouma, C, 69 b.; Olympion, 1 Megalou Alexandrou, C, 44 b.; Park, 1 31 Avgoustou, C, 105 b.

Lassi (Kefallonia) — Méditerranée (Messoghios), A, 430 b.; Irilena, C, 41 b.; Lassi, C, 61 b.; Lorenzo, C, 86 b.

Lekhaion — Corinthian Beach, C, 108 b.; Symi, C, 203 b.

Lefkanti (Crete) — Lefkandi, C, 116 b.

Lefkas — Alexandros, Nikiana, B, 51 b.; Apollon, B, 65 b.; Lefkas, 2 Panagou, B, 186 b.; Nidrio Akti, Nidri, B, 30 b.; Xenia Lefkas, B, 128 b.; Lefkatas, Vasiliki, C, 64 b.; Niricos, Ayia Mavra, C, 69 b.; Santa Mavra, 2 Sp. Vlanti, C, 38 b.

Legrena (Attic Riviera) — Amphitrite (motel), B, 58 b.; Minos, B, 72 b.

Leonidi — Dionyssos, D, 30 b.; Neon, E, 23 b.

Leptokarya — Olympian Bay (hotel and bungalows), B, 433 b.; Coral (Koralli), Paralia, C, 30 b.; Galaxy, C, 49 b.; Hera, C, 31 b.; Matos, 1 Kanari, C, 53 b.

Leros (town) — Xenon Angelou Alinda, Alinda, B, 16 b.; Alinda, C, 41 b.; Maleas Beach, C, 85 b.

Liapades (Corfu) — Elly Beach (bungalows), A, 78 b.; Liapades Beach, C, 34 b.; Liapades Beach II, D, 57 b.

Limenaria (Thasos) — Thalassies, B, 42 b.; Menel, 43 Omonias, C, 34 b.; Sgouridis, 3 Megalou Alexandrou, C, 27 b.

Limin Khersonisou — See Khersonisos

Limni (Euboea) — Avra, C, 11 b.; Limni, C, 91 b.; Plaza, 4 Ayias Triados, C, 12 b.

Lindos (Rhodes) — Lindos Bay, Vlikha, A, 364 b.; Steps of Lindos (hotel and bungalows), Vlikha, A, 310 b.; Vlicha Sandy Beach, C, 40 b.

Linoperamata (Crete)

Apollonia Beach (hotel and bungalows), A, 590 b.; Zeus Beach, P.O. Box 509, A, 717 b.

Lipsi

Kalypso, D, 28 b.

Litokhoron

Aphroditi, Platia Eleftherias, D, 56 b.; Markissia, 104 Ayiou Yeoryiou, D, 31 b.; Myrto, D, 59 b.; Park, D, 34 b.

Livadi (Paros)

Areti, B, 22 b.; Perseus (Persefs), Paralia, B, 20 b.; Maistrali, Paralia, C, 40 b.; Serifos Beach, Paralia, C, 65 b.

Livadia

Levadia, 4 Platia L. Katsoni, B, 97 b.; Helikon, Platia Yeoryiou A, C, 36 b.; Philippos, Athinon, C, 91 b.

Livadia (Tilos)

Irini, C, 35 b.; Livadia, E, 40 b.

Livanates

Achillion, Paralia, C, 44 b.; Batis, Paralia, C, 24 b.; Florakis, Paralia, C, 16 b.

Lixouri (Kefallonia)

Ionian Sea, B, 46 b.; Poseidon, C, 67 b.; Summery, C, 108 b.

Longos

Long Beach, B, 267 b.; Spey Beach, C, 72 b.

Loutra (Kythnos)

Xenia Anagenissis, C, 93 b.

Loutra Aidipsou

Aegli, 18, 25 Martiou, A, 146 b.; Avra, 16, 25 Martiou, A, 133 b.; Adonis, 21 Megalou Alexandrou, B, 47 b.; Agapi, 7A Filellinon, B, 45 b.; Alex, 31 Ermou & G. Drossini, B, 50 b.; Alina, 11 Irakleous, B, 27 b.; Argo, 2 Filellinon, B, 25 b.; Candia, 3 Thermopylon, B, 26 b.; Chalki, 25 Martiou, B, 21 b.; Chryssi Amoudia, B, 30 b.; Diana, 17 Artemisiou, B, 32 b.; Dimitra, 60 Irakleous, B, 48 b.; Dirki, 4 Megalou Alexandrou, B, 19 b.; Efstratios, 28 Vyzantinon Aftokratoron, B, 51 b.; Electra, 9 Filellinon, B, 51 b.; Elliana, 51 Irakleous, B, 40 b.; Faros, Ermou & Elkionidon, B, 22 b.; Fivos, 8 Megalou Alexandrou, B, 33 b.; Galaxias, 7 Ermou, B, 56 b.; Georgios, 15 Thermopotamou, B, 51 b.; Hara, 2 Megalou Alexandrou, B, 65 b.; Haris, 13, 25 Martiou, B, 23 b.; Hellas, 8 Thermopotamou, B, 36 b.; Heracleion, 7 Remvis, B, 69 b.; Hermes, 12 Ermou, B, 78 b.; Hydra, 22 Irakleous, B, 38 b.; Kastri, Platania, B, 23 b.; Katerina, 12 Filellinon, B, 24 b.; Kekrops, B, 50 b.; Kentrikon, 14, 25 Martiou, B, 56 b.; Lakonia, 27 Irakleous, B, 28 b.; Lykourgos, B, 21 b.; Magda, 34 Irakleous, B, 42 b.; Oceanis, 28 Irakleous, B, 27 b.; Oraei, 62 Irakleous, B, 62 b.; Semiramis, 92 Ermou, B, 48 b.; Star, 24 Vyzantinon Aftokratoron, B, 62 b.; Ta Saranta Platania, 65, 25 Martiou, B, 29 b.; Taenaron, B, 54 b.; Xenios Zeus, 27 Irakleous, B, 18 b.; Zilion, Paralia Ayiou Nikolaou, B, 38 b.; Akis, 7 Irakleous, C, 23 b.; Anessis, 7 Filellinon & Vyzantinon Aftokratoron, C, 99 b.; Angela, 1 Telethriou, C, 20 b.; Anna, 38, 25 Martiou, C, 23 b.; Antigone, 32 Vyzantinon Aftokratoron, C, 52 b.; Artemission, 5 Filellinon, C, 27 b.; Assimina, 17 Omirou, C, 34 b.; Asteri, 28, 25 Martiou, Pano Synikia, C, 26 b.; Atlantis, 31A Filellinon, C, 38 b.; Avgi, 40, 25 Martiou, C, 22 b.; Capri, 45, 25 Martiou, C, 87 b.; Corali, 20 Artemisiou, C, 37 b.; Dessykerania, 1 Irakleous, C, 32 b.; Drossia, 4 Drossini, C, 38 b.; Faidra, 61 Irakleous, C, 22 b.; Fantasia, 10 Omirou, C, 20 b.; Foula, C, 40 b.; Galini, Ayiou Nikolaou, C, 68 b.; Hellinis, 33 Omirou, C, 15 b.; Ikaros, 12 Thermopotamou, C, 32 b.; Ilion, 37 Filellinon, C, 37 b.; Iniohos, 3 Ermou, C, 18 b.; Irene, 1 Vyzantinon Aftokratoron, C, 55 b.; Istiaea, 1, 25 Martiou, C, 63 b.; Kapolos, 68 Ermou, C, 98 b.; Knossos, 19 Vyzantinon Aftokratoron, C, 71 b.; Leto,

13 Ermou, C, 60 b.; Maria, 74 Irakleous, C, 32 b.; Marianna, 29, 25 Martiou, C, 27 b.; Metropole, Miaouli & Filellinon, C, 61 b.; Mikra Epavlis, 66, 25 Martiou, C, 33 b.; Minos, 5 Vyzantinon Aftokratoron, C, 41 b.; Mito, Thermopiyon, C, 69 b.; Nefeli, 48 25 Martiou, C, 71 b.; Olympia, 11 Irakleous, C, 16 b.; Palirria, 12, 25 Martiou, C, 29 b.; Panhellinion, 3 Miaouli, C, 17 b.; Pringhipos, 27 Ermou, C, 31 b.; Stella, 38, 28 Oktovriou, C, 26 b.; Themis, 36 Irakleous, C, 26 b.; Thermae Sylla, 2 Posidonos, C, 116 b.; Valar's, 5 Okeanidon, C, 26 b.; Vassiliki, 6 Okeanidon, C, 34 b.; Zephyros, 1 Iliou, C, 24 b.

Loutra Samothrakis

Kaviros, B, 53 b.

Loutraki

Achillion, 12 E. Venizelou, A, 100 b.; Akti Loutraki, 5 G. Leka, A, 72 b.; Bacos, 4 Ikonomou, A, 80 b.; Karelion, 23 G. Leka, A, 76 b.; Paolo, 16 Korinthou, A, 140 b.; Park, 8 G. Leka, A, 115 b.; Pefkaki, A, 67 b.; Petit Palais, 48 G. Leka, A, 71 b.; Theoxenia, 17 G. Leka, A, 50 b.; Aegli, 15 G. Leka, B, 48 b.; Arion, 1 Osiou Patapiou, B, 52 b.; Atlantic, Kentriki Platia, B, 46 b.; Barbara, 50 Posidonos, B, 165 b.; Beau Rivage, 1 Posidonos, B, 70 b.; Bekiaris, 30B G. Leka, B, 24 b.; Contis, 9 Korinthou, B, 70 b.; Davarinos, 3 Yeraniou, B, 25 b.; Dritsas, 3 Ayiou Ioannou, B, 37 b.; Excelsior, 30 Platia 25 Martiou, B, 60 b.; Galanopoulos, 1 I. Mikha, B, 28 b.; Grand Hotel (Mega), 14 E. Venizelou, B, 58 b.; Holidays Angelo-Poulos, Pefkaki, B, 98 b.; Ikia Lekka, 14 G. Leka, B, 19 b.; Kamari, 3 Platia 25 Martiou, B, 12 b.; Marinos, 1 Damaskinou, B, 97 b.; Marko, 3 L. Katsoni, B, 53 b.; Palmyra, 1 Iasonos, B, 74 b.; Pappas, Pezoulia-Pefkaki, B, 153 b.; Segas, 8 Ayiou Ioannou, B, 44 b.; Vassilikon, Kentriki Platia, B, 55 b.; Xenon Andreou, 30 G. Leka, B, 32 b.; Acropole, 11 P. Tsaldari, C, 42 b.; Alcyonis, 11 Damaskinou, C, 49 b.; Alexandros, Leoforos Athinon–Loutrakiou, C, 34 b.; Avra, 56 G. Leka, C, 17 b.; Belle Vue, 37 E. Venizelou, C, 35 b.; Bretagne, 28 G. Leka, C, 34 b.; Cosmopolite, 23 Galinis, C, 69 b.; Ekonomion, Kentriki Platia, C, 48 b.; Elpis, 18 G. Leka, C, 121 b.; Galaxy, Neraïda, C, 72 b.; Gerania, 23 Periandrou & Ypsilantou, C, 33 b.; Ilion, C, 44 b.; Isthmia, 35 E. Venizelou, C, 50 b.; Marrion, 36 G. Leka, C, 87 b.; Mitzithra, 25 E. Venizelou, C, 83 b.; Mon Repos, 13 G. Leka, C, 56 b.; Olympia, 1 E. Venizelou, C, 108 b.; Plaza, 32 Platia 25 Martiou, C, 50 b.; Possidonion, 11 Kentriki Platia, C, 72 b.

Loutro Elenis

Politis, B, 50 b.; Kakanakos, C, 30 b.; Sea View, C, 42 b.

Loutropyrgos

Achillion, km 31 on the old Athens–Corinth road, D, 12 b.; Aronis, D, 29 b.

Lykoporia

Alkyon, 217 Athinon–Patron, C, 26 b.; Elatos, D, 22 b.

Magoula
(Euboea)

Holidays in Evia (hotel and bungalows), B, 659 b.; Miramare, B, 64 b.

Makryammos
(Thasos)

Makryammos (bungalows), A, 402 b.

Makrynitsa
(Pelion)

Archontikon Mousli, A, 15 b.; Archontikon Sissilianou, A, 14 b.; Archontikon Xiradakis, A, 14 b.; Tzimerou, A, 8 b.; Archontikon Diomidi, B, 26 b.; Skotinotis House, B, 14 b.

Malakonta
(Euboea)

Eretria Beach (hotel and bungalows), B, 453 b.; Malakonda Beach (hotel and bungalows), B, 298 b.; Menexelis (hotel and bungalows), B, 58 b.

Maleme (Crete)

Crete Chandris (hotel and bungalows), A, 767 b.

Malia (Crete)

Ikaros Village, A, 326 b.; Kernos Beach, A, 519 b.; Malia Beach, A, 364 b.; Sirens Beach, A, 466 b.; Anastassia, B, 44 b.; Ariadne, B, 59 b.; Calypso (bungalows), B, 78 b.; Costas, B, 64 b.; Cleo, B, 18 b.; Grammatikaki, B, 91 b.; Phaedra Beach, B, 167 b.; Sunshine, B, 22 b.; Altis, C, 33 b.; Amvrossia, C, 54 b.; Artemis, C, 45 b.; Efi, C, 35 b.; Elkomi, C, 55 b.; Dionyssos, C, 29 b.; Florella, C, 56 b.; Frixos, C, 28 b.; Helen, C, 43 b.; Hermes, C, 69 b.; Malia Holidays, C, 162 b.; Malia Mare, C, 64 b.; Minoa, C, 37 b.; Minoikos Ilios, C, 19 b.; Mistral, C, 54 b.; Neon, C, 30 b.; Sofokles Beach, C, 64 b.; Sterling, C, 34 b.; Windmill, C, 39 b.

Mandraki

Haritos, B, 24 b.

Marathokambos

Kerkis Bay, B, 48 b.

Marathon

Golden Coast, A, 457 b.; Marathon, Timvos, C, 46 b.

Marmari (Euboea)

Delfini, C, 39 b.; Marmari Bay, C, 188 b.; Michel-Marie, C, 56 b.

Marmari (Kos)

Caravia Beach (hotel and bungalows), Ayinaropi-Marmari, A, 563 b.

Marpissa (Paros)

Andromachi, B, 23 b.; Marpissa, B, 21 b.; Amaryllis Beach, C, 40 b.; Leto, C, 28 b.; Lodos, C, 20 b.; Logaras, C, 16 b.; Pisso Livadi, C, 24 b.; Vicky, C, 28 b.

Massouri (Kalymnos)

Armeos Beach, B, 61 b.; Oasis, B, 48 b.; Afroditi, C, 24 b.; Cally Beach, C, 31 b.; Continental, C, 46 b.; Massouri Beach, C, 64 b.

Mastikhari (Kos)

In Antimakhia:
Mastihari Beach, 1 E. Gika, B, 21 b.

In Mastikhari:
Faenareti, D, 35 b.; Andreas, E, 16 b.; Zevgas, E, 16 b.

Matala (Crete)

Sun, B, 54 b.; Bamboo Sands, C, 30 b.; Eva-Marina, C, 40 b.; Frangiskos, C, 69 b.; Matala Bay, C, 104 b.; Pringipissa Evropi, C, 48 b.

Mati

Mati, 33 Posidonos, A, 130 b.; Attika Beach, 32 Posidonos, B, 178 b.; Myrto, 34 Leoforos Marathonos, C, 60 b.

Megalopolis

Kokkinakis, C, 27 b.

Melissa

Xylokastron Beach, C, 154 b.

Melos

Adamas, 2 Griara, B, 22 b.; Popi, Adamas, B, 12 b.; Venus Village, B, 173 b.; Chronis (bungalows), C, 32 b.; Corali, C, 31 b.; Meltemi, Adamas, C, 24 b.; Milos, Adamas, C, 67 b.; Santa Maria, Adamas, C. 46 b.

Merikhas (Kythnos)

Possidonion, C, 158 b.

Mesolongi

Liberty, B, 231 b.; Theoxenia, Limin, B, 198 b.

Messongi (Corfu)

Gemini, B, 92 b.; Maria House, C, 35 b.; Melissa Beach, C, 56 b.; Rossis, C, 57 b.; Roulis, C, 30 b.

Metamorfosis

Golden Beach, D, 82 b.

Hotels

Methana	Avra, B, 101 b.; Pigae, 1 Triti Parallilos, B, 47 b.; Saronis, B, 70 b.; American, 26 Akti Saronikou, 4 A. Zakharatou & 5 Vas. Konstantinou, C, 49 b.; Dima, 9 Ayias Triados, C, 38 b.; Ghionis, C, 93 b.; Methanion, C, 69 b.
Methoni (Peloponnese)	Methoni Beach, B, 23 b.; Alex, Paralia, C, 38 b.
Methoni (Thermaic Gulf)	Arion, C, 74 b.; Ayannis, C, 54 b.
Metsovo	Diasselo, Kentriki Platia, A, 43 b.; Flocas, 12 Tr. Tsoumaka, B, 10 b.; Victoria, B, 64 b.; Apollon, C, 58 b.; Bitounis, C, 46 b.; Egnatia, L. Tossitsa, C, 64 b.; Galaxy, Kentriki Platia, C, 20 b.; Kassaros, Tr. Tsoumaka, C, 47 b.; Olympic, 3 I. Stamou, C, 32 b.
Mikra Mantinia	Taygetos Beach, C, 50 b.
Milina (Pelion)	Milina Beach (apartments), C, 26 b.
Mistra	Vyzantion, Vas. Sofias, B, 38 b.
Mithimna-Molyvos (Lesbos)	Molyvos I, A, 56 b.; Alkeos, B, 108 b.; Arion, B, 105 b.; Delfinia I, B, 243 b.; Molyvos II, Eftalou, B, 115 b.; Poseidon, 2 Parodos Posidonos, B, 12 b.; Sea Horse (Thalassio Alogo), B, 27 b.; Triaena, B, 18 b.
Mokhlos (Crete)	Aldiana Club, B, 262 b.; Sophia, D, 16 b.
Monemvasia	Castro, Yefyra, A, 23 b.; Malvasia, Kastro, B, 16 b.; Monemvassia, B, 18 b.; Minoa, 14 Spartis, C, 30 b.
Moraitika (Corfu)	★ Miramare Beach (hotel and bungalows), L, 285 b.; Delfinia (motel), A, 151 b.; Albatros, B, 101 b.; Alkyonis, B, 116 b.; Capodistrias (bungalows), B, 53 b.; Delfinakia, B, 71 b.; Messonghi Beach, B, 1587 b.; Salonaki, B, 33 b.; Margarita, C, 67 b.; Prassino Nissi, C, 50 b.; Sea Bird (Thalassopouli), C, 31 b.; Three Stars, C, 136 b.
Moskhaton	Alma, 10 Vas. Konstantinou, C, 78 b.; Delfini, 12 Khrysostomou Smyrnis & Kalavryton, C, 61 b.; Kriton (Crito), 1 Platonos & 53 Leoforos Posidonos, C, 100 b.; Leto (Lito), 47 Leoforos Posidonos, C, 87 b.; Mary, 41 Leoforos Posidonos, C, 61 b.; Miami, 6 Ath. Diakou, C, 56 b.; Milano, 6 Vas. Yeoryiou, C, 70 b.; Platon, 3 Platonos, C, 71 b.
Mycenae	La Petite Planète, Leoforos Khristou Tsounda, B, 56 b.; Agamemnon, 3 Leoforos Khristou Tsounda, C, 16 b.
Mýkonos (town)	Leto, A, 48 b.; Poseidon, A, 40 b.; Anastassios-Sevasti, B, 56 b.; Andronikos, B, 12 b.; Calypso, Angelika, B, 58 b.; Cavo Tagoo, B, 45 b.; Despotiko, B, 40 b.; Glastros, Glastros, B, 26 b.; Ilio Maris, Despotika, B, 41 b.; Koumeni, Tria Pigadia, B, 36 b.; Kyma, Angelika, B, 59 b.; Les Moulins, 31 Apollonos, B, 25 b.; Petassos, B, 31 b.; Poseidon B, B, 36 b.; Rohari, B, 99 b.; Theoxenia, B, 93 b.; Vassiliou, B, 24 b.; Adonis, Vida, C, 27 b.; Aeolos, Argyrena, C, 48 b.; Bellou, Megali Ammos, C, 14 b.; Frangakis, Ornos, C, 27 b.; Gorgona, Tangou, C, 33 b.; Korfos, C, 24 b.; Manoulas Beach, Ayios Ioannis-Diakofti, C, 57 b.; Manto, 1 Evangelistrias, C, 26 b.; Marianna, Glastros, C, 43 b.; Marios, 5 N. Kaloyera Limni, C, 26 b.; Matoyanni, C, 29 b.; Mykonos, Vida, C, 30 b.; Mykonos

Beach (bungalows), Megali Ammos, C, 50 b.; Pelecan, Rokhari, C, 44 b.; Vencia, Rokhari, C, 60 b.; Thomas, Khondros Gremos, C, 76 b.; Zannis, C, 36 b.; Zefyros, Paranga, C, 56 b.; Zorzis, N. Kaloyera, C, 20 b.; Apollon, D, 33 b.; Delfines, D, 26 b.; Helena, D, 41 b.; Karbonaki, D, 39 b.

Mylos Lappa (Kos)

Albatros Beach, C, 117 b.

Myrina (Lemnos)

★Akti Myrina (Myrina Beach; bungalows), L, 250 b.; Kastro Beach, B, 136 b.; Lemnos, Platia 28 Oktovriou, C, 58 b.; Sevdalis, 6 Garofalidou, C, 63 b.

Myrties (Kalymnos)

Themis, B, 19 b.; Delfini, Mesolongiou, C, 34 b.; Zephyros, C, 58 b.

Myrtos (Crete)

Esperides, C, 112 b.; Myrtos, C, 32 b.

Mystegna (Lesbos)

Petalidi, Petalidi, C, 37 b.

Mytilini (Lesbos)

Villa 1900, Tarlas, A, 19 b.; Blue Sea, 91 P. Koundourioti, B, 101 b.; Erato, B, 22 b.; Lesvion, 27 P. Koundourioti, Prokimea, B, 68 b.; Mytilana Villae, km 6 on road to Kalonis, B, 103 b.; Xenia, B, 148 b.; Rex, 3 Katsakouli Kioski, C, 30 b.; Sappho, Prokimea, C, 56 b.

Nafpaktos

Lepanto Beach, Gribovo, B, 93 b.; Lido, 15 Menekhmou Psani, B, 23 b.; Xenia, B, 96 b.; Akti, Gribovo, C, 105 b.; Rex, 16 Mesolongiou, C, 23 b.; Amaryllis, 3 Platia Limenos, D, 28 b.

Nafplion

★Xenia's Palace, Akronafplia, L, 102 b.; ★Xenia's Palace Bungalows, Akronafplia, L, 108 b.; Amphitryon, Akti Miaouli, A, 80 b.; Xenia, Akronafplia, A, 98 b.; Agamemnon, 3 Akti Miaouli, B, 74 b.; Alcyon, 43 Argous, C, 35 b.; Amalia, 93 Argous, C, 16 b.; Amymoni, 6 Diogenous & Koleti, C, 32 b.; Athina, Platia Syntagmatos, C, 26 b.; Dioscouri, 7 Zygomala & Vironos, C, 93 b.; Galini, 39 Sidiras Merarkhias & Boublulinas, C, 72 b.; Helena, 17 Sidiras Merarkhias, C, 149 b.; Hotel des Roses, 42 Argous, C, 24 b.; Nafplia, 11 Navarinou, C, 104 b.; Parartima (annexe of Hotel des Roses), 42 Argous, C, 46 b.; Park, 1 Dervenakion, C, 131 b.; Rex, 17 Bouboulinas, C, 94 b.; Victoria, 3 Spiliadou, C. 69 b.

Naousa

Christiana, Ambelas, B, 35 b.; Christina, Alonia, B, 21 b.; Hippocambus, B, 94 b.; Kontaratos Beach, B, 44 b.; Manto, B, 29 b.; Naoussa, B, 19 b.; Nireas, B, 25 b.; Aliprantis, C, 29 b.; Ambelas, Ambelas, C, 32 b.; Atlantis, C, 55 b.; Calypso, C, 46 b.; Cavos, C, 25 b.; Christianna, Ambelas, C, 35 b.; Galini, C, 22 b.; Kouros (hotel and bungalows), C, 98 b.; Mary, C, 31 b.; Minoa, C, 51 b.; Papadakis, C, 31 b.; Piperi (bungalows), C, 16 b.; Swiss Home, C, 56 b.

Naxos (town)

Aneza, B, 12 b.; Ariadne, 1 Ariadnis, B, 46 b.; Glaros, B, 22 b.; Mathiassos (bungalows), B, 204 b.; Acroyali, C, 31 b.; Aegeon, C, 40 b.; Aeolis, C, 33 b.; Anatoli, C, 43 b.; Anessi, C, 25 b.; Apollon, 61 Neofytou, C, 34 b.; Barbouni, C, 26 b.; Coronis, Paraliaki Leoforos, C, 60 b.; Grotta, C, 35 b.; Helmos, 1 Kalavryton, C, 21 b.; Hermes, 7 Protopapadaki, C, 36 b.; Iliovassilema, C, 39 b.; Kymata, C, 32 b.; Naxos Beach, C, 80 b.; Nissaki, C, 30 b.; Panorama, Amfitrytis Kastro, C, 33 b.; Renetta, C, 23 b.; Sergis, C, 54 b.; Sphinx, C, 40 b.; Zeus, C, 29 b.

Nea Artaki (Euboea)

Bel-Air (motel), B, 82 b.; Angela, 2 Vas. Pavlou, C, 112 b.; Telemachus, 30 Ayiou Nikolaou, C, 48 b.

Nea Epidavros	See Epidauros
Nea Kifissia	Lida, 103 Tatoïou, C, 38 b.; Pines, Khelidonos & Artemidos, C, 133 b.
Nea Makri	Marathon Beach, B, 296 b.; Thomas Beach, 3 Leoforos Posidonos, B, 57 b.; Zouberi, Leoforos Posidonos, Zouberi, B, 238 b.; Afroditi, km 33 on Athens–Marathon road, C, 54 b.; Nirefs (Nereus), C, 245 b.
Nea Moudania	Kouvraki, 41, 25 March, C, 37 b.
Nea Pendeli	See Penteli
Nea Peramos (Attica)	Megalo Pefko, 15, 28 Oktovriou, C, 136 b.; Hellas, D, 26 b.
Nea Styra (Euboea)	Aegilion, C, 51 b.; Aktaeon, Paralia, C, 82 b.; Delfini, C, 85 b.; Evoikon, 62 E. Mavromikhali, C, 28 b.; Kyriaki, C, 50 b.; Nektarios, C, 68 b.; Plaza, C, 47 b.; Styra Beach, 24 Bouboulinas, C, 44 b.; Sunday, C, 50 b.; Venus Beach (Akti Afroditis; bungalows), C, 180 b.
Neapolis (Crete)	Neapolis, 1 Evangelistrias, D, 20 b.
Neapolis (Lesbos)	Lesvos Beach (apartments), B, 78 b.; Neapolis Beach (apartments), B, 28 b.
Neokhorion (Rhodes)	Doretta Beach, Tholos, A, 546 b.; Athina, 27 Yeoryiou Leontos & Amalias, B, 267 b.; Villa Rhodos, 36 Yeoryiou Leontos, C, 53 b.
Neos Marmaras	See Porto Karras
Neos Pyrgos (Euboea)	Vyzantion, C, 38 b.; Acroyali, D, 46 b.; Oassis, D, 36 b.
Nikoleika	Poseidon Beach, B, 168 b.
Nisaki (Corfu)	Nissaki Beach, Krouzeri, A, 443 b.
Oia (Santorin)	Perivolas (apartments), A, 14 b.; Atlantis Villas (accommodation in restored island houses), B, 38 b.; Laouda, B, 20 b.
Olympia	Amalia, A, 272 b.; Antonios, A, 121 b.; Spap, A, 97 b.; Apollon, 13 Douma, B, 168 b.; Leonideon, 3 P. Spiliopoulou, B, 14 b.; Neda, 1 K. Karamanli, B, 75 b.; Neon Olympia, G. Douma, B, 59 b.; Olympic Village Hotel, B, 97 b.; Xenia, B, 72 b.; Xenios Zeus (motel), B, 72 b.; Achillefs (Achilles), 4 Stefanopoulou, C, 15 b.; Artemis, 2 Tsoureka, C, 28 b.; Hercules, C, 25 b.; Ilis, Prax. Kondyli, C, 102 b.; Inomaos, C, 44 b.; Kronion, 1 Tsoureka, C, 41 b.; Olympic Torch, (Olympiaki Dada), on Pyrgos–Olympia road, C, 32 b.; Phedias, 2 P. Spiliopoulou, C, 17 b.; Possidon, 9 Stefanopoulou, C, 20 b.
Omalos (Crete)	Xenia (pavilion), B, 7 b.
Orkhomenos	Elli, D, 15 b.
Ormylia	Philoxenia Bungalows, B, 72 b.; Sermili, B, 231 b.; Psakoudia, C, 26 b.
Ornos	Ornos Bay, B, 29 b.; Ornos Beach, B, 42 b.; Paralos Beach, C, 76 b.; Pigal, C, 17 b.; Skios, C, 26 b.; Yannaki, C, 75 b.

Oropos
Alcyonis, Paralia Markopoulou, C, 181 b.; Despo, Paralia Markopoulou, C, 32 b.; Flisvos, C, 113 b.

Ouranopolis
Eagles' Palace (Aeton Melathron; hotel and bungalows), Skala Neon Rodon, A, 312 b.; Xenia (motel and bungalows), B, 84 b.; Akroyali, D, 19 b.; Pyrgos, D, 31 b.; Xenios Zeus, D, 36 b.

Palaia Epidavros
See Epidauros

Palaikastro (Crete)
Hellas, B, 24 b.; Margot's House, C, 22 b.; Marina Village, C, 54 b.

Palaiokastritsa (Corfu)
Akrotiri Beach, A, 238 b.; Oceanis, B, 123 b.; Paleokastritsa, B, 293 b.; Xenia (pavilion), B, 14 b.; Apollon, C, 46 b.; Odysseus, C, 64 b.

Palaiokastron (Crete)
Rogdia, C, 42 b.

Palaiokhora
Eliros, B, 18 b.; Lissos, 12 Venizelou, C, 21 b.; Polydoros, C, 24 b.; Rea, C, 13 b.

Palaion Faliron
Coral, 35 Posidonos, B, 160 b.; Possidon, 72 Leoforos Posidonos, B, 168 b.; Avra, 3 Nireos, C, 70 b.; Nestorion, 8 Pendelis, C, 54 b.

Palaion Kalamaki
Kalamaki Beach, A, 141 b.

Palaiopolis (Samothrace)
Xenia, B, 14 b.

Paliouri
Xenia, B, 144 b.; Paliouri, E, 14 b.

Panayia (Thasos)
Chryssafis, B, 17 b.; Golden Sand, D, 20 b.; Theo, D, 35 b.

Panormos (Crete)
Lavris, B, 56 b.; Panormo Beach, C, 61 b.

Panormos (Kalymnos)
See Kalymnos

Paralia Katerinis
Afroditi, B, 26 b.; Alkyone, 2 Stratou, B, 64 b.; Alkyonis, 4 Stratou, B, 38 b.; Aktaeon, 49 Ayiou Nikolaou, C, 69 b.; Avra, 7 Ayiou Nikolaou, C, 28 b.; Dion, 13 Ayiou Nikolaou, C, 29 b.; Galini, C, 33 b.; Hellas, C, 42 b.; Kastoria, C, 64 b.; Katerina, 41 Ayiou Nikolaou, C, 18 b.; Konstantinos, 48 Ayiou Nikolaou, C, 81 b.; Muse's Beach, C, 114 b.; Stella, 10 Kyprou, C, 33 b.; Zephyros, 10 Stratou, C, 42 b.

Paralia Skotinas
El Greco, D, 7 b.; Lefkes, D, 16 b.

Paralia Tyrou
Anessis, 2 Tagmatarkhou Alevra, C, 21 b.; Apollon, Paraliaki Odos, C, 23 b.; Blue Sea, Sapouneika, C, 41 b.; Kamvyssis, C, 40 b.

Parga
Bacoli, B, 66 b.; Lichnos Beach (hotel and bungalows), B, 164 b.; Parga Beach (bungalows), Khrysoyiali, B, 152 b.; Valtos Beach, Valtos, B, 36 b.; Acropole, C, 15 b.; Alkyon, C, 28 b.; Avra, 3 Ayiou Athanasiou, C, 35 b.; Della's, C, 32 b.; Olympic, 1 Skoufa, C, 31 b.; Rezi, C, 33 b.; Torini, C, 21 b.

Parnis
Casino Mont Parnis (alt. 1050m/3450ft), A, 212 b.

Paros (town)
Aegeon, B, 69 b.; Anna, B, 14 b.; Anessis, B, 15 b.; Apollon, B, 43 b.; Arian, B, 16 b.; Dilion, B, 27 b.; Irene, B, 31 b.; Polos, B, 40 b.; Xenia, B,

44 b.; Alkyon, C, 46 b.; Argo, C, 83 b.; Argonaftis (Argonauta), C, 28 b.; Asterias, C, 69 b.; Cyclades, C, 27 b.; Galinos, C, 65 b.; Georgy, Platia Manto Mavroyenous, C, 63 b.; Grivas, C, 44 b.; Hermes, C, 36 b.; Kirki, C, 12 b.; Louiza, C, 22 b.; Nicolas, C, 83 b.; Oassis, C, 33 b.; Paros, C, 22 b.; Paros Bay, C, 87 b.; Stella, C, 38 b.; Vaya, C, 17 b.; Zannet, C, 27 b.

Patras
Astir, 16 Ayiou Andreou, A, 222 b.; Moreas, Iroon Politekhniou & Kyprou, A, 180 b.; Galaxy, 9 Ayiou Nikolaou, B, 98 b.; Koukos, 3 Theotokopoulou, B, 43 b.; Marie, 6 Gounari, B, 48 b.; Olympic, 46 Ayiou Nikolaou, B, 75 b.; Rannia, 53 Riga Fereou, B, 54 b.; Acropole, 39 Othonos & Amalias, C, 64 b.; Adonis, Zaimi & 9 Kapsali, C, 107 b.; Delfini, 102 Iroon Politekhniou & Terpsithea, C, 135 b.; El Greco, 145 Ayiou Andreou, C, 43 b.; Esperia, 10 Zaimi, C, 39 b.; Méditerranée, 18 Ayiou Nikolaou, C, 165 b.

Paxi
Paxos Beach (bungalows), Gaios, B, 84 b.; Agios Georgios, D, 30 b.

Pefkakia (Samos)
Samos Bay, Th. Sofouli, B, 74 b.; Iliokymata (Sun Waves), C, 60 b.

Pefkari (Thasos)
Kapa-Hi, B, 44 b.

Pefki (Euboea)
Amaryllis, 2B Ayion Theodoron, C, 40 b.; Galaxias, C, 49 b.; Galini, C, 57 b.; Myrtia, C, 42 b.

Penteli
Adonis, D, 25 b.

Perama (Corfu)
Alexandros (formerly Steya), 20 I, Theotoki, A, 163 b.; Aeolos Beach (bungalows), 6 Mantzarou, B, 673 b.; Akti (motel), B, 107 b.; Oasis, B, 124 b.; Aegli, C, 71 b.; Continental, C, 40 b.; Fryni, C, 34 b.; Pontikonissi, C, 84 b.

Perdika (Aegina)
Aegina Maris, B, 310 b.; Moondy Bay (bungalows), Profitis Ilias, B, 144 b.

Perissa (Santorin)
Thira Mare, C, 35 b.; Christina (Christi), D, 16 b.; Santa Irini, D, 31 b.; Zorzis, D, 19 b.

Perivolia
Eltina, C, 68 b.; Zantina Beach, C, 33 b.

Petra
Ilion, C, 60 b.; Petra, Kentriki Platia, C, 34 b.

Petrothalassa
Aquarius (hotel and bungalows), B, 786 b.

Pigadia
See Karpathos

Piraeus
Cavo d'Oro, 19 Vas. Pavlou, Kastela, B, 134 b.; Diogenis, 27 Vas. Yeoryiou A, B, 146 b.; Homeridion, 32 Kharilaou Trikoupi & 2 Alkiviadou, Pasalimani, B, 112 b.; Kastella, 75 Vas. Pavlou, B, 48 b.; Noufara, 45 Vas. Konstantinou, B, 84 b.; Park, 103 Kolokotroni & Gladstonos, Platia Terpsitheas, B, 152 b.; Savoy, 93 Vas. Constantinou, B, 136 b.; Triton, 8 Tsamadou, B, 104 b.; Acropole, 7 D. Gounari, C, 42 b.; Anemoni, Karaoli Dimitriou & 65–67 Evripidou, C, 87 b.; Anita, 25 Notara, C, 47 b.; Argo, 23 Notara, C, 47 b.; Atlantis, 138 Notara, C, 93 b.; Bella Vista, 108 Vas. Pavlou, Kastela, C, 69 b.; Capitol, Kharilaou Trikoupi & 147 Filonos, C, 91 b.; Cavo, 79–81 Filonos, C, 85 b.; Delfini, 7 Leokharous, C, 93 b.; Diana, 11 Filellinon, C, 79 b.; Glaros, 4 Kharilaou Trikoupi, C, 80 b.; Ideal, 142 Notara, C, 56 b.; Kairo, C, 17 b.; Ionion, 10 Kapodistriou, C, 41 b.; Leriotis, 294 Akti Themistokleous, C, 85 b.; Lilia,

131 Zeas, Pasalimani, C, 21 b.; Niki, 5 Yiannakou Tzelepi, Platia Ipodamis, C, 32 b.; Phedias (Fidias), 189 Koundourioti, Pasalimani, C, 44 b.; Santorini, 6 Kharilaou Trikoupi, Ayios Nikolaos, C, 63 b.; Scorpios, 156 Akti Themistokleous, C, 44 b.; Serifos, 5 Kharilaou Trikoupi, C, 59 b.; Zaharatos, 12 Evangelistrias & 1 Notara, C, 59 b.

Piskopiano (Crete)

Kalimera (apartments), B, 44 b.; Anna-Maria (apartments), C, 12 b.; Andriani, E, 24 b.

Pisso Livadi

See Marpissa

Plaka

Olympios Zeus, (bungalows and camping), B, 168 b.; Leto, on Larisa–Katerini road, C, 177 b.

Plakias (Crete)

Calypso Cretan Village (bungalows), 19 Prevelaki, A, 204 b.; Lamon, B, 46 b.; Neos Alianthos, B, 163 b.; Alianthos, Platia Ayiou Nikolaou, C, 35 b.; Livykon, C, 27 b.; Lofos, C, 27 b.; Plakias Bay, C, 48 b.; Sophia Beach, C, 48 b.

Planos (Zákynthos)

Dias, B, 63 b.; Anetis, C, 23 b.; Cosmopolite, C, 27 b.; Orea Heleni, C, 44 b.; Tsilivi, C, 105 b.

Platamon

Maxim, B, 139 b.; Platamon Beach, 101 Megalou Alexandrou, B, 323 b.; Xenia (motel), B, 8 b.; Alkyonis, 17 Kastrou, C, 62 b.; Anessis, 16 Frouriou, C, 20 b.; Artemis, C, 31 b.; Dias, 91 K. Karamanli, C, 46 b.; Olympos, 18 Frouriou, C, 42 b.

Platania (Crete)

Filoxenia, B, 18 b.; Villa Platanias, B, 32 b.

Platania (Thessaly)

Drossero Akroyali, C, 66 b.; Hotel des Roses, D, 50 b.

Platys Yialos (Kefallonia)

White Rocks (hotel and bungalows), A, 305 b.

Platys Yialos (Mýkonos)

Petassos Beach, B, 128 b.; Petinos, C, 57 b.

Platys Yialos (Sifnos)

Platys Yalos (formerly Xenia), B, 38 b.; Benakis, C, 58 b.

Plepi

Hydra Beach–Kappa Club (hotel and bungalows), A, 516 b.; Porto Hydra (hotel and bungalows), Marina, A, 508 b.

Plomárion (Lésbos)

Oceanis, C, 78 b.

Politika (Euboea)

Evoiki Akti, C, 92 b.

Polykhnitos (Lesbos)

Olympos, E, 16 b.

Poros (Crete)

Pasiphae, 1 Naxou, C, 32 b.; Poseidon, 46 Posidonos, C, 49 b.; Prince (Pringips), 44 Konitsis, C, 50 b.; Vines (Klimataries), 13 Koritsas, C, 40 b.

Poros (Kefallonia)

Hercules (Iraklis), B, 12 b.; Atros Poros, C, 18 b.; Kefalos, C, 56 b.

Poros (Poros)

Epta Adelfia, 1 Tombazi, B, 30 b.; Latsi, 74 I. Papadopoulou, B, 54 b.; Neon Aegli, Askeli, B, 132 b.; Pavlou, Neorion, B, 66 b.; Poros (formerly Xenia), B, 173 b.; Saron, Paralia, B, 46 b.; Sirene, Monastiri, B, 228 b.; Theano, B, 49 b.; Aktaeon, 6 Platia Iroon, C, 38 b.; Angyra, Neorion, C, 87 b.; Chryssi Avgi, Askeli, C, 145 b.; Manessi, Paralia, C, 25 b.

Portaria (Pelion)
Archontiko Athanassaki, A, 22 b.; Archontiko Kantartzi, A, 35 b.; Tis Marios, A, 13 b.; Xenia, B, 152 b.; Alkistis, C, 87 b.; Pelias, C, 53 b.; Kentrikon, C, 22 b.

Porto Karras (Chalcidice)
★Meliton Beach, Sithonia, L, 1012 b.; Sithonia Beach, Sithonia, A, 920 b.

Porto Kheli
Cosmos, A, 279 b.; Hinitsa Beach, A, 385 b.; Porto Heli, A, 404 b.; Galaxy, B, 325 b.; Giouli, B, 315 b.; Thermissia (formerly La Cité), B, 308 b.; Ververoda (hotel and bungalows), B, 463 b.; Alcyon, C, 171 b.; Porto (Limani), 25 Evangelistrias, C, 20 b.; Rozos, C, 42 b.

Porto Rafti
Korali, Leoforos Grezou, Ayios Spyridon, C, 28 b.; Kyani Akti, Ziki Avlaki, C, 47 b.

Porto Yermeno
Egosthenion, C, 154 b.

Posidonia (Sýros)
Delagrazia, Agathope, B, 22 b.; Poseidonion, B, 109 b.; Eleana, C, 82 b.

Potamia (Thasos)
Kamelia, B, 24 b.; Miramare, B, 45 b.; Arion, C, 11 b.; Atlantis, C, 12 b.; Blue Sea, C, 23 b.; Korina, C, 56 b.

Potamos (Corfu)
Elvira, Polikhoma, B, 76 b.; Zorbas, Yefyra, D, 31 b.

Pothea
See Kalymnos

Potokaki (Sámos)
El Coral, B, 16 b.; Hydrele Beach, B, 86 b.; Les Tamaris (formerly Armyrikia), B, 14 b.; Penelope, B, 17 b.; Potokaki, B, 21 b.; Victoria, B, 19 b.; Anthemoussa, C, 32 b.

Pounta Parikias
Holiday Sun, A, 101 b.

Preveza
Margarona Royal, B, 222 b.; Zikas, B, 99 b.; Aktaeon, 1 Kolovou, C, 30 b.; Dioni, 4 I. Kalou, C, 61 b.; Metropolis, 1 Parthenagoyiou, C, 23 b.; Minos, 11, 21 Oktovriou, C, 36 b.; Paradissos, Amoudia, C, 35 b.; Preveza City, 81–83 Ioanninon, C, 97 b.

Prinos (Thasos)
Electra, B, 51 b.; Europa, B, 24 b.; Oassis, B, 22 b.; Crystal, Dassilion, C, 22 b.

Profitis Ilias (Rhodes)
Elafos-Elafina (alt. 710m/2330ft), A, 127 b.

Prokopion (Euboea)
Anessis, E, 13 b.

Psakoudia
See Ormylia

Psalidi (Kos)
Hippocrates Palace, A, 280 b.; Oceanis, A, 651 b.; Ramira Beach, A, 500 b.; Sun Palace, A, 274 b.; Galazia Limni, C, 81 b.

Psara
Miramare, A, 50 b.

Psathopyrgos
Florida (motel), B, 156 b.

Psykhro (Crete)
Zeus, D, 14 b.

Pylos
Karalis Beach, Paralia, B, 24 b.; Miramare (formerly Nestor), B, 30 b.; Nilefs, B, 24 b.; Galaxy, Platia Trion Navarkhon, C, 62 b.; Karalis, C, 39 b.; Arvanitis, D, 32 b.

Pyrgi (Corfu)
Pyrgi, C, 106 b.; Port (Limani), C, 14 b.

Pýrgos
Ilida, 50 Patron, C, 64 b.; Letrina, 74 Patron, C, 128 b.; Marily, 48 Deliyanni & Themistokleous, C, 51 b.; Olympos, 2 Karkavitsa & Vas. Pavlou, C, 71 b.; Pantheon, 7 Themistokleous, C, 89 b.

Pythagorion (Sámos)
Doryssa Bay, A, 455 b.; Acropole, B, 13 b.; Antonios, B, 23 b.; Astyanax, B, 17 b.; Efpalinio, B, 20 b.; Fyllis, B, 34 b.; Georgios Sandalis, B, 19 b.; Kaktos, B, 19 b.; Melanthemos, B, 24 b.; Phito (bungalows), B, 154 b.; Pighassos, B, 28 b.; Samena, B, 33 b.; Tarsanas, B, 14 b.; Villa Marie, B, 23 b.; Apollon, C, 39 b.; Belvedere, C, 16 b.; Captain's House, C, 13 b.; Damo, C, 20 b.; Evelin, C, 45 b.; Frosso, C, 19 b.; Glicoriza Beach, C, 116 b.; Hera (Ira), C, 22 b.; Ilios, C, 61 b.; Labito, C, 34 b.; Polycrates, C, 22 b.; Polyxeni, C, 44 b.; Princessa, C, 98 b.; Pythagoras, C, 55 b.; Pythais, 126 L. Logotheti, C, 15 b.

Rafina
Avra, Paralia, C, 184 b.; Bravo, Kokino Limanaki, C, 35 b.

Rakhoni (Thasos)
Hara, Paralia, C, 19 b.; Argyro, D, 56 b.

Reni (Rhodes)
Eden Rock (hotel and bungalows), A, 720 b.; Paradise (Paradissos), A, 960 b.; Kallithea Sun, B, 199 b.

Rethymnon (Crete)
Creta Star, A, 625 b.; El Greco (hotel and bungalows), Kambos Piyis, A, 573 b.; Rethymno Bay, A, 129 b.; Rithimna Beach (hotel and bungalows), Adele, A, 1058 b.; Adele Beach Bungalows, Adele, B, 101 b.; Amnissos, B, 94 b.; Brascos, 1 Kh. Daskalaki & Th. Moatsou, B, 156 b.; Dias, Adele, B, 100 b.; Gortyna, B, 71 b.; Idaeon (Ideon), 10 Platia Plastira, B, 133 b.; Jo-an, 6 Dimitrakaki, B, 93 b.; Kriti Beach, S. Venizelou & Papanastasiou, B, 100 b.; Lefkoniko Beach, Kallithea, B, 141 b.; Leon, Arkadiou & 4 Vafe, B, 25 b,; Nika, Koube, B, 14 b.; Oassis, B, 22 b.; Olympic, Moatsou & Dimokratias, B, 123 b.; Orion, Kambos Adele, B, 138 b.; Rethemniotiko Spiti, B, 19 b.; Skaleta Beach, B, 216 b.; Xenia, 30 N. Sparrou, B, 50 b.; Zania, 3 P. Vlastou, B, 15 b.; Zorbas Beach, 4 A. Schweitzer, Kallithea, B, 22 b.; Astali, 172A Leoforos Koundouriotou, C, 63 b.; Golden Beach, Adele, C, 158 b.; Golden Sun, Adele, C, 74 b.; Green, Spili, C, 17 b.; Ionia, 52 Yiamboudaki, C, 50 b.; Katerina Beach, Adele, C, 92 b.; Lefteris, 26 N. Plastira, C, 11 b.; Marita, Mastambas, C, 51 b.; Minos, Kallithea, C, 252 b.; Park, 7 Igoumenou Gavriil, C, 18 b.; Rina, Adele, C, 37 b.; Sea Side Inn, Xirokamaro, C, 39 b.; Steris Beach, 1 Konstantinoupoleos, Kallithea, C, 83 b.; Valari, 84 Koundouriotou, C, 55 b.

Rhodes (town)
★ Grand Hotel Summer Palace Astir, Akti Miaouli, L, 700 b.; Belvedere, Akti Kanari, A, 394 b.; Blue Sky, Platia Psaropoulas, A, 332 b.; Cairo Palace, 28 Ethnarkhou Makariou, A, 201 b.; Chevaliers Palace, 3 Stratigou Griva, A, 346 b.; Ibiscus (Iviskos), 17 Nisirou, A, 383 b.; Imperial, 23 Vas. Konstantinou, A, 151 b.; Kambourakis (bungalows), A, 40 b.; Kamiros, 1, 25 Martiou, A, 90 b.; Mediterranean, 35–37 Ko, A,

292 b.; Park, 12 Riga Fereou, A, 153 b.; Regina, 20 Ethnarkhou Makariou, A, 144 b.; Riviera, 2 Akti Miaouli, A, 116 b.; Siravast, Platia Vas. Pavlou, A, 170 b.; Acandia, 6 Iroon Politekhniou, B, 150 b.; Aglaia, 35 Apollonos Amerikis, B, 209 b.; Alexia, 54 Orfanidou, B, 257 b.; Amphitryon, 10 A. Diakou, B, 188 b.; Angela, 7, 28 Oktovriou, B, 118 b.; Beach Hotel 33, 19 Akti Kanari, B, 319 b.; Bella Vista, Akti Miaouli & Tilou, B, 54 b.; Cactus, 14 Ko, B, 336 b.; Chryssos Tholos, B, 14 b.; Constantinos, 65 Amerikis, B, 246 b.; Continental (formerly Monte Christos), 8 Ayiou Ioannou, B, 218 b.; Corali, 28 Vas. Constantinou & Patmou, B, 217 b.; Delfini, 45 Ethnarkhou Makariou, B, 135 b.; Despo, 40 Vas. Sofias, B, 122 b.; Erato, B, 70 b., Esperia, 7 Stratigou Griva, B, 362 b.; Europa, 94, 28 Oktovriou, B, 190 b.; Jolly, 36 Lokhagou Fanouraki, B, 28 b.; Lomeniz Beach, B, 378 b.; Manousos, 25 G. Leon, P.O. Box 92, B, 212 b.; Oassis, 16–18, 25 Martiou, B, 30 b.; Olympic, 12 Platia Vas. Pavlou, B, 86 b.; Phoenix (Palm), 2 Exarkhou Panteleimonos, B, 143 b.; Plaza, 7 Ierou Lokhou, B, 244 b.; Spartalis, 2 N. Plastira, B, 141 b.; Stella, 58 Dilberaki, B, 26 b.; Thermae, Ethnarkhou Makariou, B, 210 b.; Achillion, 14 Platia Vas. Pavlou, C, 86 b.; Adonis, 7 Vas. Konstantinou, C, 26 b.; Aegli, 90 Kolokotroni, C, 69 b.; Africa, 63 A. Diakou, C, 144 b.; Als, 10 Platia Vas. Pavlou, C, 95 b.; Amaryllis, 44 Othonos & Amalias, C, 75 b.; Ambassadeur, 53 Othonos & Amalias, C, 80 b.; Anthoula, 46 A. Diakou, C, 24 b.; Aphrodite (Venus), 50 Othonos & Amalias, C, 101 b.; Arion, 17 Ethnarkhou Makariou, C, 82 b.; Astoria, 39 Vas. Sofias, C, 72 b.; Astron, 10 I. Kazouli, C, 82 b.; Athinaea, 45 Pythagora, Palaia Agora, C, 16 b.; Atlantis, 29 I. Dragoumi, C, 91 b.; Carina, 56 Stratigou Griva, C, 108 b.; Colossos, 9 Haile Selassie, C, 99 b.; Congo, 145 Dendrinou, C, 57 b.; Diana, 68 Stratigou Griva, C, 74 b.; Diethnes (International), 12 I. Kazouli, C, 78 b.; Dora, 37 Aristofanous, C, 16 b.; Egeon (Aegeon), 3 Erythrou Stavrou, C, 28 b.; El Greco, 2 Yeoryiou Efstathiou, C, 140 b.; Elite, 15 Exarkhou Panteleimonos, C, 86 b.; Embona, 61 Stratigou Griva, C, 30 b.; Filoxenia, 28 Sava Diakou, C, 25 b.; Flora, 13, 28 Oktovriou, C, 187 b.; Florida, 5 Amarandou, C, 36 b.; Four Seasons, 32 Akti Miaouli, C, 51 b.; Galatia, 2 Erythrou Stavrou, C, 20 b.; Galaxy, 76 Vas. Anna-Maria, C, 73 b.; Helena, 78 Stratigou Griva, C, 163 b.; Hermes, 5 N. Plastira, C, 64 b.; Irene, 9, 25 Martiou, C, 87 b.; Isabella, 12 Amokhostou, C, 76 b.; Kallithea Sky, C, 92 b.; Kallithea Sun (bungalows), C, 92 b.; Kypriotis, 2 Valaoritou, C, 461 b.; Lia, 66C Pythagora, C, 16 b.; Lydia, 31, 25 Martiou, C, 111 b.; Majestic, A. Zervou & I. Metaxa, C, 147 b.; Marie, 7 Ko, C, 235 b.; Massari, 42 Irodotou, C, 22 b.; Mimosa, 4 G. Efstathiou, C, 117 b.; Minos, 8 A. Diakou, C, 133 b.; Moschos, 7 Ethelonton Dodekanision, C, 64 b.; Nausika, 8 Parrodiakou Syllogou USA, Akti Khoropoulas, C, 70 b.; New York, 36 I. Dragoumi, C, 49 b.; Noufara, 35 Vas. Sofias, C, 86 b.; Parthenon, Anthoulas Zervou, P.O. Box 68, C, 150 b.; Pavlidis, 15, 28 Oktovriou, C, 96 b.; Perle (Margaritari), 15 Stratigou Griva, C, 70 b.; Petalouda (Butterfly), 49 Amokhostou, C, 75 b.; Phaedra (Fedra), 7 Arkadiou, C, 120 b.; Royal (Vassilikon), 50 Vas. Sofias, C, 107 b.; Sant'Antonio (Agios Antonios), 7 I. Dragoumi, C, 82 b.; Saronis, 51 Othonos & Amalias, C, 54 b.; Savoy, 9 Ethelonton Dodekanision, C, 87 b.; Semiramis, 18 I. Metaxa, C, 230 b.; Sylvia, 114 Kolokotroni, C, 71 b.; Tilos, 46 Ethnarkhou Makariou, C, 39 b.; Vassilia, 55 Othonos & Amalias, C, 77 b.; Victoria, 22, 25 Martiou, C, 66 b.; Xenia-Soleil, 2 Dimokratias, C, 160 b.; Zeus, 72 Ayiou Nikolaou, C, 19 b.

Rion

Porto Rio (hotel and bungalows), A, 501 b.; Georgios, 9 Ionias, C, 26 b.; Rion Beach, Akti Posidonos, C, 162 b.

Roda (Corfu)

Roda Beach, B, 685 b.; Aphroditi, C, 40 b.; Mandylas, C, 56 b.; Milton, C, 46 b.; Silver Beach, C, 63 b.; Village Roda Inn, C, 32 b.

Salandi Salandi Beach (hotel and bungalows), B, 776 b.

Salonica ★ Makedonia Palace, Leoforos Megalou Alexandrou, L, 530 b.; Capitol, 8 Monastiriou, A, 353 b.; Electra Palace, 5A Platia Aristotelous, A, 235 b.; Astoria, 20 Tsimiski & Salaminas, B, 162 b.; Athos, 20 Dagli, B, 32 b.; Capsis, 28 Monastiriou and Promitheos, B, 823 b.; City, 11 Komninon, B, 178 b.; El Greco, 23 Egnatia, B, 162 b.; Filoxenia (ex Elizabeth; motel), 293 Monastiriou, B, 40 b.; Metropolitan, 65 Vas. Olgas & 2 Fleming, B, 224 b.; Olympia, 65 Olympou, B, 208 b.; Olympic, 25 Egnatia, B, 104 b.; Palace, 12 Tsimiski, B, 83 b.; Philippion, Odos Antheon Seih Sou, Akropolis, B, 159 b.; Queen Olga, 44 Vas. Olgas, B, 261 b.; Rotonda, 97 Monastiriou, B, 142 b.; Victoria, 13 Langada, B, 127 b.; ABC, 41 Angelaki, C, 199 b.; Aegeon, 19 Egnatia, C, 112 b.; Alma, Ayios Athanasios, C, 41 b.; Amalia, 33 Ermou, C, 124 b.; Anessis, 20, 26 Oktovriou, C, 72 b.; Ariston, 5 Karaoli-Dimitriou, C, 61 b.; Continental, 5 Komninon, C, 64 b.; Delta, 13 Egnatia, C, 217 b.; Esperia, 58 Olympou & Venizelou, C, 132 b.; Mandrino, 2 Antigonidon & Egnatia, C, 136 b.; Oceanis, 35 N. Plastira, Platia Skra, C, 45 b.; Park, 81 I. Dragoumi, C, 105 b.; Pella, 65 I. Dragoumi, C, 118 b.; Rea, 6 Komninon, C, 55 b.; Rex, 39 Monastiriou, C, 111 b.; Telioni, 16 Ayiou Dimitriou, C, 118 b.; Vergina, 19 Monastiriou, C, 256 b.

Sami (Kefallonia) Ionion, 5 Khorofylakis, C, 29 b.; Skala, C, 14 b.; Tara Beach (bungalows), C, 52 b.

Sámos (town) Galaxy, C, 81 b.; Kedros, C, 35 b.

Sani Sani Beach Club (ex Robinson Club Phocea) bungalows, A, 430 b.; Sani Beach, B, 886 b.

Seliantika Panayotis, B, 18 b.; Kanelli, C, 68 b.; Kyani Akti, Paralia, C, 51 b.; Plage, 257 Miaouli, C, 44 b.

Selinia (Salamis) Akroyali, 92 Akti Themistokleous, D, 17 b.; Votsalakia, 64 Akti Themistokleous, D, 29 b.

Serrai Elpida, 66 Merarkhias, B, 152 b.; Xenia, 1 Ayias Sofias, B, 110 b.; Galaxy, 24 Merarkhias & 1 P. Tsaldari, C, 90 b.; Helena, 7 Tsalopoulou, C, 69 b.; Park, 18 Papapavlou, Platia Eleftherias, C, 114 b.

Servia Panhellinion, 8 117 Ethnomartyron, E, 30 b.

Sfakia (Crete) Xenia, Khora Sfakion, B, 23 b.

Sidari (Corfu) Afroditi Beach, C, 35 b.; Astoria, C, 36 b.; Mimoza, 32 G. Markora, C, 67 b.; Three Brothers, C, 70 b.

Sigrion Nisiopi, B, 16 b.

Sikyon Paradissos, C, 54 b.

Sinarades (Corfu) Yaliskari Palace, A, 420 b.

Sissi (Crete) Porto Sissi (apartments), A, 30 b.; Amarylis (apartments), C, 16 b.; Elena, E, 15 b.; Micro, E, 21 b.

Sitia (Crete) Sitian Beach–Kappa Club, K. Karamanli, A, 310 b.; Sunwing (hotel and bungalows), Makriyialos, A, 276 b.; Denis, 60 E. Venizelou, B, 25 b.;

Maresol (bungalows), Ayia Fotia, B, 47 b.; Sunwing II, Makriyialos, B, 191 b.; Alice, 34 Papanastasiou, C, 69 b.; Castello, 21 Rouselaki, C, 31 b.; Chryssos Ilios, C, 60 b.; Crystal, 17 Kapetan Sifi, C, 75 b.; El Greco, C, 28 b.; Elize, C, 15 b.; Helena, C, 42 b.; Itanos, Platia Venizelou, C, 138 b.; Mariana, 67 Misonos, C, 47 b.; Vai, C, 84 b.

Skafidia
Miramare Olympia Beach (hotel, bungalows and villas), A, 665 b.; Apollon, E, 16 b.

Skala (Patmos)
Kasteli, B, 81 b.; Maria, Khokhlakas, B, 24 b.; Patmion, 34 E. Xenou, B, 42 b.; Skala, B, 152 b.; Xenon Vyzantion, B, 21 b.; Astoria, C, 26 b.; Galini, C, 21 b.; Chris, C, 90 b.; Hellinis, C, 29 b.; Kalokeri, C, 40 b.; Plaza, C, 27 b.; Villa Zacharo, C, 15 b.

Skiathos
★ Skiathos Palace, Koukounaries, L, 424 b.; Esperides, Akhladies, A, 300 b.; Nostos (bungalows), Tzaneria, A, 350 b.; Alkyon, Amoudia, B, 160 b.; Mandraki (bungalows), Koukounaries, B, 55 b.; Meltemi, B, 32 b.; Orsa, Plakes, B, 14 b.; Xenia, Koukounaries, B, 64 b.; Thymis' Home, Livadia, B, 34 b.; Akti, 26 F. Yeoryiadou, C, 22 b.; Belvedere (Kali Thea; bungalows), Akhladies, C, 120 b.; Golden Beach, C, 69 b.; Koukounaries, 47 F. Yeoryiadou, C, 32 b.; Panorama, Koukounaries, C, 23 b.; Pounda, C, 68 b.; Stelina, C, 91 b.; Toxotis, C, 24 b.; Troulos Bay, C, 69 b.; Vontzos, Akhladies, C, 34 b.; Zeus, C, 28 b.

Skopelos (town)
Andromachi, A, 12 b.; Archontiko, 1 Xanthou, A, 22 b.; Kyr-Sotos, A, 24 b.; Aegeon, B, 31 b.; Amalia, B, 88 b.; Elli, B, 39 b.; Mon Repos, B, 30 b.; Panormos Beach, Panormos, B, 57 b.; Peparithos, B, 19 b.; Prince Stafylos, Livadi, B, 94 b.; Regina, 9 Parodos, B, 21 b.; Rigas, Stafylos, B, 79 b.; Xenia, B, 8 b.; Aeolos, C, 79 b.; Agnanti, C, 23 b.; Captain, Eleftherotria, C, 33 b.; Denise, C, 41 b.

Skýros
Xenia, Magazia, B, 38 b.; Aegeon, E, 7 b.; Helena, E, 22 b.

Souda (Crete)
Knossos, 31 Platia Pringipos Yeoryiou, D, 17 b.; Parthenon, Platia Pringipos Yeoryiou & 29 E. Venizelou, D, 13 b.

Soufli
Orpheus, Vas. Yeoryiou & 1 Tsimiski, C, 34 b.; Egnatia, 225 Vas. Yeoryiou, D, 14 b.

Sounion
Belvedere Park (bungalow hotel), A, 180 b.; Cape Sounion Beach (bungalows), Plakes, A, 376 b.; Egeon (Aegeon), A, 87 b.; Surf Beach Club (hotel and bungalows), Pounta Zeza, B, 521 b.; Triton, km 68 on Athens–Sounion road, B, 78 b.; Saron, on Lavrion–Sounion road, C, 52 b.

Souvala (Aegina)
Ephi, C, 59 b.; Saronikos, D, 33 b.

Sparta
Lida, B, 75 b.; Menelaion, 65 K. Palaiologou, B, 88 b.; Apollo, 14 Thermopylon, C, 82 b.; Dioscouri, 94 Lykourgou & Atridon, C, 60 b.; Lakonia, 61 K. Palaiologou, C, 62 b.; Maniatis, 60 K. Palaiologou & D. Dafnou, C, 150 b.; Sparta Inn, C, 217 b.

Spetsai
Akroyali, Ayii Anaryiri, A, 30 b.; Kasteli (hotel and bungalows), A, 122 b.; Possidonion (Poseidonion), A, 83 b.; Spetses, A, 143 b.; Roumanis, B, 65 b.; Villa Anessis, B, 15 b.; Villa Christina, B, 24 b.; Villa Martha, B, 38 b.; Faros, Kentriki Platia, C, 87 b.; Ilios (Soleil), Paralia, C, 50 b.; Myrtoon, C, 74 b.; Star, Platia Dapias, C, 68 b.

Stalida (Crete)
Anthoussa Beach, A, 259 b.; Alkyonides, B, 54 b.; Blue Sea (bungalows), B, 371 b.; Cactus Beach, B, 116 b.; Diamond Beach, B, 34 b.;

Elvira, B, 35 b.; Korina, B, 32 b.; Palm Beach, B, 40 b.; Panorama Stalidos, B, 20 b.; Smaragdine Beach, B, 16 b.; Sunny Beach, B, 55 b.; Thisvi, B, 21 b.; Zephyros Beach, B, 75 b.; Heliotrope, C, 140 b.; Pelargos, C, 8 b.

Stavros

Aristotelis, 3 Vas. Yeoryiou, C, 30 b.; Athos, 8 K. Palaiologou, Platania, C, 48 b.; Possidonion, 2 Vas. Yeoryiou, C, 14 b.

Steni (Euboea)

Dirphys, C, 35 b.; Steni (motel), C, 70 b.

Stymfalia

Stymfalia, E, 18 b.

Svoronata

See Ayia Pelayia

Symi

Aliki, A, 28 b.; Dorian, A, 20 b.; Grace, B, 13 b.; Metapontis, B, 25 b.

Thasos (town)

Amfipolis, A, 78 b.; Akti, B, 27 b.; Diamanto, B, 30 b.; Dionyssos, B, 21 b.; Elli-Maria, B, 63 b.; Galini, 1 Theagenous, B, 29 b.; Georgios, B, 23 b.; Mary, B, 17 b.; Possidon, B, 30 b.; Timoleon, B, 54 b.; Viky, B, 27 b.; Villa Nysteri, B, 18 b.; Alcyon, C, 21 b.; Angelika, C, 50 b.; Laios, C, 49 b.; Lido, 12 Megalou Alexandrou, C, 33 b.; Panorama, C, 16 b.; Villa Meressi, C, 40 b.

Thebes

Dionyssion Melathron, 7 I. Metaxa & Kadmou, B, 42 b.; Meletiou, 56–58 Epaminonda, C, 65 b.; Niobe (Niovi), 63 Epaminonda, C, 51 b.

Thera

See Thira

Thermai (Ikaria)

George, B, 16 b.; Anna, C, 29 b.; Apollon, C, 59 b.; Parthenon, C, 36 b.

Therma Lefkados (Ikaria)

Adam's, B, 12 b.; Anyfantis (hotel and bungalows), B, 288 b.; Akti, C, 27 b.; Anna, C, 16 b.; Carras, C, 19 b.; Galini, C, 27 b.; Marina, C, 20 b.

Thermi (Lesbos)

Blue Beach, B, 12 b.; Votsala (motel), Paralia, B, 94 b.

Thermopylai

Aegli, C, 86 b.; Asclepios, D, 88 b.

Thermos

Aetolia, 35 Kh. Trikoupi, D, 11 b.

Thira (Fira; Santorin)

Atlantis, A, 46 b.; Villa Renos, B, 13 b.; Antonia, C, 20 b.; Kallisti Thira, C, 64 b.; Kavalari, C, 39 b.; Panorama, C, 34 b.; Pelican, C, 34 b.; Theoxenia, C, 20 b.

Timbaki (Crete)

Agios Georgios, C, 16 b.; El Greco, E, 19 b.; Kriti, E, 30 b.

Tingaki (Kos)

Tingaki Beach, A, 309 b.; Tingaki Toulas, B, 38 b.; Konstantinos Ilios, C, 162 b.

Tinos (town)

Aeolos Bay, Angali, B, 131 b.; Alonia, Ayia Sofia, B, 64 b.; Favie Souzane, 22 Antoniou Sokhou, B, 63 b.; Theoxenia, 2 Leoforos Megalokharis, B, 59 b.; Tinion, 1 C. Alavanou, B, 47 b.; Afroditi, 23 P. Navarkhou, C, 22 b.; Argo, Angali, C, 20 b.; Asteria, Leoforos Stavrou-Kioniou, Kallithea, C, 96 b.; Avra, Paralia, C, 31 b.; Delfinia, Paralia, C, 73 b.; Leto, Paralia, C, 36 b.; Meltemi, 7 D. Filipoti, Leoforos Megalokharis, C, 77 b.; Oassis, 1 Evangelistrias, C, 43 b.; Oceanis, 3 Akti G. Drossou, C, 91 b.; Poseidonion, 4 Paralias, C, 73 b.; Vyzantion, C, 54 b.

Tolon Dolfin, 50 Aktis, B, 42 b.; Solon, B, 50 b.; Sophia, B, 100 b.; Aktaeon, 60 Aktis, C, 39 b.; Apollon, C, 88 b.; Aris, 28 Aktis, C, 58 b.; Artemis, C, 37 b.; Assini Beach, C, 16 b.; Christina, 7 Bouboulinas, C, 39 b.; Coronis, 59 Leoforos Sekeri, C, 36 b.; Electra, C, 34 b.; Electra's, 6 Bouboulinas, C, 34 b.; Epidavria, 52 Leoforos Sekeri, C, 70 b.; Esperia, C, 82 b.; Flisvos, 13 Bouboulinas, C, 54 b.; Knossos, 46A Aktis, C, 31 b.; Kyani Akti, C, 26 b.; Minoa, 56 Aktis, C, 83 b.; Pavlos, 4 Bouboulinas, C, 24 b.; Phryne (Frini), 21 Leoforos Sekeri, C, 26 b.; Possidonion, 2 Diovouniotou, C, 69 b.; Ritsa's, Psili Ammos, C, 58 b.; Romvi, 5 E. Venizelou, C, 33 b.; Spartakos, C, 18 b.; Thetis, 3 Kardamaki, C, 30 b.; Tolo, 15 Leoforos Bouboulinas, C, 72 b.; Tolo II, C, 29 b.; Tolo Inn, C, 28 b.; Zeus, C, 15 b.

Trikala (Peloponnese) Asteria, Ano Trikala, C, 25 b.; Ta Trikala, C, 41 b.

Trikala (Thessaly) Achillion, 1–3 Platia Vas. Yeoryiou, B, 122 b.; Divani, 13 Dionysiou, B, 121 b.; Dina, 38 Asklipiou & Karanasou, C, 108 b.; Palladion, 4 Vironos, C, 34 b.

Tripoli Menalon, Platia Areos, A, 58 b.; Arcadia, 1 Platia Kolokotroni, B, 85 b.; Alex, 26 Vas. Yeoryiou A, C, 59 b.; Anaktorikon, 48 Konstantinou XII, C, 58 b.; Artemis, 1 Dimitrakopoulou, C, 126 b.; Galaxy, Platia Yeoryiou B, C, 150 b.

Tsaki (Corfu) Regency, P.O. Box 158, A, 343 b.; Karina, C, 44 b.

Tsangarada (Pelion) Villa Irini-Kivotos, A, 8 b.; Kentavros (formerly Galaxy), B, 46 b.; Konaki, Ayia Paraskevi, B, 37 b.; Paradissos, B, 31 b.; Xenia, B, 84 b.; San Stefano, C, 71 b.

Tsermiades (Crete) Kourites, B, 13 b.

Vayia (Aegina) Xeni, C, 14 b.; Vaya, E, 18 b.

Valimitika Eliki, C, 278 b.

Varkitsa (Attic Riviera) Glaros, Posidonos & 1 Xenious Dios, A, 81 b.; Varkiza, 13–15 Rodou, B, 57 b.; Holidays, 22 Leoforos Posidonos, C, 65 b.; Stefanakis, 17 Afroditis, C, 79 b.

Vartholomio Alfa, C, 55 b.; Artemis, C, 20 b.; Fegarognemata, C, 30 b.

Vary (Syros) Ahladi, C, 25 b.; Akrotiri, Megas Yialos, C, 41 b.; Alexandra, Megas Yialos, C, 58 b.; Domenica, C, 43 b.; Kamelo, C, 44 b.; Romantica, C, 58 b.

Vathý (Sámos) Aeolis, 33 Themistokli Sofouli, B, 97 b.; Eleana, B, 34 b.; Odysseas, B, 28 b.; Vathy, B, 17 b.; Virtzinia, B, 42 b.; Xenia, 23 Themistokli Sofouli, B, 56 b.; Helen, 2 Gramou Katsouni, C, 45 b.; Samos, 6 Themistokli Sofouli, C, 204 b.; Sibylla, C, 38 b.; Surf Side (Kymothalasso), Roditses, C, 54 b.

Vavrona See Brauron

Vergina See Veria

Veria Polytimi, 35 Megalou Alexandrou, C, 57 b.; Vassilissa Vergina, 31 E. Venizelou, C, 42 b.; Veria, C, 116 b.; Villa Elia, 16 Elias, C, 65 b.

Volos

Aegli, 24 Argonafton, B, 68 b.; Alexandros, 3 Topali & Iasonos, B, 134 b.; Argo, 135 Dimitriados, B, 40 b.; Electra, 22 Topali, B, 71 b.; Nefeli, 10 Koumoundourou & Dimitriados, B, 100 b.; Park, 2 Deliyioryi, B, 225 b.; Admitos, 43 Vas. Konstantinou & Athanasiou Diakou, C, 53 b.; Avra, 5 Solonos, C, 57 b.; Galaxy, 3 Ayiou Nikolaou, C, 102 b.; Filippos, 9 Solonos, C, 73 b.; Iolkos, 25 Dimitriados, C, 25 b.; Kypseli, 1 Ayiou Nikolaou, C, 100 b.; Roussas, 1 I. Tzanou, C, 17 b.; Sandi, Iasonos & 13 Topali, C, 67 b.

Vonitsa

Bel Mare, C, 63 b.; Kekrops, C, 39 b.; Vonitsa, C, 65 b.

Voula (Attic Riviera)

Voula Beach, 103 Alkyonidon, A, 106 b.; Castello Beach, 8 Kerkyras & Aktis, B, 64 b.; Plaza, 17 Alkyonidon, B, 31 b.; Kabera, 8 Alkyonidon, C, 17 b.; Noufara, 2 Metaxa & Vas. Yeoryiou, C, 42 b.; Orion, 4 I. Metaxa, C, 49 b.; Palma, 9 Alkyonidon, C, 65 b.; Parthenis, 21 Alkyonidon, C, 31 b.; Rondo, 6 Dodekanisou, C, 84 b.

Vouliagmeni (Attic Riviera)

★Aphrodite Astir Palace, L, 308 b.; ★Arion Astir Palace (hotel and bungalows), L, 462 b.; ★Nafsika Astir Palace, L, 325 b.; Armonia, 1 Armonias, A, 167 b.; Costi, 2 Dios, A, 28 b.; Greek Coast, 8 Panos, A, 103 b.; Margi House, 11 Litous, A, 175 b.; ; Blue Spell, 1 Litous, B, 71 b.; Hera (Ira), 1 Iasonos, B, 73 b.; Paradise, Armonias & Danais, B, 110 b.; Strand, 14 Litous, B, 134 b.

Vrondados (Chios)

Xenios, B, 40 b.

Xanthi

Motel Natassa, B, 127 b.; Nestos, 1 Leoforos Kavalas, B, 142 b.; Xenia, 9 Vas. Sofias, B, 48 b.; Democritus, 41, 28 Oktovriou, C, 69 b.; Sissy, 14 Lefkipou, C, 31 b.; Xanthippion, 212, 28 Oktovriou, C, 95 b.

Xylokastron

Arion, 3 K. Karamanli, A, 120 b.; Apollon, 105 I. Ioannou, B, 60 b.; Fadira, 2 Ayiou Makariou, B, 92 b.; Miramare, 37 I. Ioannou, B, 42 b.; Rallis, 55 I. Ioannou, B, 132 b.; Periandros, 1 Ayiou Makariou, C, 39 b.

Yeoryioupolis (Crete)

Drossia, B, 22 b.; Gorgona, C, 70 b.

Yerolimin

Akroyali, E, 12 b.; Akrotaenaritis, E, 10 b.

Ypati (Loutra Ypatis)

Aegli, B, 39 b.; Anessis, B, 39 b.; Angelis, B, 26 b.; Anixis, B, 34 b.; Europe, B, 29 b.; Hellas, B, 84 b.; Hermes, B, 21 b.; Lux, B, 85 b.; Pigae, B, 52 b.; Rodon, B, 33 b.; Sperchios, B, 17 b.; Xenia, B, 143 b.; Acropole, C, 20 b.; Alexakis, C, 52 b.; Alfa, C, 49 b.; Ariston, C, 15 b.; Armonia, 25 Martiou, C, 32 b.; Astron, C, 49 b.; Avra, C, 43 b.; Cronos, 25 Martiou, C, 16 b.; Diana, C, 27 b.; Dido, 104 25 Martiou, C, 20 b.

Ypsos (Corfu)

Ypsos Beach, B, 114 b.; Doria, C, 39 b.; Ionian Sea, C, 14 b.; Jason, C, 67 b.; Mega, C, 61 b.; Platanos, C, 58 b.

Zagora (Pelion)

Charavgi, E, 21 b.

Zakharo

Nestor, 7 R. Station, C, 46 b.; Rex, R. Station, C, 66 b.

Zákynthos (Zante; town)

Kryoneri, 86 Kryoneriou, B, 29 b.; Lina, B, 88 b.; Strada Marina, 14 K. Lomvardou, B, 195 b.; Xenia, 60 D. Roma, B, 78 b.; Yria, 4 Kapodistriou, B, 21 b.; Adriana, 6 N. Kolyva, Ayia Trias, C, 18 b.; Aegli, 1 A. Lountzi & 12 Lomvardou, C, 16 b.; Angelika, 80 Kryoneriou, C, 32 b.; Apollon, 30 Tertseti, C, 17 b.; Astoria, 1 Rizospaston, Platia D. Solomou, C, 15 b.; Bitzaro, 46 D. Roma, C, 74 b.; Diana, 11 Kapodistriou &

Mitropoleos, C, 91 b.; Libro d'Oro, 92 Kryoneriou, C, 92 b.; Phoenix (Finix), 2 Platia D. Solomou, C, 65 b.; Plaza, C, 33 b.; Reparo, C, 28 b.; Tereza, C, 58 b.; Zenith, 44 Tertseti & 2 Martinegou, C, 14 b.

Holiday Clubs, Holiday Villages

Holiday clubs and holiday villages are becoming more and more popular. They offer a wide range of sporting activities as well as water sports, and organise a full calendar of events of all kinds.

The best known clubs are Club Méditerranée, Club Aldiana, Robinson Club as well as Sunsail-Kuhnie Tours (yacht charter and water-sports club). Detailed information from the Greek National Tourist Organisation (see information).

Information

Greek National Tourist Organisation (Ellinikós Organismós Tourismoú, EOT)

Offices outside Greece

United Kingdom

4 Conduit Street
London W1R 0DJ
Tel. (0171) 734 5997

United States

Olympic Tower
645 Fifth Avenue
New York NY 10022
Tel. (212) 421 5777

611 West Sixth Street
Los Angeles CA 90017
Tel. (213) 626 6696

168 North Michigan Avenue
Chicago IL 60601
Tel. (312) 782 1084

Canada

1233 rue de la Montagne
Montreal
Quebec H3G 1Z2
Tel. (514) 871 1535

1300 Bay Street, Main Level
Toronto
Ontario
Tel. (416) 968 2220

EOT Offices in Greece

Athens

Head office:
Amerikis 2
Tel. (01) 3 22 31 11

Ermou 1
Tel. (01) 3 25 22 67/68

Information office in National Bank,
Sýntagma Square:
Karayeoryi Servias 2
Tel. (01) 3 22 25 45

Stoa Spiromiliou (only for festival tickets)
Tel. (01) 3 22 14 59

At Ellinikó Airport:
Tel. (01) 9 70 23 95

Corfu

Odos Zavitsainou 15
Kerkyra (town)
Tel. (0661) 3 75 20 and 3 76 38–39

Crete

Odos Xanthoudidou 1
Iráklion
Tel. (081) 22 82 03, 22 82 25, 22 60 81

Odos Kriari 40
Khaniá
Tel. (0821) 2 64 26, 4 26 24

Réthymon
Tel. (0881) 2 91 48

Evzoni

At the frontier
Tel. (0343) 5 12 23

Igoumenítsa

On harbour
Tel. (0665) 2 22 27

Ioánnina

Nap. Zerva 2
Tel. (0651) 2 50 86 and 3 14 56

Kakavia/Ioánnia

At the frontier

Kavála

Platía Eleftherías 2
Tel. (051) 22 87 62 and 22 24 25

Kefalloniá

Argostoliou, at the harbour
Tel. (0671) 2 22 48, 2 44 66

Kipi/Evros

Tel. (0555) 3 12 24

Kos

Information Office
Akti Koundourioti
Tel. (0242) 2 87 24

Lamia

Laou-Square, Tel.
Tel. (0231) 3 00 65–66

Lárisa

Koumoundourou 18
Tel. (041) 25 09 19

Lésbos

At Mytilíni Harbour
Tel. (0251) 4 25 11, 4 25 13

Niki/Flórina

Tel. (0385) 4 23 03

Patras

Iroon Polytekhniou
Tel. (061) 42 03 03–5, 42 38 66, 42 90 46

Piraeus	Marina Zeas, NTOG Building Tel. (01) 4 13 47 09 and 4 13 57 16
Promakhon	Tel. (0323) 4 12 41
Rhodes	Odos Arkhiepiskopou Makariou 5 & Odos Papagou Rhodes Town Tel. (0241) 2 36 55 and 2 32 55 and 2 74 66
Salonica	Odos Mitropoleos 34 Tel. (031) 27 18 88 and 22 29 35
Samos	Odos Martiou 25 Tel. (0273) 2 85 82, 2 85 30
Sýros	Ermoúpolis Tel. (0281) 2 23 75 and 2 67 65
Vólos	Platía Riga Fereou Tel. (0421) 2 35 00, 3 62 33, 3 74 17

Cyclades

Tourist information bureaux have recently been established on twelve islands in the Cyclades. They are to be found in the offices of the communal authorities on the harbour.

Tourist Police

Information can also be obtained from the local Tourist Police (Astynomia Allodapon).
Telephone number for Athens and surrounding area: (01) 171
Where there is no Tourist Police, apply to the local police station.

Hotels

For a comprehensive list of hotels in Greece, see the entry on Hotels (above).

For advice about hotels in Athens, apply to the branch office of the Greek Chamber of Hotels:

Stadiou 2 (corner of Karayeoryi Servias)
Tel. (01) 3 23 71 93
Open: Mon.–Fri. 8.30am–8pm, Sat. 8am–2pm

Reservations

The information bureaux of the Greek National Tourist Organisation do not arrange hotel reservations.
To book rooms in private houses, apply in writing to:

Xenodokhiako Epimitirio
(Greek Chamber of Hotels)
Stadiou 24
Athens
Tel. (01) 3 23 66 41

Insurance

General

Visitors are strongly advised to ensure that they have adequate holiday insurance including loss or damage to luggage, loss of currency and jewellery.

Medical Insurance

Under European Union regulations British visitors to Greece are entitled to medical care under the Greek social insurance scheme on the

same basis as Greek citizens. Before leaving home they should apply to their local social security office for form E 111 and the accompanying leaflet on "How to get medical treatment in other European Community countries".
These arrangements may not cover the full cost of medical treatment, and it is advisable, therefore, even for EU citizens, to take out short-term health insurance. Visitors from non-EU countries should certainly do so.

Vehicles

Visitors travelling by car should ensure that their insurance is comprehensive and covers use of the vehicle in Europe.

See also Travel Documents.

Island-Hopping

Most of the Greek islands can be reached only by boat (passenger and car ferries, hydrofoils), but many of them are now also accessible by air (either by scheduled services or by air taxi: see below). The transport facilities on the various islands vary considerably: see the entries on individual islands.

Boat services

Boats to the Aegean islands mostly sail from Athens (Piraeus); there are also some services from Salonica. There are not always connections between individual islands, and if visiting a number of islands it may be necessary to return to Piraeus in between.

The Ionian Islands are connected with the mainland by services from Patras and Igoumenítsa.

Further information about boat services can be obtained from the Greek National Tourist Organisation (see Information).

Air services

Olympic Airways fly daily services from Athens/Ellinikó Airport to the principal towns in the islands.
Information from Olympic Airways offices (see Airlines).

Air taxis

Air taxis can be hired in Athens to fly to any of the islands. Further information can be obtained from the offices of Olympic Airways (for addresses see Airlines) and Aegean Aviation (Air Taxis) at the east terminal at Athens/Ellinikó Airport, tel. (01) 9 95 03 25, 9 95 09 53, 9 95 09 62.

Air charter

It is also possible to charter an 18-seater Skyvan or 9-seater Islander for a flight from Athens to the islands of Kýthira, Melos and Páros, from Kárpathos to Kásos or from Rhodes to Kárpathos, Kásos and Kos.

Warning

It should be borne in mind that the published timetables of Greek domestic air services cannot be implicitly relied on: it is advisable, therefore, to check in advance that your plane will in fact depart at the advertised time.

Language

In most parts of Greece visitors are likely to come across local people with some knowledge of English or another European language; but in the remoter parts of the country it is helpful to have at least a smattering of modern Greek.

Modern Greek

Modern Greek is considerably different from ancient Greek, though it is surprising to find how many words are still spelled the same way as in classical times. Even in such cases, however, the pronunciation is very different. This difference in pronunciation is found in both the divergent forms of modern Greek, *dimotikí* (demotic or popular Greek) and *katharévousa* (the "purer" official or literary language).

All official announcements, signs, timetables, etc., and the political pages in newspapers were formerly written in katharevousa, which approximates more closely to classical Greek and may be deciphered (with some effort, perhaps) by those who learned Greek at school. The ordinary spoken language, however, is demotic, which has been the officially accepted version of the language since 1975. This form, the result of a long process of organic development, had long established itself in modern Greek literature and in the lighter sections of newspapers. There are differences of both grammar and vocabulary between katharevousa and demotic Greek.

The Greek Alphabet

Ancient Greek			Modern Greek	Pronunciation
Α	α	alpha	alfa	a, semi-long
Β	β	beta	vita	v
Γ	γ	gamma	gamma	g; y before e or i
Δ	δ	delta	delta	dh as in English "the"
Ε	ε	epsilon	épsilon	e, open, as in "egg"
Ζ	ζ	zeta	zita	z
Η	η	eta	ita	ee, semi-long
Θ	θ	theta	thita	th as in "thin"
Ι	ι	iota	iota	ee, semi-long
Κ	κ	kappa	kappa	k
Λ	λ	lambda	lamdha	l
Μ	μ	mu	mi	m
Ν	ν	nu	ni	n
Ξ	ξ	xi	xi	ks
Ο	ο	O	o	omicron, ómikron o, open, semi-long
Π	π	pi	pi	p
Ρ	ρ	rho	ro	r, lightly rolled
Σ	σ	sigma	sigma	s
Τ	τ	tau	taf	t
Υ	υ	ypsilon	ípsilon	ee, semi-long
Φ	φ	phi	fi	f
Χ	χ	chi	khi	kh, ch as in "loch"; before e or i, somewhere between kh and sh
Ψ	ψ	psi	psi	ps
Ω	ω	omega	oméga	o, open, semi-long

There is no recognised standard system for the transliteration of the Greek into the Latin alphabet, and many variations are found.

Accents

The position of the stress in a word is very variable, but is always shown in the Greek alphabet by an accent. In the past there were three

accents – acute (´), grave (`) and circumflex (ˆ) – but since there was no difference in practice between the three only the acute accent is now used.
The "breathings" over a vowel or diphthong at the beginning of a word, whether "rough" (‘) or "smooth" (’), are not pronounced and are now little used.
The diaeresis (¨) over a vowel indicates that it is to be pronounced separately, and not as part of a diphthong.

Punctuation

Punctuation marks are the same as in English, except that the semicolon (;) is used in place of the question-mark (?) and a point above the line (·) in place of the semicolon.

Numbers

Cardinals

0	midén
1	énas, miá, éna
2	dió, dío
3	tris, tria
4	tésseris, téssera
5	pénde
6	éksi
7	eftá
8	okhtó
9	enneá
10	déka
11	éndeka
12	dódeka
13	dekatrís, dekatría
14	dekatésseris, dekatéssera
15	dekapénde
16	dekaéksi, dekáksi
17	dekaëftá
18	dekaokhtó, dekaoktó
19	dekaënneá, dekaënnéa
20	íkosi
21	íkosi énas, miá, éna
22	íkosi dió, dío
30	triánda
40	saránda
50	penínda
60	eksínda
70	evdomínda
80	ogdónda, ogdoínda
90	enenínda
100	ekató(n)
101	ekatón énas, miá, éna
153	ekatón penínda tris, tría
200	diakósi, diakósies, diakósia
300	triakósi, -ies, -ia
400	tetrakósi, -ies, -ia
500	pendakósi, -ies, -ia
600	eksakósi, -ies, -ia
700	eftakósi, -ies, -ia
800	okhtakósi, -ies, -ia
900	enneakósi, -ies, -ia
1000	khíli, khílies, khília
5000	pénde khiliádes
1,000,000	éna ekatommírio

Ordinals	1st	prótos, próti, próto(n)
	2nd	défteros, -i, -o(n)
	3rd	trítos, -i, -o(n)
	4th	tétartos, -i, -o(n)
	5th	pémptos
	6th	éktos
	7th	évdomos, evdómi
	8th	ógdoos
	9th	énnatos, ennáti
	10th	dékatos, dekáti
	11th	endékatos, endekáti
	20th	ikostós, -i, -ó(n)
	30th	triakostós, -i, -ó(n)
	100th	ekatostós, -i, -ó(n)
	124th	ekatostós ikostós tétartos
	1000th	khiliostós
Fractions	½	misós, -i, -ó(n), ímisis
	⅓	tríton
	¼	tétarton
	⅒	dékaton

Everyday Expressions

General	Good morning, good day!	Kaliméra!
	Good evening!	Kalispéra!
	Good night!	Kalí níkhta!
	Goodbye!	Kalín andámosi(n)!
	Do you speak	Omilíte
	English?	angliká;
	French?	galliká;
	German?	yermaniká;
	I do not understand	Den katalamváno
	Excuse me	Me sinkhorite
	Yes	Nè, málista (turning head to side)
	No	Okhi (jerking head upwards)
	Please	Parakaló
	Thank you	Efkharistó
	Yesterday	Khthes
	Today	Símera, símeron
	Tomorrow	Ávrio(n)
	Help!	Voíthia!
	Open	Aniktó
	Closed	Klistó
	When?	Poté;
	Single room	Domátio me éna kreváti
	Double room	Domátio me dío krevátia
	Room with bath	Domátio me loutro
	What does it cost?	Póso káni;
	Waken me at 6	Ksipníste me stis éksi
	Where is	Pou inè
	the lavatory?	to apokhoritírion;
	a pharmacy?	éna farmakíon;
	a doctor?	énas yatrós;
	a dentist?	énas odondoyatrós;
	. . . Street?	i odós (+ name in genitive);
	. . . Square?	i platía (+ name in genitive);

Travelling

Aerodrome, airfield	Aerodromíon
Aircraft	Aeropláno(n)
Airport	Aerolimín
All aboard!	Is tas thésis sas!
Arrival	Erkhomós
Bank	Trápeza
Boat	Várka, káiki
Bus	Leoforíon, búsi
Change	Allásso
Departure (by air)	Apoyíosis
(by boat)	Apóplous
(by train)	Anakhórisis
Exchange (money)	Saráfiko
Ferry	Férri-bóut, porthmíon
Flight	Ptísis
Hotel	Ksenodokhíon
Information	Pliroforía
Lavatory	Apokhoritírion
Luggage	Aposkevá
Luggage check	Apódiksis ton aposkevón
Non-smoking compartment	Dya mi kapnistás
Porter	Akhthofóros
Railway	Sidiródromos
Restaurant car	Vagón-restorán
Ship	Karávi, plíon
Sleeping car	Vagón-li, klinámaksa
Smoking compartment	Dya kapnistás
Station (railway)	Stathmós
Stop (bus)	Stásis
Ticket	Bilyétto
Ticket-collector	Ispráktor
Ticket window	Thíris
Timetable	Dromolóyion
Train	Tréno
Waiting room	Ethousa anamonís

At the post office

Address	Diéfthinsis
Air mail	Aeroporikós
Express	Epígusa
Letter	Epistolí
Letter-box	Grammatokivótio(n)
Package	Dematáki
Parcel	Déma, pakétto
Postcard	Takhidromikí kárta
Poste restante	Post restánt
Post office	Takhidromíon
Registered	Sistiméni
Stamp	Grammatósimo(n)
Telegram	Tilegráfima
Telephone	Tiléfono(n)
Telex	Tilétipo(n)

Days of the week

Sunday	Kiriakí
Monday	Deftéra
Tuesday	Tríti
Wednesday	Tetárti
Thursday	Pémpti
Friday	Paraskeví
Saturday	Sávato(n)
Week	Evdomáda

	Day	(I)méra
	Weekday	Kathimeriní
	Holiday	Skholí
Holidays	New Year's Day	Protokhroniá
	Easter	Páskha, Lámbra(i)
	Whitsun	Pendikostí
	Christmas	Khristoúyenna
Months	January	Yanouários, Yennáris
	February	Fevrouários, Fleváris
	March	Mártios, Mártis
	April	Aprílios
	May	Máyos, Máis
	June	Yoúnios
	July	Yoúlios
	August	Ávgustos
	September	Septémvrios
	October	Októvrios, Októvris
	November	Noémvrios, Noémvris
	December	Dekémvrios
	Month	Min, mínas

Manners and Customs

The people of Greece are courteous to strangers and ever ready to help them, though never over-officious. Belonging as they do to an old seafaring nation, they show a lively interest in world events and international politics; but visitors will do well to observe discretion in discussing political matters and above all to avoid thoughtless criticism of conditions in Greece.

Dress

As in many southern countries, importance is attached to correct dress, though with the development of tourism there has been some relaxation in this respect.

Athos

Special conditions apply on Mount Athos (see entry in A to Z), where men in shorts or with long hair are not admitted.

Nude bathing

See Naturism

Medical Care

Greece is well supplied with doctors, and the standard of medical care in hospitals and doctors' surgeries is in general good. Many doctors speak some English.

Police

Tel. 100 (they will pass on emergency calls).

Emergency calls

In Athens:
Emergency medical care on Sundays and public holidays: dial 105
Chemists' emergency service: dial 107
First aid: dial 166
Hospital emergency service: dial 106
Poison centre: tel. 7 79 37 77
Red Cross: dial 150
Fire service: dial 199
Tourist Police: dial 171

See Emergencies

Other emergency numbers

See Insurance

Health insurance

Motoring

Roads

The Greek road system has been considerably improved in recent years, and it is continually being developed. Greece has now a total of some 39,000km/24,000 miles of roads.
Some 14,000km/8700 miles of road are asphalted. In the remoter areas the roads will often be narrow and winding, and on the smaller islands in particular there are still many unsurfaced roads.
When driving at night it is necessary to keep a good lookout for animals and vehicles without lights.

National highways (expressways)

There are national highways (expressways) from the frontier at Evzoni to Salonica, Lamía, Athens, Corinth and Patras. Tolls are charged on the expressways, including particularly the following sections:
Athens–Lamía
Lamía–Lárisa
Lárisa–Katerini
Athens–Corinth
Corinth–Patras
Katerini–Evzoni
Corinth–Tripoli

Driving in Greece

Road signs and traffic regulations are in line with international standards. Traffic goes on the right, with overtaking on the left.
The use of the horn is prohibited in built-up areas.
Seat-belts must be worn.
In well lit built-up areas only sidelights are normally used at night. Some drivers switch their lights off altogether when meeting another vehicle.
The blood alcohol limit is 0.5 per 1000 (lower than Britain's 0.8).

Policemen with a knowledge of foreign languages bear an arm-band labelled "Tourist Police".

Parking is prohibited in Athens on yellow lines and in marked "priority streets".

Speed limits

The speed limit for cars (including cars with trailers) is 50km p.h. (31 m.p.h.) in built-up areas, 70km p.h. (43 m.p.h.) on ordinary roads and 100km p.h. (62 m.p.h.) on national highways (expressways). For motorcycles the limits are 40km p.h. (25 m.p.h.) in built up areas, 70km p.h. (43 m.p.h.) on ordinary roads and national highways.

Drivers exceeding the speed limit may have their driving licences confiscated and the car's licence plates removed.

Trailers

Size limits: see Camping and Caravanning.

Petrol

Standard grade petrol is 90 octane; premium grade is 96 octane. Lead-free petrol is available at increasing numbers of filling stations (for a list, apply to the Greek National Tourist Organisation). Diesel fuel is widely available.

Driving ban in city centres

With the object of reducing air pollution driving is banned between 7am and 8pm in much of central Athens. There are similar restrictions in Salonica.

Offenders face heavy fines and in some cases the removal of their car's licence plates.
Special regulations apply to taxis (see entry).

Assistance in Case of Breakdown or Accident

ELPA — Foreign motorists can obtain assistance from the Greek Automobile and Touring Club (ELPA), which has offices in towns throughout Greece:

Agrinion — Khar. Trikoupi 79, tel. (0641) 2 02 93

Athens — Mesoyion 2, tel. (01) 7 79 16 15 and 7 79 74 01

Corfu Town — Patr. Athinagora, tel. (0661) 3 95 04

Ioánnina — Platía Omirou 2, tel. (0651) 2 06 95

Iráklion — Leof. Knossou & G. Papandreou, tel. (081) 28 94 40

Kalamáta — Farron 155, tel. (0721) 2 11 66

Kavála — Khris. Smyrnis 8A, tel. (051) 22 97 78

Khanjá — Apokoronou & N. Sloula, tel. (0821) 2 60 59

Lamía — Miaouli 9, tel. (0231) 2 68 83

Lárisa — Papanastasiou 70, tel. (041) 22 20 20

Patras — Astigos & Korinthou 127, tel. (061) 42 54 11

Pýrgos — Ypsalanti & Patron, tel. (0621) 2 95 82

Salonica — Vas. Olgas 228, tel. (031) 42 63 19

Vólos — Eolidos 2, tel. (0421) 2 50 01

ELPA telephone service — Visitors can obtain tourist information on Greece (in English and French as well as Greek) from the ELPA telephone service, which operates daily (including Sundays and public holidays) from 7.30am to 10pm: dial 174.

ELPA frontier offices — ELPA offices are open from 7.45am to 3.30pm, Tuesday to Saturday, at Evzoni (tel. 0343/5 14 34) and Promakhon (tel. 0323/4 12 26).

OVELPA breakdown service — The main tourist routes are patrolled from April to September by the yellow vehicles of ELPA's breakdown service, OVELPA, marked ASSISTANCE ROUTIERE.
Drivers in need of assistance should indicate this by raising the bonnet of their car or waving a yellow cloth.

OVELPA centres — In case of accident, help can be obtained from OVELPA by telephoning one of the following centres:

Athens — (01) 104

Corinth — (0741) 104

Iráklion — (081) 104

Kavála
(051) 104

Khaniá
(0821) 104

Komotiní
(0531) 104

Lamía
(0231) 104

Patras
(061) 104

Salonica
(031) 104

Tragana
(9 22 99) 104

OVELPA branch offices
There are OVELPA branch offices, open daily June to September from 7am to 10pm, at Agrinion, Akrata, Alexandroupolis, Almyros, Argos, Arta, Corfu, Drama, Edessa, Florina, Ierapetra, Igoumenitsa, Ioannina, Kalamata, Kastro, Katerini, Khalkida, Kozani, Lamia, Larisa, Orestiada, Preveza, Pyrgos, Rethymnon, Serrai, Sparta, Thebes, Trikala, Triklia (Chalcidice), Tripoli, Veria, Volos and Xanthi.

Breakdown assistance is normally provided by OVELPA free of charge. There are, however, a call-out fee and a charge for towing if required.

Police
Tel. 100.

First Aid
Tel. 166.

Service Garages

There are numbers of service garages, mainly in Athens, specialising in all the well known makes of car.

Museums

Opening times
The opening times of museums and archaeological sites vary, but as a rule are from 9am to 3pm. Many are closed on Mondays, and some on Tuesday as well.

For information on the opening times of particular museums and sites apply to the local tourist information office.

Most museums and archaeological sites are closed on certain days, including January 1st, March 21st, Good Friday (some open in the morning), Easter Day and December 25th.
They are open from 8am to 12.30pm on December 24th and 31st, January 2nd, the Saturday before Carnival and the Thursday before and Tuesday after Easter.
Half-day opening on Saturday and Sunday during school holidays, January 6th, the Monday before Lent, Easter Monday, May 1st, Whit Sunday, August 15th.

Admission charges
Admission charges vary from museum to museum and site to site. Information about admission to museums and archaeological sites at reduced charges or free can be obtained from tourist information offices or local offices of the Antiquities Service (Efories Arkhaiotiton).

Photography
See entry.

National Parks

The Greek term for national park is *ethnikós drymós,* which strictly means "national oak-forest". The name is now applied more generally to areas of natural beauty and historical or cultural interest which are designated as national parks and managed by the Greek Forestry Service.

Mount Olympus was officially designated as the first Greek national park in 1938 on the initiative of the Forestry Service and the Greek Alpine Club.

A law passed in 1961 provided a statutory basis for the establishment of national parks to protect the natural flora and fauna. Further legislation in 1970 provided severe penalties for causing damage to the natural environment.

Greece now has ten national parks with a total area of 100,000 hectares/250,000 acres, and further areas are under consideration for designation as national parks. Two "marine parks" are due to be established in the Aegean.
The national parks and nature reserves (see below) contain more than 680 species of native Greek plants, bizarre rock formations, bears and rare species of waterfowl.

The main objects of the national parks are scientific research and the protection of the natural flora and fauna. To stimulate wider interest in the parks and in the protection of the natural environment the Forestry Service plans to establish information centres and nature trails in the parks.

Visitors to the national parks should have regard to the notices banning the gathering of mushrooms and berries, the picking of flowers, the felling of trees or collection of wood, shooting and fishing. Penalties for offences against the regulations are severe.
Camping is permitted only on certain sites. Visitors should take care to leave no litter.

Information

Information on the Greek national parks can be obtained by writing to:
Greek Forestry Service
Ippokratous 3–5
Athens

List of National Parks

The following list gives the date of establishment, area, location, and features of special interest in Greece's ten National Parks:

Ainos
(1962)

2862 hectares/7069 acres
Kefalloniá
Abies cephalonica (Grecian fir)

Oeti
(1966)

3010 hectares/7435 acres (including surrounding area 4200 hectares/10,375 acres)
Phthiotis
Firs; chamois

Olympos
(1938)

3998 hectares/9875 acres
Pieria
Alpine vegetation

Parnassus
(1938)

3513 hectares/8677 acres
Phocis
Firs; rock formations

Parnis
(1961)

3812 hectares/9416 acres
Attica
Firs

Pindos
(Valiakalda; 1966)

3360 hectares/8300 acres (including surrounding area 6780 hectares/16,750 acres)
Grevená
Pinus leucodermis (Bosnian pine); bears

Prespa Lakes
(1974)

4650 hectares/11,485 acres (including surrounding area 16,550 hectares/40,880 acres)
Flórina
Waterfowl reserve

Samaria Gorge
(1962)

4850 hectares/11,980 acres
Khaniá (Crete)
Capra aegagrus (wild goat)
The Samaria Gorge National Park was granted the Council of Europe's Europa Diploma (Category A) in 1979.

Soúnion
(1974)

750 hectares/1850 acres (with surrounding area 2750 hectares/6790 acres)
Attica
Pinus halepensis (Aleppo pine)

Vikos-Aoos
(1973)

3300 hectares/8150 acres
Zagoria, Epirus
Khasmofytes gorge

Nature reserves

In addition to the national parks there are other kinds of protected areas, such as "aesthetic forests" (areas of outstanding natural beauty or interesting biotopes; public access less restricted than in national parks) and nature reserves (areas containing protected species of flora and fauna, specially protected trees, rocks or other natural features).

Naturism

Naturism is tolerated in Greece in areas set apart for that purpose and not open to the general public.

Some years ago the island of Mýkonos became the first place to permit nude bathing on two public beaches, and since then it has been tolerated in some other areas; but where the local people object the police may still take action. Topless bathing, however, is now widely accepted on the beaches of Attica and in other tourist centres.

Night Life

Of particular appeal to foreign visitors are the typical Greek tavernas with bouzouki music, night spots with popular singers and other establishments specialising in folk singing or with a full programme of floor shows. Many of the big hotels have night clubs and piano bars. The main areas for night life are central Athens, the Plaka (old town) and the Coast of Apollo (Attic Riviera).

Casinos: see entry

Photography

Photography

Photography in museums with a hand-held camera is permitted with the purchase of an admission ticket. The use of a tripod is forbidden. On archaeological sites, etc. photography is allowed but special permission is required for the use of a tripod, and a charge is payable, at different rates for amateurs and professionals and varying according to the type and size of photographs. Application for a permit must be made and the appropriate fee paid in advance. For information, apply to the Greek National Tourist Organisation.

Mount Athos

Photography without a tripod and without flash is permitted on Athos, but ciné or video cameras and tape recorders are banned.

It is forbidden to photograph or film military installations.

N.B.

Visitors should make sure that valuable cameras and other photographic equipment are properly covered by insurance, and should have regard to the limits on bringing in cameras duty-free (see Customs Regulations).

Post

The post-horn with the head of Hermes is the emblem of the Greek Post Office, Elliniká Takhydromía (ΕΛΤΑ, ELTA).

Post offices are usually open from 7.30am to 7.30pm on weekdays (in Athens to 8.30pm) and from 7.30am to 1pm on Saturdays.

The principal post offices in Athens are at Odos Aiolou 100 and at the corner of Odos Mitropoleos and Sýntagma Square.

Post-boxes are yellow.

The postage on a postcard to any European country is 40 dr.; on a letter (up to 20 grams) 50 dr.

Private Accommodation ("Bed and Breakfast")

A room in a private house is the cheapest form of holiday accommodation. All over Greece, in the country as well as in the towns, visitors can find modest but clean rooms available for an overnight stay. Addresses can be obtained from the local tourist information bureau or tourist police.

Public Holidays

Statutory public holidays

The following days are statutory public holidays:
New Year's Day (January 1st); Epiphany (January 6th); Independence Day (March 25th); May 1st; Okhi Day (October 28th: "No Day", commemorating the Greek rejection of the Italian ultimatum in 1940): Christmas (December 25th and 26th).

Religious feast days

In addition to the statutory holidays there are a series of religious festivals, the most important of which are the following:

Katharí Deftéra (Monday before Lent);
Good Friday;
Easter (usually on a different date from Easter in western Europe: April 23rd in 1995, April 14th in 1996); see Events
Whitsun;
the Annunciation; and
the Dormition (Assumption).

On January 2nd and 5th, the Saturday before Carnival, Maundy Thursday, Good Friday, Easter Monday, May 1st and Whitsunday most public offices and shops are either closed or open only in the morning.

There are also numerous local patronal and other festivals.

Radio and Television

The state radio and television company, Elliniki Radiophonia Teleorassis (ERT) comprises Hellenic Radio (ERA) as well as Hellenic Television – three programmes ET1, ET2 and ET3.

ERA 5

Short news bulletins are broadcast on ERA 5 ("The Voice of Greece") Monday to Saturday at 1.30, 3.40, 8.40 and 10.40am and 12.45, 3.30, 6.40, 7.20 and 11.35pm. Sundays only at 8.40 and 10.40am and 12.35pm.

There are special weather reports and gale warnings (6–7 and over on Beaufort scale) for sailors, in Greek and English, on VHF channel 16 daily at 7.03, 9.03 and 11.33am and 5.03 and 11.03pm.

There are also weather reports for shipping, in English, on medium wave (729 kilohertz) and VHF (916 megahertz) at 6.30am Monday to Friday.

Information

Elliniki Radiophonia Teleorassis (Hellenic Radio and Television)
Messagion 432
Ayia Paraskevi, Athens
Tel. (01) 6 39 59 70–79

Elliniki Radiophonia (Hellenic Radio)
Leof. Messogion 432
Ayia Paraskevi, Athens
Tel. (01) 6 39 05 83

Private Radio and Television Companies

In addition to ERT there are several private TV transmitting companies, such as Mega Channel and Antenna TV. One of the most popular is Sky 100,4.

Railways

The Greek railway system – not surprisingly, in view of the nature of the terrain – is much more restricted in its coverage than the systems of most other European countries. It is not electrified (though there are plans to electrify the main line from Athens to the north) and is therefore relatively slow. Although less comfortable than in some other countries, it is markedly cheaper. Since the trains are usually well filled, it is advisable to book seats in advance, either at the departure station or through a travel agency. There are sleeping cars only on international routes.

Rail and Air Services

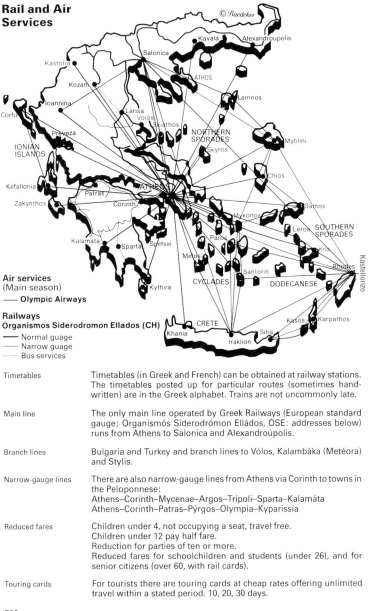

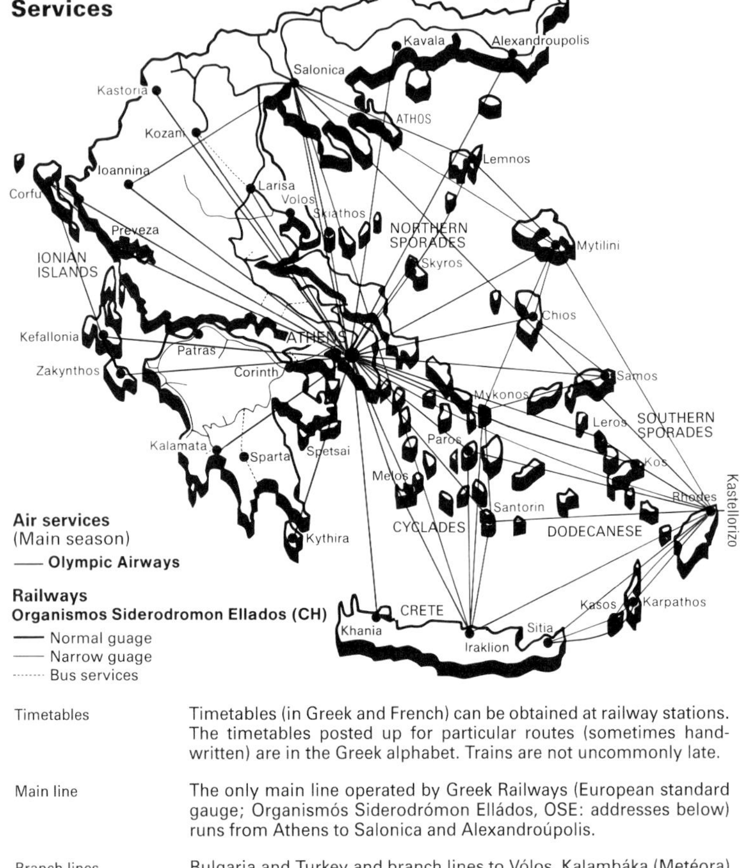

Timetables	Timetables (in Greek and French) can be obtained at railway stations. The timetables posted up for particular routes (sometimes hand-written) are in the Greek alphabet. Trains are not uncommonly late.
Main line	The only main line operated by Greek Railways (European standard gauge; Organismós Siderodrómon Elládos, OSE: addresses below) runs from Athens to Salonica and Alexandroúpolis.
Branch lines	Bulgaria and Turkey and branch lines to Vólos, Kalambáka (Metéora) and Stylis.
Narrow-gauge lines	There are also narrow-gauge lines from Athens via Corinth to towns in the Peloponnese: Athens–Corinth–Mycenae–Argos–Trípoli–Sparta–Kalamáta Athens–Corinth–Patras–Pýrgos–Olympia–Kyparissía
Reduced fares	Children under 4, not occupying a seat, travel free. Children under 12 pay half fare. Reduction for parties of ten or more. Reduced fares for schoolchildren and students (under 26), and for senior citizens (over 60, with rail cards).
Touring cards	For tourists there are touring cards at cheap rates offering unlimited travel within a stated period. 10, 20, 30 days.

There is a reduction of some 20% on return tickets (valid one month).

Return tickets

Further information can be obtained from:

Information

Greek Railways
Organismós Siderodrómon Elládos (ΟΣΕ, OSE)
Odos Karolou 1
Athens
Tel. (01) 5 24 06 46–8

Odos Sina 6
Athens
Tel. (01) 3 62 44 02–6

Restaurants

Restaurants are classified in categories, and the prices they charge are monitored by the market police.

Times of meals

The breakfast (*próyevma*) served in hotels, usually between 8 and 10am, is of the usual continental type. Lunch (*yévma*) is normally eaten between 12 and 3, dinner (*dípno*) between 8 and 11 (though in summer many restaurants are open until midnight).

The menu

The menu is often in English or another western European language as well as in Greek, though in the more modest establishments it is likely to be only in Greek, and often written by hand. Except in restaurants of the higher categories, however, it is the normal thing for clients to go into the kitchen and choose for themselves what they want to eat.

Hotel restaurants in the higher categories normally offer the standard international cuisine. Local specialities are to be found in smaller restaurants and tavernas.

During the hot months it is advisable to take your main meal in the evening. Caution should be exercised in drinking iced water.

There are no special "diet restaurants" in Greece. Visitors on a diet should discuss their requirements with the management of their hotel.

Coffee Houses

See Food and Drink

Sailing

Entry into Greece

The passengers and crew of a yacht sailing in Greek waters are officially classed as visitors in transit. On entering Greek waters the yacht must put in at a port with customs facilities for entry and exit (see map on page 592). The port authorities will then issue it with a transit log entitling it to free passage in Greek waters. During their stay in Greece the passengers and crew must spend the nights on board; any who propose to spend one or more nights ashore or to leave Greece by some other means of transport must have official entry and exit stamps entered in their passports. Yachts may remain in Greek waters without limit of time, provided that the transit log is renewed annually or on re-entering Greek waters.

There are numerous marinas with servicing and supply facilities, run by the Greek National Tourist Organisation, local authorities and private sailing clubs, and more are planned.

Sailing

Greece has more to offer sailing enthusiasts than most other countries. The Aegean in particular has ideal sailing waters.
There are sailing schools at Alexandroúpolis, Athens, Kalamáta, Salonica and Vólos and on Corfu and Sýros. For information apply to the Greek National Tourist Organisation or to:

Athens Sailing Association
Akti Navarkhou Koundourioti 7
Kastela. Tel. (01) 4 13 73 51.

1 Gouvia (Corfu)
2 Corfu Town
3 Igoumenitsa
4 Preveza
5 Vathy (Ithaca)
6 Argostoli (Kefallonia)
7 Zakynthos
8 Katakolon (for Pyrgos)
9 Patras
10 Aiyion
11 Itea
12 Pylos
13 Kalamata
14 Gythion
15 Nafplion
16 Corinth
17 Piraeus
18 Glyfada
19 Lavrion
20 Adamas (Melos)
21 Khania (Crete)
22 Iraklion (Crete)
23 Ayios Nikolaos (Crete)
24 Rhodes
25 Kos
26 Santorin (Thira)
27 Patmos
28 Samos
29 Mykonos
30 Ermoupolos (Syros)
31 Chios
32 Khalkis (Euboea)
33 Kymi (Euboea)
34 Mytilini (Lesbos)
35 Skiathos
36 Volos
37 Myrina (Lemnos)
38 Salonica
39 Kavala
40 Alexandroupolis

The Athens Sailing Association can also supply information about sailing regattas and similar events.

Small pleasure craft

Small boats brought in by road are subject to broadly the same customs regulations as private cars. They must be entered on the owner's passport and can then be used for a period of up to four months, which can be extended for a further eight months by the customs authorities on deposit of security.

Chartering boats

Charter boats sailing in Greek waters must be officially authorised and must fly the Greek flag. A copy of the charter contract and a list of the passengers and crew must be lodged with the port authorities at the port of departure, and the person in charge of the boat must carry copies of these documents.

A boat may be chartered only if the charterer and another member of the party can produce a sailing certificate or letter of recommendation from a recognised sailing club or can demonstrate their competence.

Information

Further information about chartering (charter firms, types of boat, rates, etc.) can be obtained from the Greek National Tourist Organisation.

Cruises

See entry

Wind and weather

See Facts and Figures, Climate (page 14).

Weather reports and forecasts, gale warnings

There are special weather reports and gale warnings (6–7 and over on Beaufort scale) for sailors, in Greek and English, on VHF channel 16 daily at 7.03, 9.03 and 11.33am and 5.03 and 11.03pm.

There are also weather reports for shipping, in English, on medium wave (729 kilohertz) and VHF (916 megahertz) at 6.30am Monday to Friday.

Weather forecasts for Greek sea areas can be obtained from the National Meteorological Service in Athens, 24 hours a day, by telephoning (01) 8 94 06 16.

The two Greek television channels, 1 and 2, give weather forecasts daily at 9 and 9.30pm and midnight. Although the forecasts are given in Greek, the meteorological symbols on the weather maps are easy to understand.

Self-Catering

Self-catering houses and flats are now available all over Greece. The Greek National Tourist Organisation has restored, and now lets, numbers of old houses (ranging from mansions to rock dwellings), for example at Makrinítsa and Vizitsa (near Vólos), Psará, Mesta (Chios), Areópolis (Máni), Ía (Santorin) and Papingo (Epirus); but there are also large numbers of other organisations with self-catering accommodation to let. For further information, apply to the Greek National Tourist Organisation or a travel agent.

Shopping, Souvenirs

Greece offers plenty of opportunities for acquiring interesting souvenirs. In recent years, however, mass production has taken over, and it is not always easy to find articles of good quality.

Pottery and ceramics are widely available in all price ranges, from poor imitations of ancient vases by way of good copies to the finest products of the island of Páros. Líndos, on the island of Rhodes, is famed for its plates and Arkhángelos, on the same island, for its vases; and characteristic ware is also produced on Sífnos and elsewhere. When buying pottery items it should be borne in mind that many of these must be washed with care as the colours have not been fired.

In the field of woven fabrics the folk art of Sýros, Kárpathos and Rhodes is particularly notable. Articles using ancient motifs are produced exclusively for the tourist market.

Much sought after are the knotted woollen *flokáti* rugs, looking like long-haired sheepskins, which come either in natural wool or in a wide range of colours.

Also popular are Greek costumes, embroidery (including embroidered blankets, tablecloths, handkerchiefs and slippers), lace, leather goods (particularly handbags), articles of marble, onyx and alabaster, copperware, pewter, reproductions of icons and items carved from olive-wood.

Those who have enough room in their luggage may be tempted by the elaborately carved child-sized furniture made on the island of Skýros.

Greece offers a wide variety of sweet things (aromatic honey, fig cakes soaked in ouzo, chocolate, nut pastries, etc.), dried fruit, nuts (walnuts, almonds, pistachios) and wines.

A good insight into Greek folk art can be obtained from the Museum of Folk Art in Athens (Kidathineon St.). Also worthwhile is a visit to the Athens Centre of Folk Art and Tradition (A. Hatzimihali St.).

Popular shopping streets

The shopping streets in Athens are around Sýntagma Square, Omonia Square and Monastiráki Square, as well as in Patission street; other shopping areas are in the suburb of Kifissía and Glyfáda (19km/12 miles south-east of Athens city centre).

Inexpensive handworks

In Monastiráki Square, in the north-west of the Pláka, can be found antique shops (see Antiques), as well as numerous shops offering a wide range of handwork. Inexpensive articles are for sale in the Benaki Museum (corner Vass. Soflas/Kumbari 1), in the Centre of Folk Art and Tradition (see above) and in the X.E.N. shop, Amerikis 11.

Spas

The Greek spas, situated near the sea or in a beautiful inland setting, attract many visitors.

Eleftheres
(Kavála)

Method of treatment: bathing.
Recommended for chronic rheumatism, arthritis, gynaecological disorders.

Kaiáfas

Method of treatment: bathing, drinking.
Recommmended for arthritis, gynaecological disorders, skin conditions, gallstones, hepatitis.

Kaména Voúrla
(Phthiotis)

Method of treatment: bathing.
Recommended for chronic rheumatism, rheumatoid arthritis, gout, neuritis.

Kyllíni (Elis)
Method of treatment: bathing, inhalation.
Recommended for disorders of the respiratory organs, asthma, skin diseases.

Kýthnos (Cyclades)
Method of treatment: bathing.
Recommended for rheumatism, arthritis, gynaecological disorders, sciatica, muscular pains.

Langádas (Salonica)
Method of treatment: bathing, mud baths.
Recommended for rheumatism, arthritis, general nervous system.

Lefkáda (Ikaría)
Method of treatment: bathing, drinking, electrotherapy.
Recommended for skin diseases, gynaecological disorders, rheumatism, circulatory disorders, hepatitis.

Loútra Aidipsoú (Euboea)
Method of treatment: bathing.
Recommended for rheumatism, arthritis, neuritis, sciatica, follow-up treatment of wounds, ankylosis, gynaecological disorders.

Loutráki (Corinth)
Method of treatment: bathing, drinking. Bottled water.
Recommended for disorders of the urinary tract, gravel, stones in kidney, gallstones, gout.

Methána (Saronic Gulf)
Method of treatment: bathing.
Recommended for rheumatism, arthritis, gynaecological disorders, skin diseases.

Negríta (Serrai)
Method of treatment: bathing. Bottled water.
Recommended for obesity, disorders of stomach and intestines, dyspepsia.

Platystomo (Phthiotis)
Method of treatment: bathing, drinking.
Recommended for gravel, diabetes, stones in kidney, liver disorders.

Sariza (Ándros)
Method of treatment: drinking. Bottled water.
Recommended for obesity, gravel, diabetes, stones in kidney, liver disorders.

Smokovo (Kardítsa)
Method of treatment: bathing, inhalation.
Recommended for rheumatism, arthritis, disorders of respiratory tract, gynaecological disorders, skin diseases.

Souroti (Salonica)
Method of treatment: drinking. Bottled water.
Recommended for dyspepsia and other digestive disorders, chronic intestinal trouble, chronic catarrh, functional disorders of liver, disorders of urinary tract.

Thérma Ikaría (Ikaría)
Method of treatment: bathing.
Recommended for chronic rheumatism, arthritis, gout, neuritis.

Thermopylai (Phthiotis)
Method of treatment: bathing.
Recommended for rheumatism, gynaecological disorders, general nervous system.

Vouliagméni (Attica)
Method of treatment: bathing.
Recommended for rheumatism, neuralgia, muscular pains, sciatica, gynaecological disorders.

Xino Nero (Flórina)
Method of treatment: drinking. Bottled water.
Recommended for dyspepsia and digestive disorders, chronic gastritis, stomach complaints, moderate uraemia, gravel, stones in kidney, moderate hepatic insufficiency.

Ypati
(Phthiotis)

Method of treatment: bathing.
Recommended for circulatory disorders, hypertension, coronary insufficiency, endocarditis, heart conditions, tachycardia, skin diseases, general nervous system.

Sport

A holiday in Greece provides many opportunities for sports both as a spectator and as a participant.

Spectator sports

Interesting events take place in the following Athens sports stadiums:

The Olympic Sports Centre, 10km/6 miles north-east of the city centre (tel. (01) 6 83 40 60).
The Peace and Friendship Stadium in Fáilron, Piraeus (tel. (01) 4 89 30 00).

Active Sports

Bathing

See Bathing Beaches

Climbing

The Greek Climbing Club (address below) has numerous mountain huts, mostly at altitudes between 1000m/3300ft and 2000m/6600ft, for example in the following areas:

Central Greece: Parnassus, Parnis, Iti, Vardousia, Oxia, Tymfristos, Kitheronas
Crete: White Mountains, Psiloriti
Epirus: Gamila Pindou, Mitsikeli
Euboea: Dírfys
Macedonia: Pieria, Vermion, Vrontous, Pangeo, Vitsi, Falakro
Thessaly: Pelion, Ossa, Olympus

Information on mountain huts (and winter sports):
Greek Climbing Club (EOOS)
Karayeoryi Servias 7
105 63 Athens
Tel. (01) 3 23 45 55

Greek Federation of Rambling Clubs
Dragatsaniou 4
Athens
Tel. (01) 3 23 41 07

Diving

In order to protect underwater archaeological remains diving with breathing apparatus is prohibited both in the sea and in inland lakes and rivers, with only a few exceptions.
Information about areas where diving is permitted, and about the strict regulations which must be observed, can be obtained from the Greek National Tourist Organisation. It is in any event advisable to enquire about local conditions in the nearest harbourmaster's office.

Diving tuition: see Swimming and diving tuition (below)

Fishing

Greece offers ideal conditions for anglers. Boats and equipment can be hired in almost all coastal resorts, and small boats can be hired in

Piraeus (Akti Moutsopoulou) with the permission of the harbour authorities.

An information leaflet "Fishing in the Inland Waters of Greece" is available from the Greek National Tourist Organisation (see information). Further information can be obtained from:

The Association for Fishing and Sea sports
Akti Moutsopoulou
Piraeus
Tel. (01) 4 51 57 31

Harbourmaster's Office
Piraeus
Tel. (01) 4 51 14 11

Underwater fishing: see Diving, above

Flying

Information about flying clubs in Grece is provided by the Greek National Tourist Organisation (see Information) or

The National Aeroclub of Greece–AOPA Greece
28 Hanion St, Athens
Tel. (01) 8 22 83 44

Golf

Golf is a relatively new sport in Greece. The following courses are very *popular*:

Athens area:
Glyfáda Golf Club (at Glyfáda, 16km/10 miles from Athens on the Soúnion road), 18 holes; tel. (01) 8 94 68 20 and 8 94 68 34
Hellenic Golf Club (at Varimbombi, 29km/18 miles north of Athens), 9 holes

Chalcidice:
Porto Karras Golf Club (5km/3 miles from Neos Marmaras), 18 holes; tel. (0375) 7 13 81 and 7 12 21 or in Athens (01) 3 64 41 03

Corfu:
Corfu Golf and Country Club (in Ropa plain, 17km/10½ miles from Corfu Town), 18 holes; tel. (0661) 9 42 20 or in Athens (01) 6 92 28 90

Rhodes:
Afandou Golf Club (19km/12 miles from Rhodes Town), 18 holes; tel. (0241) 5 12 55–57

Parachute jumping

Information:
Parachute-Jumping Club
Lekka 22
Athens
Tel. (01) 3 22 31 70 (afternoon only)

Riding

Information about riding can be obtained from:
The Greek Riding Club
Paradisu 18, Marussi
Tel. (01) 6 81 25 06, 6 82 61 28

Horse riding takes place at the Athens Hippodrome, Faliron, at the end of Syngrú, on Mon., Wed. and Fri. at 2.30pm. Information tel. (01) 9 41 77 61.

Sport

Rowing

Rowing boats can be hired at most rowing clubs in Greece. Rowing regattas are usually held between April and September.

Information:
Greek Rowing Club
Voukourestiou 34
Athens
Tel. (01) 3 61 21 09

Sailing

Information:
Sailing Federation
15A Xenofontos St.
Athens
Tel. (01) 3 23 68 13

Hellenic Yachting Federation (H.Y.F.)
7 Akti Navarchou Kountourioti
Piraeus
Tel. (01) 4 13 75 51–2

Swimming and diving tuition

Information on swimming and diving tuition in recognised diving schools (e.g. in Athens, Piraeus and Salonica and on Corfu):
Greek Diving Club
Athens
Tel. (01) 9 81 99 61

Tennis

There are large numbers of tennis courts attached to hotels and bathing stations, and tennis clubs in Attica, Khaniá (Crete), Ioánnina, Iráklion (Crete), Lárisa and Patras and on Corfu and Rhodes.

Information from:
Tennis Federation
89 Patisson St, Athens
Tel. (01) 8 21 04 78

Walking

Walking is becoming increasingly popular in Greece. The six-hour walk through the Samaria Gorge on Crete, for example, is an unforgettable experience, but there is unlimited scope for walks in all degrees of difficulty in every part of Greece. The European Footpath, E4, goes through Greece from Florina in the north to Githio in the south of the Peloponnes. A special travel agency organises walking holidays on some of the Aegean islands.
For information about these and other possibilities and a list of local rambling clubs, apply to the Greek National Touring Organisation.

Other sources of information:
Greek Federation of Rambling Clubs
Dragatsaniou 4
Athens
Tel. (01) 3 23 41 07

Greek Climbing Club
Karayeoryi Servias 7
Athens
Tel. (01) 3 23 45 55

Water-skiing

There are water-skiing schools at many places in Greece, including Agrinion, Attica (Lagonisi, Varkitsa, Vouliagméni), Chalcidice, Chios, Corfu, Crete, Ioánnina, Khalkís, Kýthira, Lésbos, Mýkonos, Pátmos, Póros, Pórto Khéli, Rhodes, Salonica, Skíathos, Spétsai and Vólos.

Information:
Water-Skiing Federation
Stournara 32
Athens
Tel. (01) 5 23 18 75 or 5 22 97 29

Wind-surfing

Surf-boards can be hired in all the bathing stations run by the Greek National Tourist Organisation.

Information:
Greek Wind-Surfing Club
Filellinon 7
Athens
Tel. (01) 3 23 36 06, 3 23 00 68

Winter sports

New lifts are steadily opening up the mountain regions of Greece for skiers. At heights of around 1800m/5900ft the winter sports season lasts from December to March, on Mounts Olympus and Parnassus and at higher levels in the Pindos range into May.

Information about skiing centres and mountain huts can be obtained from:
Skiing and Climbing Club
Ayiou Konstaninou 4/POB 8037
Omonia/Athens
Tel. (01) 5 24 00 57

Taxis

Taxi fares in Greece are lower than in western European countries. There are large numbers of taxis in all the larger towns, particularly in Athens, where they are to be found in all the busiest places in the city (the airport, the railway stations, the port of Piraeus, Sýntagma Square, Omonia Square, bus stations, etc.) and outside the large hotels and museums. In Athens they operate at practically any time of day or night. Taxis can be called by telephone or hailed in the street.

There are additional charges when a taxi is hired at a railway or bus station, or at an airport or seaport; for each piece of luggage over 10kg/22lb; and for journeys between 1 and 5am. Charges are increased at Easter and Christmas.

An even cheaper alternative to the ordinary taxi is provided by the communal taxis which ply in many holiday centres, taking on as many passengers as they have seats for.

In order to reduce the smog which plagues Athens in the summer months the municipal authorities have introduced new regulations for taxis. All city taxis now bear either the letter M or the letter R, and taxis with the letter M are allowed into the city centre only on even-numbered days, those with the letter R only on odd-numbered days. Travelling into Athens from the airport, therefore, make sure that you get a taxi with the right letter: otherwise you may have to change taxis en route.
An alternative means of transport from the airport is provided by the green express buses which run at 10-minute intervals round the clock.

Telephone

Most towns and islands in Greece are connected with the international direct dialling network.

	There are no public telephones in post offices; to make a call it is necessary to go to a telephone and telegraph office (OTE). There are also numerous payphones at newspaper kiosks in towns.
	The OTE office in Athens, at Odos Stadiou 15 and at Omonia Square, is open daily from 8am to midnight.
Information	Telephone information (directory enquiries): Athens: dial 131 Rest of Greece: dial 132 International: dial 162
International dialling codes	From Britain to Greece: 010 30 From the United States or Canada to Greece: 011 30 From Greece to Britain: 00 44 From Greece to the United States or Canada: 00 1
	When telephoning to Greece or to Britain the initial zero of the local dialling code should be omitted.
Speaking clock	Dial 141
Telephoning a telegram	Within Greece: dial 155 Abroad: dial 165

Time

Greece is on Eastern European Time (2 hours ahead of Greenwich Mean Time).
Summer Time (3 hours ahead of GMT) is in force from the end of March to the end of September.

Tipping

Hotels	A service charge is included in hotel bills. It is up to the guest to decide whether to give any additional tips.
Restaurants, cafés	A 15% service charge is normal in restaurants and cafés. It is usual to round up the total bill and perhaps to leave some small sum on the table.
Taxis	It is usual to round the fare up to a suitable sum.

Travel Documents

Personal papers	Visitors from the United Kingdom, Commonwealth countries and the United States require only a valid passport for a stay of up to 6 months. If they wish to stay longer than 6 months they must apply for an extension, at least 20 days before the end of the period, to the local police authorities. The formalities have recently been simplified for European Union citizens, whose passports no longer require to be stamped on entry and exit. Visitors whose passport contains any stamp or other entry by the authorities in (Turkish) Northern Cyprus may be refused entry into Greece.

Car papers

British driving licences and registration documents and those of other EU countries are accepted in Greece. Nationals of most other countries must have an international driving licence.
An international insurance certificate ("green card") valid for Greece is required. Although third party insurance is compulsory in Greece it is advisable to take out temporary insurance giving comprehensive coverage.
On entry into Greece details of the car, which must bear the usual oval nationality plate, will be entered on the owner's passport.

Visiting the monastic republic of Athos

Prospective visitors must apply to the Directorate of Religious Affairs of the Foreign Ministry, Zakola 2, Athens, tel. (01) 3 62 68 94, or the Political Affairs Division, Ministry of Northern Greece (Diikitirio), Ayiou Dimitriou, Salonica, tel. (031) 27 00 92, which will decide whether authority for a visit can be granted.

Health insurance

See Insurance
See Medical Care

Pleasure craft

See Sailing

When To Go

The best times of year for a visit to Greece, with its Mediterranean climate (see Facts and Figures, Climate), are the spring and autumn – from the second half of March to the end of May or the beginning of June and during the months of September and October and sometimes also the beginning of November. The summer months (mid June to the beginning of September) are very hot, and at this time of year the numerous insects, particularly mosquitoes, can be troublesome. From mid November to the end of March it tends to be rainy.

March to May

The months of March, April and May are mild, and all nature is in bloom. Easter, which falls within this period, is celebrated in Greece with particular ceremony (see Events).

Mid June to beginning of September

The summer months are extremely hot, particularly in the larger towns, though the dryness of the air and the *meltemi,* the prevailing wind from the north, make the heat tolerable.

During these months visitors can enjoy the numerous festivals and folk events, including wine festivals, which take place all over Greece.

Precautions

Even in summer it is advisable to take a warm coat or pullover, since on the coast and in the hills it can be quite cool in the evening. Sailing enthusiasts should have waterproof clothing, and for walkers and climbers stout footwear is essential. Sun cream and insect repellents or creams are necessary items of equipment. It is advisable to take only a light lunch and have the main meal of the day in the evening, and to avoid drinking too much iced water.

October and November

In October the temperature begins to fall, and the fine weather often continues into November. The first showers of rain are now to be expected.

Youth Hostels

Youth hostels provide reasonably priced accommodation, designed mainly for young people.

Youth Hostels

Most hostels are open throughout the year. Advance booking is advisable and during the main holiday season essential. Bookings, particularly for groups, must be accompanied by advance payment.

There are limits on the number of nights that can be spent in any one hostel. Youth hostellers must produce a membership card issued by their national youth hostels association.

There are youth hostels in Athens, Corfu Town, Delphi, Litokhoron, Mati, Nafplion, Olympia, Salonica and other towns; in Ayios Nikolaos, Iraklion, Khania, Malia, Myrthios, Plakias, Rethymnon and Sitia on Crete; and on Mts Ghiona, Kallidromon, Koziakas, Olympos, Paikon, Pelion and Vardousia.

Information

Organosis Xenonon Neotitos Ellados
(Greek Youth Hostels Association)
Odos Dragatsaniou 4
Athens
Tel. (01) 3 23 75 90

Index

Source of Illustrations:
Amberg, Archaeological Museum Iraklion, Archaeological Nationalmuseum Athens, Assimakiopulu, Baedeker-Archiv, Baier, Baumgarten, Bavaria, Birken, Bohnacker, Delta, dpa, Gärtner, Greek Centre for Tourism, Günther, Hannibal, Hellas, Historia-Photos, Kramer, Linde, Museum Delphi, Museum Olympia, Nahm, Olympic, Olympic Airways, Rogge, Schmidt-Diemitz, Spyropoulos, Stournaras, Ullstein, Uthoff, Weidleplan.